THE LEGAL ENVIRONMENT OF BUSINESS

THE LEGAL ENVIRONMENT OF BUSINESS

JOHN D. BLACKBURN, J.D.
College of Administrative Science
The Ohio State University

ELLIOT I. KLAYMAN, J.D., LL.M.
College of Administrative Science
The Ohio State University

MARTIN H. MALIN, J.D.
IIT/Chicago-Kent College of Law

Second Edition
1985

RICHARD D. IRWIN, INC.
Homewood, Illinois 60430

Cover and Interior Illustrations: Detail from the Code of Hammurabi, one of the earliest law codes, which is now located at the Louvre in Paris. Hammurabi, a Babylonian King from 1947–1905 B.C., had his code engraved on a tall diorite stela for the people to see. Before his reign, merchants in Babylon had utilized the lack of state controls to amass fortunes and impose debt slavery upon the poor. Hammurabi's Code was a reform law that established a state-controlled economy in which merchants were required to obtain a royal permit, interest was limited to 20 percent, and limits were set for commodity prices and for wages. Photo on title page and detail from Historical Pictures Service, Chicago.

ISBN 0–256–03207–6

Library of Congress Catalog Card No. 84–82472

Printed in the United States of America

2 3 4 5 6 7 8 9 0 K 2 1 0 9 8 7 6

To Our Parents

PREFACE

This second edition of *The Legal Environment of Business*, like its earlier edition, is designed to fill the need for quality teaching material for the course on the legal environment of business. The success of the first edition indicates that many of our professional colleagues who teach the legal environment of business course share our commitment to quality instruction. That commitment to quality has led us to revise the text.

Changes and developments in the legal environment of business since publication of the first edition require that the text be brought up to date. Furthermore, from our experience in teaching the legal environment of business course and from the experience that has been so generously shared with us by those with whom we have communicated, we have learned much of what students and professors desire in a textbook. This has led us to refine the book's pedagogical features.

This is a mainline legal environment of business book. Every effort has been made to be responsive to the accreditation standards of the American Assembly of Collegiate Schools of Business (AACSB). The AACSB standards define the common body of knowledge for business students as including:

> . . . a background of the economic and legal environment as it pertains to profit and/or nonprofit organizations, along with ethical considerations and social and political influences as they affect such organizations.

This book, like its predecessor, consists of 19 chapters organized into 6 parts. Part One, Legal Framework of Business, introduces the student to the legal system and presents the constitutional and administrative framework of government regulation of business. Contained in the second chapter is a discussion of the attorney-client relationship and the legal aspects of business interaction with government. Part Two, Consumer Law, includes chapters on product safety, advertising, and debtor-creditor relations. Part Three, Securities Law, consists of a chapter on the regulation of initial issues of securities and a second chapter on the regulation of securities trading. Part Four, Antitrust Law, discusses economic regulation of a business's relations with its competitors, suppliers, and costumers. It includes a chapter on franchising in addition to chapters on restraints of trade, monopolization, mergers, and price discrimination. Part Five, Labor Law, includes a chapter on labor standards and employee safety, a chapter on equal employment opportunity, and a chapter on labor relations law. Part Six, Social Environment of Business, examines business's responsibility to society. A chapter on environmental law is included as illustrative of regulation designed to protect the community from the harmful consequences of commercial activity. Special attention is given to the ethical and social influences upon managerial decision making in the chapter on business ethics and corporate social responsibility.

Adopters who used the first edition will find a reorganization of the book's six parts. The parts on consumer law and securities law have been moved forward just before Part Four's discussion of antitrust law. Our experience has shown that this provides the student with an easier transition through the book's contents. However, there is nothing sacred about the book's organization. Instructors can rearrange the sequence of the chapters without harm. For example, one of the authors consistently teaches the last chapter on business ethics and corporate social responsibility first and finds that the students respond well to that rearrangement. Some instructors may even wish to omit entire parts or chapters from their course coverage to suit their time constraints or subject preferences.

A question every legal environment of business instructor must face is whether and how to cover traditional contracts and torts material in the legal environment of business course. We believe that while today's manager must be educated in administrative regulation he or she must also have some basic background in contracts and torts. Consequently we introduce basic contracts and torts in chapter 1. We then integrate contracts and torts throughout the book to demonstrate how the law in these areas affects government regulations. Contract law is developed in chapters 5, 6, 10, and 16. Tort law is developed in chapters 5, 6, 7, 16, and 18.

Each chapter consists of approximately two-thirds text and one-third case material. We have attempted to provide a comprehensive and accurate presentation of the subject matter without being overly technical. The result is a book that is highly readable and designed for business school students.

Professors who used the first edition will find many new cases and problems in this edition. The principles of selection that we have followed for this edition are the same as those we followed in the first edition. The pedagogical qualities of a case determined its selection. Most of the cases represent current legal trends.

Each case has been carefully edited. Each case includes an editiorial introduction summarizing the facts and legal procedures and is followed by questions designed to assist student understanding.

In revising the book, we have retained some of the features that proved so successful in the first edition. Among these are the questions after cases, the problems at the end of each chapter, and the problems at the end of each part. These provide a building-block approach in the form of questions and problems whereby the student is challenged to recall and analyze legal principles through the case questions, apply what has been learned in the chapter problems, and synthesize and evaluate the various areas of law in the part problems.

A number of features have been added to the book. Among these are:

— A brief of the first court case has been provided in the Introduction.

— A part introduction precedes each part in order to orient the student to the part's subject matter and organization.

— An "Alternative Approaches" discussion concludes each chapter by presenting alternative policies and, where appropriate, international legal comparisons.

— Excerpts of statutes have been set off in the text where they are discussed so that students will not need to interrupt their reading by constantly turning to the appendix to refer to specific statutory language. Fuller versions of statutory material are provided in the appendix, which has been expanded.

— A study guide, written by Professor Alan Neff of the Illinois Institute of Technology, is available for student use. The study guide contains outlines of each chapter and practice exercises that enhance student understanding and retention of the book's content.

We have had considerable help in writing this book. We wish to especially thank professors Lynn M. Ward, Chairman of the Legal Studies Department at Bowling Green State University; Lawrence Clark of Louisiana State University, Shreveport; Mark Buchanan of St. Cloud State University; James A. Van De Bogart at University of Wisconsin, Whitewater; and Philip L. DiMarzio at Northern Illinois University for their helpful reviews. A number of student assistants deserve special mention for their valuable contribution: Anne Marie Sferra, Amy Cedarbaum, Nancy Wurst, and Jan Olexio. Several typists have had a hand in producing an accurate and readable manuscript: Barbara Maloof, Elizabeth Eichler, Susan Crowley, Mary Bartels, Deborah Kieffer, and Sharon Ford. Secretarial support services were also provided by Mary Anne Herbst and Carolyn Wilkens. Finally, we wish to thank our families for their patience while we were writing this book. None of these people is responsible for the views expressed or materials used. Any errors are our own.

John D. Blackburn
Elliot I. Klayman
Martin H. Malin

CONTENTS

Early Supreme Court Interpretation of the Commerce Clause. Supreme Court Restrictions of Congressional Commerce Power. Depression-Era Decisions. The Present Position. The Relationship between State and Federal Regulation: *The Commerce Clause. The Supremacy Clause.* Property Rights and Economic Regulation. The First Amendment and the Freedom of Speech: *Advertising and the First Amendment.* Constitutional Protections in Administrative Procedures: *Administrative Investigations.* Alternative Approaches: *Interpretivism. Noninterpretivism.*

PART TWO
CONSUMER LAW 150

PART THREE
SECURITIES LAW 256

PART FOUR
ANTITRUST LAW 324

PART FIVE
LABOR LAW   474

15 LABOR-MANAGEMENT RELATIONS   477

An Overview of the National Labor Relations Act. The National Labor Relations Board: *Board Organization. Board Procedure.* Coverage of the NLRA: *Excluded Employers. Excluded Employees.* Employer Responses to Union Organizing: *Employer Interference, Restraint, or Coercion. Company Unions. Employer Discrimination Based on Union Membership.* The Representation Process: *Appropriate Bargaining Units. Protection of Laboratory Conditions.* Negotiation of the Collective Bargaining Agreement: *The Duty to Bargain in Good Faith. Subjects of Bargaining.* Administering the Collective Bargaining Agreement: *Arbitration.* Strikes, Boycotts, and Picketing: *Illegal Job Actions. Employer Responses to Strikes.* Alternative Approaches.

16 LABOR STANDARDS AND EMPLOYEE SAFETY   510

The Evolving Common Law of Employment: *The Employment-at-Will Role. Erosion of the At-Will Rule.* Workers' Compensation: *Common-Law Background. Coverage. Benefits. Administration. Funding. Compensable Injuries.* Fair Labor Standards: *Wage and Hour Laws. Child Labor Laws. Administration and Enforcement.* Unemployment Compensation: *The Federal Law and Its Coverage. State Unemployment Insurance Programs.* Social Security: *Old-Age, Survivors, and Disability Insurance. Medicare.* Private Pension Plans: *The Employee Retirement Income Security Act.* Occupational Safety and Health Protection: *Coverage. Administration. Duties. Variance. Other Excuses for Noncompliance. Record-Keeping, Notification, and Posting Requirements. Enforcement, Inspection, and Procedure. Penalties. Employer Retaliation.* Alternative Approaches.

17 EQUAL EMPLOYMENT OPPORTUNITY   556

Title VII of the Civil Rights Act of 1964: *Disparate Treatment. Disparate Impact. Pattern or Practice of Discrimination. Exceptions. Race. Sex. Religion. National Origin. Title VII Administration and Enforcement.* The Equal Pay Act of 1963: *Equal Pay for Equal Work. Exceptions. Comparable Worth.* The Age Discrimination in Employment Act: *ADEA's Prohibitions and Requirements. Exceptions. ADEA Administration and Enforcement.* The Rehabilitation Act of 1973. The Civil Rights Act of 1866. The Executive Order Program: *Revised Order No. 4.* Alternative Approaches.

PART SIX
SOCIAL ENVIRONMENT OF BUSINESS 598

INTRODUCTION

Legal study differs from other business study. Thus, business students need an orientation to the nature of legal study before they turn to the substantive subjects of the business legal environment. This introduction provides a frame of reference from which business students can analyze, apply, synthesize, and evaluate the various areas of law affecting business. The discussion explores the objectives of legal study by business students before explaining the nature of legal study.

OBJECTIVES OF LEGAL STUDY BY BUSINESS STUDENTS

It is particularly appropriate at the beginning to inquire into the educational objectives of a book or course on the legal environment of business. Thus the following discussion focuses on the rationale and the objectives of legal study by business students.

Why Study Law in a Business School?

It is generally assumed that law is a subject taught to aspiring attorneys in a professional program within the law school. Historically, however, law was considered important to the lay public as well. In earlier days, legal study was considered part and parcel of a liberal education. Today, legal study outside the law school is gaining renewed interest. This trend is a manifestation of a simple fact of modern life: Law is too important to be left to the lawyers.

Business colleges have long recognized the importance of legal study in the curriculum. Business managers must be aware that their business relations are also legal relations. Thus, the performance or breach of a contract carries both legal and economic consequences.

In today's world it is particularly important that business students be exposed to material on law and regulation. The plethora of regulations emanating from various government agencies mandates that today's manager acquire some familiarity with the rudiments of government regulation. Today's manager deals not only with suppliers and customers but with an array of state and federal agencies. A list of the acronyms of these agencies (e.g., SEC, NLRB, FTC, OSHA, and EEOC) sounds more like an alphabet soup than a collection of government entities. Woe to the uninitiated manager who does not even know what these abbreviations stand for, let alone the shorthand jargon (e.g., "price discrimination," "bona fide occupational qualification," "tombstone ad") of the bureaucrats who work for those agencies. Today the language of business includes not only the items of the balance sheet but the legalese of government regulations.

What Are the Objectives of a Course on the Legal Environment of Business?

A course on the legal environment of business has many objectives. Some are general and resemble the objectives of other business law courses. Others are unique to a course on the legal environment of business. The following list includes both types. Two points should be noted: (1) the list is not meant to be exhaustive; and (2) the formulation of course objectives should not be an exercise which a text author or an instructor does alone, but should be a cooperative effort involving the text authors, the instructor, and the students. The following list is offered as the authors' contribution toward such an effort. A course on the legal environment of business should help the student to:

1. Apply conceptual knowledge to real-world problems. A principal goal of legal environment courses is to teach conceptual knowledge for future use in decision-making situations. This is accomplished by communicating the concepts in a case-oriented setting and by giving the student practice in applying the concepts to case problems. The use of case study makes the student sort out relevant and important facts, determine the issues involved, and reach conclusions based on known rules, regulations, standards, and principles.

2. Acquire a vocabulary of terms and concepts that will make it possible to understand further communications and so facilitate a continuation of learning beyond the limits of the classroom. A working knowledge of the legal terms and concepts used in business helps in understanding the sources that business people read every day. These sources include business papers and periodicals, technical journals, and financial reports.

3. Develop the principles of inquiry, restraint, objectivity, and regard for considerations of public policy. Understanding the "legal method" of resolving conflicts helps a person to develop restraint by not reaching conclusions too quickly on the basis of narrow thinking, to be more objective, and to consider not only the immediate issue but also the broader considerations of economic and social benefit.

4. Develop an understanding of the philosophy underlying the legal rules and regulations controlling business activity. This will result in an awareness of the individual's role in the improvement of the legal and regulatory system. Legislative bodies, administrative agencies, and courts should insure that the legal and regulatory system reflects the consensus of public thought. Therefore, everyone should think critically about the present system and the desirability of change.

5. Facilitate interdisciplinary communication in business. Accountants, financial executives, marketing experts, and other business specialists must constantly communicate with one another. Frequently the subject matter will involve legal concepts with which all of them must be familiar.

6. Develop an understanding of the principal areas of law and regulation affecting business transactions in order to do a better business management job. Legal rules and regulations affect almost every business activity. Ignorance of these rules and regulations leaves a large void in the formal education of a business manager. The fact that there is a professional field of law practice does not free managers from the need to know about the legal environment of business. Many will not have lawyers on retainer, and even those who do cannot rely on their lawyers to instruct them on every business matter in which law is involved. Almost every business decision is affected in some way by existing rules of law.

7. Develop an awareness of legal pitfalls so that professional legal assistance can be sought before losses occur.

8. Satisfy the intellectual curiosity that drives every person to learn more about the principles and concepts that give meaning to observations and experiences. Legal environment courses show how law and regulation fit into the business sector of the social order and give the student a better understanding of the relationship between business practice and social development.

NATURE OF LEGAL STUDY

The peculiar feature of legal study is the inclusion of selected legal cases in the text. These cases are unlike the business cases usually included in business school case courses. Legal cases are not really cases at all. They are legal opinions written by a judge, usually on an appellate court. These opinions resolve the legal issues in the dispute brought before the court. These written legal opinions constitute the cases presented in this book.

The cases are designed to illustrate the application of the principles of law (provided in the textual material preceding each case) to particular legal disputes. These cases, plus the text and the discussion by the instructor form the standard substance from which the student will set out to learn about the legal environment of business.

The cases selected have been chosen by the text authors for teaching purposes. Various criteria have been used in selecting them. Some cases have been selected because they proceed on unsound assumptions or somehow fail to meet the problems at hand. They provide the maximum opportunity for class discussion and criticism. Others have been included because they are the great landmark cases. From these cases the student will learn "sound law" and come into contact with dominant ideas. Some recent cases, illustrating trends in the law, have also been selected. These permit the student and instructor to evaluate the decision against the background of their own current experience.

Reading Cases

The first thing the student is expected to do is to read the textual material immediately preceding a case. This material presents the fundamental legal principles in a general manner. After this, the student must read the case following the textual presentation. Do not read a case as you would read a novel, skimming lightly for the thread of the plot. It means reading the case as carefully as you would read a page of statistics, accounting, or finance. You should read each word, looking up the unknown words in the glossary. The old proverb "To read many times is not necessarily to understand" is worth cherishing, plain as it is.

In reading cases, it is necessary to bear in mind the points of law which you are seeking. It does not suffice to read legal opinions merely as a narrative. The cases are presented to illustrate particular areas of the law, and your legal analysis of the cases should be structured to make your reading profitable. You not only must know what you are looking for; you ought also to have a method that will help you in your search. As the learned Justice Cardozo has said, "Cases do not unfold their principles for the asking. They yield up their kernel slowly and painfully."[1]

Your reading of these cases, then, must be done systematically, keeping in mind that an appellate judge does not always write his or her opinion with an eye toward functional, simple, orderly legal analysis. Our American legal system is one of the few in the world in which people are not specifically trained to become judges. Our judges have usually been trained to become lawyers (though even this is not always a prerequisite). Then, depending on the particular judicial procedure, some of these

---

[1] B. Cardozo, *The Nature of the Judicial Process* 29 (1921).

lawyers are either elected to a judgeship or appointed to this office of honor and power. When people become judges, lightning does not strike them with the knowledge and expertise necessary to write meaningful (or even lucid) legal opinions. They sometimes experience great difficulty in formulating their decisions. However, important decisions may be made in such instances. Problems in case selection arise when an important decision is contained in an opinion written by a judge who may have had great difficulty in committing his or her thoughts to paper. Often, the authors have included such cases within the text. In such instances your analysis may be impeded by obscure language. Also, many of the legal opinions in your text have been edited to conform to necessary space limitations or so that a case which in its entirety illustrates many points of law could be used to illustrate a single point.

Briefing Cases

You may be expected to prepare what is called a *brief* of the case. This is a digested version of the case. Almost every instructor has his or her own idea of what a well-formed brief should be. Sometimes your instructor will tell you how to brief cases in an introductory lecture. More frequently, you will learn what your instructor expects through criticisms of your own products in class.

Even so, let us approach the problem of briefing by examining the functions which it is to perform for you. If a brief performs these functions, then it is a useful one. The brief is intended to remind you in class of the salient facts and points of law raised and decided in the case. One timeworn request of instructors is to ask you to "state" a given case, and here a well-drawn brief will help refresh your memory. If your brief is too long, you will lose the salient points in the verbiage.

A further function of the brief is to serve as an aid in reviewing the course for examinations. Instead of attempting to accomplish the impossible task of rereading all the cases, you can recall the problems to mind by referring to your briefs. Hence, these briefs should contain enough details to help you recall the nature of the dispute, the legal principles it invokes, and their application to the facts of the case.

Topics Typically Covered in a Brief

The following is an annotated outline of the topics typically covered in a brief. The points do not always appear in the same sequence, and some may not be relevant to a particular case.

Parties   Who is suing whom? Who is the plaintiff? Who is the defendant?

Legal Proceedings	Is the litigation civil or criminal? What remedies are being sought? What was the result in the trial court? If the case was reviewed before it reached the reported appellate court, what was the result of that review? How did the case come before the appellate court?
Facts	What happened? This requires not a recitation of all the details which can be learned, but a selection of those relevant to the decision.
Issues	What issue or issues are presented for decision. These can often be presented in terms of a series of questions. Sometimes a case involves only a single issue. Other times it entails several issues. In either case, the court will attempt to resolve the issue or issues presented before it. Starting with the arguments of the contending parties is a useful way of discovering the issues of the particular controversy presented, and many judges will include the arguments of the parties in their written decision.
Holding	How were the issues decided? Who won, and what was the nature of the award? What general rule does the case lay down? The holding is the court's decision which answers these fundamental questions about the decision and its ramifications.
Rationale	What is the reasoning behind the court's decision? The court weighs the issues raised in the case and makes its decision within a conscious legal framework. On the appellate level, where these legal opinions are often presented in a formal, written format, the judges usually feel compelled to back up their decision with what they consider to be the reasons for it. The appellate court looks not only to further appellate review of its opinion (if this is possible) but also to the principle of legal precedent. In an important case a court will realize that the ramifications of its decision may be far reaching and that the case may set a precedent for decades to come. Realizing the importance of such a powerful act, a court often feels compelled to explain why the decision was reached—thus the reasons for the decision.
Concurring and Dissenting Opinions	If there are any concurring or dissenting opinions, what do they say? Concurring and dissenting opinions are the opinions of individual judges who do not join in the court's opinion. A concurring opinion is written by a judge who agrees with the court's decision but disagrees with its reasoning. A dissenting opinion is written by a judge who disagrees with the court's decision.

A Sample Brief

The following is a brief of *Smith v. Western Electric Company* which appears in chapter 1. After reading the case refer back to this example and use it as a guide for briefing the other cases in the book.

Smith v. Western Electric Co.*

643 S.W.2d 10 (Mo. App. 1982)**

Parties:
Plaintiff (employee) sued Defendant (employer) seeking an injunction (a court order ordering someone to do or not to do something) against smoking in his workplace.

Legal Proceedings:
The trial court dismissed Plaintiff's suit for failing to state a claim upon which relief can be granted. Plaintiff appealed.

Facts:
Plaintiff, a nonsmoker, shared an office with smokers. He suffered a serious reaction (nausea, blackouts, memory loss, etc.) to tobacco smoke. He complained for five years to Defendant, but Defendant moved Plaintiff to other locations and provided him with a respirator, but these measures proved ineffective. Defendant had a policy designed to separate smokers from non-smokers but refused to implement it.

Issue:
Is an employee who suffers a serious reaction to tobacco smoke entitled to an injunction requiring the employer to provide a workplace free from "second-hand smoke"?

Holding:
Yes. Plaintiff stated a claim upon which relief can be granted. The trial court's dismissal of Plaintiff's suit was reversed.

Rationale:
An employer owes a duty to provide a reasonably safe workplace and to protect employees from avoidable perils. If true, the allegations showed that Defendant was aware that second-hand smoke was hazardous to Plaintiff's health, and that Defendant had the ability to control smoking in areas requiring a smoke-free environment. Therefore, Defendant breached its duty. Injunctive relief was appropriate because Plaintiff's injury was irreparable and the risk of harm was recurrent.

---

* The title of the case reflects the parties to the lawsuit. The first name is usually the name of the party that brought the appeal, which in this case was Smith, the employee. A party who appeals a case is referred to as the *appellant*. The party who responds to the appeal is called the *appellee*. Western Electric Co. is the appellee in this case. Some courts keep the caption the same as in the trial court. In that case, the first name will be the name of the plaintiff, the party who brought the lawsuit.

** The second line in the case title contains the citation to the legal report where the case may be found in a law library. In legal citation, the first number is the volume of the publication containing the opinion,

the abbreviation is to the publication, and the number that follows is the page where the opinion is located. Thus, the case of *Smith v. Western Electric Co.* may be found in volume 643 of the *South Western Reporter*, 2d series, page 10. The abbreviation and number in the parentheses is an abbreviation of the court that decided the case and the year in which the case was decided. In the case of *Smith v. Western Electric Co.* the opinion is that of the Missouri Court of Appeals, which decided the case in 1982. Students should not need to consult the full opinion of the case by going to the library, because the authors have edited the necessary parts of the opinion and excerpted them for inclusion in the book.

General Comment

Note that in *Smith v. Western Electric Co.* terms such as plaintiff, injunction, reversed, and petition have specific legal meanings. As you read this and other cases throughout the text, consult the Glossary at the back of the book for precise definitions of key legal concepts.

Finally, class discussion may not always, or even usually, follow the outline of topics or sample brief provided above. Students may not be required to utilize these by their professor. The important thing is the result—understanding the cases—and not the technique by which that result is attained.

Managers interact with a variety of specialists, such as accountants, economists, and, increasingly, attorneys.

PART ONE

LEGAL FRAME-WORK OF BUSINESS

Modern management functions in a legal environment. Dealing with legal issues has become a central aspect of contemporary management. Consider just a few examples:

— Worker health lawsuits against the Johns-Manville Corporation force the corporation into bankruptcy.

— Unfriendly takeover attempt leads to long and costly struggle between Mobil and U.S. Steel.

— Successful antitrust suit brought by MCI Communications Corporation against the American Telephone & Telegraph Company results in a trial court damage award of $1.8 billion.

These cases and others are discussed later in this book. They stress the importance today's businesses must give to their legal environment. MCI has begun to do so and now boasts that its biggest research and development expenditure is "Legal R&D," claiming that its law department is its largest profit center.[1]

Sensitivity to legal issues must be a central part of business decision making. This does not mean that managers must be lawyers, and most

---

[1] Sturdivant and Green, "Building A Strong Corporate Legal Strategy," College of Administrative Science, The Ohio State University, Working Paper 83–70, page 5 (October 1983).

are not. However, managers must make decisions within an increasingly legalized environment, and they must often consult with attorneys. Recent surveys underscore the importance experienced managers attach to the attorney-business client relationship.[2] Reginald Jones, chairman of the board and chief executive officer of the General Electric Company from 1972 until his retirement in 1981, stated: "I used to run the world's largest law firm with incidental manufacturing facilities. I do not know how we would have run General Electric without those 400 lawyers."[3] According to a study by Arthur Young & Co., from 1979 to 1983, in-house corporate law departments grew sharply—some by as much as 50 percent. *Business Week* reports that 20 mercent of the 600,000 lawyers in the United

---

*L*itigation is the basic legal right which guarantees every
corporation its decade in court.

David Porter

States are now working directly for corporations.[4] This does not include the attorneys who practice business law in private law firms.

Ours is a litigious society. Estimates of the number of lawsuits filed in the United States range from 5 to 12 million a year. A manager is quite likely to be involved in litigation sometime during his or her career. This involvement may take a variety of forms, including being a party to a lawsuit, testifying as a witness, or compiling information for trial. A manager who understands the context of his or her participation in a lawsuit is in a better position to cooperate with counsel.

The purpose of this book is to provide an awareness of the legal environment of business. That environment has been greatly influenced by developments in consumer law, securities regulation, antitrust law, labor law, and environmental law. These topics are covered in parts two through six. Fundamental to that coverage is the material of part one: the nature of law, the legal system, constitutional law, and administrative law.

---

[2] Klayman and Nesser, "Eliminating the Disparity between the Business Person's Needs and What Is Taught in the Basic Business Law Course," 22 *American Business Law Journal* 21 (1984); Donnell, "The Businessman and The Business Law Curriculum," 6 American Business Law Journal 451 (1968); and Elliot and Wolfe, "The Need for Legal Education by Persons in Business," 19 *American Business Law Journal* 153 (1981).

[3] "Linking Executives and Educators For Business Progress," Proceedings of the First W. Arthur Cullman Symposium, sponsored by the College of Administrative Science, The Ohio State University, page 39 (June 11, 1982).

[4] *Business Week*, April 9, 1984, page 66.

Chapter 1 reviews the nature, sources, and classifications of law. Chapter 2 explores the legal system, focusing on the attorney-business client relationship, the judicial system, legal procedure, and business interaction with government. Together these two chapters lay the foundation for topics covered throughout the book.

*C*apitalism itself was brought to legal life through a succession of judicial decisions, prompted by private lawsuits that overthrew an agrarian legal order hostile to economic development.

Jethro Lieberman,
The Litigious Society

Much of today's legal environment of business is influenced by federal regulation. Chapters 3 and 4 present the constitutional and administrative framework of government regulation of business. Whenever government acts, the initial question posed is whether it has acted constitutionally. The fundamental law of the land is the United States Constitution. Government conduct, whether by Congress, the president, or an administrative agency, must conform to constitutional requirements. Thus, whenever a law is passed or an agency regulation is issued, it must be constitutional. In chapter 3, constitutional principles pertinent to business are presented.

Chapter 4 examines the procedures that federal agencies must follow. Most government activity is conducted by administrative agencies. Managers frequently must interact with agency officials, comply with agency rules, and follow other agency developments. However, administrative agencies and their officials also must obey the law.

CHAPTER 1

NATURE OF LAW

This chapter is about the nature, sources, and classification of law. It is important to start the study of the legal environment of business by looking at these subjects, because they lay the foundation for topics covered throughout this book.

WHAT IS LAW?

Each person seems to have his or her own answer to this question. Some think law is a body of rules. Others see it as a means of restricting human conduct. Still others see it as an instrument for protecting basic freedoms. A historian may regard law as a reflection of a society's mores at a particular time. A sociologist may regard it as a "social institution." Law, like other basic concepts dealing with human behavior, is susceptible to many definitions. The simple question "What is law?" leads to a complex answer that reveals the many-faceted nature of the subject. When defining law, one can refer to several schools of jurisprudence. *Jurisprudence* is the study of legal philosophy. The following discussion outlines several major philosophical conceptions of law, namely:

— Ideal conceptions
— Positivist conceptions
— Historical conceptions
— Sociological conceptions
— Realist conceptions

Ideal Conceptions: Natural Law

Natural law philosophers think of law as ordained by nature. For them, law consists of a body of higher principles existing independently of human experience. It exists as an ideal condition that is either inherent in human nature or derived from a divine source.

People cannot create natural law, but they can discover its principles through reasoned thinking. Knowledge of natural law is thus an informed intuition of what is fair and just. The principles of natural law, discoverable by reason, are universally valid. Thus, *natural law* is a body of principles of right and justice existing for all peoples irrespective of time and culture. It transcends man-made notions of what is right and just.

True law is right reason in agreement with nature; it is of universal application, unchanging and everlasting . . . And there will not be different laws at Rome or at Athens, or different laws now and in the future, but one eternal and unchangeable law will be valid for all nations and all times, and there will be one master and ruler, that is, God, over us all, for He is the author of this law.

Cicero

Positivist Conceptions: Rules of a Sovereign

In word-association exercises the word "law" often evokes the response "rules." Most people think of law as a body of rules.

Law is a rule of civil conduct, prescribed by the supreme power in a state, commanding what is right and prohibiting what is wrong.

W. Blackstone

In jurisprudential terms this is the positivist conception of law. The positivist school of jurisprudence regards law as a body of rules imposed by a sovereign. The term positivist stems from the root word "posit," which means to place, put, or lay down something. A positive law is a law laid down by the duly constituted authority.

The positivist conception of law reflects an element of injustice in that positive law is arbitrary. While at first appearing to be a disadvantage, this arbitrariness in fact has the advantage of expediency. Although arbitrary, positive law sets standards for regulating society; it facilitates decision making; it helps get things done.

Positive law and natural law are not the same thing. Natural law embodies justice and fairness. Positive law may or may not embrace these principles.

Historical Conceptions

Those who define law as the command of a political sovereign may be criticized for ignoring the many rules that bound people in the past. Because law is often older than the state, it may be argued that the state is an incidental product of the more mature legal systems rather than the distinguishing characteristic of all law.

The historical school of jurisprudence defines law as the embodiment of a society's customs. Historical jurisprudence holds that custom is the chief manifestation of law and that law develops with social development. Custom may influence and become the basis of positive law. As customs and cultural values change, so does the direction of positive law. Laws patterned after custom are likely to meet with greater social acceptance.

> **I**n the earliest times to which authentic history extends, the law will be found to have already attained a fixed character, peculiar to the people, like their language, manners and constitution.
>
> *F. K. von Savigny*

Sociological Conceptions

Closely associated with the historical view is the sociological view of law. Sociologists define law in terms of present human conduct. Thus, law is not just what the lawbooks permit but what human behavior provides. The similarity between the historical and the sociological conception is obvious. Both rely on human conduct as the source of law. However, the historical conception embodies a long-range perspective, whereas the sociological view focuses on more immediate experience.

The sociological approach to law is not necessarily in conflict with the positivist approach. Positive law may reflect current human conduct. However, where human conduct is not in accord with a formal proposition of law, those adhering to the sociological conception would change the law to bring it into line with human conduct. Stretched to its limits, this logic would reduce formal law to its lowest level if people chose to ignore it.

At the present as well as at any other time, the center of gravity of legal development lies not in legislation, nor in juristic science, nor in judicial decision, but in society itself.

E. Ehrlich

Realist Conceptions

A conception of law that is closely allied to the sociological school is the realist conception. Realism looks beyond logic and reasoning and examines what actually occurs in the legal process. Both sociological and realist jurisprudence view life experiences as affecting legal development. However, the realist conception focuses primarily on the social influences affecting the judicial process. It views law as the impact of various social influences on official discretion. The realist school flourished in the 1920s and 1930s. Its impact on legal study is still being felt.

The life of the law has not been logic; it has been experience.

Justice Oliver Wendell Holmes

 **The Case of the Speluncean Explorers***

62 HARV. L. REV. 616 (1949)

In 1949 an article appeared in the *Harvard Law Review* by Professor Lon Fuller, entitled "The Case of the Speluncean Explorers." It took the form of a fictional case decided by the Supreme Court of the mythical state of Newgarth. According to Professor Fuller, "The case was constructed for the sole purpose of bringing into a common focus certain

---

* L. Fuller, "The Case of the Speluncean Explorers," 62 Harv. L. Rev. 616 (1949). © by the Harvard Law Review Association. Reprinted in part by permission.

divergent philosophies of law and government." It presented the opinions of five fictional justices, each demonstrating different philosophical approaches to the question at hand. Read the facts of the case, excerpted below, and determine how it would be decided by justices adhering to the concepts of: (1) natural law, (2) legal positivism, (3) historical jurisprudence, (4) sociological justice, and (5) legal realism.

In The Supreme Court of Newgarth, 4300

The defendants, having been indicted for the crime of murder, were convicted and sentenced to be hanged by the Court of General Instances of the County of Stowfield. They bring [an appeal] before this Court.

The four defendants are members of the Speluncean Society, an organization of amateurs interested in the exploration of caves. Early in May of 4299 they, in the company of Roger Whetmore, then also a member of the Society, penetrated into the interior of a limestone cavern of the type found in the Central Plateau of this Commonwealth. While they were in a position remote from the entrance to the cave, a landslide occurred. Heavy boulders fell in such a manner as to block completely the only known opening to the cave. When the men discovered their predicament they settled themselves near the obstructed entrance to wait until a rescue party should remove the [debris] that prevented them from leaving their underground prison. On the failure of Whetmore and the defendants to return to their homes, the Secretary of the Society was notified by their families. It appears that the explorers had left indications at the headquarters of the Society concerning the location of the cave they proposed to visit. A rescue party was promptly dispatched to the spot.

The task of rescue proved one of overwhelming difficulty. It was necessary to supplement the forces of the original party by repeated increments of men and machines, which had to be conveyed at great expense to the remote and isolated region in which the cave was located. A huge temporary camp was established. The work of removing the obstruction was several times frustrated by fresh landslides. In one of these, ten of the workmen engaged in clearing the entrance were killed. The treasury of the Speluncean Society was soon exhausted in the rescue effort, and the sum of eight hundred thousand frelars, raised partly by popular subscription and partly by legislative grant, was expended before the imprisoned men were rescued. Success was firmly achieved on the thirty-second day after the men entered the cave.

Since it was known that the explorers had carried with them only scant provisions, and since it was also known that there was no animal or vegetable matter within the cave on which they might subsist, anxiety was early felt that they might meet death by starvation before access to them could be obtained. On the twentieth day of their imprisonment it was learned for the first time that they had taken with them into the cave a portable wireless machine capable of both sending and receiving messages. A similar machine was promptly installed in the rescue camp and oral communication established with the unfortunate men within the mountain. They asked to be informed how long a time would be required to release them. The engineers in charge of the project answered that at least ten days would be required even if no new landslides occurred. The explorers then asked if any physicians were present, and were placed in communication with a committee of medical experts. The imprisoned men described their condition and the rations they had taken with them, and asked for a medical opinion whether they would be likely to live without food for ten days longer. The chairman of the physicians told them that there was little possibility of this. The wireless machine within the cave then remained silent for eight hours. When communication was re-established the men asked to speak again with the physicians. The chairman of the physicians' committee was placed before the apparatus, and Whetmore, speaking on behalf of himself and the defendants, asked whether they would be able to survive for ten days longer if they consumed the flesh of one of their number. The physicians' chairman reluctantly answered this question in the affirmative. Whetmore asked whether it would be advisable for them to cast lots to determine which of them should be eaten. None of the physicians present was willing to answer the question. Whetmore then asked if there were among the party a judge or other official of the government who would answer the question. None of those attached to the rescue camp was willing to assume the role of advisor in this matter. He then asked if any minister or priest would answer their question, and none was found who would do so. Thereafter no further messages were received from within the cave, and it was assumed (erroneously, it later appeared) that the electric batteries of the explorers' wireless machine had become exhausted. When the imprisoned men were finally released it was learned that on the twenty-third day after their entrance into the cave Whetmore had been killed and eaten by his companions.

From the testimony of the defendants,

which was accepted by the jury, it appears that it was Whetmore who first proposed that they might find the nutriment without which survival was impossible in the flesh of one of their own number. It was also Whetmore who first proposed the use of some method of casting lots, calling the attention of the defendants to a pair of dice he happened to have with him. The defendants were at first reluctant to adopt so desperate a procedure, but after the conversations by wireless related above, they finally agreed on the plan proposed by Whetmore. After much discussion of the mathematical problems involved, agreement was finally reached on a method of determining the use of the dice.

Before the dice were cast, however, Whetmore declared that he withdrew from the arrangement, as he had decided on reflection to wait for another week before embracing an expedient so frightful and odious. The others charged him with a breach of faith and proceeded to cast the dice. When it came Whetmore's turn, the dice were cast for him by one of the defendants, and he was asked to declare any objections he might have to the fairness of the throw. He stated that he had no such objections. The throw went against him, and he was then put to death and eaten by his companions.

After the rescue of the defendants, and after they had completed a stay in a hospital where they underwent a course of treatment for malnutrition and shock, they were indicted for the murder of Roger Whetmore. The jury found the facts as related above and found the defendants guilty. On the basis of this verdict the trial judge . . . then sentenced them to be hanged, the law of [the] Commonwealth permitting him no discretion with respect to the penalty to be imposed. After the release of the jury, its members joined in a communication to the Chief Executive asking that the sentence be commuted to an imprisonment of six months. The trial judge addressed a similar communication to the Chief Executive. As yet no action with respect to these pleas has been taken, as the Chief Executive is apparently awaiting disposition of this [appeal].

[The Newgarth statute provides:] "Whoever shall willfully take the life of another shall be punished by death."

CASE QUESTION

1. How would you decide the *Case of the Speluncean Explorers?* Guilty or not guilty? Explain.

PRIMARY SOURCES OF LAW

It is often said that the legislative branch of the government makes the laws, the executive branch enforces them, and the judicial branch interprets them. While this is a valid outline of the separation of powers among the three branches of government, it is not entirely accurate. In reality, each branch "makes law." Additionally, administrative agencies, which collectively have come to be called "the fourth branch of government," are often given lawmaking authority. The following discussion focuses on the sources of law, namely:

— The legislature
— The executive
— The judiciary
— Administrative agencies

The Legislature

One source of law is the legislature. A legislature is an organized body of persons having the authority to make laws for a political unit. It often exercises other functions, such as the control of government administration.

The creation of a legislature is a development of an organized society. Early legislatures were councils consisting of aristocrats who were appointed by royal rulers to provide them with financial assistance and advice. In the 18th century, the power of legislative bodies grew in comparison with that of the royal rulers. In the 19th century they took on a republican character; that is, members of legislatures were elected by their constituencies rather than appointed by a ruler.

The legislative bodies existing today are offshoots of the English Par-

FIGURE 1-1
The Government of the United States of America

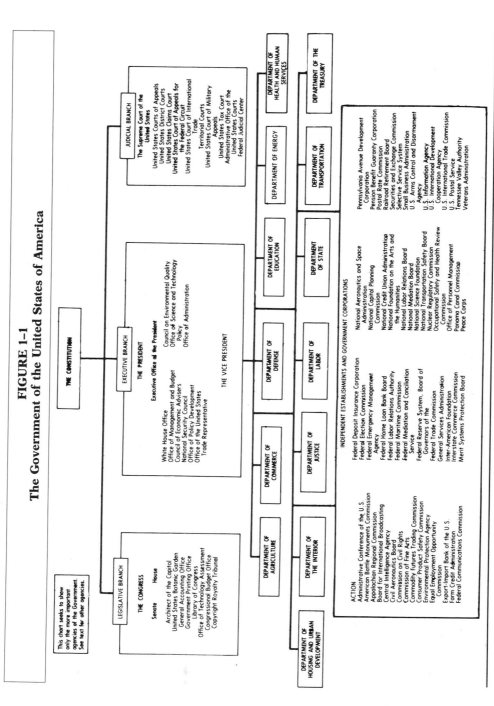

Source: *United States Government Manual 1983–1984*, p. 810.

liament. In the United States, federal and state legislative bodies have been constitutionally created.

U.S. Constitution, Article 1, Section 1

All legislative Powers herein granted shall be vested in a Congress of the United States, which shall consist of a Senate and House of Representatives.

The Legislative Process

Laws created by a legislature are called statutes, enactments, acts, or legislation. Such law is sometimes described as written law. The term *legislation* refers either to the process by which a statute is enacted or to the statute itself. Legislative acts become laws only after passing through certain formal steps in the legislature and, usually, after receiving later approval of the executive (i.e., the governor or the president). The procedure by which the U.S. Congress enacts a statute is typical of legislative procedures. A federal statute begins as a bill introduced in either the House of Representatives or the Senate. Many bills are introduced by sponsors who realize that they have little or no chance of passage. These sponsors may use the bills to satisfy constituent demands or to call public attention to particular issues.

After a bill is introduced, it is referred to the appropriate committee. Most bills die in committee from inaction. Those that receive serious consideration result in public hearings and, not infrequently, studies by the committee staff. The committee then meets in executive session to "mark up" the bill, reviewing it line by line and rewriting it. Finally, the committee sends the bill to the floor of a house of Congress. It is accompanied by a committee report that details the policy reasons for the bill and explains its intended effect on existing law. A minority report may also be included, if members of the committee disagree with the majority view. Following debate, the bill is voted on. If it receives support, it is sent to the other house of Congress for similar treatment.

If both houses pass similar but different bills, a conference committee consisting of members of both houses is established. This committee develops a compromise bill that will be acceptable to both houses and then submits it to each house for a vote.

Bills that pass both houses of Congress are forwarded to the president for signature. Pursuant to Article I, Section 7 of the U.S. Constitution, the president may sign the bill into law or may return it to the house in which it originated (i.e., veto it). If the president takes no action within

10 days following the bill's transmittal, the bill becomes law "unless the Congress by their Adjournment prevent its Return, in which case it shall not be a Law."[1] Thus, if Congress adjourns after transmitting a bill to the president, the president may "pocket-veto" the bill by simply doing nothing.

State laws are enacted through similar procedures, which are specified in state constitutions. All state laws are subject to the prohibitions of the U.S. Constitution.

Legislative Interpretation

The legislature has the primary lawmaking function. However, the meaning of a statute is not fully known until the statute is interpreted by the courts. Thus, the judicial process of legislative interpretation is another major source of the law.

In interpreting statutes, the courts attempt to determine the legislature's intent. However, the legislature may not have envisioned the particular controversy before a court, so legislative intent may be nonexistent. In this case, the court attempts to determine what the legislature would have intended to be the application of the statute in the given case.

The most obvious indication of the legislative intent is the statute's language. Where the language of a statute is clear, a court will not go beyond the plain meaning of its words to determine what it means. This is known as the *plain meaning rule*. However, a court will not apply a statute literally where doing so produces an absurd result or renders the statute unworkable.

In examining the statutory context, a court considers the statute as a whole, not merely the particular clause at issue in the case. In this way the court avoids considering a particular statutory clause out of context. Thus courts do not divorce a single phrase or section of a statute from its other portions.

Where the context of the statutory language does not reveal legislative intent, courts frequently consider legislative history. This includes the social conditions that gave rise to the legislative response and any documents such as committee reports, proceedings, and records of legislative debates. For example, knowing the history of race relations in the United States before 1964 is helpful in understanding the legislative purposes of the federal Civil Rights Act of 1964.

Frequently, the committee that reports a bill to the floor of the legislature will attempt to express its legislative intent in an accompanying report. At the state level, this is usually not done. Formal committee reports are found more frequently in the legislative history of federal statutes. Courts often rely on these reports and published proceedings of committee hearings to find congressional intent. Congressional committee reports for

---

[1] U.S. Constitution, Article I, Section 7.

enacted laws are published in the *U.S. Code, Congressional News and Administrative Report.* Proceedings of congressional committee hearings, published by the U.S. Government Printing Office, may be found in libraries that are repositories of government documents.

Occasionally, a congressional enactment is unaccompanied by a committee report. This occurred with the 1964 Civil Rights Act, which was considered by several committees. For that act, the only evidence of the legislative history is the congressional debates which, like all federal legislative debates, were published in the *Congressional Record.* The *Congressional Record* is published daily.

Legislative history is an imprecise instrument of interpretation. For example, the *Congressional Record* does not contain a verbatim transcript of the debates. Members of Congress may edit their remarks before they are published in the *Congressional Record.* This editing may add to their remarks or change them entirely. Of course, the editing may merely clarify what the individual speaker intended to convey. However, it would be an overstatement to say that edited legislative remarks have persuaded members of Congress to vote one way or another.

The *Congressional Record* often includes remarks that are not relevant to the interpretation of a particular statute. In the case of the 1964 Civil Rights Act, its opponents filibustered against its enactment. If one were to refer to the entire record of the filibuster one would find an occasional poem and several recipes for Southern cooking.

Constitutional Limitations

The legislature's authority to make law is limited by the constitution. Congress is limited by the U.S. Constitution; state legislatures are limited by both their state constitution and the U.S. Constitution.

Congressional legislative authority is prescribed by Article I, Section 8 of the U.S. Constitution. That section empowers Congress to, among other things, lay and collect taxes, provide for the common defense and general welfare, regulate commerce, and "make all Laws which shall be necessary and proper for carrying into Execution the foregoing Powers, and all other Powers vested by this Constitution in the Government of the United States, or in any Department or Officer thereof."

The Constitution also contains certain prohibitions against congressional legislation. Most of these are contained in the first 10 amendments, commonly known as the Bill of Rights. For example, the First Amendment provides: "Congress shall make no law respecting an establishment of religion, or prohibiting the free exercise thereof; or abridging the freedom of speech, or of the press; or the right of the people peaceably to assemble or to petition the Government for a redress of grievances."

If Congress or a state legislature enacts a statute that violates the Constitution, the court may declare it to be unconstitutional. Judicial review of the constitutionality of U.S. legislation is not expressly provided by the Constitution. Nevertheless, the Supreme Court's decision in *Marbury v. Madison* established that Court as the final arbiter of the Constitution's meaning as it relates to legislation.[2]

The Executive

The executive branch of government also is a source of law. However, its lawmaking authority is limited.

Article II of the U.S. Constitution provides that "the executive Power shall be vested in a President." The executive branch of the government consists of the president, the Cabinet, and the agencies and bureaus that operate under the president's authority. The president's exercise of official discretion is a source of law. In addition, the Constitution gives the president limited authority to make law in foreign and domestic affairs.

Presidential Authority over Foreign Affairs

The president's ability to make law regarding foreign affairs derives from the president's power, subject to the advice and consent of two-thirds of the Senate, to make treaties. By virtue of the supremacy clause in Article VI, treaties confirmed by the Senate become part of the supreme law of the land, along with the Constitution and congressional enactments. Judges of every state are bound by a treaty, notwithstanding any state law or state constitution to the contrary. The treaty controls whether its ratification precedes or follows the enactment of state law.

Treaties are an important source of law for international businesses. They are often used to determine the type and quantity of goods that may be sold in foreign markets.

Presidential Authority over Domestic Affairs

The president's authority over domestic affairs is yet another source of law. It is a more limited source than his authority in foreign affairs. Executive lawmaking in domestic affairs is exemplified by the executive orders issued and implemented by presidents throughout U.S. history.

Presidential power to make law has been limited by the Supreme Court's interpretation of the Constitution. For example, during the Korean conflict President Truman directed seizure of the nation's steel mills to prevent a threatened strike. The Supreme Court held the seizure unconstitutional[3] for two reasons: First, there was no constitutional basis for the seizure; second, Congress had rejected the conferring of such authority upon the president. The Court stated that the president's power to issue an executive order must stem from an act of Congress or from the Constitution itself.

Many executive orders are currently in operation. Executive orders germane to the business community require affirmative action and equal opportunity. Executive Order No. 11246 requires that government contrac-

---

[2] *Marbury v. Madison,* 5 U.S. (1 Cranch) 137 (1803).
[3] 72 S. Ct. 863 (1952).

tors take "affirmative action" to ensure that their hiring and promotion practices are nondiscriminatory.

The Judiciary

Courts are also a source of law. When a court decides a dispute, it makes law. Through the application of general legal principles to actual controversies, these principles are refined and shaped into a more precise statement of law. A court's application of a statute to a particular case gives meaning to the statute. In the absence of legislative guidance, a court will decide a dispute by applying to the present case the reasoning of past judicial decisions in similar cases. Sometimes a court must decide an issue with no statute or prior judicial decision to guide its determination. When this occurs, the court is faced with a *case of first impression*. A court confronted with this novel situation must determine what the law should be. The court is truly creating new law when it decides such cases.

Doctrine of Stare Decisis

The doctrine under which past judicial decisions are applied to a present controversy is called *stare decisis* (let the decision stand). A rule of law decided by the highest court of a jurisdiction is binding on all lower courts within that jurisdiction. It is also binding on the same court's later decisions. Unless that court overrules itself, the decision will be followed in all future cases presenting the same legal issue. The decision is not binding on courts in other jurisdictions. However, they may find its reasoning persuasive and follow it when considering similar cases in their jurisdictions. For example, although the Supreme Court of California is not bound by the decisions of the Supreme Court of Pennsylvania, it may adopt the Pennsylvania court's reasoning in a particular case.

> **A**dherence to precedent must . . . be the rule rather than the exception if litigants are to have faith in the evenhanded administration of justice in the courts.
>
> *Benjamin Cardozo*

The purpose of *stare decisis* is to provide stability and discipline in the judicial system. It prevents lower court judges from making arbitrary decisions. It does this by compelling them to follow the appellate court decisions in their jurisdictions or face reversal.

Similarly, some consistency in judicial lawmaking is provided by the fact that the same appellate court must generally follow its earlier decisions. This prevents fluctuations that might otherwise result from changes in court personnel. However, the court may overrule an earlier case where there is good reason to do so. For example, technological change or changes in social conditions may dictate that the law be changed; or events occurring after an earlier decision may prove that the decision was wrong. It would be ironic if appellate courts, which are empowered to correct the errors of lower courts, lacked the power to correct their own errors. If appellate courts could not correct erroneous precedents, the law would stagnate.

When an appellate court decides a case, it usually states its reasons in an opinion. This practice of issuing and publishing its opinions subjects the appellate court's decision to public criticism. Any interested person can ascertain what the appellate court decided and its reason for the decision.

Stare decisis is important to the business community. Because of this doctrine, business managers can rely on court decisions in conducting their affairs.

Administrative Agencies

Administrative agencies have the power to affect the right of private parties. Administrative agencies are housed in the executive branch of government but are created by the legislature. An administrative agency may have functions that are traditionally executive, such as investigating, administering, and prosecuting. It may also have functions that are traditionally legislative or judicial, such as rulemaking and adjudication.

Later chapters discuss lawmaking by administrative agencies in more detail. However, it is helpful to realize that administrative agencies may make law in much the same way that the legislative, executive, and judicial branches do. For example, if Congress confers rule-making authority upon an agency, that agency's duly authorized rules and regulations create law as if Congress itself had acted on the matters.

Interaction among the Various Sources of Law

The various sources of law in the United States do not operate in a vacuum. There is frequent interaction among the three branches of government. This interaction provides a system of checks and balances. As already noted, a congressional enactment needs presidential approval to become law, and a treaty negotiated by the executive branch needs Senate ratification.

It is often thought that the judiciary stands isolated from the other two branches and has the final word on any issue. Students often accept appellate court opinions in their casebooks as the final word on the law. In reality, a dynamic interaction occurs between the judiciary and the other branches of government. Congress, for example, can "overrule" a Supreme Court decision by statutory or constitutional amendment. The judicial opinions presented in this book should be critiqued carefully. Students should question not only what the law is, but what it should be.

SECONDARY SOURCES OF LAW

Books and articles sometimes contain discussions about a particular area of law. Books and articles *about* law are not law; they represent merely the opinion of the author. These references are known as secondary sources of law. Although these sources are not law, they sometimes influence legal development. Some of the more common secondary sources are:

— Books and treatises
— Law reviews
— Model and uniform laws

Books and Treatises

Sometimes a legal subject is given in-depth treatment in book form. These books, referred to as treatises, are usually written by professors who devote their careers to a particular legal area. For example, the late Professor Arthur Corbin, formerly of the Yale Law School, became an authority on the subject of contract law and wrote an eight-volume treatise on the subject. *Corbin on Contracts* has been cited in countless cases as the authoritative statement of contract law.

Probably the most influential secondary source in book form is the series entitled *Restatements*. Each volume (e.g., the *Restatement of Contracts*) purports to restate the law in a particular area. The *Restatements* are published by the American Law Institute, which is a private organization of lawyers, law professors, and judges. The group meets regularly to discuss changes in the law and to revise its *Restatements*. These books are frequently cited by courts as authoritative descriptions of law.

Law Reviews

Law reviews are legal periodicals. They include articles by professors, lawyers, and judges. They also contain articles by law students, usually on current legal developments. Law review articles usually cover a topic in depth and contain suggestions for reform.

Model and Uniform Laws

From time to time, groups propose drafts of statutes or codes, hoping to change the law on a particular subject. Their efforts spur change by pointing up emerging problems in the current law.

The most influential organization for the development of model or uniform laws is the National Commission on Uniform State Laws. This organization includes lawyers from the American Bar Association and the American Law Institute. The Commission proposes uniform laws, which are laws it seeks to have enacted by all the states to provide uniform legal treatment of an area. Although these uniform and model laws are intended to influence legislatures, courts frequently find that the proposals offer suggestions for judicial change in the law as well.

CLASSIFICATION OF LAW

Law is classified into several categories. When discussing a case, for example, one may discuss a topic as *common law* as opposed to *statutory law*. Or a legal development may be described as *state law* rather than *federal law*. And sometimes a case may be said to fall under the *criminal law* instead of the *civil law*. These and other categories are discussed briefly below.

Statutory Law and Common Law

As previously discussed, statutory law is law enacted by a legislature. It is written law. It is legislation. It is contained in the code books.

Common law is judge-made law or case law. Following the Norman conquest of England, William the Conqueror sent his court officials throughout the realm to keep the king's peace. These officials resolved disputes by applying custom. William's purpose was to bring the various parts of his newly conquered country under one law. Thus, there developed in England a body of judicial decisions that constituted the country's "common law." Without a Parliament (which did not come into existence until later) and without a written constitution, these decisions became the law of England. Today the term common law refers to those areas of law that have been principally developed by the courts and are not the product of legislative enactments.

State Law and Federal Law

Law may be classified as either state or federal. This is because the Constitution of the United States divides governmental responsibility between the federal government and the states.

The Tenth Amendment to the U.S. Constitution

The powers not delegated to the United States by the Constitution, nor prohibited by it to the States, are reserved to the States respectively, or to the people.

The concept of dividing governmental responsibility is known as *federalism*. Under this concept, the federal government may act only in those areas delegated to it by the Constitution, and the states are free to rule in all other areas.

Because there are 50 states, the federalism concept means that there are literally 50 bodies of state law. However, this is not as confusing as it first appears, for most states follow a general rule of law.

Criminal Law and Civil law

Criminal law defines offenses against the state and provides for their punishment. Only the state may bring a criminal proceeding against an alleged offender of the criminal law. A prosecutor will bring the case against the defendant on behalf of the state, and the claim will be described as "the State versus the defendant." If the defendant is found guilty, the state imposes punishment in the form of a fine or imprisonment, or both. The defendant pays the fine to the state, not to the victim.

Civil law exists for deciding the disputes of private parties. For example, the victim of a crime may be able to bring a civil suit against the criminal. By doing so, the victim may recover money to compensate for the injuries caused by the crime.

Contract Law and Tort Law

Private civil law is divided into two broad classifications: the law of contracts and the law of torts. Both concern private redress of wrongdoing. Contract law deals with private wrongs arising from a failure to perform duties that have been agreed upon. Tort law deals with private wrongs resulting from the breach of duties imposed by law, irrespective of one's consent to perform them.

Both contract and tort law are common law in their origin and development. However, during the twentieth century Congress and state legislatures enacted statutes supplanting the common law of contracts and torts in several areas—particularly in antitrust law, consumer law, securities law, labor law, and environmental law. While legislation has virtually taken over these areas, knowledge of the common law of contracts and torts is essential for the following reasons:

— Knowing that a statute is aimed at responding to a particular common-law rule sheds light upon what the statute is intended to accomplish.
— Although a statute may serve to change the common-law rule, the language used in a statute may involve common-law terms.
— Many statutes do not repudiate the common law of torts and contracts; rather they create public agencies to enforce what were private rights at common law.
— Common-law actions are available in many areas to supplement statutory and administrative regulation.

In-depth treatment of contracts and torts is beyond the scope of this book, but both are referred to throughout the text. It is important to begin with an explanation of their basic principles and recent trends.

Principles of Contract Law

A contract is an agreement that a court will enforce. The elements of a contract are:

— An agreement
— Consideration
— Persons with contractual capacity
— Legal subject matter
— Legal form

The agreement is the foundation of a contract. An agreement occurs when one party (the offeror) makes an *offer* to enter into a contract with another party (the offeree), which the offeree accepts. An offer is an expression of the offeror's intent to enter a contract. It contains the terms upon which the offeror will enter into a contract with the offeree. To be effective, an offer must be:

— Made with contractual intent
— Definite
— Communicated

Since an offer must be made with contractual *intent*, mere invitations to negotiate or statements made in jest or anger are not considered offers. Requests for bids, advertisements, price lists, and supplier catalogs are normally treated not as offers, but as invitations to enter into negotiations. Whether a statement manifests contractual intent is determined by giving the statement a reasonable interpretation under the circumstances. If a reasonable person would believe that the person making the statement intends to enter a contract, then contractual intent exists. This is true even though the speaker may not have actually intended to enter a contract.

The requirement that an offer be *definite* allows a court to formulate a remedy for breach of contract. Thus, the offer must be definite enough for the court to enforce.

The offer must be *communicated.* This means that the offeree must know or have reason to know of its terms.

An agreement results when the offeree accepts the offer. The *acceptance* is the offeree's manifestation of assent to the terms of the offer. The acceptance must comply with the terms of the offer and must be communicated to the offeror.

Before an agreement can become a contract, it generally must be supported by *consideration.* Consideration is what flows between the parties in exchange for their promises. It is their intended exchange. For example, if someone offers to sell certain goods to another for $100, and that person accepts, the consideration consists of the goods and the money.

Before a person can be held to a contract, he or she must have *contractual capacity*. Contractual capacity is the legal ability to make a contract. By law, minors and people who have been determined incompetent by a court cannot be held to the agreements they make.

An agreement that is not *legal* as to its subject matter cannot be a contract. Thus an agreement, the formation or performance of which is a crime, a tort, or is otherwise opposed to public policy, cannot be a contract.

Finally, some agreements must be in a particular legal form to be binding as contracts. The required form is a *writing*. A statute called the Statute of Frauds (because it was intended to stop fraudulent proof of contracts in court by perjured testimony) requires that certain contracts must be evidenced by a writing. The most important contracts are those:

— Involving interests in land
— That cannot be fully performed within one year
— For the sale of goods for a price of $500 or more

A party who fails to perform its contract duties is in *breach of contract*. A party in breach of contract is liable to the innocent party for that breach, unless it can be shown that the duty of performance was discharged.

Trends in Contract Law

The current trend in contract law is to use public interest criteria rather than consent as the basis for enforcing contract rights.[4] This may be seen by looking at some social and legal changes that have occurred over the last three centuries.

In the eighteenth century, society was basically agricultural and feudal. Religious and ethical standards controlled transactions. For example, the Church rule requiring a "just price" for contracts was followed.

The Industrial Revolution in the nineteenth century transformed society from an agricultural to an industrial economy. Activity at this time was primarily individual rather than corporate. Trading between makers and users of goods and services was done directly, without the involvement of complex distribution networks. Labor-management relations were characterized by personal, close-knit dealings between workers and shop owners. The social values of the time emphasized equality, individuality, and less government involvement in people's lives. The dominant legal, political, and economic philosophy at the time was *laissez-faire*. Laissez-faire

---

[4] This discussion draws heavily upon the discussion of social change and its relation to contract law in Metzger and Phillips, "Promissory Estoppel and the Evolution of Contract Law," 18 AM. BUS. L. J. 139 (1980).

is a French expression meaning "let the people do or make what they choose."

In contract law, this philosophy translated into court reluctance to declare that a contract had been made. However, once satisfied of a contract's existence, the courts made it difficult for parties to avoid their obligations.

With the twentieth century came the age of science and technology and the rise of large corporations and other large groups. Society became more complex and interdependent. With the rise of large groups came disparity of bargaining power. This in turn gave rise to governmental intervention to protect the weaker party. The cry for freedom of contract gave way to the cry for the public interest.

In contract law, this translated into court willingness to protect consumers by reading implied terms into contracts and by being more responsive to claims by consumers that they should be discharged from their contracts. For example, the courts fashioned the concept of unconscionability, under which a contract term considered to be overly harsh would not be enforced.

Principles of Tort Law

A *tort* is a civil wrong other than a breach of contract for which a court will provide a remedy. The purpose of tort law is to compensate injured persons who have been wronged. Tort law is concerned with the allocation of losses arising from human conduct. It seeks to answer the question of who pays when an injury occurs. Tort law answers this question by weighing the conduct causing the injury against the interests of the victim that have been invaded by the *tortfeasor*, a person who commits a tort. Also considered are the social consequences of a particular decision. Tort law thus reflects society's determination of which injuries should be compensated, which interests protected, and which conduct deterred.

Tort law is divided into three areas of liability. These include:

— Intentional torts
— Negligence
— Strict liability

Intentional torts are those that involve voluntary wrongdoing. Several intentional torts exist. The one most relevant to this text is the tort of fraud or deceit. This tort may be defined as a knowing and intentional misrepresentation of a material fact. It consists of the following elements:

— A false representation of fact
— Knowledge by the person making the representation that it is false
— An intent to induce the listener to rely upon the representation
— Justifiable reliance upon the representation by the listener
— Damage to the duped party resulting from such reliance

Negligence is conduct that falls below the standard of care that is necessary to protect others against exposure to an *unreasonable* risk of a *foreseeable* injury. The elements of negligence are:

— The existence of a *duty* to exercise the degree of care that a reasonable and prudent person under the same or similar circumstances would have exercised
— A breach of that duty by a failure to adhere to the standard of *reasonable conduct*
— The unreasonable conduct must have *caused* the victim's injury
— Actual *injury* to the victim

The existence of a duty of care is for a court to determine. However, the duty may be created by a statute. In that case, the violation of the statute is called *negligence per se,* which means that the violation of the statute is, by itself, considered unreasonable.

A person's liability for negligence may be reduced in most states by showing that the victim's own negligence contributed to his or her injuries. This is known as *contributory negligence.* In most states, the jury may compare the relative fault of the parties and allocate the damage award accordingly. The use of the victim's contributory negligence to apportion recovery is known as the doctrine of *comparative negligence.* In the few states that have not adopted comparative negligence, the victim's contributory negligence is a complete defense.

Another defense to negligence is *assumption of the risk.* A victim who voluntarily assumes the risk of injury may not recover for the tort of negligence. Assumption of the risk is a complete defense.

By emphasizing the factors of voluntary intent and reasonable conduct, the areas of intentional torts and negligence use a *fault* standard to determine liability. The third area of tort law, *strict liability,* does not emphasize fault. Liability is strictly imposed in certain situations even if the actor does not intend to do the act and exercises all reasonable care.

Strict liability applies to ultrahazardous activities, such as blasting operations. It also applies to injuries caused by defective products which, because of their defects, are unreasonably dangerous.

Trends in Tort Law

Until the 19th century, the basis for liability in tort was the strict liability standard. Strict liability reflected the social order of that time. Peace and order were the dominant objectives. Liability rested on the person whose dangerous activity disturbed the status quo.

A leading authority on tort law made the following observation about the development of the negligence or fault standard during the 19th century:

With the rise of the industrial revolution, a philosophy of individualism and *laissez-faire* ushered in a different set of values. The activity of the entrepreneur, often dangerous, assumed a high place among social objectives. It was not unduly to be burdened. Strict liability, which was seen to burden it, gave way. The rule of negligence took its place. This rule conferred on the actor—including the entrepreneur—the privilege of injuring and killing people so long as this was done carefully in the course of lawful pursuits. Looked at another way, the rule of negligence meant that the progress of the Industrial Revolution was in part subsidized by the limbs and lives of those who were the casualties of dangerous but careful conduct—usually engaged in for the profit or pleasure of the actor.[5]

Starting in the middle 20th century the trend has been back toward greater application of strict liability. This shift resulted from a recognition that human failures are an inevitable consequence of a complex society. According to this thinking, the costs of compensating injured consumers and workers would be treated as just another cost of doing business. As with other costs, the costs of compensating injured victims are ultimately paid by consumers in the form of higher prices for goods and services. Firms that experience higher costs as a result of their harmful activity will operate at a competitive disadvantage. The result may be that firms with poor safety performance records will be driven from the marketplace by firms with safer products and services.

Although the trend has been toward greater acceptance of strict liability, the fault standard continues as a standard of tort liability. The two theories stand side by side.

Common Law and Equity

As used earlier, the term *common law* meant judge-made law. However, that term has a different meaning when it is used in contrast to the term equity. Similarly, the term equity normally means fairness, but when used in contrast to common law, it means something else.

Early in English history, kings sent special officers throughout the realm to be their representatives in deciding disputes. This action launched the English legal system. The courts of this system were called *law courts*, or *courts of law*. The body of law that developed through their decisions was called the *common law*. The remedies the courts granted were called *remedies at law*, or *legal remedies*. The usual legal remedy was an award for monetary damages.

Early English kings kept a tight rein on their judicial officers. They did not want an independent judiciary. Thus, before the king's courts

---

[5] F. James, "Practical Changes in the Field of Negligence," 4 PRAC. LAW. 11 (1958).

could hear a case, a writ had to be obtained from the chancellor, the highest member of the king's council. A writ is a written order.

The writ system served to control the cases that the king's courts heard. Over the years, the English government grew to the point that the courts were no longer connected to the council. Thus, in time, an independent judiciary did develop. However, before a court would hear a case, it would still require that the case fit one of the established writs.

The writ system created a rigid legal system. As society evolved, creating new issues to be resolved, the common law courts were not responsive to new claims for relief. Parties rebuffed by the law courts started taking their cases to the chancellor.

At first, the chancellor took these cases before the king in council, but over the years the chancellor started granting relief without this formality. In time, he delegated this authority to others. From this there evolved a system of chancery courts, which were separate from the law courts.

The chancery courts developed their own rules. Unlike the courts of law, chancery courts were less concerned with the form of pleading and more concerned with substance. Procedures were informal. The judge, called the chancellor, sat without a jury and dispensed equity. The courts came to be called equity courts. The law they applied was called equity. In contrast to the courts of law, which provided monetary remedies, equitable remedies took the form of injunctions, which are court orders commanding that someone either do or not do some act, and specific performance, which is an order requiring someone to perform his or her part of a contract. Because equity courts developed to provide remedies that were not available through the law courts, they required that the party seeking an equitable remedy show that it did not have an adequate remedy available at law.

The English legal system was transported to the American colonies and continued to exist long after the Revolution. Today, virtually all the states have merged the law and equity courts into one unified legal system. However, the historic distinctions between law and equity have not disappeared. There continue to be principles of law and principles of equity. For example, actions which have been traditionally viewed as equitable in nature require trial by a judge, not a jury.

Traditionally, equitable remedies were available only in the absence of an adequate legal remedy; hence, someone seeking an equitable remedy today must show that the legal remedy of monetary damages is not adequate. To obtain an injunction, for instance, one must show that a monetary award would not provide complete redress.

In the following case, the court considered whether a petition seeking an injunction against smoking in the workplace presented a valid claim upon which relief could be granted. A brief of the case was provided in the Introduction to this book along with a discussion of how to read cases.

Smith v. Western Electric Co.

643 S.W. 2d 10 (Mo. App. 1982)

Smith (plaintiff) was employed by Western Electric Co. (defendant). He filed a petition (a type of pleading to initiate a lawsuit) seeking an injunction to prevent his employer from exposing him to tobacco smoke in the workplace and from affecting his pay or employment conditions because of his medical reaction to tobacco smoke. The trial court dismissed Smith's petition on the ground that it failed to state facts that would entitle him to relief. Smith appealed the decision, arguing that the trial court erred in dismissing his petition. He contended that his petition invoked principles entitling him to injunctive relief. The Missouri Court of Appeals reversed the trial court decision.

Judge Dowd

The petition includes the following allegations. Plaintiff has been employed by defendant since 1950 and has worked in defendant's Missouri branch since 1967. He is a nonsmoker sharing an open office area with other employees, many of whom smoke tobacco products as they work. In 1975 plaintiff began to experience serious respiratory tract discomfort as a result of inhaling tobacco smoke in the workplace. A subsequent medical evaluation determined that plaintiff suffers a severe adverse reaction to tobacco smoke. His symptoms include sore throat, nausea, dizziness, headache, blackouts, loss of memory, difficulty in concentration, aches and pains in joints, sensitivity to noise and light, cold sweat, gagging, choking sensations, and lightheadedness. After a sufficient period of non-exposure to smoke, plaintiff's symptoms abate somewhat. The symptoms have become increasingly severe over the years, however. Doctors evaluating and treating plaintiff have advised him to avoid contact with tobacco smoke whenever possible.

The petition further alleges that plaintiff first complained to defendant about the tobacco smoke in the workplace in 1975. Defendant thereafter moved plaintiff to different locations within the plant, but no improvement resulted because each location contained significant amounts of tobacco smoke. In 1978 plaintiff was informed that he should no longer submit complaints about the smoke through defendant's anonymous complaint procedure since defendant would not process them. In response to recommendations of the National Institute for Occupational Safety and Health, defendant adopted a smoking policy in April 1980. The declared policy was to protect the rights of both smokers and nonsmokers by providing accommodations for both groups and by making a reasonable effort to separate the groups in work areas. Because defendant has failed to implement its policy by making such a reasonable effort, improvement of the air in the workplace has not resulted.

According to the petition, in August

1980 plaintiff filed with defendant a Handicapped Declaration Statement that he was handicapped by his susceptibility to tobacco smoke. Refusing to segregate smokers or to limit smoking to non-work areas, defendant informed plaintiff he could either continue to work in the same location and wear a respirator or apply for a job in the computer room (where smoking is prohibited). The latter option would entail a pay decrease of about $500 per month. Defendant thereafter provided plaintiff with a respirator that has proven ineffective in protecting plaintiff from tobacco smoke.

The petition states that plaintiff has exhausted all avenues of relief through defendant; he has no adequate remedy at law; he is suffering and will continue to suffer irreparable physical injuries and financial losses unless defendant improves working conditions. The petition alleges that defendant is breaching its common law duty as an employer to provide plaintiff a safe place to work, and that defendant has available reasonable alternatives to avoid the continuing breach of duty, as demonstrated by defendant's ability to protect its computer equipment from tobacco smoke. The petition further states that, although "second-hand smoke" is harmful to the health of all employees, defendant is permitting them to be exposed in the workplace to this health hazard which is neither related to nor a necessary by-product of defendant's business.

We must determine whether [these allegations] invoke principles of law entitling him to relief.

It is well-settled in Missouri that an employer owes a duty to the employee to use all reasonable care to provide a reasonably safe workplace and to protect the employee from avoidable perils. Whether the employer has fulfilled its duty depends upon the facts of each case.

The allegations of the instant case, taken as true, show that the tobacco smoke of co-workers smoking in the work area is hazardous to the health of employees in general and plaintiff in particular. The allegations also show that defendant knows the tobacco smoke is harmful to plaintiff's health and that defendant has the authority, ability, and reasonable means to control smoking in areas requiring a smoke-free environment. Therefore, by failing to exercise its control and assume its responsibility to eliminate the hazardous condition caused by tobacco smoke, defendant has breached and is breaching its duty to provide a reasonably safe workplace.

* * * * *

If plaintiff's petition establishes defendant's failure to provide a safe place for plaintiff to work, we must next consider whether injunctive relief would be an appropriate remedy. An injunction may be issued to prevent the doing of any legal wrong whatever, whenever in the opinion of the court an adequate remedy cannot be afforded by an action for damages. Injunctive relief is unavailable unless irreparable harm is otherwise likely to result.

The petition alleges that plaintiff's continuing exposure to smoke in the workplace is increasingly deleterious to his health and is causing irreparable harm. Assuming the allegations and reasonable inferences therefrom to be true, we think it is fair to characterize deterioration of plaintiff's health as "irreparable" and as a harm for which money damages cannot adequately compensate. This is particularly true where the harm has not yet resulted in full-blown disease or injury. Money damages, even though inadequate, are the best possible remedy once physical damage is done, but they are certainly inadequate to compensate permanent injury which could have been prevented. Plaintiff should not be required to await the harm's fruition before he is entitled to seek an inadequate remedy.

Moreover, the nature of plaintiff's unsafe work environment represents a recurrent risk of harm that would necessitate a multiplicity of lawsuits. Finally, the petition states that plaintiff has no adequate remedy at law and alleges facts indicating that prior to this action plaintiff unsuccessfully pursued relief, both through his employer's in-house channels and through administrative agencies. Viewing the petition favorably, as we must to determine its sufficiency, we find that injunction would be an appropriate remedy.

*   *   *   *   *

We conclude that plaintiff has stated a claim upon which relief can be granted and that the trial court therefore erred in dismissing the petition. Plaintiff should be allowed the opportunity to prove his allegations.

CASE QUESTIONS

1. It should be noted that the court in *Smith v. Western Electric Co.* did not hold that an injunction should be awarded; it merely sent the case back to the trial court (what is called a "remand" of the case) for findings on the issue. What findings will the lower court have to make in order to issue the injunction? If the trial court finds in Smith's favor, how might you expect it to frame the injunction? That is, what might the court require Western Electric Co. to do?

2. As a result of *Smith v. Western Electric Co.*, will employers in general be required to provide all of their nonsmoking employees with a smoke-free workplace? Explain.

3. Should the resolution of the conflicting interests of smokers and nonsmokers be determined by the courts on a case-by-case basis, or should the matter be resolved more broadly by legislation? Would you favor a federal statute in this area instead of state legislation?

4. Put yourself in the position of Smith's supervisor. How would you have confronted the problem?

ALTERNATIVE APPROACHES

Western cultures rely more upon formal or written law than other cultures. To provide a contrast to the Western legal tradition, consider the following discussion of the role of law in China.

China's Developing Environmental Law: Policies, Practices and Legislation*

Unlike Western legal systems, which have based social regulation, dispute settlement and much public policy on statutes, regulations and the decisions of courts, China has historically resorted to written law only for limited purposes or when other methods of social control have failed.

Before 1911 the Chinese concept of social order was based upon the teachings of Confucius. Central to this philosophy was the concept of social harmony based upon ordered relationships and a hierarchy of classes and persons. Education and the ex-

* Ottley and Valauskas, "China's Developing Environmental Law: Policies, Practices and Legislation," 6 BOS. COLL. INT'L & COMP. L. REV. 81, 86–89 (1983). Reprinted by permission.

ample set by wise leaders provided man with rules of conduct necessary for the preservation of this equilibrium. As a result, Confucianism placed little emphasis on written rules ("fa"). Instead, it stressed social regulation through "li," ethical norms which focused on man's duties based upon his relative position in society rather than on his rights as an individual.

In conflict with Confucianism was the Legalist School. According to that view, man is by nature selfish and therefore the only way to preserve social order is to impose order from above. This school encouraged the ruler to promulgate unyielding written laws and to enforce them strictly with harsh penalties. Although the Legalist School was briefly in the ascendancy in China, the harshness of its written laws and punishments resulted in the virtual adoption of Confucianism as the state ideology in traditional China.

The adoption of Confucianism did not mean, however, that written law was nonexistent. The Chinese admitted that under certain circumstances written law was necessary to regulate relations between the individual and the state. Thus, a number of dynastic codes were adopted. These codes made no distinction between what Western legal systems classify as criminal and civil matters. Instead, they relied upon punishment in order to produce the desired governmental results. Yet, even when the dynastic codes were in force, disputes between individuals which did not affect the state were still resolved according to custom through extra-legal organizations such as the family, village, or clan.

During the Republican period in China, from 1911 to 1949, the government made attempts to introduce Western concepts of law into China. Although those efforts produced European-style codes and a Western-trained legal profession and judiciary, their influence was limited to the ma-

jor cities. The overwhelming majority of the people continued to live their lives according to traditional Confucianist norms.

The victory of the Communist Party in 1949 brought about the abolition of the [existing] legal system. Since the country's new leaders had little knowledge about Western law, their initial efforts to construct a new legal system were patterned on Soviet models. Those attempts, however, were brief, and legislation played a limited role in China between 1949 and 1979. In its place was a legal system which possessed many of the same characteristics as that of traditional China.

The first point of similarity between the traditional Chinese legal system and that of the People's Republic during its first thirty years is that social order in both systems was, for the most part, based upon unwritten rules which reflected official norms of behavior. While in traditional China those norms were the Confucian teachings, in the People's Republic they were the political considerations that were reflected in Communist Party policy. Victor Li has pointed out that in the People's Republic, as in Confucian China, the

> [p]roper modes of behavior [were] taught not through written laws but through a lengthy and continuing educational process whereby a person first learn[ed] and then internaliz[ed] the socially accepted values and norms. Compliance [was] obtained not through fear of governmental punishment, but from a genuine understanding and acceptance of the proper rules of conduct.

Second, as in traditional China, the People's Republic recognized that for certain purposes written rules were required. As a result, a number of statutes, regulations and directives were adopted between 1949 and 1979. Those laws, however, were not the usual method of social regulation. In a 1957 speech, "On the Correct Handling of Contradictions Among the People," Mao Zedong stated that written laws were only necessary to resolve conflicts between the "enemy" and the "people." Thus, the vast majority of the written laws were penal in nature or aimed at "counter-revolutionaries."

Finally, just as relations between individuals that did not affect the government were not subject to written laws in traditional China, "nonantagonistic" conflicts "among the people" in the People's Republic were resolved by neighborhood or workplace committees using education, persuasion and conciliation. Despite statements attributed to Mao Zedong in the early 1960's

concerning the need for a formal legal system, a civil code was never adopted. Instead, when the Cultural Revolution swept China between 1966 and 1976, all thought of codified law was abandoned.

With the conflicts of the Cultural Revolution and the upheavals that followed the death of Mao Zedong now over, China's leaders have concluded that, to prevent future excesses of the type experienced during that decade, to promote rapid economic development and to encourage foreign investment, major changes in the legal system are necessary. The result has been the adoption of a number of new laws and regulations since 1979.

CHAPTER PROBLEMS

1. What conception of law is embodied in the following statement from the Declaration of Independence:

When in the Course of human events it becomes necessary for one people to dissolve the political bonds which have connected them with another, and to assume among the powers of the earth, the separate and equal station to which the Laws of Nature and of Nature's God entitle them, a decent respect to the opinions of mankind requires that they should declare the causes which impel them to the separation. We hold these truths to be self-evident, that all men are created equal, that they are endowed by their Creator with certain unalienable Rights, that among these are Life, Liberty and the pursuit of Happiness.

2. In 1973 the U.S. Supreme Court was called upon to decide the constitutionality of a state statute making it a crime to obtain an abortion. In deciding that the statute was unconstitutional, the Court stated:

We forthwith acknowledge our awareness of the sensitive and emotional nature of the abortion controversy, of the vigorous

opposing views, even among physicians, and of the deep and seemingly absolute convictions that the subject inspires. One's philosophy, one's experiences, one's exposure to the raw edges of human existence, one's religious training, one's attitudes toward life and family and their values, and the moral standards one establishes and seeks to observe, are all likely to influence and to color one's thinking and conclusions about abortion. . . . Our task, of course, is to resolve the issue by constitutional measurement free of emotion and predilection.

What conception of law best describes the Court's statement? Do you think that the Court can resolve the issue "by constitutional measurement free of emotion and predilection?"

3. Martin Luther King Jr. once wrote: "I think we all have moral obligations to obey just laws. On the other hand, I think we have moral obligations to disobey unjust laws because noncooperation with evil is just as much a moral obligation as cooperation with good." Lewis F. Powell, associate justice of the Supreme Court of the United States, when he was president of the American Bar Association, deplored the doctrine "that only 'just' laws need be obeyed and that every man is free to determine for himself the question of 'justness.'" "An ordered society cannot exist," he added, "If every man determines which laws he will obey." Which conception of law was Dr. King reflecting? Which conception of law was Justice Powell expressing? Which position do you agree with?

4. The president of the United States concludes a commercial treaty with the Soviet Union. The treaty is subsequently ratified by the U.S. Senate. After ratification, a group of citizens file a lawsuit in a federal court attacking the treaty as unconstitutional. Will the citizens win? Explain.

5. The Federal Trade Commission, a federal agency, brings action against Conglomerate Car Company as a result of a complaint filed with the commission by Bigdome Car Company. After reviewing the complaint, the commission concludes that Conglomerate is guilty. The commission's opinion provides its reasons for reaching this conclusion. Is the commission's opinion law? Explain.

6. Arthur and Ava Strunk have two sons, Tommy, age 28, and Jerry, age 27. Tommy is married, employed, and a part-time college student. He suffers from a fatal kidney disease and is being kept alive by frequent dialysis treatment, a procedure that cannot be continued much longer. Jerry is incompetent and has been legally committed to a state institution for the mentally retarded. He has an IQ of approximately 35, which corresponds to a mental age of approximately six years. He is further handicapped by a speech defect that makes it difficult for him to communicate with people who are unacquainted with him. When it was determined that Tommy would need a kidney transplant in order to survive, doctors looked for a donor. Possible donors include cadavers as well as live persons. Because of compatibility of blood type and tissue, the only acceptable live donor is Jerry. The parents petitioned a court for authority to proceed with the operation. The case is one of first impression: There are no statutes, or prior case law to guide the court's determination. How should the court decide?

7. Kenneth Allen, an insurance agent, contracted to place several advertisements in the Flint, Michigan classified telephone directory. Michigan Bell Telephone Company (Michigan Bell) accepted the order and agreed to publish the listing in its 1963 yellow pages—but failed to do so. Allen sued Michigan Bell to recover damages. As a defense, Michigan Bell presented the contract between it and Allen, which contained the following clause:

> Telephone Company (a) will not be bound by any verbal agreements or (b) will not be liable to Advertiser for damages resulting from failure to include all or any of said items of advertising in the Directories or from errors in the advertising printed in the Directories, in excess of the agreed prices for such advertising for the issues in which the error or omission occurs.

Michigan Bell argued that it may lawfully require those who want to advertise in the yellow pages to agree to a limitation of liability in the event of an omission or error in the yellow pages. In essence, Michigan Bell argued that the concept of freedom of contract requires the court to uphold the contract's disclaimer of liability provision. Do you agree with Michigan Bell? Explain. If Michigan Bell's defense is not successful, what theories of liability could Allen possibly recover upon against Michigan Bell? Explain.

8. A Chrysler dealer sold a new car to Mr. Smith. When Mrs. Smith took the car for a ride, a steering knuckle snapped. She lost control of the car and was severely injured. The new car warranty expressly limited recovery to replacement of defective parts. Mrs. Smith sued the Chrysler Corporation, which manufactured the car, and the dealer from whom the car was purchased. Both assert the warranty as a defense, claiming that it was part of the contract for sale. Should Mrs. Smith win or lose? Explain.

9. Oliver Wendell Holmes once said, "The state might conceivably make itself a mutual insurance company against accidents, and distribute the burden of its citizens' mishaps among all its members." Would you agree to a proposal to substitute a socialized compensation system in place of the tort-litigation system? Why or why not?

10. Compare Eastern and Western legal traditions. What cultural differences might account for the greater reliance upon formal law and legal institutions in the United States?

CHAPTER 2

BUSINESS AND THE LEGAL SYSTEM

Now that the nature and sources of law have been examined, it is appropriate to explore the legal system within which business operates. Businesses come into contact with various components of the legal system. Disputes with suppliers or customers may result in lawsuits that bring the business manager face to face with the judicial system and its process. Businesses also interact with other branches of government. Government regulation brings them in contact with administrative agencies. Businesses may also deal with the legislative and executive branches of government in their efforts to influence political action. These contacts with the legal system create a need for legal advice and representation by attorneys.

This chapter will familiarize the reader with the business firm's interaction with the legal system—the judiciary as well as other branches of government. First, however, it is important to understand the role of the business attorney.

THE FIRM AND ITS ATTORNEY

With the advent of increased government regulation, businesses are more apt to call upon lawyers to assist them through the "red tape." In the past, a business usually did not contact lawyers until a problem arose—when it was sued for example, or when a distributor would not pay an outstanding debt. However, more and more businesses are concerned with preventive law. By contacting lawyers early and implementing legal advice, companies attempt to avoid the consequences that accompany uninformed business practices. Business managers today have a more ongoing relationship with lawyers than they had in the past; hence, they need to know more about how lawyers function.

Lawyers have a common base of education: law school. In law school lawyers receive generalized training that enables them to adapt to a wide range of tasks. The average person thinks that lawyers know the law, but it is more accurate to say that lawyers are versed in legal principles. They are trained to find the relevant law and to apply it to particular circumstances. This general training and ability equip a lawyer for various specialized duties.

Counselor

The lawyer practices preventive law by counseling the business client. Wise counsel can avoid a host of problems; for example, advising a corporation regarding the legal consequences of a merger might avert potential antitrust problems. As a counselor, the business lawyer must be imaginative, perceiving a range of alternatives and the probable legal consequences of each. To do this, the business lawyer must be versed in the multidimensional operations and activities of the business firm. It is the business manager's responsibility to help educate the lawyer about those operations and activities.

Investigator

The role of investigator is often preliminary to the role of counselor or advocate. The lawyer needs to accumulate useful information and extract the data pertinent to the particular task. This takes cooperation with the business client who knows how the firm operates and where to find specific documents. During the course of the investigation, the attorney may uncover damaging information or even evidence of criminal activity. The attorney owes an allegiance to the client. An attorney is deemed an officer of the court and cannot counsel a client to participate in illegal activities. Nonetheless, the canons of ethics, as constituted at present, do not require the attorney to "blow the whistle."

Drafter

The business lawyer drafts documents for the firm. This activity draws the attorney into a close working relationship with the business person. Contracts, deeds, corporate instruments, and securities registration statements are just a few of the documents that are commonly prepared by lawyers with the help of the business client. Good drafting is important to avoid adverse legal consequences. In this respect drafting is a form of preventive law.

Negotiator

The lawyer possesses negotiating skills. The role of the negotiator is akin to that of the advocate. The lawyer presents the client's strongest arguments in order to achieve the best result. Negotiation may be necessitated by a dispute with a regulatory agency, another business, or a customer. Successful negotiation resulting in a settlement often avoids costly suits, work stoppages, and other undesirable economic consequences.

Advocate

In the capacity of an advocate, the lawyer is called upon to represent the client's interest. This may occur in a court, before an administrative agency or a legislative body, or in another arena. The lawyer's duty as an advocate is to present the facts and the law in the light most favorable to the client. Of course, the opponent's lawyer will be doing the same. This adversary system enables the judge or other hearing officer to examine the full range of arguments before arriving at a reasoned decision.

Selecting a Lawyer

No lawyer is an expert in all of the above roles or in every substantive area of the law. Some lawyers concentrate their practice in the area of counseling, while others develop specialized skills in advocacy. Some attorneys concentrate on antitrust law, while others specialize in tax law. For these reasons, it might seem desirable for the corporate client to choose a lawyer based on the specific problem that arises. However, this is not always feasible. First, lawyers do not normally hang "specialty shingles," and in most states they are prohibited from doing so. Consequently it is difficult for the business manager to know whom to call upon among the ranks of the specialists. Second, specialists have a narrow focus and often fail to see the big picture. Selecting a generalist as corporate counsel has its advantages. The general practitioner can effectively handle most of the routine problems that confront a business firm. When a problem calls for a specialist, the general corporate practitioner can refer the client to one and then brief the specialist on the problem.

Large companies hire lawyers and establish their own inside law firm. In-house lawyers have the advantage of being closer to and more familiar with the business. They are in a better position than outside counsel to identify and react to potential legal pitfalls and to render on-the-spot advice. Problems that require specialized attention can be referred to outside counsel.

Communicating with Lawyers

A lawyer is not permitted to solicit clients by direct contact. A person needing a lawyer's services must take the initiative and should contact counsel early, before the problem intensifies. It is better to have a lawyer draft a contract than to call in a lawyer to remedy a problem arising from a contract poorly drafted by the client. If a firm has an ongoing professional relationship with counsel, its attorney can take the initiative with regard to a law that will affect the firm's business. This is not solicitation, which is prohibited, because a lawyer-client relationship already exists.

It is important that the client make a full disclosure of the facts relevant to the question at hand. If an attorney's opinion is based on anything less, the opinion is incomplete. A general understanding of the law affecting the business will help a client detail the material facts and avoid irrelevancies when communicating with a lawyer. Understanding the lawyer's role will also facilitate communications.

The client should not take a passive role but should actively assist the lawyer's search for solutions. The client needs to inform the lawyer of the company goals so that the lawyer will seek solutions compatible with those goals. Finally, the client should expect high-quality service from counsel and should communicate that expectation. After all, the client is paying the bill.

Corporate Legal Strategy

There has been a long-standing tension between lawyers and business people. Lawyers tend to be conservative in their advice and often dampen a business's desire to do creative things. Many business executives believe that an attorney should be consulted only to find out what cannot be done. Because they use attorneys only on an *ad hoc* basis, they do not know how to incorporate them into their business organization charts.

Some businesses, however, do recognize the need to develop a corporate legal strategy. A *preventive strategy* employs attorneys to review new programs and documents with an eye to avoiding legal problems. An *enforcive strategy* involves legal activity to protect a company against patent infringement and other violations of its rights. A *creative strategy* employs legal counsel to help formulate corporate goals. It is an active strategy that brings the manager and the attorney together to explore various ways of achieving those goals—through, for example, a takeover of another corporation, legal loopholes, or a change in the law. The preventive, enforcive, and creative corporate legal strategies may be used together, depending upon the circumstances that confront the company.[1]

The Attorney-Client Privilege

The law encourages clients to communicate fully with their counsel by protecting such communication from disclosure to a third person. The attorney-client privilege gives the client the right to conceal matters relating to counsel's advice. The canon of ethics does not permit an attorney

---

[1] This discussion of corporate legal strategy is derived from F. Sturdivant and C. Green, *Building a Strong Corporate Strategy*, College of Administrative Science, The Ohio State University, Working Paper Series 83–70 (October 1983).

to disclose communications regarding legal advice to the client. The client may, however, waive the privilege and authorize the attorney to make disclosure. The privilege applies only to confidential communications. It does not include statements made to an attorney in the presence of third parties other than the client's agents or employees. The attorney-client privilege is examined in the following case.

Upjohn Co. v. United States

449 U.S. 383 (1981)

Upjohn sells pharmaceuticals. During an audit it was discovered that one of Upjohn's foreign subsidiaries made payments to officials of foreign governments in order to obtain government business. The accountants communicated this finding to Gerald Thomas, Upjohn's vice president, secretary, and general counsel. Thomas contacted outside counsel, and an internal investigation began. The attorneys drafted a questionnaire and sent it to the relevant managers. The questionnaire was designed to compile full information on the extent of the payments made to foreign governmental officials. As part of the investigation, Thomas and the outside counsel interviewed the questionnaire recipients and 33 other officers and employees.

Upjohn disclosed its findings of "questionable payments" to the Securities and Exchange Commission and the Internal Revenue Service (IRS). The IRS began its own investigation and issued a summons to Upjohn demanding "all files relative to the investigation conducted under the supervision of Gerald Thomas," including the questionnaires and the notes of interviews. The company refused to comply with the summons, maintaining that those items were protected from disclosure by the attorney-client privilege. The United States sought enforcement in the district court, which determined that Upjohn must comply with the summons. The petitioner appealed to the court of appeals, which held that under the "control group test" the attorney-client privilege was not applicable to communications made by persons "not responsible for directing [Upjohn's] actions in response to legal advice." The Supreme Court reversed and remanded.

Justice Rehnquist

The attorney-client privilege is the oldest of the privileges for confidential communications known to the common law. Its purpose is to encourage full and frank communication between attorneys and their clients and thereby promote broader public interests in the observance of law and administration of justice. The privilege recognizes that sound legal advice or advocacy serves public ends and that such advice or advocacy depends upon the lawyer being fully informed by the client. . . .

The Court of Appeals, however, considered the application of the privilege in the corporate context to present a "different problem," since the client was an inanimate entity and "only the senior management, guiding and integrating the several operations, . . . can be said to possess an identity analogous to the corporation as a whole." The first case to articulate the so-called "control group test" adopted by the court below . . . reflected a similar conceptual approach. . . . Such a view, we think, overlooks the fact that the privilege exists to protect not only the giving of professional advice to those who can act on it but also the giving of information to the lawyer to enable him to give sound and informed advice. . . .

In the case of the individual client the provider of information and the person who acts on the lawyer's advice are one and the same. In the corporate context, however, it will frequently be employees beyond the control group as defined by the court below—"officers and agents . . . responsible for directing [the company's] actions in response to legal advice"—who will possess the information needed by the corporation's lawyers. Middle-level—and indeed lower-level—employees can, by actions within the scope of their employment, embroil the corporation in serious legal difficulties, and it is only natural that these employees would have the relevant information needed by corporate counsel if he is adequately to advise the client with respect to such actual or potential difficulties. . . .

The control group test adopted by the court below thus frustrates the very purpose of the privilege by discouraging the communication of relevant information by employees of the client to attorneys seeking to render legal advice to the client corporation. The attorney's advice will also frequently be more significant to noncontrol group members than to those who officially sanction the advice, and the control group test makes it more difficult to convey full and frank legal advice to the employees who will put into effect the client corporation's policy.

The narrow scope given the attorney-client privilege by the court below not only makes it difficult for corporate attorneys to formulate sound advice when their client is faced with a special legal problem but also threatens to limit the valuable efforts of corporate counsel to ensure their client's compliance with the law. In light of the vast and complicated array of regulatory legislation confronting the modern corporation, corporations, unlike most individuals, "constantly go to lawyers to find out how to obey the law," . . . particularly since compliance with the law in this area is hardly an instinctive matter. . . . The test adopted by the court below is difficult to apply in practice, though no abstractly formulated and unvarying "test" will necessarily enable courts to decide questions such as this with mathematical precision. But if the purpose of the attorney-client privilege is to be served, the attorney and client must be able to predict with some degree of certainty whether particular discussions will be protected. . . .

The communications at issue were made by Upjohn employees to counsel for Upjohn acting as such, at the direction of corporate superiors in order to secure legal advice from counsel. As the magistrate found, "Mr. Thomas consulted with the Chairman of the Board and outside counsel and thereafter conducted a factual investigation to determine the nature and extent of the questionable payments *and to be in a position to give legal advice to the company with respect to the payments."* Information, not available from upper-echelon management, was needed to supply a basis for legal advice concerning compliance with securities and tax laws, foreign laws, currency regulations, duties to shareholders, and potential litigation in each of these areas. The communications concerned matters within the scope of the employees' corporate duties, and the employees themselves were sufficiently aware that they were being questioned in order that the corporation could obtain legal advice. The questionnaire identified Thomas as "the company's General Counsel" and referred in its opening sentence to the possible illegality of payments such as the ones on which information was sought. A statement of policy accompanying the questionnaire clearly indicated the legal implications of the investigation. The policy statement was issued "in order that there be no uncertainty in the future as to the policy with respect to the practices which are the subject of this investigation." It began "Upjohn will comply with all laws and regulations," and stated that commissions or payments "will not be used as a subterfuge for bribes or illegal payments" and that all payments must be "proper and legal." Any future agreements with foreign distributors or agents were to be approved "by a company attorney" and any questions concerning the policy were to be referred "to the company's General Counsel." This statement was issued to Upjohn employees worldwide, so that even those interviewees not receiving a questionnaire were aware of the legal implications of the interviews. Pursuant to explicit instructions from the Chairman of the Board, the communications were considered "highly confidential" when made, and have been kept confidential by the company. Consistent with the underlying purposes of the attorney-client privilege, these communications must be protected against compelled disclosure.

* * * * *

The Court of Appeals declined to extend the attorney-client privilege beyond the limits of the control group test for fear that doing so would entail severe burdens on discovery and create a broad "zone of silence" over corporate affairs. Application of the attorney-client privilege to communications such as those involved here, however, puts the adversary in no worse position than if the communications had never taken place. The privilege only protects disclosure of communications; it does not protect disclosure of the underlying facts by those who communicated with the attorney. . . .

. . . [W]e conclude that the narrow "control group test" sanctioned by the Court of Appeals in this case cannot, consistent with "the principles of the common law as . . . interpreted . . . in light of reason and experience," govern the development of the law in this area.

Our decision that the communications by Upjohn employees to counsel are covered by the attorney-client privilege disposes of the case so far as the responses to the questionnaires and any notes reflecting responses to interview questions are concerned.

CASE QUESTIONS

1. What does the attorney-client privilege protect? What is the purpose of this privilege?
2. What is the "control group" test? Why did the Supreme Court reject the "control group" test? Did the Court announce an alternative test?
3. What test would you formulate to deter-

mine whether an attorney's communications with a corporation's employees are protected?

4. Assume that several employees inform in-house counsel of their concern about safety violations in the company. Should these communications be protected by the attorney-client privilege? How does this contact differ from the employee-attorney contact in *Upjohn?*

Codes of Professional Conduct

Every state has ethical codes of conduct that govern lawyers. Lawyers have certain responsibilities to their clients, to the legal system, and to their own conscience. These responsibilities often result in ethical dilemmas. The American Bar Association, a national organization of attorneys, has approved The Model Rules of Professional Conduct (Model Rules). The Model Rules are offered for state adoption in order to provide national guidelines for professional responsibility and standards for resolving ethical conflicts.

The Model Rules require the lawyer to provide competent representation to a client. Competent representation "requires the legal knowledge, skill, thoroughness and preparation reasonably necessary for the representation." In determining whether to take a case, the lawyer should analyze its complexity, his or her training and experience in the particular field, and the amount of attention the lawyer can devote to the case. Having decided to take a case, the lawyer is bound by the rules to act with reasonable diligence and promptness in representing the client. The lawyer must act with commitment to the client's interests and with zeal in advocating the client's cause. This must be accomplished while abiding by the client's decision regarding the objectives of the representation and while exercising candor to the tribunal before which the case is pending.

The Model Rules require a lawyer to keep a client reasonably informed about the case. The attorney must communicate with the client about matters necessary to permit the client to make informed decisions about the representation. All serious offers made by an opponent must be communicated to the client.

Under the rules, a lawyer must keep confidential all information relating to the representation unless the client consents to its disclosure. If a lawyer knows that a client intends to commit a criminal act that would result in death or substantial bodily harm, the lawyer is free from the confidentiality rule.

The rules permit a lawyer to withdraw from a case if a client refuses to cooperate with the lawyer, uses the lawyer's services to perpetrate a crime, or insists on pursuing an objective the lawyer finds imprudent. A client has a right to discharge a lawyer with or without cause. Upon termination, the lawyer must take steps to protect a client's interest. That includes cooperating with the client or the client's new attorney in releasing the file and refunding any unearned money.

Violation of any of the rules of professional conduct adopted by the state may result in disciplinary action by the proper authority. Penalties range from reprimand to disbarment, depending upon the severity of the violation.

THE JUDICIAL SYSTEM

The judicial system in the United States consists of the federal system and the judicial systems of the 50 states. This means that there are 51 distinct judicial systems. It is not unusual for a firm to do business in a number of states and hence to be subject to the judicial processes in many jurisdictions. It thus behooves the business manager to have a general understanding of the workings of the state and federal judicial systems.

The Federal System

The federal judicial system derives from the U.S. Constitution. Article III provides that "the judicial Power of the United States shall be vested in one supreme Court, and in such inferior Courts as the Congress may from time to time ordain and establish." Pursuant to Article III, Congress has created 13 circuit courts of appeal and 94 district courts (see figure 2–1).

District Courts The basic federal trial court is the U.S. district court. There is at least one district in every state and territory. Many states are divided into more than one district, depending on size, population, and number of lawsuits filed.

The district court has jurisdiction to hear basically two types of cases: *federal question* and *diversity of citizenship*. Jurisdiction is the power of a court to hear a case and is discussed in greater detail later in this chapter. Federal question cases include any claim arising under a federal statute, a treaty, or the U.S. Constitution. Hence, it is proper for a federal district court to hear a case that involves a substantial issue of federal law. Cases involving robbery of federal banks, federal antitrust violations, and interpretations of U.S. treaties with foreign nations are all properly heard by a federal district court because they present federal questions.

Diversity jurisdiction extends to controversies between citizens of different states where the amount in contest exceeds $10,000. A corporation is considered a citizen of the state in which it is incorporated and in which it has its principal place of business. Hence, for purposes of diversity jurisdiction, a corporation holds dual state citizenship.

There must be complete diversity of citizenship; no plaintiff may be a citizen of the same state in which any defendant is a citizen. (A plaintiff is the one who sues another. The defendant in a lawsuit is the one who is being sued.) If there are multiple plaintiffs, each must claim, in good faith, damages exceeding $10,000 not counting interest or court costs. Although plaintiffs may bring a suit in the federal district court when diversity of citizenship is present, they are not required to and may elect instead to file suit in a proper state court. This is because in diversity of citizenship cases the district court has *concurrent jurisdiction*, along with the state courts, as opposed to *exclusive jurisdiction*. However, if plaintiffs sue in a state court, the defendant may have the case removed to the federal district court if the case could have originally been brought in that court. This is referred to as *removal jurisdiction*.

Assume that eight individual plaintiffs sue ABC, Inc. because wastes it dumped into a waterway ultimately polluted the plaintiffs' property. Seven of the plaintiffs are citizens of Ohio, and the eighth is a citizen of Michigan. ABC, Inc. is incorporated under the law of Delaware and has its principal place of business in Michigan. Here, diversity of citizenship is not present because a plaintiff and a defendant are citizens of Michigan. If the Michigan plaintiff was eliminated from the suit, then diversity jurisdiction would be present, assuming that each plaintiff satisfied the jurisdictional amount of more than $10,000. Even then, the plaintiffs may elect to sue in a state court. ABC could, however, have the case removed to the federal district court.

The federal district court sitting in a diversity of citizenship case will apply the law of the state in which it sits. This is known as the *Erie* doctrine, named after a case in which this principle was first announced.[2] The court will, however, apply its own procedural rules, such as rules of evidence and rules of conduct regarding the administration of the trial.

Courts of Appeals

Appeals from the district courts are heard by the U.S. circuit courts of appeals. They also hear appeals from the Tax Court and review administrative agency actions. The Tax Court hears disputes involving tax deficiencies assessed against a taxpayer. Administrative agencies are discussed later in this chapter and more fully in Chapter 4.

The Federal Court Improvements Act established the Court of Appeals for the Federal Circuit. This court hears appeals from specialized tribunals such as the U.S. Court of Claims and the Court of International Trade. The Court of Claims has jurisdiction over cases against the United States, except tort actions against the government are brought in the district court. The Court of International Trade handles cases involving import and export transactions. Additionally, the Court of Appeals for the Federal Circuit hears appeals of cases brought in the district court involving patents, trademarks, copyrights, and federal contracts (see Figure 2–1).

Supreme Court

Sitting atop the federal legal system is the U.S. Supreme Court. Review in the Supreme Court is not usually automatic; in fact, it is very limited. Parties seeking review must normally file a petition for a *writ of certior-*

---

[2] *Erie Railroad Co. v. Tompkins*, 304 U.S. 64 (1938).

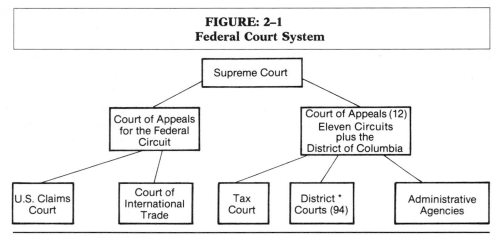

FIGURE: 2–1
Federal Court System

* Cases involving patents, trademarks, copyrights, and contract claims against the United States are reviewed by the Court of Appeals for the Federal Circuit.

ari—that is, a request that the Court hear the case. The Court has absolute discretion to grant or deny the writ, and it rarely gives a reason for a denial. The denial of *certiorari* does not establish a precedent. *Certiorari* is granted if any four of the nine Supreme Court justices are in favor of it. *Certiorari* is likely to be granted when a constitutional issue of national importance is posed or when an issue has been decided in a conflicting manner by the circuit courts of appeals.

A few types of cases are reviewed in the Supreme Court by appeal rather than *certiorari*. For example, there is an appeal from a court of appeals decision declaring a federal statute unconstitutional. In these cases the Court has no discretion but must decide the merits of the appeal.

In rare instances the Supreme Court sits as a court of *original jurisdiction*. In these cases, however, the Court delegates the trial to a "special master" who hears the case and reports findings to the Court. The Court has original and exclusive jurisdiction over all controversies between two or more states and over cases where a foreign ambassador is sued. This means that the U.S. Supreme Court is the only court empowered to hear these cases. In a few other types of cases the Supreme Court has original but not exclusive jurisdiction. That means that the Supreme Court is not the only court empowered to hear these cases. For example, cases in which a state sues the citizens of another state or foreign citizens may be decided in a state court. The U.S. Supreme Court, however, is primarily an appellate tribunal and expressed that perception when it wrote:

> This Court is . . . structured to perform as an appellate tribunal, ill-equipped for the task of factfinding and so forced, in original cases, awkwardly to play the role of factfinder without actually presiding over the introduction of evidence. Nor is the problem merely our lack

of qualifications for many of these tasks potentially within the purview of our original jurisdiction; it is compounded by the fact that for every case in which we might be called upon to determine the facts and apply unfamiliar legal norms we would unavoidably be reducing the attention we could give to those matters of federal law and national import as to which we are the primary overseers.[3]

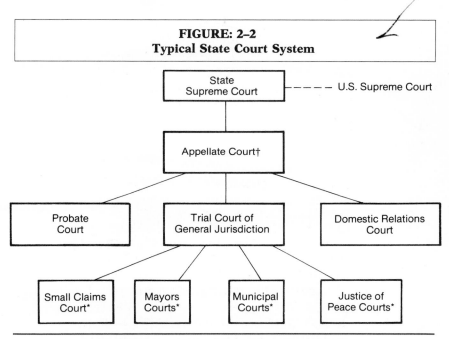

FIGURE: 2–2
Typical State Court System

* In some cases, appeals are made directly to the Appellate Court.
† Not present in the system in smaller, less populous states.

The State System

State trial courts consist of courts of general and limited jurisdiction. A court of general jurisdiction is one which can hear any type of case unless specifically prohibited by statute. Thus, many cases that can be brought in the federal district courts may also have been properly commenced in a state court. Among the exceptions are admiralty, bankruptcy, and patent infringement actions, which may only be brought in federal court. Most state trial courts of general jurisdiction are organized at the county level. Their names vary from state to state. The most popular names are circuit court, court of common pleas, and superior court.

State trial courts of limited jurisdiction are those that can hear only

---

[3] *Ohio v. Wyandotte Chemical Corp.*, 401 U.S. 493, 498 (1971).

specific types of cases. A probate court cannot hear a divorce case; a small claims court cannot try a felony case. Some courts are limited in that they can only hear disputes up to a maximum monetary ceiling.

Many states have a court of appeals, similar to the federal circuit courts of appeals. Following decision by the court of appeals, review may be sought in the state supreme court, which, like the U.S. Supreme Court, reviews most cases by *certiorari.* In the smaller and less populous states, appeals from the trial court are taken directly to the state supreme court, since there is no intermediate court of appeals.

A state supreme court is the highest authority on the law of its state. The U.S. Supreme Court has no power to decide issues of state law. State supreme court decisions interpreting federal statutes, treaties, and the U.S. Constitution are, however, subject to Supreme Court review.

Jurisdiction

Jurisdiction is the power of a court to hear and decide a controversy. In order to exercise this power, a court generally must have jurisdiction over both the *subject matter* of the dispute and the *parties* to the dispute. Jurisdiction over the subject matter is accomplished by selecting a court empowered to hear the type of dispute that it is called upon to decide. State courts of general jurisdiction are usually empowered to hear any type of dispute. The federal courts, as previously observed, have limited subject matter jurisdiction.

Jurisdiction over the person, called *in personam* jurisdiction, may be accomplished by serving the defendant with notice of the suit within the state in which the court is located. The notice is called a *summons.* Personal service was the only authorized method in the early days of our court system. This required a process server to slap the summons in the defendant's hand. Nothing short of that was deemed good service. There are thrilling stories about brave process servers who climbed tall buildings and shuffled along windowsills to serve a defendant with process. There are other stories of less heroic process servers who refused to play cat-and-mouse. Instead, they avoided the "sport" by "sewer service"—filing an affidavit of return of service stating that the defendant had been served when in fact the process server had been unable to locate the defendant. In response, states adopted other methods of service designed to inform the defendant within the state of the suit. Residential service and certified mail service are two of the more common methods. Residential service occurs when the process server leaves the summons with a responsible person at the defendant's residence. Sending the summons by certified mail to the defendant's address has also been adopted as a way of obtaining service. Under certain circumstances publication in a newspaper is an acceptable means of securing service over a defendant.

The requirement that the process be served on the defendant in the state in which the court is located poses a severe limitation. Suppose a defendant who lived in Alaska struck a pedestrian while operating a motor vehicle in Florida. If the Alaskan resident returned home, the injured pedestrian would be forced to sue in Alaska. To combat this shortcoming states enacted *long arm statutes*. A long arm statute is a means of gaining service over an out-of-state defendant. Most states have long arm statutes that subject an out-of-state defendant to the jurisdiction where the defendant is doing business or has committed a civil wrong. Long arm statutes are subjected to constitutional due process scrutiny. In considering the application of a long arm statute, the landmark decision of *International Shoe Co.* v. *Washington* held that the U.S. Constitution requires a defendant, if not present within the territory, to have certain minimum contacts with the territory where the suit is maintained.[4] The next case illustrates the application of the due process standard laid out in *International Shoe.*

Helicopteros Nacionales DE Colombia, S.A. v. Elizabeth Hall

52 U.S.L.W. 4491 (1984)

Helicopteros Nacionales de Colombia (Helicol) (petitioner) is a Colombian corporation having its principal place of business in the city of Bogota. It provides helicopter transportation services for oil and construction companies in South America. Four U.S. citizens were killed when one of Helicol's helicopters crashed in Peru.

The crash victims were working for Consorcio/WSH at the time of the crash. Consorcio/WSH was building a pipeline in Peru and needed helicopters to move personnel, materials, and equipment to and from the construction area.

About two years before the accident, the chief executive officer of Helicol traveled to Houston, Texas, and conferred with representatives of Consorcio/WSH. They negotiated a contract that was later signed in Peru. It stated that controversies arising out of the contract would be decided by the Peruvian courts. It also provided that Consorcio/WSH would make payments to Helicol's bank account with Bank of America in New York. Over $5 million in payments received in these accounts were drawn on a Texas bank. Over about a seven-year period Helicol purchased helicopters and spare parts for more than $4 million from Bell Helicopter Company in Fort Worth. Helicol sent pilots for training to Fort Worth. It also sent management and maintenance personnel to visit Bell Helicopter in Fort Worth.

---

[4] 326 U.S. 310 (1945).

Elizabeth Hall and others, representing the decedent's estates (petitioners), sued Helicol in Texas for wrongful death.* Helicol moved to dismiss the action for lack of *in personam* jurisdiction. The motion was denied and a jury returned a verdict in favor of the decedent's representatives. The Texas Court of Civil Appeals reversed the judgment. The Supreme Court of Texas reversed the judgment of the court of appeals and reinstated the jury's award. The Supreme Court of the United States found in favor of Helicol and reversed the judgment of the Supreme Court of Texas.

Justice Blackmun

The Due Process Clause of the Fourteenth Amendment operates to limit the power of a State to assert *in personam* jurisdiction over a nonresident defendant. Due process requirements are satisfied when *in personam* jurisdiction is asserted over a nonresident corporate defendant that has "certain minimum contacts with [the forum] such that the maintenance of the suit does not offend 'traditional notions of fair play and substantial justice.'" When a controversy is related to or "arises out of" a defendant's contacts with the forum, the Court has said that a "relationship among the defendant, the forum, and the ligitation" is the essential foundation of *in personam* jurisdiction.

Even when the cause of action does not arise out of or relate to the foreign corporation's activities in the forum State, due process is not offended by a State's subjecting the corporation to its *in personam* jurisdiction when there are sufficient contacts between the State and the foreign corporation. . . .

All parties to the present case concede that respondents' claims against Helicol did not "arise out of," and are not related to, Helicol's activities within Texas. We, thus, must explore the nature of Helicol's contacts with the State of Texas to determine whether they constitute . . . continuous and systematic general business contacts. . . .

It is undisputed that Helicol does not have a place of business in Texas and never has been licensed to do business in the State. Basically, Helicol's contacts with Texas consisted of sending its chief executive officer to Houston for a contract-negotiation session; accepting into its New York bank account checks drawn on a Houston bank; purchasing helicopters, equipment, and training services from Bell Helicopter for substantial sums; and sending personnel to Bell's facilities in Fort Worth for training.

The one trip to Houston by Helicol's chief executive officer for the purpose of negotiating the transportation-service contract with Consorcio/WSH cannot be described or regarded as a contact of a "continuous and systematic" nature . . . and, thus, cannot support an assertion of *in personam* jurisdiction over Helicol by a Texas court. Similarly, Helicol's acceptance from Consorcio/WSH of checks drawn on a Texas bank is of negligible significance for purposes of determining whether Helicol had sufficient contacts in Texas. There is no indication that Helicol ever requested that the checks be drawn on a Texas bank

---

* A wrongful death suit is brought on behalf of a deceased person's beneficiaries alleging that the death was caused by the willful or negligent act of another.—Au.

or that there was any negotiation between Helicol and Consorcio/WSH with respect to the location or identity of the bank on which checks would be drawn. Common sense and everyday experience suggest that, absent unusual circumstances, the bank on which a check is drawn is generally of little consequence to the payee and is a matter left to the discretion of the drawer. Such unilateral activity of another party or a third person is not an appropriate consideration when determining whether a defendant has sufficient contacts with a forum State to justify an assertion of jurisdiction. . . .

The Texas Supreme Court focused on the purchases and the related training trips in finding contacts sufficient to support an assertion of jurisdiction. We do not agree with that assessment. . . . [P]urchases and related trips, standing alone, are not a sufficient basis for a State's assertion of jurisdiction.

* * * * *

. . . [W]e hold that mere purchases, even if occurring at regular intervals, are not enough to warrant a State's assertion of *in personam* jurisdiction over a nonresident corporation in a cause of action not related to those purchase transactions. Nor can we conclude that the fact that Helicol sent personnel into Texas for training in connection with the purchase of helicopters and equipment in that State in any way enhanced the nature of Helicol's contacts with Texas. The training was a part of the package of goods and services purchased by Helicol from Bell Helicopter. The brief presence of Helicol employees in Texas for the purpose of attending the training sessions is [not] a significant contact. . . .

We hold that Helicol's contacts with the State of Texas were insufficient to satisfy the requirements of the Due Process Clause of the Fourteenth Amendment.

CASE QUESTIONS

1. What were the contacts between Helicol and the state of Texas?

2. Why were the contacts insufficient to confer personal jurisdiction over Helicol in Texas?

3. What additional contacts would have met the minimum contacts test?

4. Is there a relationship between the heli-copter crash and the contacts between Helicol and Texas? Would it make a difference if the crash occurred as a result of the negligence of a pilot who was trained in Texas? Explain.

5. What if Consorcio/WSH sued Helicol for breach of contract? Could Consorcio/WSH use the long arm statute to gain personal jurisdiction over Helicol in Texas? Explain.

Jurisdiction must be distinguished from *venue*. Venue is concerned with the geographic locality within the jurisdiction where an action should be tried. Venue is specified by statute. Many courts within a particular state may have jurisdiction, but all may not meet the venue requirements. For example, venue may require that the case be heard in the county where the defendant resides or where the property that is the subject of the action is located. When there are multiple defendants, several geographic localities may be proper, and the plaintiff may be authorized to make the selection. When the location of a trial would result in an inconvenience and a hardship, the doctrine of *forum non conveniens* permits a defendant to transfer the case to another geographic location where venue is proper.

THE CIVIL PROCESS

A dispute must involve a *case or controversy* before a court will adjudicate it. Courts do not act when there is no real dispute; otherwise they would be embroiled in unnecessary litigation. Courts are best equipped to decide a case when the parties have a personal stake in the outcome. Under these circumstances the parties have the incentive to expend their best efforts in prosecuting or defending a case. This is the adversary system. In this adversarial environment, courts are in the best position to examine the arguments, find the truth, and apply justice.

TABLE 2–1 Civil versus Criminal Cases		
	Civil	*Criminal*
Who institutes the action?	Individual or business enterprise	Sovereign
Who has been wronged?	Individual or business enterprise	Society
What is the burden of proof?	Preponderance of the evidence*	Beyond a reasonable doubt†
What is the remedy?	Damages, injunction, or other private relief	Punishment (fine and/or imprisonment)

* By the greater weight of the evidence.

† To satisfy this burden the trier of the facts (judge or jury) must have an abiding conviction amounting to a moral certainty of the guilt of the accused. This is a greater burden of proof than "preponderance of the evidence."

Table 2–1 contrasts civil and criminal cases. When an event triggers a dispute, the potential for a lawsuit exists. A lawsuit is a civil case. The civil process is the sequence of events from the beginning of the suit to the end. It consists of three distinct stages: the pleading stage, the discovery stage, and the trial stage. (See figure 2–3.)

The Pleading Stage

A lawsuit begins when the suing party, or *plaintiff*, files a *complaint* with the court. The complaint is a document that identifies the parties and

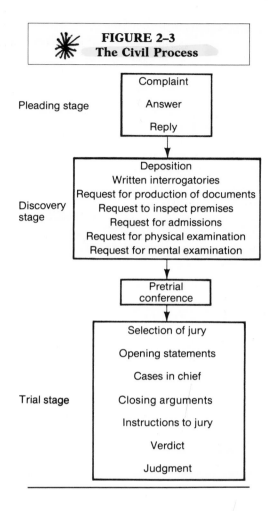

FIGURE 2–3
The Civil Process

Pleading stage
- Complaint
- Answer
- Reply

Discovery stage
- Deposition
- Written interrogatories
- Request for production of documents
- Request to inspect premises
- Request for admissions
- Request for physical examination
- Request for mental examination

- Pretrial conference

Trial stage
- Selection of jury
- Opening statements
- Cases in chief
- Closing arguments
- Instructions to jury
- Verdict
- Judgment

states the basis for the court's jurisdiction, the factual basis of the plaintiff's claim (cause of action), and the remedy the plaintiff seeks. The complaint is served on the *defendant*.

The defendant must then file an *answer*. The answer will admit, deny, or state an inability to admit or deny the particular allegations of the complaint. The defendant may also raise *defenses* to the action in the complaint. For example, in a complaint for breach of contract, the defendant might claim *lack of capacity* to enter into a contract. The defendant may also assert a *counterclaim* against the plaintiff, alleging that the plaintiff, in fact, breached the contract. When the answer sets up a counterclaim, the plaintiff must normally reply by admitting, denying, or stating an inability to admit or deny the particular allegations in the counterclaim. If there are two or more defendants, one of them may assert a *cross claim* against another for any action he or she may have against that defendant. Defendants may also *implead* persons not original parties to the suit who they believe are liable. In a proper case, a person not named as a party to the suit may *intervene*.

Class Action Suits

Under certain circumstances a person may maintain a suit on behalf of a class of people who have been similarly injured. This is known as a *class action suit.* For example, assume that members of the public have been injured as a result of illegally inflated utility prices. It may not be feasible for every injured person to sue the utility company individually. Not everyone may be aware of the illegal activity. The cost of maintaining the suit also may be a deterrent, especially if the amount of potential recovery is too small to be worth the effort. The law in this case may permit one or more persons to undertake a suit against the utility company on behalf of all the injured customers. By consolidating in one suit the claims of many, the class action suit avoids the potential for multiple litigation.

Although the rules on class actions differ from state to state, most states have adopted the rule that prevails in federal courts. The federal class action rule requires:

— A class so numerous that joining all members is not practical
— Questions of law and fact common to each person's claim
— The claim of the representative to be typical of all members within the class

Generally, each member of the class is entitled to notice of the suit. Any member may request to be excluded from the class or may choose his or her own counsel for representation. No class action may be dismissed or settled without court approval.

Class actions have involved thousands and even hundreds of thousands of people. The administration of a class suit is often very difficult because of the number of persons involved. The distribution of the proceeds of a settlement or judgment may be equally difficult. Not all members of the class may be identified or found. Additionally, the amount of distribution to each individual may be disputed. Some courts, aware of this problem, have ordered that damages be distributed to benefit the public. For example, in a case where a utility company charges illegally high rates, a court might order the company to reduce its rates to all consumers for a period of time.

Motions

During the pleading stage, each party (plaintiff or defendant) may make *motions* in an attempt to win the case. Motions are requests to the court to rule on questions of law. Three common motions interposed at this stage are: the motion to dismiss, the motion for judgment on the pleadings, and the motion for preliminary injunction.

Motion to Dismiss	This motion is filed by the defendant. It argues that even if the allegations of the complaint are true, the defendant is entitled to judgment as a *matter of law.* Assume that the plaintiff files suit in a federal district court against a defendant, alleging diversity of citizenship and a debt of $5,000 owed to the plaintiff. Defendant's motion to dismiss the complaint would be granted because the amount in controversy does not exceed $10,000. Hence, the district court lacks jurisdiction over the subject matter and, as a matter of law, the defendant must prevail.
Motion for Judgment on the Pleadings	This motion may be made by either party after all the pleadings have been filed. It argues that on the face of the pleadings the moving party is entitled to judgment as a matter of law. Assume, for example, that the plaintiff files a complaint alleging that the plaintiff entered into a contract with the defendant and was damaged because the defendant did not perform the contract. The defendant then answers by admitting the allegations. Judgment in favor of the plaintiff would be proper because it is clear from the pleadings that the defendant breached the contract.
Motion for Preliminary Injunction	Most people sue for monetary damages, but in some cases a plaintiff will ask the court for an *injunction*—an order compelling the defendant to do something or to refrain from doing something. The plaintiff will not be entitled to a permanent injunction until the end of the case. However, the plaintiff may, in a proper case, obtain a preliminary injunction by demonstrating that (1) the plaintiff is very likely to win on the merits of the case, (2) the plaintiff will suffer irreparable harm if the preliminary injunction is not issued, (3) the injunction will not be unjustly harsh on the defendant, and (4) the injunction is in the public interest.

The Discovery Stage

Parties may participate in discovery proceedings prior to trial. In *discovery* each party seeks to obtain information that is under the control of the other. This information enables the parties to evaluate the strengths and weaknesses of their opponent's case. It is also helpful in preparing for trial and for settlement negotiations.

Discovery may be accomplished by: *interrogatories* (written questions addressed to the other party, who must answer the questions in writing under oath), *requests for documents, requests to admit specific facts,* and *requests to inspect premises.* A *request for a physical* or *mental examination* is permitted when the physical or mental condition of the party is at issue. One of the more frequently used and flexible discovery tools is the *deposition,* whereby potential witnesses (including the parties) are examined under oath by a party's attorney before a court reporter. The deposition gives the parties an idea of how the witnesses will testify at trial. It may also be used at trial to impeach the credibility of a witness whose testimony varies from that given at the deposition.

During the discovery stage, it is not uncommon for a party to make a motion to the court for *summary judgment.* This motion argues that there are no disputed issues of material fact and, therefore, there is no need for a trial. It contends that the moving party is entitled to judgment as a matter of law.

Before trial, there is normally a *pretrial conference.* The judge meets with the attorneys to discuss the issues that must be tried, the length of trial, and the possibility of settlement.

The Trial Stage

If the plaintiff is seeking *legal relief,* that is, monetary damages, the parties are ordinarily entitled to a trial by jury. They may waive this right and try the case to the court. If the plaintiff is seeking *equitable relief* such as an injunction or other court order, the parties are not ordinarily entitled to a jury trial.[5]

The plaintiff has the burden of proving the case by a preponderance of the evidence. Preponderance of the evidence means by the greater weight of the evidence. To sustain that burden of proof, the plaintiff must convince the judge or jury that the facts are probably as the plaintiff alleges. If at the end of the case the trier of the facts is undecided, then the defendant will win.

After selection of the jury (if a jury trial is proper and not waived), counsel for the plaintiff makes an *opening statement,* explaining what he or she intends to prove. Defense counsel may make an opening statement immediately thereafter or reserve the statement until the close of plaintiff's case. Plaintiff then presents the *case-in-chief* by calling witnesses who present testimony and by presenting other evidence, such as business records, photographs, or other tangible objects called *exhibits.* The defendant is given the opportunity to cross-examine the plaintiff's witnesses. The admissibility of the evidence is decided by the judge, based on the law of evidence. The plaintiff rests after completing the case-in-chief.

The defendant frequently makes a *motion for directed verdict* after the plaintiff's case-in-chief. The motion will be granted if, on the basis of the plaintiff's case, reasonable minds cannot differ as to the outcome. If the motion is granted, which rarely happens, the defendant wins. If it is denied, the defendant proceeds with an opening statement, if previously reserved, and presents his or her case-in-chief. When all the evidence has been offered, the defendant may renew the motion for directed verdict. The plaintiff may make a similar motion, arguing that reasonable minds cannot differ as to the outcome and that the plaintiff is entitled to judgment as a matter of law. If these motions are denied, the parties make closing

---

[5] For a fuller treatment of law and equity, see the discussion in chapter 1, beginning on page 34.

arguments. The *closing arguments* attempt to persuade the judge or jury by reasoning from the evidence.

Witnesses often have conflicting versions of a particular event. Other evidence also may be in conflict. If the case was tried to the court, the judge must resolve the conflicts, find the facts, apply the law, and render judgment. If the case was tried to a jury, the judge *instructs the jury* on the applicable law and tells the jury to resolve the factual issues and apply the law to reach a *verdict.* Following the jury's verdict, the losing party may move for *judgment notwithstanding the verdict* (sometimes referred to in the Latin form as *judgment non obstante verdicto,* or abbreviated *judgment n.o.v.*), again arguing that he or she is entitled to judgment as a matter of law. The losing party may also move for a *new trial,* arguing that the verdict is against the clear weight of the evidence. If, however, reasonable minds could reach the same conclusion as the jury, the verdict will not be set aside. The judge then enters a *judgment* in accordance with the verdict. The following case illustrates the application of these trial motions.

James Gibbons Co. v. Hess

407 A.2d 782 (Md. Ct. App. 1979)

Grady Garland was employed by the James F. Gibbons Company (appellant). He died as a result of a work-related accident. Shirley Hess (claimant) filed a workers' compensation action* against Gibbons on behalf of her two children, who were born out of wedlock to Garland and Hess. The Workmen's Compensation Commission denied benefits on the basis that the children were not dependents of the decedent. Hess appealed the finding to the Baltimore City Court, where the question of "dependency" was heard by a jury. At the end of Hess's case Gibbons made a motion for direct verdict, which was denied. The case was submitted to the jury, which found that the children were "wholly dependent upon the deceased." Gibbons thereafter made a motion for judgment notwithstanding the verdict and new trial, which the court overruled. Gibbons appealed those rulings. The Maryland Court of Special Appeals affirmed.

---

* By statute in Maryland, as well as other states, fixed awards are provided to employees for their dependents in case of employment related accidents and diseases. Claims are determined by a state commission, which in Maryland is called the Workmens' Compensation Commission. The commission's decisions may be appealed to the courts, where the case is retried. The subject of Worker's Compensation is discussed further in chapter 16.—Au.

Liss, Judge

The issue raised by this appeal is: Whether the Baltimore City Court erred in denying the employer and insurer's motions for a directed verdict and allowing to stand the jury's verdict that the claimants were wholly dependent upon the deceased at the time of his accidental injury and death.

To a substantial extent, the facts in the case are undisputed. Shirley Hess and the deceased, Grady Garland, were never married, but they were the parents of two children, Angela, born on July 20, 1968, and Grady Scott, born on June 22, 1975. These two children, Mrs. Hess, and Mrs. Hess's four other children from a previous marriage lived with the deceased from 1967 to 1975. In September of 1975, after an argument between Mrs. Hess and Mr. Garland, Mr. Garland left the home to live with his sister. It is undisputed that from September of 1975 until Garland's death on December 16, 1976 the parties did not live together.

The evidence presented at trial showed that Shirley Hess and Grady Garland entered into a paternity agreement in September of 1975 by which Garland agreed to pay the sum of $15.45 per week for the support of each of the children, a total payment of $138.27 per month. A decree was entered evidencing this agreement. Mrs. Hess was then receiving a grant from the Department of Social Services in the amount of $308.00 for the support of the members of her family. As a condition for the continuation of her Social Services grant, Mrs. Hess was required to sign a "form 80" allowing the agency to receive support payments on her behalf, the payments to come out of the weekly payments to be made by the deceased pursuant to the paternity decree. The evidence also indicated that during the period of the deceased's separation from his children he would visit them two or three times a week, and on those occasions Mr.

Garland and Mrs. Hess would "go shopping for groceries, medicine, if the children needed them, anything that they needed," and "Mr. Garland also brought the children clothing, birthday presents . . . generally anything . . . that they needed."

A number of payments were made pursuant to the decrees, and at the time of his death the decedent was in arrears on the required payments. An agent for the Maryland Parole and Probation Department testified that the Department of Social Services grant was made subject to the understanding that when Garland made any payments pursuant to the paternity decree, these funds would be paid to the Social Services Department without any increase or decrease in the grant.

*　*　*　*　*

There was additional testimony by Mrs. Hess that there was a possibility that she and Mr. Garland might resume living together, but she conceded there were "a few little problems we had yet, and besides, he was living in Reisterstown." In any case, no date had been set for the resumption of their previous living arrangement.

In reviewing the propriety of the trial judge's action in denying a directed verdict or judgment n.o.v., we are required to resolve all conflicts in the evidence in favor of the plaintiff, to assume the truth of all credible evidence presented in support of the plaintiff, and to accept as true all inferences naturally and legitimately arising from the evidence which tend to support the plaintiff's right to recover. If there is competent evidence, however slight, tending to support the plaintiff's right to recover, the case should be submitted to the jury and the motion for judgment n.o.v. denied.

Appellant urges that the trial court erred in denying appellant's motions for a directed verdict and by allowing the jury's verdict that the claimants were wholly dependent on the deceased to stand.

Maryland Code . . . provides: "In all cases, questions of dependence, in whole, or in part, shall be determined by the Commission in accordance with the facts in each particular case existent at the time of the injury resulting in death of such employee. . . ." Appellant argues that this section requires the Commission to consider only the facts existent at the time of the injury and to determine from those facts whether the claimant was actually receiving the necessities of life from the decedent. . . .

There [are], however, . . . cases that [suggest] that dependency may be found when the facts existent at the time of injury reveal that the claimant had in the past substantially received the necessities of life from the workman, that a temporary lapse had occurred in the workman's support of the claimant, and that a reasonable probability existed that the support of the claimant would resume in the near future. . . .

*   *   *   *   *

It is our function in this case to determine whether there was evidence legally sufficient to be submitted to the jury. We are convinced that there was. We conclude that based on the evidence in this case the question of dependency was a question of fact, not of law. There was evidence from which the jury might have found that the deceased after separation remained in the area at a known address and phone number; that he continued to be employed in the immediate area; that he regularly visited the children; that in addition to signing a paternity decree in which he obligated himself to pay support for the children on a monthly basis, he regularly purchased groceries, clothing, medicine and other needs of the children; that the deceased made regular payments on the order in the paternity cases from November 24, 1975 until February 3, 1976, though he was substantially in arrears when he died in December, 1976; that deceased did not marry anyone or arrange to live with another woman; that at the time of his death the deceased and Mrs. Hess were actively engaged in discussing a reestablishment of their family. These facts were sufficient to require the trial court to deny appellant's motion for directed verdict and to deny its motion for judgment n.o.v. or for a new trial.

CASE QUESTIONS

1. What issue does this case present?

2. Does the court's concept of "dependency" line up with yours? Explain. What was the claimant's legal theory? What facts supported that theory?

3. What would this court have done if the jury in this case had returned in favor of Gib-bons? What do a motion for directed verdict and a motion for judgment notwithstanding the verdict have in common?

4. How could you modify the facts in this case so that the appellant's motions should be granted?

Once the trial court makes a final judgment in the case, the losing party may appeal to an appellate court. The losing party may not, however, institute a new suit against the same parties involving the same issues.

This would be barred by a doctrine called *res judicata* (the matter has been decided).

Appeals

The legal system provides an opportunity for a party to ask a higher court to review a case for error committed by the trial court judge. The basis for such a request might be that the judge's ruling on a motion was wrong or that the judge's instruction to the jury misstated the law. The courts that review trial court decisions are called *appellate courts*. These courts review the trial record to determine whether or not a party's claim that a serious error was made is true. An appellate court does not hold a new trial, nor does it hear additional evidence; it merely reviews the record of the trial and listens to the arguments of the party (called the *appellant*) claiming some serious error in that trial. The appellate court also listens to the arguments of the opposing party (called the *appellee*), who may be claiming that no serious error occurred.

After reviewing the record of the trial and the arguments of the parties involved, the appellate court has several alternatives. It can (1) *affirm* the verdict of the trial court, that is, accept it as is and change nothing; (2) *reverse* the verdict, which is to decide that the outcome of the trial was wrong; (3) *modify* the legal remedy provided by the trial court; or (4) *remand* the case to the trial court level for further proceedings.

The great majority of trial cases never reach the appellate level, since the parties involved simply accept the verdict of the trial court. When cases are appealed, the appellate court judges often decide to write down the reasons for their decision, as a guide to the parties involved and also as a guide to anyone who may have a similar problem in the future. These written decisions create precedent.

The appeal is decided by at least three appellate judges. A majority vote decides the issues. One judge is usually assigned to write the majority's opinion, which constitutes the *opinion of the court*. A judge may disagree with the majority by writing a *dissenting opinion*. A *concurring opinion* may be written by a judge who agrees with the result but for different reasons. These written legal opinions constitute almost all the cases presented in this book.

THE CRIMINAL PROCESS

The criminal process begins when a *sworn affidavit* is filed with the court charging a defendant with the commission of a crime. Depending upon the nature of the offense charged, the defendant will be arrested (if not already in custody) or merely summoned to appear in court to answer the charge. When arrested, the defendant is given an opportunity to post a bond and be released pending the next court appearance. The only purpose of the bond is to insure the defendant's appearance at trial; it is not designed to punish the accused. A failure to appear results in a forfeiture of the amount of the bond. If the judge is convinced that a bond is not necessary to insure the defendant's appearance, the judge may release the defendant on his or her *own recognizance*.

In felony cases many states provide for a *preliminary hearing* to determine whether there is probable cause to bind the defendant over to the grand jury. The grand jury usually consists of 15 to 23 jurors, depending upon the locality, who sit to determine whether there is sufficient evidence to require the defendant to stand trial. Absent sufficient evidence, the grand jury will *ignore* the case and the defendant will go free. If the grand jury determines that there is sufficient evidence, then it will *indict*, and the defendant must stand trial. A defendant can waive the grand jury procedure and request the prosecution to proceed on a *bill of information*, a simpler procedure. After indictment or a bill of information, the defendant is *arraigned* before a judge. At that time the defendant is called upon to enter a *plea*. The most common pleas are guilty, not guilty, and not guilty by reason of insanity. Some states recognize the plea of *nolo contendere* (no contest), a plea that admits the facts in the indictment but questions whether the defendant is guilty under those facts.

If a plea of guilty is entered, then the judge will *sentence* the defendant. Many states provide for a *presentence report*. The presentence report is compiled by the probation department or other office of the court. It contains a profile of the defendant and aids the judge in providing detailed information about the defendant. If a *nolo contendere* plea is entered, then the judge must decide whether the facts as contained in the indictment constitute the crime as charged. If a plea of not guilty or not guilty by reason of insanity has been entered, then the defendant will be afforded a full trial.

The format of the criminal trial is very similar to that of the civil trial. A defendant is ordinarily entitled to a jury trial unless this has been waived. The prosecutor has the burden of proof to show the defendant's guilt beyond a reasonable doubt. This is accomplished through the presentation of testimony and tangible evidence. At the end of the prosecutor's case-in-chief the defendant may move for a *judgment acquittal* on the basis that the prosecutor failed to produce sufficient evidence to sustain a conviction. If the motion is overruled, then the defendant has an opportunity to present evidence. The defendant does not have to testify because there is a constitutional privilege against self-incrimination. In fact, the jury is instructed by the judge not to draw an unfavorable inference from the failure of the defendant to take the stand and testify.

After the defendant's case-in-chief, closing arguments, and instructions to the jury, the jury retires to deliberate. In most states, the verdict of the jury must be unanimous. If a jury cannot reach a verdict, then the jury is referred to as *hung* and the defendant must be retried or the case dismissed. Normally the jury deliberates and reaches a verdict of acquittal or conviction. If convicted, the defendant will be sentenced. The conviction is subject to review by the appellate courts.

THE REGULATORY PROCESS

Both the federal government and state government perform various functions. Those functions include regulating private conduct. Government employs the administrative process and administrative agencies to accomplish this end. An administrative agency is not a court, yet it often possesses the power to make law by deciding cases. An administrative agency is not a legislative body, yet it is often empowered to enact rules and regulations, which have the force of law. An administrative agency is established by the legislative or executive branch of government, and as such it is an agent of its creator. In many instances it is vested with the power to enforce statutes and agency rules through criminal and civil sanctions.

Administrative agencies run the gamut from those that exact taxes, such as the Internal Revenue Service, to those that disburse monies, such as the Social Security Administration. In between are the administrative agencies that have been created to regulate certain activities and industries. Price fixing, product safety, creditor practices, securities, labor-management relations, and pollution are a few of the areas regulated by specific administrative agencies.

Administrative agencies are established to perform specialized tasks. They are usually heavily staffed and organized along hierarchical lines. These agencies are well suited for their assigned tasks because of their expertise and experience. The Environmental Protection Agency, for example, analyzes highly technical data involving the impact of various potential pollutants and activities on the environment. The agency's expertise in this area is greater than that of the courts or Congress; hence, presumably, it can do the work more efficiently. The regulatory process via administrative agencies is detailed in chapter 4 and will be considered throughout this book.

THE FIRM'S INTERACTION WITH GOVERNMENT

Corporate activities which are perceived as socially undesirable often provoke governmental regulatory responses. Businesses therefore frequently attempt to influence government action.

Efforts to Influence Political Campaigns and Elections

Many state governments have enacted laws regulating political campaigns in general and political contributions in particular. These laws apply to state and local election campaigns and are as varied as the state governments that have enacted them.

Federal elections are governed by the Federal Election Campaign Act (FECA). The act specifically prohibits federal election campaign contributions by national banks, federally chartered corporations, and labor unions. It further prohibits contributions by businesses and others that enter into or are negotiating contracts with the federal government. All other persons and businesses are limited in the amount of the federal campaign contributions they can make. Individual contributions may not exceed $1,000 to any one candidate and $25,000 in total during any calendar year.

A phenomenon which is changing the face of American politics is the rise of political action committees (PACs). PACs are organizations formed by corporations, labor organizations, trade associations, or other groups of persons to receive money and distribute it to political candidates. PACs are not necessarily aligned with a political party but rather with an interest or a cause.

FECA permits individuals to contribute up to $5,000 per year to PACs. A PAC may distribute $5,000 per candidate per election with no aggregate maximum. PACs are becoming an increasingly more important source of political contributions. They enable individuals to indirectly give more than their $1,000 per candidate limit. And, candidates looking for money may find it easier to solicit funds from an identifiable group than from an amorphous mass of individuals. In 1984 PAC money donated to the presidential candidates for their campaigns represented a very significant percentage of the total contributions to the candidates.

Lobbying

Lobbying is the act of influencing government. It is as old as government and is a constitutionally protected right. Today there are over 9,000 individuals and 600 law and public relations firms strategically located in Washington for the purpose of representing their own or their client's best interest. This does not include, of course, the manifold more working at the state and local level of government. Lobbyists represent an array of clientele and interests including trade and professional associations, labor unions, corporations, special interest groups and issues.

Lobbying has taken on new dimensions since the seamy 19th century practice when it was quite individualized: the representative sought something of value from the state on behalf of its client, for example, charters, subsidies, loans, or other favored treatment. Today governmental influence has added the flavor of associational lobbying. Groups with common interests, often economic competitors, band together to achieve a purpose for the collective good. Lobbying is marked by a rise of special interest and single issue organizations seeking cooperatively to further causes by the passage of laws or the blocking of their passage.

The Federal Regulation of Lobbying Act (FRLA) regulates lobbying activities. FRLA defines lobbyists as those who, for pay, attempt to influence the passage or defeat of legislation before Congress. The act does not cover individuals who engage in lobbying on their own behalf or who confine their lobbying activities to testifying before Congress. It also does not cover individuals who are not paid for their lobbying activities.

Under the FRLA every lobbyist is required to register with both houses of Congress. The registration must include the lobbyist's name and address, the lobbyist's employer, the amount and source of the lobbyist's compensation and expense account, the types of expenses that the employer reimbursed, and the duration of the lobbyist's employment. Each lobbyist is also required to file quarterly reports detailing a financial accounting of monies received and expended, the purposes of the receipts and payments, and other information pertaining to the lobbyist's activities.

Persons and organizations that solicit contributions used to support or defeat legislation before Congress are also required to file quarterly reports. These reports must include the name and address of persons contributing $500 or more and other pertinent financial data.

The First Amendment to the Constitution guarantees the right to free speech, press and the right to petition the government. Many activities designed to influence governmental action, which might otherwise be illegal, are protected by the First Amendment.

For example, the Sherman Antitrust Act, as discussed in Chapter 10, prohibits two or more companies to conspire together to restrain trade. Companies may, however, lobby the legislature and administrative agencies to pass laws that would injure those companies' competitors without violating the Sherman Act. In fact, this would still be protected conduct even if the sole intent of the company was to eliminate their competitors. However, there are limits. Companies which band together to deliberately prevent a competitor from using the political process will not find protection in the First Amendment as the next case well illustrates.

 **California Motor Transport Co. v. Trucking Unlimited**

404 U.S. 508 (1972)

Trucking Unlimited and others (respondents) are highway carriers. They sued California Motor Transport Co. and others (petitioners) who are also highway carriers. Trucking Unlimited charged California Motor Transport with conspiracy to monopolize trade and commerce in the transportation of goods in violation of the Sherman Antitrust Act. (That act is discussed in detail in chapters 10 and 11.) Respondents alleged that petitioners engaged in concerted action to institute state and federal proceedings to resist and defeat applications by respondents to acquire operating rights or to transfer or register those rights. The district court dismissed the complaint. The court of appeals reversed. The U.S. Supreme Court affirmed the court of appeal's decision.

Justice Douglas

The present case is akin to *Eastern Railroad Conference v. Noerr Motor Freight* where a group of trucking companies sued a group of railroads to restrain them from an alleged conspiracy to monopolize the long-distance freight business in violation of the antitrust laws and to obtain damages. We held that no cause of action was alleged insofar as it was predicated upon mere attempts to influence the Legislative Branch for the passage of laws or the Executive Branch for their enforcement. We rested our decision on two grounds:

1. "In a representative democracy such as this, these branches of government act on behalf of the people and, to a very large extent, the whole concept of representation depends upon the ability of the people to make their wishes known to their representatives. To hold that the government retains the power to act in this representative capacity and yet hold, at the same time, that the people cannot freely inform the government of their wishes would impute to the Sherman Act a purpose to regulate, not business activity, but political activity, a purpose which would have no basis whatever in the legislative history of that Act."
2. "The right of petition is one of the freedoms protected by the Bill of Rights, and we cannot, of course, lightly impute to Congress an intent to invade these freedoms."

The same philosophy governs the approach of citizens or groups of them to administrative agencies (which are both creatures of the legislature, and arms of the executive) and to courts, the third branch of Government. Certainly the right to petition extends to all departments of the Government. The right of access to the courts is indeed but one aspect of the right of petition.

We conclude that it would be destructive of rights of association and of petition to hold that groups with common interests may not, without violating the antitrust laws, use the channels and procedures of state and federal agencies and courts to advocate their causes and points of view respecting resolution of their business and economic interests [with relation to] their competitors.

We said, however, in *Noerr* that there may be instances where the alleged conspiracy "is a mere sham to cover what is actually nothing more than an attempt to interfere directly with the business relationships of a competitor and the application of the Sherman Act would be justified."

In that connection the complaint in the present case alleged that the aim and purpose of the conspiracy was "putting their competitors, including plaintiff, out of business, of weakening such competitors, of destroying, eliminating, and weakening existing and potential competition, and of monopolizing the highway common carriage business in California and elsewhere."

More critical are other allegations, which are too lengthy to quote, and which elaborate on the "sham" theory by stating that the power, strategy, and resources of the petitioners were used to harass and deter respondents in their use of administrative and judicial proceedings so as to deny them "free and unlimited access" to those tribunals. The result, it is alleged, was that the machinery of the agencies and the courts was effectively closed to respondents, and petitioners indeed became "the regulators of the grants of rights, transfers and registrations" to respondents—thereby depleting and diminishing the value of the businesses of respondents and aggrandizing petitioners' economic and monopoly power.

Petitioners rely on our statement in *Pennington* that *"Noerr* shields from the Sherman Act a concerted effort to influence public officials regardless of intent or purpose." In the present case, however, the allegations are not that the conspirators sought "to influence public officials," but that they sought to bar their competitors from meaningful access to adjudicatory tribunals and so to usurp that decisionmaking process. It is alleged that petitioners "instituted the proceedings and actions . . . with or without probable cause, and regardless of the merits of the cases. . . ."

There are many . . . forms of illegal and reprehensible practice which may corrupt the administrative or judicial processes and which may result in antitrust violations. Misrepresentations, condoned in the political arena, are not immunized when used in the adjudicatory process. Opponents before agencies or courts often think poorly of the other's tactics, motions, or defenses and may readily call them baseless. One claim, which a court or agency may think baseless, may go unnoticed; but a pattern of baseless, repetitive claims may emerge which leads the factfinder to conclude that the administrative and judicial processes have been abused. That may be a difficult line to discern and draw. But once it is drawn, the case is established that abuse of those processes produced an illegal result, [namely], effectively barring respondents from access to the agencies and courts. Insofar as the administrative or judicial processes are involved, actions of that kind cannot acquire immunity by seeking refuge under the umbrella of "political expression."

* * * * *

. . . [W]hen applied to the instant controversy, the following conclusions [are] clear: (1) that any carrier has the right of access to agencies and courts, within the limits, of course, of their prescribed procedures, in order to defeat applications of its competitors for certificates as highway carriers; and (2) that its purpose to eliminate an applicant as a competitor by denying him free and meaningful access to the agencies and courts may be implicit in that opposition.

First Amendment rights may not be used as the means or the pretext for achieving "substantive evils" which the legislature has the power to control. A combination of entrepreneurs to harass and deter their competitors from having "free and unlimited access" to the agencies and courts, to defeat that right by massive, concerted, and purposeful activities of the group are ways of building up one empire and destroying another. . . . If these facts are proved, a violation of the antitrust laws has been established. If the end result is unlawful, it matters not that the means used in violation may be lawful.

CASE QUESTIONS

1. What activity was alleged to be a violation of the antitrust laws? What branches of government were employed to defeat competition?

2. What limitations did the Court place upon attempts to influence governmental action?

3. Formulate a legally protected campaign designed to gain a competitive advantage by influencing government.

4. In light of *California Transport,* what policies would you suggest for a company seeking to engage in influencing government?

Other Business Efforts to Influence Government Action

The federal criminal code establishes two types of offenses—bribery and gratuities—for the giving of money or anything else of value to government employees. A person convicted of bribery is subject to a maximum penalty of 15 years in prison and three times the amount of the bribe. A person convicted of offering or giving a gratuity is subject to a maximum penalty of two years in prison and a $10,000 fine. Similar penalties are imposed upon government employees convicted of soliciting or receiving bribes and gratuities.

The bribery and gratuity prohibitions encompass the giving or promising of anything of value to a government employee. A *bribe* is a payment or promise that is intended as an exchange for official action that might otherwise not be undertaken. A *gratuity* is any payment or promise, regardless of whether it is specifically designed to procure official action. Thus, gratuities encompass payments made to administrative officials to speed up the approval of applications which would have been approved anyway.

Prohibitions against outright gifts do not eliminate the opportunities for more subtle influences upon government officials. Consequently, other regulatory and statutory provisions have been designed to bolster the anti-bribery law. It is a criminal offense for a former government employee to represent a client (other than the United States) in a matter before any agency, department, committee, or court (involving the United States) in which that employee participated personally and substantially while so employed. Violations of this provision subjects the former employee to a prison sentence of up to two years and a fine of up to $10,000. A partner of a former government employee is subject to similar prohibitions. The partner may be imprisoned up to one year and fined up to $5,000.

It is a civil offense for any elected or appointed official or any employee of any branch of the federal government to accept any honorarium of more than $2,000 for a speaking engagement.

Efforts to Influence Foreign Government

In response to many disclosures of corporate acts of foreign bribery, Congress enacted the Foreign Corrupt Practices Act. The act specifies accounting methods and disclosures to be made by companies that the Securities and Exchange Commission regulates.

The act also criminalizes certain corrupt practices perpetrated in foreign countries and in dealings with foreigners. It specifically prohibits giving anything of value to any foreign official for the purpose of influencing any official action by a foreign government. The act also prohibits gifts to any foreign political party or candidate for the purpose of influencing the outcome of a foreign election, where the motivation is to gain a business advantage. The act restricts the class of illegal payments to those made to foreign officials, rather than all employees of foreign governments, and to those intended to influence the performance of official acts. The act does not appear to prohibit "grease" payments to speed up routine matters.

ALTERNATIVE APPROACHES

In recent years there has been an explosion in the number of lawsuits. Both federal and state judicial structures are being overtaxed. The Supreme Court of the United States receives about 5,000 new filings per year and selects less than 200 cases to hear. The circuit courts of appeals receive more than three times that number and do not normally have the discretion to deny a hearing. Federal trial court dockets have increased every year at a staggering rate over the last decade. In some state courts the docket control problem has been even greater.

It has been suggested that the surge in litigation is due to the increase in population. The population of the United States grew from about 130 million in 1940 to about 215 million in 1980. Although the population growth rate appears to have declined, it is expected to accelerate in the future. The increase in the number of people heightens the potential for conflict.

The passage of new legislation is another possible reason for the trend toward litigation. For example, the Consumer Credit Protection Act, Fair Credit Reporting Act, Consumer Product Safety Act, and other recent legislative enactments have expanded consumer rights and created new causes of action.

The availability of legal services has also contributed to the groundswell in litigation. The federal government provides grants to private corporations that serve clients through legal assistance programs at hundreds of offices throughout the United States. Nonprofit public interest law firms have been increasing in number. These firms concentrate on litigation involving such public policy concerns as environmental and consumer protection, land and energy use, health care, welfare benefits, and corporate responsibility. Through their efforts more and more people have become conscious of their legal rights and have exercised those rights through litigation. Traditionally, attorney's fees were paid by each individual litigant, and this discouraged some potential litigants from instituting suits. However, statutory authorization of attorney's fees to victorious plaintiffs has become common. The Fair Labor Standards Act, the Securities Act of 1933, and the Fair Debt Collection Practices Act are a few of the acts that extend this right to plaintiffs. This creates an incentive to litigate.

One possible solution to the impending litigation crisis is to expand the judiciary. However, there are obstacles to this solution. For example, the funds for additional judges may be unavailable.

Some advocate eliminating the diversity jurisdiction of the federal courts. This measure could eliminate up to 50 percent of a given district court's case load. Although the measure would add to the case load at the state level, its impact would be spread over many state courts, so that the diversion would hardly be noticeable.

Another possible solution is to encourage the use of available dispute resolution procedures outside the court system. One such procedure is the use of *neighborhood mediation centers* through which local residents could handle local disputes. *Mediation* involves an intermediary to assist in bringing the parties to a resolution of the conflict. Although mediation is a means of assisting the parties in reconciling a dispute, the mediator has no power to force a solution.

Another means for relieving the pressure on the judicial system is compulsory and binding *arbitration*. An arbitrator acts like a judge, decides a dispute, and binds the parties to the judgment. Courts could delegate the resolution of cases to private arbitration panels. Arbitration is swifter and less costly than court litigation. Rules of evidence are relaxed, and the proceedings are normally less formal than those employed by a judge. Arbitrators can be selected on the basis of their particular areas of expertise. An alternative procedure is to require arbitration in certain cases (for example, cases involving a controversy of less than $50,000) as a prerequisite to invoking the judiciary; any dissatisfied party could proceed to the proper court.

The U.S. Arbitration Act provides for arbitration of maritime disputes, and certain contract disputes where the parties had previously agreed to submit the matter to arbitration. Most states have statutes that provide for binding arbitration under certain circumstances. The use of judicially mandated arbitration could be legislatively expanded to include more types of cases. Voluntary arbitration is available through the American Arbitration Association and other private arbitration associations. The use of this service could be increased by making its availability better known.

Some have suggested that administrative tribunals be established to curb the rising tide of cases. These tribunals would hear cases that involve repetitious factual issues arising out of specialized legislation. The tribunals could maintain flexibility by conducting hearings informally and without counsel when feasible. Appeals from the tribunal's decisions could be processed by the appellate courts in the same manner that they now process appeals from administrative agency decisions. The tribunals would gain expertise in handling complex factual issues that recur in cases dealing with, for example, energy, safety, and health. This would free courts of their overload. At least one scholar[6] has suggested that:

> Alternatively one might envision by the year 2000 not simply a court house but a Dispute Resolution Center, where the grievant would first be channelled through a screening clerk who would then direct him to the process (or sequence of processes) most appropriate to his type of case. The room directory in the lobby of such a Center might look as follows:

Screening Clerk	Room 1
Mediation	Room 2
Arbitration	Room 3
Fact Finding	Room 4
Malpractice Screening Panel	Room 5
Superior Court	Room 6

Perhaps the resolution of the growing litigation crisis lies not in any one method but in a combination.

---

[6] Frank E. A. Sander, *Varieties of Dispute Processing,* 70 F.R.D. 111, 131 (1976).

CHAPTER PROBLEMS

1. Plastic Corporation manufactures plastic containers that are sold to bottling companies. The bottling companies fill the containers with liquid and secure them with leak-proof caps. John T. purchased from Ace Hardware a bottle of Prevention Plus, a sulfuric acid based liquid drain unstopper. While carrying the bottle home, it leaked, causing severe burns about John T.'s body. The container was manufactured by Plastic Corporation and the Prevention Plus was bottled by Sure Bottle Company. John T. threatens to sue. Plastic Corporation seeks to hire an attorney. How should Plastic Corporation select an attorney? As a managerial executive in Plastic

Corporation, what is your objective in this conflict? Assume that your lawyer informs you that John T. is willing to settle the case for $10,000. What other information do you need in order to determine whether to settle or not?

2. J. P. Honey was a licensed real estate sales associate. He worked for the real estate brokerage firm of Decade Today Realtors as an office manager. As office manager, J. P. handled customers' monies. These monies were to be deposited in escrow accounts in strict accordance with the State Division of Real Estate Regulations. J. P. delegated this task to his assistant manager and brother-in-law Brad Stinson.

(J. P.'s wife, Angela Honey, was Stinson's sister.) Stinson often signed J. P.'s name to ledger sheets and deposit accounts in order to accomplish the task. J. P. was aware of this practice. Stinson mishandled $50,000. Instead of depositing the $50,000 in the appropriate escrow account, he lost the money at the race track. Then, in desperation, Stinson called upon his sister to help him out of the financial mess.

Angela, sympathetic to her brother's plight, went to the bank and borrowed $50,000 on an open end credit arrangement that she and her husband had with the bank. She gave the $50,000 to her brother who placed it in the escrow accounts to make up the deficit. Stinson signed his brother's-in-laws name to the deposit slips.

Two months later, during a company audit, the misappropriation was discovered. Stinson admitted to his wrongdoing and was immediately fired. The vice president of operations, who is in charge of the audit, finds it very difficult to believe that J. P. was unaware of the $50,000 shortage and did not know his wife borrowed the money to help her brother cover up the shortage. J. P. Honey has turned a very good profit for the company in the 12 years he has been working for Decade Today Realtors. A clause in the contract between Honey and the company states "In the event Honey is discharged for any reason, Honey is entitled to $10,000 severance pay."

The vice president of operations recommends that Honey be terminated. The vice president of finances recommends that Honey be retained. The president of the company consults with in house counsel, vice president in charge of finance, and vice president of operations to determine what to do about J. P. Honey.

As president of the company, explore the relevant considerations and formulate a plan of action.

3. Al Ladin, attorney for Spray Lawn, Inc., suspected that two of Spray Lawn's lower echelon employees were diverting the corporation's funds to their own use. Ladin confronted the employees with his suspicions, and they both confessed. At Ladin's insistence the employees wrote a detailed account of their activities involving the diversion of company funds. Their employment was then terminated. Subsequently the IRS conducted an audit of Spray Lawn, Inc., and issued a summons for the written statements in Ladin's possession. Must Ladin produce the statements? Explain. Could the IRS derive the desired information in any other way?

4. American Cyanamid Company is suing Hercules Powder Company for infringement of its Daniel Patent No. 2,595,935. American alleges that Hercules' sales of resin products under its Keim patents infringe the Daniel patent. Each party is attempting to obtain documents from the other; however, each is also resisting the discovery of the other by invoking the attorney-client privilege. Hercules asserts that communications from Peverill, a lawyer in its employ, are protected by the privilege. The documents in question were prepared by Peverill, however, they do not pertain to legal matters but contain information regarding prior patents and the manufacture of certain resins.

American contends that letters received by it from Hoxie and Kelton, two New York lawyers working as outside counsel for American, are protected from disclosure by the attorney-client privilege. The letters, prepared for American prior to the sale of its Keim patent resins, concern an analysis of whether the employment of these resins in producing paper infringes the claims of the Daniel patent.

Are the communications between American and its lawyers and between Hercules and its lawyer protected by the attorney-client privilege? Explain.

5. Sadler was indebted to Balcon, Inc. as a result of a business transaction in Maryland. Balcon, Inc. instituted suit in North Carolina against Sadler. Sadler was not a resident of North Carolina. He did, however, own real estate in North Carolina. How may the North Carolina court obtain *in personam* jurisdiction over Sadler? Explain.

6. Harry and Kay Robinson purchased a new Audi in New York. The Robinsons, who were residents of New York, thereafter left the state, in their Audi, for a new home in Arizona. While they were passing through the state of Oklahoma, their Audi was rear-ended by another automobile. Mrs. Robinson and her two children were severely burned in the accident. The Robinsons brought suit against the Audi manufacturer

(Audi), its importer (Volkswagen), its regional distributor (Worldwide), and its dealer (Seaway), claiming that the injuries resulted from a defective design and placement of Audi's gas tank. Audi is a foreign corporation. Volkswagen, Worldwide, and Seaway all have their principal place of business in New York and are incorporated in the State of New York. None of the defendants does business in Oklahoma, ships or sells any products to that state, or advertise in any media calculated to reach Oklahoma. What is the outcome of the suit and why?

7. UHF, Inc., a citizen of the state of California, manufactured a weather insulation. It sold the insulation to contractors who installed it in buildings throughout the United States. The insulation was found to be hazardous to health. Thousands of people suffered injury as a result. Hundreds of thousands more have been exposed to the insulation. What are the potential consequences to UHF, Inc.?

8. Professor Ephraim Cross is employed by New York University to teach French, Spanish, and Romance linguistics. In June 1954 he and his wife sailed from New York for France via Portugal, Morocco, Algeria, and Italy. Upon arriving in Marseilles, they split up. Mrs. Cross continued to tour, and Mr. Cross, though not pursuing a formal course of study, visited schools, courts of law, churches, book publishers, and restaurants; read magazines; listened to radio broadcasts; conversed with students and teachers; and attended political meetings. Cross and his wife returned to New York in September, in time for Cross to resume his teaching schedule at NYU. In 1955 Cross filed his income tax return and deducted the full cost of the trip he and his wife took to Europe.

The IRS objected to the deduction and brought suit against Cross, demanding payment of the amount he allegedly underpaid. Cross contended that the deduction was pursuant to the Internal Revenue Code provision that allows deductions for all expenses incurred in carrying on a trade or business. Cross presented affidavits

of other professors that indicated the desirability and necessity of foreign travel for a professor of foreign languages. He then motioned for a summary judgment. Cross contended that the summary judgment was appropriate under the circumstances.

Do you agree? What is the criterion for granting a summary judgment? What if Cross listed separately the expenses incurred by his wife and himself and sought to deduct only his own expenses? Would additional information still be required? Explain.

9. The American Medical Association (AMA), comprised of over 200,000 medical doctors, was engaged in efforts to prevent chiropractors from furnishing care in hospitals. Toward that end the AMA adopted a resolution asserting:

> It is the position of the medical profession that chiropractic is an unscientific cult whose practitioners lack the necessary training and background to diagnose and treat human disease.

The AMA was heavily involved in legislative work at state and national levels to accomplish its goal of eliminating chiropractors from the health care industry. Five chiropractors sued the AMA charging them with illegal attempts to restrain trade. At the trial the judge instructed the jury as follows:

> The AMA's advocacy activity directed to the legislative and administrative agencies or bodies is protected if the AMA undertook such efforts to influence governmental bodies with a sincere purpose to obtain the governmental actions that they sought.

Did the judge correctly instruct the jury? Explain.

10. What comprehensive legislation would you propose to reduce court congestion in the federal courts? state courts? Analyze the impact of each legislative recommendation on the courts, business, consumers, and society.

CHAPTER 3

CONSTITUTIONAL LAW

The U.S. government derives its power to regulate business from the Constitution of the United States. Thus, a preliminary question underlying any attempt to regulate business is whether the regulation is consitutional. This chapter focuses on the constitutional provisions that are especially important to business.

CONSTITUTIONALISM, THE CONSTITUTION, AND THE SUPREME COURT

Constitutionalism is a concept that government power is limited by a higher law. Its central principle is that government officials are not free to do as they please. In the United States, this higher law is the U.S. Constitution. This document establishes and empowers the federal government. It also contains a Bill of Rights in the form of its first ten amendments. In the words of the late Justice William O. Douglas, the purpose of the Bill of Rights and other constitutional safeguards is "to take the government off the backs of the people."

The Nature of the U.S. Constitution

The Constitution establishes the federal government and distributes its powers among three branches: the legislative branch, the executive branch, and the judicial branch. This division of governmental powers is known as the concept of *separation of powers*. The Constitution's drafters feared the tyranny of unbridled power in one person or group. Therefore, they separated governmental powers into three branches, with each serving as a check and balance against the other. The interrelationship of the three branches is called the *doctrine of checks and balances*.

The legislative power, the power to enact laws, resides in Congress.

Congress consists of two bodies or houses: the Senate and the House of Representatives. The executive power, which is the power to execute or carry out the law, resides in the Office of the President. The judicial power, which is the power to interpret the law, resides in the Supreme Court and the lower courts.

The Constitution enumerates (lists) the powers of the federal government. Thus, the federal government is said to be one of *enumerated or limited power.* The Constitution expressly reserves the powers not delegated to the federal government to the states or to the people. This concept of dividing governmental responsibility between the federal government and the states is called *federalism.*

Although the U.S. Constitution is the governing document for the federal government, each state has its own constitution. The U.S. Constitution originally applied only to the federal government. However, after the Civil War, the Thirteenth, Fourteenth, and Fifteenth amendments were directed toward the states. These Reconstruction Era amendments outlawed slavery, established rights of citizenship, and protected the right to vote, respectively.

The Supreme Court has interpreted the Fourteenth Amendment as incorporating or absorbing those liberties provided in the Bill of Rights that are fundamental and necessary to the ordered liberty of a free society. By doing so, the Court has interpreted these provisions as limitations upon the states. While not every right contained in the first ten amendments is applied against the states, most are. This process of applying those provisions of the U.S. Constitution to the states through the Fourteenth Amendment is known as the *incorporation doctrine.*

Although the Constitution reflects certain fundamental values of American society, it is important to remember that it limits only government conduct. Government conduct is frequently called *state action.* The Constitution does not apply to purely private conduct. Thus, while the government cannot interfere with a person's freedom of speech, a private employer can forbid its employees to talk while working.

The Role of the Supreme Court

The task of interpreting the Constitution was assumed by the Supreme Court in the 1803 decision of *Marbury v. Madison.*[1] There the Supreme Court reserved for itself the power to declare laws enacted by Congress to be unconstitutional. This is known as the power of *judicial review.* This means that the court can prevent the enforcement of laws or other governmental decisions that it determines to be in violation of the Constitution.

The body of Supreme Court cases interpreting the Constitution makes

---

[1] 1 Cranch 137 (U.S. 1803).

up constitutional law. The Supreme Court is said to be the final arbiter of what the Constitution means. However, the Constitution can be amended with the approval of two-thirds of both houses of Congress and three-fourths of the states. In this way, the people actually possess the final word on any constitutional issue.

THE HISTORICAL CONTEXT OF THE U.S. CONSTITUTION

Before the American Revolution, the 13 colonies exhibited a degree of autonomy. Although created by crown charters and governed by royal governors, the colonies developed substantial experience in self-governance through their legislative assemblies.

When difficulties between Great Britain and the colonies developed in June 1774, the Massachusetts and Virginia assemblies called for an intercolonial meeting of delegates from all the colonies. That September the first Continental Congress met in Philadelphia. When fighting started in Lexington, the Continental Congress became a de facto revolutionary government, coordinating the colonial military effort and declaring independence from Britain in 1776. After this declaration, the Congress began preparing a formal plan of government. In 1778 the states approved a plan of confederation. The plan was contained in the Articles of Confederation. By this plan the 13 states joined in a "firm league of friendship," and little more.

Weaknesses in the Articles of Confederation soon became apparent. For example, Congress had no authority to regulate foreign or interstate commerce. Legislation in this area was left to the individual states.

The U.S. Constitution was a response to the weaknesses of the Articles of Confederation. In place of a loose confederation of states with no central authority over commerce arose a plan for a strong federal government with power "[t]o regulate Commerce with foreign Nations, and among the several States."

FEDERAL POWER TO REGULATE COMMERCE

Every power exercised by the government must be authorized by the Constitution. Thus, whenever the federal government seeks to regulate business activity, the first issue posed is: What is the constitutional basis for the regulation? The Constitution's commerce clause is the most frequent answer.

Article I, section 8, clause 3 of the Constitution provides that Congress shall have power "[t]o regulate Commerce with foreign Nations, and among the several States." Foreign commerce involves imports from and exports to foreign nations. The following discussion concentrates on congressional power to regulate domestic commerce, that is, commerce "among the several States."

Early Supreme Court Interpretation of the Commerce Clause

In 1824, the Supreme Court decided the landmark case of *Gibbons v. Ogden*.[2] New York State had granted Ogden exclusive rights to operate steamboats between New York City and New Jersey. Ogden obtained an injunction against Gibbons's operation of steamboats on the same route. The Supreme Court reversed, because Gibbons had licensed and enrolled his boats pursuant to a federal statute. In sustaining the constitutionality of the federal statute, Chief Justice John Marshall wrote:

> Commerce, undoubtedly, is traffic, but it is something more: it is intercourse. It describes the commercial intercourse between nations, and parts of nations, in all its branches, and is regulated by prescribing rules for carrying on that intercourse. . . .
>
> . . . The word "among" means intermingled with. . . . Commerce among the States cannot stop at the external boundary line of each State, but may be introduced into the interior. . . .
>
> . . . This power [to regulate interstate commerce] . . . is complete in itself, may be exercised to its utmost extent, and acknowledges no limitations other than are prescribed in the Constitution.

Despite the generally broad interpretation of *Gibbons v. Ogden*, Congress rarely exercised its full powers under the commerce clause until 1887, when it passed the Interstate Commerce Act. This was followed by the Sherman Antitrust Act in 1890.

Supreme Court Restrictions of Congressional Commerce Power

Toward the turn of the twentieth century, the Supreme Court restricted the scope of congressional power under the commerce clause. The case of *Hammer v. Dagenhart* (The Child Labor Case) represents the Court's most restrictive view of the commerce clause.[3] A federal statute prohibited the interstate transportation of goods made in factories that employed children. Although phrased in terms of prohibiting the transportation of goods made by child labor, the statute left no doubt that its real purpose was to suppress child labor. The Court held the statute unconstitutional by finding that manufacturing was an internal state affair not subject to regulation under the commerce clause. This position dominated the Court until the administration of Franklin D. Roosevelt.

Depression-Era Decisions

With the economic depression of the 1930s, there emerged increased public pressure for federal solutions. Congress responded by passing legislation

[2] 22 U.S. 9 (Wheat) 1 (1824).
[3] 247 U.S. 251 (1918).

regulating business activity and labor-management relations. The National Industrial Recovery Act of 1933 (NIRA) provided for industry codes of self-regulation of production, prices, wages, and work hours. The National Labor Relations Act of 1935 (NLRA) forbade unfair labor practices.

In *Schechter Poultry Corp. v. United States*[4] (the Sick Chicken Case), the Court held that the NIRA, as applied to New York poultry slaughterhouses, was unconstitutional. The Court held that Congress exceeded its power under the commerce clause. The decision prompted President Roosevelt's unsuccessful effort to "pack" the Court. Roosevelt called for legislation to allow for an additional appointment whenever a Supreme Court justice reached the voluntary retirement age but refused to retire. Because six members of the Court were past the voluntary retirement age, this would have given Roosevelt six new appointments. Although the "Court-packing" plan failed to get congressional approval, Roosevelt's influence was felt. Chief Justice Hughes, worried about a potential confrontation with the executive branch, lobbied two justices to change their positions on the scope of the commerce clause.

By 1937 the Court's majority had changed. That year the Court decided *NLRB v. Jones & Laughlin Steel Corp,*[5] which upheld the constitutionality of the NLRA. In what represented a turning point in commerce clause interpretation, the Court rejected the argument that manufacturing was not commerce. It held instead that congressional power was no longer limited to commerce moving across state lines, but included all activities, "if they have a close and substantial relation to interstate commerce." This power included many activities that might be intrastate when considered alone.

The Present Position

In 1941 *Hammer v. Dagenhart* was formally overruled in *United States v. Darby.*[6] There the Court upheld the constitutionality of the Fair Labor Standards Act (FLSA). This statute established minimum wages and maximum hours for employees producing goods in interstate commerce. The Court decided that the production of goods "affected" interstate commerce even though the activity took place entirely within one state. Congress has the power to regulate any activity that has any appreciable effect upon interstate commerce. This is called the *affectation doctrine.* When applying the affectation doctrine, the Court today uses a very narrow analysis that usually results in finding federal economic legislation constitutional. The following case is a classic illustration of commerce clause power.

---

[4] 295 U.S. 495 (1935).

[5] 301 U.S. 1 (1937).

[6] 312 U.S. 100 (1941).

Heart of Atlanta Motel, Inc. v. United States

375 U.S. 241 (1964)

The owner of the Heart of Atlanta Motel (appellant) sued for a declaratory judgment that Title II of the Civil Rights Act of 1964 was unconstitutional. Title II forbids racial discrimination in public accommodations (e.g., theaters, hotels, restaurants). The district court upheld the statute as an authorized exercise by Congress of the commerce clause. A direct appeal was taken to the Supreme Court, which affirmed the district court decision.

The Heart of Atlanta Motel had 216 rooms available to transient guests. It was located on Courtland Street, two blocks from downtown Peachtree Street. It was readily accessible to interstate highways 75 and 85 and state highways 23 and 41. The motel advertised in national media and maintained over 50 billboards and highway signs within Georgia. It accepted convention trade from outside Georgia and approximately 75 percent of its registered guests were from out of state. Before passage of the Civil Rights Act, the motel had refused to rent rooms to blacks, and it intended to continue this practice.

Justice Clark

The sole question posed is . . . the constitutionality of the Civil Rights Act of 1964 as applied to these facts. The legislative history of the Act indicates that Congress based the Act on its power to regulate interstate commerce.

* * * * *

While the Act as adopted carried no congressional findings, the record of its passage through each house is replete with evidence of the burdens that discrimination by race or color places upon interstate commerce. This testimony included the fact that our people have become increasingly mobile with millions of all races traveling from state to state; that Negroes in particular have been the subject of discrimination in transient accommodations, having to travel great distances to secure the same; that often they have been unable to obtain accommodations and have had to call upon friends to put them up overnight; and that these conditions had become so acute as to require the listing of available lodging for Negroes in a special guidebook which was itself "dramatic testimony of the difficulties" Negroes encounter in travel. These exclusionary practices were found to be nationwide, the Under Secretary of Commerce testifying that there is "no question that this discrimination in the North still exists to a large degree" and in the West and Midwest as well. This testimony indicated a qualitative as well as quantitative effect on interstate travel by Negroes. The former was the obvious impairment of the Negro traveler's pleasure and convenience that resulted when he continually was uncertain of finding lodging. As for the latter, there was evidence that this uncertainty stemming from racial discrimination had the effect of discouraging travel on the part of a substantial portion of the Negro community. The voluminous testimony presents overwhelming evidence that discrimination by hotels and motels impedes interstate travel. . . .

The same interest in protecting interstate commerce which led Congress to deal with segregation in interstate carriers and the white slave traffic has prompted it to extend the exercise of its power to gambling, to deceptive practices in sale of products, to fraudulent security transactions, to misbranding of drugs, to discrimination against shippers, to the protection of small business from injurious price cutting, and to racial discrimination by owners and managers of terminal restaurants.

That Congress was legislating against moral wrongs in many of these areas rendered its enactments no less valid. In framing Title II of this Act, Congress was also dealing with what it considered a moral problem. But that fact does not detract from the overwhelming evidence of the disruptive effect that racial discrimination has had on commercial intercourse. It was this burden which empowered Congress to enact legislation, and, given this basis for the exercise of its power, Congress was not restricted by the fact that the particular obstruction to interstate commerce with which it was dealing was also deemed a moral and social wrong.

It is said that the operation of the motel here is of a purely local character. But, assuming this to be true, "if it is interstate commerce that feels the pinch, it does not matter how local the operation which applies the squeeze." Thus, the power of Congress to promote interstate commerce also includes the power to regulate the local incidents thereof, including local activities in both the states of origin and destination, which might have a substantial and harmful effect upon that commerce. One need only examine the evidence which we have discussed above to see that Congress may— as it has—prohibit racial discrimination by motels serving travelers, however "local" their operation may appear.

. . . The commerce power invoked here by the Congress is a specific and plenary one authorized by the Constitution itself. The only questions are: (1) whether Congress had a rational basis for finding that racial discrimination by motels affected commerce, and (2) if it had such a basis, whether the means it selected to eliminate that evil are reasonable and appropriate. If they are, appellant has no "right" to select its guests as it sees fit, free from governmental regulation.

*   *   *   *   *

We therefore conclude that the action of the Congress in the adoption of the Act as applied here to a motel which concededly serves interstate travelers is within the power granted it by the Commerce Clause of the Constitution, as interpreted by this Court for 140 years.

CASE QUESTIONS

1. What was the purpose of the Civil Rights Act of 1964? What was the basis for congressional enactment of Title II of the Civil Rights Act of 1964?

2. What approach does the Court follow in reviewing federal economic legislation challenged under the commerce clause? Is the Court's decision in *Heart of Atlanta Motel* consistent with Chief Justice John Marshall's definition of commerce in *Gibbons v. Ogden?*

3. If none of the motel's customers had been interstate travelers, would the Court have reached the same result? Explain.

4. Do you think that it is appropriate to use the commerce clause as a basis for enacting "social" legislation? Explain.

THE RELATIONSHIP BETWEEN STATE AND FEDERAL REGULATION

The previous discussion focused on federal regulatory power in national and local matters. Now the discussion turns to the power of the states to regulate business. The individual states have a strong interest in protecting the health, safety, and morals of their people. When they so act, they are said to be exercising their *police power*. That power, though broad, is not unlimited. It may not be exercised in a manner contrary to the Constitution.

Some state activity is specifically prohibited by the Constitution. For example, only the federal government has the power to coin money, declare war, and impose tariffs. Other provisions of the Constitution impliedly limit state action. The following discussion focuses on two such provisions: the commerce clause and the supremacy clause.

The Commerce Clause

The commerce clause not only contains an express grant of federal power over interstate commerce, but by implication it limits the authority of states to regulate in a manner that unduly restricts the free flow of interstate commerce. Without the commerce clause, individual states could establish regulatory barriers against interstate commerce in order to give local commercial interests an economic advantage.

When Congress remains silent and a state enacts legislation on a subject of interstate commerce, the Supreme Court sits as umpire of the competing national and state interests. In distinguishing between legitimate exercises of a state's police power and unconstitutional restraints upon interstate commerce, the Court balances the need for national uniformity in law against the state's interest in protecting its people from health and safety hazards. On some occasions the court has carved out areas of exclusive federal control, and on other occasions it has struck down state statutes that discriminate against or obstruct interstate commerce.

Exclusive Federal Areas

Generally, when Congress is silent on a subject of interstate commerce, the states are free to regulate the area. Thus, states possess some power to govern local matters that affect interstate commerce. Congress may remove this permissible area of state regulation by enacting legislation. However, some subjects of interstate commerce are exclusively federal.

This means that state regulation is unconstitutional even in the absence of congressional legislation. An exclusively federal area is one where national uniformity in regulation is necessary. Congress possesses exclusive power over such an area. No state can regulate in the area. If regulation is needed, it must come from Congress.

Most cases raising the issue of federal exclusivity have involved state transportation regulation. For example, the Court struck down an Arizona law making it illegal to operate within Arizona a train of more than 14 passenger cars or 70 freight cars.[7] Although the statute was a safety measure designed to reduce railroad accidents, the Court concluded that the length of trains was an area in which national uniformity was indispensable. Efficient interstate train operation would be impeded if trains were forced to stop and reassemble upon entering and leaving each regulating state.

Obstruction of and Discrimination against Interstate Commerce

Even though an area of interstate commerce is not exclusively federal, a state is not free to use its regulatory authority to obstruct interstate commerce. Similarly, a state may not enact discriminatory laws designed to protect or aid local business in its competition with interstate commerce. For example, license fees that are required only from nonresidents or from businesses bringing in goods from outside the state have been held to burden the free flow of interstate commerce.

The Pike Test

In determining whether state regulation violates the commerce clause either because it regulates in an area exclusively reserved for the federal government or because it obstructs or discriminates against interstate commerce, the Court uses a balancing test: It weighs the regulation's burdens on interstate commerce against its local benefits. The Court summarized its analysis in *Pike v. Bruce Church, Inc.*,[8] where it stated:

> [W]here the statute regulates evenhandedly to effectuate a legitimate local public interest, and its effects on interstate commerce are only incidental, it will be upheld unless the burden imposed on such commerce is clearly excessive in relation to the putative local benefits. If a legitimate local purpose is found, then the question becomes one of degree. And the extent of the burden that will be tolerated will of course depend on the nature of the local interest involved, and on whether it could be promoted as well with a lesser impact on interstate activities.[9]

The Supremacy Clause

The previous section on the commerce clause discussed to what extent a state can regulate an area of interstate commerce when Congress is

---

[7] *Southern Pacific Co. v. Arizona* 323 U.S. 761 (1945).

[8] 397 U.S. 137 (1970).

[9] 397 U.S. 137 at 142 (1970).

silent. Where both Congress and a state enact laws regulating a field of interstate commerce, which law controls? Must managers obey both laws? If complying with one law means violating the other, which law should be followed? The answers are in the supremacy clause of the Constitution, which embodies the *preemption doctrine.* When Congress enters a field of regulation, the extent that a state may also regulate that field depends on whether Congress intends to preempt state law in the whole field or only in part.

Supremacy Clause, Article VI

This Constitution, and the Laws of the United States which shall be made in Pursuance thereof; . . . shall be the supreme Law of the Land; and the Judges in every State shall be bound thereby, any Thing in the Constitution or Laws of any State to the Contrary notwithstanding.

Sometimes Congress specifically declares state regulation to be preempted. At other times Congress specifically declares that it does not intend to preempt state regulation.

Absent explicit preemptive language, determination of congressional intent to preempt state law is left to the courts. The following case shows the judicial approach for determining whether congressional preemptive intent is present.

Silkwood v. Kerr–McGee Corporation

104 S.Ct. 615 (1984)

Karen Silkwood was a laboratory analyst for Kerr–McGee Corp. (appellee) at its Cimmaron plant near Crescent, Oklahoma. The plant fabricated plutonium fuel pins for use as reactor fuel in nuclear power plants. The plant was subject to licensing and regulation by the Nuclear Regulatory Commission (NRC) pursuant to the Atomic Energy Act.

During a three-day period of November 1974, Silkwood was contaminated by plutonium from the Cimmaron plant. Contamination was detected on her hands, arms, neck, hair, nostrils, and in samples of her urine and feces. Contamination was also found in her apartment. Silkwood was sent to the Los Alamos Scientific Laboratory to determine the extent of contamination in her vital body organs. She returned to work on November 13. That night she was killed in an unrelated automobile accident.

Bill Silkwood (appellant), Karen's father, sued Kerr–McGee in his capacity as administrator of the estate. The suit was brought in federal district court as a diversity of citizenship action. The suit was based on common-law tort principles of strict liability and negligence under Oklahoma law. The jury returned a verdict in favor of Silkwood, finding actual damages of $505,000 ($500,000 for personal injuries and $5,000 for property damage) and punitive damages* of $10,000,000. The trial court entered judgment against Kerr–McGee in that amount. Kerr–McGee then moved for a judgment notwithstanding the verdict or a new trial, which the trial court denied. The court of appeals reversed the punitive damages award, finding that because of federal statutes regulating the Kerr–McGee plant, "punitive damages may not be awarded." The Supreme Court reversed.

Justice White

[S]tate law can be preempted in either of two general ways. If Congress evidences an intent to occupy a given field, any state law falling within that field is preempted. If Congress has not entirely displaced state regulation over the matter in question, state law is still preempted to the extent it actually conflicts with federal law, that is, when it is impossible to comply with both state and federal law, or where the state law stands as an obstacle to the accomplishment of the full purposes and objectives of Congress. Kerr–McGee contends that the award in this case is invalid under either analysis. We consider each of these contentions in turn.

A

In *Pacific Gas & Electric*, an examination of the statutory scheme and legislative history of the Atomic Energy Act convinced

us that "Congress . . . intended that the federal government regulate the radiological safety aspects involved . . . in the construction and operation of a nuclear plant." Thus, we concluded that "the federal government has occupied the entire field of nuclear safety concerns, except the limited powers expressly ceded to the states."

* * * * *

Kerr–McGee submits that because the state-authorized award of punitive damages in this case punishes and deters conduct related to radiation hazards, it falls within the prohibited field. However, a review of the same legislative history which prompted our holding in *Pacific Gas & Electric*, coupled with an examination of Congress' actions with respect to other portions of the Atomic Energy Act, convinces us that the preemption field does not extend as far as Kerr–McGee would have it.

* * * * *

[T]here is no indication that Congress even seriously considered precluding the use of such remedies either when it enacted

---

* Punitive damages are damages awarded to a plaintiff which are greater than the amount necessary to compensate his or her loss. Generally, punitive damages are granted where the wrong involved intent, malice, recklessness, or other aggravated circumstances.—Au.

the Atomic Energy Act in 1954 and or when it amended it in 1959. This silence takes on added significance in light of Congress' failure to provide any federal remedy for persons injured by such conduct. It is difficult to believe that Congress would without comment, remove all means of judicial recourse for those injured by illegal conduct.

More importantly, the only congressional discussion concerning the relationship between the Atomic Energy Act and state tort remedies indicates that Congress assumed that such remedies would be available. After the 1954 law was enacted, private companies contemplating entry into the nuclear industry expressed concern over potentially bankrupting state-law suits arising out of a nuclear incident. As a result, in 1957 Congress passed the Price–Anderson Act, an amendment to the Atomic Energy Act. That Act established an indemnification* scheme under which operators of licensed nuclear facilities could be required to obtain up to $60 million in private financial protection against such suits. The government would then provide indemnification for the next $500 million of liability, and the resulting $560 million would be the limit of liability for any one nuclear incident.

The discussion preceding [the Price–Anderson Act's] enactment and subsequent amendment indicates that Congress assumed that persons injured by nuclear accidents were free to utilize existing state tort law remedies.

*   *   *   *   *

In sum, it is clear that in enacting and amending the Price–Anderson Act, Congress assumed that state-law remedies, in whatever form they might take, were available to those injured by nuclear incidents.

---

* Indemnification means to reimburse someone for a loss already sustained.—Au.

This was so even though it was well aware of the NRC's exclusive authority to regulate safety matters. No doubt there is tension between the conclusion that safety regulation is the exclusive concern of the federal law and the conclusion that a state may nevertheless award damages based on its own law of liability. But as we understand what was done over the years in the legislation concerning nuclear energy, Congress intended to stand by both concepts and to tolerate whatever tension there was between them. We can do no less. It may be that the award of damages based on the state law of negligence or strict liability is regulatory in the sense that a nuclear plant will be threatened with damages liability if it does not conform to state standards, but that regulatory consequence was something that Congress was quite willing to accept.

[I]nsofar as damages for radiation injuries are concerned, preemption should not be judged on the basis that the federal government has so completely occupied the field of safety that state remedies are foreclosed but on whether there is an irreconcilable conflict between the federal and state standards or whether the imposition of a state standard in a damages action would frustrate the objectives of the federal law. We perceive no such conflict or frustration in the circumstances of this case.

B

The United States, as *amicus curiae*,* contends that the award of punitive dam-

---

* *Amicus curiae* is Latin for "friend of the court." An individual, a corporation, or, in this case, the government, may petition a court for permission to file a brief because of a strong interest in a case. Usually a court will allow this if the person petitioning to file an amicus curiae brief wishes to address an issue that is not being addressed by one of the parties. In this case, the federal government was allowed to file an amicus curiae brief to present an argument beneficial to Kerr–McGee.—Au.

ages in this case is preempted because it conflicts with the federal remedial scheme, noting that the NRC is authorized to impose civil penalties on licensees when federal standards have been violated. However, the award of punitive damages in the present case does not conflict with that scheme. Paying both federal fines and state-imposed punitive damages for the same incident would not appear to be physically impossible. Nor does exposure to punitive damages frustrate any purpose of the federal remedial scheme.

Kerr–McGee contends that the award is preempted because it frustrates Congress' express desire "to encourage widespread participation in the development and utilization of atomic energy for peaceful purposes." . . . Indeed, the provision cited by Kerr–McGee goes on to state that atomic energy should be developed and utilized only to the extent it is consistent "with the health and safety of the public." Congress therefore disclaimed any interest in promoting the development and utilization of atomic energy "by means that fail to provide adequate remedies for those who are injured by exposure to hazardous nuclear materials. Thus, the award of punitive damages in this case does not hinder the accomplishment of the purpose stated in [the Act].

CASE QUESTIONS

1. What basic principles regarding preemption guided the Court's decision?

2. How did the Court reach the conclusion that an award of punitive damages did not fall within the prohibited field regulated by the Atomic Energy Act?

3. How did the Court reach the conclusion that an award of punitive damages did not conflict with the Atomic Energy Act?

4. What are the implications of the *Silkwood* decision for nuclear safety regulation?

PROPERTY RIGHTS AND ECONOMIC REGULATION

All governments have historically enjoyed the right of *eminent domain*. Eminent domain is the right of a government to take, or to authorize the taking of, private property for public use. The Fifth Amendment recognizes this basic governmental right but requires that *just compensation* be given to the owner. It provides that private property may not "be taken for public use, without just compensation." Thus, if government wants to convert a privately owned building into a post office or to build a dam that will flood nearby land, it must compensate owners for the losses resulting from these activities.

Under the Supreme Court's interpretation of the Fifth Amendment, compensation is required only for a governmental *taking* of property and not for losses occasioned by mere regulation. Where government engages in business regulation, courts usually decide that the economic loss suffered by the private citizen is merely an incident of the lawful exercise of police power and is not compensable.

In deciding whether government action is a "taking" or merely regulation, the Court usually balances the character of the governmental action against its economic impact, as the following case illustrates.

Penn Central Transportation Company v. New York

438 U.S. 104 (1978)

Under New York City law, advance approval must be obtained from the New York City Landmarks Preservation Commission before exterior changes can be made on property that is designated a landmark. In 1967 the commission designated Grand Central Terminal a landmark. The Penn Central Transportation Company (appellant), which owned the terminal, sought permission in 1968 to construct a 55-story office building above it. Penn Central submitted two plans—one requiring a cantilevered building resting on the terminal's roof, the other necessitating the destruction of the terminal's south facade. Both plans were rejected. New York City's law also provided owners of landmark sites additional opportunities to transfer development rights to adjacent parcels on the same city block. This is known in land-use planning as a "transfer development rights program." Because of this program and because full development of the terminal site was prohibited, Penn Central was entitled to exceed zoning limits on the development of other parcels of land. Penn Central challenged the Landmarks Preservation Law, alleging that its property had been taken without just compensation in violation of the Fifth and Fourteenth Amendments. The New York trial court enjoined enforcement of the law. The Appellate Division reversed. The New York Court of Appeals, the highest court in the State of New York, affirmed the Appellate Division. Penn Central appealed to the U.S. Supreme Court, which also affirmed.

Justice Brennan

The question of what constitutes a "taking" for purposes of the Fifth Amendment has proved to be a problem of considerable difficulty. While this Court has recognized that the "Fifth Amendment's guarantee . . . is designed to bar Government from forcing some people alone to bear public burdens which, in all fairness and justice, should be borne by the public as a whole," this Court, quite simply, has been unable to develop any "set formula" for determining when "justice and fairness" require that economic injuries caused by public action be compensated by the government, rather than remain disproportionately concentrated on a few persons. Indeed, we frequently observed that whether a particular restriction will be rendered invalid by the government's failure to pay for any losses proximately caused by it depends largely "upon the particular circumstances in that case."

In engaging in these essentially ad hoc, factual inquiries, the Court's decisions have identified several factors that have particular significance. The economic impact of the regulation on the claimant and, particularly, the extent to which the regulation has interferred with distinct investment-backed expectations are, of course, relevant considerations. So, too, is the character of the governmental action. A "taking" may more readily be found when the interference with property can be characterized as a physical invasion by government than when interference arises from some public program adjusting the benefits and burdens of economic life to promote the common good.

* * * * *

In contending that the New York City law has "taken" their property in violation of the Fifth and Fourteenth Amendments, appellants make a series of arguments, which . . . essentially urge that any substantial restriction imposed pursuant to a landmark law must be accompanied by just compensation if it is to be constitutional.

* * * * *

They first observe that the airspace above the Terminal is a valuable property interest. They urge that the Landmarks Law has deprived them of any gainful use of their "air rights" above the Terminal and that, irrespective of the value of the remainder of their parcel, the city has "taken" their right to this superadjacent airspace, thus entitling them to "just compensation" measured by the fair market value of these air rights.

. . . [T]he submission that appellants may establish a "taking" simply by showing that they have been denied the ability to exploit a property interest that they heretofore had believed was available for development is quite simply untenable. . . . "Taking" jurisprudence does not divide a single parcel into discrete segments and attempt to determine whether rights in a particular segment have been entirely abrogated. In deciding whether a particular governmental action has effected a taking, this Court focuses rather both on the character of the action and on the nature and extent of the interference with rights in the parcel as a whole—here, the city tax block designated as the "landmark site."

Secondly, appellants, focusing on the character and impact of the New York City law, argue that it effects a "taking" because its operation has significantly diminished its value of the Terminal site.

* * * * *

Stated baldly, appellants' position appears to be that the only means of ensuring that selected owners are not singled out to endure financial hardship for no reason is to hold that any restriction imposed on individual landmarks pursuant to the New York City scheme is a "taking" requiring the payment of "just compensation." Agreement with this argument would, of course, invalidate not just New York City's law, but all comparable landmark legislation in the Nation. We find no merit in it.

* * * * *

[A]ppellants' repeated suggestions that are solely burdened and unbenefited is factually inaccurate. This contention overlooks the fact that the New York City law applies to vast numbers of structures in the city in addition to the Terminal—all the structures contained in the 31 historic districts and over 400 individual landmarks, many of which are close to the Terminal. Unless we are to reject the judgment of the New York City Council that the preservation of landmarks benefits all New York citizens and all structures, both economically and by improving the quality of life in the city as a whole—which we are unwilling to do—we cannot conclude that the owners of the Terminal have in no sense been benefited by the Landmarks Law.

* * * * *

We now must consider whether the interference with appellants' property is of such a magnitude that "there must be an exercise of eminent domain and compensation to sustain it." That inquiry may be narrowed to the question of the severity of the impact of the law on appellants' parcel, and its resolution in turn requires a careful assessment of the regulation on the Terminal site.

[T]he New York City law does not interfere in any way with the present uses of the Terminal. Its designation as a landmark not only permits but contemplates that appellants may continue to use the property precisely as it has been used for the past 65 years: as a railroad terminal containing office space and concessions. So the law does not interefere with what must be regarded as Penn Central's primary expectation concerning the use of the parcel. More importantly, on this record, we must regard the New York City law as permitting Penn Central not only to profit from the Terminal but also to obtain a "reasonable return" on its investment.

Appellants, moreover, exaggerate the effect of the law on their ability to make use of the air rights above the Terminal in two respects. First, it simply cannot be maintained, on this record, that appellants have been prohibited from occupying *any*

portion of the airspace above the Terminal. While the Commission's actions in denying applications to construct an office building in excess of 50 stories above the Terminal may indicate that it will refuse to issue a certificate of appropriateness for any comparably sized structure, nothing the Commission has said or done suggests an intention to prohibit *any* construction above the Terminal. The Commission's report emphasized that whether any construction would be allowed depended upon whether the proposed addition "would harmonize in scale, material and character with the Terminal." Since appellants have not sought approval for the construction of a smaller structure, we do not know that appellants will be denied any use of any portion of the airspace above the Terminal.

Second, to the extent appellants have been denied the right to build above the Terminal, it is not literally accurate to say that they have been denied all use of even those pre-existing air rights. Their ability to use these rights has not been abrogated; they are made transferable to at least eight parcels in the vicinity of the Terminal, one or two of which have been found suitable for the construction of new office buildings. Although appellants and others have argued that New York City's transferable developments-right program is far from ideal, the New York courts have supportably found that, at least in the case of the Terminal, the rights afforded are valuable. While these rights may well not have constituted "just compensation" if a "taking" had occurred, the rights nevertheless undoubtedly mitigate whatever financial burdens the law has imposed on appellants and, for that reason, are to be taken into account in considering the impact of regulation.

On this record, we conclude that the application of New York City's Landmarks Law has not effected a "taking" of appellants' property. The restrictions imposed are substantially related to the promotion of the general welfare and not only permit reasonable beneficial use of the landmark site but also afford appellants opportunities further to enhance not only the Terminal site proper but also other properties.

CASE QUESTIONS

1. What approach did the court use in determining whether there had been a taking of private property? Could this approach be characterized as a "test?"

2. Were Penn Central's transferable development rights (TDRs) with regard to the adjacent property as commercially valuable as the airspace over the Terminal? Does that make a difference? Explain. Suppose that as a result of the commission's rejection of Penn Central's development plans for the Terminal, Penn Central had been deprived of earning a reasonable return on its investment. Would the Court have reached the same result? Explain.

3. Suppose that the New York City Landmark Preservation Commission orders a business to change from its present use of a property designated as a landmark and to return to using the property as it was used at some point in the past. Would such a decision fall within the *Penn Central* holding and not constitute a taking?

4. As a result of the Court's decision, do you think that developers will be more likely or less likely to invest in historically significant properties? Explain.

THE FIRST AMENDMENT AND THE FREEDOM OF SPEECH

This discussion of the First Amendment focuses on freedom of speech in a commercial context. The Supreme Court does not consider the First Amendment's guarantee of freedom of speech to be absolute. Justice Holmes said in *Schenck v. United States,* "The most stringent protection of free speech would not protect a man in falsely shouting fire in a theatre and causing panic."[10] What speech, then, is protected by the Constitution, and what speech may be prohibited or punished? These questions have not been easy ones for the Court.

The First Amendment of the Constitution

Congress shall make no law respecting an establishment of religion, or prohibiting the free exercise thereof; or abridging the freedom of speech, or of the press; or the right of the people peaceably to assemble, and to petition the Government for a redress of grievances.

---

[10] 249 U.S. 47 (1919).

Although frequently thought of in connection with speech in a political context, the First Amendment also applies to speech in a commercial context. The following discussion focuses on one area of commercial speech: advertising.

Advertising and the First Amendement

The First Amendment to the Constitution protects freedom of speech and freedom of the press from infringement by the government. As the advertising industry expanded, courts faced the issue of whether these protections extended to advertising.

In 1942 the Supreme Court decided *Valentine v. Chrestensen.*[11] Chrestensen distributed a handbill advertising a submarine he operated as an amusement attraction. He was advised that an ordinance prohibited the distribution of commercial material in the street. Chrestensen revised the handbill, printing his advertisement on one side and a protest against the ordinance on the other. He was restrained from distributing the handbill. The Court upheld the prohibition, reasoning that Chrestensen's purpose in printing the protest was to avoid the ordinance. The Court sustained the constitutionality of the ordinance, holding that commercial speech was not entitled to First Amendment protection.

Although *Chrestensen* was a unanimous opinion, several state supreme courts interpreted their state constitutions as protecting commercial speech. Later, the *Chrestensen* decision was limited when the Court held that paid political advertisements[12] and abortion advertisements[13] were protected by the Constitution.

In *Virginia Pharmacy Board v. Virginia Citizens Commerce,* the Supreme Court was again confronted by a claim that purely commercial speech was protected by the Constitution.[14] A Virginia statute prohibited licensed pharmacists from advertising their prices for prescription drugs. The Commerce Council, a consumer group, challenged the law's constitutionality. The Court examined the interests of the parties to the advertisement, noting that the advertiser's motivation was purely economic. However, after reviewing decisions rendered after *Chrestensen,* it concluded that this did not necessarily disqualify the advertisement from constitutional protection.

The Court then focused on the consumer's interests, which had not been represented before the Court in *Chrestensen* 24 years earlier. The consumer's interest in the free flow of commercial information was at least as strong as the consumer's interest in political debates. Information about drug prices facilitates the well-informed private economic decisions

---

[11] 316 U.S. 52 (1942).

[12] *New York Times v. Sullivan,* 376 U.S. 255 (1964).

[13] *Bigelow v. Virginia,* 421 U.S. 809 (1975).

[14] 425 U.S. 746 (1976).

responsible for allocating resources in a predominantly free enterprise economy. The consumer's interests, although not considered in *Chrestensen*, were also protected by the First Amendment. Thus, the Virginia statute was declared unconstitutional.

The Court indicated, in *Virginia Pharmacy*, however, that reasonable restrictions on the time, place, and manner of commercial speech are permissible where such restrictions are justified by a significant governmental interest and where ample alternative channels of communication remain available. By this qualification the Court in *Virginia Pharmacy* indicated that there was still life in the commercial speech doctrine. Lest any doubt remain, however, the Court applied the doctrine two years later in *Ohralik v. Ohio State Bar Association*, upholding the suspension of an attorney's license to practice law where the attorney solicited clients.[15]

The following case illustrates the constitutional analysis involved in commercial speech cases.

Central Hudson Gas and Electric Corp. v. Public Service Commission of New York

447 U.S. 557 (1980)

Central Hudson Gas and Electric (appellant) brought suit in a New York State court to challenge the constitutionality of a regulation of the New York Public Service Commission (appellee) that completely barred promotional advertising by the utility. The regulation prohibited private electric utilities from engaging in promotional advertising intended to stimulate sales. The order was necessary, the commission maintained, to further energy conservation. The regulation was upheld by the trial court and at the intermediate appellate level. On appeal by the utility, the New York Court of Appeals sustained the regulation. The U.S. Supreme Court reversed.

Justice Powell

The Commission's order restricts only commercial speech, that is, expression related solely to the economic interests of the speaker and its audience. The First Amend-

ment, as applied to the States through the Fourteenth Amendment, protects commercial speech from unwarranted governmental regulation. Commercial expression not only serves the economic interest of the speaker, but also assists consumers and fur-

---

[15] 436 U.S. 447 (1978).

thers the societal interest in the fullest possible dissemination of information. In applying the First Amendment to this area, we have rejected the "highly paternalistic" view that government has complete power to suppress or regulate commercial speech. "[P]eople will perceive their own best interests if only they are well enough informed, and . . . the best means to that end is to open the channels of communication rather than to close them."

Nevertheless, our decisions have recognized "the 'common-sense' distinction between speech proposing a commercial transaction, which occurs in an area traditionally subject to government regulation, and other varieties of speech." The Constitution therefore accords a lesser protection to commercial speech than to other constitutionally guaranteed expression. The protection available for particular commercial expression turns on the nature both of the expression and of the governmental interests served by its regulation.

The First Amendment's concern for commercial speech is based on the informational function of advertising. Consequently, there can be no constitutional objection to the suppression of commercial messages that do not accurately inform the public about lawful activity. The government may ban forms of communication more likely to deceive the public than to inform it, or commercial speech related to illegal activity.

If the communication is neither misleading nor related to unlawful activity, the government's power is more circumscribed. The State must assert a substantial interest to be achieved by restrictions on commercial speech. Moreover, the regulatory technique must be in proportion to that interest. The limitation on expression must be designed carefully to achieve the State's goal. Compliance with this requirement may be measured by two criteria. First, the restriction must directly advance the state interest involved; the regulation may not be sustained if it provides only ineffective or remote support for the government's purpose. Second, if the governmental interest could be served as well by a more limited restriction on commercial speech, the excessive restriction cannot survive.

* * * * *

The second criterion recognizes that the First Amendement mandates that speech restrictions be "narrowly drawn." The regulatory technique may extend only as far as the interest it serves. The State cannot regulate speech that poses no danger to the asserted state interest nor can it completely suppress information when narrower restrictions on expression would serve its interest as well. . . .

In commercial speech cases, then, a four-part analysis has developed. At the outset, we must determine whether the expression is protected by the First Amendment. For commercial speech to come within that provision, it at least must concern lawful activity and not be misleading. Next, we ask whether the asserted governmental interest is substantial. If both inquiries yield positive answers, we must determine whether the regulation directly advances the governmental interest asserted, and whether it is not more extensive than is necessary to serve that interest.

The Commission does not claim that the expression at issue either is inaccurate or relates to unlawful activity.

* * * * *

The Commission offers two state interests as justifications for the ban on promotional advertising. The first concerns energy conservation. Any increase in demand for electricity—during peak or off-peak periods—means greater consumption of energy. The Commission argues . . . that the

State's interest in conserving energy is sufficient to support suppression of advertising designed to increase consumption of electricity. In view of our country's dependence on energy resources beyond our control, no one can doubt the importance of energy conservation. Plainly, therefore, the state interest asserted is substantial.*

* * * * *

Next, we focus on the relationship between the State's interests and the advertising ban. . . .

. . . [T]he State's interest in energy conservation is directly advanced by the Commission order at issue here. There is an immediate connection between advertising and demand for electricity. Central Hudson would not contest the advertising ban unless it believed that promotion would increase its sales. Thus, we find a direct link between the state interest in conservation and the Commission's order.

We come finally to the critical inquiry in this case: whether the Commission's complete suppression of speech ordinarily protected by the First Amendment is no more extensive than necessary to further the State's interest in energy conservation. The Commission's order reaches all promotional advertising, regardless of the impact of the touted service on overall energy use. But the energy conservation rationale, as important as it is, cannot justify suppressing information about electric devices or services that would cause no net increase in total energy use. In addition, no showing has been made that a more limited restriction on the content of promotional advertising would not serve adequately the State's interests.

Appellant insists that but for the ban, it would advertise products and services

that use energy efficiently. These include the "heat pump," which both parties acknowledge to be a major improvement in electric heating, and the use of electric heat as a "back-up" to solar and other heat sources. Although the Commission has questioned the efficiency of electric heating before this Court, neither the Commission's Policy Statement nor its order denying rehearing made findings on this issue. In the absence of authoritative findings to the contrary, we must credit as within the realm of possibility the claim that electric heat can be an efficient alternative in some circumstances.

The Commission's order prevents appellant from promoting electric services that would reduce energy use by diverting demand for less efficient sources, or that would consume roughly the same amount of energy as do alternative sources. In neither situation would the utility's advertising endanger conservation or mislead the public. To the extent that the Commission's order suppresses speech that in no way impairs the State's interest in energy conservation, the Commission's order violates the First and Fourteenth Amendments and must be invalidated.

The Commission also has not demonstrated that its interest in conservation cannot be protected adequately by more limited regulation of appellant's commercial expression. To further its policy of conservation, the Commission could attempt to restrict the format and content of Central Hudson's advertising. It might, for example, require that the advertisements include information about the relative efficiency and expense of the offered service, both under current conditions and for the foreseeable future. In the absence of a showing that more limited speech regulation would be ineffective, we cannot approve the complete suppression of Central Hudson's advertising.

Our decision today in no way dispar-

---

* The Court's discussion of the second state interest is omitted.—Au.

ages the national interest in energy conservation. We accept without reservation the argument that conservation, as well as the development of alternate energy sources, is an imperative national goal. Administrative bodies empowered to regulate electric utilities have the authority—and indeed the duty—to take appropriate action to further this goal. When, however, such action involves the suppression of speech, the First and Fourteenth Amendments require that the restriction be no more extensive than is necessary to serve the state interest. In this case, the record before us fails to show that the total ban on promotional advertising meets this requirement.

CASE QUESTIONS

1. Should the Court treat commercial speech differently than political speech? Explain.

2. In a dissenting opinion in the *Virginia Pharmacy* case (discussed in the text on p. 96), Justice Rehnquist included the following fictional ads by a hypothetical pharmacist:

"Pain getting you down? Insist that your physician prescribe Demerol. You pay a little more than for aspirin, but you get a lot more relief."

"Can't shake the flu? Get a prescription for Tetracycline from your doctor today."

"Don't spend another sleepless night. Ask you doctor to prescribe Seconal without delay."

What would be required today to justify government regulation of such ads?

3. Suppose the public Service Commission of New York adopts a regulation prohibiting "utilities from using bill inserts to discuss political matters, including the desirability of future development of nuclear power." Would such a regulation be constitutional?

CONSTITUTIONAL PROTECTIONS IN ADMINISTRATIVE PROCEDURES

Most governmental regulation of business is accomplished through administrative agencies. Administrative agencies are established by the legislature, which delegates to them the authority to pursue the public interest as it is legislatively defined. In this way, the legislature frees itself from the day-to-day aspects of economic regulation by empowering agencies staffed by experts to administer legislatively defined regulatory objectives.

Increasing governmental regulation has made the relationship between administrative power and individual rights more important in modern society. The following discussion focuses on the rights of individual members of the business community *vis-á-vis* the administrative process. The discussion examines agency efforts to acquire information about the subjects of their regulation.

Administrative Investigations

Administrative agencies need information in order to exercise their rule-making and enforcement powers intelligently.[16] Regulation of businesses cannot be intelligently undertaken unless the regulators have access to information that only the businesses can supply. Indeed, private parties supply most of the information that agencies acquire for these rulemaking and enforcement activities. For example, there is an enormous flow of information to the Internal Revenue Service in the form of tax returns and to the Securities and Exchange Commission in the form of registration statements. Nevertheless, some protection against governmental meddling is provided by the Fourth Amendment's prohibition against "unreasonable searches and seizures" and by the Fifth Amendment's prohibition against compelling any person "in any criminal case to be a witness against himself."

The Fourth and Fifth Amendments

The right of the people to be secure in their persons, houses, papers, and effects, against unreasonable searches and seizures, shall not be violated, and no Warrants shall issue, but upon probable cause, supported by Oath or affirmation, and particularly describing the place to be searched, and the persons or things to be seized.

Nor shall any person . . . be compelled in any criminal case to be a witness against himself. . . .

Agencies obtain information through (1) record-keeping and reporting requirements, (2) the inspection of records and premises, and (3) the subpoena of witnesses and documents.

Record-Keeping and Reporting Requirements

In a country where regulation is a fundamental fact of economic existence, record-keeping and reporting requirements span the entire business spectrum. An agency generally requires a regulated business to keep records and to file reports with the agency so that the agency can monitor its compliance with the law.

---

[16] Some agencies are authorized to issue rules that have the force of law. This rulemaking power is discussed in chapter 4.

The Supreme Court has held that records required to be kept by law are considered public records and hence are not shielded from agency inspection by the Fifth Amendment.[17] For regulated businesses, the effect of this approach is to remove the protection against self-incrimination contained in the Fifth Amendment with regard to any relevant records that a regulating agency might require them to keep.

Similarly, the Court has held that the Fifth Amendment does not protect a business against a report requirement.[18] Under the Court's present approach, the public interest in obtaining information outweighs the private interest in opposing disclosure.

Administrative Inspections

Inspection is an indispensable aspect of any agency's enforcement procedures. The major issue with regard to administrative inspection of business premises pertains to the Fourth Amendment's prohibition against warrantless, unreasonable searches and seizures.

In *See v. City of Seattle,* the Court recognized the constitutional right of a business premise not to be subjected to an administrative inspection without a search warrant.[19] In 1970, the Court created an exception to the *See* warrant requirement, holding that it was not applicable to a closely regulated business, such as a liquor establishment.[20] In such a business the legislature may validly authorize warrantless inspection by relevant regulatory agencies. If the legislature is not restricted in the area of liquor regulation, it might be presumed that it is likewise unrestricted in other fields of economic activity subjected to pervasive regulation. However, as is shown by the following case the Court refused to expand this exception to the warrant requirement.

Marshall, Secretary of Labor v. Barlow's, Inc.

436 U.S. 307 (1978)

Section 8(a) of the Occupational Safety and Health Act of 1970 (OSHA or act) empowers agents of the secretary of labor (secretary) to search the work area of any employment facility within the act's jurisdiction. The purpose of the search is to inspect for safety hazards and violations of OSHA regulations. No search warrant or other process is expressly required under the act.

---

[17] *Shapiro v. United States,* 335 U.S. 1 (1948).

[18] *Byers v. California,* 402 U.S. 424 (1971).

[19] 387 U.S. 541 (1967).

[20] *Colonnade Catering Corp. v. United States,* 397 U.S. 72 (1970).

On the morning of September 11, 1975, an OSHA inspector entered the customer service area of Barlow's, Inc. (appellee), an electrical and plumbing installation business in Pocatello, Idaho. The president and general manager, Errol B. Barlow, was on hand. After showing his credentials, the OSHA inspector informed Barlow that he wished to search the working areas of the business. Barlow asked if a complaint had been received about his company. The inspector answered no, explaining that Barlow's, Inc., had simply turned up in the agency's selection process. Barlow then asked to see a search warrant, but the inspector had none. Relying on his Fourth Amendment rights, Barlow refused to allow the inspector to enter the employee area of his business.

Three months later, the secretary of labor petitioned the U.S. District Court for the district of Idaho to issue an order compelling Barlow to admit the inspector. The requested order was issued on December 30, 1975, and was presented to Barlow on January 5, 1976. Barlow again refused admission, and he then sought injunction relief against the warrantless searches assertedly permitted by OSHA. On December 30, 1976, a three-judge district court ruled in Barlow's favor. It held that the Fourth Amendment required a warrant for the type of search involved here and that the statutory authorization for warrantless inspections was unconstitutional. The court also entered an injunction against searchers or inspections pursuant to section 8(a). The secretary of labor (appellant) appealed to the U.S. Supreme Court, which affirmed the district court's judgment.

Justice White

The Secretary urges that warrantless inspections to enforce OSHA are reasonable within the meaning of the Fourth Amendment. Among other things, he relies on §8(a) of the Act, . . . which authorizes inspection of business premises without a warrant and which the Secretary urges represents a congressional construction of the Fourth Amendment that the courts should not reject. Regretably, we are unable to agree.

This Court has already held that warrantless searches are generally unreasonable, and that this rule applies to commercial premises as well as homes.

*   *   *   *   *

The Fourth Amendment prohibition against unreasonable searches protects against warrantless intrusions during civil as well as criminal investigations. . . . The reason is found in the "basic purpose of this amendment . . . which is to safeguard the privacy and security of individuals against arbitrary invasions by government officials." . . . If the government intrudes on a person's property, the privacy interest suffers whether the government's motivation is to investigate violations of criminal laws or breaches of other statutory or regulatory standards. It therefore appears that unless some recognized exception to the warrant requirement applies, *See v. Seattle* would require a warrant to conduct the inspection sought in this case.

The Secretary urges that an exception from the search warrant requirement has been recognized for "pervasively regulated business[es]," . . . and for "closely regulated" industries "long subject to close supervision and inspection." . . . These cases are indeed exceptions, but they represent responses to relatively unique circumstances. Certain industries have such a history of government oversight that no reasonable expectation of privacy . . . could exist for a proprietor over the stock of such an enterprise. Liquor and firearms are industries of this type; when an entrepreneur embarks upon such a business, he has voluntarily chosen to subject himself to a full arsenal of government regulations.

Industries such as these fall within the "certain carefully defined classes of cases." . . . The element that distinguishes these enterprises from ordinary businesses is a long tradition of close government supervision, of which any person who chooses to enter such a business must already be aware. "A central difference between those cases . . . and this one is that businessmen engaged in such federally licensed and regulated enterprises accept the burdens as well as the benefits of their trade, whereas the petitioner here was not engaged in any regulated or licensed business. The businessman in a regulated industry in effect consents to the restrictions placed upon him."

* * * * *

The critical fact in this case is that entry over Mr. Barlow's objection is being sought by the Government agent. Employees are not being prohibited from reporting OSHA violations. What they observe in their daily functions is undoubtedly beyond the employer's reasonable expectation of privacy. The Government inspector, however, is not an employee. Without a warrant he stands in no better position than a member of the public. What is observable by the public is observable, without a warrant, by the Government inspector as well. The owner of a business has not, by the necessary utilization of employees in his operation, thrown open the areas where employees alone are permitted to the warrantless scrutiny of Government agents. That an employee is free to report, and the Government is free to use, any evidence of noncompliance with OSHA that the employee observes furnishes no justification for federal agents to enter a place of business from which the public is restricted and to conduct their own warrantless search.

* * * * *

The Secretary submits that warrantless inspections are essential to the proper enforcement of OSHA because they afford the opportunity to inspect without prior notice and hence to preserve the advantages of surprise. While the dangerous conditions outlawed by the Act include structural defects that cannot be quickly hidden or remedied, the Act also regulates a myriad of safety details that may be amendable to speedy alteration or disguise. The risk is that during the interval between an inspector's initial request to search a plant and his procuring a warrant following the owner's refusal of permission, violations of this latter type could be corrected and thus escape the inspector's notice. To the suggestion that warrants may be issued *ex parte** and executed without delay and without prior notice, thereby preserving the element of surprise, the Secretary expresses concern for the administrative strain that would be experienced by the inspection system, and by the courts, should *ex parte* warrants issued in advance become standard practice.

We are unconvinced, however, that requiring warrants to inspect will impose seri-

---

* A warrant that is issued by a court *ex parte* is one that is issued on the application of the government only, without notice to the party to whom the warrant applies—Au.

ous burdens on the inspection system or the courts, will prevent inspections necessary to enforce the statute, or will make them less effective. In the first place, the great majority of businessmen can be expected in normal course to consent to inspection without warrant; the Secretary has not brought to this Court's attention any widespread pattern of refusal. . . .

Whether the Secretary proceeds to secure a warrant or other process, with or without prior notice, his entitlement to inspect will not depend on his demonstrating probable cause to believe that conditions in violation of OSHA exist on the premises. Probable cause in the criminal law sense is not required. For purposes of an administrative search such as this, probable cause justifying the issuance of a warrant may be based not only on specific evidence of an existing violation but also on a showing that "reasonable legislative or administrative standards for conducting an . . . inspection are satisfied with respect to a particular [establishment]." . . . A warrant showing that a specific business has been chosen for an OSHA search on the basis of a general administrative plan for the enforcement of the Act derived from neutral sources such as, for example, dispersion of employees in various types of industries across a given area, and the desired frequency of searches in any of the lesser divisions of the area, would protect an employer's Fourth Amendment rights. We doubt that the consumption of enforcement energies in the obtaining of such warrants will exceed manageable proportions.

* * * * *

Nor do we agree that the incremental protections afforded the employers' privacy by a warrant are so marginal that they fail to justify the administrative burdens that may be entailed. The authority to make warrantless searches devolves almost unbridled discretion upon executive and administrative officers, particularly those in the field, as to when to search and whom to search. A warrant, by contrast, would provide assurances from a neutral officer that the inspection is reasonable under the Constitution, is authorized by statute, and is pursuant to an administrative plan containing specific neutral criteria. Also, a warrant would then and there advise the owner of the scope and objects of the search, beyond which limits the inspector is not expected to proceed. These are important functions for a warrant to perform, functions which underlie the Court's prior decisions that the Warrant Clause applies to inspections for compliance with regulatory statutes. . . . We conclude that the concerns expressed by the Secretary do not suffice to justify warrantless inspections under OSHA or vitiate the general constitutional requirement that for a search to be reasonable a warrant must be obtained.

We hold that Barlow's was entitled to a declaratory judgment that the Act is unconstitutional insofar as its purports to authorize inspections without warrant or its equivalent and to an injunction enjoining the Act's enforcement to that extent.

CASE QUESTIONS

1. Is it true that after *Barlow's* most employers will consent to an OSHA inspection without requiring a warrant? What "reasonable legislative or administrative standards" for conducting an inspection would constitute probable cause for issuing a warrant? Who pays the ultimate price for the Court's decision? Must an OSHA official who observes a serious OSHA violation in the public area of an employer's premises first obtain a warrant before inspecting the remainder of the premises or causing a citation to be issued?

2. Suppose a magistrate issues a batch of warrants to an inspector, leaving blank the description of the premises to be searched. If refused consent to an inspection, may the inspec-

tor on the spot fill in the blanks of the warrant and thereby compel entry?

3. Does the warrant requirement significantly hamper inspectors? Does it significantly protect employers?

4. Does a business premise have the same privacy interest as a residential premise?

The Subpoena Power

Administrative investigatory power is supported by the authority to issue a subpoena. A subpoena is an official order commanding an individual to appear and testify or to produce specified documents. However, by itself an agency subpoena is merely a piece of paper. It has no legal effect until it is enforced by a court.

The constitutional concept of separation of powers requires that an agency apply to a court for enforcement of a subpoena. If an agency vested with the subpoena power issues a subpoena and the subject of the subpoena fails to appear or to produce the required documents, the agency must apply for a court order. Violation of the court order is punishable as a contempt of court.

The Supreme Court has established four criteria that must be met before an agency's subpoena will be judicially enforced.[21] These criteria, require the agency to (1) show that the investigation will be conducted pursuant to a *legitimate purpose,* (2) that the inquiry may be *relevant* to the purpose, (3) that the information sought is not already in the agency's *possession,* and (4) that the *administrative steps* required by law have been followed. These criteria establish a standard of fairness in administrative investigations to assure that the agency does not arbitrarily abuse the subpoena process to gain advantage beyond that contained in the powers delegated to the agency by Congress. Administrative procedures are discussed in detail in Chapter 4.

ALTERNATIVE APPROACHES

The debate over the proper role of the courts in interpreting the Constitution comes to the fore when a Supreme Court appointment is announced or when the Supreme Court announces a decision that touches the values

---

[21] 379 U.S. 48 (1964).

held dear by many Americans. Supreme Court nominations spur speculation on how the nominee might interpret the Constitution. Significant constitutional decisions touching upon the personal values of many Americans generate heated public debate. For example, the Supreme Court's decisions in the areas of prayer in public schools, abortion, and women's rights have recently led to attempts to amend the Constitution.

Critics of what are viewed as overly broad constitutional decisions claim that such decisions represent "judicial legislation," and that the Court is "rewriting the Constitution." Critics of decisions that appear to stand in the path of progress portray the Court as "applying the dead hand of the past" to the need for a living Constitution.

The debate between those who adhere to a "strict" interpretation of the Constitution and those favoring a "broad"construction is known formally as the debate between "interpretivism" and "noninterpretivism." Loosely described, those favoring strict interpretation are interpretivists; those favoring broader interpretation are noninterpretivists.

Interpretivism

Interpretivism is a theory of constitutional law that maintains that judges must decide cases according to the intent of the framers. It holds that judges should confine themselves to enforcing values that are stated or clearly implicit in the written Constitution. Such values are found by interpreting the Constitution's text, referring when necessary to the intent of the framers. It is essentially an historical inquiry. Under interpretivism, the Supreme Court reaches its decisions by "interpreting" the textual provision of the Constitution, which embodies the value judgment that the Court should apply.

To the interpretivist, the values to be applied to particular cases are embedded in the Constitution. As John Marshall, the third Chief Justice of the Supreme Court admonished, "We should never forget that it is *a constitution* we are expounding." The important value choices have already been made by the framers. It is up to the Court to apply those values, not substitute some other set of values in their place.

Interpretivists see their theory as protecting society against judicial tyranny. They point to the fact that federal judges are appointed for life. Although they can be impeached for bad behavior, impeachment is rare. Interpretivists also point to the difficulties of amending the Constitution as a method to override Court decisions. The Constitution has been amended only 26 times in almost 200 years, and the first ten amendments came into effect at the same time shortly after the Constitution's ratification.

Although interpretivists concede that the framers may not have given any specific thought to an issue, they argue that certain "important objects" may nevertheless be discerned to govern judicial decision making. Thus, the framers' intent serves to provide the broad contours around which the Supreme Court must confine its decision making.

Noninterpretivism

Noninterpretivism holds that the Supreme Court may make the determination of constitutionality by referring to values other than those constitutionalized by the framers. Such review is noninterpretive because the Court reaches its decision without really interpreting any provision of the Constitution, although, to be sure, the Court may explain its decision with language designed to create the illusion that it is merely "interpreting" or "applying" some provision.

Noninterpretivists argue the legitimacy of judicial creativity by pointing to the difficulties of determining the framers' intent and by pointing to acceptance of noninterpretivism by the American public. They argue that the boundaries of permissible constitutional interpretation are subject to continuous adjustment, not embedded in the intent of the framers. They maintain that the meaning of the Constitution is not fixed; rather it changes over time to accommodate altered circumstances and evolving values. To noninterpretivists, constitutional law is not an expression of values written into the Constitution by the framers, but is the product of a continuing process of valuation carried on by those to whom the task of constitutional interpretation has been entrusted. Noninterpretivists cite with approval Woodrow Wilson's description of the Supreme Court as "a Constitutional Convention in continuous session." Constitutional law thus emerges as a process by which each generation gives formal expression to the values it holds fundamental in the operation of government.

In arguing the difficulties in fathoming the framers' intent, noninterpretivists assert that historical materials are incomplete and fail to yield answers with sufficient clarity. They also point to another difficulty in the form of determining which framer's intent matters. Another problem pointed to is the fact that the Constitution was ratified by the people through their state ratifying conventions, and an examination of these debates fails to reveal any consensus of original intent. Noninterpretivists argue that the framers could not have even considered the possibility of certain issues arising. For example, they could not have contemplated the application of the Fourth Amendment's search and seizure provision to wiretapping and aerophotography.

Noninterpretivists also point to the acceptance that noninterpretivist interpretation has achieved with the American public. The fact that the American people have not repudiated these decisions by constitutional amendment directed at abolishing either the rule created or the Court itself evidences the legitimacy of such decisionmaking. To the argument that interpretivism protects the public from judicial tyranny, noninterpretivists respond by pointing to the appointment and impeachment procedures that apply to federal judges.

CHAPTER PROBLEMS

1. Congress passed the Agricultural Adjustment Act of 1938 in an effort to stabilize agricultural production so that farmers could obtain reasonable minimum prices. With regard to wheat, the secretary of agriculture issued an annual proclamation of a national acreage allotment that was apportioned among the states and ultimately among individual farms. Filburn was a small farmer who kept chickens and dairy cattle and raised a small amount of winter wheat. Some of the wheat was sold, but most of which was used by his family or as feed for his livestock. Filburn's quota for 1941 was set 11.1 acres but he sowed and harvested 23 acres. The secretary of agriculture fined him $117.11. Filburn brought suit against the secretary, seeking an injunction against enforcement of the penalty. He claimed that the regulation was beyond the reach of the commerce clause because the production of wheat for farm and family use was a purely local activity. Is Filburn right?

2. Like many states, Iowa imposes a 60-foot length limit on trucks operating within the state. It allows 55-foot single-trailer trucks and 60-foot doubles (a tractor pulling two trailers). However, unlike other western and midwestern states, Iowa, by statute, prohibits the use of 65-foot doubles within state borders. Consolidated Freightways, a trucking company which carries commodities through Iowa on interstate highways, sued, alleging that the Iowa statute unconstitutionally burdened interstate commerce. Because Consolidated cannot use its 65-foot doubles to move through Iowa, it must use shorter truck units, detach the trailers of a 65-foot double and shuttle each through Iowa separately, or divert 65-foot doubles around Iowa. Iowa defends the law as a reasonable safety measure, asserting that 65-foot doubles are more dangerous than 55-foot singles and that the law promotes safety and reduces road wear by diverting much truck traffic to other states. What result and why?

3. The state legislature is considering a bill that will ban the retail sale of milk in plastic nonreturnable, nonrefillable containers, but will permit such sale in other nonreturnable, nonre- fillable containers such as paperboard milk cartons. The bill's proponents argue that it will promote resource conservation, ease solid waste disposal problems, and conserve energy. Relying on the results of several studies, they stress the need to stop introduction of the plastic nonreturnable container before it becomes established in the market.

You are the vice president of marketing for the Clover Leaf Creamery. If the bill is enacted into law, your company stands to lose a great deal of money because it is the only dairy in the state that is already marketing its milk in nonreturnable plastic containers. The company invested large amounts of capital in plastic container production.

Studies conducted by the state Milk Producers Association, your industry trade association, present empirical evidence that the proposed legislation will not promote the goals asserted by its proponents, but will merely increase costs of retail milk products and prolong the use of ecologically undesirable paperboard milk cartons.

Develop a strategy to respond to this legislative proposal. If the bill is enacted into law, what arguments can your company advance to challenge the legislation's constitutionality? Could your local United States congressman or senator be of any assistance to your company? In what way? Explain.

4. As vice president for acquisitions for MITE Corporation, you have targeted the Chicago Rivet and Machine Co., an Illinois corporation, for acquisition. You and other members of MITE's management team decide to have MITE make a tender offer for all of the outstanding shares of Chicago Rivet at a price that includes a premium over the market price per share. In this way you hope to entice Chicago Rivet shareholders into accepting your offer. You ask in-house counsel to advise you of any legal problems that might be encountered in the takeover bid. Counsel reports that MITE will need to comply with the federal Williams Act, which requires that certain disclosure forms must be filed with the federal Securities and Exchange Commission. Counsel also advises you of an Illinois statute that regulates corporate takeover bids through tender offer. The statute forbids the making of tender offers in the state until the offeror files a statement of intent with a state official and the target company and agrees to participate in any hearings required by a state agency. Counsel warns that complying with the Illinois statute will involve delays that are not likely to be encountered with the Williams Act. These delays may jeopardize the success of the takeover if Chicago Rivet's management decides to resist the bid and compete with MITE for the stock of Chicago Rivet's shareholders.

Formulate a takeover strategy that takes into account what to do about the federal and state laws.

5. A New York statute provides that landlords must permit a cable television company (CATV) to install its facilities upon their property and may not demand payment from any tenant or CATV company in excess of an amount determined by a state commission to be reasonable. The purpose of the statute is to facilitate the installation of CATV facilities for tenants. The commission ruled that a one-time $1 payment was a reasonable fee.

After purchasing an apartment building, Jean Loretto discovered that Teleprompter Manhattan CATV Corp. had installed cables on the building. Loretto sued for damanges and sought an injunction in a New York state court. She alleged that Teleprompter's installation was a trespass and, insofar as Teleprompter relied on the state law, a taking without compensation in violation of the Fifth and Fourteenth amendments of the U.S. Constitution. Is Loretto correct? Explain.

6. Imagine you are the manager of the PruneYard Shopping Center. PruneYard is a privately owned shopping center that contains over 75 commercial establishments and is open to the public. One Saturday afternoon you observe a group of high school students setting up a table in a corner of PruneYard's central courtyard. The security guard informs you that the students are soliciting support for their opposition to a United Nations resolution. They are asking people to sign their peititions against the resolution, which they are then going to forward to state and federal government representatives as well as to the United Nations. The students have copies of the state constitution, which protects petitioning, reasonably exercised, in shopping centers even when the centers are privately owned. PruneYard has traditionally maintained a no-solicitation policy. Several proprietors in the shopping center phone you to complain about the violation of this policy. They want to know what you intend to do about it. Describe in detail how you will respond to the situation, and include in your decision an analysis of the constitutional considerations that will affect that decision.

7. The federal Surface Mining Control and Reclamation Act of 1977 is a comprehensive statute designed "to establish a nationwide program to protect society and the environment from the adverse effects of surface mining operations." The act establishes a regulatory program for surface coal mining that is enforced by the secretary of the interior. Under the act, the secretary is to adopt a regulatory program for each state, either by approval of a state program that meets federal minimum standards, or by the adoption of a federal program for any state that chooses not to submit a program. Enforcement rests either with the participating states or with the secretary for nonparticipating states. The Virginia Surface Mining and Reclamation Association, Inc., an association of coal producers engaged in coal mining operations in Virginia, sued the Secretary in federal district court, seeking a judgment declaring the act unconstitutional and enjoining its enforcement. The association alleges that the act violates the commerce clause and the just compensation clause of the Fifth Amendment. Will the association prevail? Why or why not?

8. Title VII of the Civil Rights Act of 1964 prohibits employers from discriminating according to race, color, sex, national origin, or religion in any employment advertisement. Is this statutory restriction on employment advertising constitutional? Explain.

9. In December 1977, as part of a continuing investigation of emissions from powerhouses located inside the Dow Chemical Company's (Dow) 2,000 acre Midland, Michigan, plant, the Environmental Protection Agency (EPA) requested entry to Dow's plant to inspect the powerhouses. The EPA had been admitted to the plant in the past and had received schematic drawings of the powerhouses from Dow. When the agency informed Dow that it intended to photograph the facility this time, the company objected and denied the EPA's entry request.

Rather than obtain a search warrant or institute civil proceedings to compel entry, the EPA contracted with a private firm for aerial photographs of the powerhouses. On February 7, 1978, the private contractor flew over Dow's plant and, using a sophisticated aerial mapping camera, took approximately 75 photographs at various altitudes over the plant. Some of these photographs showed parts of the Dow complex other than the powerhouses. The high degree of resolution in the photographs would reveal, if enlarged and magnified, details of equipment, pipes, and power lines as small as one-half inch in diameter. Many of these details, surrounded by buildings and structures in the internal regions of the plant, would be virtually unobservable from anywhere but directly above the facility.

The firm used by the EPA, which also did work for Dow, informed Dow of the overflights. Fearing that the photographs revealed trade secrets and would be available to competitors and the public, Dow brought a civil suit against the EPA. In its suit, Dow claimed that the EPA overflight and aerial photography were an unreasonable search in violation of the Fourth Amendment, and that the aerial photography was a taking in violation of the Fifth Amendment. What result and why?

10. When interpreting the Constitution, should justices of the Supreme Court adhere to the intentions of those who drafted the Constitution or should they be free to read other values into it? Explain.

CHAPTER 4

ADMINISTRATIVE PROCEDURES

The United States is a regulated society. Virtually every activity engaged in by organizations and individuals is subject to administrative regulation. Business managers must be particularly alert to the impact of administrative agencies upon their lives and careers. For example, administrative agencies are charged with:

— Regulating the safety of products
— Establishing requirements for the sale and purchase of securities to protect investors
— Preventing unfair methods of competition, unlawful pricing practices, and market monopolization
— Protecting workers' rights to engage in union activities, to work in a safe workplace, and to be treated by their employers without regard to their race, sex, or age
— Ensuring that companies do not pollute the environment

The list could continue. The point is that the regulations of administrative agencies are a major topic of study in the legal environment of business.

The chapters contained in Parts Two through Six of this book examine the regulatory activities listed above. However, before examining the specific areas of government regulation of business, it is necessary to look at some basic legal principles that apply to administrative agencies in general. This chapter focuses on administrative agencies, their creation, their structure, and their general procedures.

CREATION OF AN AGENCY

Much of the maze of government regulations with which business must contend emanates from administrative agencies. An *administrative agency* is a governmental body other than a court or legislature that takes action affecting the rights of private parties. Agencies may be called boards, commissions, agencies, administrative departments, or divisions. They may consist of single individuals, or they may be large bureaucratic structures employing hundreds of persons. But each administrative agency implements government policy in specifically defined fields.

In a complex technological society it is inefficient, and perhaps impossible, for Congress to immerse itself in the intricacies of each regulated activity. Congress has neither the time nor the expertise to do so. It therefore sets general goals and policies and delegates the task of applying them to administrative agencies composed of experts in the regulated areas.

Enabling Legislation

Congress creates an administrative agency by passing a statute. The statute, called the enabling legislation, specifies the name, composition, and powers of the agency. The Federal Trade Commission Act (FTCA) is an example of a typical enabling statute.

Section 1 of the FTCA creates the agency. Section 5 declares certain practices unlawful and empowers the agency to prohibit these practices. Section 5 goes on to describe the hearing procedure (called adjudication) to be used by the agency in prohibiting illegal trade practices and to provide for judicial review of agency orders in the federal courts of appeals. Another section of the FTCA authorizes the agency to issue rules specifying practices that the agency interprets the statute to prohibit. This section also sets out the procedures (called rulemaking) to be followed by the agency in formulating these rules. The section also provides for judicial review of the agency's rulemaking in the federal courts of appeals, and establishes the standards applied by a court in the course of such review.

Federal Trade Commission Act

§1: A commission is created and established, to be known as the Federal Trade Commission, which shall be composed of five commissioners, who shall be appointed by the President, by and with the advice and consent of the Senate.

§5: Unfair methods of competition in or affecting commerce, and unfair or deceptive acts or practices in or affecting commerce, are hereby declared unlawful.

Other sections of the FTCA describe the agency's internal procedures and provide for such powers as that of conducting investigations and requiring reports from corporations.

Constitutional Status of Administrative Agencies

Administrative agencies, often referred to as "the fourth branch of government," frequently engage in activities typical of the three branches of government. When an agency investigates, administers, or prosecutes, it acts like the executive. When it issues regulations, it acts like a legislature. When it engages in adjudication, it resembles a court.

The Constitution separates the executive, legislative, and judicial functions of government. The delegation of judicial and legislative functions to administrative agencies has been challenged as violating this separation of powers. At one time this challenge posed a significant problem for Congress. Congress could not delegate legislative authority to administrative agencies in such a broad manner as to indicate that it was abdicating its policymaking function.

In theory, Congress states in general terms what activity is prohibited or in what manner a class of activities is to be regulated. It is the agency's function to determine whether particular situations are specific instances of the general activity Congress sought to regulate or prohibit. Although such fact-finding may be the product of quasi-legislative rulemaking or quasi-judicial adjudication, it does not transgress the Constitution's separation of powers if the delegation enables the courts, the public, and Congress to determine whether the agency has exceeded its authority.

At one time Congress was required to provide very specific standards and guidelines for the exercise of agency discretion. For example, the Emergency Price Control Act of 1942 was upheld against constitutional attack, even though it delegated to the Office of Price Administration the power to set maximum rents and commodity prices. The act directed that prices be based on those prevailing at a specific date and enumerated the factors the agency could consider in deviating from those levels.[1]

Some states still require their legislatures to provide rigid guidelines for the exercise of administrative discretion. Federal courts and most states today, however, have stretched the requirement of standards and guidelines to sustain very broad delegations of power, such as those enabling the Federal Trade Commission to prohibit "unfair methods of competition" and the Federal Communications Commission to license radio broadcasters to operate in the "public interest, convenience, and necessity."

The current approach views delegation as requiring Congress to express an "intelligible principle" to which an agency must adhere. Thus, whereas the 1942 Emergency Price Control Act specified base dates and a detailed list of factors to justify deviating from them, the Economic

---

[1] *Yakus v. United States*, 321 U.S. 414 (1944).

Stabilization Act of 1970 simply delegated to the president the power to "issue such orders and regulations as he may deem appropriate to stabilize prices, rents, wages and salaries at levels not less than those prevailing on May 25, 1970." It also authorized the president to redelegate the task to any subordinate officer or agency that he might deem appropriate. The courts had little trouble in sustaining the statute's constitutionality.[2]

AGENCY TYPE AND ORGANIZATION

Administrative agencies exist at all levels of government. State and local governments have agencies that perform strictly local functions, such as zoning boards and liquor control commissions. Some agencies on the state and local levels, such as state environmental protection agencies, are counterparts to federal agencies. This chapter will concentrate primarily on federal administrative agencies.

Executive versus Independent Agencies

Many administrative agencies exist within the Executive Office of the President or within the executive departments comprised by the president's cabinet. These are called *executive agencies.* Congress has given the president general authority to delegate to subordinate officials functions vested in him by law. Cabinet officials receive authority delegated to them by the president or by statutes Congress enacts. These cabinet officials frequently redelegate such functions to agencies under their command. Other agencies under their command are established by Congress to administer particular statutes.

The first administrative agency was created by Congress on July 31, 1789, but it was not until 1887 that the Interstate Commerce Commission (ICC) was established as the first independent regulatory agency. Congress created the ICC because it was reluctant to vest the regulatory authority in President Benjamin Harrison, who had formerly been a railroad lawyer. The ICC has served as a model for the numerous other independent regulatory agencies that have followed.

Much of the administrative regulation businesses (see Table 4–1) must deal with emanates from the independent regulatory agencies. The *independent agency* is usually headed by a board or commission whose members are appointed for a term of years by the president with the advice and consent of the Senate. During their tenure these commissioners or board members may be removed by the president only for statutorily defined cause. Thus, independent agencies differ from executive agencies in that the president may appoint and remove the heads of executive agencies at will.

---

[2] *Amalgamated Meat Cutters v. Connolly,* 337 F. Supp. 737 (D.D.C. 1971).

> **TABLE 4–1**
> **Independent Agencies Affecting Business**
>
> Federal Trade Commission (FTC)
> Small Business Administration (SBA)
> Consumer Product Safety Commission (CPSC)
> National Transportation Safety Board (NTSB)
> National Labor Relations Board (NLRB)
> Equal Employment Opportunity Commission (EEOC)
> Securities and Exchange Commission (SEC)
> Environmental Protection Agency (EPA)
> Nuclear Regulatory Commission (NRC)

Agency Organization

An agency's organization varies with its functions and powers. Because all agencies have specialized functions, they develop bureaucratic hierarchies to implement and monitor regulations within their jurisdictions. Set forth in Figure 4–1, to provide a flavor of this bureaucracy, is the organizational structure of the Federal Trade Commission. The FTC was selected because it regulates many of the substantive areas covered in later chapters of this book. These include antitrust, advertising, consumer credit, and product safety.

The FTC consists of five commissioners appointed by the president with the advice and consent of the Senate for seven-year terms. The FTC staff is divided into three bureaus. The Bureau of Competition is responsible for enforcing the antitrust laws. The Bureau of Consumer Protection is responsible for controlling unfair and deceptive trade practices. The Bureau of Economics gathers data, conducts surveys, and provides expert support services for the other two bureaus.

AGENCY FUNCTIONS AND POWERS

Most administrative activities are informal. Agencies administer grants-in-aid and other assistance programs. They undertake investigations, gather and analyze data, issue reports, and provide advice to governments and private parties. The ability to give informal advice is one of the strongest powers an agency has. For example, if an inspector from the Occupational Safety and Health Administration suggests that a particular condition at a plant is unsafe, the employer, fearing a citation and fine, will be very reluctant to ignore the suggestion. Similarly, broadcasters hesitate to ignore informal suggestions from the FCC, fearing that their actions may harm them when their licenses must be renewed.

Many agencies promulgate regulations that have the force and effect of law. This process is known as *rulemaking*. Agencies may also conduct administrative proceedings to determine whether a particular individual or corporation has violated a statute or regulation. The proceedings are called *adjudications*.

FIGURE 4-1
The Federal Trade Commission

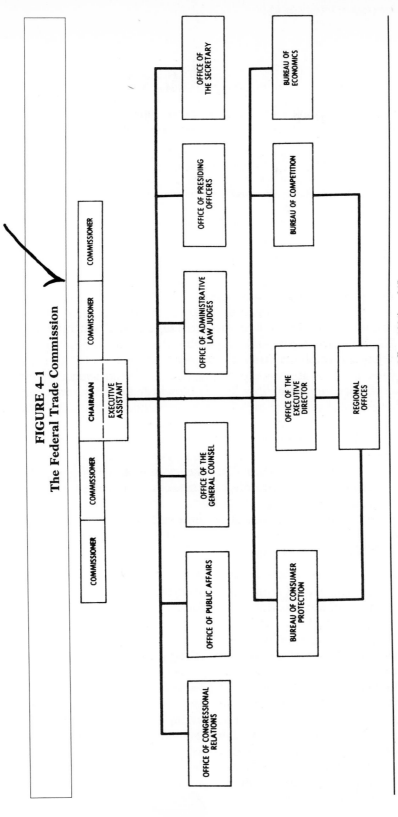

Source: *U.S. Government Manual, 1984–85* (Washington, D.C.: U.S. Government Printing Office, 1984), p. 845.

Adjudication enables an agency to make law and policy on a case-by-case basis in much the same way as a court. Adjudication gives an agency considerable flexibility in developing an area of regulation. Rule-making, on the other hand, results in regulations of greater certainty and consistency and allows for broader public input.

An agency may use adjudication even where it wishes to announce new principles or to overturn prior decisions. The choice between rule-making and adjudications is initially at the agency's discretion, and a court will overturn the agency's choice only if the agency has been arbitrary or capricious.

Standardizing Administrative Procedure

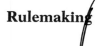

When engaging in rulemaking and adjudication, federal agencies must follow the procedures provided in their enabling legislation and in another federal statute, the Administrative Procedure Act (APA). Enacted in 1946, the APA was a congressional response to criticism of the vast discretion and power afforded numerous agencies. The act specifies the procedures agencies must follow and establishes standards and prerequisites for judicial review of agency action. The APA applies to all federal agencies. The APA does not supercede stricter procedural requirements imposed on an agency in its enabling legislation. However, if an agency's enabling legislation is silent as far as procedures are concerned, the APA applies.

Rulemaking

The APA defines a *rule* as "an agency statement of general or particular applicability and future effect designed to complement, interpret or prescribe law or policy." Rulemaking is the process of promulgating rules. In other words, rulemaking is the enactment of regulations that will be generally applicable in the future. All such regulations are compiled in the *Code of Federal Regulations*. There are three types of administrative rules:

— Procedural rules
— Interpretive rules
— Legislative rules

Procedural and Interpretive Rules

Procedural rules describe how an agency will proceed in various matters. Interpretive rules are statements that express an agency's understanding of the statutes it administers. These rules are intended to advise the public of the agency's positions on particular issues. They are not legally binding on the agency, the courts, or the public. Nevertheless, when courts construe the underlying legislation, they frequently find such agency interpretations persuasive. Courts give great weight to an agency's interpretive rule, even though such rules are not legally binding on courts. This is because the agency is usually the body closest to the legislation and has developed a particular expertise in interpreting it.

IRS Procedural Rule

(b) *Investigative procedure.*

(1) A witness when questioned in an investigation conducted by the Criminal Investigation Division may have counsel present to represent and advise him. Upon request, a copy of an affidavit or transcript of a question and answer statement will be furnished a witness promptly, except in circumstances deemed by the Regional Commissioner to necessitate temporarily withholding a copy.

(2) A taxpayer who may be the subject of a criminal recommendation will be afforded a district Criminal Investigation conference when he requests one or where the Chief, Criminal Investigation Division, makes a determination that such a conference will be in the best interests of the Government. At the conference, the IRS representative will inform the taxpayer by a general oral statement of the alleged fraudulent features of the case, to the extent consistent with protecting the Government's interests, and, at the same time, making available to the taxpayer sufficient facts and figures to acquaint him with the basis, nature, and other essential elements of the proposed criminal charges against him.

(c) *Processing of cases after investigation.* The Chief, Criminal Investigation Division, shall ordinarily notify the subject of an investigation and his authorized representative, if any, when he forwards a case to the Regional Counsel with a recommendation for prosecution. The rule will not apply if the case is with a United States Attorney.

Source: 26 Code of Federal Regulations Sec. 601.107 (b) and (c).

EEOC Interpretive Rule

Pre-employment inquiries as to sex: A pre-employment inquiry may ask "Male . . . , Female . . ."; or "Mr. Mrs. Miss," provided that the inquiry is made in good faith for a nondiscriminatory purpose. Any pre-employment inquiry in connection with prospective employment which expresses directly or indirectly any limitation, specification, or discrimination as to sex shall be unlawful unless based upon a bona fide occupational qualification.

Source: 29 Code of Federal Regulations, Sec. 1604.7

Interpretive and procedural rules are exempt from the rulemaking requirements of the APA. The APA's requirements apply, however, to legislative rules.

Legislative Rules

Legislative rules must be enacted in accordance with the APA. When such rules are consistent with the APA, the enabling legislation, and the Constitution, they have the force and effect of law. As such, they are binding on the agency, the courts, and the public.

The APA sets forth two methods for rulemaking: informal and formal (see Table 4–2). Informal rulemaking is used by most agencies. Formal rulemaking is only used when an agency's enabling legislation requires that its rulemaking be conducted "on the record." Each method is considered in detail below.

Informal Rulemaking

Informal, or "notice and comment," rulemaking is begun when an agency publishes a "Notice of Proposed Rulemaking" in the *Federal Register*. The notice must contain a statement of the time, place, and nature of the proceedings, the legal authority, usually a citation to the enabling legislation, and either the terms of the proposed regulation or a description of the subjects or issues involved. The notice provides the public sufficient information to participate in the proceedings. It need not parrot the language of the regulation eventually enacted. The agency need not even have any particular wording in mind. A simple, brief description of the subject matter is all that is usually required.

Following publication of the notice of proposed rulemaking, the agency provides interested parties time to submit written comments. The agency may hold public hearings, but it is not required to do so.

After the agency receives and considers the comments, it may publish the final version of the regulation in the *Federal Register* or discontinue proceedings. The agency must include a summary and discussion of the major comments received. However, it is not restricted to evidence produced in a formal manner. In addition to the comments received, it may consider information in its files, general knowledge in the field, material prepared by other agencies, and its own expertise. Where the agency in-

TABLE 4–2 **APA Rulemaking Procedures**	
Informal	*Formal*
Publication of notice of proposed rulemaking in *Federal Register*	Publication of notice of proposed rulemaking in *Federal Register*
Comment period: agency may limit parties to written comments	Comment period: agency must conduct formal hearings.
Publication of final rule in *Federal Register*	Publication of formal findings and final rule in *Federal Register*

tends to rely upon outside documents, it should so indicate in the *Federal Register* and make them available for inspection by interested parties. The regulation may take effect no sooner than 30 days following its publication.

Responding to complaints from small businesses about the burdens of federal regulation, Congress enacted the *Regulatory Flexibility Act of 1980*, amending the APA's informal rulemaking process. The act's purpose is to assure that agencies fit regulations issued through informal rulemaking to the scale of the businesses they regulate. To achieve this goal, agencies are required to solicit and consider "flexible regulatory proposals." As part of the informal rulemaking procedure, agencies must prepare a "regulatory flexibility analysis" (RFA) describing the impact upon small entities of any proposed or final rule. The RFA must be provided to the Small Business Administration. It must also be published in the *Federal Register* along with the required notices of informal rulemaking. The act also requires that agencies periodically review their rules that significantly affect small entities. The RFA further requires agencies to publish twice yearly regulatory agendas describing the rules they propose to consider as well as rules under consideration.

The principal advantage of informal rulemaking is efficiency. The lack of required hearings minimizes the opportunities for delay. But efficiency is obtained at a great cost: members of the public have minimal opportunity to be heard on the desirability of the proposed regulations.

The opportunity to be heard is particularly important in legitimizing a regulation. Individuals who have that opportunity are less likely to view the regulation as being forced upon them and consequently are more likely to comply voluntarily. There is a much greater opportunity to be heard when an agency is required to use formal rulemaking.

Formal Rulemaking

Like informal rulemaking, formal, or "on the record," rulemaking begins when the agency publishes a "Notice of Proposed Rulemaking" in the *Federal Register.* The notice must set a date, time, and place for a public hearing. The agency must hold formal trial-type hearings where all its evidence justifying the proposed regulation is presented. Interested parties have the right to examine the agency's exhibits and to cross-examine its witnesses. They may also introduce their own exhibits and call their own witnesses. These exhibits and witnesses are subject to examination and cross-examination by the agency and all other interested parties. The agency must then make formal, written findings, based on the evidence adduced at the hearings. The court of appeals for the appropriate circuit may review the findings and may set them aside if they are not supported by substantial evidence in the record as a whole.

The requirement of formal hearings enables parties that might be adversely affected by a proposed regulation to delay its implementation. Opportunities to do so exist at every stage of the rulemaking process. Such parties frequently flood the agency with issues they claim should be considered at the formal hearings. During prehearing conferences designed to simplify the issues, these parties can raise countless trivial procedural issues. Finally, they can drag the hearings out for years by cross-examining agency witnesses and by parading a seemingly endless supply of their own witnesses before the agency.

The most notorious example of such delays occurred when the federal Food and Drug Administration proposed a regulation requiring peanut butter to contain at least 90 percent peanuts. The peanut butter industry resisted the regulation, insisting that the appropriate amount was 87 percent. The rulemaking began in 1959 and did not end until 1968. The industry sought judicial review, and the Third Circuit Court of Appeals approved the regulation in 1970. The matter was finally laid to rest in late 1970, when the Supreme Court denied *certiorari*.

Adjudication

The APA defines adjudication as any process, including licensing, that results in an order. An *order* is defined as a final disposition other than a regulation. From this cryptic definition, adjudication has developed as a primary means of enforcing agency statutes and regulation. An agency prosecutes an alleged violator and affords the violator a trial before it. Since the same agency serves as prosecutor and judge, there are obvious problems. The APA attempts to deal with these problems by requiring agencies to separate their prosecutorial and judicial functions.

Separation of Functions

The adjudicatory hearing is presided over by an agency employee known as an administrative law judge (ALJ). The APA prohibits ALJs from consulting *ex parte* (privately) with any person or party involved in the proceeding. It also requires that ALJs not be responsible to or subject to the supervision or direction of any persons in the prosecutorial or investigative divisions of the agency. The APA thus attempts to split the agency into somewhat autonomous judging and prosecutorial divisions. For example, the chart on Figure 4–1 shows that the FTC's administrative law judges are structurally separate from the enforcement sections of the Bureaus of Competition and Consumer Protection.

Agency prosecutorial and investigative powers are frequently formidable. Agencies often can subpoena business records and require companies being investigated to present evidence of their compliance with the law.

A Typical Adjudication

The National Labor Relations Board is fairly typical of an agency with adjudicatory enforcement powers. The prosecutorial division of the NLRB is headed by the general counsel, who is appointed by the president. The general counsel has final authority over all prosecutions. Under his or her supervision are the regional directors and their staffs.

The board itself consists of five persons who serve staggered five-year terms after appointment by the president and confirmation by the Senate. The board appoints administrative law judges. They may be removed only after a hearing by the Civil Service Commission, at which good cause for removal must be established.

To understand the adjudication process, consider the following example (Figure 4–2). The XYZ Widget Corporation employed Harold Worker as a stock clerk. Harold had been very active in attempting to unionize the employees of XYZ. He had also been late for work on a few occasions, and once he called in sick when he was not ill. He was fired from his job. Section 8(a)(1) of the National Labor Relations Act prohibits employer restraint, interference, or coercion of employees exercising their rights to organize and bargain collectively. Harold believed that he had been fired because of his union activities, and thus his employer had violated section 8(a)(1).

If Harold wishes to prosecute the XYZ Widget Corporation, he must file a charge with the regional director, whose staff will investigate the complaint. If the regional director finds reasonable cause to believe a violation has occurred, he will advise XYZ and will try to settle the matter informally. The settlements are entered in the form of "consent decrees" or "consent orders." Frequently they provide for the respondent to deny the alleged violation but to agree to take the action demanded by the agency. If a settlement is unattainable, the regional director must file a complaint with the board.

The complaint is served on XYZ, which may file an answer admitting or denying the allegations. The case is assigned to an administrative law judge (ALJ). Then there are prehearing proceedings. These are similar to pretrial court proceedings, but less formal and with less extensive discovery.

The matter comes to trial before the ALJ. The trial is less formal

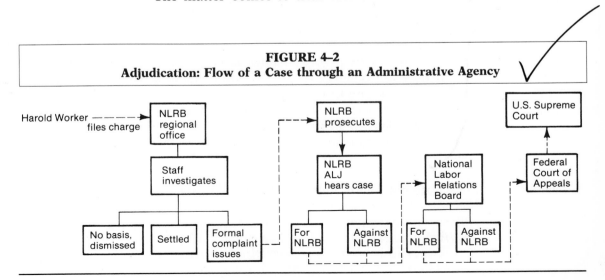

FIGURE 4–2
Adjudication: Flow of a Case through an Administrative Agency

than a court trial. For example, the rules of evidence are relaxed. Hearsay and other types of evidence frequently not admissible in court are admissible before the ALJ.

The parties may present both written and oral arguments to the ALJ, who then examines the hearing transcript and prepares a decision that includes findings of fact, conclusions of law, and a recommended order. The losing party may appeal to the full board.

Public Disclosure of Agency Information

Concern over secretive agency operations and the misuse of agency information led Congress to enact three statutes:

— The Freedom of Information Act of 1966 and the 1974 Amendments (FOIA)
— The Privacy Act of 1974
— The Government in the Sunshine Act of 1976

The Freedom of Information Act (FOIA)

The FOIA requires all federal administrative agencies to make all agency documents publicly available upon request unless the documents qualify for one of the following nine specific exemptions:

1. Documents classified by the president in the interest of national security.
2. Documents related to an agency's internal personnel practices.
3. Documents whose disclosure is prohibited by other statutes.
4. Documents containing trade secrets or commercial and financial information.
5. Interagency and intraagency memoranda which contain advisory opinions or recommendations or otherwise reflect the deliberative process of policy formulation.
6. Personnel, medical, and similar files if the disclosure "should constitute a clearly unwarranted invasion of privacy."
7. Law enforcement records where disclosure would interfere with enforcement proceedings, jeopardize an individual's right to a fair trial, reveal a confidential source or investigative techniques, or endanger the lives of law enforcement personnel.
8. Documents regarding the operation of financial institutions.
9. Geological and geophysical maps and data.

The act provides for indexing certain documents, sets time limits and uniform fees for handling requests for documents, and subjects any agency employee to disciplinary action for arbitrarily refusing a request for a document.

The FOIA has been used by businesses to obtain sensitive information about competitors. This type of information is often found in agency files because of the numerous reports companies are required to file. An FOIA request is directed to an agency. The act does not state whether the party that supplied the information may prevent the agency from disclosing it. This issue is considered in the following case.

Chrysler Corp. v. Brown

441 U.S. 281 (1980)

In order to be eligible for a federal government contract, Chrysler Corporation was required to furnish the Defense Logistics Agency (DLA) with reports on its affirmative action programs and on the general composition of its work force at several plants. Executive Orders 11246 and 11375 empowered the secretary of labor to request and evaluate such reports to ensure that government contract holders were providing equal employment opportunity regardless of race or sex. When the DLA informed Chrysler that it was about to release this information to third parties who had requested it under the Freedom of Information Act, Chrysler objected and secured a temporary restraining order in federal district court. At trial, Chrysler argued that disclosure was barred by the Freedom of Information Act. Although the district court held that the FOIA prohibited release of some of the Chrysler material, the third Circuit Court of Appeals reversed. The U.S. Supreme Court vacated (set aside) this reversal.

Justice Rehnquist

In contending that the FOIA bars disclosure of the requested equal employment opportunity information, Chrysler relies on the Act's nine exemptions and argues that they require an agency to withhold exempted material. In this case it relies specifically on Exemption 4:

> [FOIA] does not apply to matters that are . . . (4) trade secrets and commercial or financial information obtained from a person and privileged or confidential. . . .

Chrysler contends that the nine exemptions in general, and Exemption 4 in particular, reflects a sensitivity to the privacy interests of private individuals and nongovernmental entities. That contention may be conceded without inexorably requiring the conclusion that the exemptions impose affirmative duties on an agency to withhold information sought. In fact, that conclusion is not supported by the language, logic or history of the Act.

The organization of the Act is straightforward. Subsection (a) places a general obligation on the agency to make information available to the public and sets out specific modes of disclosure for certain classes of information. Subsection (b), which lists the exemptions, simply states that the specified material is not subject to the disclosure obligations set out in subsection (a). By its terms, subsection (b) demarcates the limits of the agency's obligation to disclose; it does not foreclose disclosure.

That the FOIA is exclusively a disclosure statute is, perhaps, demonstrated most convincingly by examining its provision for judicial relief. Subsection (a)(4)(B) gives federal district courts "jurisdiction to enjoin the agency from withholding agency records and to order the production of any agency records improperly withheld from the complainant." That provision does not give the authority to bar disclosure, and thus fortifies our belief that Chrysler, and courts which have shared its view, have incorrectly interpreted the exemption provisions to the FOIA. The Act is an attempt to meet the demand for open government while preserving workable confidentiality in governmental decisionmaking. Congress appreciated that with the expanding sphere of governmental regulation and enterprise, much of the information within Government files has been submitted by private entities seeking Government contracts or responding to unconditional reporting obligations imposed by law. There was sentiment that Government agencies should have the latitude, in certain circumstances, to afford the confidentiality desired by these submitters. But the congressional concern was with the agency's need or preference for confidentiality; the FOIA by itself protects the submitters interest in confidentiality only to the extent that this interest is endorsed by the agency collecting the information.

CASE QUESTIONS

1. Was Chrysler able to prevent release of the information by the DLA? Explain.

2. Do you agree with the Court's decision? Explain.

3. How did Chrysler learn that the agency intended to release the information? Will all companies know beforehand that information about them is to be released?

The Privacy Act

While the FOIA seeks to protect access to agency files, the Privacy Act seeks to protect the confidentiality of certain information supplied to government agencies. The Privacy Act restricts agencies from gathering unnecessary information about individuals. However, it does not prevent agency officials from using agency records for official purposes. The Privacy Act provides individuals with a right of access to agency files maintained on them and a right to request a correction. Agencies must respond to these requests in ten days either by making the correction or explaining the reasons why the correction was not made.

The Privacy Act forbids unwarranted disclosure of information that an agency maintains on someone. That is, the act forbids an agency from disclosing individual records to any other person or agency without the permission of the individual involved. The act provides that permission is not needed in 11 situations. Disclosure is allowed where it is:

1. To agency employees who need the record to perform their duties.
2. Required under the Freedom of Information Act.
3. The routine use of information.
4. To the Census Bureau.
5. To an individual for statistical research and the record is not individually identifiable.
6. To the National Archives.
7. To an agency for criminal and civil law enforcement.
8. To a person showing compelling circumstances affecting the health or safety of an individual.
9. To Congress.
10. To the General Accounting Office.
11. Pursuant to a court order.

The Government in the Sunshine Act

The Sunshine Act requires that all meetings of an independent agency be open to the public. The agency may close a meeting to the public if the meeting qualifies for one of several exemptions. These exemptions closely parallel those of the FOIA.

CONTROLLING ADMINISTRATIVE AGENCIES

Businesses affected by administrative action may want to influence agency decisionmaking. With regard to agency rulemaking and adjudication, this is done by participating, when possible, in the agency's procedures. Companies often belong to trade associations, who alert their members of an agency's proposal to issue a rule. The trade association and its membership then will communicate with the agency during the comment period or during any formal public hearings conducted by the agency.

After an agency has issued a rule or after the agency has held a hearing and issued an order, businesses or others affected by the agency decision may wish to change that decision. To do so, they turn to Congress, the president, or the courts.

Congressional Control of Administrative Agencies

The control of agencies by Congress takes several forms. The Senate confirms agency appointments. Congress may amend enabling legislation or include restrictions in legislation appropriating funds to the agency. Each house of Congress has oversight committees that review the work of agencies, hold hearings, and propose action regarding appointments, amendments to the enabling statute, and appropriations.

An example of congressional control of agency conduct can be seen in the treatment of the FTC by Congress in the late seventies and early eighties. During this time Congress considered riders to FTC appropriation bills forbidding expenditures on particular matters. For example, in 1980 Congress amended the FTCA and directed the allocation of agency funds with regard to FTC regulation of the funeral industry. Funeral industry lobbying prompted Congress' actions.

The FTC had proposed to issue a rule regarding trade practices in the funeral industry in 1975. Before the rule was actually issued, Congress enacted the Federal Trade Commission Improvement Act in 1980, amending the FTCA. One provision of the amendments stated, "the Federal Trade Commission shall not have any authority to use any funds . . . to . . . issue the funeral trade regulation rule in final form." By doing this, Congress effectively cut off funds to the FTC for that particular rule. The amendment went on to describe the basic provisions of a rule governing the funeral industry that would meet congressional approval and for which the agency could spend funds. The FTC finally issued its funeral industry rule in 1982.

Another method of congressional oversight is sunset legislation. Sunset legislation provides that an agency's authority shall expire on a given date unless Congress extends it.

The legislative veto was a method of oversight popular with Congress. Legislative veto provisions in enabling legislation provided that an agency's regulation could not take effect for a specified time period after issuance, usually 60 or 90 days. During that time Congress could pass a resolution of disapproval, vetoing the regulation. Legislative veto provisions had been enacted into over 200 enabling statutes, many affecting agencies that regulated business activity. Some legislative veto provisions required the veto resolution to be passed by both houses of Congress. Others allowed either house to act unilaterally. Legislative vetoes differed from amendments to enabling legislation in two ways: they were not presented to the president for signature; and, in some cases, they were approved by only one house. In the following case, the Supreme Court considered whether the legislative veto provision of the Immigration and Nationality Act was constitutional. The case has enormous repercussions with regard to the legislative veto provisions in many other statutes directly involving business regulation.

 **Immigration and Naturalization Service v. Chadha**

103 S. Ct. 2764 (1983)

Section 244(c)(2) of the Immigration and Nationality Act authorized either house of Congress to veto the decision of the Attorney General to allow a deportable alien to remain in the United States. Chadha (appellee-respondent), an alien lawfully admitted to the U.S. on a nonimmigrant student visa, remained in the U.S. after his visa had expired. He applied for a suspension of his deportation. An immigration judge, acting on behalf of the Attorney General, ordered the suspension and reported the suspension to Congress, as the act required. The House of Representatives passed a resolution vetoing the suspension. When the immigration judge reopened the deportation proceedings, Chadha moved to terminate the proceedings on the ground that the act's legislative veto provision was unconstitutional. The immigration judge ordered Chadha deported. Chadha appealed the deportation to the Court of Appeals, which held the legislative veto unconstitutional and ordered the Attorney General to cease attempting to deport Chadha. The Supreme Court affirmed.

Chief Justice Burger

[T]he fact that a given law or procedure is efficient, convenient, and useful in facilitating functions of government, standing alone, will not save it if it is contrary to the Constitution. Convenience and efficiency are not the primary objective—or the hallmarks—of democratic government and our inquiry is sharpened rather than blunted by the fact that Congressional veto provisions are appearing with increasing frequency in statutes which delegate authority to executive and independent agencies.

*   *   *   *   *

Justice White undertakes to make a case for the proposition that the one-House veto is a useful "political invention," and we need not challenge that assertion. . . . But policy arguments supporting even useful "political inventions" are subject to the demands of the Constitution which defines powers and, with respect to this subject, sets out just how those powers are to be exercised.

Explicit and unambiguous provisions of the Constitution prescribe and define the respective functions of the Congress and of the Executive in the legislative process.

Since the precise terms of those familiar provisions are critical to the resolution of this case, we set them out verbatim. Art. I provides:

> "All legislative Powers herein granted shall be vested in a Congress of the United States, which shall consist of a Senate *and* a House of Representatives." Art. I, § 1. (Emphasis added).

> "Every Bill which shall have passed the House of Representatives *and* the Senate, *shall*, before it becomes a Law, be presented to the President of the United States; . . ." Art. I, § 7, cl. 2. (Emphasis added).

> *Every* Order, Resolution, or Vote to which the Concurrence of the Senate and House of Representatives may be necessary (except on a question of Adjournment) *shall be* presented to the President of the United States, and before the Same shall take, Effect, *shall be* approved by him, or being disapproved by him, *shall be* repassed by two thirds of the Senate and House of Representatives, according to the Rules and Limitations prescribed in the Case of a Bill." Art. I, § 7, cl. 3. (Emphasis added).

These provisions of Art. I are integral parts of the constitutional design for the separation of powers. . . .

The records of the Constitutional Convention reveal that the requirement that all legislation be presented to the President before becoming law was uniformly accepted by the Framers. . . .

It is beyond doubt that lawmaking was a power to be shared by both Houses and the President . . .

The President's role in the lawmaking process also reflects the Framers' careful efforts to check whatever propensity a particular Congress might have to enact oppressive, improvident, or ill-considered measures.

* * * * *

By providing that no law could take effect without the concurrence of the prescribed majority of the Members of both Houses, the Framers reemphasized their belief . . . that legislation should not be enacted unless it has been carefully and fully considered by the Nation's elected officials. . . .

The President's participation in the legislative process was to protect the Executive Branch from Congress and to protect the whole people from improvident laws. The division of the Congress into two distinctive bodies assures that the legislative power would be exercised only after opportunity for full study and debate in separate settings. The President's unilateral veto power, in turn, was limited by the power of two thirds of both Houses of Congress to overrule a veto thereby precluding final arbitrary action of one person. It emerges clearly that the prescription for legislative action in Art. I §§ 1, 7 represents the Framers' decision that the legislative power of the Federal government be exercised in accord with a single, finely wrought and exhaustively considered procedure.

* * * * *

Since it is clear that the action by the House under § 244(c)(2) was an exercise of legislative power, that action was subject to the standards prescribed in Article I. [These standards] were intended to erect enduring checks on each Branch and to protect the people from the improvident exercise of power by mandating certain prescribed steps. To preserve those checks, and maintain the separation of powers, the carefully defined limits on the power of each Branch must not be eroded. To accomplish what has been attempted by one House of Congress in this case required action in conformity with the express procedures of the Constitution's prescription of legislative action: passage by a majority of both Houses and presentment to the President.

The veto authorized by § 244(c)(2) doubtless has been in many respects a convenient shortcut; the "sharing" with the Executive by Congress of its authority over aliens in this manner is, on its face, an appealing compromise. In purely practical terms, it is obviously easier for action to be taken by one House without submission to the President; but it is crystal clear from the records of the Convention, contemporaneous writings and debates, that the Framers ranked other values higher than efficiency. The records of the Convention and debates in the States preceding ratification underscore the common desire to define and limit the exercise of the newly created federal powers affecting the states and the people. There is unmistakable expression of a determination that legislation by the national Congress be a step-by-step, deliberate and deliberative process.

The choices we discern as having been made in the Constitutional Convention impose burdens on governmental processes that often seem clumsy, inefficient, even unworkable, but those hard choices were consciously made by men who had lived under a form of government that permitted arbitrary governmental acts to go unchecked. There is not support in the Constitution or decisions of this Court for the proposition that the cumbersomeness and delays often encountered in complying with explicit Constitutional standards may be avoided, either by the Congress or by the President. With all the obvious flaws of delay, untidiness, and potential for abuse, we have not yet found a better way to preserve freedom than by making the exercise of power subject to the carefully crafted restraints spelled out in the Constitution.

We hold that the Congressional veto provision § 244(c)(2) is servable from the Act and that it is unconstitutional.

Justice White, dissenting

Today the Court not only invalidates § 244(c)(2) of the Immigration and Nationality Act, but also sounds the death knell for nearly 200 other statutory provisions in which Congress has reserved a "legislative veto." For this reason, the Court's decision is of surpassing importance. . . .

*   *   *   *   *

The reality of the situation is that the constitutional question posed today is one of immense difficulty over which the executive and legislative branches—as well as scholars and judges—have understandably disagreed. That disagreement stems from the silence of the Constitution on the precise question: The Constitution does not directly authorize or prohibit the legislative

veto. Thus, our task should be to determine whether the legislative veto is consistent with the purposes of Art. I and the principles of Separation of Powers which are reflected in Article I and throughout the Constitution. We should not find the lack of a specific constitutional authorization for the legislative veto surprising, and I would not infer disapproval of the mechanism from its absence. From the summer of 1787 to the present the government of the United States has become an endeavor far beyond the contemplation of the Framers. Only within the last half century has the complexity and size of the Federal Government's responsibilities grown so greatly that the Congress must rely on the legislative veto as the most effective if not the only means to insure their role as the nation's lawmakers. But the wisdom of the Framers was to anticipate that the nation would grow and new problems of governance would require different solutions. Accordingly, our Federal Government was intentionally chartered with the flexibility to respond to contemporary needs without losing sight of fundamental democratic principles. . . .

This is the perspective from which we should approach the novel Constitutional questions presented by the legislative veto. In my view, neither Article I of the Constitution nor the doctrine of separation of powers is violated by this mechanism by which our elected representatives preserve their voice in governance of the nation.

CASE QUESTIONS

1. Why did the Supreme Court's majority conclude that the legislative veto was unconstitutional? Why did Justice White dissent? With whom do you agree?

2. What effect will the *Chadha* decision have on the ability of business to lobby Congress

for relief from an agency's regulation? Is there any continued role for legislative veto resolutions after *Chadha?* Explain.

3. Will *Chadha* result in greater or lesser congressional control of administrative agencies? Explain.

4. What role should Congress play in responding to administrative action? Should Congress defer to the expertise of regulators or should Congress be involved in specific regulatory issues? Having lost a battle with an agency, should special interest groups be able to turn to Congress and obtain relief? Explain.

Presidential Involvement in Agency Decisionmaking

Recent presidential administrations have sought to influence administrative decisionmaking beyond the usual influence of agency appointments. This involvement has taken place with regard to review of proposed regulations.

Executive Order 12291 requires all executive agencies to perform cost-benefit analysis of all proposed major regulations and to choose the least costly alternative. The Office of Management and Budget (OMB) monitors compliance with the executive order. All proposed and final major regulations are submitted to the OMB, which reviews and analyzes them, subject to review by the president. Thus, much agency rulemaking has been brought under the control of the president. The executive order does not apply to the independent agencies.

Executive Order 12291 reflects an attempt to modify agency rulemaking procedures. Its legality is debatable. Supporters of the presidential order argue that it is a valid exercise of executive authority to oversee the execution of the laws. Critics argue that it violates the Administrative Procedure Act and encroaches on the legislative prerogative in violation of the constitutional separation of powers principle.

Judicial Review of Administrative Action

Although oversight of administrative agencies occurs in Congress and by the president, the primary task of ensuring agency compliance with the law has fallen on the courts. Judicial review of agency action is provided for by the APA. Although a few agency decisions are reviewed in the U.S. district courts, most agency decisions are reviewed in the circuit courts of appeal.

The Right to Judicial Review

Not all complaints about agency action receive judicial attention. To challenge agency action in court, a party seeking judicial review must take the initiative. Such a party must meet the threshold requirements of:

— Reviewability
— Standing
— Exhaustion of administrative remedies

Reviewability   The APA creates a strong presumption that final agency action is subject to judicial review. This presumption may be overcome if Congress specifies that a particular action shall be exempt from judicial review. This requires interpreting the enabling legislation to determine the congressional intent. Congress must be clear and specific in indicating its intent to preclude judicial review.

Standing   Article III of the Constitution limits the jurisdiction of the federal courts to actual "cases and controversies." Thus a federal court has no power to act except when it is necessary to resolve a dispute. It may not render an advisory opinion or entertain a case that has become moot as a result of subsequent events. A federal court which acted in the absence of a live dispute would intrude into the provinces of the executive and legislative branches, thereby violating the principle of separation of powers.

Similarly, a court case must be brought by a party that actually has a dispute with the defendant. Such a party is said to have standing. The requirement of standing also ensures that the court will have two parties that are sufficiently antagonistic to develop a full record and present full arguments. Thus standing is usually thought of as requiring the party seeking judicial review of agency action to have a stake in the outcome.

Initially courts responded to the issue of standing in order to challenge agency action by requiring litigants to demonstrate a legal interest in the action. A party seeking judicial review thus had to show that the action infringed a right granted that party by the constitution, a statute, or the common law.

As agency regulation expanded, courts became more liberal in finding standing. The current test requires a party challenging an agency action to allege (1) a resulting injury that (2) falls within the zone of interests protected by the statute or the constitutional provision which the action is claimed to contravene. The most concrete type of injury is an economic loss resulting from the action. Less concrete injuries, however, will suffice. Thus the harm may be emotional, spiritual, environmental, or aesthetic. But a mere interest in the subject matter of the action is not sufficient to confer standing. The following case illustrates the standing concept.

 **Tax Analysts and Advocates v. Blumenthal**

566 F.2d 130 (D.C. Cir. 1977)

Tax Analysts and Advocates, a tax reform organization, and its executive director, Thomas F. Field (appellants) sought judicial review of IRS regulations allowing tax credits* for payments made to foreign nations in connection with oil extraction and production. They claimed the regulations violated the Internal Revenue Code. Field claimed standing because he owned a currently producing domestic oil well and competed with those companies that were granted tax credits.

Wilkey, Circuit Judge

Appellant alleges two injuries in his capacity as a competitor. As the first injury appellant Field alleges that the IRS rulings "result in his obtaining lower prices for his oil production than he would receive if the international companies could only deduct and not credit their oil production related payments." The rulings at issue in this case enable the international companies to pay far less income tax to the United States than if these payments were merely deductible. A substantial portion of the oil produced in Saudi Arabia, Libya, Kuwait, Iran and Venezuela by United States companies is exported to the United States. The prices charged by the international companies largely determine the market price for uncontrolled crude oil received by independent producers such as appellant Field. According to appellants, the lower taxes paid by the international companies allow these companies to sell their foreign oil in the United States at lower prices than would prevail if the companies could only deduct and not credit their foreign income tax payments. Thus, as a consequence, appellant Field contends that the IRS rulings result in competitive injury due to the loss of potential income in the sale of his domestically produced oil.

The second injury of a competitive nature alleged by appellant Field concerns the

impact of the challenged rulings on the value of his operating interest in his domestic oil well. According to appellant Field, the challenged IRS rulings increase the net income from foreign oil production over what it would be if the foreign payments could only be deducted from gross income for federal tax purposes. Thus, as a result of the rulings, foreign oil production yields higher investment returns and investors are more willing to invest in foreign oil production than they would be if the rulings had not been promulgated. The value of foreign oil well investments is therefore increased relative to similar domestic investments, to the alleged competitive detriment of appellant Field.

*   *   *   *   *

The standing doctrine has two sources: the "case or controversy" requirement of Article III of the Constitution, and judicially imposed rules of self-restraint known as "prudential limitations." The Article III constitutional requirement is one of "injury in fact, economic or otherwise"; such injury is the constitutional minimum which must be present in every case. If a court finds that there is no injury in fact, "no other inquiry is relevant to consideration of . . . standing." The vast majority of the case law on standing at all levels of the federal court system has been directed at defining this constitutionally based concept of injury in fact.

Prudential limitations, on the other hand, are not constitutional requirements;

---

* A tax credit is applied directly against a taxpayer's tax liability. A tax deduction is taken against a taxpayer's *income*. A deduction results in lower tax liability, but not to the degree that a credit does.—Au.

these limitations are developed and imposed by the Supreme Court in its supervisory capacity over the federal judiciary. . . . The first of these limitations to be enunciated . . . is the so-called "zone test": "whether the interest sought to be protected by the complainant is arguably within the zone of interests to be protected or regulated by the statute or constitutional guarantee in question." . . .

Injury in Fact

We conclude that appellant Field has suffered injury in fact in his capacity as a competitor. Although appellant's economic injury is relatively small in magnitude, this does not negate our finding of injury in fact. Appellant Field has alleged "a distinct and palpable injury to himself" which meets the requirements of Article III of the Constitution; given that the constitutional hurdle has been surmounted, we must now proceed to examine appellant's claim in light of the zone test.

Zone of Interests

The zone test admittedly presents the courts with an ambiguous and imprecise standard to apply. . . .

The zone test serves no independent purpose but, rather, constitutes one method to ensure that the basic purposes and policies of the standing doctrine itself are effectuated. . . . The first purpose, or basic policy, is to ensure the complete adversarial presentation of the issues before the court. The second purpose concerns the "proper—and properly limited—role of the courts in a democratic society." That is, the standing doctrine can be employed to define the proper judicial role relative to the other major governmental institutions in the society. As the Court has stated, the "prudential rules of standing . . . serve to limit the role of the courts in resolving public disputes."

We believe that the zone test is particularly suited to the task of furthering the second stated purpose of the standing doctrine relating to the role of the federal judiciary. The zone test, by its very language, implicates the relationship between the legislative and judicial branches as the predominant factor in its operation—"the zone of interests to be protected or regulated by the statute . . . in question." Thus, the zone test serves the purpose of allowing courts to define those instances when it believes the exercise of its power at the instigation of a particular party is not congruent with the mandate of the legislative branch in a particular subject area.

By its choice of language, the Supreme Court has indicated that the zone test is a quite generous standard; on the other hand, the test is obviously meant to serve as a limitation on those who can use the federal courts as a forum for grievances emanating from agency action taken pursuant to a particular statutory mandate. These competing considerations serve to frame the bounds of a court's discretion in applying the zone test. The discretion of a court to deny standing on the basis of the zone standard is not undefined; the zone test limitation is grounded in Congressional action as embodied in the statute. The zone test therefore cannot be used arbitrarily to deny access to the courts; it is based on discerned Congressional purpose, a purpose which can be more clearly or differently defined as Congress wishes.

* * * * *

Application of Zone Test to Appellant Field

Having described what we believe to be the purpose of the zone test and the manner in which it should operate, it is now possible to formulate with precision the relevant zone test inquiry with respect to appellant Field's standing as a competitor: did Congress arguably legislate with respect to competition in Section 901 of the Code so as to protect the competitive interests of domestic oil producers?

We answer the posed query in the negative for the following reasons. The purpose of the tax credit provision of Section 901 of the Code is to prevent the double taxation of any United States companies operating abroad. This purpose is clear from the fact of the statute itself, and has been consistently confirmed in the case law dealing with this particular provision in other contexts. The tax credit envisioned in Section 901 is also available to U.S. companies operating outside the sphere of oil extraction and production, with the same purpose of avoiding the double taxation of United States taxpayers, whether such companies have domestic competition or not. Given this purpose, it is obvious that the protective intent of the statutory section extends to all those U.S. companies doing business abroad and paying foreign income taxes.

In addition it cannot be said that parties in the position of appellant Field are arguably intended to be regulated by the provision granting tax credits; that is, appellant Field cannot be said to fall within the regulatory field of concern without stretching the concept of regulation to implausible limits. Therefore, we conclude that the interests being asserted by appellant Field as a competitor are not the interests arguably intended to be protected by the tax credit provision of Section 901 which is the statutory basis for the challenge in this case. The congruence between the purpose of the statute (to prevent the double taxation of particular parties) and the interests asserted by appellant (competitive interest in fairness) is not sufficient to invoke the federal judicial power.

* * * * *

. . . Every decision by a government agency generates consequences and various forms of impact on a wide range of valid interests held by a diverse range of parties. There is no doubt that the decisions embodied in the challenged revenue rulings have had an impact on appellant Field. But the concepts of consequence and impact are not the proper guideposts to define the relevant zone of interests; reference to these concepts does not aid greatly in determining whether a protected interest exists, but rather serves as part of the vocabulary in defining the relationship between an alleged injury and an asserted interest.

* * * * *

We recognize that as the result of our decision in this case it is likely that the revenue rulings at issue in the case may go unchallenged in federal court due to the lack of a proper party to sue. This eventuality does not, however, operate in favor of granting standing to the parties in this case. The standing doctrine should not be manipulated to guarantee that there is a party to bring any action in court that some persons may think desirable to have adjudicated.

CASE QUESTIONS

1. What was Field's injury? Why did it not come within the zone of protected interests?

2. What is the difference between the injury requirements and the zone of interests requirements? What functions do these requirements serve?

3. Who might be injured by the IRS regulation and have standing to challenge it?

Exhaustion of Administrative Remedies

Administrative agencies are created when Congress believes that a particular type of activity must be regulated by an expert body. In reviewing agency action, courts generally defer to agency expertise in technical matters. To ensure having the benefit of agency expertise, courts require that an agency action be in final form before it is subjected to judicial review. Courts also require that a party seeking judicial review first exhaust the available administrative remedies.

The exhaustion requirement generally applies even though the complaining party contends that the agency has exceeded its authority. For example, section 5 of the Federal Trade Commission Act empowers the FTC to order persons employing unfair or deceptive trade practices or unfair methods of competition to cease and desist using such practices, where such an order is in the public interest. If a FTC complaint counsel charges a party with violating section 5, that party must file an answer, proceed to trial before an administrative law judge, and appeal to the full commission before the matter will be subject to judicial review.

The Scope of Judicial Review

When a case meets the requirements of reviewability, standing, and exhaustion, a court may overturn an agency's action for any of the following reasons:

1. The agency failed to comply with the procedures detailed in its enabling legislation or the APA.
2. The agency's action exceeds the scope of its authority provided by its enabling legislation.
3. The agency's decision is premised on an erroneous interpretation of the law. Courts are never bound by an agency's legal interpretations, though they may find such interpretations persuasive.
4. The agency's action conflicts with the Constitution. For example, a regulation prohibiting a certain type of advertising may violate the First Amendment's guarantee of free speech. The Constitution's limitations on government regulation of business were explored in Chapter 3.
5. The agency erred in the substance of its action. The APA contains several standards that courts may apply in reviewing the substance of an agency's action. These standards vary in strictness and in the degree of discretion they afford the agency.

The strictest standard employed by a court is *de novo review,* which means examining anew the agency decision as if it had not been made before. Here, the court is not bound by the agency's findings of fact, but instead holds an entirely new hearing and makes independent findings. De novo review is provided for in only a few statutes. De novo review in the U.S. district courts is provided for challenges of agency action under the Freedom of Information Act, the Privacy Act, and the Government in the Sunshine Act. A court will also review an agency's findings de novo where the agency held adjudicatory hearings but its fact finding procedures were inadequate or where factual issues not considered by the agency are raised in court.

Enabling statutes frequently provide that agency *findings of fact* must be supported by *substantial evidence on the record as a whole.* In applying the substantial evidence standard, a reviewing court will not receive new evidence. The court examines the record and weighs the evidence supporting an agency's finding against the evidence contradicting it. The finding will be set aside only if the contradictory evidence substantially outweighs the supporting evidence. The Administrative Procedure Act requires courts to apply the substantial evidence standard to the review of formal rulemaking and adjudication. Both formal rulemaking and adjudication involve trial-type hearings.

The standard affording agencies the widest degree of discretion provides that agency findings not be set aside unless they are *arbitrary and capricious.* In applying this standard, a court must determine whether the agency considered all relevant factors and whether it made a clear error in judgment. The arbitrary and capricious standard of judicial review is applied to informal agency action, such as informal rulemaking.

In the following case, the Supreme Court reviews an agency decision to withdraw a rule.

 ## Motor Vehicle Manufacturers Association v. State Farm Mutual Automobile Insurance Co.

103 S. Ct. 2856 (1983)

In 1967, the National Highway Transportation Safety Administration (NHTSA) (Petitioner) issued Motor Vehicle Safety Standard 208, requiring the installation of seatbelts in all automobiles. It soon became clear that the use of manual lap seatbelts was too low to reduce traffic injuries to an acceptable level. In 1970, Standard 208 was changed to require installation of "passive restraints"—safety devices that do not depend for their effectiveness upon any action taken by the vehicle's occupants. The 1970 standard required inflatable airbag crash restraints. In 1971, although NHTSA presumed that manufacturers would continue to meet the Standard primarily by installing airbags, the agency revised the Standard again to permit the use of automatic seatbelts. Automatic seatbelts are fastened to the inside of a car door and deploy automatically to protect the passenger when the door is closed. In 1977, after repeated delays in the implementation of the rule, NHTSA issued Modified Standard 208, which required that passive restraints be phased in by car size starting in 1982.

By 1981, however, it became apparent that car manufacturers intended to comply with Standard 208 by installing detachable automatic seatbelts, rather than airbags, in virtually all new cars. The industry's plans led NHTSA to conclude that it could no longer reliably predict a significant increase in the use of passive restraints, and that only minimal safety benefits would result from application of Standard 208. The agency therefore rescinded the rule altogether.

State Farm Mutual Automobile Insurance Company (Respondent) sought review of the rescission in the Court of Appeals for the District of Columbia. That court held that NHTSA's rescission of Standard 208 was arbitrary and capricious. The Supreme Court affirmed the circuit court's judgment.

Justice White

Both the Motor Vehicle Safety Act and the 1974 Amendments concerning occupant crash protection standards indicate that motor vehicle safety standards are to be promulgated under the informal rulemaking procedures of the Administrative Procedure Act. The agency's action in promulgating such standards therefore may be set aside if found to be "arbitrary, capricious, an abuse of discretion, or otherwise not in accordance with law." We believe that the rescission or modification of an occupant protection standard is subject to the same test. Section 103(b) of the Motor Vehicle Safety Act states that the procedural and judicial review provisions of the Administrative Procedure Act "shall apply to all orders establishing, amending, or revoking a Federal motor vehicle safety standard," and suggests no difference in the scope of judicial review depending upon the nature of the agency's actions.

. . . [A]n agency changing its course by rescinding a rule is obligated to supply a reasoned analysis for the change beyond that which may be required when an agency does not act in the first instance. . . .

. . . If Congress established a presumption from which judicial review should start, that presumption—contrary to petitioners' views—is not *against* changes in current policy that are not justified by the rulemaking record. . . .

. . . The scope of review under the "arbitrary and capricious" standard is narrow and a court is not to substitute its judgment for that of the agency. Nevertheless, the agency must examine the relevant data and articulate a satisfactory explanation for its action including a "rational connection between the facts found and the choice made." . . .

*   *   *   *   *

The ultimate question before us is whether NHTSA's rescission of the passive restraint requirement of Standard 208 was arbitrary and capricious. We conclude, as did the Court of Appeals, that it was. We also conclude, but for somewhat different reasons, that further consideration of the issue by the agency is therefore required. We deal separately with the rescission as it applies to airbags and as it applies to seatbelts.

A

The first and most obvious reason for finding the rescission arbitrary and capricious is that NHTSA apparently gave no consideration whatever to modifying the Standard to require that airbag technology be utilized.

* * * * *

Given the effectiveness ascribed to airbag technology by the agency, the mandate of the Safety Act to achieve traffic safety would suggest that the logical response to the faults of detachable seatbelts would be to require the installation of airbags. At the very least this alternative way of achieving the objectives of the Act should have been addressed and adequate reasons given for its abandonment. But the agency not only did not require compliance through airbags, it did not even consider the possibility in its 1981 rulemaking. Not one sentence of its rulemaking statement discusses the airbags-only option. . . . We have frequently reiterated that an agency must cogently explain why it has exercised its discretion in a given manner.

* * * * *

We do not require today any specific procedures which NHTSA must follow. Nor do we broadly require an agency to consider all policy alternatives in reaching decision. . . . But the airbag is more than a policy alternative to the passive restraint standard; it is a technological alternative within the ambit of the existing standard. We hold only that given the judgment made in 1977 that airbags are an effective and cost-beneficial life-saving technology, the mandatory passive-restraint rule may not be abandoned without any consideration whatsoever of an airbags-only requirement.

B

Although the issue is closer, we also find that the agency was too quick to dismiss the safety benefits of automatic seatbelts. NHTSA's critical finding was that, in light of the industry's plans to install readily detachable passive belts, it could not reliably predict "even a 5 percentage point increase as the minimum level of expected usage increase."

* * * * *

In this case, the agency's explanation for rescission of the passive restraint requirement is *not* sufficient to enable us to conclude that the rescission was the product of reasoned decisionmaking. . . .

[T]here is no direct evidence in support of the agency's finding that detachable automatic belts cannot be predicted to yield a substantial increase in usage. The empirical evidence on the record, consisting of surveys of drivers of automobiles equipped with passive belts, reveals more than a doubling of the usage rate experience with manual belts. Much of the agency's rulemaking statement—and much of the controversy in this case—centers on the conclusions that should be drawn from these studies. The agency maintained that the doubling of seatbelt usage in these studies could not be extrapolated to an across-the-board mandatory standard because the passive seatbelts were guarded by ignition interlocks and purchasers of the tested cars are somewhat atypical. Respondents insist these studies demonstrate that Modified Standard 208 will substantially increase seatbelt usage. We believe that it is within the agency's discretion to pass upon the generalizability of these field studies. This is precisely the type of issue which rests within the expertise of NHTSA, and upon which a reviewing court must be most hesitant to intrude.

But accepting the agency's view of the field tests on passive restraints indicates only that there is no reliable real-world experience that usage rates will substantially increase. To be sure, NHTSA opines that "it cannot reliably predict even a 5 percentage point increase as the minimum level of increased usage." But this and other statements that passive belts will not yield substantial increases in seatbelt usage apparently take no account of the critical difference between detachable automatic belts and current manual belts. A detached passive belt does require an affirmative act to reconnect it, but—unlike a manual seat belt—the passive belt, once reattached, will continue to function automatically unless again disconnected. Thus, inertia—a factor which the agency's own studies have found significant in explaining the current low usage rates for seatbelts—works in *favor* of, not *against*, use of the protective device. Since 20 to 50% of motorists currently wear seatbelts on some occasions, there would seem to be grounds to believe that seatbelt use by occasional users will be substantially increased by the detachable passive belts. Whether this is in fact the case is a matter for the agency to decide, but it must bring its expertise to bear on the question.

* * * * *

The agency also failed to articulate a basis for not requiring nondetachable belts under Standard 208. It is argued that the concern of the agency with the easy detachability of the currently favored design would be readily solved by a continuous passive belt, which allows the occupant to "spool out" the belt and create the necessary

slack for easy extrication from the vehicle. The agency did not separately consider the continuous belt option, but treated it together with the ignition interlock device* in a category it titled "option of use-compelling features." The agency was concerned that use-compelling devices would "complicate extrication of [a]n occupant from his or her car." "To require that passive belts contain use-compelling features," the agency observed, "could be counterproductive given . . . widespread, latent and irrational fear in many members of the public that they could be trapped by the seat belt after a crash." In addition, based on the experience with the ignition interlock, the agency feared that use-compelling features might trigger adverse public reaction.

By failing to analyze the continuous seatbelts in its own right, the agency has failed to offer the rational connection between facts and judgment required to pass muster under the arbitrary and capricious standard.

------

* The ignition interlock device prevents a car from starting until the driver's seatbelt has been fastened. In response to public reaction against an earlier NHTSA rule requiring ignition interlock devices in automobiles, Congress had amended the Safety Act to prohibit any such requirement.—Au.

CASE QUESTIONS

1. What standard of review did the Court use in judging NHTSA's decision to rescind Standard 208? Why?

2. In order for an agency to meet the standard of judicial review used by the Court in *State Farm*, what must an agency do?

3. Why was the standard not met in *State Farm?*

4. Does the Court's decision mean that NHTSA's deregulation effort is completely aborted? Why or why not?

5. How far should a court go in deferring to an agency's decision to issue or withdraw a rule? Explain.

ALTERNATIVE APPROACHES

A continuous public debate abounds over the role of administrative agencies. It has been going on ever since the number of agencies mushroomed in the 1930s as part President Franklin Roosevelt's New Deal. At times, the public mood has been to encourage administrative efforts to solve social problems. At other times, the public sentiment has been skeptical of administrative solutions.

From this public debate, four views may be identified. One view favors giving agencies greater flexibility to carry out their public policy mandates. Another favors requiring that agencies follow more formal procedures when implementing public policy. A third view focuses on making agencies more politically responsive by requiring greater public participation in the administrative process. Still another view emphasizes the result of agency action and would require that agency decisions be efficient. These views sometime overlap.

Administrative Flexibility

Those who champion giving agencies broad flexibility to act with minimum procedural limitations have in mind a model of an independent agency consisting of experts. The expertise of administrative agencies should be given freedom to act. Although this sentiment may seem strange in today's climate of deregulation, this view dominated during the first half of the twentieth century and continues to play a prominent part in today's administrative law.

The view favoring administrative flexibility is reflected in administrative law in several places:

— In court decisions upholding broad delegations of agency authority in enabling legislation
— In court decisions allowing agencies broad discretion in choosing between rulemaking and adjudication when implementing policy
— In the fact that agencies may issue interpretive rules without following the APA's rulemaking procedures, and the fact that courts will give such rules great weight and deference
— In the APA's relatively relaxed procedures for informal rulemaking
— In the deference given by courts to agency rulemaking and adjudication when such agency action is judicially reviewed

Adherents of administrative flexibility argue that sound reasons exist for maintaining regulatory programs, including: remedying market failures, maximizing consumer welfare, and protecting the public interest. They argue that centralized decisionmaking and rulemaking in agencies whose members have the expertise to make technical decisions is necessary to carry out these programs. Furthermore, they assert public controversies may be diffused by transferring responsibility for policy resolution to administrative agencies. These agencies, they argue, should be free of political and public pressures that prevent them from performing their legislatively established responsibilities.

Formal Procedures

In contrast to the view favoring administrative flexibility is the view that favors requiring more formal administrative procedures. More formal procedures coupled with greater judicial review of agency action would allow interested parties to challenge the factual bases and policy choices of administrative agencies. Adherents of this view are skeptical of administrative "expertise." They voice concern that agencies have become too powerful. They charge that vague general statutes creating discretion in agencies threatens the legitimacy of agency action because major policy questions are decided by officials who are not accountable to the electorate. Advocates of this view seek to constrain agency discretion by imposing more formal procedures on its exercise.

In the 1970s and 1980s the proponents of formal administrative procedure succeeded in getting some of their proposals enacted into law. Some changes in administrative law requiring more formal agency procedures have been:

— The Regulatory Flexibility Act's requirement that agencies publish rulemaking agendas, review existing and proposed rules for impact on small entities, and share their impact studies with the Small Business Administration
— Provisions in the enabling legislation of some agencies, such as the FTC, requiring a form of rulemaking known as hybrid rulemaking, which requires the agency to hold hearings when issuing rules. Trial-type hearings are required for inquiries involving specific actors. Legislative-type hearings (the type congressional committees use) must be used for inquiries into general policy issues
— The requirement of Executive Order 12291 that all proposed major rules by executive agencies be reviewed by the Office of Management and Budget
— The 1970 National Environmental Policy Act's requirement that all agencies formulate environmental impact statements before undertaking any major federal action[3]

In addition to the procedures required by the above laws, several administrative formalization proposals have been given serious consider-

---

[3] This is discussed in detail in Chapter 18.

ation by Congress during the 1980s. Among them have been proposed amendments to the APA that would:

— Increase the amount of information an agency must include in its rulemaking notices required to be published in the *Federal Register*
— Provide specific procedures to be followed by agencies when undertaking informal rulemaking
— Require agencies to review every major rule within 10 years after being issued
— Remove the presumption in favor of the correctness of an agency's interpretive rule

Political Responsiveness

Adherents to the view that agencies should be more politically responsive would require greater public participation in the administrative process. Their underlying premise is that agencies should make policy by reconciling conflicting demands of competing interest groups. The intellectual foundations of this premise are the concepts of democracy and fairness. It is assumed that agency decisions will better match the "public interest" if those whose interest are affected participate in them. Furthermore, the process of public involvement encourages confidence in administrative fairness. It is fair that the interested or aggrieved person participate in the process.

Proponents of the political responsiveness of administrative agencies have received recognition in the 1970s and 1980s, as seen by the following:

— The Regulatory Flexibility Act's requirement that agency informal rulemaking procedures include public hearings on the rule's impact on small entities
— The Government in the Sunshine Act, which opens up the work of federal agencies to public scrutiny
— Sunset legislation, which increases congressional involvement in government agencies by requiring reconsideration of their existence
— The relaxation of the standing requirement for challenging agency action in court
— The FTC Improvement Act of 1975, which authorized the FTC to pay the expenses of persons participating in its proceedings who "would not otherwise be represented in such a proceeding"

Measures for increasing public participation in agency policymaking that have recently received serious congressional consideration include the following proposals:

— A requirement that agencies provide interested persons at least 60 days to submit written comments on a proposed rule.
— An amendment to the APA to extend the practice embodied in the FTC Improvement Act of paying the expenses of participants in FTC proceedings to all federal agencies.

The political responsiveness view of administrative procedure assumes that the regulatory process should mirror the best aspects of the legislative process, in minature. Under this view, the "best" decision is one that is most politically acceptable to the greatest number of participants. The model of agency that this view has in mind is not necessarily that of an agency consisting of experts, but an agency that acts as an arbiter or referee of competing interests.

Economic Efficiency or Impact

Many argue that agency policies should be "efficient," that is, agency policy making should maximize public welfare. And the public welfare is to be determined by assessing the costs and benefits of agency policies.

In recent years, Congress and the executive branch have required agencies to evaluate the economic impact of regulations. At least 40 laws in the areas of health, transportation, housing, and the environment have called for evaluation of the economic impact of rules proposed under them. Several rules specifically authorize funding for these evaluations. Similarly, recent presidential administrations have pursued economic impact analysis.

In the 1980s Congress has given serious consideration to a proposed amendment to the APA that would modify agency rulemaking procedure to require agencies to:

— Conduct an analysis of the costs and benefits of any proposed or final rule
— Describe all reasonable alternatives to the rule
— Explain why the rule chosen is more cost effective than the alternatives

The courts have been less responsive to the economic efficiency viewpoint. The Supreme Court upheld a regulation issued by the Occupational Safety and Health Administration (OSHA) limiting occupational exposure to cotton dust, which induces "brown lung" disease.[4] In doing so, the Court rejected the argument of the American Textile Manufactures Institute that Congress intended OSHA to support its choice of rule by cost-benefit analysis.

---

[4] American Textile Manufacturers Institute, Inc. v. Donovan, 452 U.S. 490 (1981).

CHAPTER PROBLEMS

1. A statute creates an Industrial Accident Commission (IAC), provides a comprehensive scheme to compensate employees for work-related injuries and states that the IAC shall award such compensation after conducting hearings. The findings of the IAC are subject to judicial review and reversal only if the IAC acts outside its powers or if the award is not supported by substantial evidence on the record taken as a whole. What is the nature of the power exercised by the IAC in making awards? Is it constitutional to confer such power on an administrative agency? Explain. Suppose that the statute expressly made the IAC's determinations final and unreviewable by a court. Would such a provision be constitutional?

2. In an adjudicatory proceeding, the National Labor Relations Board (NLRB) confronted the question of whether an employer must supply a union with a list of employees eligible to vote in an election between the employer and the union. In the course of the proceedings, the NLRB invited certain interested parties to file briefs and to participate in oral arguments of the issue. Various employer groups and unions did so. After these proceedings, the board issued its decision. It purported to establish the general rule that employee lists must be provided. However, the NLRB did not apply its new rule to the company involved in the case before it. Instead, it held that the new rule would apply only in elections held 30 days from the date of its decision.

You are vice president of employee relations of the Wyman–Gordon Company. A union has petitioned the board to conduct an election to determine whether your company's employees want it to represent them in collective bargaining negotiations. Must you comply with the previous NLRB's decision that an employee list be provided? Explain. If you decide to challenge the NLRB's rule laid down earlier, how would you do it? What arguments could you make against the rule? Would they be successful? Explain. If your company were not currently undergoing a NLRB election proceeding, could you challenge the NLRB's rule? Explain.

3. You are the president of a restaurant trade association. The FTC issued a notice of proposed rulemaking stating that its studies found many restaurants misrepresented the food they served. Dishes described on menus and in advertising as "veal" often contained substantial amounts of beef and soy. "Hamburgers" contained large percentages of soy and similar additives, and "fresh vegetables" were often frozen. The notice proposed regulations detailing specific requirements when these and similar terms were used on menus or in ads. The association's members oppose the proposed regulations. How will you respond to the notice?

4. You are the personnel manager for XYZ Corporation. The company president has given you a copy of a complaint served on the company by the regional director of the NLRB. The complaint charges that the company fired two employees because they were involved in union organizing activities. Your records show that both employees were active union organizers but that they were fired because each had 15 unexcused absences over the past year. Prepare a memorandum for the president outlining the procedures that the NLRB will use in processing the complaint and recommending a course of action.

5. The Equal Employment Opportunity Commission (EEOC) has charged that Willie's Widget Works refused to hire an applicant because she was female. Willie's claims that the applicant did not meet specified qualifications for the job. The EEOC subpoenas Willie's book of job descriptions. Willie's complains that the book is confidential and resists the subpoena. The parties settle. Willie's agree to turn over the book and the EEOC agrees not to copy it, to keep it confidential, and to return it when it is no longer needed. Can Willie's competitors use the FOIA to obtain the book while it is in the EEOC's possession?

6. The secretary of the interior granted Walt Disney Enterprises a use permit to develop a ski resort in the Mineral King Valley of the Sequoia National Forest. The Sierra Club sought review of this decision in a federal court of appeals. The Sierra Club alleged that it was interested in preserving Mineral King in its undeveloped state, but the club did not allege that any of its members used Mineral King or would suffer any specific injury from the development of the ski resort. Does the Sierra Club have standing to challenge the secretary of the interior's decision? Explain.

7. The National Motor Vehicle Safety Act empowers the secretary of transportation to issue regulations establishing practicable standards that meet the need for motor vehicle safety. The secretary proposes a regulation requiring that all retread tires contain permanent labeling of tire size, maximum inflatable pressure, ply rating, tubeless or tube type, and bias belted or radial construction. During the notice and comment period, tire retreaders seek modification of the proposal to eliminate the requirement of permanency. They claim that two thirds of all the tire casings they receive either lack labels or have labels that are obliterated during the retread process. They further argue that furnishing permanent labels will require the use of mold plates. Unlike a tire manufacturer who mass produces large batches of tires to the same specifications, retreaders deal with small batches of different sizes and construction. This means that the mold plates will have to be changed frequently by employees working with hand tools at temperatures up to 300°F. The retreaders produce a study showing that the labeling process is 80 percent effective and adds 30 percent to the cost of retreads. If the secretary promulgates the regulation, will it be sustained in court? Explain.

8. The Clear Air Act authorizes the Environmental Protection Agency to regulate gasoline additives whose emissions "will endanger the public welfare." EPA promulgates regulations requiring a stepwise reduction of the lead content of gasoline. Scientific and clinical evidence shows that high concentrations of lead in the body are toxic, that lead can be absorbed from ambient air, and that 90 percent of the lead in the air comes from automobiles. However, air is only one of several lead sources absorbed by the body. Furthermore, since all humans breathe the same air, it is impossible to conduct a controlled experiment. Consequently it is impossible to identify the precise level of airborne lead that will endanger human health, and no single dispositive study fully supports the EPA's position. Will a court overturn the rule? Explain.

9. The Economic Development Administration is empowered to award communities with high unemployment rates grants for use in community projects designed to create jobs. To fund a project that will compete with local private businesses, EDA must find that there is sufficient demand to support the funded project as well as the local businesses. EDA, relying on data from the Department of Labor which show a 15 percent unemployment rate in and around Duluth, Minnesota, makes a substantial grant to the city of Duluth for operation of a ski resort at nearby Spirit Mountain. EDA projects future demand by using a formula based on an average of demand for the preceding five years. It, therefore, refuses to consider reports from the National Weather Service predicting an abnormally warm winter in the upper Great Lakes region. It also makes a mathematical error in applying its formula, resulting in an underestimation of the demand. If the competing private ski resorts sue EDA and the city of Duluth, will they succeed in having the grant set aside? Explain.

10. Which view or views of administrative procedures discussed under "Alternative Approaches" do you most agree with? Explain.

PART PROBLEMS

1. Congress established the Federal Communications Commission (FCC) to regulate broadcasting in the "public interest, convenience and necessity." Congress authorized the FCC to pass rules and regulations to accomplish its legislative objective. The FCC passed Regulation G prohibiting cable television stations from broadcasting: feature films less than three years old, live sports events, and series programs.

In its statements of the final rule published in the *Federal Register,* the FCC expressed that the rule was necessary to prevent cable companies from buying up programs and removing them from the conventional free broadcasting networks. It reasoned that, if this "siphoning" occurred, only those who could afford cable would be able to view prime programming; that sponsors would abandon conventional television; and that conventional television would ultimately be displaced by cable television.

There are 24 cable companies in the state of Kansas. They have banned together and formed Kansas Cable Broadcasters (KCB) for the purpose of promoting cable broadcasting in Kansas. The association has one general secretary, a lobbyist, and one paid attorney on its staff. It has also hired an advertising firm to "promote the cablecasters' image and undermine conventional television broadcasting."

Several of the cable companies in Kansas do not fully comply with Regulation G; they purchase and air programs prohibited by that regulation. This was brought to the attention of the attorney for KCB at an annual convention. The station manager of WAKW, a member of the association, informed the association's attorney that Regulation G was unrealistic; that his station was airing first run feature movies and series and that other member broadcasters were doing the same. The association's attorney in response sent out a questionnaire to each of the station managers, designed to uncover the extent of the violations. Fifteen companies responded to the questionnaire prepared by the association's attorney.

The FCC has been investigating the extent of noncompliance with Regulation G in Kansas and has become aware of the questionnaire prepared by the association's attorney. It has issued a summons to the attorney demanding the responses to the questionnaires.

a. Discuss the legality of Regulation G and include a constitutional analysis.

b. As manager for one of the cable stations, how would you suggest attacking the regulation?

c. As owner of the advertising firm hired by KCB, develop a lawful plan to "promote the cablecasters' image and undermine conventional broadcasting."

d. What is the attorney's responsibility regarding release of the questionnaires?

e. As a compliance officer with the FCC what course of action would you recommend in the event you were unable to obtain the questionnaires?

2. The following notice recently appeared in the *Federal Register:*

Notice of Proposed Rulemaking— Federal Trade Commission

The FTC staff has conducted an initial study of real estate sales personnel and has found that many salespersons are incompetent. The use of incompetent salespersons has harmful effects on consumers who rely on these persons for information concerning the law, the market, and what to look for in buying a house. Accordingly, the commission proposes the following regulation:

Section 1. Authority for this regulation may be found in section 5 of the Federal Trade Commission Act which empowers the FTC to enact regulations designed to prevent unfair methods of competition and unfair and deceptive trade practices in interstate commerce.

Section 2. The Commission finds that the use of inadequately trained real estate salespersons is an unfair and deceptive trade practice which affects interstate commerce.

Section 3. No person may sell real estate anywhere in the United States unless he or she has obtained an FTC Real Estate Sales License (RESL).

Section 4. To apply for a RESL, an individual must hold at least an Associate of Arts degree in real estate from an accredited university, college, or junior college. The applicant's program of study must include courses in real estate law, real estate finance, the real estate market, and elementary architecture.

Section 5. Each applicant, upon passing a comprehensive examination with a score of 65 percent or higher, will be issued a license. The license will be subject to renewal five years after it is issued. A licensee must pass a renewal examination at that time. Interested persons may submit comments until March 15th. A hearing will be held at FTC headquarters in Washington, D.C., on March 19 at 9:00 A.M.

You are the president of the American Real Estate Trade Association (ARETA). The membership of your association is vehemently opposed to this new regulation. You must prepare a report to the membership. In your report, be sure to include the following:

a. What action, if any, should ARETA take to oppose the proposed regulation?

b. If the regulation is enacted, how should ARETA proceed? Would ARETA be successful if it challenged the regulation in court? Explain.

In the 1980s many are wondering whether government has intervened too deeply into the affairs of business.

PART TWO

CONSUMER LAW

There was a time when consumers did not need the protection of law. Technology was not complex. Products were few. The economy was simple. Mass marketing was nonexistent. Those were the days when seller-buyer relations were personal. Sellers sold locally. As such they were especially sensitive to "bad press" and were prone to satisfy the buyer. Consumers were in a good position to protect themselves. The rule of the day was "buyer beware"—and they were.

By the post–Civil War period, it was a different world. Assembly lines resulted in increased production. Technological advances were responsible for complex products, unfamiliar to buyers. Growth in the transportation system made mass distribution possible. Sellers were no longer confined to local markets. Seller-buyer relations became highly impersonal. No longer were consumers in a position to fend for themselves, and many were taken advantage of by sellers. Upton Sinclair's book, *The Jungle,* exposed one aspect of the abuse—the filthy conditions that existed in the meat packing industry. The climate was ripe for government regulation.

Federal regulation is normally preceded by common law and state statutory protections, which prove inadequate. This was true in the area of federal consumer law legislation. In 1906 the Food and Drugs Act and the Meat Inspection Act were passed to curb abuses. The Federal Trade Commission, created in 1914 to combat antitrust activity, was also authorized to supervise the marketplace for other unfair methods of competition. In the 1920s and 1930s additional consumer legislation was passed.

The Federal Trade Commission Act was amended to give consumers added protection against the growing number of deceptive practices.

Disregard for consumer needs and rights had reached disturbing heights in the 1950s. Credit extension and related activities altered the nature of the economy. Advertisers were utilizing psychological strategies to influence the consumer's will. A drug called thalidomide, which was

---

It is better to have a fence around the top of a cliff than to have an ambulance in the valley below.

National Commission on Product Safety Hearings

---

found to cause birth defects, heightened consumer awareness of the dangers of unregulated products. Cries for reform were heard. In his book, *Unsafe at Any Speed,* Ralph Nader exposed the lack of safety consciousness in the automobile industry. He became a prominent figure championing the cause of the consumer. President John F. Kennedy gave impetus to the growing consumer movement. In a 1962 congressional address entitled "Protecting the Consumer Interest," he expressed the need to recognize the rights of the consumer. In particular he listed four consumer rights that needed legislative and administrative protection:

— the right to safe products
— the right to be informed about products
— the right to definite choices in selecting products
— the right to be heard regarding consumer interests

It was not until the 1960s that "consumerism" produced a flurry of federal legislation. Consumer legislation and administrative activity in the 1960s and 1970s was a response to unsafe products, deceptive advertising, and abusive credit practices. The Consumer Product Safety Commission was established to regulate product safety. The Federal Trade Commission's authority was further expanded to police credit activities.

In the 1980s many are wondering whether government has intervened too deeply into the affairs of business. Worried about the high cost of regulation and its inflationary nature, the federal government has made some significant moves toward cutting back on consumer regulation. To some extent, the pendulum has swung back. Many federal laws adopt a framework that encourages states to displace federal regulation. And, recognizing that government regulation is a product of a lack of self-policing, manufacturers, advertisers, and members of the credit industry have increased self-regulatory activities. Deregulation, which may be the wave of the future, has occurred in some industries. Nevertheless, business managers continue to operate today in an environment of consumer regulation.

The chapters that follow highlight the significant areas of consumer law. Chapter 10 examines consumer laws related to products. Chapter 11 explores the laws that affect the advertising of those products. Chapter 12 covers the laws as they relate to credit extension, collection, and bank-

---

*I*ndividuals and agencies have competed . . . to be on the crest of the wave of consumer protection.
. . . [Y]et the short-term political advantage offered by spectacular but unsound consumer legislation can do lasting damage to the very consumers it purports to help.

James M. Roche, Chairman
General Motors

---

ruptcy. Together these chapters provide an up-to-date treatment of the consumer laws that impact business.

CHAPTER 5

PRODUCT SAFETY

Hairdryers, microwave ovens, garage door openers, toasters, blenders, snow blowers, and other household products make life more comfortable. They usually perform to the satisfaction of the consumer, but when they are defective they may cause both inconvenience and injury.

Manufacturers do not want to produce defective products. In fact, many belong to associations that subject their members to minimum product safety standards. Nonetheless, injuries arising from product defects account for over one million lawsuits per year. Some of the largest monetary judgments are awarded to injured plaintiffs based on successful suits lodged against manufacturers and distributors. Many of these awards are highly publicized. This provides an incentive for other consumers to prosecute similar claims. Faced with rising costs for legal defense and payment of judgment awards, most businesses now insure against their liability. Insurance companies have increased their rates to reflect the sharp increase in claims payments. Businesses pass these additional costs on to the public in the form of higher retail prices. In the end the consumer pays for the injury.

The government has intervened to prevent product injury. Federal administrative agencies have been created to supervise the market and establish product safety standards. These government agencies work closely with business in an effort to create a safer environment for the consumer.

This chapter examines state and federal laws governing product liability and safety. These laws are applicable to small businesses and giant corporations alike. It is essential for those who operate in the business world to be aware of their legal responsibilities and the standards imposed on their conduct.

PRODUCT LIABILITY—STATE LAW

A product liability action results when a plaintiff sues because of an injury caused by a defective product. Defects may occur in construction, design, and labeling.

A *construction defect* results when a product falls short of the manufacturer's own established standards. Many household products are produced on assembly lines. Quality control becomes very important. Because of human frailty, an overcarbonized bottle or a defectively wired television set may go unnoticed—omissions that could result in injury to product users.

A *design defect* occurs when the product meets the manufacturer's standards but the standards are inferior. A football helmet or a radial tire may conform to the manufacturer's specifications, yet their inability to absorb shock may invite injury.

A *labeling defect* occurs when the manufacturer fails to provide adequate warning of the risks associated with product exposure or proper procedures for using a product. Failure to include a warning against a particular medicine's hazard to diabetics may constitute a labeling defect.

There are several theories of recovery under which a plaintiff may proceed against the party responsible for a defective product that caused injury. The most common theories are negligence, strict liability, and warranty.

Negligence

Through the process of the common law, courts have carved out certain recognized wrongs. These wrongs are commonly referred to as torts. An introduction to torts is contained in chapter 1. A tort is a civil wrong other than a breach of a contract. One tort recognized in the law is negligence. Negligence occurs when a person fails to exercise a standard of care in a situation that causes harm to another.

A plaintiff must prove certain elements to recover against a defendant under the tort of negligence. These elements are: a duty of care owed to the plaintiff, a breach of that duty, which proximately causes injury to the plaintiff.

Duty of Care

The law imposes a duty of ordinary care upon people's conduct. To gauge this ordinary care standard of conduct the law created a fictitious being—"the reasonable person"—who always acts prudently under existing circumstances. One whose conduct falls below that of the reasonable person has breached the duty of care imposed by law.

Breach of Duty

Those who fail to conform to the reasonable person standard risk liability to plaintiffs who are injured as a result. A breach of a duty of care may result from the commission or omission of an act. An automobile dealer may commit a *negligent act* by overinflating a spare tire. A manufacturer's failure to test a boiler after assembly is an example of a *negligent omission*.

The type of conduct that is considered reasonable may change with circumstances. In 1982 several deaths and injuries occurred when Tylenol capsules were laced with cyanide. The packaging made it quite easy for this to happen. Now many manufacturers of over-the-counter drugs, including the makers of Tylenol, are using tamperproof containers that are difficult, if not impossible, to penetrate without detection. Failure to use a tamperproof container may now be considered a breach of ordinary care.

Res Ipsa Loquitur

Of course, not every product defect is caused by a negligent act or omission; some occur even though the manufacturer exercises prudent care. In a highly industrialized society it is often extremely difficult for a plaintiff to prove that the product defect resulted from the manufacturer's breach of a duty of care. The plaintiff is normally not privy to inside information regarding the manufacturer's operation. Moreover, when a manufacturer produces 10,000 widgets a day, it is unlikely that even the manufacturer would know why one widget proved defective.

To help injured plaintiffs through the difficult task of establishing a breach of duty of care, courts developed a rule of evidence referred to as *res ipsa loquitur* ("the thing speaks for itself"). *Res ipsa loquitur* permits the natural inference of negligence to be drawn from the fact that a product is defective. The rule applies when the injury is one that ordinarily does not occur except where someone has been negligent, and where the instrumentality causing the injury was within the defendant's exclusive control. If a rat's tail is found in a pop bottle or poison in baking flour, a common-sense presumption arises that their presence resulted from someone's negligence. *Res ipsa loquitur* requires the defendant to explain away that presumption. Because of this rule, many plaintiffs are able to establish their case without any direct evidence of negligence.

Res ipsa loquitur, however, is far from absolute in helping a plaintiff recover for negligence. Because the manufacturer is in control of its plant operations, it is usually in a good position to dispel the inference created by *res ipsa loquitur*. It may do so by presenting evidence to show that it used reasonable quality control standards to guard against product defects. A pop bottle may explode in a consumer's hands because it was overcarbonized at the plant, or because it was rustled in transit by a wholesaler. The plaintiff must trace the custody of the product to show that it left the defendant's plant in a defective condition.

Negligence Per Se

In many states the defendant's conduct will be deemed negligence *per se* ("by itself") without the necessity of inquiring into the nature of the defendant's conduct or the standard of care. These cases involve violation of a statute. In order for the violation of the statute to fall under the negligence *per se* category two conditions must be met: (1) the plaintiff must be within the particular class of persons the statute is designed to protect, and (2) the plaintiff's injury must be the type which the statute is designed to prevent.

Assume, for example, that a statute prohibits the mislabeling of any drug. Jim Plaintiff purchases a drug from his local pharmacy which is labeled aspirin but in reality is a poisonous substance. If he becomes violently ill as a result of ingesting the mislabeled drug, the manufacturer would be negligent *per se*. Jim Plaintiff is a consumer, a person within the class the statute was designed to protect, and the statute is designed to prevent the very type of injury that occurred.

However, assume that a local health ordinance requires a restaurant to have smooth flooring. One Star Restaurant violates the statute by having corrugated flooring. Jill Patron trips and injures herself when her high heel lodges within a riveted portion of the floor. Here, the violation of the statute would not constitute negligence *per se*. The statute is for sanitation purposes and is not designed to protect patrons against the type of injury that befell Jill.

Proximate Cause

The plaintiff must also prove that the defendant's negligence (breach of the standard of ordinary care) was the direct or *proximate cause* of the injury. Proximate cause has to do with the likelihood (foreseeability) of injury. In *MacPherson v. Buick Motor Co.*, an auto manufacturer negligently failed to inspect a defective wheel made by another manufacturer. The car was sold by a dealer to the plaintiff, who was injured when the wooden spokes of a car wheel crumbled.[1] In holding that defendant's negligence proximately caused plaintiff's injury the court said:

> Beyond all question, the nature of an automobile gives warning of probable danger if its construction is defective. . . . Unless its wheels were sound and strong, injury was almost certain.

If the injury sustained by the plaintiff could not be reasonably foreseen by the defendant at the time of the negligent act or omission, then no recovery is available.

Injury

Generally, injury includes damage to property or person. A plaintiff who sustains physical injury is entitled to recover for damages including medical expenses, loss of wages, and even pain and suffering.

Defenses

Even when the plaintiff can successfully prove the elements constituting negligence, defenses can be raised to defeat recovery. Comparative negligence and assumption of the risk are two of the more common defenses.

Comparative Negligence

Most states have adopted comparative negligence as a defense. Under this principle recovery will be reduced by the percentage that the plaintiff's

---

[1] 217 N.Y. 382, 111 N.E. 1050 (1916).

negligence contributed to his or her injury. Assume, for example, that the defendant negligently designed a refuse bin so that it was unstable. The plaintiff purchased the bin and negligently placed it on an irregular and inclined surface. When the bin overturned in a windstorm, the plaintiff was injured. If the jury determines that the plaintiff's damages are $40,000 and that the defendant was only 75 percent at fault, the plaintiff's recovery would be reduced by 25 percent to $30,000. In some states, the plaintiff's contributory negligence in the above example would bar any recovery.

Assumption of the Risk

Assumption of the risk prevents a plaintiff from recovering against a negligent defendant. Assumption of the risk consists of a voluntary exposure to a known risk. It differs from contributory negligence in that contributory negligence is based on carelessness, whereas assumption of the risk is based on voluntary exposure. A plaintiff who continues to drive an automobile with full knowledge that it has defective brakes is deemed to have assumed the risk of injury that is likely to result. If the plaintiff does not know about the defective brakes, but should know, then he or she is guilty of contributory negligence.

Strict Liability

Although the concept of strict liability was being developed as early as the 1930s, it was not until 1963, in *Greenman v. Yuba Power Products, Inc.*, that it emerged as an independent tort.[2] In *Greenman* plaintiff was seriously injured while using a defective combination power tool. The Supreme Court of California imposed strict liability on the manufacturer without the necessity of proving it was negligent. In its opinion the court said:

> A manufacturer is strictly liable in tort when an article he places on the market, knowing that it is to be used without inspection for defects, proves to have a defect that causes injury to a human being. . . .

> *   *   *   *   *

> . . . The purpose of such liability is to insure that the costs of injuries resulting from defective products are borne by the manufacturers that put such products on the market rather than by the injured persons who are powerless to protect themselves.

Section 402A

Since *Greenman,* courts have followed its lead in developing product liability law along the lines of strict liability. The strict liability standard has been set down in the *Restatement (Second) of Torts.* The *Restatement* is a scholarly synthesis and summary of the law as perceived by the American

---

[2] 50 Cal. 2d 57, 377 P.2d 897 (1963).

Law Institute. It does not have the force of law, though courts often rely heavily on it and adopt its provisions as the law of their jurisdiction.

Section 402A of the *Restatement* imposes liability. Under this section, liability for injury exists even if the "seller has exercised all possible care in the preparation and sale of his product."

Restatement of Torts, Second, § 402A(1)

One who sells any product in a defective condition unreasonably dangerous to the user or consumer or to his property is subject to liability for physical harm thereby caused to the ultimate user or consumer, or to his property, if:

    a. the seller is engaged in the business of selling such a product, and

    b. it is expected to and does reach the user or consumer without substantial change in the condition in which it is sold.

Strict liability applies only against those regularly engaged in selling the product. It is not intended to reach the occasional seller, such as the person who makes an isolated sale of a hunting rifle to a friend. The word *seller*, however, has been liberally construed by courts to encompass, for example, lessors, and those performing services. In order to recover under strict liability in most states the plaintiff must prove that:

— The product was defective.
— The product left the defendant in a defective condition.
— The defect caused the product to be unreasonably dangerous.
— The defect was the proximate cause of injury.

Experts will often be called upon to determine whether a product is defective. An engineer may be needed to assess the stress potential of a lawn mower foot guard that broke and caused injury. An expert may have to reconstruct an accident and render an opinion as to whether it was caused by the driver's negligence or defective brakes. Failure to warn a buyer of a product's hidden danger may also make the product defective. In absence of proof of a defective product there can be no recovery under strict liability.

Although it is often difficult to prove the condition of a product when it left the defendant, it can be established by circumstantial evidence. Assume, for example, that Wanda Consumer purchases a bottle of Liquid

Drain Unstopper from the local hardware store. On her way home, the bottle leaks and the liquid burns her skin. An examination of the bottle shows that its safety cap was defective. In a suit against the manufacturer under strict liability, Wanda will need to trace the custody of the bottle from the store back through to the manufacturer. She must show that the cap was not tampered with after it left the manufacturer's control. Recovery for damages due to injury would not be limited to the manufacturer. Everyone in the distributive chain is liable, including the wholesaler and retailer. Their liability, like the manufacturer's, is not dependent on their conduct. Even when a defective component is integrated into a larger product, any seller of the final product may still be strictly liable as long as it left that seller's control in a defective condition.

Additionally, the defect must make the product unreasonably dangerous. A defectively manufactured tire is a classic case of strict liability. It is reasonably foreseeable that a defect in a tire would cause the tire to be unduly dangerous. Tires support cars that travel at high speed. If a tire blows because of defective tread, there is a reasonable likelihood of injury to its occupants. Food, drugs, automobiles, power tools, water heaters, and gas stoves are just a few of the many products that are unreasonably dangerous if defective. In contrast, a defectively manufactured transistor radio would not normally present an unreasonably dangerous risk of injury to the user and hence would not be the subject of strict liability. Paper clips, pens, window shades, and music boxes are other examples of products not ordinarily the subject of strict liability.

Injury must proximately result from the defective product; i.e., the injury must be directly attributable to the defendant's negligence and be foreseeable. Recovery is not limited to buyers. The trend in the law has been to extend recovery to family members and those users and bystanders whose injury is reasonably foreseeable.

Defenses

Economics, not fault, is the basis for holding a manufacturer liable under strict liability. The manufacturer is ordinarily in a better position than the plaintiff to cover the loss for injury. Hence, a plaintiff's contributory negligence will not affect recovery. Misuse of the product, however, is a bar to recovery when the misuse contributes to the plaintiff's injury. For example, a person who uses a power saw as a fingernail clipper cannot recover for loss of a finger even if the saw was defective. This misuse cannot reasonably be foreseen by the seller. Assumption of the risk also bars recovery. A person who knows of a dangerous defect in a swimming pool slide, but uses it nonetheless, assumes the risk of injuries caused by the defect.

Recently, questions have arisen as to whether a manufacturer can be held strictly liable for injury caused by a defective product that was not scientifically known to be defective at the time of manufacture. The next case involving exposure to asbestos examines this "state-of-the-art defense."

Beshada v. Johns–Manville Products Corp.

90 N.J. 187, 447 A.2d 537 (1982)

Beshada and others (plaintiffs) are workers and survivors of deceased workers who complained of having been exposed to asbestos on the job. As a result of that exposure they allegedly contacted asbestosis (scarring of the lungs), mesothelioma (a rare cancer), and other asbestos-related illnesses. Plaintiffs instituted suit under a theory of strict liability for failure to warn of these health hazards. Defendant Johns–Manville asserted that no one knew or could have known of the danger when the exposure first occurred in the 1930s. Plaintiffs moved to strike this state-of-the-art defense. The trial court overruled the motions and the cases were ultimately appealed to the Supreme Court of New Jersey, which reversed the trial court decision and struck the state-of-the-art defense.

Justice Pashman

The sole question here is whether defendants in a product liability case based on strict liability for failure to warn may raise a "state of the art" defense. Defendants assert that the danger of which they failed to warn was undiscovered at the time the product was marketed and that it was undiscoverable given the state of scientific knowledge at that time. . . .

*   *   *   *   *

. . . For purposes of analysis, we can distinguish two tests for determining whether a product is safe: (1) does its utility outweigh its risk? and (2) if so, has that risk been reduced to the greatest extent possible consistent with the product's utility? The first question looks to the product as it was in fact marketed. If that product caused more harm than good, it was not reasonably fit for its intended purposes. We can therefore impose strict liability for the injuries it caused without having to determine whether it could have been rendered safer. The second aspect of strict liability, however, requires that the risk from the product be reduced to the greatest extent possible without hindering its utility. Whether or not the product passes the initial risk-utility test, it is not reasonably safe if the same product could have been made or marketed more safely.

Warning cases are of this second type. When plaintiffs urge that a product is hazardous because it lacks a warning, they typically look to the second test, saying in effect that regardless of the overall cost-benefit calculation the product is unsafe because a warning could make it safer at virtually no added cost and without limiting its utility. . . .

*   *   *   *   *

As it relates to warning cases, the state-of-the-art defense asserts that distributors of products can be held liable only for injuries resulting from dangers that were scientifically discoverable at the time the product was distributed. Defendants argue that the question of whether the product can be made safer must be limited to consideration of the available technology at the time the product was distributed. Liability would be absolute, defendants argue, if it could be imposed on the basis of a subsequently discovered means to make the product safer since technology will always be developing new ways to make products safer. Such a rule, they assert, would make manufacturers liable whenever their products cause harm, whether or not they are reasonably fit for their foreseeable purposes.

* * * * *

. . . Essentially, state-of-the-art is a negligence defense. It seeks to explain why defendants are not culpable for failing to provide a warning. They assert, in effect, that because they could not have known the product was dangerous, they acted reasonably in marketing it without a warning. But in strict liability cases, culpability is irrelevant. The product was unsafe. That it was unsafe because of the state of technology does not change the fact that it was unsafe. Strict liability focuses on the product, not the fault of the manufacturer. . . .

When the defendants argue that it is unreasonable to impose a duty on them to warn of the unknowable, they misconstrue both the purpose and effect of strict liability. By imposing strict liability, we are not requiring defendants to have done something that is impossible. In this sense, the phrase "duty to warn" is misleading. It implies negligence concepts with their attendant focus on the reasonableness of defendant's behavior. However, a major concern of strict liability—ignored by defendants— is the conclusion that if a product was in fact defective, the distributor of the product should compensate its victims for the misfortune that it inflicted on them.

* * * * *

The most important inquiry . . . is whether imposition of liability for failure

to warn of dangers which were undiscoverable at the time of manufacture will advance the goals and policies sought to be achieved by our strict liability rules. We believe that it will.

Risk Spreading

One of the most important arguments generally advanced for imposing strict liability is that the manufacturers and distributors of defective products can best allocate the costs of the injuries resulting from those products. The premise is that the price of a product should reflect all of its costs, including the cost of injuries caused by the product. This can best be accomplished by imposing liability on the manufacturer and distributors. Those persons can insure against liability and incorporate the cost of the insurance in the price of the product. In this way, the costs of the product will be borne by those who profit from it: the manufacturers and distributors who profit from its sale and the buyers who profit from its use. . . .

* * * * *

. . . [S]preading the costs of injuries among all those who produce, distribute and purchase manufactured products is far preferable to imposing it on the innocent victims who suffer illnesses and disability from defective products. The basic normative premise is at the center of our strict liability rules. It is unchanged by the state of scientific knowledge at the time of manufacture.

Finally, contrary to defendants' assertion, this rule will not cause the price and production level of manufactured products to diverge from the so-called economically efficient level. Rather, the rule will force the price of any particular product to reflect the cost of insuring against the possibility that the product will turn out to be defective.

Accident Avoidance

. . . The "state-of-the-art" at a given time is partly determined by how much industry invests in safety research. By imposing on manufacturers the costs of failure to discover hazards, we create an incentive for them to invest more actively in safety research.

Fact Finding Process

The analysis thus far has assumed that it is possible to define what constitutes "undiscoverable" knowledge and that it will be reasonably possible to determine what knowledge was technologically discoverable at a given time. In fact, both assumptions are highly questionable. The vast confusion that is virtually certain to arise from any attempt to deal in a trial setting with the concept of scientific knowability constitutes a strong reason for avoiding the concept altogether by striking the state-of-the-art defense.

Scientific knowability, as we understand it, refers not to what in fact was known at the time, but to what *could have been* known at the time. In other words, even if no scientist had actually formed the belief that asbestos was dangerous, the hazards would be deemed "knowable" if a scientist could have formed that belief by applying research or performing tests that were available at the time. Proof of what could have been known will inevitably be complicated, costly, confusing and time-consuming. Each side will have to produce experts in the history of science and technology to speculate as to what knowledge was feasible in a given year. We doubt that juries will be capable of even understanding the concept of scientific knowability, much less be able to resolve such a complex issue. Moreover, we should resist legal rules that will so greatly add to the costs both sides incur in trying a case.

* * * * *

. . . The burden of illness from dangerous products such as asbestos should be placed upon those who profit from its production and, more generally, upon society at large, which reaps the benefits of the various products our economy manufactures. That burden should not be imposed exclusively on the innocent victim. Although victims must in any case suffer the pain involved, they should be spared the burdensome financial consequences of unfit products. At the same time, we believe this position will serve the salutary goals of increasing product safety research and simplifying tort trials.

CASE QUESTIONS

1. What is the state-of-the-art defense?

2. Would the result in this case be different if only negligence principles were invoked? Explain.

3. What goals and policies are sought by the strict liability rule? How does the court's ruling advance those goals?

4. Is it fair to place liability against the defendants for failing to warn of dangers undiscoverable at the time of manufacture? Explain.

5. What proof burden do plaintiffs in this case still bear, even in the absence of the state-of-the-art defense?

Market Share Liability

Generally, an injured plaintiff must identify the defective product that caused the injury and the defendant that produced or distributed that product. This is true whether the plaintiff sues under negligence or strict liability theories of recovery. In some cases, however, this is virtually impossible to do.

For example, one type of foam insulation used in residences has been found to produce harmful effects in occupants exposed to it. Hundreds of manufacturers produce this type of insulation. An injured homeowner may not be able to identify the company that manufactured the specific foam insulation in his or her home. This may be true because the foam is fungible—it all looks the same—and because it may have already been in the house when the owner moved in. Under traditional rules, the injured occupant would be denied recovery. However, under these circumstances, courts have carved out exceptions to the rule requiring the plaintiff to identify the particular manufacturer in order to recover.

Where the whole industry has produced defective homogeneous products, some states shift the burden to the defendants to prove their product did not cause the injury. The following case involving a harmful drug illustrates the "market share liability" approach to the problem.

Sindell v. Abbott Laboratories

163 Cal. Rptr. 132, 607 P.2d 924 (1980)

Judith Sindell (plaintiff) sued 11 drug companies (defendants) engaged in the business of distributing diethylstilbestrol (DES), a drug prescribed for use by plaintiff's mother to prevent miscarriages. Plaintiff alleged that she developed a cancerous tumor and suffered from adenosis (precancerous vaginal and cervical growths) as a result of her mother's ingestion of DES. Plaintiff predicated her complaint upon various theories of recovery, including negligence and strict liability. In her complaint she alleged that the defendants marketed DES and knew or should have known that it was a cancer-causing substance. She was unable to identify which company manufactured the precise drug that caused the injury. Consequently, the trial court dismissed the action against the defendants. The Supreme Court of California reversed.

Justice Mosk

We begin with the proposition that, as a general rule, the imposition of liability depends upon a showing by the plaintiff that his or her injuries were caused by the act of the defendant or by an instrumentality under the defendant's control. . . .

There are, however, exceptions to this rule. Plaintiff's complaint suggests several bases upon which defendants may be held liable for her injuries even though she cannot demonstrate the name of the manufacturer which produced the DES actually taken by her mother. . . .

Plaintiff places primary reliance upon cases which hold that if a party cannot identify which of two or more defendants causes an injury, the burden of proof may shift to the defendants to show that they were not responsible for the harm. This principle is sometimes referred to as the "alternative liability" theory.

The celebrated case of *Summers v. Tice*, a unanimous opinion of this court, best exemplifies the rule. In *Summers*, the plaintiff was injured when two hunters negligently shot in his direction. It could not be determined which of them had fired the shot which actually caused the injury to the plaintiff's eye, but both defendants were nevertheless held jointly and severally liable for the whole of the damages. We reasoned that both were wrongdoers, both were negligent toward the plaintiff, and that it would be unfair to require plaintiff to isolate the defendant responsible, because if the one pointed out were to escape liability, the other might also, and the plaintiff-victim would be shorn of any remedy. In these circumstances, we held, the burden of proof shifted to the defendants, "each to absolve himself if he can." We stated that under these or similar circumstances a defendant is ordinarily in a "far better position" to offer evidence to determine whether he or another defendant caused the injury.

* * * * *

Nevertheless, plaintiff may not prevail in her claim that the *Summers* rationale should be employed to fix the whole liability for her injuries upon defendants, at least as those principles have previously been applied. There is an important difference between the situation involved in *Summers* and the present case. There, all the parties who were or could have been responsible for the harm to the plaintiff were joined as defendants. Here, by contrast, there are approximately 200 drug companies which made DES, any of which might have manufactured the injury-producing drug.

* * * * *

In our contemporary complex industrialized society, advances in science and technology create fungible goods which may harm consumers and which cannot be traced to any specific producer. The response of the courts can be either to adhere rigidly to prior doctrine, denying recovery to those injured by such products, or to fashion remedies to meet these changing needs. . . .

* * * * *

From a broader policy standpoint, defendants are better able to bear the cost of injury resulting from the manufacture of a defective product. . . . As was said by Justice Traynor in *Escola*, "[t]he cost of an injury and the loss of time or health may be an overwhelming misfortune to the person injured, and a needless one, for the risk of injury can be insured by the manufacturer and distributed among the public as a cost of doing business." The manufacturer is in the best position to discover and guard against defects in its products and to warn of harmful effects; thus, holding it liable for defects and failure to warn of harmful effects will provide an incentive to product safety. These considerations are particularly significant where medication is involved, for the consumer is virtually help- less to protect himself from serious, sometimes permanent, sometimes fatal, in- juries caused by deleterious drugs.

Where, as here, all defendants pro- duced a drug from an identical formula and the manufacturer of the DES which caused plaintiff's injuries cannot be identified through no fault of plaintiff, a modification of the rule of *Summers* is warranted. . . . [A]n undiluted *Summers* rationale is inap- propriate to shift the burden of causation to defendants because if we measure the chance that any particular manufacturer supplied the injury-causing product by the number of producers of DES, there is a pos- sibility that none of the . . . defendants in this case produced the offending substance and that the responsible manufacturer, not named in the action, will escape liability.

But we approach the issue of causation from a different perspective: we hold it to be reasonable in the present context to mea- sure the likelihood that any of the defen- dants supplied the product which allegedly injured plaintiff by the percentage which the DES sold by each of them for the pur- pose of preventing miscarriage bears to the entire production of the drug sold by all for that purpose. . . .

If plaintiff joins in the action the man- ufacturers of a substantial share of DES which her mother might have taken, the in- justice of shifting the burden of proof to defendants to demonstrate that they could not have made the substance which injured plaintiff is significantly diminished. . . .

The presence in the action of a sub- stantial share of the appropriate market also provides a ready means to apportion damages among the defendants. Each de- fendant will be held liable for the propor- tion of the judgment represented by its share of that market unless it demonstrates that it could not have made the product which caused plaintiff's injuries. . . .

*   *   *   *   *

We are not unmindful of the practical problems involved in defining the market and determining market share, but these are largely matters of proof which properly cannot be determined at the pleading stage of these proceedings. . . . [U]nder the rule we adopt, each manufacturer's liability for an injury would be approximately equiva- lent to the damages caused by the DES it manufactured.

CASE QUESTIONS

1. Explain the alternative liability theory. Does it place an undue burden upon the defen- dant? How can the defendant avoid liability?

2. What is the distinction between *Sindell* and *Summers*?

3. Should the rule of this case be confined to drugs and similar inherently dangerous prod- ucts, or should it be expanded? Explain.

4. What is the reasoning behind the rule of this case? Does this case adopt a no-fault stan- dard? Explain. Do you feel it is unfair to hold a defendant liable who has not caused the wrong? Explain.

5. Assume that the case went to trial and the jury came back with the following findings:

a. Verdict in favor of plaintiff against man- ufacturers A, B, C, and D.

b. A had 10 percent of the market; B had 20 percent of the market; C had 15 percent of the market; and D had 20 percent of the market.

c. Plaintiff sustained injuries amounting to $500,000. What is the liability of each defendant? Are you bothered by the possibility that none of these defendants were directly responsible for the injury? Why or why not?

Warranties

A warranty is a promise that a product will perform in a certain way. It is part of a contract. A plaintiff who proves that the defendant breached a warranty may recover damages. The plaintiff does not have to prove that the defendant was negligent, only that injury occurred because the product did not conform to the warranty.

Early case law required *privity* between the plaintiff and the defendant before the plaintiff could recover for injury based on warranty; i.e., there had to be a contractual relationship. Since warranty is based on contract principles, courts were quick to rule that an injured consumer could not recover against a remote manufacturer. Under the privity doctrine the injured plaintiff could recover only from the immediate seller. Intervening distributors of the product insulated the manufacturer from liability. The privity requirement, however, has been abandoned in most states. Some states extend the warranty to family, household members, and guests of the buyer. Others include any person reasonably expected to use or be affected by the product. Warranties may be expressly made or implied.

Express Warranty

Often, in an effort to make a product more attractive to the consumer, a seller makes express warranties or representations concerning the product. The product will be expected to live up to the representations. If it does not, a plaintiff who sustains injury as a result of the breach of an express warranty may recover damages against the warrantor. A warranty need not be couched in formal language. Section 2–313 of the Uniform Commercial Code (UCC) recognizes that any statement of fact or promise which is part of the bargain creates an express warranty.

Uniform Commercial Code § 2–313(1)(a)

Express warranties by the seller are created as follows:
Any affirmation of fact or promise made by the seller to the buyer which relates to the goods and becomes part of the basis of the bargain creates an express warranty that the goods shall conform to the affirmation or promise.

An express warranty or representation must be distinguished from a statement of opinion. A statement of the value of the goods or commendation of the goods does not create a warranty. It is to be expected by consumers that a lawn mower salesperson or any merchant interested in selling a product is prone to make exaggerated claims about the product. A claim couched in terms of a general opinion, such as "This lawn mower is the safest on the market," will normally not be the subject of a warranty. On the other hand, if more specific factual claims are made, such as "The blades in this lawn mower are built to last five years," then a breach of that representation results in liability.

 **Implied Warranty**

 Under UCC section 2–314, a seller of goods implicitly warrants that those goods are fit for *ordinary purposes*. This is known as the implied warranty of merchantability. In selling a hamburger, the seller impliedly warrants

---

Uniform Commercial Code § 2–314(1)

Unless excluded or modified . . . a warranty that the goods shall be merchantable is implied in a contract for their sale if the seller is a merchant. . . .

---

that it is fit for consumption. If the hamburger is rotten, the seller has breached the implied warranty of merchantability and is liable for resulting injury. This rule of law is consistent with the expectations of the consumer. It is only reasonable for a consumer to expect that a product placed on the market is safe for its intended use.

 The implied warranty of merchantability applies only to merchants. A merchant is one who customarily deals in the goods which are the subject of the sale or has a particular expertise regarding these goods. One who engages in an isolated sale of goods is not a merchant. Such a seller would not normally be totally familiar with the mechanics of the product, and the buyer would not reasonably expect a nonmerchant to imply that the product sold is merchantable.

In addition to the implied warranty of merchantability, the UCC affords an injured plaintiff the protection of section 2–315. This section grants the purchaser an implied warranty that goods are fit for a *particular purpose*.

Uniform Commercial Code § 2–315

Where the seller at the time of contracting has reason to know any particular purpose for which the goods are required and that the buyer is relying on the seller's skill or judgment to select or furnish suitable goods, there is unless excluded or modified . . . an implied warranty that the goods shall be fit for such purpose.

The particular purpose warranty is more specific than the merchantability warranty. It involves situations in which the seller has been informed of a particular use as opposed to a customary use. The customary use of shoes would be for normal walking; a particular use would be for mountain climbing. If a customer asks for a pair of shoes that would be suitable for mountain climbing and relies upon the seller's recommendation, the implied warranty of fitness for a particular purpose comes into play. Like the implied warranty of merchantability, it is only applicable when the seller is a merchant.

Damages
Ordinarily, when there is a breach of warranty the injured person may recover damages—the difference between the value of the goods received and their value had they been as warranted.

Suppose Seth purchases a jackhammer from the local hardware store for $25. An express warranty states that all parts are in working order, but in reality the safety latch is defective. The warranty has been breached, and Seth is entitled to damages. If the value of the hammer in its defective condition is $20, Seth has incurred damages in the amount of $5 and may recover that amount in a breach of warranty suit.

Buyers also are entitled to personal injury damages proximately resulting from any breach of warranty. Suppose, in our example, that Seth was unaware that the jackhammer's safety latch was inoperative. Had he been injured as a result, he would be entitled to damages, including compensation for doctor and hospital expenses, loss of wages, disability, cosmetic disfigurement, and pain and suffering related to the injury. In most jurisdictions, family members who are injured as a result of the defective safety switch can also recover their damages for personal injury.

Warranty Limitations
Under UCC section 2–316 the seller can exclude both express and implied warranties. Any disclaimer, however, must be clear and comply with the terms of the UCC. Ambiguities will be resolved in favor of the consumer. Suppose that Crop Harvester, Inc. sold pesticide with a tag marked "safe

for crop dusting" but that a contract covering the sale of that pesticide stated "no warranties." The conflict here would be resolved in favor of the existence of the warranty.

The UCC sets out the procedure for disclaiming implied warranties. To effectively disclaim an implied warranty of merchantability, the disclaimer must specifically mention merchantability and, if in writing, must be conspicuous. To disclaim an implied warranty of fitness, the disclaimer again must be by a conspicuous writing. A conspicuous writing is one that a reasonable person would take notice of. A written disclaimer should appear in larger letters than the surrounding print.

The UCC further specifies that all implied warranties may be excluded by expressions like "as is," "with all faults," or other language that clearly communicates the intention of disclaiming implied warranties. There is no implied warranty under the code with respect to defects that an inspection could have revealed. An injured purchaser who refused the seller's request to inspect the goods may be without warranty protection. In a sense, contributory negligence, a tort concept, has crept into the law of warranty.

The UCC also permits parties to limit the remedies. For example, a merchant may include a term in a contract which limits the consumer remedy, in the event of breach of warranty, to repair and replacement. As the following landmark case indicates, however, any disclaimer or limitation is strictly scrutinized by the courts when it relates to personal safety.

Henningsen v. Bloomfield Motors, Inc.

32 N.J. 358, 161 A.2d 69 (1960)

Clause Henningsen (plaintiff) purchased a Plymouth automobile for his wife (plaintiff) as a Mother's Day gift. The automobile was manufactured by Chrysler (defendant) and sold by Bloomfield Motors, Inc. (defendant). The purchase agreement was a printed form. Most of the front side of the form was printed in 12-point block type and easy to read, but a smaller portion in 6-point type read:

> The front and back of this Order comprise the entire agreement affecting this purchase and no other agreement or understanding of any nature concerning same has been made or entered into, or will be recognized. . . .
>
> I have read the matter printed on the back hereof and agree to it as a part of this order the same as if it were printed above my signature.

On the back of the purchase agreement, in the seventh paragraph, there was a clause disclaiming all express and implied warranties except the following:

> The manufacturer warrants each new motor vehicle . . . , chassis or parts manufactured by it to be free from defects in material or workmanship under normal use and service.

The provision went on to limit the manufacturer's obligation to replacement of defective parts returned to the manufacturer, transportation prepaid, within 90 days of the original delivery or 4,000 miles, whichever occurred first. Mr. Henningsen did not read the back of the purchase contract or the paragraphs that referred to it.

The Henningsens drove the vehicle for 10 days without mishap. On the 11th day Mrs. Henningsen was driving on a paved, smooth road at 20–22 miles per hour when she heard a loud noise "from the bottom, by the hood. It felt as if something cracked." The steering wheel spun and the car veered to the right before crashing into a brick wall. The vehicle was a total loss, and Mrs. Henningsen was injured.

The Henningsens sued for damages on the theories of negligence and breach of express and implied warranties. The case was submitted to the jury on the issue of implied warranty of merchantability, and verdicts were returned against both defendants. Defendants appealed to the Supreme Court of New Jersey, which affirmed the trial court's decision.

Justice Francis

The Effect of the Disclaimer and Limitation of Liability Clauses on the Implied Warranty of Merchantability

*　*　*　*　*

. . . [W]hat effect should be given to the express warranty in question which seeks to limit the manufacturer's liability to replacement of defective parts, and which disclaims all other warranties, express or implied? In assessing its significance we must keep in mind the general principle that, in the absence of fraud, one who does not choose to read a contract before signing it, cannot later relieve himself of its burdens. And in applying that principle, the basic tenet of freedom of competent parties to contract is a factor of importance. But in the framework of modern commercial life and business practices, such rules cannot be applied on a strict, doctrinal basis. The conflicting interests of the buyer and seller must be evaluated realistically and justly, giving due weight to the social policy evinced by the Uniform Sales Act [the predecessor of the Uniform Commercial Code], the progressive decisions of the courts engaged in administering it, the mass production methods of manufacture and distribution to the public, and the bargaining position occupied by the ordinary consumer in such an economy. This history of the law shows that legal doctrines, as first expounded, often prove to be inadequate under the impact of later experience. In such case, the need for justice has stimulated the necessary qualifications or adjustments.

* * * * *

. . . In a society such as ours, where the automobile is a common and necessary adjunct of daily life, and where its use is so fraught with danger to the driver, passengers and the public, the manufacturer is under a special obligation in connection with the construction, promotion and sale of his cars. Consequently, the courts must examine purchase agreements closely to see if consumer and public interests are treated fairly.

* * * * *

The traditional contract is the result of free bargaining of parties who are brought together by the play of the market, and who meet each other on a footing of approximate economic equality. In such a society there is no danger that freedom of contract will be a threat to the social order as a whole. But in present-day commercial life the standardized mass contract has appeared. It is used primarily by enterprises with strong bargaining power and position. "The weaker party, in need of the goods or services, is frequently not in a position to shop around for better terms, either because the author of the standard contract has a monopoly (natural or artificial) or because all competitors use the same clauses. His contractual intention is but a subjection more or less voluntary to terms dictated by the stronger party, terms whose consequences are often understood in a vague way, if at all.". . .

* * * * *

The warranty before us is a standardized form designed for mass use. It is imposed upon the automobile consumer. He takes it or leaves it, and he must take it to buy an automobile. No bargaining is engaged in with respect to it. . . .

* * * * *

It is undisputed that the president of the dealer with whom Henningsen dealt did not specifically call attention to the warranty on the back of the purchase order. The form and the arrangement of its face, as described above, certainly would cause the minds of reasonable men to differ as to whether notice of a yielding of basic rights stemming from the relationship with the manufacturer was adequately given. The words "warranty" or "limited warranty" did not even appear in the fine print above the place for signature, and a jury might well find that the type of print itself was such as to promote lack of attention rather than sharp scrutiny. . . .

* * * * *

But there is more than this. Assuming that a jury might find that the fine print referred to reasonably served the objective of directing a buyer's attention to the warranty on the reverse side, and, therefore, that he should be charged with awareness of its language, can it be said that an ordinary layman would realize what he was relinquishing in return for what he was being granted? Under the law, breach of warranty against defective parts or workmanship which caused personal injuries would entitle a buyer to damages even if due care were used in the manufacturing process. Because of the great potential for harm if the vehicle was defective, that right is the most important and fundamental one arising from the relationship. Difficulties so frequently encountered in establishing negligence in manufacture in the ordinary case make this manifest. Any ordinary layman of reasonable intelligence, looking at the phraseology, might well conclude that Chrysler was agreeing to replace defective parts and perhaps replace anything that went wrong because of defective workmanship during the first 90 days or 4,000 miles of operation, but that he would not be entitled to a new car. It is not unreasonable to believe that the entire scheme being conveyed was a proposed remedy for physical deficiencies in the car. *In the context* of this warranty, only the abandonment of all sense of justice would permit us to hold that, as a matter of law, the phrase "its obligation under this warranty being limited to making good at its factory any part or parts thereof" signifies to an ordinary reasonable person that he is relinquishing any personal injury claim that might flow from the use of a defective automobile. . . .

* * * * *

. . . From the standpoint of the purchaser, there can be no arms length negotiating on the subject. Because his capacity for bargaining is so grossly unequal, the inexorable conclusion which follows is that he is not permitted to bargain at all. He must take or leave the automobile on the warranty terms dictated by the maker. He cannot turn to a competitor for better security.

Public policy is a term not easily defined. Its significance varies as the habits and needs of a people may vary. It is not static and the field of application is an ever increasing one. A contract, or a particular provision therein, valid in one era may be wholly opposed to the public policy of another. Courts keep in mind the principle that the best interests of society demand that persons should not be unnecessarily restricted in their freedom to contract. But they do not hesitate to declare void as against public policy contractual provisions which clearly tend to the injury of the public in some way.

* * * * *

. . . In the framework of this case, illuminated as it is by the facts . . . we are of the opinion that Chrysler's attempted disclaimer of an implied warranty of merchantability and of the obligations arising therefrom is so inimical to the public good as to compel an adjudication of its invalidity.

CASE QUESTIONS

1. The cause of action for negligence was dismissed by the court. Why? What doctrine could help to prove negligence in this case?

2. What was the express warranty? What did it attempt to do? What is the implied warranty of merchantability that accompanies the sale of a car?

3. Did the court hold that the disclaimer was ineffective because Mr. Henningsen did not read it? What is the holding in this case? Is it limited to automobiles?

4. Can a manufacturer or supplier effectively disclaim warranties? Under what circumstances? Explain your answer.

5. Does this decision undermine freedom of contract? Why or why not?

REGULATION OF PRODUCTS—FEDERAL LAW

State product liability laws have not been totally effective in combatting product hazards and injury. One notable weakness is that they are not applicable until after injury occurs. The federal government has intervened to prevent injury by passing laws to inform consumers about the products they buy and to impose safety standards on products. Two noteworthy federal acts are the Magnuson–Moss Warranty Act and the Consumer Product Safety Act.

Magnuson–Moss Warranty Act

A task force on appliance warranties and service concluded that the consumer was unfairly treated and inadequately protected in the area of product servicing, repair, and durability. The prime abuse was found to be in the manufacturer's use of disclaimers to restrict its liability. It was common for the manufacturer to disclaim the product's implied warranty of fitness and merchantability by using a vague or deceptive written warranty that appeared to give the consumer something extra. Written warranties were often stated in language incomprehensible to the average consumer, and many manufacturers failed to honor them.

As a result, Congress passed the Magnuson–Moss Warranty Federal Trade Commission Improvement Act. The stated purpose of the act is to "improve the adequacy of information available to consumers, prevent deception, and improve competition in the marketing of consumer products." Toward these ends the act requires certain disclosures in connection with written warranties, imposes restrictions upon disclaimers of implied warranties, and establishes a procedure through which consumers may more effectively enforce their warranty rights.

Magnuson–Moss is administered by the Federal Trade Commission (FTC). The act covers products normally used for personal, family, or household purposes and is applicable only when a seller offers a written warranty.

Disclosure

The manufacturer or seller does not have to make any warranties. But if a written warranty is made in connection with a consumer product costing over $15, it must "fully and conspicuously disclose in simple and readily understandable language the terms and conditions of the warranty."[3] The specific contents of disclosures under the act are entrusted to the FTC. The FTC has the power to promulgate rules requiring that the writing clearly inform the purchaser of the terms of the warranty. For example, one FTC rule provides that any exclusion, such as a limitation of liability for personal injury or property damage, must be accompanied by the following statement:

> Some states do not allow the exclusion or limitation of . . . damages, so the above limitation or exclusion may not apply to you.

---

[3] Although the act authorizes the FTC to promulgate rules requiring disclosure on warranties pertaining to products that cost over $5, the FTC only requires disclosure for products costing over $15.

Full and Limited Warranty

Magnuson–Moss also requires that any written warranty involving a product that costs more than $10 must clearly and conspicuously contain the tag "full" or "limited." The "full" tag is properly employed only if the warranty is consistent with at least the four following federal standards:

— In case of a defect, malfunction, or failure to conform to the warranty, the warrantor must fix the product within a reasonable time without charge.
— The warrantor may not impose any limitation on the duration of an implied warranty on the product.
— The warrantor may not exclude or limit damages (including personal injury damages) for breach of warranty on the product *unless the exclusion appears conspicuously on the face of the warranty.*
— After a reasonable number of failed attempts to remedy the defects in the product, the warrantor must permit the customer to elect a refund or replacement of the product without charge.

If a warranty does not meet these federal standards, then it must conspicuously be designated as "limited." Note that under the above standards the seller may absolve itself from any personal injury liability resulting from the breach of warranty; confine the remedies to refund or replacement; and still depict the warranty as full.

Limitation of Disclaimer

Under the Magnuson–Moss Act a seller who extends a written warranty or a service contract may not disclaim implied warranties. This provision does not stop a seller from disclaiming implied warranties when the sale of the product is not connected with a written warranty or a service contract. Consequently, it is possible for a supplier to except all implied warranties by selling "as is." Furthermore, a supplier may limit the duration of implied warranties to the duration of a written warranty as long as the limitation is conscionable (fair) and conspicuously disclosed. An express warranty that restricts the duration of the implied warranty must be designated as "limited."

Remedies

Consumers may sue warrantors that violate the Magnuson–Moss Act or otherwise breach express or implied warranties. A successful plaintiff may recover damages plus the costs of the suit, including an award of reasonable attorney fees.

The warrantor may establish an informal dispute resolution procedure that conforms to FTC rules and may include within the written warranty a requirement that the consumer use this procedure before pursuing legal action under the act. The consumer will be bound by this provision. The Magnuson–Moss Act also requires that the warrantor be afforded a reasonable opportunity to rectify its failure to comply before a suit may be instituted.

The Consumer Product Safety Act

In 1967 the National Commission on Product Safety was established to investigate the adequacy of consumer protection against unreasonable risks caused by "hazardous household products." In its report to the president and Congress, the commission observed that "the exposure of consumers to unreasonable consumer product hazards is excessive by any standard of measurement." The commission took particular note of products that were notorious for presenting unreasonable hazards, including color TV sets, fireworks, glass bottles, infant furniture, lawn mowers, and un-

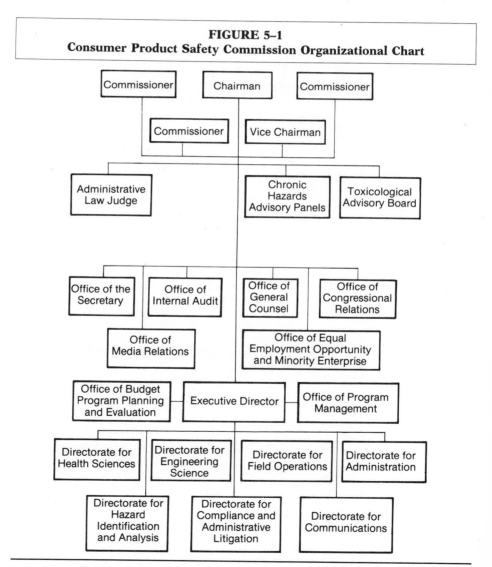

FIGURE 5–1
Consumer Product Safety Commission Organizational Chart

Source: Michael R. Lemov, *Consumer Product Safety Commission,* Shepard's/McGraw Hill, 1983.

vented gas heaters. The commission believed that the industries producing these products were too profit-conscious to engage in the type of self-regulation that would adequately protect consumers. It recommended the creation of a federal regulatory agency with broad authority to insure the safety of consumer products by imposing mandatory safety standards. In response to these recommendations, Congress passed the Consumer Product Safety Act (CPSA), which established the Consumer Product Safety Commission (CPSC).[4] The CPSC consists of five commissioners appointed by the president—one of whom the president appoints as chairperson—with the advice and consent of the Senate. The commissioners are appointed for seven-year terms. (See Figure 5–1.)

Consumer Products

The commission has jurisdiction over consumer products. The definition of a consumer product is broad. It includes products that are customarily sold to consumers and used in the home, at school, or for recreation. A product need not be sold directly to a consumer to be considered a consumer product as long as it was produced or distributed for consumer use. Likewise, a product need not be intended for exclusive use or control by a consumer in order to be classified as a consumer product. For example, vending machines placed in schools, workplaces, or other public places are deemed consumer products.

Information Gathering

As directed by the act, the CPSC maintains an Injury Information Clearinghouse to collect and analyze injury reports. The National Electronic Injury Surveillance System (NEISS) assists the CPSC in the collection of the data.

NEISS is a computerized record compilation system that accumulates injury data from hospitals located throughout the United States. These reports are transmitted immediately by NEISS to the commission in Washington, D.C. NEISS provides examples of product-related injuries to help the commission determine which products pose the most serious risks of injury. The higher the risk of injury, the faster a product will receive attention from the CPSC.

The commission is also authorized to require manufacturers to keep records and supply it with information regarding products. Pursuant to proper procedure, the CPSC may inspect the premises or records related to the manufacture of consumer products. It can also require a manufacturer to furnish it with notice of any new consumer products before making them available to the public. To facilitate its information-gathering function, the commission may conduct hearings and inquiries regarding consumer product safety.

---

[4] The CPSA transferred to the CPSC the administration of several other acts related to consumer safety. These were the Federal Hazardous Substances Act, the Poison Prevention Packaging Act, the Flammable Fabrics Act, and the Refrigerator Safety Act.

Safety Standards

In its attempt to remove products that present unreasonable risks of injury, the CPSC issues consumer product safety standards in the form of performance or labeling specifications. A *performance standard* specifies minimum performance criteria, such as the number of pounds of pressure a glass window must withstand. A *labeling standard* may require warning labels. When no safety standard adopted by the commission could adequately protect the public from unreasonable risk of injury, the commission can seek to ban a product.

Before implementing a mandatory standard, the CPSC must find that voluntary standards would not adequately reduce the risk of injury. It must also find that the product presents an unreasonable risk of injury. Any standard must be "reasonably necessary" to mitigate or eliminate that risk. To make this determination the commission and courts engage in a type of cost-benefit analysis, weighing the effectiveness of the standard against its effect on the cost of the product. The following case concerning swimming pool slides offers some insight into a court's approach to determining whether a standard meets the "reasonably necessary" test.

 **Aqua Slide 'N' Dive v. CPSC**

569 F.2d 831 (5th Cir. 1978)

The Consumer Product Safety Commission established safety standards for swimming pool slides. One standard required that signs warning of paralysis be placed on the steps of the ladder and in the water. Aqua Slide filed a petition in the 5th Circuit Court of Appeals challenging the standard. The court found in favor of Aqua Slide and struck down the standard.

Roney, Circuit Judge

Reasonable Necessity

The Act requires a finding that the standard is "reasonably necessary to eliminate or reduce an unreasonable risk of injury." Aqua Slide argues that substantial evidence does not support the Commission's conclusion, that this standard is "reasonably necessary," [since] . . . the warning signs have not been tested, may not work, and may be so explicit as to deter slide use unnecessarily. . . .

* * * * *

The Act does not define the term "reasonably necessary," and apparently Congress intended the Commission and the courts to work out a definition on a case-by-case basis. The legislative history, and the holdings of other cases decided under similar statutes, do discuss the meaning of "unreasonable risk," and indicate that term is interrelated with the "reasonably necessary" requirement. The necessity for the standard depends upon the nature of the risk, and the reasonableness of the risk is a function of the burden a standard would impose on a user of the product.

* * * * *

In this case, the severity of the risk is so terrible that virtually any standard which actually promised to reduce it would seem to be "reasonably necessary.". . . [T]he Commission . . . concentrated [its] fact-gathering efforts on an attempt to identify the precise nature of the risk. After surveying slide accidents, and considering the result of scientific studies of slide dynamics, the Commission identified a risk of "quadriplegia and paraplegia resulting from users . . . sliding down the slide in a head first position and striking the bottom of the pool." The risk is greater than an inexperienced "belly-slider" would anticipate, because improper head-first entry can cause an uncontrollable "snap rotation of the body" that "allows the arms to clear the bottom prior to head impact." Also, a curved slide can disorient persons who are using it for the first time. Without question, paraplegia is a horrible injury.

The risk of paraplegia from swimming pool slides, however, is extremely remote. More than 350,000 slides are in use, yet the Commission could find no more than 11 instances of paraplegia over a six-year period. According to . . . figures, the risk, for slide users, is about one in 10 million, less than the risk an average person has of being killed by lightning. . . . Aqua Slide argues that, because of the low frequency, this Court should hold the risk to be "reasonable" and set aside the entire standard. . . .

Given the severity of the injury, however, and the precedent of other cases, it seems likely that a standard which actually promised to reduce the risk without unduly hampering the availability of the slides or decreasing their utility could render this risk "unreasonable." The question then is whether the specific provisions of the standard which Aqua Slide challenges have been shown to accomplish that task.

* * * * *

Given the infrequency of the risk, it was incumbent upon the . . . Commission to produce evidence that the standard actually promised to reduce the risk. Instead, . . . the Commission gave the matter short shrift. To begin with, the standard only applies to new slides. It does not affect slides now in use, despite [a] . . . finding that "[t]here are many more slides in use than produced per year by a factor of ten to one." It is odd that the Commission chose this limited method of addressing the risk rather than deciding to use its power to conduct a public education campaign, which could reach far more slide users. A Red Cross representative [said] that its safety courses could inform 3,000,000 people a year of the risk of slide injury.

Furthermore, the record contains only the most ambiguous of indications that the warning signs would actually be heeded by slide users. The Commission did not test the signs.

* * * * *

. . . In the preamble to the proposed standard, [the Commission] could do no more than say the signs "may achieve" a reduction in dangerous belly slides. Certainly the evidence of actual injuries bespeaks the kind of foolhardiness for which proper instructions would provide no cure. One accident victim had been drinking, and a jury apparently concluded he had hit a chair floating in a pool. Another dove through a hoop. Still a third went down a slide improperly installed in only three feet of water. Another went down on his knees, a position about which the proposed warning sign is silent. While Congress intended for injuries resulting from foreseeable misuse of a product to be counted in assessing risk, that does not warrant adoption of a standard which has not been shown to prevent misuse.

* * * * *

In short, the Commission provided little evidence that the warning signs would benefit consumers. The risk is remote. The evidence that the signs would reduce the risk rests more on inference than it does on proof. In weighing the "reasonable necessity" for the signs, the crucial question then, is whether the benefit has a reasonable relationship to the disadvantages the sign requirement imposes.

In this case, the prime disadvantage to which Aqua Slide points is the warning's effect on the availability of the slides. Because the Commission did not test the signs, it provided little evidence of whether the signs were so explicit and shocking in their portrayal of the risk of paralysis as to constitute an unwarranted deterrent to the marketing of slides, and, hence, their availability to users. The record provides only scant assurance that purchasers would not be so alarmed by the warning signs that they would unnecessarily abstain. The signs do not indicate paralysis is a one in 10 million risk. The only evidence concerning the marketing impact the Commission's signs would have is a Commission staff report, based on [a research institute study]. The Commission report was developed to satisfy a required statutory finding concerning the economic impact of the standard. It was based on interviews with persons active in the industry; however, it did not test the reaction of slide buyers.

The Commission report indicated 20 percent of total sales would be lost over six years. Perhaps as much as half of the 42 percent drop in slides sales from 1973 to 1974 could be attributed just to uncertainty about what the standard would say. The Commission apparently thought that, because, absent the standard, the industry was expected to grow each year by 51 percent, the net effect would be merely to slow the industry's rate of growth and harm investment. . . . The Commission's economic report constitutes the only record evidence concerning the economic impact of the standard. As such it is the "basic data" upon which the Commission relied. . . .

Certainly, on this record, the economic finding is crucial. The only way to tell whether the relationship between the advantages and disadvantages of the signs is reasonable is to know exactly what those disadvantages are. Yet the Commission's study of the standard's economic impact lacks the indicia of reliability. At the same time, the proof that signs will significantly reduce the risk is weak. We consequently hold that the Commission has failed to provide substantial evidence to demonstrate the reasonable necessity of the warning signs. We set aside the warning sign requirement. . . .

CASE QUESTIONS

1. What standard did the CPSC enact? What risks was it designed to eliminate?

2. Why did the court determine that the agency failed to demonstrate that the warning signs were not a reasonable necessity?

3. What could the agency have done to substantiate the need for the warning signs?

4. What factors determine whether a risk of injury is unreasonable?

Imminent Hazards

When the CPSC determines that a consumer product presents an imminent hazard, there is a need for a quicker mechanism for eliminating the hazard than the normal safety standard and ban procedures. The commission may sue in the federal district court seeking seizure of the imminently hazardous product. It may also seek an injunction against the manufacturer. The district court may require the manufacturer either to recall the product or to notify product owners of the risk associated with it.

In one case the commission instituted an action against the manufacturer of a baseball pitching machine that the commission alleged to be an imminent hazard. The case was terminated when the manufacturer agreed to a decree whereby it would manufacture the machines with a metal screen guard enclosing the trajectory of the arm to prevent wild pitches from injuring the consumer.

Substantial Product Hazard

A substantial product hazard is one that creates a substantial risk of injury to the public. Manufacturers, distributors, and retailers of consumer products must immediately notify the commission of such hazards. Failure to comply with this reporting requirement is excused if the manufacturer or other appropriate party knows that the commission has already been adequately informed about the problem.

Certain guidelines are used to determine whether a product presents a substantial hazard. These include a consideration of the risk of injury, need for the product, and the population exposed to the product. The commission learns of such hazards not only through reports from manufacturers, distributors, and retailers, but also through consumer complaints, news media stories, and NEISS data.

Once the commission is satisfied that a substantial product hazard exists, it may require the firm to submit a corrective action plan. It may or may not accept the plan, but it deems voluntary action to be the most expedient way to avoid costly delay while achieving the desired consumer protection. If voluntary compliance cannot be reached, then the commission can initiate formal enforcement proceedings. Once there is a formal finding that a consumer product constitutes a substantial hazard, the commission may require the firm to give notice to known customers who purchased the product. In addition to notification, or in lieu of it, the commission may require the manufacturer, distributor, or retailer to remedy the hazard, repair or replace the product, or refund the purchase price.

Remedies

The CPSA authorizes various enforcement procedures, including product seizure and injunctions. Other remedies include civil and criminal penalties, private suits to enforce the act, and private damage actions.

A civil penalty of up to $2,000 may be assessed against a person who knowingly violates any CPSA provisions. "Knowingly" is not confined to actual knowledge. It includes knowledge that a reasonable person would possess by exercising reasonable diligence to discover truth.

A manufacturer that knowingly sells banned products commits a separate civil offense for each product sold. However, the commission cannot impose multiple civil penalties totaling more than $500,000, and it is authorized to reduce a penalty to less than the prescribed amount at its discretion. The CPSC will take the size of the offender's business and the gravity of the offense into consideration when exercising this discretion.

A person who knowingly and *willfully* commits an act prohibited by the CPSA, after being notified by the commission of its prohibition, is subject to a criminal penalty of up to $50,000 and one-year imprisonment.

Any interested person may institute a private suit in order to enforce the CPSA. The individual must first notify the CPSC, the attorney general, and the alleged violator of the intention to sue. This notification affords the commission or the attorney general an opportunity to take appropriate civil or criminal action and gives the alleged offender an opportunity to resolve the complaint. If the commission or the Department of Justice files suit within 30 days, the individual is barred from suing.

An individual who has been injured as a result of a knowing or willful violation of a commission rule or order may seek damages in a federal district court when the amount in controversy exceeds $10,000. (Otherwise, the injured party is left solely to state remedies.) The aggrieved individual may recover damages, the costs of the suit, and reasonable attorney fees.

The remedies under the CPSA are not exclusive. They are in addition to common-law and statutory remedies provided under state law.

ALTERNATIVE APPROACHES

As presently constituted, product liability law lacks uniformity. It is possible for a victim to recover for product injury in one state but not in another. Each state has its own common and statutory law governing product liability cases. For example, although *Sindell v. Abbott Laboratories,* discussed in this chapter, is good law in California, several jurisdictions have rejected the market share liability approach. Hence, in many states plaintiffs seeking to recover for DES injury have a greater burden than they do in California.

Even within states, product liability law is often uncertain. This seems to be an area where courts take giant leaps rather than small steps. They are prone to overrule long-standing decisions in their desire to "find a deep pocket" against which to compensate injured victims. This tendency to change is causing widespread confusion. Manufacturers argue that they have no consistent guidelines to help them in their operations to avoid liability. The lack of uniformity in state product liability law has caused serious problems for many manufacturers who distribute products in various states. Attorneys representing injured consumers often find it difficult to evaluate a product liability case because of these disparities.

Uncertainty breeds higher product liability insurance rates because losses are not predictable. Insurance companies tend to base their rates on a "worst case" scenario, and many are reluctant to underwrite product liability. Consequently, product liability insurance is becoming difficult to obtain—and increasingly expensive. This added cost of doing business is incorporated into the price of the product and passed on to the consumer.

The Risk Retention Act has attempted to solve the insurance product liability crisis by eliminating the legal restrictions that prohibited sellers from grouping together to insure. It was hoped that private rate setting and risk retention by these seller groups would pressure commercial insurance carriers to lower their rates to more realistic levels. Although the act has had some effect, it is not a panacea to the problem.

One approach to the problem of uncertainty is a uniform state law. In fact, in 1979 the U.S. Department of Commerce proposed a Model Uniform Product Liability Act (ULPA) for voluntary adoption by the states. However, the states have not been very responsive. They have taken a piecemeal approach to the problem, addressing particular issues rather than enacting comprehensive legislation such as the ULPA. In fact, no state has yet adopted the act in its entirety. Even if some states were to adopt it, there would be no interstate uniformity until all states did so. Even then, each would be free to legislatively modify provisions in the act, and judicial interpretations of the statute would undoubtedly vary from state to state.

Some have strongly advocated a federal law that would preempt state law. They feel that this approach would provide uniformity, certainty and the predictability necessary to stabilize insurance rates and promote settlements. Congress has been pressed to pass such a federal bill, called the Products Liability Act (PLA). The substantive provisions of the bill are an attempt to balance the relative interests of the product manufacturer, supplier, and consumer.

Under the proposed act, the plaintiff must prove that a product was unreasonably dangerous and that it proximately caused injury to him or her. The statute adopts a strict liability standard to products that possess construction defects or do not conform to an express warranty. In these cases a manufacturer is better able to avoid defects and nonconforming warranties because they would constitute violations of its own preselected standards. The consumer has a reasonable expectation that a product is free from construction flaws and conforms to representations. Because it is unlikely that a plaintiff would be able to point to a specific negligent act or omission that caused the construction defect, in the absence of a strict liability standard, plaintiffs would bear the loss. A strict liability standard also encourages honest representation in warranties.

In contrast, the PLA applies a negligence standard to products that possess a defective design or an inadequate warning label. The reasoning here is that when a product is held to violate these standards, liability covers the whole product line. A strict liability standard could financially wipe out a manufacturer, even though it made a wise choice at the time of manufacture. It was also felt that a strict liability standard would thwart innovation and experimentation. A negligence standard still encourages new ideas and rewards manufacturers who exercise greater care.

Many feel that enactment of the proposed federal legislation is necessary to promote certainty and uniformity and avert the liability insurance crisis. They feel that it fairly adjusts the interests of manufacturers and consumers.

CHAPTER PROBLEMS

1. Mary Domany was descending from the second to the first floor of the Sears, Roebuck store when the escalator she was riding came to an abrupt stop. She fell several steps to the floor below. The escalator was purchased from and installed by Otis Elevator Company. It was serviced and maintained by Otis under a contract with Sears which provided that the escalator was under Sears's exclusive control. The place where the escalator mechanism was housed, while not locked, was actually under the exclusive control of Otis. Pursuant to the contract, Otis inspected and serviced the escalator regularly and responded to service requests from Sears. Domany, who was severely injured by the abrupt stop, claims Sears is responsible. Do you agree? Explain.

2. John Lindsay was killed in the crash of an F4B jet aircraft he was piloting in the course of naval maneuvers. The aircraft was the product of the McDonnell Douglas Corporation, a large supplier of such aircraft to the U.S. government. The aircraft in question crashed in the

ocean and was never recovered, so no conclusive evidence is available regarding the cause of the crash.

It is agreed that the aircraft involved was first flown by a McDonnell Douglas test pilot. During that flight the cooling light came on twice, indicating overheating. Overheating also occurred during the second and third flights. McDonnell Douglas delayed delivery of the aircraft to the government to correct this and other deficiencies it discovered through careful inspection. Lindsay's widow has brought suit against McDonnell Douglas. What is her best theory, and what must she prove in order to recover? McDonnell Douglas contends that it is not liable for any injury caused by the crash because it conducted a scrupulous examination. Do you agree? Explain.

3. Norma Corley suffered from breast cancer necessitating partial removal of her breasts. In connection with the surgery the surgeon implanted a silicone prosthesis manufactured by Dow Corning Corporation and distributed by

Mueller Co., Inc. When the surgical wound failed to heal properly, it was discovered that a tear in the implant caused silicone to spill out and hinder the healing process. The implant was surgically removed and replaced with another, but the second implant was also torn and had to be removed. What types of evidence would help Dow and Mueller avoid liability for Corley's injury.

4. Irma Carter was hospitalized at Memorial Hospital for abdominal surgery that necessitated a blood transfusion. Thereafter Carter was diagnosed as having acquired immune deficiency syndrome (AIDS), a fatal condition she contracted from a bad blood transfusion. Memorial Hospital attracted blood donors from the general public by offering $25 a pint. Every donor was required to fill out a form that asked, "Have you ever had or do you now have AIDS?" Those who did were immediately disqualified from selling blood. At the time, there was no scientific method of detecting AIDS in the blood. Discuss the various theories under which Carter may proceed against Memorial Hospital. What policies might the hospital implement to minimize the risk of future liability?

5. Josh Dowell was injured when a defective foil broke while he was fencing. After the accident the weapon was lost, and Dowell could not remember which of two manufacturers produced it. He sued both manufacturers under strict liability and sought the application of *Sindell.* What is the result?

6. Louise Hauter purchased a "Golfing Gizmo" from House of Zog, the manufacturer, and gave it to her son Fred on Christmas. The Gizmo is a training device designed to improve the unskilled golfer's game. The company describes the Gizmo as follows:

The Gizmo is a simple device consisting of two metal pegs, two cords—one elastic, one cotton—and a regulation golf ball. After the pegs are driven into the ground approximately 25 inches apart, the elastic cord is looped over them. The cotton cord, measuring 21 feet in length, ties to the middle of the elastic cord. The ball is attached to the end of the cotton cord. When the cords are extended, the Gizmo resembles

the shape of a large letter "T," with the ball resting at the base.

Both the label on the shipping carton and the cover of the instruction booklet urge players to "drive the ball with full power," and state: "Completely safe. Ball will not hit player." A picture of a golfer on the instructions shows the proper way to stand and hit the ball. Fred approached the Gizmo with a seven iron and took a normal beginner's swing. The ball struck him in the left temple, causing brain damage. Under what theories is House of Zog liable? Explain.

7. Orange Electronics manufactures computers. A brochure accompanies the sale of an Orange computer. In big easy to read print it includes the following language:

1. The manufacturer will remedy any defects within one year of purchase. After 3 failed attempts the customer may elect a refund or replacement of the product without charge.

2. The manufacturer will not be liable for any personal injury sustained by the customer as a result of computer malfunction.

3. Before instituting suit against the manufacturer the customer must submit to the arbitration procedure established by the manufacturer.

May Orange Electronics include these terms without violating the Magnuson-Moss Warranty Act? If so, what type of warranty designation is proper?

8. The Consumer Product Safety Commission found that urea-formaldehyde foam insulation (UFFI) in residences posed an unreasonable risk of injury from acute irritant effects and cancer. In arriving at this conclusion the CPSC:

— Conducted a study of 1,164 homes. 827 of these homes contained occupants who complained of UFFI-related health problems.
— Conducted a study on a number of commercial UFFI products in simulated wall panels which reflected conditions similar to an unheated home without air conditioning.

— Exposed 240 rats to an average of 14.3 parts per millimeter of formaldehyde five days a week for six hours a day. After two years, 103 rats developed nasal cancer.

Based on its findings, the CPSC seeks to ban UFFI. What arguments might the industry make against the ban?

9. Kaiser Aluminum and Chemical Corporation manufactures aluminum branch circuit wiring systems. These systems conduct electric current from fuses or circuit breakers to terminals within a residence, such as light fixtures and wall plug outlets. Kaiser sells the systems to wholesalers who sell it to contractors for installation in residences. The Consumer Product Safety Commission, concerned about reports of electrical failures and overheating of the systems, commenced proceedings to adopt a consumer product safety standard regulating the systems. How should Kaiser respond? How would you refute Kaiser's argument?

10. List the advantages and disadvantages of a product liability system based on a model uniform state law as compared to one based on a federal products liability law.

CHAPTER 6

ADVERTISING

The earliest advertisements to appear in America may have been those contained in the *Boston Newsletter* in 1704. In fact, most early American advertising was confined to local newspapers. However, as the American economy expanded, so did advertising.

The national railroad system built in the late nineteenth century hastened the development of magazines with national circulations. These magazines carried a good deal of advertising, most of it for medicines. Modern mass production and marketing techniques caused a tremendous expansion in the advertising industry. Brokers who sold magazine space to advertisers gave way to advertising agencies providing a wide range of services. Advertising expenditures increased from $5.7 billion in 1950 to $54.7 billion in 1980. By 1983 they reached $75.1 billion.

This chapter explores the laws governing advertising. It looks at private remedies for false advertising available to both consumers and competitors, and it examines government regulation of advertising by the Federal Trade Commission (FTC). Constitutional protections for advertisers are discussed in chapter 3.

PRIVATE REMEDIES FOR FALSE ADVERTISING

False advertising harms consumers by unfairly influencing them to buy goods and services that they might otherwise avoid. It also harms competitors by diverting potential customers. Not surprisingly, both consumers and competitors have sought relief from false advertising.

Consumer Remedies

Consumer remedies for false advertising are provided by both common law and statute. Common-law actions exist for *breach of contract* and for the tort of *deceit,* but these protections are more theoretical than real. Likewise, a statutory remedy for *breach of express warranty* provides only limited consumer protection against false advertisements.

Breach of Contract

A contract is an agreement a court will enforce. For an agreement to exist, there must be an *offer* and an *acceptance.* Advertisements are not normally offers. An offer details its terms, whereas advertisements are usually vague. They do not specify quantities available and often do not give price information. For these reasons, courts generally hold that advertisements are not offers to enter contracts, but invitations to make offers. A consumer who responds to an ad makes rather than accepts an offer to contract. This means that the advertiser is free to reject that offer.

At common law an advertiser may "bait" the consumer with advertisements of goods it does not intend to sell and then "switch" to more expensive goods at the time of sale. An advertiser may even refuse to sell at the advertised price.

Consider this example: A reader of an advertisement for an electric shaver goes to the store that placed the ad but is told by the merchant that the product will be sold at a price higher than that advertised. Can the reader win in an action against the advertiser for breach of contract? The general answer at common law is no.

If an advertisement is complete and reflects an intent to contract it can be construed as an offer. For example, the following ad was held to be an offer:[1]

```
┌─────────────────────────────┐
│     Saturday 9 A.M. Sharp    │
│        3 Brand New           │
│           Fur                │
│          Coats               │
│           · · ·              │
│        First Come            │
│        First Served          │
│            $1                │
│           Each               │
└─────────────────────────────┘
```

Thus, certainty of sale terms and words of promise can turn an advertisement into an offer. This is especially true, when, as in the above ad, it is clear from the terms that only a limited number of people can take advantage of it. Ads requiring the reader to do some act, in return for a reward are also considered offers. However, these represent the rare exceptions to the rule. In response to the common law, some cities have passed

---

[1] *Lefkowitz v. Great Minneapolis Surplus Store, Inc.,* 251 Minn. 188, 86 N.W. 2d 689 (1957).

ordinances requiring advertisers to stock sufficient inventories and to honor their ads.

Tort of Deceit

When the advertiser misrepresents the quality of goods or services, the consumer may recover for the common law tort of deceit. To do so, he or she must prove the following:

— A misrepresentation of a material fact
— Knowledge by the seller that the misrepresentation is false
— The seller's intent that the buyer rely on the misrepresentation
— The buyer's justified reliance on the misrepresentation
— Damage to the buyer

The tort of deceit gives limited protection to buyers because it is difficult to prove these elements. Consider the plight of the buyer of a used car who finds out that the odometer has been rolled back. In a suit for deceit the buyer must prove that the dealer either rolled back the odometer or knew that this had been done. This is hard to prove because of the possibility that the previous owner rolled back the odometer before delivering it to the dealer.

Frequently, statements intended to induce a sale do not constitute deceit because they express opinion, not fact. Obvious exaggerations are considered "puffing," and reliance on such statements is not justified. Reliance on the seller's statements is also unjustified where the buyer should know better or had a chance to inspect the goods before purchase.

Uniform Commercial Code

Besides common-law remedies for false advertising a buyer may have a statutory remedy under the Uniform Commercial Code (UCC). The UCC, as explained in chapter 5, has been adopted, at least in part, by all states. Article 2 of the UCC governs sales of goods. Section 2–313 provides that any statement, sample, or model may constitute an express warranty, as long as it is part of the basis of the bargain.

Advertising terms may be express warranties. If the goods do not conform to the representation, the purchaser may sue for breach of warranty. However, courts require that the buyer reasonably rely upon these terms; puffing will not create an express warranty under the UCC. A seller can avoid liability by disclaiming express warranties in the sales contract. Thus, the puffing defense and disclaimer clauses have weakened the action for breach of warranty under the UCC.

Competitor Remedies

Competitors, like consumers, may be harmed by false advertisements. Injury may result from the sale of inferior goods misrepresented as the goods of the competitor or from false statements made about the competitor. Competitors can sue for the torts of palming off, defamation, and disparagement. These actions, like the common-law remedies for consumers, are highly restrictive. A federal statute, the Lanham Act, provides a more expansive private remedy for competitors.

Palming Off

If an advertiser represents its goods in a way that deceives the average buyer into believing them to be the goods of a competitor, the advertiser is liable to that competitor for palming off. The misrepresentation may involve imitating the trademark, labels, containers, appearance of business, or any other distinctive characteristic of the competitor.

Assume that a local company which sells cheap wristwatches stamps the name "Bulova" (a quality watch) on the face of its watches and advertises them as such. This would amount to unlawful passing off—a practice that would injure Bulova in two ways. First, it would take away customers who would purchase the watches thinking that they were made by Bulova. Secondly, it would injure Bulova's image by associating the inferior watch with its name. Here, Bulova could obtain both an injunction restraining the company from misrepresenting its goods and damages for loss of business.

Palming off is not the only type of false advertising that injures competitors. Most often, false advertisements misrepresent the quality, price, or nature of the advertised goods. These misrepresentations harm competitors by taking customers away from them. Nevertheless, tort law leaves the competitor powerless against such claims.

This view dates to a 1900 decision in *American Washboard Co. v. Saginaw Manufacturing Co.*[2] American, a manufacturer of aluminum washboards, filed a suit alleging that Saginaw was selling zinc washboards by representing that they were made of aluminum. The Sixth Circuit Court of Appeals affirmed the trial court judgment for Saginaw. The court reasoned that the purpose of the common law was to protect property rights. Since there was no palming off, no property right was threatened. A different result, the court argued, would give American a property right in the use of the word aluminum.

A few cases have held that a competitor may recover against an advertiser who attributes to its merchandise qualities that it does not in fact possess. However, most courts still follow the *American Washboard* rule.

Defamation

False statements that hold a competitor's business reputation up to the contempt or ridicule of the community amount to defamation. If these statements are written, they constitute libel; if made orally, they are slander. In either case, a court will presume that the statements are untrue and that the competitor was damaged. When the statements are made with malice (evil intent), the injured party may recover punitive (or exemplary) damages. Punitive damages are amounts intended to punish the

---

[2] 103 F. 281 (6th Cir. 1900).

wrongdoer and compensate the plaintiff for the defendant's intentional misconduct. The defendant may successfully defend by proving that the statements made were in fact true.

Disparagement

False statements that injure a person's interest in property, as opposed to one's reputation, amount to disparagement. For example, assume that X accuses Y, a butcher, of selling spoiled meat. Since this statement tends to injure Y's reputation, it would be defamatory. Assume, however, that X falsely informs potential customers that Y went out of business. This does not directly injure Y's reputation; however, it injures the business by keeping potential buyers away from Y. This statement may constitute disparagement.

Disparagement is harder to prove than defamation. Competitors must prove that the statements were false and malicious and that they resulted in monetary loss by, for example, causing certain customers to avoid dealing with them.

The Lanham Act

In 1946 Congress enacted the Lanham Trademark Act. Section 43(a) of the act prohibits the use of "any false description or representation" in connection with any goods or services introduced into commerce. It provides a claim for any competitor likely to be damaged by the false representation.

Lanham Act, § 43(a)

Any person who shall . . . use in connection with any goods or services . . . a false . . . description or representation . . . shall be liable. . . .

Section 43(a) was hailed by many as creating a new federal tort for false advertising. Early decisions, however, did not broadly interpret the statute. Courts restricted its prohibitions to false representations that resulted in palming off the goods of the defendant as those of the plaintiff. Most federal circuits now hold that section 43(a) does enable one competitor to sue another for misrepresentation of a product. The clear trend is to interpret the Lanham Act to encompass a claim of false advertising, even where no palming off occurs.

The following case involving two giant orange juice producers and an Olympic gold medalist illustrates the application of the Lanham Act.

Coca-Cola Co. v. Tropicana Products, Inc.

690 F.2d 312 (2d Cir. 1982)

Tropicana Products, Inc. (appellee) aired a new television commercial for its Premium Pack orange juice. In it, American Olympic decathlon athlete Bruce Jenner squeezes an orange while saying, "It's pure, pasteurized juice as it comes from the orange." Jenner then pours the juice he squeezed into a Tropicana carton. The audio states "It's the only leading brand not made with concentrate and water." Coca-Cola Co. (Coke) (appellant), producer of Minute Maid orange juice, sued Tropicana for false advertising in violation of section 43(a) of the Lanham Act. Coke claims the commercial to be false because it represents that Premium Pack contains unprocessed, fresh-squeezed juice; in fact, the juice is heated and sometimes frozen before packaging. Coke sought an injunction to prevent Tropicana from continuing this advertisement.

The district court found in favor of Tropicana and denied the injunction. The circuit court of appeals reversed and sent the case back to the district court for issuance of the injunction.

Cardamone, Circuit Judge

A proverb current even in the days of ancient Rome was "seeing is believing." Today, a great deal of what people see flashes before them on their TV sets. This case involves a 30-second television commercial with simultaneous audio and video components. We have no doubt that the byword of Rome is as valid now as it was then. And, if seeing something on TV has a tendency to persuade a viewer to believe, how much greater is the impact . . . when he both sees and hears a message at the same time?

*   *   *   *   *

Perhaps the most difficult element to demonstrate when seeking an injunction against false advertising is the likelihood that one will suffer irreparable harm if the injunction does not issue. It is virtually impossible to prove that so much of one's sales will be lost or that one's goodwill will be damaged as a direct result of a competitor's advertisement. Too many market variables enter into the advertising-sales equation. Because of these impediments, a Lanham Act plaintiff who can prove actual lost sales may obtain an injunction even if most of his sales decline is attributable to factors other than a competitor's false advertising. In fact, he need not even point to an actual loss or diversion of sales.

*   *   *   *   *

. . . [I]f consumers are misled by Tropicana's commercial, Coca-Cola probably would suffer irreparable injury. Tropicana and Coca-Cola are the leading national competitors for the chilled (ready-to-serve) orange juice market. If Tropicana's advertisement misleads consumers into believing that Premium Pack is a more desirable product because it contains only fresh-squeezed unprocessed juice, then it is likely that Coke will lose a portion of the chilled juice market and thus suffer irreparable injury.

Evidence in the record supports the conclusion that consumers are likely to be misled in this manner. A consumer reaction survey conducted by ASI Market Research, Inc. and a Burke test, measuring recall of the commercial after it was aired on television, were admitted into evidence. . . . Our examination of the Burke test results leads to the . . . conclusion . . . that a not insubstantial number of consumers were clearly misled by the defendant's ad. Together these tests provide sufficient evidence of a risk of irreparable harm because they demonstrate that a significant number of consumers would be likely to be misled. . . .

*　*　*　*　*

Coke is entitled to relief under the Lanham Act if Tropicana has used a false description or representation in its Jenner commercial. When a merchandising statement or representation is literally or explicitly false, the court may grant relief without reference to the advertisement's impact on the buying public. When the challenged advertisement is implicitly rather than explicitly false, its tendency to violate the Lanham Act by misleading, confusing or deceiving should be tested by public reaction.

In viewing defendant's 30-second commercial at oral argument, we concluded that the trial court's finding that this ad was not facially false is an error of fact. Since the trial judge's finding on this issue was based solely on the inference it drew from reviewing documentary evidence, consisting of the commercial, we are in as good a position as it was to draw an appropriate inference. We find, therefore, that the squeezing-pouring sequence in the Jenner commercial is false on its face. The visual component of the ad makes an explicit representation that Premium Pack is produced by squeezing oranges and pouring the freshly-squeezed juice directly into the carton. This is not a true representation of how the product is prepared. Premium Pack juice is heated and sometimes frozen prior to packaging. Additionally, the simultaneous audio component of the ad states that Premium Pack is "Pasteurized juice as it comes from the orange." This statement is blatantly false—pasteurized juice does not come from oranges. Pasteurization entails heating the juice to approximately 200° Fahrenheit to kill certain natural enzymes and microorganisms which cause spoilage. Moreover, even if the addition of the word "pasteurized" somehow made sense and effectively qualified the visual image, Tropicana's commercial nevertheless represented that the juice is only squeezed, heated and packaged when in fact it may actually also be frozen.

*　*　*　*　*

. . . The purpose of the Act is to insure truthfulness in advertising and to eliminate misrepresentations with reference to the inherent quality or characteristic of another's product. The claim that Tropicana's Premium Pack contains only fresh-squeezed, unprocessed juice is clearly a misrepresentation as to that product's inherent quality or characteristic. . . .

CASE QUESTIONS

1. Was Coke accusing Tropicana of "palming off"? Explain.

2. What was misleading about the commercial? Was it misleading visually? Audially?

3. How would Coca-Cola be injured by Tropicana's ad? Was it necessary for Coke to introduce the consumer reaction survey?

4. What percentage of consumers must be misled by the advertisement before it is considered misleading? What impact would the Tropicana ad have on you?

5. What if Tropicana aired another television commercial in which Bruce Jenner takes a drink of the juice and, smacking his lips, says, "Tropicana . . . the juice that champions are made of." Would this violate the Lanham Act? Why or why not?

An advertisement may be literally true but may still violate section 43(a) because of its tendency to mislead the reasonably intelligent consumer. In *Vidal Sassoon, Inc. v. Bristol–Meyers Co.*, the defendant ran TV commercials in which a model claimed that "in shampoo tests with over 900 women like me, Body on Tap got higher ratings than Prell for body. Higher than Flex for conditioning. Higher than Sassoon for strong, healthy looking hair."[3] The plaintiff, Sassoon, cited a marketing study showing that consumers interpreted the ad to mean that each of the 900 women had tried all of the mentioned products. The majority believed that the tests showed Body on Tap to be superior than the other brands. In fact, this perception was false. The 900 women were divided into groups of about 200. Each group tested only one product. And, the tests did not reveal a statistically significant difference between Body on Tap and Sassoon. Finding in favor of the plaintiff the court held that the Lanham Act is not only applicable to blatant falsehoods, but also implicit misrepresentations—subtle suggestions that result in consumer misapprehension.

FTC Regulation of False Advertising

The weakness of private remedies for false advertising has placed the burden of regulation on government agencies. Several federal agencies regulate advertising, including the Federal Communication Commission, the Food and Drug Administration, and the Federal Trade Commission (FTC). The FTC has been the most active.

History of the FTC

In 1914 Congress enacted the Federal Trade Commission Act. Section 5 of the act empowered the FTC to initiate actions and, after hearings and findings, to order violators to stop engaging in unfair methods of competition. Although the statute's legislative history indicated that Congress was primarily concerned with more effective enforcement of the antitrust laws, the FTC interpreted the statute as empowering it to proceed against deceptive advertisers.

---

[3] 661 F.2d 272 (2d Cir. 1981).

One advertisement attacked by the FTC was used by the Raladam Company to promote its product Marmola. Raladam claimed that Marmola would cure obesity. The FTC found that the product could not be used safely without the supervision of a physician. It concluded that the advertisement deceived the public, and it ordered Raladam to stop making the claim. The U.S. Supreme Court, however, held that the commission had exceeded its authority because it failed to establish that the advertisement injured competition. Consumer protection was not recognized as an independent objective of the statute.[4]

In 1938, seven years after Raladam, Congress enacted the Wheeler-Lea Act, which amended section 5. The amendment enlarged the prohibitions of section 5 by including "unfair or deceptive practices." Congress

---

Federal Trade Commission Act, § 5(a) (1)

Unfair methods of competition . . . and unfair or deceptive acts or practices . . . are hereby declared unlawful.

---

made it clear that it intended to protect the consumer injured by unfair trade practices as well as the merchant or manufacturer injured by the unfair methods of a dishonest competitor.

For 35 years after the passage of the Wheeler-Lea Act the FTC attacked deceptive advertising on a case-by-case basis. Although the commission asserted that it had rulemaking authority as well, some courts disagreed. Congress removed the uncertainty by enacting the FTC Improvements Act of 1975. This act specifically gave the commission power to enact rules to prevent unfair and deceptive trade practices.

Dissatisfaction soon developed over the commission's exercise of its new powers. The FTC embarked upon rulemaking proceedings that aroused considerable criticism. Its most controversial action was a proposed ban on all television advertising aimed at children. The FTC Improvements Act of 1980 terminated the proceedings against children's advertising and limited the commission's subsequent rulemaking powers. Since then, the FTC has proceeded against violators of the act on a case-by-case basis.

FTC Structure and Adjudicatory Procedure

The FTC consists of five commissioners who are appointed by the president and confirmed by the Senate for seven-year terms. The FTC's Bureau of

---

[4] *FTC v. Raladam Co.*, 283 U.S. 643 (1931).

Consumer Protection (Bureau) is responsible for controlling unfair and deceptive advertising. (See page 117 for FTC organizational chart.)

When a deceptive advertisement is brought to the attention of the FTC, the staff investigates the alleged violation. After the investigation, if the Bureau's director finds reasonable cause to believe a violation exists, the director will attempt to negotiate a consent order with the alleged violator. A *consent order* is an agreement to cease activities that the government claims are illegal.

If the parties cannot agree to a consent order, the FTC Complaint Counsel may file a complaint against the alleged violator, who is now called the respondent. The case will be tried before an administrative law judge (ALJ). The ALJ is empowered to order a respondent to cease and desist from engaging in deceptive advertising. The losing party may appeal the ALJ's decision to the full commission. If the commission finds against the respondent, the respondent may appeal to the appropriate U.S. court of appeals. The court of appeals reviews the decision to determine whether it is supported by substantial evidence on the record. (Administrative procedures are discussed in Chapter 4.)

Deceptive Price Advertising

Advertisements dealing with price were among the first to be scrutinized by the FTC. An ad offering free goods or services to customers who make a purchase is lawful only if the goods to be bought are sold at the advertiser's regular price—the price at which they were sold before the advertisement. They are deceptive if the advertiser recovers the cost of the free merchandise by marking up the price of the merchandise to be bought. Similarly, when ads offer "two for the price of one," the two units must be sold at the regular price of one unit before the ad was run.

Price reductions, such as "one-third off" or "25 percent below the suggested retail price," also present a potential for false advertising. When an advertisement claims that prices have been reduced, they must be reduced from their former regular prices. If they have been reduced from prices that were artificially inflated to facilitate the "reductions," the ad violates section 5.

With price comparisons which offer, for example, "a $10 retail value for $7.50," the comparable price must be one charged in a substantial number of sales in the area. If only a few isolated outlets charge $10, while most other outlets charge between $7 and $8, the advertisement would violate section 5. Manufacturers often preticket merchandise to suggest retail prices. If the manufacturer's suggested price does not reflect the prevailing price in the area, an advertiser may not lawfully use it as a basis for comparison.

Another deceptive advertising scheme akin to false price comparisons is the "bait and switch." Section 5 is violated if one product is advertised in order to lure customers into a store to buy other, more expensive products, when the advertiser has no intention of selling the advertised product. This practice is examined in the following case.

Tashof v. F T C

437 F.2d 707 (D.C. Cir. 1970)

Leon Tashof (appellant) is in the retail trade conducting business as New York Jewelry Co. (NYJC). The store is located in a neighborhood that serves low-income consumers, many of whom have no bank or charge accounts. Eighty-five percent of NYJC's sales are made on credit.

The FTC charged NYJC with falsely advertising the availability of discount eyeglasses and misrepresenting its prices and credit practices. The hearing examiner (administrative law judge) dismissed the charges. The commission rejected the examiner's findings and found Tashof guilty of unfair and deceptive advertising practices in violation of the Federal Trade Commission Act. The FTC ordered Tashof to cease and desist (stop) the practices. Tashof sought review of the order claiming that the evidence was not sufficient to support the commission's findings, and that the FTC order was unjustified. The court of appeals upheld the findings and the order.

Bazelon, Chief Judge

A. False Advertising of Eyeglasses

The Commission first found that NYJC employed a "bait and switch" maneuver with respect to sales of eyeglasses. The evidence showed that NYJC advertised eyeglasses "from $7.50 complete," including "lenses, frames and case." The newspaper advertisements, but not the radio advertisements, mentioned a "moderate examining fee." During this period NYJC offered free eye examinations by a sign posted in its store, and through cards it mailed out and distributed on the street. NYJC claimed that it offered $7.50 eyeglasses only to persons with their own prescriptions. But we have no doubt that the record amply supports the Commission's finding that the advertising campaign taken as a whole offered complete eyeglass service for $7.50.

That much shows "bait." There was no direct evidence of "switch"—no direct evidence, that is, that NYJC disparaged or discouraged the purchase of the $7.50 eyeglasses, or that the glasses were unavailable on demand, or unsuited for their purpose. The evidence on which the Commission rested its finding was a stipulation that out of 1,400 pairs of eyeglasses sold each year by NYJC, less than 10 were sold for $7.50 with or without a prescription. NYJC claims that this evidence does not support the finding. We disagree.

It seems plain to us that the Commission drew a permissible inference of "switch" from the evidence of bait advertising and minimal sales of the advertised product. At best only nine sales—64/100 of one percent of NYJC's eyeglass sales—were made at $7.50. The record leaves unexplained why NYJC's customers, presumably anxious to purchase at as low a price as possible, would so consistently have bought more expensive glasses if suitable glasses at $7.50 were available. Further, NYJC continued to advertise the $7.50 glasses for a year and a half despite the scarcity of sales, a fact which tends to support a finding of a purpose to bring customers into the store for other reasons. This evidence, we think, was sufficient to shift the burden of coming forward to the respondent. But NYJC offered no evidence to negate the inference of "switch." The relevant facts are in NYJC's possession, and it was in the best position to show, if it could be shown at all that $7.50 glasses were actually available in the store. Yet the most NYJC could produce was its sales manager's denial that the $7.50 glasses were disparaged. NYJC never did point to even a single sale of the advertised product.

B. False Advertising of Discount Prices

There is no dispute that NYJC claimed to be a discount seller of eyeglasses. Nor is there any question that the sales slips introduced by the FTC were sufficient to show NYJC's actual prices. . . .

The Commission's staff presented the only evidence of prevailing prices: the testimony of Dr. Zachary Ephraim, an optometrist. Since optometrists are a major retail outlet for eyeglasses and perform a service closely comparable to that provided by NYJC—examining eyes and filling prescriptions—Dr. Ephraim was well qualified to testify about prevailing prices. We hold that his uncontradicted testimony was a sufficient basis for the Commission's findings.

The Commission determined the generally prevailing prices of eyeglasses on the basis of Dr. Ephraim's testimony of the usual price charged by most optometrists in the trade area. NYJC first claims that the Commission erroneously ignored the expert's statements that some sellers might charge higher prices. We disagree, because Dr. Ephraim referred only to some extremely high prices that a relatively few sellers might charge. Thus the record as a whole supports the Commission's finding of generally prevailing eyeglass prices, i.e., the prices to which NYJC's must be compared in considering the charge that its representations of discount prices were false. NYJC's second claim concerns the Commission's refusal to include in the prevailing price the amount which the consumer would have had to pay for an eye examination. Since NYJC offered "free" eye examinations, it could be argued that no adjustment for examinations was required. But the Commission did make allowance for NYJC's actual cost of the examination. We cannot say that this treatment was unreasonable. It is worth noting that even if the prevailing prices were computed as NYJC has urged, NYJC's customers still paid a higher than prevailing price more often than not.

*   *   *   *   *

. . . The Commission ordered NYJC to cease and desist from representing that it sells "any article of merchandise" at a discount price . . . unless it first takes a "statistically significant survey" which shows that the prevailing price is "substantially" above NYJC's. The order apparently subjects NYJC to civil penalties if it advertises discount prices without having taken the survey, even if the advertisement is true. The Commission claims that this remedy constitutes "reasonable action . . . calculated to preclude the revival of the illegal practices." We agree. NYJC was shown to have taken little account of the true level of prices in the trade area. We think the FTC may enter an order to ensure that this is not repeated in the future, without having to determine whether respondent's previous conduct was due to inadvertence, bad faith, or a kind of inattention or negligence involving some intermediate culpability. Where a businessman has wrought a wrong on the public, he may be held to a reasonable business procedure that will prevent repetition of that wrong, and in view of his past record he will not be permitted to object that his own approaches might also avoid this wrong in the future, perhaps by happenstance and perhaps only on occasion.

NYJC has offered nothing either here or before the Commission to support its assertion that the statistical survey requirement is unduly burdensome. The requirement does not appear onerous on its face. Thus the order must be enforced.

Robb, Circuit Judge (concurring in part, dissenting in part):

. . . In my judgment the Commission exceeds its authority when it requires NYJC to conduct a "statistically significant survey" of relevant prices in its trade area before advertising a "discount price." This requirement shifts to NYJC the burden of proving its innocence; and as the majority opinion concedes, might subject NYJC to heavy civil penalties even if its advertisement is true. I would affirm after eliminating this part of the order.

CASE QUESTIONS

1. What was the evidence of the bait? What was the evidence of the switch?

2. What could Tashof have done to avoid being charged with using bait and switch tactics?

3. What inquiries should an advertiser make to insure that it will not violate section 5 when advertising that its goods are being sold at discount prices?

4. What must Tashof now do in order to advertise "discount prices"? Do you agree with Judge Robb? Why or why not?

5. Suppose Tashof had advertised "easy credit," but pursued a vigorous collection policy that often resulted in the garnishment of a buyer's wages. Would he have been in violation of section 5?

Testimonials and Mock-Ups

Testimonials and endorsements by well-known personalities sometimes violate the act. An advertisement is deceptive if it represents that a product is endorsed by a person who does not, in fact, use the product or prefer it. Advertisements are also deceptive if they imply falsely that the endorser has superior experience or training. For example, it is deceptive for an athlete to imply falsely that he or she is an expert in nutrition and praise the energy content of a cereal.

In television advertising, mock-ups are necessary because the medium cannot effectively transmit the real product. For example, on a black and white TV screen white appears grey and coffee looks like mud. Advertisers often use mock-ups to counter the distortion or improve the effectiveness of their ad. If the viewing public is led to believe that it is seeing a real product or experiment, the advertisement will violate the FTC act. The use of mock-ups must be disclosed.

Quality Claims

Advertisers frequently make quality claims. Some of these claims are considered trade puffing and do not violate the act. Where quality claims exceed the bounds of permissible puffing, two issues frequently arise: (1) What claim did the advertiser make? (2) Was the claim false or deceptive?

Identifying Quality Claims

Quality claims may be expressly made in an advertisement, or they may be implied from its language. The burden of proving that a claim is implied in an ad rests on the FTC. When the FTC interprets an advertisement to determine its meaning, it may rely upon its own expertise in the area. If it chooses to do so, it will simply view the ad and, aided by the arguments of counsel, draw its conclusions. The commission frequently supplements its expertise with testimony from experts and with consumer surveys.

Consumer surveys are considered by the FTC when they are reliable and probative. In determining the weight to be given to a survey, the commission considers the reputation of the organization that ran it, the training and experience of the persons who conducted it, the sampling techniques used, the use of controls and validation procedures, and the incentives to bias the results. The weight of surveys is greatly enhanced where two or more independent surveys confirm each other. The cautious advertiser should therefore consider previewing advertisements before representative audiences, to evaluate potential audience perceptions.

From 1964 to 1970, advertisements appeared on national television depicting a child eating Wonder Bread and growing rapidly from a very young child to a 12-year-old. The words **protein, mineral, carbohydrates,** and **vitamins** flashed above the child, while the announcer narrated:

These are the Wonder Years, the formative years 1 through 12 when your child develops in many ways, actually grows to 90 percent of her adult height.

To help make the most of these Wonder Years, serve nutritious Wonder Enriched Bread. Wonder helps build strong bodies in 12 ways. Carefully enriched with foods for body and mind, Wonder Bread tastes so good, and is so good for growing child, for active adult.

Help make the most of her Wonder Years, her growth years. Serve Wonder Bread. Wonder helps build strong bodies 12 ways.

The FTC complaint counsel alleged that this advertisement implied that Wonder Bread was unique in providing nutrients far superior to those of all other breads. The commission, however, reviewed conflicting consumer surveys and expert testimony and concluded that complaint counsel had failed to establish the existence of the implied claim.[5]

Deceptive Quality Claims

Once it has been ascertained that a claim is made in an advertisement, the FTC must determine whether the claim is deceptive. The FTC considers an act or practice deceptive if it misleads reasonable consumers to their detriment. Advertisers must possess adequate *substantiation* for their claims at the time they are made. It is deceptive advertising to make a product claim without substantiation. All quality claims imply that the advertiser has a reasonable basis, or substantiation, for making them. What constitutes a reasonable basis will vary greatly with the type of product and the type of claim. The reasonable basis or substantiation requirement stems from the commission's view that highly technical and complex information places the consumer at a distinct disadvantage compared to the advertiser in evaluating product claims.

An illustration of why advertisers must be careful to avoid making implied claims, without evidence of substantiation, is provided by the next case involving a leading manufacturer of painkillers.

American Home Products Corp. v. F.T.C.

695 F.2d 681 (3rd Cir. 1982)

American Home Products (AHP) (petitioner) manufactures drugs. One drug, Anacin, is an over-the-counter (nonprescription) analgesic (pain-killer). It contains two ingredients: aspirin and caffein. Aspirin is Anacin's only pain-killing component. For years petitioner advertised its products through various news media, including magazines and television.

The FTC issued a complaint against AHP charging that AHP falsely advertised that Anacin (1) has a unique pain-killing formula and (2) is proven to be superior to all other nonprescription analgesics. AHP denied that it made any false claims. An administrative law judge (ALJ) heard the case and ordered AHP to: (1) stop falsely representing that its nonprescription analgesics are established to be superior to competitors, and (2) not represent the superiority of its nonprescription analgesics unless it can support it with at least two well-controlled clinical studies. The

---

[5] *ITT Continental Baking Co.*, 83 F.T.C. 865 (1973).

FTC adopted these findings and the order of the ALJ. AHP appealed, but the court of appeals affirmed that portion of the commission's order.

Adams, Circuit Judge

How Advertising Is to Be Interpreted

"[T]he tendency of the advertising to deceive must be judged by viewing it as a whole, without emphasizing isolated words or phrases apart from their context.". . .

* * * * *

In the present proceeding, the Commission analyzed not only the words used, but also, with respect to the television advertisements, the messages conveyed through the "aural-visual" pattern. The Commission's right to scrutinize the visual and aural imagery of advertisements follows from the principle that the Commission looks to the impression made by the advertisements as a whole. Without this mode of examination, the Commission would have limited recourse against crafty advertisers whose deceptive messages were conveyed by means other than, or in addition to, spoken words. . . .

* * * * *

We have no hesitation in affirming the Commission's determination that AHP represented that the superiority of Anacin had been proven or established, and that such representation was deceptive.

1. Were the Establishment Claims Made?

* * * * *

One advertisement which appeared in virtually identical form in several magazines is entitled "News about headache relief you probably missed (unless you read medical magazines)." Beneath what was designed to resemble a clipping from a medical journal, the body of the advertisement informed readers:

> In clinical tests on hundreds of headache sufferers, it has now been proven beyond a doubt that today's Anacin delivers the same complete headache relief as the leading pain relief prescription. This advertisement in leading medical journals [i.e., the clipping] told the complete story. Doctors know Anacin contains more of the specific medication they recommend most for pain than the leading aspirin, buffered aspirin, or extra-strength tablet. Is it any wonder that last year physicians and dentists distributed over 25 million packets of Anacin tablets to their patients?
>
> Now you know that Anacin gives you the same complete headache relief as the leading pain relief prescription. Next headache, see how fast Anacin relieves your pain.

The advertisement . . . proclaims that Anacin has been clinically proven to be as effective as the leading prescription analgesic, and that Anacin is known by doctors to have more of the pain reliever they recommend most than do the other leading non-prescription analgesics. There is no explicit representation that Anacin has been clinically proven to be more effective than any other non-prescription analgesics. . . . [T]he fundamental objection to the advertisement is that consumers . . . will be likely to combine the claim of *proven* equivalence to the leading prescription drug, and the claim that doctors know that Anacin has more pain reliever than the other non-prescription products, into a claim that

Anacin's superiority to the other non-prescription products has been proven.

* * * * *

The Commission, despite primary reliance on its own knowledge in interpreting the advertisements, weighed all the survey evidence in the record. Although AHP produced several types of empirical data, only one type—the Audience Studies, Inc. (ASI) tests—was relevant to determining the meaning of particular advertisements, as AHP's expert admitted. ASI had conducted tests on behalf of AHP's advertising agency to measure the effectiveness of some advertisements. These tests involved none of the print or radio advertisements but rather were limited to thirty of those that appeared on television. A sample of consumers was shown films . . . of the advertisements. Thirty or forty minutes later, the consumers wrote down what they recalled, and these responses were then tabulated and coded. AHP's expert, Dr. Smith, apparently found no consumers who thought that an "establishment" claim was made in the advertisements. The Commission, however, for a number of reasons discounted this result as being of limited usefulness. Dr. Smith's analysis was found to be flawed [for various technical reasons]. . . .

* * * * *

We cannot say that the Commission's appraisal of this evidence was unsupported. It is also significant that there was considerable record evidence of a widespread consumer belief in Anacin's superior efficacy. . . . In view of the inability of consumers to discriminate objectively between competing analgesics, . . . the Commission was "convinced that the primary source of this consumer belief in Anacin's superiority is the advertising of the product." . . . The Commission also concluded that consumers' belief in superiority, and their implicit belief in established superiority, would be likely to persist unless AHP carried out the directives of the Commission's Order.

2. Were the Establishment Claims Deceptive?

Having upheld the Commission's determination that certain of AHP's advertisements should be read as making the "establishment" claim, we proceed to consider whether the Commission could have found that claim misleading. On this issue as well it is clear that the Commission must be sustained. Even though AHP's advertisements never disclosed the presence of aspirin in Anacin, the claim to superior effectiveness appears to be based on the belief that a somewhat larger dosage of aspirin, such as Anacin contains, is more effective in the relief of pain than "ordinary" aspirin.

The Commission carefully considered, and rejected, the evidence that Anacin's superiority had been established or proven. It found that there was "no real dispute as to the type of evidence scientists require before they regard it as having been proven (established) that one drug is more effective than another."

* * * * *

Quite apart from the argument that the word "established" is of uncertain meaning, AHP asserts that two studies performed for it by Dr. Gilbert McMahon meet the standard of two well-controlled clinical studies; but the Commission found numerous defects in these studies. The Commission objected that the results were not statistically significant; that the drug product tested against aspirin was not shown to be equivalent to commercially-available Anacin; and that the studies failed to deal with headache pain, which AHP's witnesses conceded to be different from other types of pain. The ALJ, in a closely reasoned analysis of the

McMahon studies, made additional points, including that bias was introduced into the studies by the ongoing "peeking" at and evaluation of data by AHP. We are unable to hold that the Commission acted unreasonably in refusing to assign to these studies the probative force that AHP wishes for them.

*   *   *   *   *

A number of expert witnesses testified that Anacin's superior efficacy has not been established, and some expressed the view that Anacin was *not* superior. Far from concluding that Anacin's superiority had been proven, the ALJ suggested that Anacin might be less effective than "ordinary" aspirin. The possibility that the caffeine in Anacin could actually *heighten* awareness of pain was not ruled out. Moreover, there was evidence that caffeine exacerbated aspirin's gastrointestinal side effects, and "in terms of chronic use, the record evidence strongly suggest[s] that more aspirin may be worse [in its side effects] than less aspirin."

There are numerous appellate decisions upholding the Commission's right to require substantiation of advertising claims. In a case involving non-prescription weight-reducing tablets . . . the court refused to strike down an order prohibiting, among other things, representations that *any* product of the advertiser could achieve *any* result, "unless the representation is, when made, substantiated by competent scientific and medical tests and studies." This prohibition was more far-reaching than . . . the present Order. . . .

CASE QUESTIONS

1. What explicit claims did AHP make about Anacin in its advertisement? Did the FTC contend these claims were false?

2. What impact do you think this advertisement would have on the average consumer? Do you agree with the court?

3. Why were Anacin's claims determined to be deceptive?

4. Is it unfair to require AHP to substantiate its claims with two clinical studies? What is wrong with one good study?

5. Assume that well-documented consumer surveys proved that the vast majority of people who had taken various over-the-counter pain killers believed Anacin to be superior. Would evidence of those surveys change the result in this case? Explain.

Comparative Advertising

Advertisements comparing one product with a competing product have increased over the last two decades. Originally, comparative advertising was subtle. The competitor was not named but was referred to instead as "Brand X," or by a name that implicitly identified the competitor. For example, in the mid-1960s Avis initiated a successful comparative advertising campaign against "Number One." Although the target of the campaign was not expressly mentioned, it was clear that "Number One" was Hertz. Advertisers were reluctant to name their competitors, not wanting to give them free advertising nor place them in a sympathetic light. They were also fearful of competitor or FTC reprisal. In any event, most television networks refused to accept comparative ads that expressly named competing products.

In 1972, however, the FTC encouraged the networks to air comparative ads. The FTC believed that such advertising was necessary in order to give the public fuller information about products. Since then, comparative advertising has become a widely acceptable marketing tool. About one out of every four television ads are comparative, claiming superiority to competing products.

Competitors who are the target of deceptive comparative advertising are susceptible to injury. If its product is disparaged, a company can seek a private common-law remedy. Or, if the advertiser misrepresents its own product, the competitor can bring suit for violation of the Lanham Act.

The consumer also may be injured by deceptive comparative advertising, but private consumer remedies are practically nonexistent. The FTC, however, is charged with acting in the public interest to prevent such deceptive advertising.

Unfair Advertising

Section 5 prohibits *"unfair* or deceptive acts."* This raises the issue of whether that section empowers the FTC to regulate ads that it finds unfair even in the absence of deception. Proponents of such a power call for a broad interpretation of section 5, noting that the FTC has been allowed much flexibility in adapting to new practices that are contrary to public policy. Opponents argue that Congress never intended the FTC to regulate ads that were not deceptive and that such regulation would violate the First Amendment.[6]

Had the FTC limited the development of the unfairness doctrine to an adjudicatory context, the issue might not have gained much attention. However, after obtaining rulemaking authority in 1975, the FTC sought to give the doctrine broader application by promulgating industrywide trade regulation rules. The FTC initiated proceedings to develop rules to ban all children's television advertising. It reasoned that even if such ads are truthful, they may be considered unfair because they are aimed at a particularly vulnerable audience.

The breadth of the unfairness doctrine and the fear of abuse prompted Congress to enact the FTC Improvements Act of 1980, which terminated the proceedings on children's advertising. Furthermore, the act declared that unfairness might not be used as a basis for a trade regulation rule. It forbade the FTC to use any funds to initiate rulemaking proceedings that might result in regulating ads on the basis that they constitute unfair acts or practices. This moratorium on rulemaking is still in effect.

---

[6] For a discussion of the constitutionality of commercial speech regulation, see Chapter 3.

The restriction applies only to FTC rulemaking power. The agency remains free to challenge acts or practices, including unfair commercial advertising, in an adjudicatory context. It just cannot apply the unfairness standard on an industrywide basis through rulemaking.

FTC Orders

The FTC is authorized to issue cease and desist orders to violators of section 5. These orders instruct those who are engaged in unfair or deceptive acts or practices to stop using such methods.

Since 1970 the FTC has claimed the authority to order affirmative disclosures to dissipate the residual effects of an advertiser's deception. These disclosures are called "corrective advertising." False claims will linger in the public's mind for a long time; therefore, corrective statements may be needed over a period to dispel these residual effects. In the following case, the circuit court of appeals applies the concept of corrective advertising.

Warner–Lambert Co. v. FTC

562 F.2d 749 (D.C. Cir. 1977)

Warner–Lambert (petitioner) has been marketing Listerine, a mouthwash, since 1879. The formula has remained the same. Over the years, petitioner has represented to the public that Listerine relieves colds, cold symptoms, and sore throats. The FTC issued a complaint against petitioner charging that its advertisements misrepresented the qualities of Listerine. It ordered petitioner to stop advertising that Listerine prevents, cures, or alleviates the symptoms of a cold. The FTC order further required Warner–Lambert to make the following disclosure in future Listerine advertisements: "Contrary to prior advertising, Listerine will not help prevent colds or sore throats or lessen their severity." Petitioner sought a review of the FTC order in the court of appeals. The order was affirmed but modified to delete from the required disclosure the phrase "contrary to prior advertising."

J. Skelly Wright, Circuit Judge

Listerine has been on the market since 1879. Its formula has never changed. Ever since its introduction it has been repre-sented as being beneficial in certain respects for colds, cold symptoms, and sore throats. Direct advertising to the consumer, including the cold claims as well as others, began in 1921.

* * * * *

The first issue on appeal is whether the Commission's conclusion that Listerine is not beneficial for colds or sore throats is supported by the evidence. The Commission's findings must be sustained if they are supported by substantial evidence on the record viewed as a whole. We conclude that they are.

Both the ALJ and the Commission carefully analyzed the evidence. They gave full consideration to the studies submitted by petitioner. The ultimate conclusion that Listerine is not an effective cold remedy was based on six specific findings of fact.

First, the Commission found that the ingredients of Listerine are not present in sufficient quantities to have any therapeutic effect. This was the testimony of two leading pharmacologists called by Commission counsel. The Commission was justified in concluding that the testimony of Listerine's experts was not sufficiently persuasive to counter this testimony.

Second, the Commission found that in the process of gargling it is impossible for Listerine to reach the critical areas of the body in medically significant concentration. The liquid is confined to the mouth chamber. Such vapors as might reach the nasal passage would not be in therapeutic concentration. Petitioner did not offer any evidence that vapors reached the affected areas in significant concentration.

Third, the Commission found that even if significant quantities of the active ingredients of Listerine were to reach the critical sites where cold viruses enter and infect the body, they could not interfere with the activities of the virus because they could not penetrate the tissue cells.

Fourth, the Commission discounted the results of a clinical study conducted by petitioner on which petitioner heavily relies. Petitioner contends that in a four-year study school children who gargled with Listerine had fewer colds and cold symptoms than those who did not gargle with Listerine. The Commission found that the design and execution of the "St. Barnabas study" made its results unreliable. For the first two years of the four-year test no placebo was given to the control group. For the last two years the placebo was inadequate: the control group was given colored water which did not resemble Listerine in smell or taste. There was also evidence that the physician who examined the test subjects was not blinded from knowing which children were using Listerine and which were not, that his evaluation of the cold symptoms of each child each day may have been imprecise, and that he necessarily relied on the non-blinded child's subjective reporting. Both the ALJ and the Commission analyzed the St. Barnabas study and the expert testimony about it in depth and were justified in concluding that its results are unreliable.

Fifth, the Commission found that the ability of Listerine to kill germs by millions on contact is of no medical significance in the treatment of colds or sore throats. Expert testimony showed that bacteria in the oral cavity, the "germs" which Listerine purports to kill, do not cause colds and play no role in cold symptoms. Colds are caused by viruses. Further, "while Listerine kills millions of bacteria in the mouth, it also leaves millions. It is impossible to sterilize any area of the mouth, let alone the entire mouth."

Sixth, the Commission found that Listerine has no significant beneficial effect on the symptoms of sore throat. The Commission recognized that gargling with Listerine could provide temporary relief from a sore throat by removing accumulated debris irritating the throat. But this type of relief can also be obtained by gargling with salt water or even warm water. . . . It was reasonable to conclude that "such temporary relief does not 'lessen the severity' of a sore throat any more than expectorating or blowing one's nose 'lessens the severity' of a cold."

* * * * *

Petitioner contends that even if its advertising claims in the past were false, the portion of the Commissioner's order requiring "corrective advertising" exceeds the Commission's statutory power. The argument is based upon a literal reading of Section 5 of the Federal Trade Commission Act, which authorizes the Commission to issue "cease and desist" orders against violators and does not expressly mention any other remedies. The Commission's position, on the other hand, is that the affirmative disclosure that Listerine will not prevent colds or lessen their severity is absolutely necessary to give effect to the prospective cease and desist order; a hundred years of false cold claims have built up a large reservoir of erroneous consumer belief which would persist, unless corrected, long after the petitioner ceased making the claims.

* * * * *

The Commission has adopted the following standard for the imposition of corrective advertising:

> [I]f a deceptive advertisement has played a substantial role in creating or reinforcing in the public's mind a false and material belief which lives on after the false advertising ceases, there is clear and continuing injury to competition and to the consuming public as consumers continue to make purchasing decisions based on the false belief. Since this injury cannot be averted by merely requiring respondent to cease disseminating the advertisement, we may appropriately order respondent to take affir-

mative action designed to terminate the otherwise continuing ill effects of the advertisement.

We think this standard is entirely reasonable. It dictates two factual inquiries: (1) did Listerine's advertisements play a substantial role in creating or reinforcing in the public's mind a false belief about the product? and (2) would this belief linger on after the false advertising ceases? It strikes us that if the answer to both questions is not yes, companies everywhere may be wasting their massive advertising budgets. Indeed, it is more than a little peculiar to hear petitioner assert that its commercials really have no effect on consumer belief.

For these reasons it might be appropriate in some cases to presume the existence of the two factual predicates for corrective advertising. But we need not decide that question, or rely on presumptions here, because the Commission adduced survey evidence to support both propositions. . . .

We turn next to the specific disclosure required: "Contrary to prior advertising, Listerine will not help prevent colds or sore throats or lessen their severity." Petitioner is ordered to include this statement in every future advertisement for Listerine for a defined period. In printed advertisements it must be displayed in type size at least as large as that in which the principal portion of the text of the advertisement appears and it must be separated from the text so that it can be readily noticed. In television commercials the disclosure must be presented simultaneously in both audio and visual portions. During the audio portion of the disclosure in television and radio advertisements, no other sounds, including music, may occur.

These specifications are well calculated to assure that the disclosure will reach the public. It will necessarily attract the notice of readers, viewers, and listeners, and be plainly conveyed. Given these safeguards, we believe the preamble "Contrary to prior advertising" is not necessary. It can serve only two purposes: either to attract attention that a correction follows or to humiliate the advertiser. The Commission claims only the first purpose for it, and this we think is obviated by the other terms of the order. The second purpose, if it were intended, might be called for in an egregious case of deliberate deception, but this is not one. While we do not decide whether petitioner proffered its cold claims in good faith or bad, the record compiled could support a finding of good faith. On these facts, the confessional preamble to the disclosure is not warranted.

Finally, petitioner challenges the duration of the disclosure requirement. By its terms it continues until respondent has expended on Listerine advertising a sum equal to the annual Listerine advertising budget for the period April 1962 to March 1972. That is approximately ten million dollars. Thus if petitioner continues to advertise normally the corrective advertising will be required for about one year. We cannot say that is an unreasonably long time in which to correct a hundred years of cold claims. But, to petitioner's distress, the requirement will not expire by mere passage of time. If petitioner cuts back its Listerine advertising, or ceases it altogether, it can only postpone the duty to disclose. The Commission concluded that correction was required and that a duration of a fixed period of time might not accomplish that task, since petitioner could evade the order by choosing not to advertise at all. The formula settled upon by the Commission is reasonably related to the violation it found.

CASE QUESTIONS

1. Would evidence of consumer satisfaction provide a reasonable basis for the Listerine ads?

2. What conditions must be present before the FTC will order corrective advertising?

3. Do you agree that the preamble "contrary to prior advertising" is not necessary?

4. How did the FTC arrive at the formula for the duration of the disclosure?

5. Is corrective advertising punitive in nature? If so, should it be outside the FTC's authority to order such advertising? Do corrective advertising orders present any constitutional problems? Explain.

ALTERNATIVE APPROACHES

Three alternative approaches to the existing regulation of advertising may be identified. Some critics of the current system opt for deregulation; others would rely upon self-regulation; while a third group would like to see some regulatory reform.

Deregulation

Those who oppose governmental regulation of advertising argue that the marketplace is a self-equilibrating mechanism which, if left alone, will satisfy consumer needs better than any alternative involving regulation or control. Freedom of choice is one of the most cherished and fundamental American values. Historically, freedom of choice has been defined as the seller's right to enter a market and the worker's right to choose an occupation or a specific type of job. Free market philosophers argue that consumers should be free to spend more or less in their purchases. They will buy from those who provide the needed product or service at the optimum price.

Opponents to regulation argue that deterrents to fraud exist in the form of:

— Consumer knowledge and intelligence (some claims simply will not be believed)
— The cost to the seller of developing a reputation for dishonesty
— Competition (another seller's advertisement may correct a fraudulent claim)

However, there are limits to the ability of market forces to deter fraud. Some consumer groups lack sufficient knowledge or education to judge advertised claims. The costs of developing a reputation for dishonesty are not a deterrent to fly-by-night sellers with no fixed locale or stable clientele. Competitors cannot be expected to discredit all fraudulent claims, and private legal remedies are not attractive to individual consumers of small items.

The market system is conducive to fraud in some areas. The costs of getting product information—what economists call "search costs"—for some inexpensive goods may be so prohibitive that buyers are forced to rely upon sellers for that information. Free market economic philosophy assumes that the consumer possesses the ability to appraise the costs and benefits of various purchasing alternatives, but in reality the seller has a strong informational advantage over the consumer. Thus, the argument can be made that regulation is needed to accommodate the consumer's need for information and industry's willingness to provide such information.

Self-Regulation

Some critics believe that a strong system of self-regulation would balance consumer and industry needs. In fact, some form of self-regulation of advertising already exists. Each major broadcasting network has a Broadcast Standards Department which reviews all ads for truthfulness, substantiality of claims, and conformance with both legal and network advertising standards. These departments also review ads for compliance with the National Association of Broadcasters (NAB) Television Standards Code. The NAB Code prohibits ads for certain goods and services (e.g., fortune-telling), regulates ads for others (e.g., no beer drinking in beer commercials), and has special standards for ads aimed at children. Ads for some products (e.g., toys and mood drugs) must be presubmitted to the National Advertising Review Board. A procedure exists for complaints to be heard by the consuming public.

Many believe that self-regulation can be effective, but others are less hopeful about the responsiveness of self-regulatory institutions. They point to inadequate public awareness of existing self-regulatory institutions, the delays that are prevalent in self-regulatory systems, and the difficulty of formulating adequate standards.

Regulatory Reform

Some critics would like to see regulatory reform. Two topics under discussion are the FTC substantiation program and the FTC remedies against violators.

The existing substantiation program for product claims requires advertisers to substantiate their claims, whether true or not. Some argue that the substantiation program increases the amount and availability of information to consumers. A prominent critic of the program is Richard Posner, a former professor at the University of Chicago Law School, and now a federal court of appeals judge. He argues:

> The consumer is interested in whether the claim is true, not in the evidence the seller has collected to support it. If a product claim, although unsubstantiated when made, turns out to be true, the consumer who purchased the product on the strength of the claim suffers no harm.[7]

The substantiation program may be justified as a method of reducing the FTC's administrative costs. The costs of prosecution are lowered by shifting the burden of proof onto sellers to substantiate their claims. However, Judge Posner contends that this is apt to discourage the advertising of claims that are costly to substantiate, thus reducing the flow of information to consumers. He adds that the costs of substantiation will also reduce new market entry by increasing costs to new firms or firms with new products.

However, "the cardinal deficiency in the legislative framework," according to Judge Posner, "is in the area of remedies. Specifically it is the absence of any provision for money damages, compensatory or punitive." The fact that the FTC cannot award monetary reparation to consumers weakens consumer incentive to lodge complaints with the commission. This deprives the FTC of substantial private assistance. It also weakens sellers' incentive to comply with the law since they are only obliged to cease and desist their practices and are permitted to keep any profits obtained during the period of violation.

---

[7] R. Posner, *Regulation of Advertising by the FTC* (1973), p. 23.

CHAPTER PROBLEMS

1. On July 31, 1966, Lee Calan Imports advertised a 1964 Volvo station wagon for sale in the *Chicago Sun-Times*. Lee Calan instructed the newspaper to advertise the price at $1,795, but the paper erroneously ran it as $1,095. O'Brien visited Lee Calan Imports and agreed to buy the car for $1,095. The salesperson at first agreed but then refused to sell the car for the erroneous price listed in the advertisement. O'Brien contends that the advertisement represents an offer by Lee Calan Imports which he duly accepted and that the parties thus formed a binding contract. Is O'Brien correct? Has Lee Calan violated section 5 of the Federal Trade Commission Act? Explain.

2. Sun TV runs the following advertisement in a newspaper of general circulation which has about 500,000 readers:

WIDE SCREEN
COLOR
TVs
$1,139.95
WHILE THEY LAST
SATISFACTION GUARANTEED

When Wilma Budoff went to purchase a wide screen TV, the item was out of stock. The TVs were in when she returned the following day, but they were marked up to $1,339.95. She complained to the store manager about the price. He noted that the advertisement said "while they last" and that this was part of a new stock. She purchased the wide screen TV anyway because it was still a lower price than any in town. Her husband was upset about Sun's sales practices and insisted that she return it, but the store refused to take it back even though Wilma explained that the TV caused much dissatisfaction. Will Wilma be successful in a suit against Sun TV? Explain.

3. The Seven-Up Company sells a lemon-lime soft drink under the trademark 7Up, which it has advertised since 1968 as "the uncola." Seven-Up displays its product in a specific section of supermarkets and in vending machines. It markets 7Up nationally. The No-Cal Corpora-

tion sells a lemon-lime diet soft drink called "Shape-Up," which it advertises as "the unsugar." At no time has No-Cal advertised Shape-Up without identifying it as a product of No-Cal, and at no time has it used the term "unsugar" without mentioning No-Cal as its source. Although sold in supermarkets, Shape-Up is not sold in vending machines. Seven-Up sues No-Cal under the Lanham Act, seeking to enjoin the distribution and advertising of Shape-Up. Will Seven-Up win? Explain.

4. Bohsei Enterprises imports screws, nuts, bolts, and other industrial fasteners into the United States. Porteous Fastener also imports fasteners into the United States and competes with Bohsei. Porteous repackages the fasteners and labels some of them "United States" or imprints upon the packages the names of cities where it operates fastener packaging facilities. Most of its packages, however, contain no geographical designation. Bohsei contends that Porteous' repackaged fasteners create a false impression that the fasteners are made in the United States. It sues Porteous under the Lanham Act, seeking an order requiring Porteous to label all packages with their true country of origin. Will Bohsei win? Explain.

5. Standard Oil Company of California advertised its product F-310, a gasoline additive, on television commercials from January 9 to June 9, 1970. The commercials were based on visual comparison of automobile exhaust before and after F-310 was used. A large, clear balloon was attached to the exhaust pipe of an idling automobile. The balloon was shown inflating with black, opaque vapor while the announcer described it as "filling with dirty exhaust emissions that go into the air and waste mileage." The announcer then stated that "Standard Oil of California has accomplished the development of a remarkable gasoline additive, Formula F-310, that reduces exhaust emissions from dirty engines." He informed the viewers that the same car was run on six tankfuls of Chevron F-310 and the result was "no dirty smoke, cleaner air."

To prove the point, a clear balloon was again shown being attached to the car. This time the balloon inflated with transparent vapor. In conclusion the viewers were told: "Chevron F-310 turns dirty smoke into good, clean mileage." The FTC advised Standard that it objected to the ads because these had not made clear that the car depicted in the before segment of each commercial had been driven previously with a gasoline that had been deliberately formulated to accelerate carbon deposits, resulting in an especially dirty engine. Has Standard violated section 5? Explain.

6. The Colgate–Palmolive Company set out to prove to the television viewing public that its shaving cream, Rapid Shave, outshaved them all. It used a one-minute commercial designed to show that Rapid Shave could soften even the toughness of sandpaper. The commercial contained a "sandpaper test." The announcer informed the audience that "to prove Rapid Shave's super moisturizing power, we put it right from the can onto this tough, dry sandpaper. It was apply . . . soak . . . and off in a stroke."

While the announcer was speaking, Rapid Shave was applied to a substance that appeared to be sandpaper, and immediately thereafter a razor was shown shaving the substance clean. Sandpaper of the type depicted in the commercials could not be shaved immediately following the application of Rapid Shave, but required a substantial soaking period of about 80 minutes. The substance resembling sandpaper in the commercial was in fact a simulated prop made of plexiglas to which sandpaper had been applied. The FTC claimed that the commercials violated section 5 of the Federal Trade Commission Act.

Colgate–Palmolive argued that Rapid Shave could shave sandpaper, even though not in the short time represented by the commercials. It noted that if real sandpaper had been used in the commercials the inadequacies of television transmission would have made it appear to viewers to be nothing more than plain, colored paper. Who is right? Discuss.

7. United States Way advertises its pop-up wafers as "a new, exciting breakfast for kids . . . higher energy than the leading breakfast cereals." The advertisements are run on Saturday mornings and depict favorite cartoon characters eating the pop-up wafers and saying, "Makes you strong. Better than cereal." The advertising campaign is designed to shift the focus of breakfast for children from cereal to pop up wafers. The wafers consist of two thin dough crusts held together by one of several jelley-type flavors. The pop-up wafer is then heated in a toaster and served. The main ingredients of the product are sugar, corn syrup, preservatives, and artificial coloring and flavoring. The FTC seeks to stop United States Way from continuing the advertisements. What arguments can the FTC make? What are United's counterarguments?

8. Wendy's, a national fast-food chain, airs a commercial in which three patrons are seen standing at the food counter in a fast-food store with a large sign in the background which reads: "Home of the Big Bun." A very small hamburger on a large bun is on the counter in front of the patrons. One of the three picks up the bun, puts it to her ear, and rattles it a bit. Another, a hard-of-hearing elderly woman, proclaims loudly: "Where's the beef?" There is no response from the fast-food management, and after two more queries the patron says in disgust, "I don't think there's anybody back there." Then a big juicy hamburger is seen on the screen and the audio portion says: "At Wendy's you get a full quarter-pound hamburger."

Burger King and McDonalds, Wendy's two leading competitors, sue under the Lanham Act to stop the ads. The FTC files a complaint charging Wendy's with unfair and deceptive advertising practices. Discuss the outcome of the suits.

9. The Campbell Soup company advertises its soup on television. In its commercials Campbell's soups appear to be quite rich. This effect is achieved by adding marbles to the soups before showing them in the commercials. This ploy displaces the solid ingredients and gives the products a deceptively rich appearance. Campbell has been doing this for years. Should consumers who relied upon the apparently bounteous nature of the soups be informed of Campbell's past deception through corrective advertising? Explain.

10. Evaluate the economic costs and benefits of advertising regulation by the FTC. Develop a comprehensive alternative plan that would balance the interests of consumers, advertisers, and competitors.

CHAPTER 7

DEBTOR-CREDITOR RELATIONS

In this age of rapid technological advancement, there are a growing number of products available to the public. Consumers are borrowing money or purchasing on credit to realize their new-found "dreams." They now owe over $1.5 trillion. A spate of federal laws have been enacted to accommodate these debtor-creditor relationships. (The debtor is the person who owes money; the creditor is the person to whom money is owed.) Some of these laws are part of the Consumer Credit Protection Act. Those laws discussed in this chapter are outlined in table 7–1.

These laws directly affect businesses. As such, they demand the attention of business managers and those responsible for regulatory compliance. This chapter will discuss these federal laws and state regulation of consumer credit. Debtor financial failure is also on the rise, not only among individuals and small businesses, but among large corporations as well. The Bankruptcy Reform Act, designed to relieve debtor failures, will be covered at length in this chapter.

THE TRUTH IN LENDING ACT

 Congress passed the Truth in Lending Act (TILA) to ensure that consumers have adequate information about the cost of credit. To promote the informed use of credit, Congress required lenders to disclose certain credit terms in a standard way. TILA does not dictate credit terms. Rather it requires *creditors* to disclose and express credit terms uniformly when involved in *consumer credit* transactions.

Various administrative authorities enforce TILA. For example, the administrator of the National Credit Union Administration is empowered to enforce the act with respect to any federal credit union. The Federal Trade Commission enforces the act with respect to all transactions not covered by another agency.

TABLE 7-1
Federal Consumer Credit Laws

Law	*Description*
Truth in Lending Act	Encourages informed use of credit
Equal Credit Opportunity Act	Promotes nondiscrimination in the extension of credit
Fair Credit Reporting Act	Regulates the content and use of credit reports
Fair Credit Billing Act	Sets out procedures for the resolution of billing errors
Electronic Funds Transfer Act	Clarifies the rights and liabilities of electronic funds transfer users
Fair Debt Collection Practices Act	Limits deceptive and abusive conduct of bill collectors
Title III Restrictions on Garnishment	Places restrictions on garnishment of wages

Creditor

A creditor under TILA is one who regularly extends consumer credit and requires a finance charge or repayment in more than four installments. Assume, for example, that Connie Consumer borrows $50 from John Friend and agrees to repay $55 next payday. Although John is requiring a finance charge for the loan, unless he regularly extends credit he is not considered a creditor. Consequently, he would not need to make TILA disclosures.

A *credit arranger* is also a creditor and is required to make TILA disclosures. A credit arranger is one who regularly arranges for the extension of consumer credit *for a person or business that does not regularly extend consumer credit*. Assume that Connie Consumer purchases a new Eldorado from DS Cadillac Dealer (DS) for $30,000. DS prepares and processes loan papers supplied by General Motors Acceptance Corporation (GMAC) and receives a fee from GMAC for each loan processed. DS is not a "credit arranger" as defined by TILA, because DS is arranging for credit from GMAC, which is regularly engaged in the credit extension business. GMAC will be required to give Connie TILA disclosures, but DS will not.

Consumer Credit

Consumer credit is credit that is extended primarily for personal, family, or household purposes. Credit extended to corporations does not qualify as consumer credit; neither does credit extended primarily for business, commercial, or agricultural purposes. Assume that Connie Consumer borrows $1,000 from First Member Bank for the purpose of opening a shoe repair store. Since the purpose of the loan is commercial, First Member

Bank is exempt from the TILA and its disclosure requirements. In creating this exemption, Congress believed that debtors involved in these transactions are capable of protecting themselves. Under the same reasoning, most credit transactions, other than home financing, are exempt when the total amount to be financed exceeds $25,000.

Disclosure

The specific type of disclosure required under the TILA is applicable to both *open-end* and *closed-end* credit transactions. Open-end credit involves accounts such as MasterCard and VISA; the customer may enter into a series of credit transactions and may choose to pay the balance in installments. Closed-end credit involves transactions such as loans, where a specific amount of credit is extended for a definite time. In closed-end transactions the borrower agrees to repay the amount in predetermined installments with the balance due by a specific date.

Open-end transactions require fewer initial disclosures than closed-end transactions. However, TILA requires large merchants in open-end credit transactions to make ongoing disclosure in the form of periodic statements detailing each such transaction.

In both open- and closed-end transactions a creditor must conspicuously disclose to the consumer the key terms of the transaction. These generally include the total amount financed, the finance charges, schedule of payments, penalty charges, and the annual percentage rate of interest (APR).

The APR is determined by computing the annualized interest paid on the amount of money actually used during a given time. For example, assume that a creditor borrows $1,000 for one year and the lender charges a total interest of $100 for the loan. If the borrower has the use of the entire $1,000 for one year, then the APR is 10 percent. But if the $1,100 (principal plus interest) is repaid over the year in equal installments, then the borrower only has the average use of about one half of the $1,000. In this case the $100 interest charge translates into an APR of almost 20 percent.

The finance charges used to compute the APR consist of the total of all charges for the loan. These charges include interest, service charges, loan fees, and in most instances fees for credit reports. Since lenders must quote the costs of loans in terms of the APR, consumers can more easily compare prices among lending institutions. Consumers presumably benefit from the competition that arises from more informed credit shopping.

The board of governors of the Federal Reserve System provides model disclosure forms. The forms use simplified language to help the borrower understand the transaction. Creditors need not use these forms, but doing so ensures compliance. Figure 7–1 is an example of a model form.

TILA also applies to credit advertising. An advertisement that lists

FIGURE 7–1
Model Truth in Lending Disclosure Form

Big Wheel Auto   Alice Green

ANNUAL PERCENTAGE RATE The cost of your credit as a yearly rate.	FINANCE CHARGE The dollar amount the credit will cost you.	Amount Financed The amount of credit provided to you or on your behalf.	Total of Payments The amount you will have paid after you have made all payments as scheduled.	Total Sale Price The total cost of your purchase on credit, including your downpayment of $ _1500 –_
14.84 %	$1496.80	$6107.50	$7604.30	$9129.30

You have the right to receive at this time an itemization of the Amount Financed.

☐ I want an itemization.   ☒ I do not want an itemization.

Your payment schedule will be:

Number of Payments	Amount of Payments	When Payments Are Due
36	$211.23	Monthly beginning 6-1-81

Insurance

Credit life insurance and credit disability insurance are not required to obtain credit, and will not be provided unless you sign and agree to pay the additional cost.

Type	Premium	Signature
Credit Life	$120 –	I want credit life insurance. *alice green* Signature
Credit Disability		I want credit disability insurance. Signature
Credit Life and Disability		I want credit life and disability insurance. Signature

Security: You are giving a security interest in:

☒ the goods being purchased.

☐ _____ .

Filing fees $ _12.50_   Non-filing insurance $ _____

Late Charge: If a payment is late, you will be charged $10.

Prepayment: If you pay off early, you

☐ may   ☐ will not   have to pay a penalty.

☒ may   ☐ will not   be entitled to a refund of part of the finance charge.

See your contract documents for any additional information about nonpayment, default, any required repayment in full before the scheduled date, and prepayment refunds and penalties.

I have received a copy of this statement.

alice Green _____   5-1-81
Signature   Date

_____
e means an estimate

Source: Regulation Z Truth in Lending; 12 CFR 226, Appendix H at p. 662 (1984).

any credit terms must also include other significant terms, including the APR and terms of repayment.

Cancellation of Credit Agreements

Under certain circumstances a debtor may cancel a credit transaction. When a person's home is used as security for a loan, the borrower may cancel the transaction within three business days. (This right does not apply to a first mortgage given to secure the financing of a home.) The creditor must inform the borrower in writing of this right to cancel. Cancellation is accomplished when written notice is communicated to the creditor. Upon cancellation the borrower is not liable for any finance charges. Also, any security interest given by the borrower is cancelled. The creditor has 20 days to return any money the borrower has paid.

Because of this right of the owner to cancel the credit agreement, contractors normally will wait three days after an agreement to begin work. However, the homeowner may waive the right to cancel by notifying the contractor in writing that there is a real emergency and credit is needed immediately to finance repairs. In that event the contractor may start the work immediately without fear of cancellation.

Consumer Leasing

TILA provisions also regulate *consumer leases.* They require disclosure of lease terms.

A consumer lease involves a lessor who regularly leases personal property for personal, family, or household use when (1) the leasehold period exceeds four months and (2) the amount of the lease does not exceed $25,000. An automobile leased for personal use would be covered under TILA; an automobile leased for business purposes would be excluded.

Every lessor covered under the act must supply the lessee with a dated written statement. The statement must identify the lessor and the lessee and disclose in a clear and conspicuous manner: the leased property; an itemization of the charges; the express warranties; insurance information and responsibility; periodic payment details; the lessee's liability at the end of the lease term; and the conditions and consequences for terminating the lease before it expires.

Penalties

The law provides for both criminal and civil liability for violation of the disclosure provisions of TILA. Willful violations of the act carry a fine of up to $5,000 and imprisonment up to one year. A creditor who fails to disclose required information may also be civilly liable to a consumer. The liability is limited to twice the amount of the finance charge. In the case of a lease the maximum liability is $1,000. The successful debtor is also entitled to reasonable attorney fees and court costs.

Creditors may avoid liability for errors by correcting them within 60 days after discovery. They may also escape liability by showing that the violation was unintentional and resulted from a good faith error. An example of a good faith error would be one resulting from a computer malfunction.

Credit Cards

Over 70 million credit cards are reported lost or stolen each year, and about 20,000 cards are used fraudulently each day. The credit card industry is losing about $1 billion dollars a year as a result of credit card misuse.

TILA regulates the issuance and use of credit cards. It provides that no credit cards may be issued without a request. This provision prevents unsolicited credit cards.

TILA also limits the cardholder's liability to $50 if another person uses the credit card without authorization. This could happen, for example, if the card were lost or stolen. The cardholder can avoid all liability by notifying the issuer of the card's loss or theft before the unauthorized use occurs. The next case examines the question of "unauthorized use" by a spouse.

Walker Bank & Trust Co. v. Jones

672 P.2d 73 (Utah 1983)

Betty Jones (defendant) opened VISA and MasterCharge accounts with Walker Bank (plaintiff). Pursuant to her request, credit cards were issued to herself and her husband. Jones later informed the bank that she would no longer honor charges made by her husband. (The case is silent as to why she made this request.) The bank revoked the accounts and requested that the cards be returned. In spite of numerous requests, both Jones and her husband continued to use the cards. After the bank's employee visited Jones's place of employment she surrendered her card. At that time the balance owed on the accounts was $2,685.70. At least a portion of that amount represented charges made by defendant's husband after the bank was requested to not honor his charges. Jones refused to pay the balance and the bank sued her to recover the amount.

Gloria Harlan (defendant) requested that her husband be added to her VISA account as an authorized user. The bank complied. Thereafter the parties separated and Harlan requested that the account be closed or that her husband be denied further extensions of credit. Harlan did not immediately return her card. After her request to the bank, several charges were made on the account by her husband. The bank sued Harlan to recover these amounts.

In both cases the trial court granted summary judgment in favor of the bank. The cases were consolidated on appeal to the Supreme Court of Utah. That court affirmed the trial court's judgment.

Chief Justice Hall

Defendants' sole contention on appeal is that the Federal Truth in Lending Act (hereinafter "TILA") limits their liability, for the *unauthorized use of the credit cards* by their husbands, to a maximum of $50. . . . [Emphasis added]

* * * * *

The Bank's rejoinder is that . . . defendants' husbands' use of the credit cards was at no time "unauthorized use" within the meaning of the statute. Whether such use was "unauthorized," as that term is contemplated by the statute, is the pivotal question in this case.

The term "unauthorized use" is defined as:

> [U]se of a credit card by a person other than the cardholder who does not have actual, implied, or apparent authority for such use and from which the cardholder receives no benefit.

A "cardholder" is described as:

> [A]ny person to whom a credit card is issued or any person who has agreed with the card issuer to pay obligations arising from the issuance of a credit card to another person.

Defendants contend that they alone occupied the status of "cardholder," by reason of their request to the bank that credit cards be issued to their husbands and their assumption of liability therefor. Accordingly, they maintain that their husbands were no more than authorized users of defendants' accounts.

Defendants' further aver that the effect of their notification to the Bank stating that they would no longer be responsible for charges made against their accounts by their husbands was to render any subsequent use (by their husbands) of the cards unauthorized. This notification, defendants maintain, was all that was necessary to revoke the authority they had once created in their husbands and thereby invoke the . . . limitations on cardholder liability.

The Bank's position is that unauthorized use . . . is precisely what the statutory definition says it is, to wit: "[U]se . . . by a person . . . who does not have actual, implied, or apparent authority. . . ," and that notification to the card issuer has no bearing whatsoever on whether the use is unauthorized, so as to entitle a cardholder to the statutory limitation of liability. We agree with this position.

. . . [T]he liability of the cardholder for unauthorized charges is limited to $50 regardless of any notification to the card issuer. . . . Unless and until the unauthorized nature of the use has been established, the notification provision, as well as the statute itself, is irrelevant and ineffectual.

The language of the statute defining unauthorized use is clear and unambiguous. It excludes from the category of unauthorized users, any person who has "actual, implied, or apparent authority."

The Bank maintains that defendants' husbands clearly had "apparent" authority to use the cards, inasmuch as their signatures were the same as the signatures on the cards, and their names, the same as those imprinted upon the cards. Accordingly, it contends that no unauthorized use was made of the cards, and that defendants therefore cannot invoke the limitations on liability provided by the TILA.

Again, we find the Bank's position to be meritorious. Apparent authority exists:

> [W]here a person has created such an appearance of things that it causes a third party reasonably and prudently to believe that a second party has the power to act on behalf of the first person. . . .

As previously pointed out at defendants' request their husbands were issued cards bearing the husbands' own names and signatures. These cards were, therefore, a representation to the merchants (third parties) to whom they were presented that defendants' husbands . . . were authorized to make charges upon the defendants' . . . accounts. This apparent authority conferred upon defendants' husbands by reason of the credit cards thus precluded the application of the TILA.

In view of our determination that the TILA has no application to the present case, we hold that liability for defendants' husbands' use of the cards is governed by their contracts with the Bank. The contractual agreements between defendants and the Bank provided clearly and unequivocally that *all* cards issued upon the accounts be returned to the Bank in order to terminate defendants' liability. Accordingly, defendants' refusal to relinquish either their cards or their husbands', at the time they notified the Bank that they no longer accepted liability for their husbands' charges, justified the Bank's disregard of that notification and refusal to terminate defendants' liability at that time.

CASE QUESTIONS

1. What, if anything, could the defendants have done to avoid legal responsibility for their husbands' charges?

2. What is apparent authority? Do you agree that there was apparent authority after the defendants notified the bank? Explain.

3. Does this case encourage estranged spouses to engage in unlimited charge card usage? Explain.

4. Assume that the use was deemed unauthorized? Would the defendants have any liability? Explain.

5. Assume that a wife, without permission, uses her husband's department store credit card. What other facts would you want to know to determine the husband's liability?

Penalties   Anyone who uses a counterfeit, altered, forged, lost, stolen, or fraudulently obtained credit card incurs criminal liability under TILA if:

— The unauthorized usage was in a transaction affecting interstate or foreign commerce
— The obtained goods or services, or both, have a retail value of $5,000 or more

A violation carries a penalty of up to $10,000 and imprisonment of up to five years. State laws also provide for criminal penalties for using a credit card under similar unlawful circumstances, regardless of the value of the obtained goods or services.

THE EQUAL CREDIT OPPORTUNITY ACT

Market forces were unable to ensure that credit was equally available to all creditworthy customers. Prejudices affected decision making. Credit extenders often based their decisions on factors such as race or marital status. The Equal Credit Opportunity Act (ECOA) prohibits discrimination in credit extension on the basis of:

— race
— color
— religion
— national origin
— marital status
— age

— sex
— receipt of income from public assistance programs
— good faith exercise of a right under the act

The act forbids a creditor from asking credit applicants certain questions. For example, a creditor may not ask whether any of the income stated in the application is derived from alimony or child support. Neither may a creditor ask the race, color, religion, or national origin of an applicant (except for statistical monitoring purposes).

A creditor must notify the applicant of its decision within 30 days of the application. If the decision is unfavorable, the applicant is entitled to a statement of the specific reasons. Unfavorable action includes a denial or revocation of credit or an undesirable change in the terms of the existing credit arrangement.

Violators of ECOA are liable to credit applicants for their actual damages. Punitive damages not to exceed $10,000 may also be recovered. Where members of a discriminated group bring a class action against a creditor, recovery is limited to the lesser of $500,000 or one percent of the net worth of the creditor. Costs and reasonable attorney fees are added to the damage award. In some cases a court will grant an injunction prohibiting the creditor from further acts of discrimination.

Like under the TILA, various agencies enforce the act, depending upon the applicant and the subject matter of the credit transaction. The Federal Trade Commission enforces the act with respect to transactions not policed by any other agency.

THE FAIR CREDIT REPORTING ACT

Computer technology now permits the storage and instant retrieval of enormous amounts of information. When a lender considers a loan application, the logical place to start the investigation is at a credit information storage house, termed a *credit bureau*. Credit bureaus compile information to help potential creditors make intelligent decisions as to the credit risks of applicants.

Credit bureaus maintain massive files of information on over 100 million Americans, and every year they receive that many requests for credit reports. Because of the increased number of reported abuses, Congress enacted the Fair Credit Reporting Act (FCRA) to regulate consumer reporting agencies.

Consumer Reporting Agencies

The FCRA regulates consumer reporting agencies. These agencies assemble and evaluate consumer credit information for the purpose of furnishing consumer reports to those requesting them. A business may escape the regulations of the act if it assembles credit information for its own use as opposed to use by another.

Permissible Activities

A consumer reporting agency may furnish consumer reports only for the purposes specified in the act. It may legitimately supply information:

— in response to a valid court order
— upon the written request of a consumer to whom it relates
— for use in determining a consumer's eligibility for credit, insurance, employment, or other legitimate business purposes

Obsolete Information

The consumer reporting agency is obliged to keep its files up to date. Generally, the agency may not report stale information about bankruptcies, suits, judgments, tax liens, bad debts, and criminal records. This limitation does not apply to reports used in connection with a credit transaction involving $50,000 or more, or with the employment of an individual at an annual salary of at least $20,000.

Compliance

Every consumer reporting agency is required to maintain reasonable procedures to avoid violations of the act. The reporting agency must take measures to ensure that those requesting information identify themselves and certify the intended use of the information. It must act reasonably to verify statements made by a new user.

The reporting agency must also maintain reasonable procedures to assure the accuracy of its consumer reports and the completeness of public information reported for employment purposes. Otherwise, the reporting agency must notify the consumer each time it supplies such information. The notification must include the name and address of the person to whom the report was sent.

Investigative Consumer Reports

Consumer reporting agencies often accumulate information about a consumer's character, reputation, or mode of living. This information, gathered through personal interviews with neighbors, friends, associates, or others, is called an *investigative consumer report.* Although Congress recognized that abuses occurred because of the gathering of irrelevant information, it did not regulate the type of information that could be gathered and reported. Instead it defined the permissible use of this information.

No unfavorable private information based on an investigative report that is at least three months old may be included in a consumer report unless reverified. The consumer must be informed when an investigative consumer report is requested or prepared. The consumer has a right to an accurate disclosure of the nature and scope of the investigation if a written report has been requested. This right does not apply if the investigative report is to be used to consider the consumer's suitability for a job for which the consumer did not specifically apply.

Disclosure

Consumers are entitled to disclosure of the information (except medical) about them that is in the files of the reporting agency. The agency, however, need not disclose the sources of information used solely to prepare investigative consumer reports. Generally, consumers are also entitled to the names of those to whom the agency supplied consumer reports.

Disputes

A consumer may dispute the accuracy of information in the reporting agency's files. In such case the reporting agency may be required to reinvestigate the accuracy of the information. If the reinvestigation fails to confirm the validity of the information, then the reporting agency must delete the information from its files. If the reinvestigation fails to resolve the dispute, the consumer is permitted to file a brief written statement giving his or her side of the story. On all future reports containing the information the agency must point out that the information is disputed and supply the consumer's statement or an abstract of it. The consumer may insist that any deleted or disputed information be brought to the attention of persons who received a report.

Requirements on Users of Reports

An unfavorable consumer report may result in denial of credit, insurance, or employment or in higher finance charges or insurance premiums. In such cases, the user of the report is required to advise the consumer of the name and address of the consumer reporting agency that supplied the report. Sometimes consumer credit is denied or the charge for consumer credit is increased because of information received from a source other than a consumer reporting agency. When this occurs, the user of the information, upon written request, must inform the applicant of the nature of the information that resulted in the unfavorable action.

Remedies

The FTC is empowered to enforce the act by cease and desist orders against violators not committed under the act to another specified governmental agency. The act also provides for criminal penalties, for example, against persons who obtain information about a consumer from a consumer reporting agency under false pretenses. Violators may be fined up to $5,000 and imprisoned up to one year.

Civil liability under the act is divided into two categories. First, any consumer reporting agency or user that *willfully* violates the act is liable to the consumer for actual damages, punitive damages, court costs, and reasonable attorney's fees. Second, a reporting agency or user of information that *negligently* fails to comply with the act is liable to the consumer for the actual damages, court costs, and reasonable attorney's fees.

The following case, involving a computer mixup, illustrates the need to employ reasonable controls over credit information to ensure accuracy and avoid liability.

 **Thompson v. San Antonio Retail Merchants Association**

682 F.2d 509 (5th Cir. 1982)

The San Antonio Retail Merchants Association (SARMA) (defendant), a computerized credit reporting agency, provides service to local business subscribers. These subscribers feed credit information into SARMA's computers. They also have access to SARMA's credit information files. To obtain information about a consumer a subscriber must feed identifying information from its own computer terminal into SARMA's central computer. SARMA's computer displays on the subscriber's terminal the history file of the consumer who most nearly matches the identifying information.

If the subscriber accepts the file as that of the particular consumer, SARMA's computer automatically captures any information from the subscriber's terminal that it did not already have.

William Daniel Thompson, Jr. opened an account with Gordon's Jewelers (Gordon's) in November 1974. He listed his social security number as 457–68–5778, his address as 132 Boxter, marital status as single, and his occupation as a truck loader. He charged $77.25 at Gordon's which he failed to pay. Gordon's reported the debt to SARMA who placed the information and a bad credit rating in file number 5867114. It failed to include any social security number.

William Douglas Thompson, III (plaintiff) applied for credit in early 1978 with Gulf and with Ward's in San Antonio. He gave his social security number as 407–86–4065, his address as 6929 Timbercreek, his wife as Deborah C., and his occupation as grounds keeper. Gulf's terminal operator mistakenly accepted file number 5867114 as the plaintiff's, and SARMA's computer automatically captured information about William Douglas Thompson, III into file number 5867114. That information included plaintiff's social security number. The original file on William Daniel Thompson, Jr. became an amalgam of information on both William Daniel Thompson, Jr. and the plaintiff. It included plaintiff's social security number.

When Ward's ran a check on plaintiff, the terminal operator was given the garbled data and accepted file number 5867114 as that of the plaintiff. It contained adverse information about Gordon's delinquent account. Ward's denied credit to the plaintiff. In May 1979 plaintiff applied again and was rejected.

Gulf requested a revision of file number 5867114 in February 1978. SARMA apparently contacted Gordon's to verify the credit information but failed to check the social security number of Gordon's delinquent customer. The adverse information stayed in the file under plaintiff's social security number, and Gulf denied him credit.

Plaintiff thought that he was rejected because of a felony conviction for burglary in 1976. When he learned that his adverse credit rating was due to a bad debt at Gordon's, he and his wife went to the jeweler. After a two-hour wait they were informed of the mistake—that his credit record was for William Daniel Thompson, Jr.

Plaintiff and his wife then went to SARMA to straighten out the problem. They showed birth records and a driver's license revealing his name to be William Douglas Thompson, III. The process took three hours. Afterwards, SARMA mailed the plaintiff a letter addressed to William Daniel Thompson, III. Plaintiff and his wife made two additional visits to SARMA on separate occasions. Each was followed by a letter from SARMA addressed incorrectly to William Daniel Thompson, III. SARMA's policy was to send corrections to subscribers who had made inquiry within the last six months, but it failed to notify Ward's.

Plaintiff sued SARMA under the FCRA for failing to employ reasonable care in reporting credit information. The district court awarded plaintiff $10,000 actual damages and $4,485 attorney's fees. SARMA appealed to the Fifth Circuit Court of Appeals which affirmed the district court decision.

Opinion of the Court

[The FCRA] . . . does not impose strict liability for any inaccurate credit report, but only a duty of reasonable care in preparation of the report. That duty extends to updating procedures, because "preparation" of a consumer report should be viewed as a continuing process and the obligation to insure accuracy arises with every addition of information. The standard of conduct by which the trier of fact must judge the adequacy of agency procedures is what a reasonably prudent person would do under the circumstances.

Applying the reasonable-person standard, the district court found two acts of negligence in SARMA's updating procedures. First, SARMA failed to exercise reasonable care in programming its computer to automatically capture information into a file without requiring any minimum number of "points of correspondence" between the consumer and the file or having an adequate auditing procedure to foster accuracy. Second, SARMA failed to employ reasonable procedures designed to learn the disparity in social security numbers for the two Thompsons when it revised file number 5867114 at Gulf's request. . . .

With respect to the first act of negligence, George Zepeda, SARMA's manager, testified that SARMA's computer had no minimum number of points of correspondence to be satisfied before an inquiring subscriber could accept credit information. Moreover, SARMA had no way of knowing if the information supplied by the subscriber was correct. Although SARMA did conduct spot audits to verify social security

numbers, it did not audit all subscribers. With respect to the second act of negligence, SARMA's verification process failed to uncover the erroneous social security number even though Gulf made a specific request for a "revision" to check the adverse credit history ascribed to the plaintiff. . . . In light of this evidence, this Court cannot conclude that the district court was clearly erroneous in finding negligent violation of [the FCRA].

* * * * *

The district court's award of $10,000 in actual damages was based on humiliation and mental distress to the plaintiff. Even when there are no out-of-pocket expenses, humiliation and mental distress do constitute recoverable elements of damage under the Act. . . .

SARMA asserts that Thompson failed to prove any actual damages, or at best proved only minimal damages for humiliation and mental distress. There was evidence, however, that Thompson suffered humiliation and embarrassment from being denied credit on three occasions. Thompson testified that the denial of credit hurt him deeply because of his mistaken belief that it resulted from his felony conviction. . . . Further, the inaccurate information remained in SARMA's files for almost one and one-half years after the inaccurate information was inserted. Even after the error was discovered, Thompson spent months pressing SARMA to correct its mistakes and fully succeeded only after bringing a lawsuit against SARMA. This Court is of the opinion that the trial judge was entitled to conclude that the humiliation and mental distress were not minimal but substantial.

CASE QUESTIONS

1. Describe SARMA's method for supplying and gathering credit information? What is the advantage of such a system? What is the disadvantage?

2. What acts of negligence did the district court find? Can you find any others?

3. What should SARMA have done once Gulf made a request to check the adverse credit information concerning plaintiff?

4. How can SARMA avoid the problem in the future?

5. How does a judge or jury evaluate the value of damages based on humiliation and mental distress? In this case would $20,000 have been excessive? $30,000? $100,000?

THE FAIR CREDIT BILLING ACT

The Fair Credit Billing Act was enacted to protect the consumer against inaccurate and unfair billing practices. The act regulates procedures for resolving billing errors. It applies to creditors that issue credit cards, to creditors that regularly extend credit payable in more than four installments, and to those that assess a finance charge. These creditors must advise consumers of their rights and responsibilities when an account is opened and at semiannual intervals thereafter. They also must disclose on the periodic billing statement where to address billing inquiries.

Any creditor that receives written notice of a billing error must respond in writing. If the creditor agrees that an error exists, then it must adjust the account and notify the consumer. If the creditor concludes that the billing statement is correct, it must give the consumer reasons supporting its conclusion. The creditor must include documentary evidence of the debt if the consumer requests it.

The creditor may not institute any action to collect the debt until it makes the proper response. However, the creditor may continue to send periodic statements reflecting the disputed amount. The creditor may not close or restrict the consumer's account before it responds, but it may use the amount of the dispute to determine whether the consumer has exceeded credit limits.

A creditor may not give a bad credit report concerning the disputed amount until at least 10 days after the creditor informs the consumer of its belief in the accuracy of its bill. This allows the consumer time to respond. If the consumer continues to dispute the billing statement, the creditor must indicate that dispute on future reports.

A creditor that violates the act forefeits the right to collect the disputed amount and finance charges of up to $50 for each disputed item. For extenders of large amounts of credit this is a small price to pay for noncompliance. In fact, it may be economically justified for large firms to ignore billing complaints and suffer the forfeiture. Ethical considerations, however, are also relevant.

ELECTRONIC FUNDS TRANSFER ACT

The use of electronic funds transfer (EFT) services increases annually. Over one million electronic transfers occur daily. Automated teller machines, electronic deposits, telephone payment services, and point-of-sale transfers threaten to replace the traditional methods of money transfer. Congress enacted the Electronic Funds Transfer Act (EFTA) in 1978 in order to establish the rights and responsibilities of the parties involved in electronic transfers. Congress recognized the potential consumer benefits that electronic systems provided and felt that regulation would instill greater consumer confidence in the systems.

Disclosure

The act requires financial institutions to disclose to customers the terms and conditions of the EFT service. The disclosure must include the consumer's liability for unauthorized fund transfers, who to notify in the event of an unauthorized transfer, any charges for electronic funds transfers, and the procedure necessary to stop payment.

Because electronic funds transfers dispense with the use of paper, Congress required that users be given receipts for each transaction. Periodic statements identifying each transaction are also required. These detailed documentation requirements have been criticized on the basis that the amount of paperwork involved defeats the reason for EFT and retards progress.

Error Resolution

The act contains a comprehensive procedure for resolving errors. The financial institution is required to investigate all consumer allegations of errors and notify the consumer of its findings within ten days. The institution may extend the investigation to 45 days if it credits the consumer's account pending the outcome of the investigation. If the institution, upon examination, determines that there is an error, it must reverse the error within one business day. Failure to comply with the error-resolution procedure may result in treble damages against the noncomplying institution.

Remedies

Under the act, consumers may be liable for unauthorized use of an EFT card. Liability is limited to $50 as long as the consumer gives prompt notification of the unauthorized use to the institution. Financial institutions are liable to consumers for all damages resulting from the institution's failure to make an electronic funds transfer ordered by the consumer. There are certain specified exceptions, for example, when the transfer would exceed an established credit line. The institution is also liable for damages caused by a failure to stop payment when properly instructed to do so by the consumer. Failure to otherwise comply with the act may result in liability to the consumer for actual damages plus additional damages not less than $100 nor more than $1,000.

In addition to civil penalties, any knowing and willful violations of the act constitute a crime. Administrative enforcement of the act is specifically committed to various federal agencies. The Federal Trade Commission is authorized to enforce cases that have not been specifically committed to another agency. The board of governors of the Federal Reserve System is authorized to prescribe regulations to carry out the act.

DEBT COLLECTION

When a debtor defaults, the creditor will naturally attempt to collect. The initial attempts usually take the form of letters and phone calls. Sometimes these communications are extremely harsh and threatening. If these efforts fail, the creditor may employ a third party to collect the debt. Professional collection agencies often invoke novel techniques to force payment, but they cannot go beyond certain defined permissible limits in pursuing the debtor. A creditor's conduct is governed by the common law and by federal and state statutes.

Common Law

Common law offers the debtor some protections against unreasonable collection activities. They consist of actions for defamation, invasion of privacy, and intentional infliction of mental distress. Although these remedies are available, they are not usually applicable to ordinary aggressive credit collection activities.

Defamation is the publication of statements that discredit another's reputation. Since truth is a defense to defamation, this action is generally successful only where allegations of a debt or of unwillingness to pay a debt are in fact false. Privilege is another defense to defamation. As long as there is no malicious intent, the creditor is privileged to communicate statements to another who has a legitimate interest in the information.

Employers of debtors are popular targets for debt collectors. Some courts hold that employers have a legitimate interest in knowing of their employees' delinquencies and hence deem these communications privileged.

Invasion of privacy may be a basis for recovery for damages against an overenthusiastic bill collector. Some courts grant recovery where the creditor publishes the debt in a newspaper or makes repetitive and harassing calls to the debtor's employer or to the debtor. Generally, reasonable communications do not form a basis for an invasion of privacy suit.

Some states recognize a cause of action for *intentional infliction of mental distress.* In most states that recognize this common-law tort, the collection activity must be outrageous and the resulting distress severe.

Because of the inadequate protection provided by the common law against abusive collection tactics, Congress responded with legislation that regulates creditors' collection activities.

The Fair Debt Collection Practices Act

The Fair Debt Collection Practices Act (FDCPA) covers debt collectors who are in the business of collecting debts for others. The act also applies to those who process their own debts when they do so under other names. Attorneys who collect debts for their clients are not deemed debt collectors under the act.

Communications

Under the act, a covered debt collector may contact a person other than the debtor, the debtor's spouse, or the debtor's parents (if the debtor is a minor) only for the purpose of obtaining "location information." This includes the debtor's home telephone number, place of residence, and place of employment. Obviously, if the collector knows the debtor's location, then no communication with third parties is necessary or permissible.

When talking to a third party, the debt collector cannot volunteer the nature of his or her business. That information may be supplied only if it is expressly requested. Even then, the collector is not permitted to inform the third party that a debt is owed. The debt collector cannot communicate with the same third party more than once unless the party so requests or the collector reasonably believes that the information received from that party was erroneous or incomplete.

The debt collector may not contact the debtor at a time or place "which should be known to be inconvenient." In the absence of knowledge as to convenient times or places, the act specifies as convenient the hours between 8:00 A.M. and 9:00 P.M. at the debtor's location. Any other hours are considered inconvenient. The debt collector may not contact the consumer on the job if the collector is aware that the employer prohibits such communications.

As soon as the collector becomes aware that the debtor is represented by an attorney, further contacts with the debtor must cease. They may be resumed only if the attorney fails to respond to the debt collector's inquiry within a reasonable time or if the attorney permits direct communications with the client. Contacts with the debtor must also cease if the debtor communicates, in writing, a refusal to pay or a request that the contacts end. This communication then normally leads the creditor to sue the debtor.

Prohibitions

The collector may not harass, oppress, or abuse any person in connection with the collection of a debt. For example, a debt collector may not make repeated or obscene phone calls to the debtor or advertise the debt for sale.

Debt collectors cannot make false or misleading statements in collection efforts. They cannot, for example, falsely claim to be an attorney or a governmental official. Collectors also may not threaten to take action which they cannot legally take or do not intend to take. For example, a creditor may not ordinarily take a debtor's property without legal process. Any threat to do so violates the act. In addition, collectors cannot engage in unfair practices. Attempting to collect a debt that is not authorized by law and concealing charges for collection are examples of unfair practices.

Validation of Debts

A consumer may dispute the debt and refuse to pay. In this case its validity would ultimately be decided by a court.

Under the act, the debt collector is required to give the consumer written notice of the details of the debt, and the consumer has a right to dispute it in writing. Upon receipt of the writing, the creditor must cease collection efforts and verify the debt.

The following case illustrates the application of the validation requirements and other aspects under the FDCPA.

Baker v. G.C. Services Corp.

677 F.2d 775 (9th Cir. 1982)

Ken Baker (appellee) owed money to two oil companies. These past due accounts were given to G.C. Services Corp. (appellant) for collection. Appellant sent three form letters in an effort to collect the money owed. One letter stated:

> It is our policy to attempt to settle these matters out of court before making any decision whether to refer them to an attorney for collec-

tion. . . . Unless we receive your check or money order, we will proceed with collection procedures.

* * * * *

Verification of this debt, a copy of judgment or the name and address of the original creditor, if different from the current creditor, will be provided if requested in writing within 30 days. Otherwise the debt will be assumed to be valid.

Baker filed suit claiming G.C. Services violated the Fair Debt Collection Practices Act. Each party filed a motion for summary judgment. The judge found in favor of Baker and awarded $100 in damages and $800 in attorney's fees. G.C. Services appealed from that award. The court of appeals affirmed the decision.

Skopil, Circuit Judge

The act is designed to protect consumers who have been victimized by unscrupulous debt collectors, regardless of whether a valid debt actually exists. Section 1692k, which governs a debt collector's civil liability under the Act, provides in pertinent part that "any debt collector who fails to comply with any provision of this subchapter with respect to any person is liable to such person." The statute does not make an exception for liability under section 1692g when the debtor does in fact owe the entire debt.

* * * * *

Section 1692g(a) of the Act provides that a debt collector must send the debtor a written notice. . . .

The clear language of the statute explicitly requires that a debtor shall be given notice that he may "dispute the validity of the debt, or any portion thereof. . . ."

* * * * *

The district court found that the notice "does not inform [the debtor] that he may dispute only a portion of the debt," and thus violated section 1692g(a) (3). . . .

The notice sent by appellant barely in-forms the debtor that he may even dispute the entire debt. Appellant's notice does contain a statement that verification of the debt will be provided if requested in writing. . . . However, the only statement referring to a dispute regarding the validity of the debt . . . is the sentence "[o]therwise the debt will be assumed to be valid." . . . The language of the notice is simply not sufficient to put a debtor on notice that he could dispute a portion of the debt. A debtor who does owe a valid obligation to the creditor but could dispute finance charges, interest, or have some valid defense, might not be put on notice that he could dispute these additional charges. . . .

The Act prohibits a debt collector from using "any false, deceptive, or misleading representation or means" to collect a debt. Among the specific types of conduct prohibited by section 1692e is

"(5) The threat to take any action that cannot legally be taken or that is not intended to be taken."

* * * * *

. . . Appellant's policy, as stipulated in the pretrial order, was not to take legal action in these types of cases, but only to proceed with further telephone and mail solicitation.

The district court found that the language of the notice "create[d] the impression that legal action by defendant is a real possibility . . . [and] a consumer could legitimately believe that 'further collection procedures' meant court action when defendant had no intention of pursuing such a course of action." . . . We cannot say this finding is clearly erroneous, and therefore we affirm the court's conclusion that appellant's letter violated section 1692e(5).

The Act provides a debt collector with a "bona fide error" defense. . . .

*   *   *   *   *

. . . The only evidence presented by appellant in support of the bona fide error defense is the following stipulation:

> "Defendant obtained the advice and assistance of counsel on the meaning of and compliance with the Fair Debt Collection Practices Act and the correctness of the contents of the letter [containing the disputed language]. Defendant's attorneys have, from time to time, met with the staff of the Federal Trade Commission to discuss compliance with the Act."

Reliance on advice of counsel or a mistake about the law is insufficient by itself to raise the bona fide error defense. "Section 1692k(c) does not immunize mistakes of law, even if properly proven."

CASE QUESTIONS

1. What provisions of the FDCPA was the debt collector charged with violating? In what ways did the debt collector violate the act? Assume that the oil companies would have attempted to collect the debt in the same way. Would that have been a violation? Explain.

2. Why should Baker be entitled to notice that he could dispute the debt when, in fact, he owed the money?

3. What is the bona fide error defense? Why is it not applicable in this case?

4. Redraft the letter to make it legal.

Penalties and Enforcement

Any debt collector who violates the act is liable to the debtor for actual damages. Actual damages might occur if an employer fires the debtor after learning of the debt. The debt collector may be assessed additional damages of up to $1,000, depending upon the nature of the violation. Malicious, repeated violations are more likely to result in maximum penalties than are isolated, nonmalicious violations. Reasonable attorney's fees and court costs are also recoverable.

The Federal Trade Commission is charged with the administration and enforcement of the FDCPA, except where the enforcement is committed to another agency. A violation of the FDCPA is deemed to be an unfair or deceptive act or practice under the Federal Trade Commission Act.

In addition to the FDCPA, state laws have been enacted to protect debtors from the unscrupulous techniques of creditors and their agents. If the commission determines that the law in a given state grants adequate protection to the consumer, it may exempt the debt collectors in that state from the operation of the act.

Postjudgment Collection

When "peaceable" means of debt collection are unsuccessful, a creditor might resort to a court to aid in the collection process. Even if a creditor receives a court *judgment,* the debtor might still refuse to pay. A court judgment is reflected by an entry signed by a judge acknowledging the amount awarded to the winning party. If the debtor is "judgment proof," that is, has no assets, then the court entry will not help the creditor. However, if the uncooperative debtor has property, the creditor may attach it. Under *attachment* a sheriff seizes the property, the property is sold, and the proceeds are distributed to the creditor to the extent necessary to satisfy the judgment and related expenses. Any excess funds derived from the sale are returned to the debtor.

Garnishment is another remedy available to a judgment creditor. Garnishment is a way of reaching debtors' property that is held by third parties. Bank accounts and wages are the most commonly garnisheed property. (In certain circumstances a creditor may attach or garnishee a debtor's property before a judgment; many states permit this when it pears that the debtor intends to leave the jurisdiction to avoid creditors.) Each state has enacted its own statute to regulate the creditor's right to garnishee a debtor's wages. In the past, the garnishment process was loosely controlled and subject to abuse. Under many state statutes the ease with which wages could be garnisheed invited lenders to extend credit without adequate inquiry into the borrower's credit background.

When a creditor garnisheed a debtor's wages, the employer usually fired the debtor immediately. This caused widespread disruption of employment, production, and consumption, but employers had two primary reasons for firing these debtors. First, they simply did not want to be party to a court process that entailed paperwork and administrative expense. Secondly, employees whose wages are being garnisheed are often less motivated to work to full capacity because of the reduction in their paycheck.

To curb the impact of unrestricted garnishment practices and discharge because of garnishment, Congress passed Title III of the Consumer Credit Protection Act. Title III does not supplant state garnishment statutes but merely places limitations upon them.

A state statute providing for garnishment procedure must be at least as restrictive as Title III. The act limits the percentage of a debtor's *disposable earnings* that is subject to garnishment. Disposable earnings are the wages that an employee receives after certain withholdings are deducted. These withholdings include federal, state, and local taxes; social security payments; and deductions for pension plans required by state law for government employees. Under the act, the maximum amount that may be garnisheed for any work week, is generally (1) 25 percent of an employee's disposable earnings for the week *or* (2) the amount that the disposable earnings for the week exceeds 30 times the federal minimum hourly wage, whichever is less.

Assume, for example, that Rocky Hound receives a court judgment against Ron Debtor in the amount of $500. Ron Debtor, a business law professor, earns $400 each week. Assume that the federal minimum hourly wage is $3.50. Deductions from Debtor's pay each week amount to: taxes, $100; social security, $50; credit union, $10; Blue Cross-Blue Shield, $20; and alimony, $50.

Debtor's Weekly Disposable Income

Earnings:		$400.00
Required Withholdings:		
Taxes	$100.00	
Social Security	50.00	150.00
Total weekly disposable income:		$250.00

Although the total deductions are $230, the total required deductions are only $150, leaving a total disposable income of $250 ($400 − $150). The maximum amount that Hound may garnishee for the week would be $62.50 (25 percent of $250), since this amount is less than the difference between Debtor's disposable income and 30 times the federal minimum hourly wage as given ($250 − $105 = $145). Hound will have to attach or continue to garnishee Debtor's property to satisfy the remaining $437.50 unless satisfactory arrangements can be made for payment. Many state statutes restrict the number of permissible garnishments to one per month.

The act also places restrictions on discharge from employment by reason of garnishment. An employer may not discharge an employee whose earnings have been subjected to garnishment for any one indebtedness. An employer who violates this provision may be fined up to $1,000 and imprisoned for one year. Even if a creditor garnishees an employee's wages 12 times in a year, the debtor-employee is afforded protection as long as this is for the same debt. The secretary of labor, acting through the Wage and Hour Division of the Department of Labor, enforces the provisions of Title III.

STATE LAWS

In addition to federal legislation, each state has its own consumer credit laws. These laws differ from state to state.

Usury

All states have usury laws that set limits on the maximum rate of interest a lender may charge. The maximum permitted rates vary within a particular state depending upon the nature of the loan. For small loans (generally ranging from $1,000 to $50,000), the rate ceilings may be as high as 36 percent per annum. On other types of loans the maximum legal rates generally range from 5 percent to 18 percent. In some states there is no ceiling for corporate borrowers. In some cases federal law fixes interest rates. For example, state laws would not apply to loans secured by first liens on residential real property.

The penalty for violating usury laws also varies from state to state. Some states provide for a forfeiture of the interest. Others provide for forfeiture of double or triple the amount of interest paid. Still others provide for a forfeiture of all or a portion of the principal as well as the interest. Violators are also subject to criminal penalties.

Uniform Consumer Credit Code

The Uniform Consumer Credit Code (UCCC) is a proposed consumer code for state adoption. It is designed to replace existing state laws in the consumer credit area and to provide uniformity of regulation among the states. Ten states have enacted the entire UCCC or a substantial portion of it.[1] Consumer advocates originally criticized the UCCC because it did not adequately protect the consumer. Recent drafts have adopted a more consumer-oriented posture.

The UCCC requires certain disclosures and specifically regulates rate ceilings, creditors' remedies, referral sales, and fine print clauses. The UCCC has been streamlined by incorporating the federal Truth in Lending Act by reference.

Under the UCCC the consumer has the right to cancel a home solicitation credit sale within three days. Most states grant the consumer this right independent of UCCC adoption. Furthermore, a rule of the Federal Trade Commission makes it a deceptive trade practice to fail to give a consumer three days to cancel when the purchase price is at least $25. This FTC rule includes cash sales and leases that do not occur at the seller's place of business.

THE BANKRUPTCY REFORM ACT

Individuals and businesses are confronted with serious financial hardship daily. This usually boils down to the simple fact that they cannot meet their creditors' legitimate demands. The failure of a business means loss of jobs for its employees and a financial loss to its creditors. Shareholders and others that have an interest in the business may lose their investment, and customers may lose a supplier. Whatever the reason for the failure,

---

[1] The adopting states are Colorado, Idaho, Indiana, Iowa, Kansas, Maine, Oklahoma, South Carolina, Utah, and Wyoming.

there is a need for debtor relief to lighten the burden. Those affected must be treated fairly.

Debtors can seek relief not only through state statutes, but also through federal bankruptcy laws enacted by Congress. The first comprehensive federal Bankruptcy Act was enacted in 1898. The Bankruptcy Reform Act of 1978 repealed all prior bankruptcy legislation. It represented the first major overhaul of bankruptcy legislation in 40 years.[2]

This section is concerned with three types of debtor relief under the Bankruptcy Reform Act. These include liquidation (chapter 7), reorganization (chapter 11), and adjustment of the debts of an individual with regular income (chapter 13).

Liquidation

Liquidation is sometimes referred to as straight bankruptcy or as a chapter 7 proceeding. Generally, a liquidation involves the sale of the debtor's assets, distribution of the proceeds to creditors, and the discharge of the debtor's remaining liabilities. Liquidation is consistent with the philosophy of allowing an honest debtor to get a fresh start. Individuals, partnerships, or corporations that are insolvent may be the subject of a liquidation.

Insolvency for the purpose of liquidation means that the debtor cannot meet financial obligations as they become due. This differs from the ordinary *balance sheet* concept of insolvency under which liabilities exceed assets. It is not uncommon for a debtor to possess assets in excess of liabilities yet still be unable to meet the liabilities as they mature. The assets might be in the form of unmarketable securities, slow-moving inventory, or real property. The nonliquid state of these assets might prevent the debtor from meeting day-to-day debts.

Voluntary and Involuntary Petitions

Liquidation may be voluntary or involuntary. In a voluntary liquidation the debtor files a bankruptcy petition. The petition acts as an *order for relief* and gives the court jurisdiction to administer the liquidation. Railroads, governmental units, banks, insurance companies, and savings and loan associations may not initiate voluntary petitions in bankruptcy. These industries are subject to rigid supervision and control by regulatory agencies.

A debtor may be forced into liquidation by creditors. (Farmers, charitable corporations, and the aforementioned industries may not be targets of involuntary liquidations.) To force a debtor into liquidation, the creditor(s) must file an involuntary petition. If the debtor has more than 12 creditors, at least three must join in filing the petition. If there are fewer than 12 creditors, then at least one creditor must file the petition. In either case, the petitioning creditors must have unsecured claims totaling at least

---

[2] Congress, more recently, has enacted the Bankruptcy Amendments and Federal Judgeship Act of 1984, which amendments are incorporated into this discussion.

$5,000. For example, assume that Janet Milestone is doing business as the Corner Drugstore. She has four creditors, as follows:

Blue		$ 5,000
Green		4,000
Hazel		2,000
Rose		1,000
	Total	$12,000

Since Milestone has fewer than 12 creditors, only one need sign the involuntary petition. However, since the signing creditor must have at least a $5,000 claim, only Blue qualifies. If Green and Hazel or Green and Rose both sign the involuntary petition, then the $5,000 requirement would also be satisfied. The petitioning creditors are granted an order for relief if they can prove that (1) the debtor is insolvent or (2) someone was appointed to take possession of the debtor's property within 120 days before the petition was filed.

Both voluntary and involuntary debtors are required to file a list of creditors, a schedule of assets and liabilities, and a statement of financial affairs. Each creditor and other interested party receives notice of the filing of the petition.

Automatic Stay

The filing of a petition in bankruptcy causes an automatic stay (suspension) of most attempts by creditors to collect on their indebtedness. Government agencies acting to enforce their regulatory powers are excepted from the stay, as are creditors pursuing alimony or child support.

In some cases, creditors that are not excepted from the stay may be granted relief upon application to the bankruptcy court. If the applicant can show that an interest in specific property held as collateral on a debt is jeopardized by the stay, the court will relieve the applicant unless adequate protection can otherwise be afforded by the applicant. Adequate protection is discussed below under the heading "The Trustee's Powers and Responsibilities."

Interim and Permanent Trustees

After an order for relief is granted, an interim trustee is appointed to take over the debtor's property. The takeover is not usually physical at this stage, although the interim trustee does possess the legal rights of ownership. The interim trustee conducts a first meeting of creditors. The debtor appears at the meeting and is questioned by the creditors and the trustee about assets and other matters. At this stage, creditors are generally most concerned about the whereabouts of the debtor's property. The creditors may elect a permanent trustee; otherwise the interim trustee continues to serve. The debtor's property passes to the trustee, who converts it to cash to the extent necessary to pay creditors.

Exemptions

An individual debtor is entitled to exempt certain property from distribution to creditors. The debtor may elect to take exemptions provided by either the state or the federal law. State law, however, may restrict the debtor to state exemptions. Federal exemptions are more liberal than those granted in most states. Consequently, debtors usually choose the federal exemptions where state law does not prohibit them from doing so. The following assets are exempt under federal law:

— Equity in a residential home not exceeding $7,500 (homestead exemption)
— Equity in a motor vehicle not exceeding $1,200
— Household items, wearing apparel, and other property for personal use whose value is $200 or less (There is a $4,000 aggregate monetary limitation for this category.)
— Jewelry not exceeding $500
— Property selected by a debtor of up to $400 in value in addition to up to $3,750.00 of any unused portion of the homestead exemption mentioned above
— Trade tools not exceeding $750 in value
— Interests in life insurance policies
— Health aids
— State and federal benefits, such as social security, unemployment, alimony, and pensions, to the extent reasonably necessary for support.

A husband and wife may be joint petitioners, and each may claim exemptions. If they do not own a residence, each spouse may, under the federal exemptions, select $4,150 of otherwise nonexempt personal property to be held exempt from distribution. This means that the joint petitioners may retain $8,300 in personal property in addition to the other specified exemptions. With these liberal federal exemptions, some debtors feel that they cannot afford *not* to go bankrupt.

The Trustee's Powers and Responsibilities
The debtor's estate includes all property in which the debtor has an interest. Anyone holding estate property must turn it over to the trustee. However, anyone having an interest in the property, such as a secured creditor, may insist upon adequate protection from the trustee before doing so. A secured creditor possesses a security interest in specific property as collateral for a debt. This creditor is entitled to be paid out of the proceeds of the sale of the secured property. Consequently, a secured creditor has a strong interest in protecting the secured property from depreciation or other loss. The trustee may provide such a creditor with adequate protection by, for example, agreeing to make cash payments to the creditor in an amount equal to the periodic depreciation of the secured property.

Preferential and Fraudulent Transfer
The trustee has the power to avoid a preferential transfer of property made by the debtor. A preferential transfer is (1) a transfer of property made for the benefit of a creditor (2) to pay a preexisting debt (3) when the debtor is insolvent under a balance sheet test and (4) made during

the 90-day period before the petition is filed (5) which gives a creditor a *greater percentage* of the debt than would have been received under the distribution provision of the act.

Assume that Ham owes his creditors the following amounts:

Round	$ 500
Square	1,000
Pentagon	2,500
Total	$4,000

Ham's total assets equal $3,000, making him insolvent under a balance sheet test since his liabilities exceed his assets. On February 1, 1987, Ham pays Square $750. Sixty days later he files bankruptcy, listing assets of $3,000 and exemptions amounting to $1,000. Because the transfer was preferential, the trustee in bankruptcy may recover the $750 transfer to Square and include it in Ham's bankruptcy estate.

The first four criteria of a preferential transfer are easy to see in this case. Square also received a greater percentage of the debt than he would be entitled to under bankruptcy law. The transfer gave Square 75 percent of the amount due. However, under the act Square would be entitled only to 25 percent of the indebtedness since that is the percentage that the amount due him ($1,000) bears to the amount due all the creditors ($4,000).

Under these circumstances, trustees also may avoid transfers to an insider if the transfers were made within one year before the filing of the petition and the insider reasonably believed that the debtor was insolvent. An insider is one who is in a close relationship to the debtor, e.g., a spouse, relative, partner, corporate officer, or director. Some types of transactions cannot be avoided by the trustee even if they appear to be preferential. The trustee cannot, for example, set aside the payment of a debt incurred within the ordinary course of the debtor's business.

The trustee may set aside certain fraudulent transfers that were made within one year of the filing of the petition. Fraudulent transfers include those intended to hinder, delay, or otherwise defraud creditors.

Distribution The trustee is charged with distributing the cash realized from the liquidation to satisfy the allowed claims of creditors. There are three classes of creditors: secured creditors, priority creditors, and general creditors. Secured creditors are paid out of the proceeds of the sale of the collateral in which they have an interest. If those proceeds are insufficient to satisfy the debt, then the secured creditor is a general creditor for the balance due.

Certain unsecured claims are entitled to *priority* in distribution. These claims are paid before the claims of other unsecured creditors. Priority claims are grouped into the following categories:

1. Administrative expenses, including court costs, trustee and attorney fees

2. Claims that arise against the debtor between the time a petition is filed and the time an order for relief is issued or a trustee appointed.
3. Claims of up to $2,000 per employee for wages earned within 90 days before the petition is filed
4. Employee claims, arising within 180 days prior to the filing of the petition, for unpaid contributions to employee benefit plans, to the extent of the unused limitation in the preceding priority category
5. Claims of up to $900 per claimant for deposits on consumer goods or services that were never received
6. Claims for federal, state, and local taxes

Each category of priority creditors must be paid in full before the next is entitled to be paid. If there are insufficient funds to satisfy the claims of all the creditors within a category, then each one in that category receives a *pro rata* share.

After the claims of the priority creditors have been satisfied, any remaining nonexempt assets are distributed among the general (unsecured) creditors. Any assets remaining after distribution to the general creditors are delivered to the debtor.

Discharge

An individual debtor may be afforded a discharge in bankruptcy. A discharge excuses the debtor from the obligation to pay the remaining dischargeable unpaid debts. Unpaid creditors may contest the discharge in bankruptcy on any one of several grounds, including the following: concealment of assets, commission of a bankruptcy crime, and a prior discharge in bankruptcy within the last six years. Certain claims are nondischargeable—they must ultimately be paid by the debtor. These include:

— Certain taxes
— Claims for property obtained under false pretenses
— Debts not listed by the debtor in the schedule of debts
— Certain claims arising from theft or fraud
— Claims for alimony and child support
— Claims arising from willful and malicious torts
— Claims arising from a prior bankruptcy when the debtor was denied a discharge for grounds other than the six-year limitation
— Claims for certain student loans that have been due and owing for less than five years, unless repayment would cause undue hardship
— Debts arising from court awards due to drunken driving
— Certain debts incurred for the purchase of luxuries

Reaffirmation

A debtor may agree to pay an obligation that has been discharged through bankruptcy. A debtor may reaffirm a debt so that the creditor will continue to deal with the debtor, or so that the creditor will not take secured property to satisfy the debt. Because creditors are in a position to exert undue influence upon unsuspecting debtors, the act places certain restrictions upon these reaffirmation agreements.

To be valid, a reaffirmation agreement must be filed with the court and entered into before the discharge of the debt. The agreement may be rescinded by the debtor before discharge or within 60 days after it is filed with the court, whichever is later. In addition, the court must warn the debtor about the consequences of reaffirmation at a discharge hearing. Finally, where the debtor was not represented by an attorney when entering into the agreement, the court must approve the reaffirmation unless the debt is secured by real property. The court will not approve the agreement unless it is in the best interests of the debtor.

Reorganization

Except for stockbrokers and commodities brokers, the same individuals and entities that are eligible for chapter 7 liquidation treatment are also eligible for reorganization (chapter 11). The purpose of reorganization is to allow a financially disturbed business to continue while arrangements for the adjustment of debts are made with creditors of the business. Reorganizations may be voluntary or involuntary. Generally, the same rules that apply to liquidation cases apply to reorganization, including trustee powers, exemptions, preferential transfers, and discharges.

After issuing the order for relief, the court appoints creditors' and stockholders' committees. The committees' task is to represent their respective interest groups. The committees are charged with investigation of the financial condition and activities of the debtor as well as participation in the formulation of a reorganization plan. They may also request the appointment of a trustee to replace the debtor in possession, if no trustee was previously appointed.

When no trustee has been appointed, the debtor has the exclusive right to submit a reorganization plan for the first 120 days after the order for relief. If a trustee has been appointed or if the debtor fails to submit a plan which is accepted by each class of creditors, then any interested party may submit a proposed plan for reorganization. Interested parties include the debtor, the trustee, and the committees.

Creditors are afforded an opportunity to accept or reject reorganization plans. A class of creditors accepts a plan when it is approved by a majority of the creditors within the class that represents at least two thirds of the allowed claims. A class of stockholders accepts a plan when at least two thirds of the shares within the class approve the plan.

The court will confirm a plan which is accepted by the various classes of creditors and stockholders as long as the plan is fair and reasonable. Even if a class has failed to accept the plan, the court may still confirm the plan if the plan treats the nonaccepting class fairly and equitably. A confirmed plan is binding upon all interest holders and discharges all debts not provided for under the plan.

Under certain circumstances a debtor may convert a reorganization into a liquidation. The court may, at its own option, convert a reorganization into a liquidation or dismiss the case in the best interest of the creditors.

The next case illustrates a company's use of reorganization to ease a major crisis.

In Re Johns–Manville Corp.

36 Bankruptcy Rptr. 727 (S.D.N.Y. 1984)

Johns–Manville's (debtor), a successful Fortune 500 Company, shocked the business community when it filed for reorganization under the Bankruptcy Code. Johns–Manville's sole reason for filing was the number of health suits brought against it. These suits were a result of exposure to Johns–Manville's products containing asbestos, a lethal substance. As of the date of the filing under the code there were about 16,000 such suits pending, and it is estimated that over the next 20 to 30 years many more asbestos health claims will be filed. Johns–Manville's total liability as a result of these asbestos claims is estimated at $1.9 billion. The Committee of Asbestos-Related Litigants (the Asbestos Committee) filed a motion to dismiss the Johns–Manville's petition. It maintains that the petition was entered in bad faith to avoid liabilities and that the company concocted false evidence to show economic distress. The district court dismissed the Asbestos Committee's motion.

Lifland, District Judge

. . . The Asbestos Committee premises its motion to dismiss the petition on what it contends is Manville's "bad faith" in filing for protection under Chapter 11. . . .

. . . Manville has credibly analyzed its position in its counter to the Asbestos Committee's allegations of fraud contained in its submission of a . . . Compendium.* . . .

_____
* A brief summary of a larger work.

*   *   *   *   *

. . . The Compendium relates the testimony of Manville officers and supports the inference accepted herein that these petitions were filed only after Manville undertook lengthy, careful and detailed analysis. For example, Manville commissioned and strictly scrutinized the results of studies by two separate epidemiological groups. . . . According to Manville, the results of the studies by ERI and SERC corroborated each other's projections of runaway asbestos health costs within the foreseeable future.

In addition, the Compendium cites to testimony of Manville officers which details the slow and deliberate process of data commissioning and review and "soul-searching" antedating the filing. . . . The data submitted by Manville also supports the accepted inference that the $1.9 billion projected debt figure ratified by Manville was the result of careful, conservative, and perhaps understated projections.

* * * * *

Manville was advised by Robert O. F. Bixby of the Price Waterhouse accounting firm that it was necessary to book a $1.9 billion reserve for contingent liability according to the accrual principle. . . . On balance, Manville's decision to follow this advice was neither unreasonable, illogical, nor in any sense fraudulent.

* * * * *

1. The Code's Policies of Open Access and Liquidation Avoidance

In determining whether to dismiss . . . a court is not necessarily required to consider whether the debtor has filed in "good faith" because that is not a specified predicate under the Code for filing. . . .

A "principal goal" of the Bankruptcy Code is to provide "open access" to the "bankruptcy process". . . . Thus, Congress intended that "there should be no legal barrier to voluntary petitions." Another major goal of the Code, that of "rehabilitation of debtors," requires that relief for debtors must be "timely". . . .

Accordingly, the drafters of the Code envisioned that a financially beleaguered debtor with real debt and real creditors should not be required to wait until the economic situation is beyond repair in order to file a reorganization petition. The "Con-

gressional purpose" in enacting the Code was to encourage resort to the bankruptcy process. This philosophy not only comports with the elimination of an insolvency requirement, but also is a corollary of the key aim of Chapter 11 of the Code, that of avoidance of liquidation. The drafters of the Code announced this goal, declaring that reorganization is more efficient than liquidation because "assets that are used for production in the industry for which they were designed are more valuable than those same assets sold for scrap." Moreover, reorganization also fosters the goals of preservation of jobs in the threatened entity.

In the instant case, not only would liquidation be wasteful and inefficient in destroying the utility of valuable assets of the companies as well as jobs, but, more importantly, liquidation would preclude just compensation of some present asbestos victims and all future asbestos claimants. . . . Manville must not be required to wait until its economic picture has deteriorated beyond salvation to file for reorganization.

* * * * *

2. Manville's "Good Faith" Filing Is Measured by the Existence of Massive Unmanageable Real Debt Owed to Real Claimants

* * * * *

. . . In *Manville*, it is undeniable that here has been no sham or hoax perpetrated on the Court in that Manville is a real business with real creditors in pressing need of economic reorganization. Indeed, the Asbestos Committee has belied its own contention that Manville has no debt and no real creditors by quantifying a benchmark settlement demand approaching one billion dollars for compensation of approximately 15,500 prepetition asbestos claimants. . . . This huge asserted liability does not even take into account the estimated 6,000 new asbestos health claims which have arisen in only the first 16 months since the filing date. The number of post-filing claims increases each day as "future claims back into the present."

Moreover, asbestos related property damage claims present another substantial contingent and unliquidated liability. Prior to the filing date, various schools initiated litigation seeking compensatory and punitive damages from . . . Manville for their unknowing use of asbestos containing products in ceilings, walls, structural members, piping, ductwork and boilers in school buildings. . . .

* * * * *

Accordingly, it is clear that Manville's liability for compensatory, if not punitive, damages to school authorities is not hypothetical, but real and massive debt. A range

of $500 million to $1.4 billion is the total projected amount of Manville's real debt to the school creditors.

* * * * *

. . . The economic reality of Manville's highly precarious financial position due to massive debt sustains its eligibility and candidacy for reorganization.

* * * * *

In sum, Manville is a financially beseiged enterprise in desperate need of reorganization of its crushing real debt, both present and future. The reorganization provisions of the Code were drafted with the aim of liquidation avoidance by great access to Chapter 11. Accordingly, Manville's filing does not abuse the jurisdictional integrity of this Court. . . .

CASE QUESTIONS

1. Why do you think Manville chose reorganization as opposed to liquidation? Are there any other alternatives available to Manville?

2. What evidence led the court to believe that Manville filed for reorganization in good faith? Does Manville's motivation make any difference? Explain.

3. Why do you think the Asbestos Committee wanted the petition dismissed?

4. Name some possible proposals in a plan

for reorganization that would deal with the massive quantity of asbestos claimants.

5. What if Johns–Manville filed a petition for reorganization for the sole purpose of avoiding a collective bargaining agreement with its union? Would this be considered bad faith? To determine good faith should there be an inquiry as to how and why the company wound up in a financially distressed condition?

Adjustment of Debts for Individuals

Individuals with regular income, except stockbrokers and commodities brokers, may file a voluntary petition to adjust their debts (chapter 13). This includes wage earners and individuals engaged in business. To qualify for chapter 13 status, a debtor's unsecured debts may not exceed $100,000 and his or her secured debts may not exceed $350,000. A chapter 13 resembles a reorganization, but it may be sought only by individuals. Unlike the debtor in a liquidation, a chapter 13 debtor does not surrender assets.

Creditors may not force a debtor into a chapter 13. As long as the debtor is complying with the plan, creditors may not compel the conversion of a chapter 13 into a chapter 7 or 11.

The chapter 13 debtor files a plan for repaying creditors. It may be a *composition* plan or an *extension* plan. In a composition plan the creditors receive a percentage of the indebtedness, and the debtor is discharged of the remaining obligation. Under an extension plan the creditors receive the entire indebtedness, but the payments extend past the due date. Both plans provide for completion within three years unless the court approves a longer period, not to exceed five years.

Unsecured creditors do not have to accept the plan for it to be implemented; however, they must receive at least as much as they would have received under a liquidation. Priority claimants must be paid in full under the plan unless a partial payment is agreed upon. The plan may be confirmed without the consent of the secured creditors when they are assured of full payment on the debt or when the debtor surrenders the secured property to the creditor.

A trustee is appointed by the court to administer the plan. The debtor normally pays a monthly sum to the trustee directly or by payroll deduction. The trustee then apportions the payment to creditors in accordance with the plan.

Assume that Joe files a chapter 13 petition for adjustment of the following debts:

Hi-Rise Bank	$1,500
Lenox Department Store	500
Doctor	1,200
Shell Oil	400
Total	$3,600

Joe earns $1,000 a month. He is unable to pay the $3,600 indebtedness now due. Under a chapter 13 extension plan, he could pay $100 a month to the trustee over 36 months. The trustee would distribute an apportioned share to each of the creditors, and they would be paid in full at the end of 36 months. This is a simplified example; in reality, administrative expenses, attorney's fees, and interest on the indebtedness would be added into the plan. Joe's monthly payments over 36 months would be a bit more than $100.

In many instances the court order prevents a chapter 13 debtor from incurring further debt without the consent of the court during the administration of the plan. At the completion of the plan a chapter 13 debtor receives a discharge from all debts covered by the plan. Even when the debtor has not completed the payments within the prescribed period, the court may still extend a discharge, as long as the failure was due to circumstances beyond the debtor's control.

ALTERNATIVE APPROACHES

Many believe that the current Bankruptcy Code is too generous to debtors. Critics maintain that exemptions, discharges, and other features, slanted in favor of the debtor, actually encourage bankruptcy. They cite this bias as a major cause for the rise in bankruptcies.

For this reason, the proposed Bankruptcy Improvements Act (BIA) is being heavily backed by a coalition of banks, finance companies, credit unions, and other consumer creditors. The proposal would modify the existing code so that a debtor who could pay off a significant portion of his or her debts over a five-year period would be excluded from chapter 7 liquidation. Only chapter 13 would be available to that debtor. Proponents of this reform measure cite a study which indicated that 29 percent of those who were discharged under a chapter 7 proceeding could have repaid 100 percent of the debt within five years. According to the study another 8 percent could have repaid 50 percent of the debt.

The BIA also proposes to modify the code so that debtors would have access only to state exemptions. This would generally result in less generous exemptions for the debtor than under the present system.

Opponents to the BIA sharply criticize its provisions, arguing that it would be a retreat from the American "fresh start" philosophy. Although the battle rages, it is unlikely that any major overhaul of the Bankruptcy Reform Act will occur in the near future.

CHAPTER PROBLEMS

1. Linda Glaire purchased a seven-year membership in a health club owned and operated by LaLanne. The price of the membership was $408, regardless of whether the sum was paid in cash at the outset or over a two-year period in monthly installments of $17 each. Glaire elected to pay over time, as do most of LaLanne's customers. She entered into a standard contract which stated that no finance charge would be assessed for the extension of credit. In accordance with its usual practice LaLanne then sold Glaire's contract to Universal Guardian Acceptance Corporation at a discount of 37.5 percent. LaLanne thus immediately received $255 in cash. Glaire became obligated to Universal for the full $408, payable over two years. LaLanne and Universal are interlocking corporations with common ownership and con-trol. Universal regularly assists LaLanne in its financing by accepting contracts at a discount. Upon learning of the arrangement between LaLanne and Universal, Glaire filed suit against LaLanne. She alleged violations of the Truth in Lending Act.

Is the act applicable to LaLanne? Why? Has LaLanne violated the act? Who, if anyone, is required to make TILA disclosures to Glaire?

2. James C. Jenkins, after moving from Washington, D.C., to St. Louis, applied for auto insurance with the Fireman's Fund Insurance Company. Several days after his application was filed, Jenkins was informed by Fireman's that his background would be investigated in connection with the policy. A few days later, he learned that his application had been rejected because of information contained in a report compiled by Accurate Reports. Jenkins learned that the information was based on interviews between Accurate's representative and Jenkins's neighbors in Washington. Jenkins requested that he be allowed to see the report and that he be told to whom the representative had spoken. The Accurate representative in St. Louis denied both requests.

Jenkins learned of the content of the report from Fireman's and thereupon contacted Accurate once again. He disputed the accuracy of the information in the file and requested an explanation. Accurate's representative refused to discuss the matter with Jenkins. Is the refusal justified? Explain.

3. Joe T. Morris (plaintiff) was denied credit on several occasions because of an unfavorable credit report communicated by the Credit Bureau of Cincinnati. The bad credit rating was based upon a bankruptcy and two unpaid department store accounts. The delinquent accounts belonged to his wife, who had filed bankruptcy before they were married. They erroneously wound up in Joe Morris's credit file.

After Morris personally informed the credit bureau of the mistake, they purged his file of the inaccurate information. Thereafter, another inquiry was made about the plaintiff's credit history in the name of Joseph T. Morris (instead of Joe T. Morris). The credit bureau opened up a new file on Joseph T. Morris and the same inaccurate information regarding the bad accounts and bankruptcy turned up in the file. Morris was again denied credit on the basis of that information. Morris sought damages under the Fair Credit Reporting Act for injury to his reputation, his family, his work, and his sense of well-being. What is the result? Explain.

4. Glen Wood, an executive vice president of SAR Manufacturing Company, checked into the Holiday Inn in Phenix City, Alabama and tendered a Gulf Oil Company credit card to pay for his room. After an imprint of the card was made, it was returned to Wood. Gulf Oil Company monitors the accounts of its cardholders on an ongoing basis and cancels a customer's credit if it determines that he or she cannot afford to pay. Gulf furnishes National Data Corporation with a list of all credit cancellations and

authorizes it to disburse credit information to inquirers that are authorized to extend credit to Gulf cardholders.

Gulf noticed that Wood had been charging large amounts in comparison to his income. (Gulf was unaware that Wood had been using the card to charge business expenses.) Although Wood's account was not in arrears, Gulf canceled his credit and directed National Data Corporation to give the following report to those seeking approval of his credit card use:

> Pick up travel card. Do not extend further credit. Send card to billing office for reward.

When the night auditor at Holiday Inn checked with National Data Corporation he received the above communication. The auditor then went to Wood's room at 5:00 A.M. and awakened him on the pretense that he needed Wood's credit card because the "imprinting" had not taken. Wood inquired at the front desk when the credit card was not returned. He was told that the card had been "seized upon the authority of National Data." Wood left the motel, but his anger over the incident caused a heart attack.

Wood sued Gulf, alleging that it negligently failed to comply with the Fair Credit Reporting Act as a consumer reporting agency. He also sued National Data Corporation and Holiday Inn, alleging that they negligently failed to comply with the Fair Credit Reporting Act as users of a consumer report. Do you agree with Wood? Explain. Should Gulf alter its policy regarding credit card practices? If so, in what way?

5. Robert Cragin and his wife submitted a written application for a $2,000 property improvement loan to First Federal Savings. Mr. and Mrs. Cragin signed the application as joint applicants. The loan was approved by First Federal, and the Cragins were informed of the approval in a letter from Arthur Barnett, a loan manager of the bank. Thereafter Barnett informed Mr. Cragin that several documents would have to be signed by both Mr. and Mrs. Cragin and notarized. Mr. Cragin informed Barnett that it would be extremely inconvenient for his wife to sign the documents before a notary since she took care of two small children and could not get away from the house. When Barnett insisted that this procedure be followed, Cragin asked if he could apply for the loan in his own name. Barnett responded by saying, "You will have to submit a new application in writing as required by the bank's procedure." Cragin refused and sued First Federal, alleging a violation of the Equal Credit Opportunity Act based on sexual and marital status discrimination. Who will prevail? Why?

6. Luella Davis was indebted to Public Finance Corporation. She informed Public Finance that she was no longer employed, was on public aid, and was unable to make payments on the indebtedness. Over an eight-month period, in attempts to collect the debt, employees of Public Finance called Mrs. Davis several times a week, sometimes more than once a day, and frequented her home weekly. On one occasion an agent of Public Finance telephoned Mrs. Davis at the hospital where she was visiting her sick daughter. On another occasion an employee of Public Finance persuaded Mrs. Davis to write a check on the promise that the check would not be cashed. The employee then informed an acquaintance of Mrs. Davis that she was writing bad checks. On still another occasion a Public Finance employee went to Mrs. Davis's home and took an inventory of her household furnishings, refusing to leave until her son entered the room. Public Finance was aware that Mrs. Davis suffered from hypertension and a nervous condition. Both of these ailments were aggravated as a result of Public Finance's conduct.

Discuss the possible remedies that Mrs. Davis has against Public Finance. What cause of action affords her the best chance of recovery?

7. Lady Cosmetics, a wholesaler of cosmetics, engaged in a rigorous collection campaign in an effort to reduce its bad debt expense. Jerry Swartz, an employee of the company, was assigned 900 accounts which amounted to accounts receivable of $10 million. He was required by the company to make some contact with each delinquent account at least once every nine days. Republic Department Store sued Lady Cosmetics and Jerry Swartz under the Fair Debt Collection Practices Act. Republic alleged that on one occasion Swartz contacted the accounting office of Republic and threatened to "sue the pants off of the store" if it did not make payment

immediately. Republic further alleged that "Swartz showed up repeatedly at the store, insisted on talking to high-level officers and refused to leave until he was paid, causing embarrassing scenes in front of customers of Republic on several occasions." Assuming that Republic's allegations are true, will it be successful? Explain.

8. Lynn Handsome was a student at Rutgers University from 1968 through 1974. During this time she borrowed $4,600 in the form of federally guaranteed student loans. Health problems necessitated her withdrawal from college in January 1975, and because of large medical bills she was unable to meet the repayment schedule on the loans. Consequently, Rutgers obtained a default judgment against the plaintiff for $4,991.75 plus costs and interest.

Handsome filed a petition in bankruptcy in April 1977. The liabilities listed in her petition were in excess of $25,000, including the indebtedness to Rutgers University. Her assets totaled $368.75. Handsome was discharged of all indebtedness, including the debt to Rutgers. Thereafter she attempted to reenroll at Rutgers. Although her admission was approved on scholastic grounds, a "place hold" notice was put upon her records since she was "more than three months delinquent in [her] debts to the university." She was prevented from registering and was unable to obtain a release of her transcripts.

Handsome filed a complaint against Rutgers University alleging that its actions violated the Constitution and the Bankruptcy Reform Act. The court granted a temporary restraining order that directed Rutgers to allow plaintiff to register. The court was then presented with the question of whether the restraining order should be made permanent. How should the court decide? Why?

9. Continental Airlines Corporation (debtor) lost over $500,000,000 since the airlines were deregulated in 1978. One cause of the loss was that its competitors have lower labor costs and are able to charge lower fares.

Continental was not able to pay its debts as they became due. As a result, some of its creditors threatened to cut off services. The debtor made efforts to adjust its collective bargaining agreements by reducing pay and work benefits for employees, but no agreement could be reached with the unions.

Debtor filed a voluntary petition for reorganization. In connection with this Chapter 11 proceeding, the debtor sought to reject its collective bargaining agreements and other related employee contracts. The unions argued that the petition was grounded in bad faith because it was filed for the sole purpose of avoiding its employee contracts. On this basis they filed a motion to dismiss the petition. Discuss.

10. Do you favor the current bankruptcy laws? What are their advantages? Disadvantages? How would you modify the bankruptcy code?

PART PROBLEMS

1. Dietic Pound Watchers (DPW) pioneered the development of a substitute for food. The food substitute was a synthetic compound called ingesterone and it contained all of the needed daily minerals, vitamins, carbohydrates, fats, and proteins. DPW added other chemicals giving the final product the quality of removing any hunger pain feelings. This was accomplished by two time-released chemicals: one was a mild anesthetic (pain reliever) and the other mixed with the hydrochloric stomach acid to form a gas that expanded to give the diet conscious consumer a bloated feeling. The FDA approved the compound for marketing. DPW marketed the compound under the name "Slims." It adopted a comprehensive advertising campaign designed to impress upon the consumer that "Slims" are safe. The campaign included testimonials of various movie stars, Olympic athletes, and famous personalities who, in their slim-looking bodies, sang praises of the virtues of "Slims." Although all of those who testified had actually taken "Slims," only one had lost weight through the "Slims" program. The others had A-type bodies not prone to overweight. The Federal Trade Commission has started an investigation of DPW's advertising practices.

Several other drug producers started manufacturing and distributing similar type food-substitute-hunger-suppressant drugs. Babcock Laboratories marketed a drug called "Thin Again," which also contained ingesterone, but achieved the hunger suppressant effect by an amphetamine (stimulant) additive. Two other companies, Jackson and Jackson, and Ravenol also entered the food substitute market with drugs containing ingesterone, though using other additives to achieve the suppressant effect. By 1985 there were over 50 companies marketing ingesterone-based food substitutes. In that year the share of the market was as follows:

Company	Percent Share of Market
Dietic Pound Watchers	40
Babcock Laboratories	20
Jackson & Jackson	10
Ravenol	5
Others	25

All of the companies marketed their drugs nationwide. In 1986 all drugs containing ingesterone were taken off the market because of their linkage to stomach and intestinal cancer.

It is believed that several million people were taking ingesterone-based food substitutes on a regular basis while it was on the market. Already several hundred suits have been filed against the various manufacturers. Eleven suits have come to trial. Eight suits resulted in verdicts against the defendants averaging $1 million dollars each. Three suits were dismissed because the plaintiff was unable to recall which brand of ingesterone she took. Two of these are on appeal. Currently there are over 200 suits pending that name DPW as defendant. Suits are now being filed at the rate of 100 per month, and this rate is expected to increase over the next five years.

DPW has been experiencing a financial crisis for the last eighteen months. It is having serious difficulty repaying bank loans and many of its suppliers are threatening to cut DPW off unless it pays a substantial portion of amounts in arrearage. DPW feels that it can survive the short run. However, DPW is particularly concerned about "ingesterone" suits since its insurance has a $100 million ceiling.

Assume you are the vice-president of financial affairs and have been appointed by the chief executive officer of DPW to head a committee to make a recommendation to her.

a. What legal questions would you want to ask in-house counsel?

b. Outline the possible courses of action available to DPW. Analyze and describe the consequences of each.

c. What is your recommendation to the chief executive officer?

2. The Computer Complex, Inc. (CCI) is a manufacturer of small home computers. They range in price from $1,000 to $150,000. CCI offers financing at the maximum rate allowed by state usury laws for consumer transactions. These rates are below the prime rate. CCI has an aggressive collections department that frequently calls delinquent debtors and threatens lawsuits, writes nasty letters to employers, and causes general embarrassment. It persists in doing so even if the consumer contests the debt. It frequently ignores letters from consumers claiming billing errors.

CCI's chief electrical engineer recently discovered a defect in the wiring of the most expensive model. The defect could result in an electrical short or fire in one out of every 10,000 units. The engineer resigned in protest over CCI's refusal to take corrective action or warn purchasers of the danger.

CCI advertises on television. Its ad shows a happy teenage boy using a home computer. The computer used in the ad is not a CCI model but is manufactured by Competitor Corporation. The narrator says:

> CCI turns computers into child's play. Computers are the way of the future. Your child should be prepared. Buy a CCI home computer. You can use it yourself in tax planning, managing the family budget, playing games, and dozens of other ways. And your children will enjoy it, too, as you teach them the wonders of computers. Liberal financing is available below the skyrocketing prime rate. Hurry! Act today!

You have just been hired by CCI. Your first assignment is to prepare a report to the president discussing all of the legal concerns raised by the above facts.

3. The Electric Factory manufactures toys for mature children. Its research and development department produced a bicycle that is designed to operate by sprockets, springs, or motor. The bicycle is called the Chameleon. The standard model 10-speed sprocket-control bike sells for $149.95. By means of the #666 adaptable spring kit, which sells for $99.99, the bicycle can be made to self-propel. The springs self-wind when the operator peddles the bicycle. If the op-

erator then flicks a switch to engage the springs, they will propel the bicycle. The #777 adaptable motor attachment, which sells for $499, converts the Chameleon into a motorbike.

The Electric Factory markets the Chameleon through 37 exclusive dealerships in various parts of the country. It places all Chameleon advertisements and is running the following advertisement concerning the Chameleon:

THE CHAMELEON
A CHAMPION'S 10-SPEED BICYCLE
FOR RACERS
$149.95
AND IT'S STURDIER, SAFER,
LIGHTER, AND LESS
EXPENSIVE THAN ITS COMPETITORS
EASY TO ASSEMBLE

When customers inquire about the Chameleon, they are first made aware of the spring and motor attachments. Most of the dealerships use high-pressure techniques to persuade customers to purchase the attachments. Customers are offered a 10 percent discount if they buy the spring or motor attachment within 30 days after they purchase the standard model. The standard model contains a written warranty, portions of which read:

> The company agrees to fix any movable defective parts within 60 days of sale when said parts are delivered or sent postage prepaid to the plant.

> The company disclaims liability for any injuries sustained as a result of manufacturer's defects.

> This warranty is in lieu of all other warranties, express or implied.

In reality, the standard-model Chameleon without attachments is two pounds heavier than the average weight of its 10-speed competitors, although it is lighter than all of its spring bike and motorbike competitors. The bike comes unassembled in two boxes and includes a booklet for "easy assembly." The standard model is assembled in 47 steps; 26 additional steps are required to assemble the spring attachment, and 34 additional steps are required to assemble the motor attachment. The steps are clearly explained with explicit diagrams. In order to assemble even the standard model, 16 standard-size sprocket wrenches are needed, in addition to Phillips screwdrivers, pliers, a hammer, and a vise.

Swan manufactures a $139.95 bicycle that competes with the Chameleon standard model. Through its legal office, Swan has contacted the Electric Factory and has threatened suit unless the Electric Factory removes or alters its present advertisement. The Federal Trade Commission has already filed a complaint alleging unfair and deceptive advertising against the Electric Company and has stated that it will accept a consent order only if the order includes a corrective advertising order that says, "contrary to prior advertisements, the Chameleon is not lighter or less expensive than all of its competitors."

Through the National Electronic Injury Surveillance System the Consumer Product Safety Commission has become aware of several injuries sustained on the Chameleon because the sprockets disengage when the operator is peddling, causing the rider to lurch forward and fall off the bike. The Consumer Product Safety Commission may seek a ban of the product because it poses an imminent threat of injury to consumers.

An accident occurred while Jimmy Jones, age 15, was assembling the motor attachment to the Chameleon he had recently purchased. Apparently, while the motor was hanging from an A-frame by a double-strand rope in accordance with the instructions, a sharp edge of the motor mounting sliced through the rope. The motor fell on his brother's chest, fracturing three ribs. There was no warning in the instructions or otherwise of this danger. Jimmy's parents have initiated suit against the Electric Company.

John Moore made $1,200 a month at the Electric Factory. His take-home pay after the normal federal, state, and local deductions was $1,000. He owes $200 to Jan Ross, a lawyer who handled an accident case for him. She called him twice on the job and left messages with his employer for John to return the call. On one occasion she called John at home at 7:30 A.M. and demanded payment. Every week she sends a bill to John's home; the envelope gives her name and address and identifies her as an attorney at law. John also owes Sears department

store $500. International Revenue Corporation has been collecting for Sears. John recently moved to get away from his hounding creditors. International conducted an investigation in John's old neighborhood to ascertain his whereabouts. When it found out his new address it phoned his wife and said "Your husband is a deadbeat. If he doesn't pay by tomorrow, we are going to sue him for everything he has." In addition, a $1,000 judgment against John was awarded to Jim McNeil as a result of an auto accident. Jim hired a lawyer who garnisheed John's wages for the months of January, February, and March and obtained the entire indebtedness. As a result, the Electric Factory fired John.

James Auser, a divorced Electric Company employee, is unable to meet his day-to-day debts. His balance sheet looks like this:

Assets

Cash	$ 1,200
Inventory	2,000
Automobile	3,000
House	63,500
Household furnishings	15,000
Jewelry	1,000
Business tools	3,000
Life insurance policies	3,050
	$91,750

Liabilities

Doctors	$ 3,000
Paris Finance Company	56,000
Master Card	2,500
Sears	1,000
Food Fast, Inc.	6,000
Taxes	12,000
Payroll	1,000
Alimony	2,500
Student loan	2,500
	86,500
Owner's equity	5,250
	$91,750

The Paris Finance Company holds a $56,000 mortgage on James's house. The household furnishings consist of 22 pieces of furniture, of which 15 are valued at $200 apiece and the remaining 7 at over $200 apiece. James owes the taxes to the IRS because he failed to pay last year's income tax. He incurred the student loan six years ago. The administrative expenses (court costs) of any bankruptcy proceeding are $200. The state exemptions are: homestead, $5,000; jewelry, $2,000; motor vehicle, unlimited; and tools of trade, $500. James went to the Electric Company's in-house counsel to discuss the problem.

You are being interviewed for a position with the Electric Company as a general executive manager. The interviewer is aware that you have taken a legal environment of business course that includes product safety, advertising, and debtor-creditor relations. The interviewer asks you to discuss the relevant issues contained in the data presented above.

*T*he sale of stocks, bonds, and other securities
is a prime method for raising capital.

PART THREE

SECURITIES LAW

Businesses need to raise money in order to function. Normally they can
use the available cash and assets on hand to meet their needs. However,
a new enterprise needs start-up capital; an existing business, to expand
its operations or undertake a special project, must raise money to do
so. The sale of stocks, bonds, and other securities is a prime method for
raising capital. Businesses sell securities to investors. Investors purchase
these securities with hopes of earning a profit or deriving some other
benefit. Once these securities are in the hands of investors, they may resell
them to other investors. Part Three is about the laws that govern these
sales and purchases. Before examining those laws, it is helpful to examine
the nature of the business organizations that sell securities to raise capital.

*   *   *   *   *

Selecting a particular form of business organization requires a careful
analysis of factors such as management control, risk exposure, and capital
needs. Three types of business organizations are commonly used: sole
proprietorship, partnership, and corporation.

The *sole proprietorship* is the simplest form of business organization.
It involves one person who owns and operates a business. Theoretically,
any business, regardless of size, can operate in this form. However, a
sole proprietorship is usually confined to small businesses.

The sole proprietorship enjoys the advantage of combining management and control in the owner. As the business expands, the owner needs
to employ agents to assist in its operation. An *agent* is one who is authorized to act for another. An employee is a type of agent. Because of this

agency relationship, the employer is responsible for acts of the agents committed within the scope of employment.

A major disadvantage of the sole proprietorship is that its creditors may satisfy their claims out of the personal assets of the owner. For example, assume a business patron slipped on a wet floor and was injured. If the owner's employee failed to warn the patron of the hazard, the patron might sue and collect damages against the owner. Unlimited liability can be a high price to pay for being your own boss.

The *partnership* is an association of two or more persons who carry on a business for profit. It is formed by agreement of the parties. Normally, each partner contributes money or property to the partnership to initially fund the business. The Uniform Partnership Act (UPA), adopted by most states, governs the operation of partnerships.

Although a partnership is an association of individuals, it is considered a separate legal entity for some purposes. For example, a partnership can own and convey property in its own name. It can sue or be sued. However, for other purposes the partnership is not considered a legal entity. For example, it is not taxed. Individual partners are taxed on their share of earnings as defined in the partnership agreement.

On the distribution of profits, if the partnership agreement is silent, each partner is entitled to an equal share. Absent an agreement to the contrary, each partner bears an equal share of losses. Each partner has the right to use partnership property for partnership purposes. Each partner possesses equal rights in the management and control of the partnership's affairs unless the partnership agreement specifies otherwise. Each partner is an agent of the partnership.

The agency relationship creates fiduciary duties upon partners. A *fiduciary duty* is one that requires a high standard of good faith and loyalty. A partner may not act against the interests of the partnership to promote his or her own interests. Partners are "held to something stricter than the morals of the marketplace."[1] Any breach of this fiduciary responsibility results in liability. For example, a partner who fails to inform other partners about a business opportunity, related to the partnership and instead takes advantage of it, is liable to the partnership for the value of the benefit.

A major disadvantage of the partnership form of business is that, like the sole proprietorship, partners are exposed to unlimited liability. After exhausting the partnership assets, creditors can turn to the individual partner's assets for satisfaction.

The *limited partnership* was created to counter the undesirable characteristic of unlimited liability. The Uniform Limited Partnership Act (ULPA), adopted by most states, governs the operation of limited partnerships. Limited partnerships must have at least one partner whose liability is unlimited. The other partners, designated limited partners, are shielded

---

[1] *Meinhard v. Salmon,* 294 N.Y. 458, 164 N.E. 545 (1928).

from personal liability. In return for this protection, the limited partners surrender the right to exercise management powers. Limited partners are passive investors who contribute money, expecting to earn a profit. Their investment may be evidenced by limited partnership interests. These interests, like stock in a corporation, are a type of security. The sale of limited partnership interests is a popular means of raising capital for projects ranging from the purchase and development of land to the purchase of prized race horses for breeding.

*M*anipulative price-control methods were . . .
practiced by corporate officers . . . who utilized the
stock exchange facilities to advance their . . . schemes.

Congressman Wolverton (1934)

The *corporation* is the usual organizational form employed by large businesses. A corporation is a separate legal entity, taxed on its earnings and liable for its debts. Every state has laws that govern the creation, operation, and termination of corporations. Corporations consist of a board of directors, officers, and shareholders. The board of directors is normally elected by the shareholders to direct the management of the corporation. The board appoints officers and delegates day-to-day management functions to them. Chief executive officer (CEO) is the usual title assigned to the highest officer in a corporation. Officers are normally authorized to hire employees. Like partners in a partnership, directors and officers of a corporation are fiduciaries. They owe to the corporation and its shareholders the duties of loyalty, full disclosure, and good faith. Any breach of these duties may result in liability.

The shareholders, or stockholders, are the owners of the corporation. They invest in the corporation by purchasing shares of stock. Known as *equity securities,* these shares represent ownership interest in the corporation. Stockholders may receive a return on their investment by way of dividends and capital appreciation. A dividend is a distribution of profits to shareholders. Capital appreciation results when a shareholder sells stock for a higher price than originally paid.

The main attraction of the corporate form is that the owner, or shareholders, of the business enjoy limited liability. The most they can lose is their investment. Creditors of the corporation must satisfy their claims from the corporate assets and may not look to the individual shareholders to satisfy those claims.

In addition to issuing stock, corporations often raise money by issuing bonds. Those who invest in bonds are called bondholders. They are really lending money to the corporation. These bonds are known as *debt securities* because they represent a debt of the corporation.

* * * * *

The history of the securities laws indicates that Congress was concerned about investors who purchased securities from large corporations. When corporations were small and there was real personal contact among owners, managers, and shareholders, there was no need for securities regulation. But when the corporation enlarged to a place where contacts between owners and investors were nonexistent and impersonal, abuses occurred that many believe contributed to the stock market crash of 1929 and finally government regulation of the securities industry.

> *F*ederal [s]ecurities law did not spring full grown from the brow of any New Deal Zeus. It followed a generation of state regulation and several centuries of legislation in England. For the problems at which modern securities regulation is directed are as old as the cupidity of sellers and the gullibility of buyers.
>
> *Professor Louis Loss,*
> *Harvard Law School*

The Great Depression of the 1930s undermined public confidence in the securities markets. Federal securities laws were enacted to restore that confidence. They are administered and enforced by the Securities and Exchange Commission (SEC). The federal securities laws consist of specialized securities laws, the Securities Act of 1933 (Securities Act), and the Securities Exchange Act of 1934 (Exchange Act). All are designed to protect the investing public.

The *Public Utility Holding Company Act* of 1935 was designed to correct abuses that existed among the gas and electric public utility holding companies. The act requires public utility holding companies to simplify and fully disclose their financial, organizational, and operational behavior.

The *Trust Indenture Act* of 1939 regulates the public sale of bonds and other debt securities in excess of $1 million when these are issued pursuant to a trust indenture. A *trust indenture* is a document whose terms and conditions govern the responsibility of the issuer (seller) and the rights of the bondholder (buyer). The trust indenture designates a trustee to carry out the terms of the indenture. The Trust Indenture Act imposes high standards of conduct on the trustee to ensure that the rights of the bondholders are adequately safeguarded.

The *Investment Company Act* of 1940 regulates publicly owned companies engaged in the business of investing and trading in securities. These companies must comply with registration and disclosure requirements designed to safeguard the public. The *Investment Advisers Act* of 1940 empowers the SEC to regulate persons and firms that are in the business of rendering investment advice to clients. The act requires that investment advisers register with the Securities and Exchange Commission (SEC).

Under the *Bankruptcy Reform Act* the SEC may render expert advice and assistance to the bankruptcy courts in connection with the reorganization of certain debtor corporations. The advice is designed to assist these courts in affording fair treatment to creditors and investors while assuring that the corporations emerge from the reorganization in sound financial condition.

The *Securities Investor Protection Act* of 1970 empowers the Securities Investor Protection Corporation (SIPC) to supervise the liquidation of securities firms in financial trouble. SIPC, a nonprofit corporation whose members are brokers, also protects investors from losses due to the financial failure of brokerage firms.

*   *   *   *   *

Most of the states were operating under securities laws before the enactment of the first federal securities laws. However, the state securities laws required that a security have merit before it could be sold. State examiners would closely evaluate the worth of the security before permitting its sale within the state. In contrast, Congress adopted a system that permitted securities to be sold and traded on exchanges, regardless of merit, as long as the issuer filed a registration statement containing full disclosure about the securities.

The *Securities Act* requires that securities be *registered* with the SEC before being offered for sale. The registration process affords investors a full disclosure of the information about the securities and the company offering them. The act also provides for criminal and civil penalties for misstatements or fraudulent practices in connection with the sale of securities and the preparation of the registration statements. The Securities Act covers the original issuance of securities. The details of this act are treated in chapter 8.

The *Exchange Act* extends the disclosure requirements to securities traded on securities exchanges. Under this act, the trading firm is required to file a registration statement with the SEC and to make periodic reports to the commission. The act includes provisions designed to prevent fraud. The Exchange Act covers the secondary sale of securities. (See Figure 9–1 on page 295). The details of this act are treated in chapter 9.

CHAPTER 8

ISSUING SECURITIES

Securities are different from most of the "merchandise" familiar to the average person. A consumer who purchases a loaf of bread in the grocery store can touch and smell the bread and evaluate its worth by comparing it with other brands on the shelf. This is not the case with securities. The worth of a share of stock depends on the worth of the enterprise that issued it. Evaluating this worth requires knowledge of that enterprise's operations. This information is ordinarily beyond the investor's reach. An alternative is to rely on the issuer's claims about the enterprise. In the past, this means of ascertaining value often tempted those issuing stocks and other securities to exaggerate the financial status and future prospects of their enterprise. Unsuspecting investors were enticed with fanciful promises of "pie in the blue sky."[1] This practice made legislators aware of the need for investor protection.

At the turn of the nineteenth century a few states enacted laws designed to protect investors. By 1933 virtually every state was operating under some type of securities regulation.[2] These state laws varied. Some prohibited misrepresentations in the sale of securities. Others required registration of securities or of those engaged in the securities business. Still others contained a combination of these regulatory devices.

State regulations proved inadequate to protect investors. First, they lacked uniformity. Opportunists preyed upon consumers in the states that had permissive securities laws. Also, it was often possible to avoid state securities laws altogether by operating on a purely interstate basis or by falling under liberal state exemptions.

---

[1] The term *blue sky laws* refers to state securities regulations intended to protect investors from "speculative schemes which have no more basis than so many feet of blue sky." *Hall v. Geiger Jones, Co.,* 242 U.S. 539 (1917).

[2] Nevada was the sole exception.

Many Americans lost their life's savings in the 1929 stock market crash. By 1933 Congress observed that billions of dollars had been lost due to the flotation of worthless securities. The securities industry was blamed for the debacle. Many made alluring promises of easy wealth without informing investors of the facts necessary to estimate the value of the security. Recognizing that federal intervention was needed to restore public confidence in securities and their markets, Congress passed the Securities Act of 1933 (Securities Act). This was the first of several federal laws regulating securities.

Federal securities laws are based on the philosophy that the best protection for an investor is access to complete information regarding the contemplated investment. The Securities and Exchange Commission (SEC), which administers the federal securities laws, may not pass on the worth of a security or even decide whether its issuance would be in the public interest. As long as full disclosure is provided, the securities may "float," regardless of their worth. The final determination of their desirability is left to the investor. Congress did not, however, disturb the states' regulation of securities. As a result, state and federal securities laws operate side by side and often necessitate dual compliance.

This chapter begins with a brief look at the SEC. It then focuses on how to identify a security and the marketing of securities. Registration of securities and exemptions from the registration process are treated next. Finally, the chapter concentrates on the remedial provisions of the Securities Act.

THE SECURITIES AND EXCHANGE COMMISSION

The SEC is an administrative agency created by Congress to administer the securities laws. Its five members are appointed by the president and serve five-year terms. No more than three of the members may be affiliated with the same political party. The terms are staggered so that one member's term expires each year. Most of the commission's staff is located in Washington, and the remainder is situated in nine regional and eight branch offices in key cities throughout the country (see Figure 8–1).

The SEC has broad rulemaking powers, and its rules have the force of law. Informal SEC releases define the attitudes and policies of the agency, although they do not have the effect of law. In addition, the SEC responds to specific questions by advising the inquirers of its opinion on proposed transactions. These responses are sometimes referred to as *no action* letters. They often state that the SEC will not take any action against the inquirer based on the facts and the intended action outlined in the inquirer's letter.

IDENTIFYING A SECURITY

Perhaps one of the greatest tasks that faced Congress when it was drafting securities legislation was to define a security. The definition had to be

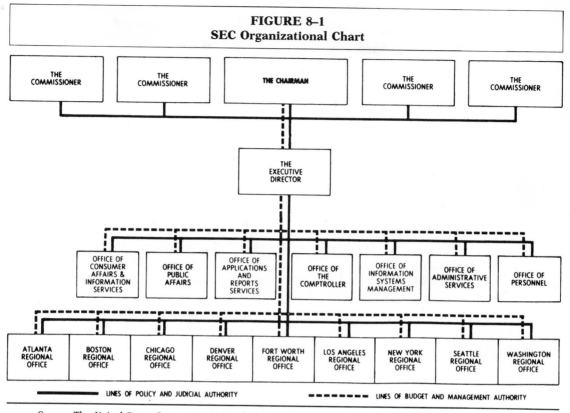

FIGURE 8–1
SEC Organizational Chart

Source: The *United States Government Manual*, 1983–1984.

specific enough for common instruments to be readily identified as securities, yet general enough to allow for the inclusion of new instruments or interests. The Securities Act adopts a very expansive definition of a security, which includes notes, stocks, bonds, investment contracts, and other interests "commonly known as a security."

Securities Act

§2(1). . . . [U]nless the context otherwise requires . . . the term "security" means any note, stock, . . . bond, debenture, evidence of indebtedness, certificate of interest or participation in any profit-sharing agreement, . . . transferable share, investment contract, . . . certificate of deposit for a security, fractional undivided interest in oil, gas or other mineral rights, . . . or, in general, any interest or instrument commonly known as a "security". . . .

This definition has been interpreted broadly. Courts focus on the substance of a transaction rather than its form. In *SEC v. W. J. Howey Co.* the Supreme Court adhered to this principle and established the general test for a security.[3] In that case, the W. J. Howey Company (Howey), which owned 500 acres of citrus groves in Florida, offered 250 acres to the public. The company sold each purchaser a narrow strip of the grove (one sale, for example, consisted of about two thirds of an acre) on a land installment contract, with the deed to be delivered to the buyer when the last installment was paid. Howey also offered a service contract for maintaining the acreage. This contract required pooling the proceeds of the whole crop and distributing those proceeds *pro rata* to the individual investors. The Supreme Court held that the combination of the land contract, service contract, and deed as a package constituted an "investment contract," which is specifically named as a security under the definition. In arriving at its findings, the Court listed the following three characteristics of a security: (1) A contract, transaction or scheme whereby a person invests money in a common enterprise, (2) whose investors have reasonable expectations of profit, and (3) whose profits are derived solely from the efforts of persons other than the investors.

Investment of Money in Common Enterprise

The first characteristic stipulated by the *Howey* definition requires that *money* be invested in a *common enterprise.* An investment of labor will not satisfy.[4] A common enterprise has been defined as "one in which the fortunes of the investor are interwoven and dependent upon the efforts and success of those seeking the investment." Some courts have held that it is sufficient if the success of each investor is tied to the efforts of the promoter. For these courts it is not necessary for an investor's return to be linked to other investors' participation in the scheme.

Expectation of Profit

The second prong of the *Howey* definition requires that investors have reasonable expectations of profit. For example, stock purchased by low-income investors in a low-rent cooperative project has been held not to be a security. The stock was not purchased with an expectation of profit but to acquire subsidized low-cost housing. The context of the transaction excluded this stock from being deemed a security.[5]

---

[3] 328 U.S. 293 (1946).

[4] *International Brotherhood of Teamsters v. Daniel,* 439 U.S. 551 (1979).

[5] *United Housing Foundation v. Foreman,* 421 U.S. 837 (1975).

Derivation of Profits

The third element of the *Howey* test of a security requires that the profits be derived solely from the efforts of those other than the investors. Investors who are actively involved in the operation of the enterprise normally do not need the assistance of the securities law. They are in a position to protect themselves.

Slight investor activity will not remove an investment from the category of a security. In *SEC v. Glenn Turner Enterprises,* Dare to Be Great, a wholly owned subsidiary of Glenn Turner Enterprises, offered sales courses.[6] Purchasers paid for the privilege of receiving lessons aimed at self-improvement and sales ability plus the *opportunity to help sell the course to others* in return for a commission. The Ninth Circuit Court of Appeals found that what was being sold was not the usual "business motivation" course; instead, the buyer was purchasing the possibility of deriving profits from the sale of Dare to Be Great courses. The court applied the *Howey* test and wrestled with the requirement that profits must be derived *solely* from the efforts of others. In examining the nature of the Securities Act, the court recognized the policy of affording broad protection to the investor. In adhering to this policy, the court interpreted the third prong of the *Howey* test to be satisfied if the promoters' efforts are significant— "those essential managerial efforts which affect the failure or success of the enterprise."

The following case, involving the sale of a business by transfer of its stock, applies the principles of identifying a security.

Frederiksen v. Poloway

637 F.2d 1147 (7th Cir. 1981)

North Shore Marina (NSM) sold, serviced, and provided storage facilities for boats. Jefferey Frederiksen (appellant) and Emerald City Corporation (ECC) (appellant) bought the assets and stock of NSM from Edward Poloway, the president and sole shareholder of NSM. The agreement between ECC and NSM provided that ECC would employ Poloway for five years. In return for Poloway's assistance and expertise he was to receive $32,000 a year plus 20 percent commission on the sale of boats and other related activities.

A management agreement gave ECC authority to operate and manage

---

[6] 474 F.2d 476 (9th Cir. 1973).

the marina facilities and receive 50 percent of the gross income from the operation of the marina. The remainder of the revenues were to be applied to the corporation's expenses.

ECC terminated its employment agreement with Poloway before the expiration of the five years. Poloway filed suit against ECC and Frederiksen in the state court for breach of contract. ECC and Frederiksen filed a suit in the U.S. District Court alleging that Poloway's conduct in connection with the sale of stock violated the federal securities laws. Poloway moved to dismiss the suit. The court granted the motion on the grounds that the sale of the stock did not involve a sale of a security. The Seventh Circuit Court of Appeals affirmed the dismissal.

Sprecher, Circuit Judge

The critical legal issue in this case is whether the plaintiffs' acquisition of North Shore Marina involves a "security" within the meaning of the . . . securities acts. . . .

* * * * *

We now turn to plaintiffs' claim that the interest they acquired in NSM constitute "securities" within the meaning of the federal securities laws. First, plaintiffs argue that ECC's purchase of NSM stock falls under the literal wording of the federal securities laws and, for that reason, a legal presumption exists that a security was sold. There are several problems with this "literal application" theory.

The first problem is that the language in the securities acts is not as broad as the plaintiffs contend. . . . The definition of "security" in the Securities Act of 1933 is prefaced by [the phrase "unless the context otherwise requires"].

The second problem is that it is not the case that any conduct within the theoretical reach of a statute is necessarily governed by that statute. . . .

It is a familiar rule, that a thing may be within the letter of the statute and yet not within the statute, because not within its spirit, nor within the intention of its makers.

The third problem with the plaintiffs' "literal application" argument is that the [U.S. Supreme Court has] specifically rejected that argument. . . .

"[I]n searching for the meaning and scope of the word 'security' . . . form should be disregarded for substance and the emphasis should be on economic reality.". . .

* * * * *

. . . Here, in contrast, the transaction did not involve a sale of corporate stock to raise capital for profitmaking purposes. The plaintiffs sought to acquire NSM's business in its entirety. The "stock" sale was a method used to vest ECC with ownership of that business. There was no offer of investment "securities." The stock of NSM merely was passed incidentally as an indicia of ownership of the business assets sold to ECC. For the above reasons, we reject the plaintiffs' "literal application" theory.

Plaintiffs' second argument is that the transaction here meets the requirements of a securities investment under the "economic reality" test. . . . The "economic reality" test for determining the existence of a security involves three elements: (1) an investment in a common venture; (2) premised on a reasonable expectation of profits;

(3) to be derived from the entrepreneurial or managerial efforts of others. The first and third elements of this analysis are in issue here.

The first element of the "economic reality" test is whether there is an investment in a common venture. . . .

. . . [A] sharing or pooling of funds is required to satisfy the test for a common enterprise. Plaintiffs suggest that because Mr. Poloway received a 20% commission on NSM sales, they and Mr. Poloway "shared" their profits, and, thus, there was an investment in a common enterprise. But merely stating the plaintiffs' argument reveals its hollowness. After the sale, Mr. Poloway was an employee of ECC, not a participant in an enterprise whose profits were shared. The fact that an employee receives partial compensation in commissions on sales does not transform an employment contract into a securities investment.

The third element of the "economic reality" test—that profits be derived from efforts of others—presents an even more difficult hurdle for the plaintiffs. Plaintiffs argue that they had no experience in the business of selling and servicing boats and that they relied completely on the managerial efforts and expertise of Mr. Poloway. The first problem with this argument is that it is contradicted by materials in the record on appeal.

Contrary to plaintiffs' argument, the record discloses that the plaintiffs, not Mr. Poloway, were responsible for the continued management of NSM. . . .

The second problem with the plaintiffs' attempt to meet the source-of-profit requirement of the "economic reality" analysis is that the employment relationship they created with Mr. Poloway is not legally sufficient to meet that requirement. . . . As the Ninth Circuit stated . . . the test for determining whether the reliance element has been met is "whether the efforts made by those other than the investor are the undeniably significant ones, those essential managerial efforts which affect the failure or success of the enterprise.". . .

To be sure, ECC expected, and by contract required, Mr. Poloway to give his "best efforts" and "expertise" to NSM and ECC. But Mr. Poloway, as an employee, was not responsible for those "essential managerial decisions," . . . affecting the conduct of the business. Indeed, Mr. Poloway's "best efforts" were specified by the employment agreement to be "within the goals, guidelines, directives, policies, and procedures" of ECC.

Because ECC so strongly assumed management control when it purchased NSM, the ECC efforts were clearly not "nominal or limited.". . . Although ECC certainly depended on Mr. Poloway to be a good employee, the fact that plaintiffs took over and operated the business clearly demonstrates that they were not "relying" on Mr. Poloway within the concept of a securities investment.

For the above reasons, we find that this matter does not properly come within the scope of the federal securities laws, under either the "literal application" or the "economic reality" theory.

CASE QUESTIONS

1. What is the "literal application" theory? Why was that theory not applicable to the sale of the NSM stock? Do you agree with the court? Explain.

2. What is the "economic reality" theory? Why was the stock not considered a security under that theory?

3. What if ECC had purchased only 51 percent of the outstanding stock in NSM? Would that constitute a sale of a security? What about the purchase of an amount less than 50 percent which constitutes a controlling interest?

4. Assume that Poloway would have been given shared managerial responsibilities with Frederiksen. Would that fact change the outcome of the case?

5. Assume that Frederiksen purchased 100 percent of the stock from Poloway and that Frederiksen did not intend to manage the company but entrusted the management to Poloway. Then later Frederiksen takes a more active role in the management. Does the purchase transaction involve a sale of a security? At the time of the sale? When Frederiksen became more active? What problems do you see in applying this "sale of business doctrine?"

MARKETING SECURITIES

Within the normal process of distributing securities there are issuers, underwriters, dealers, and investors. They perform similar roles as manufacturers, wholesalers, retailers, and ultimate consumers in the area of product distribution (see Figure 8–2). The issuer is generally the person or entity that originates the securities. These securities are ultimately offered and sold to investors. Underwriters are often employed to aid in the distribution effort. Underwriters sell securities for issuers or purchase securities from issuers for resale. Banks, investment institutions, and underwriting firms perform underwriting services. The underwriter's outlet is brokers and dealers (broker-dealer). Brokers purchase and sell securities for others. Dealers are in the business of purchasing and selling securities for themselves. A broker-dealer may be a small local business with one employee or a large national brokerage firm employing thousands, like Merrill Lynch and E. F. Hutton.

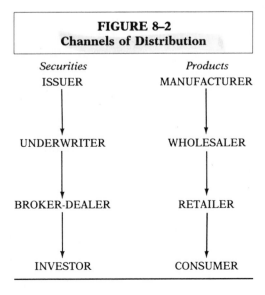

FIGURE 8–2
Channels of Distribution

Securities	*Products*
ISSUER	MANUFACTURER
↓	↓
UNDERWRITER	WHOLESALER
↓	↓
BROKER-DEALER	RETAILER
↓	↓
INVESTOR	CONSUMER

There are basically two types of underwriting: firm commitment and best efforts.

Firm Commitment

Under a firm commitment the underwriter is obligated to purchase a designated number of shares of securities from the issuer at a specified price. An underwriter that makes such a commitment prearranges to sell the securities through brokers at a markup. The brokers then sell the securities at retail to the public. To illustrate this process, assume that an underwriter makes a firm commitment to buy 100,000 shares of stock from an issuer, XYZ, Inc., at $31 a share. The underwriter sells the stock to brokers at $32 a share, and the brokers in turn sell the stock to the investing public at $33 a share. The underwriter's gross profit is $100,000, and the brokers enjoy a gross profit of $1 times the number of shares they sell. If the underwriter is unable to sell all or any portion of its undertaking, it must assume the loss. There is no recourse against the issuer under firm commitment underwriting.

Best Efforts

Under a best efforts commitment the underwriter acts for the issuer and expends its best efforts to sell the securities to brokers. In return the underwriter receives a commission on the sales it makes. Under this type of distribution the underwriter is not obligated to sell any designated quantity of securities.

REGISTRATION

All securities must be registered with the SEC unless they are exempt.

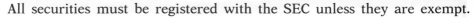

Securities Act
§5(a)(1). Unless a registration statement is in effect . . . it shall be unlawful for any person . . . to . . . use . . . any means . . . of . . . interstate commerce or . . . the mails to sell [a] security. . . .

A security may not be offered for sale until a registration statement is filed and becomes effective. The registration statement is designed to assure that a person selling securities discloses all material information related to the sale. Investors may use the information contained in the registration statement to make an informed decision.

The SEC examines the statement to make sure that there has been disclosure about the company and the securities it intends to offer for sale. As long as the statement is complete, the commission cannot deny the registration. The commission, however, does not vouch for the financial condition of the company or the fairness of the terms of the securities offering. The investor, not the commission, bears the burden and the risk of evaluating the worth of the security. Neither does the commission guarantee the accuracy of the information contained in the registration statement. There are, however, criminal laws that prohibit a registrant from making false or misleading representations under pain of fine and imprisonment. In addition, an investor who suffers financial injury due to a material misrepresentation in the registration statement may pursue civil remedies, discussed later in this chapter.

The registration statement offers detailed information about the registrant's business and properties; the management, control, and operation of the business; the securities that are to be offered for sale; and the company's financial condition. This information is available for public inspection. Additionally, a prospectus must be given to each person to whom a security is offered for sale. A *prospectus* is a pamphlet that capsulizes the information contained in the registration statement. Figure 8–3 illustrates the contents of a typical prospectus. Sometimes the registration statement and the prospectus are referred to collectively as the "registration statement." Preparation of these documents is very costly. It involves the work of lawyers, accountants, financial analysts, management specialists, and other experts.

The registration process may be divided into the prefiling, waiting, and posteffective periods.

Prefiling Period

The prefiling period is the time before a registration statement is filed. The Securities Act prohibits offers to buy or sell during the prefiling period. The act does not prohibit preliminary negotiations or agreements between issuers and underwriters. Thus, during this prefiling stage the issuer may begin to set up its network for distribution of the securities in anticipation of its eventual offering.

Offers are not confined to formal proposals. The SEC considers unusual publicity about the proposed securities or the issuer's business to be part of a sales effort to condition the public. Offers disguised as speeches or writings are considered "gun jumping," which is prohibited by the act during this stage. An SEC rule does permit an issuer to release news of a proposed offering that contains only the name of the issuer and the purpose and terms of a proposed issue. The name of the underwriters may not be mentioned in the news release.

FIGURE 8–3
Table of Contents—Prospectus

TABLE OF CONTENTS

No person is authorized to give any information or to make any representations other than those contained or incorporated by reference in this Prospectus and, if given or made, such information or representations must not be relied upon as having been authorized. This Prospectus does not constitute an offer to sell or a solicitation of an offer to buy any securities other than the securities to which it relates. This Prospectus does not constitute an offer to sell or a solicitation of an offer to buy such securities in any circumstances in which such offer or solicitation is unlawful. Neither the delivery of this Prospectus nor any sale made hereunder shall, under any circumstances, create any implication that there has been no change in the affairs of the Company since the date hereof or that the information herein is correct as of any time subsequent to its date.

Archer-Daniels-Midland Company

$250,000,000
7% Debentures due May 15, 2011

$125,000,000
16% Sinking Fund Debentures
due May 15, 2011

Goldman, Sachs & Co.

Kidder, Peabody & Co.
Incorporated

Merrill Lynch White Weld
Capital Markets Group
Merrill Lynch, Pierce, Fenner & Smith Incorporated

Representatives of the Underwriters

Figure 8–4
Tombstone Ad

2,000,000 Shares

Common Stock
($.10 par value)

Price $15 Per Share

Upon request, a copy of the Prospectus describing these securities and the business of the Company may be obtained within any State from any Underwriter who may legally distribute it within such State. The securities are offered only by means of the Prospectus, and this announcement is neither an offer to sell nor a solicitation of any offer to buy.

Goldman, Sachs & Co.

Alex. Brown & Sons
Incorporated

Piper, Jaffray & Hopwood
Incorporated

Bear, Stearns & Co.　　The First Boston Corporation　　Becker Paribas　　Dillon, Read & Co. Inc.
Incorporated

Drexel Burnham Lambert　　Hambrecht & Quist　　E. F. Hutton & Company Inc.
Incorporated　　　　　　　　Incorporated

Kidder, Peabody & Co.　　Lazard Frères & Co.　　Lehman Brothers
Incorporated　　　　　　　　　　　　　　Shearson Lehman/ American Express Inc.

Merrill Lynch Capital Markets　　Paine Webber　　Prudential-Bache　　Robertson, Colman & Stephens
Incorporated　　Securities

L. F. Rothschild, Unterberg, Towbin　　Salomon Brothers Inc　　Smith Barney, Harris Upham & Co.
Incorporated

Wertheim & Co., Inc.　　Dean Witter Reynolds Inc.　　Dain Bosworth
Incorporated

ABD Securities Corporation　　Advest, Inc.　　Allen & Company　　Arnhold and S. Bleichroeder, Inc.
Incorporated

Atlantic Capital　　Robert W. Baird & Co.　　Bateman Eichler, Hill Richards　　William Blair & Company
Corporation　　Incorporated　　Incorporated

Blunt Ellis & Loewi　　Boettcher & Company, Inc.　　J. C. Bradford & Co.　　Butcher & Singer Inc.
Incorporated　　　　　　　　　　　　　　Incorporated

Cowen & Co.　　F. Eberstadt & Co., Inc.　　A. G. Edwards & Sons, Inc.　　Eppler, Guerin & Turner, Inc.

EuroPartners Securities Corporation　　First Southwest Company　　Robert Fleming
Incorporated

Gruntal & Co., Incorporated　　Interstate Securities Corporation　　Janney Montgomery Scott Inc.

Josephthal & Co.　　Kleinwort, Benson　　Ladenburg, Thalmann & Co. Inc.　　Legg Mason Wood Walker
Incorporated　　Incorporated　　　　　　　　　　　　　　　　　Incorporated

McDonald & Company　　Moseley, Hallgarten, Estabrook & Weeden Inc.　　The Ohio Company
Securities. Inc.

Oppenheimer & Co., Inc.　　Prescott, Ball & Turben, Inc.　　Rauscher Pierce Refsnes, Inc.

Robinson Humphrey/American Express Inc　　Rotan Mosle Inc.　　Rothschild Inc.

Sogen Securities Corporation　　Sutro & Co.　　Swiss Bank Corporation International Securities Inc.
Incorporated

Tucker, Anthony & R. L. Day, Inc.　　Underwood, Neuhaus & Co.　　Wheat, First Securities, Inc.
Incorporated

Bacon Stifel Nicolaus　　The Chicago Corporation　　Craig-Hallum, Inc.
Stifel. Nicolaus & Company, Incorporated

J. J. B. Hilliard, W. L. Lyons, Inc.　　John G. Kinnard and Company　　Manley, Bennett, McDonald & Co.
Incorporated　　　　　　　　　　Incorporated

Newhard, Cook & Co.　　Parker/Hunter　　Scherck, Stein & Franc, Inc.
Incorporated　　　　Incorporated

June 6, 1984

Waiting Period

The interlude between filing and the time when the registration becomes effective is called the waiting period. During this period the SEC examines the registration to ensure its completeness. Sales are not permitted during this period. Oral offers can be made, but written offers are expressly prohibited unless they conform to SEC requirements. The most common form of compliance is a preliminary prospectus that summarizes the information contained in the registration statement. This prospectus is commonly referred to as a *red herring prospectus* because it requires a special legend printed in red. The legend states that the securities may not be sold and offers to buy may not be accepted before the registration statement becomes effective. The SEC further requires that copies of the preliminary prospectus be distributed to persons intending to solicit customers and to any customers requesting a copy.

During the waiting period the SEC also permits the distribution of notices which include identifying information and legends specifying that they are not an offer to sell or a solicitation of an offer to buy the securities. These notices appear in newspapers. Because they are often bordered in black, they are termed *tombstone ads.* Figure 8–4 is an example of a tombstone ad.

Posteffective Period

The registration becomes effective 20 days after filing unless the registration process is accelerated or postponed by the commission. On that date, underwriters and dealers are free to offer and sell the securities. Before a registration becomes effective, the original registration statement, including the preliminary prospectus, must be amended to include prices and other information that may have been omitted. A prospectus must accompany a written offer to sell a security or a confirmation of its sale.

As the next case illustrates, any material developments after the effective data must be reported by amending the prospectus to include them.

Securities & Exchange Commission v. Manor Nursing Centers, Inc.

458 F.2d 1082 (2d Cir. 1972)

Ira Feinberg (appellant) owned a nursing home called 133 County Road. Together with Ivan Ezrine (appellant), an attorney, they decided to issue securities to raise public financing for Feinberg's nursing home business.

They formed a new corporation named Manor Nursing Centers, Inc. (Manor). Manor (appellant) acquired the assets of 133 County Road. Ezrine and Feinberg then determined that Manor and some of its shareholders would offer 450,000 shares of common stock at $10/share. They hoped to raise close to $4 million to fund the operation of the nursing home.

Ezrine prepared and filed the registration statement. According to the terms of the prospectus, the offering was made on condition that all 450,000 shares would be sold. The proceeds were to be received within 90 days; otherwise all funds were to be returned to the purchasers. The registration statement also affirmed that the shares would be sold for cash only and that no brokerage commissions would be paid unless the issue was fully subscribed (that is, all 450,000 shares were sold). The prospectus did not disclose that any special compensation beyond the normal commissions was to be given to any brokers for their agreement to participate in the offering.

From the outset the underwriter experienced difficulty in selling the shares. As a result, brokers were given special compensation by way of Manor shares and a loan guarantee as an enticement to participate in the offering. Ezrine and Feinberg paid their broker and attorney in shares of stock rather than cash, and Manor creditors were given shares of stock in lieu of outstanding indebtedness. Before the offering was fully subscribed, commissions and payments to sellers were made. Also the underwriter issued checks to Manor and the selling stockholders.

Erzine amended the registration statement and prospectus and filed them with the SEC. The amendment stated that the entire Manor issue had been sold, though it had not. It failed to mention the special compensation paid to brokers.

The SEC brought an action against the appellants, alleging, among other offenses, that they violated the prospectus-delivery requirement of the 1933 Securities Act. The district court found the appellants in violation, and the court of appeals affirmed that finding.

Timbers, Circuit Judge

Section 5(b)(2) prohibits the delivery of a security for the purpose of sale unless the security is accompanied or preceded by a prospectus which meets the requirements of . . . the 1933 Act. . . . To meet the requirements . . . a prospectus must contain, with specified exemptions, all "the information contained in the registration statement. . . ." In turn, the registration statement . . . must set forth certain information specified in . . . the 1933 Act. . . .

Among the items of information [the Act] requires the registration statement, and therefore the prospectus, to contain are the use of proceeds, the estimated net proceeds, the price at which the security will be offered to the public and any variation therefrom, and all commissions or discounts paid to underwriters, directly or indirectly.

The Manor prospectus purported to disclose the information required by the above items. . . . The evidence adduced at trial showed, however, that developments subsequent to the effective date of the registration statement made this information false and misleading. Moreover, Manor and its principals did not amend or supplement the prospectus to reflect the changes which had made inaccurate the information which [the Act] required the prospectus to disclose. We hold that implicit in the statutory provision that the prospectus contain certain information is the requirement that such information be true and correct. A prospectus does not meet the requirements . . . if information required to be disclosed is materially false or misleading. Appellants violated §5(b)(2) by delivering Manor securities for sale accompanied by a prospectus which did not meet the requirements of [the Act] in that the prospectus contained materially false and misleading statements with respect to information required . . . to be disclosed.

Manor contends, however, that §5(b)(2) does not require that a prospectus be amended to reflect material developments which occur subsequent to the effective date of the registration statement. This contention is premised on the assumptions that the prospectus spoke only as of the effective date of the registration statement and that the prospectus contained no false or misleading statements as of the effective date. . . .

In support of their argument that the prospectus need not be amended or supplemented to reflect post-effective developments, appellants cite an administrative decision in which the SEC held that it will not issue a stop order with respect to a registration statement which becomes misleading subsequent to its effective date because of material post-effective events. Under this line of SEC decisions, a registration statement need not be amended after its effective date to reflect post-effective developments. These decisions, however, are not apposite here. Assuming that the registration statement does speak as of its effective date and that Manor did not have to amend its registration statement, appellants were obliged to reflect the post-effective developments referred to above in the prospectus. Even those SEC decisions holding that the registration statement need not be amended to reflect post-effective developments recognize that the prospectus must be amended or supplemented in some manner to reflect such changes. . . . There is no authority for the proposition that a prospectus speaks always as of the effective date of the registration statement.

We hold that appellants were under a duty to amend or supplement the Manor prospectus to reflect post-effective developments; that their failure to do so stripped the Manor prospectus of compliance with [the Act].

CASE QUESTIONS

1. Name some items a prospectus must contain. What is the reason for each?

2. What change occurred in the terms of the offering after the registration statement was filed? Did Manor do anything to reflect those changes? Explain.

3. What argument did Manor make in its contention that it did not violate the act? Why was that argument rejected?

4. Name some ways Manor could have avoided legal problems.

Shelf Registration

The SEC has adopted a rule that permits issuers to delay the effective registration period for up to two years. Under this shelf registration procedure the issuer is in a better position to time an offering with the market conditions. The issuing firm may file a single registration with the SEC and place designated securities "on the shelf" to be issued at a later date. Then, when the market conditions are favorable for issuance, the firm can enter the market, taking the securities "off the shelf." The issuer need not publish a new registration statement or detailed prospectus. Shelf registration is available only to large companies. Studies have shown that the primary benefit of shelf registration is the substantial cost savings to registrants.

EXEMPTIONS

The filing of a registration statement is very costly, as it involves careful preparation by accountants, attorneys, and other professionals. These cost considerations tend to discourage the issuance of securities as a means of raising capital, unless they can be issued under an exemption. Some exemptions are made for securities issued by the government or charitable institutions. The following are the exemptions most relevant to the businessperson:

— Transactions by persons other than issuers and underwriters
— Private placements
— Limited offerings
— Intrastate offerings

It must be noted, however, that qualifying under an exemption does not relieve the issuer from the antifraud provisions of the securities laws (discussed later in this chapter and in chapter 9).

Persons Other than Issuer

Section 4(1) exempts "transactions by any person other than an issuer, underwriter or dealer." Since most transactions by dealers are exempt, under another section, almost all offerings other than the first offering are free from the registration requirements of the Securities Act. The resale, or secondary trading, of a security may, however, be subject to registration under the Securities Exchange Act of 1934, which is treated in the next chapter.

Private Placements

Section 4(2) of the Securities Act exempts "transactions by an issuer not involving any public offering." In order to qualify for this preferred exempt status, an offering must be confined to selected purchasers that have access to the same type of information provided by registration. These purchasers also must be sophisticated enough to evaluate the merits of the offering. This category includes insurance companies, pension funds, and other institutional investors that meet the "access" and "sophistication" criteria. Sales to these investors pose no threat to the public and are routinely honored as legitimate private placement exemptions by the SEC. In fact, these institutional investors are normally able to command more information from the issuer than is required for registration.

The private placement exemption is also used in corporate securities offerings to employees of the corporation. In *SEC v. Ralston Purina Co.*[7] the Supreme Court clarified that the validity of a private offering exemption is determined by whether the offerees need the protection of the Securities Act. If they have sufficient information, knowledge, and skill to fend for themselves, then they do not need the disclosures registration provides. In *Ralston* "key employees" were given the option of purchasing treasury stock in the corporation.[8] A key employee was defined as "one who is eligible for promotion, an individual who especially influences others or who advises others, a person whom the employees look to in some special way, an individual, of course, who carries some special responsibility, who is sympathetic to management and who is ambitious and who the management feels is likely to be promoted to a greater responsibility." Employees from a variety of job positions, including artist, bakeshop foreman, electrician, stenographer, and veterinarian, responded to the opportunity to purchase the stock. The Supreme Court, in denying that this constituted a private offering under section 4(2), ruled that Ralston failed to show that the employees had "access to the kind of information which registration would disclose."

Under Section 4(2) and the cases interpreting that section there is no magic formula that will ensure the exempt status of a promotional offering. The following case, involving limited partnership interests in cable television systems, illustrates the restrictiveness of the private placement exemption under section 4(2).

Securities and Exchange Commission v. Murphy

626 F.2d 633 (9th Cir. 1980)

Stephen Murphy (appellant) organized and controlled Intertie. Intertie, in connection with International Securities Corporation (ISC), a securities

---

[7] 346 U.S. 119 (1953).

[8] Treasury stock is usually issued to shareholders and then repurchased by the corporation. Sometimes it includes authorized but unissued shares of stock. This was the case in *Ralston.*

brokerage firm, promoted about 30 limited partnerships to which it sold cable television systems.

Intertie would first buy a cable television system. It would make a cash down payment on the system and finance the remainder. Then it would sell the system to one of the limited partnerships for a cash down payment and notes promising to repay the balance. Finally, Intertie would lease the system back from the partnership.

Neither Intertie nor ISC registered the limited partnership interests as securities. They relied on the private offering exemption of section 4(2) of the Securities Act.

The SEC brought suit, charging Murphy with fraud and failure to register a security. The district court granted summary judgment in favor of the SEC and granted an injunction against Murphy. The court of appeals affirmed the district court decision.

Ferguson, Circuit Judge

Elements of a Section 5 Violation

Section 5 of the 1933 Act forbids the offer or sale of unregistered securities in interstate commerce, but §5 does not apply if the securities are exempt from registration as a private offering. . . .

*   *   *   *   *

Not Exempt from Registration

Murphy contends that the limited partnership interests were exempt from registration under the private offering exemption in §4(2) of the 1933 Act, which . . . exempt[s] certain private placements. [This exemption] from registration [is] . . . construed narrowly. . . . Once the SEC introduces evidence that a defendant has violated the registration provisions, the defendant then has the burden of proof in showing entitlement to an exemption.

*   *   *   *   *

A court assessing the availability of a private offering exemption focuses upon the issuer and the offerees, paying particular attention to the relationship between the two. This assessment often requires a careful inquiry into the facts surrounding the offering . . . and, of course, it requires knowledge of who was the issuer of the securities. [The court found that Intertie was the issuer of the securities.—Au.]

*   *   *   *   *

Private Offering Exemption: §4(2)

For nearly 30 years, the Supreme Court's opinion in *SEC v. Ralston Purina Co.* . . . has provided the framework for private offering analysis. In *Ralston Purina*, the Court held: "[T]he applicability of [§4(2)] should turn on whether the particular class of persons affected needs the protection of the Act. An offering to those who are shown to be able to fend for themselves is a transaction 'not involving any public offering.'". . .

Building on these concepts, courts have developed flexible tests for the private offering exemption, focusing upon: (1) the number of offerees; (2) the sophistication of the offerees; (3) the size and manner of the offering; and (4) the relationship of the offerees to the issuer. . . . The party claiming the exemption must show that it is met not only with respect to each purchaser, but also with respect to each offeree.

1. The Number of Offerees

The *Ralston Purina* decision made it clear that there was no rigid limit to the number of offerees to whom an issuer could make a private offering. Nonetheless, while the number of offerees, itself, is not decisive, "the more offerees, the more likelihood that the offering is public." Murphy introduced no evidence below to suggest that the number of offerees was small or that there was even any attempt to monitor the number of offerees at all.

The SEC introduced Murphy's deposition, in which he stated that offering memoranda were not numbered. Apparently, then, no one knows how many offerees ISC contacted on any of the partnership offerings. Once the SEC provided evidence that there was no control placed on the number of offerees, it was incumbent upon Murphy . . . to rebut that evidence. . . .

*   *   *   *   *

. . . When we look at the number of purchasers in the aggregate, as we must, their number—400—clearly suggests a public offering rather than a private placement.

2. The Sophistication of the Offerees

It was also incumbent upon Murphy to introduce evidence to rebut the inferences of lack of investor sophistication that the court could have drawn from Murphy's deposition testimony. His statement that 60 percent of the investors used offeree representatives suggests at least that the majority of the purchasers, if not the majority of the offerees, lacked the sort of business acumen necessary to qualify as sophisticated investors. Moreover, Murphy's admission that offeree representatives who were also sales-

men and general partners in the cable systems did not disclose this relationship to prospective investors suggests the inadequacy of the representatives. His further testimony that some of the offeree representatives whom he met were incompetent reveals both that the investors needed the protection of the Act and that Murphy and Intertie were not concerned about investor sophistication. Intertie did not obtain information about the investors in the limited partnerships, nor did it insist that ISC do so. Murphy merely stated that Intertie relied on ISC to qualify the investors, but he did not produce evidence suggesting that ISC actually took any such steps.

*   *   *   *   *

3. The Size and Manner of the Offering

If an offering is small and is made directly to the offerees "rather than through the facilities of public distribution such as investment bankers or the securities exchange," a court is more likely to find that it is private. The SEC's evidence shows that the amounts invested in individual systems varied, but that the purchase price for several of the systems was more than $1 million each. Viewed individually, these offerings cannot automatically be labeled small; and there is reason to believe that they should not be viewed individually in any case. When we consider the placements as one integrated offering, we are confronted with a sale of $7.5 million in securities. Without question, that is a sizeable offering, and it is one that we are inclined to consider as public, absent a significant showing that the investors did not need the protection of the Act. . . .

4. The Relationship between the Issuer and the Offeree

A court may only conclude that the investors do not need the protection of the Act if all the offerees have relationships with the issuer affording them access to or disclosure of the sort of information about the issuer that registration reveals. As with the other requirements discussed, after the SEC demonstrated that the requisite relationship did not exist, it was incumbent upon the defendant to produce evidence that the offerees had available the necessary information. . . . Included in [the required] information is the use of investor funds, the amount of direct and indirect commissions, and accurate financial statements. Intertie supplied almost none of this required information. In addition, there were a number of general facts of enormous importance regarding Intertie's operations that were omitted. Operating memoranda purported to show cash flow projections for individual systems but did not reveal that no system would be self-sustaining; thus, offerees did not know that because of Intertie's large short-term debt obligations, the continued viability of Intertie depended upon a consistent influx of new capital. These omissions contrast sharply with the Act's requirements for provision of information.

CASE QUESTIONS

1. Describe the arrangement between Intertie and its investors. How did that benefit Intertie? What was the benefit to investors?

2. What factors are relevant in determining whether an offering is exempt under section 4(2)?

3. Why did the offering fail to qualify as a private exempt offering? Explain.

4. What precautions could Murphy, Intertie, and ICS have taken to ensure private offering status?

Limited Offerings

Certain small issues are exempt from full registration. Section 3(b) of the Securities Act authorizes the SEC to exempt offerings not exceeding $5 million when "by reason of the small amount involved or the limited character of the public offering" registration is not necessary.

Regulation A   Pursuant to section 3(b) the SEC adopted Regulation A. To qualify for this limited exemption the issue cannot exceed a total amount of $1,500,000 within a one-year period. The exemption is not available to those who have been convicted of securities offenses.

Regulation A provides a faster and less expensive procedure than full registration. Instead of filing a registration statement with the SEC in Washington, an issuer files a notice and an offering circular at a regional office at least 10 days before the proposed offering. The offering circular is a "mini-registration" form. Financial statements need not be audited, nor is a prospectus required. However, an offering circular must be given to every offeree.

Regulation D   The SEC has enacted Regulation D, which contains rules simplifying the exemptions for limited offerings. These exemptions are designed to make it easier for small businesses to qualify for exemption and hence raise capital to meet their needs. An important term related to Regulation D rules is *accredited investor*. Accredited investors include:

— Certain institutional investors such as banks, insurance companies, and charitable institutions
— Directors, officers, or general partners of the issuer
— Persons who purchase at least $150,000 of the securities offered for sale as long as the purchase price does not exceed 20 percent of the purchaser's net worth
— Any person whose net worth exceeds $1,000,000
— Persons with an annual income exceeding $200,000

These accredited investors do not need the full protection of registration. In many instances they are in a position to obtain more information than registration requires. Nonaccredited investors are those who do not meet the above qualifications.

Generally, the issuer may not publicly advertise securities sold under a Regulation D exemption. The issuer must also take precautions to ensure that the purchasers do not resell the securities without registering them or meeting another exemption from registration.

Rule 504   This rule under Regulation D permits a sale of up to $500,000 of securities within any 12-month period to any number of purchasers, accredited or nonaccredited. The issuer need not furnish information to the purchasers.

Rule 505   Under this rule an issuer may sell up to $5 million of securities within any 12-month period to an unlimited number of accredited purchasers and up to 35 nonaccredited purchasers. If there are any nonaccredited purchasers, then all purchasers are entitled to information.

Rule 506   An issuer under Rule 506 is permitted to sell an unlimited amount of securities to accredited investors and up to 35 nonaccredited purchasers. To take advantage of this rule, the issuer must reasonably believe that each nonaccredited purchaser, or purchaser's representative, has sufficient knowledge or experience to evaluate the merits of the risk of the investment. If there are any nonaccredited purchasers, then all purchasers must be furnished information.

Intrastate Offerings

The Securities Act provides an exemption for any security offered and sold only to residents within a single state or territory. To qualify, the issuer of the security must be a resident and doing business within the state or territory. If the issuer is a corporation, it must be incorporated and doing business within the state or territory. The exemption is quite narrow, as the SEC and the courts have been very strict in their interpretation of "doing business within the state." To take advantage of this exemption, the issuer must do substantial business in the state. In addition, each *offeree* of the securities must be a resident of the same state. Offering the security to a nonresident of the state will invalidate the exemption for the whole issue. This virtually precludes the use of general advertising in the offering because of the possibility of communicating the offer to an out-of-state resident. This exemption was designed for purely local financing for local businesses accomplished by local investment.

Rule 147

To provide more objective standards for compliance with the intrastate exemption, the SEC adopted Rule 147, which defined some of the terms contained in the Securities Act's intrastate exemption.

*Person
Resident*

Rule 147 clarifies that the issuer of the securities be a resident of the state in which it is incorporated, or organized, or if an individual, the state in which the issuer has its principal residence. An offeree or purchaser must be a resident of the state in which the individual has his or her principal place of residence, or, if a corporation, where its principal office is located.

*Doing Business
Within*

An issuer is deemed to be doing business within the state if (1) it receives at least 80 percent of its gross revenues within the state, (2) at least 80 percent of its assets are within the state, (3) it intends to use at least 80 percent of the net proceeds from the offering within the state, and (4) its principal office is in the state.

Coming to Rest

An intrastate exemption is lost in the event that a security comes to rest in a nonresident. Under Rule 147 no part of an issue may be offered or resold outside the state for nine months following the date of the last sale by the issuer. Rule 147 also requires the issuer to take steps to prevent resale outside the state.

Compliance with Rule 147 is not the only way to qualify for the intrastate exemption, but it is the most secure way. Absent compliance with Rule 147, the case law and SEC interpretations prior to Rule 147 must be consulted to determine if the exemption is appropriate.

INTEGRATION

Rules of integration determine the relationship of one security to another. If securities are part of the same issue, they are *integrated*. If not for the rules of integration, an issuer could qualify for small offering status or private placement exemption status by dividing a larger issue into smaller components. The following are guidelines for determining whether the SEC will require offerings to be integrated:

— The issues are part of a single plan of financing
— The issues involve the same class of securities
— The issues were made at or about the same time
— The issues involve the same type of pricing
— The issues were made for the same general purpose

PRIVATE REMEDIES

Within the act there are sections that impose liability against specified persons who violate the Securities Act. These sections offer injured investors certain private remedies.

Misrepresentation in Registration Statement

Section 11 of the Securities Act imposes liability upon certain persons if the registration statement contains material untruths or omissions. Section 11 liability applies only when a registration statement has been filed. To recover under section 11, the purchaser must prove (1) a material misstatement in or omission from the registration statement and (2) monetary damages. Generally, it is not even necessary to prove reliance on the misstatement or omission. A person may recover despite having failed to examine the registration statement. The right of action exists even for secondary purchasers—those who did not buy the security as part of the initial offering.

The omission or untrue statement must concern a material fact. A material fact is one which, if correctly stated or disclosed, might have discouraged a prudent investor from purchasing the securities in question. Such facts might include impending litigation or new acquisitions, customers' delinquencies, proposed government controls that would affect the company, and loans to corporate officials.

Persons Liable   Section 11 imposes absolute liability on an issuer for violation of its provisions.[9] In addition, the following persons also may be liable:

— Every person who signed the registration statement
— Every director of the issuer at the time of registration
— Every person who consented to being named as a director or a future director
— Every accountant, engineer, appraiser, attorney, or other expert whose statement was used in the preparation of the registration statement
— Every underwriter

---

[9] The Securities Act imposes vicarious liability on "[e]very person who, by or through stock ownership, agency, or otherwise, . . . controls any person liable under sections [11 or 12] . . . unless the controlling person had no knowledge or reasonable grounds to believe in the existence of the facts by reason of which the liability of the controlled person is alleged to exist." 15 U.S.C § 77 (0) (1982).

Their liability is joint and several, so that the injured purchaser of the security may enforce a judgment against any one or any combination of the above defendants who are found liable.

Defenses

Several defenses are available to defendants under section 11. An action under section 11 must be brought within one year after discovery has been made by the exercise of reasonable diligence. In no event may an action be brought more than three years from the date of the original offer.

If a defendant can prove that the plaintiff knew of the untruth or omission, the claim will be defeated. In addition, before liability attaches, a relationship must be established between the decline in value of the security and the material untruth or omission. If the two are wholly unrelated and the defendant can demonstrate that the reduced value of the security resulted from other causes, such as economic trends, the claim will be defeated.

The most popular defense is the *due diligence defense.* This defense is available to all persons other than the issuer. It is the subject of the following case, which involves plaintiffs who purchased stock in a corporation constructing "bowling centers."

Escott v. BarChris Construction Corp.

283 F. Supp. 643 (S.D.N.Y. 1968)

BarChris, a company that built and sold bowling alleys, was founded by Vitolo and Pugliese, two men of limited education. They employed Russo, an accountant, who acted as chief executive officer; Kircher, a certified public accountant, who first became comptroller and then treasurer; Birnbaum, who was hired as house counsel and became secretary; Auslander, who sat on the board of directors; and Peat, Marwick, an accounting firm. Early in 1961 BarChris sold securities because it needed additional working capital. At the same time, it was having trouble collecting amounts due from some of its customers. It continued to build bowling alleys, but the industry was overbuilt. In May 1967 it made a futile effort to rehabilitate its financial condition by the sale of common stock. It then filed a bankruptcy petition and defaulted on the interest due on the securities.

Escott and other investors (plaintiffs) sued BarChris Construction Corporation, its directors, executive officers, legal counsel, and auditors (defendants) for material misrepresentations contained in the registration statement filed with the SEC. The district court awarded judgment to the plaintiffs.

McLean, District Judge

It is a prerequisite to liability under Section 11 of the Act that the fact which is falsely stated in a registration statement, or the fact that is omitted when it should have been stated to avoid misleading, be "material." The regulations of the Securities and Exchange Commission pertaining to the registration of securities define the word as follows:

> The term 'material' when used to qualify a requirement for the furnishing of information as to any subject, limits the information required to those matters as to which an average prudent investor ought reasonably to be informed before purchasing the security registered.

What are "matters as to which an average prudent investor ought reasonably to be informed"? It seems obvious that they are matters which such an investor needs to know before he can make an intelligent, informed decision whether or not to buy the security.

*   *   *   *   *

Judged by this test, there is no doubt that many of the misstatements and omissions in this prospectus were material. This is true of all of them which relate to the state of affairs in 1961, i.e., the overstatement of sales and gross profit for the first quarter, the understatement of contingent liabilities as of April 30, the overstatement of orders on hand, and the failure to disclose the true facts with respect to officers' loans, customers' delinquencies, application of proceeds, and the prospective operation of several alleys.

*   *   *   *   *

This leaves for consideration the errors in the 1960 balance sheet figures. . . . Current assets were overstated by approximately $600,000. Liabilities were understated by approximately $325,000. [There were other significant misstatements and omissions in the balance sheet—Au.].

*   *   *   *   *

. . . On all the evidence I find that these balance sheet errors were material within the meaning of Section 11.

*   *   *   *   *

I turn now to the question of whether defendants have proved their due diligence defenses. The position of each defendant will be separately considered.

Russo

Russo was, to all intents and purposes, the chief executive officer of BarChris. . . . He was familiar with all aspects of the business. . . . He acted on BarChris's behalf in making the financing agreements. . . . He talked with customers about their delinquencies. . . . He was thoroughly aware of BarChris's stringent financial condition. . . . He had personally advanced large sums to BarChris of which $175,000 remained unpaid. . . .

In short, Russo knew all the relevant facts. He could not have believed that there were no untrue statements or material omissions in the prospectus. Russo has no due diligence defenses.

Vitolo and Pugliese

They were the founders of the business who stuck with it to the end. Vitolo was president and Pugliese was vice president. . . .

Vitolo and Pugliese are each men of limited education. It is not hard to believe that for them the prospectus was difficult reading, if indeed they read it at all.

But whether it was or not is irrelevant. The liability of a director who signs a registration statement does not depend upon whether or not he read it or, if he did, whether or not he understood what he was reading.

And, in any case, Vitolo and Pugliese were not as naive as they claim to be. They were members of BarChris's executive committee. At meetings of that committee BarChris's affairs were discussed at length. They must have known what was going on. Certainly they knew of the inadequacy of cash in 1961. They knew of their own large advances to the company which remained unpaid. They knew that they had agreed not to deposit their checks until the financing proceeds were received. They knew and intended that part of the proceeds were to be used to pay their own loans.

. . . They could not have believed that the registration statement was wholly true and that no material facts had been omitted. And in any case, there is nothing to show that they made any investigation of anything which they may not have known about or understood. They have not proved their due diligence defenses.

Kircher

Kircher was treasurer of BarChris and its chief financial officer. He is a certified public accountant and an intelligent man. He was thoroughly familiar with BarChris's financial affairs. . . . He knew of the customers' delinquency problem. . . .

Moreover, as a member of the executive committee, Kircher was kept informed as to those branches of the business of which he did not have direct charge. He knew about the operation of alleys, present and prospective. . . . Kircher knew of the infirmities in customers' contracts included in the backlog figure.

Kircher worked on the preparation of the registration statement. . . .

Kircher's contention is that he had never before dealt with a registration statement, that he did not know what it should contain, and that he relied wholly on [experts] to guide him. He claims that it was their fault, not his, if there was anything wrong with it. . . .

. . . Knowing the facts, Kircher had reason to believe that the expertised portion of the prospectus, i.e., the 1960 figures, was in part incorrect. He could not shut his eyes to the facts and rely on Peat, Marwick for that portion.

As to the rest of the prospectus, knowing the facts, he did not have a reasonable ground to believe it to be true. On the contrary, he must have known that in part it was untrue. Under these circumstances, he was not entitled to sit back and place the blame on the lawyers for not advising him about it.

Kircher has not proved his due diligence defenses.

*   *   *   *   *

Birnbaum

Birnbaum was a young lawyer . . . who, after brief periods of employment by two different law firms and an equally brief period of practicing in his own firm, was employed by BarChris as house counsel and assistant secretary in October 1960. . . . He signed the later amendments, thereby becoming responsible for the accuracy of the prospectus in its final form.

*   *   *   *   *

It seems probable that Birnbaum did not know of many of the inaccuracies in the prospectus. He must, however, have appreciated some of them. In any case, he made no investigation and relied on the others to get it right. . . . [H]e was entitled to rely upon Peat, Marwick for the 1960 figures, for as far as appears, he had no personal knowledge of the company's books of account or financial transactions. . . . As a lawyer, he should have known his obligations under the statute. He should have known that he was required to make a reasonable investigation of the truth of all the statements in the unexpertised portion of the document which he signed. Having failed to make such an investigation, he did not have reasonable ground to believe that all these statements were true. Birnbaum has not established his due diligence defenses except as to the audited 1960 figures.

Auslander

Auslander was an "outside" director, i.e., one who was not an officer of Bar-Chris. . . .

In February and early March 1961, before accepting Vitolo's invitation, Auslander made some investigation of BarChris. He obtained Dun & Bradstreet reports which contained sales and earnings figures for periods earlier than December 31, 1960. He caused inquiry to be made of certain of BarChris's banks and was advised that they regarded BarChris favorably. . . .

On March 3, 1961, Auslander indicated his willingness to accept a place on the board. Shortly thereafter, on March 14, Kircher sent him a copy of BarChris's annual report for 1960. Auslander observed that BarChris's auditors were Peat, Marwick. . . . He thought well of them.

Auslander was elected a director on April 17, 1961. . . .

* * * * *

In considering Auslander's due diligence defenses, a distinction is to be drawn between the expertised and nonexpertised portions of the prospectus. As to the former, Auslander knew that Peat, Marwick had audited the 1960 figures. He believed them to be correct because he had confidence in Peat, Marwick. He had no reasonable ground to believe otherwise.

As to the non-expertised portions,

however, Auslander is in a different position. He seems to have been under the impression that Peat, Marwick was responsible for all the figures. This impression was not correct, as he would have realized if he had read the prospectus carefully. Auslander made no investigation of the accuracy of the prospectus. . . .

* * * * *

I find and conclude that Auslander has not established his due diligence defense with respect to the misstatements and omissions in those portions of the prospectus other than the audited 1960 figures.

* * * * *

Peat, Marwick

* * * * *

[Peat, Marwick was the accounting firm that audited BarChris's 1960 figures. The actual work was delegated to Berardi, the senior accountant. Berardi was not versed in the bowling industry, and this particular assignment was an extremely difficult one for someone as uninitiated as he. Berardi asked questions in order to prepare portions of the registration statement, and accepted the answer without independent verification—Au.].

* * * * *

Accountants should not be held to a standard higher than that recognized in their profession. I do not do so here. Berardi's review did not come up to that standard. He did not take some of the steps which Peat, Marwick's written program prescribed. He did not spend an adequate amount of time on a task of this magnitude. Most important of all, he was too easily satisfied with glib answers to his inquiries.

This is not to say that he should have made a complete audit. But there were enough danger signals in the materials which he did examine to require some further investigation on his part. Generally accepted accounting standards required such further investigation under these circumstances. It is not always sufficient merely to ask questions.

Here again, the burden of proof is on Peat, Marwick. I find that that burden has not been satisfied. I conclude that Peat, Marwick has not established its due diligence defense.

CASE QUESTIONS

1. What were the material omissions in the BarChris statement? What is the test of materiality?

2. What is the difference in obligation when relying upon nonexpert portions of the registration statement as compared to relying upon expert portions? What is the reason for the distinction?

3. What is the difference between an "inside director" and an "outside director?"

4. Are you less inclined to become a board member of a corporation after BarChris? Why?

5. Do you think the *BarChris* decision affected the cost of malpractice insurance for attorneys and accountants? What effect would an increase in such costs have on the cost of preparing the registration statement? Who pays in the long run?

Failure to File Registration Statement

Any person who sells a nonexempt security without complying with the registration requirements is liable to purchasers for rescission under section 12(1). An action under section 12(1) must be brought within one year of the violation and no more than three years from the date of the original offer.

Assume that the Bogus Company is incorporated under the laws of the state of Virginia and conducts all of its business in that state. Bogus makes a public offering of one million shares of common stock, advertising such in *The Wall Street Journal* at $6 per share. The company fails to file a registration statement in accordance with section 5. Mack Donaldson, a resident of Virginia, is a sophisticated investor who is intimately aware of the operations of Bogus Company. He purchases 500 shares of its stock for $1,500, but the stock price then drops to $3 per share.

Mack Donaldson may seek rescission of the transaction and receive a full refund on the purchase price upon returning the stock. The stock was not exempt from registration because the issue did not qualify as either a private offering or an intrastate offering within the meaning of the act.

Misrepresentation and Fraud in Sale of Securities

Section 12(2) imposes liability on any person who offers or sells a security by means of any communication which misstates or omits a material fact that would have prevented the statement from being misleading. Section 12(2) is applicable whether or not the security was registered.

An action under section 12(2) must be brought within one year after discovery of the untrue statement or omission or after discovery should have been made by the exercise of reasonable diligence. In no event may an action be brought more than three years after the sale. Also, the seller will not be liable if it can establish that it exercised reasonable care and did not discover the misstatement or omission.

Section 17 prohibits fraud in the offer or sale of securities and is commonly the basis for criminal sanctions and injunctive relief. It has been used successfully by aggrieved purchasers to recover against persons who defrauded them in the sale of securities. In this respect it affords a defrauded purchaser an implied remedy free of section 11 and section 12 restrictions, such as the statute of limitations.

PUBLIC REMEDIES

In addition to private actions, persons who violate the Securities Act are subject to public remedies, which include administrative stop orders, court injunctions, and criminal penalties.

Stop Orders

The act provides an administrative remedy against fraudulent offerings or sales of securities. If the registration statement appears to be materially incomplete, inaccurate, or otherwise defective, the SEC will ordinarily inform the registrant and provide an opportunity to clarify or amend the problematic portions. If the registrant fails to comply, the commission may proceed to a hearing to determine the facts. Upon finding that material representations are misleading, inaccurate, or incomplete, the commission may suspend the effectiveness of a registration statement by issuing a stop order. The commission may also issue a stop order, after a hearing, even after the sale of securities has begun. Once the statement is properly amended, the stop order must be lifted and the effectiveness of the registration affirmed.

Injunction

The SEC also has the power to seek an injunction in the federal district courts to prevent violations of the act or its rules or regulations. An injunction will be granted to stop persons from using the mails or instruments of interstate commerce to sell nonexempt securities when the proper registration has not been filed or a prospectus supplied pursuant to section 5.

Criminal Penalties

Any person who willfully violates any provision of the act or any rules and regulations enacted by the commission is guilty of a criminal offense. Similarly, any person who willfully makes an untrue statement about a material fact or omits to state any material fact in connection with the offering or sale of a security is guilty of a crime.

The SEC does not have the power to adjudicate guilt or impose penalties. It may transmit evidence of a violation to the attorney general, who may prosecute an alleged offender. Conviction for an offense may carry a penalty of up to $10,000 and five years imprisonment. There is a five-year statute of limitations for prosecuting criminal actions against offenders.

ALTERNATIVE APPROACHES

Federal securities laws do not preempt the states' right to regulate securities, even when those securities are the subject of interstate activity. Since all states and the District of Columbia have laws pertaining to securities, an issuer that floats a new issue of securities on a national level has to contend with 52 distinct bodies of securities laws. This multipronged registration requirement can be a major obstacle to the offering of public securities. In some instances the cost and complication of the various procedures discourage the issuance of securities among the states. For this reason, recent moves to standardize and streamline registration procedures among the states have been gaining impetus.

In 1956, the Commission on Uniform State Laws created a Uniform Securities Act (USA) for adoption by the states. More than 30 states have adopted at least portions of the USA, which includes provisions for securities registration, exemptions, and sanctions for offenders. States are free to adopt the USA in full, to reject it, or to adopt it in part or with amendments. The states' approach to securities regulation provides a contrast to federal securities regulation in some areas.

Registration of Securities

Most states require registration of securities, but the methods of registration vary from state to state. Many states use one or a combination of the procedures available under the USA.

By Qualification

In sharp contrast to the federal securities laws, practically all state securities laws contain qualification requirements for registration. These laws include standards against which the quality of securities must be measured. Under this approach, the states maintain the discretion, based on guidelines, to refuse registration to securities that do not qualify as bona fide and nonfraudulent. The issuer that must register a security files a statement similar to that required under the Securities Act. The statement becomes effective and the security becomes available for sale upon approval by the administrator. The USA authorizes the issuance of a stop order denying effectiveness to the registration if the administrator finds that such an order would be in the public interest and that the offering would tend to work a fraud upon purchasers.

By Notification

Registration by notification is a simplified method of registering on the order of a federal Registration A statement. It is available for certain securities that have a proven track record and, thus, are considered less risky. The specific standards vary from state to state. In most states that permit registration by notification, registration is effective upon filing.

By Coordination

To register by coordination, the registrant simply files the same registration statement with the state that was filed with the SEC. The registration, if in full compliance, will take effect at the same time that the federal registration becomes effective. A majority of the states have adopted registration by coordination. This is happy news for issuers and underwriters who "blue sky" public securities offerings among the several states, as it affords them an efficient way to effect registration in many states at the same time. However, the administrator may stop the issuance if the securities do not qualify as bona fide and nonfraudulent, regardless of what the SEC does.

Exemptions

Exemptions from registration similar to those afforded by the Securities Act also exist in several states. These include exemptions for government securities and for securities issued by companies subject to special regulatory statutes (e.g., banks and common carriers), for limited offerings and those restricted to sophisticated investors.

Some have advocated the enactment of a state statute which would exempt all offerings registered with the SEC. Others have advocated that Congress enact legislation preempting the states from regulating securities altogether. This would result in instant uniformity of securities regulation.

CHAPTER PROBLEMS

1. The Weavers bought a $50,000 certificate of deposit (CD) from the Marine Bank. The CD earned 7½ percent interest, matured in six years, and provided for a penalty for early withdrawal.

The Weavers then pledged the CD to Marine Bank to guarantee repayment of a $65,000 loan that the bank made to Columbus Packing Co. (Columbus). Columbus was a wholesale slaughterhouse owned by the Piccirillos.

Because the Weavers guaranteed the loan for Columbus, the Piccirillos entered into an agreement with the Weavers. Under the agreement, the Weavers were to receive 50 percent of Columbus's net profits and $100 a month. They were also permitted to use Columbus's barn and pasture and to veto future borrowing by Columbus.

Is the CD pledged by the Weavers a security? Why or why not? Does the agreement between the Weavers and the Piccirillos constitute a security? Explain.

2. Frank Jones and James Jamerson were involved in a trucking business called Evergreen Investors. It was in financial trouble.

Jones and Jamerson teamed up with several small investors and together purchased Krimbel Trucking, a company that hauled loads between Washington and California. Jamerson was Krimbel's president and Jones was its vice president.

Krimbel was operating at a loss. Jones approached potential investors, telling them that Krimbel was undergoing expansion and showed great promise. He presented a "package" to these investors that permitted them to buy trailers from Evergreen and lease them back to Krimbel. Investors made low down payments on the equipment and borrowed the rest through bank loans. Krimbel made the monthly payments on its lease obligations to the bank. The bank applied the payments to the investor's loan balances, and the excess was deposited to their accounts. Jones collected a commission on each trailer sale.

The terms of the investment also gave Krimbel an option to purchase the trailer at the end of the lease term. Exercise of the option would result in a profit to the investors. Were the sale-leaseback transactions securities? Discuss.

3. Koscot Interplanetary, Inc. has set up a multilevel network of independent distributors engaged in selling a line of cosmetics. The beauty advisor is at the lowest level. Beauty advisors may purchase products from Koscot at 45 percent discount. At the second level is a beauty supervisor. For a $1,000 investment the supervisor receives a 55 percent discount on products. A supervisor receives $600 for introducing a prospect who buys into the program at the beauty supervisor level. At the top of the program is a beauty distributor. For an investment of $5,000 the distributor may purchase products at 65 percent discount. The distributor is also entitled to $600 or $3,000, respectively, for bringing in prospects who later buy into a supervisor or distributor position.

Those who have invested in the Koscot plan bring prospects to "opportunity meetings," where they are introduced to the program. At that meeting Koscot employees sell the prospects on the program, and investors sometimes participate directly in the sales pitch. They are required to follow a manual prepared by Koscot, which instructs them to drive to the meetings in expensive cars, dress fashionably, and flaunt large sums of money. Those who do not follow the manual verbatim can be dismissed from participation.

Analyze the scheme and explain why a security is being offered. How could Koscot avoid registration?

4. The Bangor Punta Corporation was contemplating issuing a block of securities. Bangor prepared to file a registration statement covering the proposed distribution under the Securities Act. Before filing, Bangor issued a press release announcing its intention to issue the securities. The release also stated that "in the judgment of the First Boston Corporation, each share of Bangor stock has a value of not less than $80." The SEC filed suit against Bangor, claiming that the press release violated section 5 of the Securities Act. Is the SEC correct? Explain.

5. Johnson devised a plan whereby his corporation issued notes to investors and purportedly used the proceeds from the notes to import industrial wine. He did not file a registration statement. Johnson sold the notes through intermediaries to sophisticated, wealthy businesspeople. He did not advertise, and at no time were the notes held by more than 30 investors. The enterprise turned out to be a fraud. The money Johnson received from investors was used not to import wine, but to pay off previous investors who were lured into the scheme. Mower, a sophisticated investor, became interested in the plan and invested large sums of money with Johnson. When it finally became known that Johnson had defrauded his investors, Mower brought suit under the Securities Act, claiming violations of its antifraud provisions.

In his defense Johnson asserts that the act is inapplicable because the notes (which he concedes to be securities) were issued pursuant to a section 4(2) exemption. Is Johnson's assertion valid? Explain.

6. Truckee Showboat, Inc. was organized in the state of California. All of its directors and officer are residents of California. It does 90 percent of its business in that state.

Truckee placed an ad in the *Los Angeles Times* offering to sell 4,080 shares of its stock at $1,000 per share exclusively to bona fide residents of California. The proceeds from the sales were to be used to purchase, improve, and operate the El Cortez Hotel in Las Vegas, Nevada.

Truckee Showboat received a permit to issue the securities from the Commissioner of Corporations of California. No stock was actually purchased.

May Truckee take advantage of the intrastate offering exemption? Explain.

7. McGuire owned oil and gas leases on 300,000–500,000 acres in northern Ohio. In need of cash to pay the rental for the leases, he proposed to raise capital by selling investment interests in them. He organized three Delaware corporations to accomplish this: Asta-King, Tamarac, and Haratine. Each corporation had a board of directors and officers who were McGuire's relatives and employees. All three corporations were controlled by McGuire, and each sold securities amounting to $1 million. The securities were registered with the SEC pursuant to Regulation A. What advantage did McGuire achieve? Were McGuire's actions lawful? Explain.

8. Winter & Hirsch, Inc. (WH), a consumer finance company, issued short-term promissory notes amounting to $1,612,500. Forty-two investors purchased these notes through John Nuveen & Co., Inc., an underwriting firm. Nuveen prepared "commercial paper reports" on the WH paper and distributed them to investors.

WH issued fraudulent financial statements. They overstated the accounts receivable by $14,000,000 and omitted $750,000 of its indebtedness. The registration statements filed by WH reflected these misrepresentations and omissions. Nuveen was not aware of the fraud. Its commercial paper reports reflected the false WH financial statements.

WH defaulted on the notes. The buyers of the notes now seek a return of the purchase price. Discuss the possible remedies against WH and Nuveen.

9. Andrew and Mary Tell are real estate developers. They arranged with the Usedco Corporation, through its president, Roghbard, to sell certain lands and buildings to Usedco. It was subsequently agreed that, in lieu of cash, Usedco would issue 93,333 shares of its stock to the Tells. No registration statement was filed under the Securities Act with regard to the issuance or sale of the stock.

Bromberg and Cravitz were attorneys for Usedco, and Cravitz's family held all the shares of DJ&M Investment Company. On the advice of Cravitz, DJ&M bought 61,000 of the shares issued to the Tells and subsequently resold them to various brokers, including Murray J. Ross & Company. Ross sold a block of 5,000 shares to Aaron and Ruth Winter. The Winters alleged that Ross effected the sale by making material misrepresentations concerning Usedco's profitability and by omitting pertinent facts as to Usedco's financial condition. If the Winters sue to recover damages, what must they prove to succeed? Who may be liable for violating which section of the Securities Act? What damages are possible?

10. Explain the key differences between the federal and state approaches to securities regulation.

CHAPTER 9

TRADING SECURITIES

As discussed in chapter 8, the Securities Act of 1933 regulates the offering of original securities by requiring that they be registered. The Federal Trade Commission was responsible for its enforcement until Congress passed the Securities Exchange Act of 1934 (Exchange Act). That act created the Securities and Exchange Commission (SEC) to administer federal securities laws. The Exchange Act regulates the secondary trading of securities (as opposed to their original sale) by regulating those involved in the securities industry (see Figure 9–1). This chapter explores several specific areas regulated by the Exchange Act, including:

— Stock exchange and over-the-counter markets
— Registration of securities traded in secondary markets
— Securities brokers
— The use of proxies
— Attempts to take over corporate control
— Corporate insiders
— Fraudulent activities
— Remedies for violations

SECURITIES MARKETS

A market is a place where buyers and sellers meet to transact business. There are two types of securities markets in the United States: securities exchanges and over-the-counter markets.

Securities Exchanges

The New York Stock Exchange is the largest and most well-known securities exchange, trading 50 million or more shares of stock each day. These

---

FIGURE 9–1
Primary and Secondary Sale of Securities

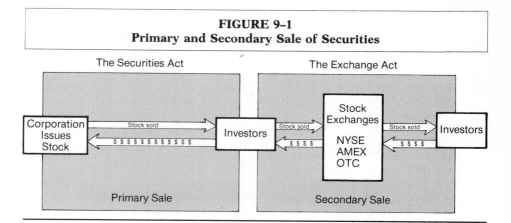

The Securities Act   The Exchange Act

Corporation Issues Stock — Stock sold → Investors — Stock sold → Stock Exchanges NYSE AMEX OTC — Stock sold → Investors

$ $ $ $ $ $ $ $ $ $ $ $ $ $ $ $ $ $ $ $

Primary Sale   Secondary Sale

---

shares are traded on a "floor" at a physical facility. Trading procedures on the New York Stock Exchange are much like those used on other national or regional securities exchanges. Trading begins when a customer contacts a broker with an order to buy or sell a certain quantity of a specific security. The broker transmits the order to the brokerage firm's order room at the exchange. There the order is communicated to a floor broker who offers to buy or sell as instructed. Upon completing the purchase or sale, the broker notifies the central office of the brokerage firm. The customer is then informed of the purchase or sale price, the stock certificates are exchanged, and the transaction is complete.

Securities exchanges are required to register with the SEC. To do so, an exchange must be capable of complying with the Exchange Act and of policing its members (brokerage firms) and their personnel. The exchange must meet strict reporting requirements concerning market transactions. It also must adopt rules that enforce standards regarding:

— Admission to membership
— Prevention of fraud
— Protection of investors and the public
— Fair procedures for members charged with violations
— Discipline of members and their associates for offenses

The commission has complete authority over the activities of securities exchanges. It may deny registration until it determines that an exchange conforms with the Exchange Act and SEC regulations. In some cases it may require modifications of an exchange's rules. The commission has the power to suspend or withdraw the registration of any exchange, expel or suspend exchange members, and suspend the trading of any security listed on an exchange.

Over-the-Counter Markets

An over-the-counter market handles securities transactions that do not take place on an organized exchange. There is no exchange floor. Most over-the-counter trading occurs through the National Association of Securities Dealers Automated Quotations (NASDAQ). NASDAQ is a computerized system that collects and stores data on over-the-counter transactions. Up-to-the-minute data are projected on video terminal units in each over-the-counter broker establishment. Many brokerage firms act as dealers and trade stocks "over the counter" that are not listed on exchanges.

The National Association of Securities Dealers (NASD) supervises the conduct of the over-the-counter market. Established pursuant to the Exchange Act, it is the only self-regulatory organization which the commission has approved to supervise this market. NASD is required to have self-governing rules that prevent fraud and promote fair principles of trade in over-the-counter transactions. NASD has adopted rules regulating the conduct of its members. One rule, for example, prohibits brokers from recommending securities not consistent with the client's financial situation.

Most brokerage firms are members of NASD, but a brokerage firm may deal in over-the-counter securities without belonging to NASD. The SEC imposes rules on NASD nonmembers that are similar to the rules adopted by NASD.

SECURITIES REGISTRATION AND REPORTING

The Exchange Act requires that, unless exempt, any equity or debt security be registered in order to be traded on a national securities exchange. An *equity security* is any stock or similar security that evidences an ownership interest in the issuing company. A *debt security* is any bond or similar security that evidences a debt of the issuing company. The issuer of these securities must file a registration statement with the exchange and the SEC.

The Exchange Act also requires the registration of any equity security that is to be traded in the over-the-counter market if the issuer (1) is engaged in a business that affects interstate commerce or uses interstate facilities for trading in the security, (2) has more than $3 million in assets, and (3) has at least 500 shareholders. Registration must be filed with the SEC.

A security that was registered under the Securities Act must still be registered under the Exchange Act if it is to be traded in a secondary market. The Securities Act registration permits the initial sale of the security. The Exchange Act registration permits the security to be traded in secondary markets.

Generally, there are two forms for registration: general and simplified. The general form requires detailed information about the registrant's business holdings, securities, finances, management, and relationship to all parent companies and subsidiaries. The information it requires is very similar to that required under the Securities Act. A company qualifies for a simplified registration if it has previously registered under the Exchange Act or the Securities Act. The contents of this registration include a description of the class and character of the securities to be registered and a list of the exhibits incorporated into the registration. These include specimens of the securities, bylaws, and financial reports. Registration contents are available for public inspection.

Periodic Disclosure

The Exchange Act was designed to assure the continuing availability of adequate information about publicly traded securities, since trading is ongoing. To further that design, the registrant must update its registration with annual, quarterly, and current reports. Generally, SEC Form 10–K must be filed within 90 days after the end of the fiscal period. It includes current audited financial statements and information regarding the operations of the business and the status of its securities. Form 10–Q must be filed quarterly. It includes an unaudited summary of the financial changes that have occurred in the registrant's finances, management, and securities since the preceding report was made. Much of the information to be included in Forms 10–K and 10–Q may incorporate by reference the company's annual and quarterly shareholders report. Form 8–K must be filed in order to disclose materially important events such as a change in the control of the registrant, a change in the registrant's certifying accountants, bankruptcy, or the resignation of a director.

Integration of Disclosure

Until recently, the registration and disclosure requirements of the Securities Act and Exchange Act were duplicative and uncoordinated. Companies that reported periodically under the Exchange Act would have to duplicate their filing efforts when registering new securities under the Securities Act. To some extent, the separate disclosure requirements have been integrated by standardizing the disclosure forms required under each act. Companies that are issuing securities and have been reporting under the Exchange Act for at least three years are permitted to incorporate information by reference to their periodic reports or their annual reports to shareholders. This saves them time and money.

BROKER-DEALER REGISTRATION

The Exchange Act requires brokers and dealers to register with the commission. A broker, for purposes of the act, transacts business in securities for customers' accounts. A dealer regularly transacts business in securities for his or her own account. Brokers and dealers (broker-dealers) are held to high standards of professional conduct.

Broker-dealers may be liable to a customer. One area on which the SEC has focused is the possible conflict of interest between the broker-dealer and the customer. Where such a possibility is present, the broker-dealer is required to make full disclosure to the customer. In fact, a broker is required to supply customers with a written confirmation of each transaction. This confirmation must disclose whom the broker represented in the transaction (customer, dealer for own account, or broker for another). These full disclosure requirements are designed to protect the customer.

A broker is entitled to a commission on every transaction performed for a customer, whether it involves a gain or a loss to the customer. The more transactions a broker completes for a customer, the greater are the commissions. A broker is not permitted to influence a customer to engage in excessive trading just for the purpose of boosting commissions. This practice is called *churning*. Churning is fraudulent and subjects the broker to liability.

The public looks upon the broker as an expert. By "hanging a shingle," the broker implies that there is an adequate basis for his or her opinions regarding stock transactions. A broker is prohibited from offering opinions about a security unless these are based on reliable information. A broker may not recommend the purchase of a stock for the purpose of inflating its value so that the broker, who had purchased the same stock previously, capitalizes on its sale. This practice is termed *scalping*. Scalping is fraudulent and subjects the broker to liability.

PROXY RULES

The Exchange Act regulates the common corporate practice of proxy solicitation. A *proxy* is a document that grants an agent authority to vote for a shareholder. This is the principal method of voting corporate shares in the United States. Specific SEC rules govern the content of proxies. Figure 9–2 is an example of a proxy that conforms to these rules.

The Exchange Act and the commission rules regulate proxy solicitation in order to prevent management and others from obtaining or maintaining corporate control through deception or inadequate disclosure. The Exchange Act also requires certain disclosures to be made to shareholders even if no proxies are solicited.

Proxy Statement

Under the commission's rules, no proxies may be solicited unless the solicitor furnishes prescribed information to the shareholders in the form of a proxy statement. Some of the information is general, for example, items dealing with the persons making the solicitation, the interests of the solicitors regarding the matters to be considered at the shareholders meeting, and the vote required on specific matters. Other required disclosure concerns specific proposals, such as information about nominees and direc-

FIGURE 9–2
Proxy

ISELDORF, INC

This Proxy is Solicited on Behalf of Management.

The undersigned hereby designates Ashley Brown and Norman Howard, or either of them in the absence of the other, with power of substitution to act as my lawful authorized attorney and proxy to act in my stead to attend the shareholder's meeting of ISELDORF, INC., to be conducted at 305 Doris Court Englewood, Ohio, at 9:30 a.m., on March 15, 1988, and thereto vote the shares of ISELDORF, INC., which I own, with all powers which I would possess if present at such meeting regarding:

☐ 1. **The election of directors.**
☐ 2. **A merger with Amalgum, Inc.**
    ☐ For   (Management recommends
    ☐ Against a vote for this proposal.)

☐ 3. **For every other matter that may
    come before the meeting to vote
    in the best interest of the company.**

IN THE EVENT THAT NO SPECIFIC DIRECTION IS GIVEN ON ITEMS 1 and 2, THE PROXY WILL VOTE FOR THE SLATE OF CANDIDATES NAMED IN THE PROXY STATEMENT AND FOR THE MERGER.

DATE: _____

_____
Signature

Any stockholder who wishes to revoke this proxy and vote in person may do so by written instrument or as modified by state law.

tors when an election of board members is on the agenda of the shareholders meeting.

Proxy solicitation may be a battleground for control of the corporate enterprise. It is often used to gain control of a corporation by electing a new board of directors.

Proxy contests necessitate the filing of additional information, and special procedures govern the fight for management control. The opponents to management are required to file a proxy statement and information about those participating in the fight. Management must provide the opponents with a list of the shareholders or mail the proxy material to the shareholders at the opponents' expense. It is unlawful to solicit proxies by means of a proxy statement that is false or misleading with respect to a *material fact*. The United States Supreme Court defined a material fact in the next case.

 **TSC Industries, Inc. v. Northway, Inc.**

426 U.S. 438 (1976)

National Industries, Inc. (petitioner) acquired 34 percent of TSC Industries, Inc.'s (petitioner) stock from Charles Schmidt and his family.

Schmidt, the founder and principal shareholder of TSC resigned from the board of directors. Five National nominees were placed on TSC's board. Stanley Yarmuth, National's president and chief executive officer, was named chairman of TSC's board. Charles Simonelli, National's executive vice president, was placed in an executive position in TSC.

The TSC board (with the National nominees not voting) approved a proposal to sell all of TSC's assets to National. The proposal involved an exchange of TSC stock for National stock. TSC and National sent a joint proxy statement to their shareholders recommending the proposal. With proxies the proposal was approved. TSC was liquidated and dissolved. The shares were exchanged.

Northway (respondent), a TSC shareholder, sued TSC and National, claiming that their proxy statement was materially misleading. Northway moved for summary judgment in its favor. The district court denied Northway's motion. The court of appeals reversed the district court and found in favor of Northway. The U.S. Supreme Court reversed the court of appeals decision and found in TSC's favor.

Justice Marshall

. . . [Section] 14(a) of the Securities Exchange Act "was intended to promote 'the free exercise of the voting rights of stockholders' by ensuring that proxies would be solicited with 'explanation to the stockholder of the real nature of the questions for which authority to cast his vote is sought.' " . . . There was no need to demonstrate that the alleged defect in the proxy statement actually had a decisive effect on the voting. So long as the misstatement or omission was material, the causal relation between violation and injury is sufficiently established . . . if "the proxy solicitation itself . . . was an essential link in the accomplishment of the transaction." . . .

*　*　*　*　*

The Court of Appeals in this case concluded that material facts include "all facts which a reasonable shareholder might consider important." . . . This formulation of the test of materiality has been explicitly rejected by at least two courts as setting too

low a threshold for the imposition of liability. . . .

*　*　*　*　*

In formulating a standard of materiality . . . we are guided, of course, by the recognition . . . of the Rule's broad remedial purpose. That purpose is not merely to ensure by judicial means that the transaction, when judged by its real terms, is fair and otherwise adequate, but to ensure disclosures by corporate management in order to enable the shareholders to make an informed choice. As an abstract proposition, the most desirable role for a court in a suit of this sort, coming after the consummation of the proposed transaction, would perhaps be to determine whether in fact the proposal would have been favored by the shareholders and consummated in the absence of any misstatement or omission. But . . . such matters are not subject to determination with certainty. Doubts as to the critical nature of information misstated or omitted will be commonplace. And particularly in view of the prophylactic purpose of the Rule and the fact that the content of the proxy statement is within management's control, it is appropriate that these doubts be resolved in favor of those the statute is designed to protect.

We are aware, however, that the disclosure policy embodied in the proxy regulations is not without limit. Some information is of such dubious significance that insistence on its disclosure may accomplish more harm than good. The potential liability for . . . violation [of the Rule] can be great indeed, and if the standard of materiality is unnecessarily low, not only may the corporation and its management be subjected to liability for insignificant omissions or misstatements, but also management's fear of exposing itself to substantial liability may cause it simply to bury the shareholders in an avalanche of trivial information—a result that is hardly conducive to informed decision-making. Precisely these dangers are presented, we think, by the definition of a material fact adopted by the Court of Appeals in this case—a fact which a reasonable shareholder might consider important. . . .

The general standard of materiality that we think best comports with the policies of [the] Rule . . . is as follows: An omitted fact is material if there is a substantial likelihood that a reasonable shareholder would consider it important in deciding how to vote. . . . It does not require proof of a substantial likelihood that disclosure of the omitted fact would have caused the reasonable investor to change his vote. What the standard does contemplate is a showing of a substantial likelihood that, under all the circumstances the omitted fact would have assumed actual significance in the deliberations of the reasonable shareholder. Put another way, there must be a substantial likelihood that the disclosure of

the omitted fact would have been viewed by the reasonable investor as having significantly altered the "total mix" of information made available. . . .

*   *   *   *   *

The omissions found by the Court of Appeals to have been materially misleading as a matter of law involved two general issues—the degree of National's control over TSC at the time of the proxy solicitation, and the favorability of the terms of the proposed transaction to TSC shareholders. . . .

*   *   *   *   *

The proxy statement prominently displayed the facts that National owned 34% of the outstanding shares in TSC, and that no other person owned more than 10%. It also prominently revealed that 5 out of 10 TSC directors were National nominees, and it recited the position of those National nominees with National—indicating, among other things, that Stanley Yarmuth was president and a director of National, and that Charles Simonelli was executive vice president and a director of National. These disclosures clearly revealed the nature of National's relationship with TSC and alerted the reasonable shareholder to the fact that National exercised a degree of influence over TSC. In view of these disclosures, we certainly cannot say that the additional facts that Yarmuth was chairman of the TSC board of directors and Simonelli chairman of its executive committee were, on this record, so obviously important that reasonable minds could not differ on their materiality.

*   *   *   *   *

The proxy statement revealed that the investment banking firm of Hornblower & Weeks–Hemphill, Noyes had rendered a favorable opinion on the fairness to TSC shareholders of the terms for the exchange of TSC shares for National securities. In that opinion, the proxy statement explained, the firm had considered, "among other things, the current market prices of the securities of both corporations, the dividend and debt service requirements of both corporations, . . . the substantial premium over current market values represented by the securities being offered to TSC stockholders, and the increased dividend income."

* * * * *

In summary, none of the omissions claimed to have been in violation of [the] Rule . . . were, so far as the record reveals, materially misleading as a matter of law.

CASE QUESTIONS

1. What is a material fact? How did the Supreme Court's definition differ from the court of appeal's definition?

2. What is the danger of requiring disclosure in proxy materials to be too extensive.

3. What did Northway claim were material nondisclosures? What was the court's response?

4. Name some nondisclosures that would be material.

Information Statement

Corporations with securities registered under the Exchange Act are required to make disclosures to their shareholders even if no proxies are solicited. These disclosures are made in the form of an information statement. The statement includes a notice of the date, time, and place of the shareholders meeting and states that proxies are not being solicited. It also discloses the interests of certain persons involved in any matter to be voted on and presents the proposals of security holders.

At least 10 days before mailing the proxy or information statement to the shareholders, the issuer is required to send the SEC a preliminary copy. The SEC reviews it for completeness and may issue a letter of comment requiring changes before the statement is mailed. Copies of the proxy or information statement actually mailed to shareholders must be filed with the commission and the securities exchanges where the securities are registered.

When a proxy or information statement relates to voting for directors, stockholders must be supplied an annual report, including financial statements for the last two years. An agenda of the proposals that are expected to be considered at the shareholders meeting also must be included in the statement, along with a place for the shareholder's approval or disapproval for each proposal.

Shareholder Proposals

The Exchange Act gives a shareholder the right to make a proposal at the shareholders meeting. The shareholder must notify management of the proposal. Management must include the proposal in the proxy statement and give the shareholders a right to vote on it. If management opposes the proposal, then the shareholder is entitled to include a 200-word rationale for the proposal in the proxy statement.

Management may exclude a proposal from consideration if it:

— Violates the law
— Is a personal, political, or social grievance not related to the corporation's business
— Relates to ordinary business operations
— Relates to elections
— Is similar to a recent proposal that was defeated by a wide margin

TAKEOVER BIDS

Various techniques may be used to acquire a controlling interest in a company. A proxy contest may divest current management of its control, but such contests are expensive and usually unsuccessful. An alternate strategy involves publicly offering cash or securities to stockholders in return for their stock. This action is called a takeover bid or tender offer. The subject of the takeover attempt is called the *target company*. The company attempting the takeover is referred to as the *tender offeror*. Takeover attempts may result in bitter contests between the tender offeror and the target company. Corporate officials often resist takeovers for fear of losing their jobs if the takeover is successful.

A target company faced with the threat of a takeover may deploy a host of defensive tactics to neutralize the outside threat. Shareholders can be warned of the takeover attempt and solicited not to sell their shares. The target company may buy up its own shares on the open market or issue additional shares to management and its allies. It might also announce a dividend increase or a stock split to boost the market price of the stock. This would make the takeover more expensive for the tender offeror. Targets sometimes merge with other companies that are less threatening. On a few occasions targets have responded by attempting to take over the attacker.

Shareholders are often the pawns of takeover contests, courted with inflated purchase offers for their stock. The tender offeror may or may not be interested in the welfare of the target company. If the target company has fallen prey to the tender offeror because of its own mismanagement, the takeover could benefit the target company's shareholders and its market. In any case, market manipulation, coercion, and confusion are natural by-products of takeover contests.

A tender offeror that attempts to take over a company by making a public offer to exchange its own securities for the stock of the target company is governed by the Securities Act and must comply with its registration requirements. However, until 1968 federal securities laws did not regulate the acquisition of control by cash tender offers. In that year Congress passed the Williams Act as an amendment to the Exchange Act. The Williams Act regulates tender offers.

Under the Williams Act, a person or group that acquires more than five percent of a class of securities registered under the Exchange Act is required to file a statement with the SEC and the issuer of the securities. The act also stipulates that no one may make a tender offer for more than five percent of a class of securities without first filing a statement with the SEC. The statement in both cases must include:

— The background of the person or entity
— The number of shares owned
— The source of the funds for the acquisition
— The purpose of the acquisition
— The tender offeror's plans for the target company
— Information regarding agreements between the tender offeror and any person relevant to the target company

The target company that is attempting to ward off its attacker must also comply with the filing and disclosure provisions.

Under the Williams Act it is unlawful to omit any material facts; to make any untrue or misleading statements of such facts; or to engage in "fraudulent, deceptive, or manipulative acts or practices" in extending or opposing a tender offer. The following case involving takeover attempts of a major oil company raises questions about what constitutes a manipulative act in connection with a tender offer.

 **Mobil Corporation v. Marathon Oil Co.**

669 F.2d 366 (6th Cir. 1981)

Mobil Corporation (appellant) sought to take over Marathon Oil Company (appellee). It announced its intention to purchase 40 million shares of stock for $85 a share. It conditioned its offer on receipt of at least 30 million shares, which represented slightly over one-half of the outstanding Marathon shares.

The Marathon board of directors was alarmed. The board decided to seek a "white knight"—a company that is more attractive to merge with since it poses less threat to management.

Marathon negotiated with several companies. United States Steel Corporation offered to pay $125 a share for 30 million shares of Marathon stock. Its plan called for a follow-up merger with its subsidiary U.S.S. Corporation (USS). The Marathon directors voted to recommend the offer to its shareholders, and on the same day U.S. Steel, USS, and Marathon all signed a formal agreement. USS made its tender offer to Marathon shareholders the next day.

The USS offer had two conditions: (1) an irrevocable option to purchase ten million shares of common stock for $90 a share and (2) an option to purchase 48 percent of the oil and mineral rights in the Yates Field for $2.8 billion. (Yates Field was owned by Marathon and has been referred to as its "crown jewel.") According to the agreement, this option could only be exercised if USS's tender offer did not succeed, and another tender offer did.

Mobil filed suit in the United States District Court for the Southern District of Ohio, in an attempt to stop the option agreements and USS's tender offer. Meanwhile, Mobil announced a new tender offer of $126 per share. It conditioned its offer on a finding that the USS option to buy the Yates Field was invalid.

The district court judge refused to grant Mobil an injunction stopping Marathon and USS from following through with the tender offer or option agreement. Mobil appealed to the Sixth Circuit Court of Appeals, which reversed the district court decision.

Engel, Circuit Judge

. . . [W]e now consider Mobil's claim that the Yates Field and stock options granted by Marathon to USS, the wholly owned subsidiary of U.S. Steel, constitute a "manipulative act or practice" in connection with the USS tender offer . . . in violation of [the Williams Act]. . . .

. . . [W]e . . . conclude that the Yates Field option and the stock option individually and together are "manipulative" as that term is used in [the act].

The term "manipulative" is not defined in either the Securities Exchange Act or the Williams Act. "Manipulation" in securities markets can take many forms, . . . but the Supreme Court has recently indicated that manipulation is an affecting of the market . . . by artificial means, i.e., means unrelated to the natural forces of supply and demand. . . . In our view, it is difficult to conceive of a more effective and manipulative device than the "lock-up" options employed here, options which not only artificially affect, but for all practical purposes completely block, normal healthy market activity and, in fact, could be construed as expressly designed solely for that purpose.

The types of options demanded and

received by USS in this case are relatively new to the world of tender offer takeover contests, and we are unaware of any Supreme Court or Court of Appeals case confronting the question of whether these particular techniques are "manipulative" within the meaning of . . . the Williams Act. However, courts have recognized that the term "manipulative" must remain flexible in the face of new techniques which artificially affect securities markets. . . .

* * * * *

We are of the opinion that under the circumstances of this particular case, Mobil has shown a sufficient likelihood of ultimately establishing that the Yates Field option and the stock option had the effect of creating an artificial price in the tender offer market for Marathon common shares, and that the options therefore are "manipulative acts or practices" in connection with a tender offer in violation of . . . the Williams Act.

There is ample evidence in the record to support [the district court judge's] finding that Marathon's Yates Field interest is a unique and significant asset. We believe there is also sufficient evidence in the record to indicate that this asset is a very important attraction to Mobil and other potential bidders for control of Marathon. The Yates Field option which USS demanded and received in connection with its tender offer of $125 per share greatly dampens the demand by Mobil and other potential bidders in the tender offer market, because a successful takeover by any bidder other than USS will give USS the right to exercise its option and purchase the Yates Field interest for $2.8 billion. This presents a significant threat to other bidders that even if they gain control of Marathon they will lose the Yates Field oil reserves.

The district court found that the $2.8 billion which Marathon would receive from

USS in exchange for the Yates Field oil reserves is a fair price, but there was evidence that the field might be worth as much as $3.639 billion. We point this out . . . to illustrate that potential tender offerors may value the Yates Field reserves at a higher figure than $2.8 billion, especially in today's world of ever-depleting oil supplies and the volatile, unpredictable nature of oil prices over the long term. Oil companies and other companies like USS seeking to invest in the oil industry may believe that long-term oil reserves, not cash or other assets, will best ensure long-term profits. As a result, we cannot say that Mobil and other potential bidders for control of Marathon would not be willing to make tender offers reflecting a Yates Field valuation far greater than $2.8 billion, were it not for the Yates Field option which USS possesses. Only the open market contemplated by the act provides a means to measure its value.

* * * * *

The particular facts before us also indicate that the stock option that USS demanded and received in connection with its tender offer prevents all others from competing on a par with USS for control of Marathon. In our opinion, the stock option was large enough in this takeover contest to serve as an artificial and significant deterrent to competitive bidding for a controlling block of Marathon shares.

* * * * *

The size and price of the stock option, together with the fact that it was granted to USS, a tender offeror, prevented all others from competing on a par with USS for a controlling block of Marathon shares, and tipped the scales decidedly in favor of USS. In our opinion, the stock option artificially and significantly discouraged competitive bidding for the Marathon stock.

The Yates Field option and the stock

option, both individually and in combination, have the effect of circumventing the natural forces of market demand in this tender offer contest. Were this contest a straight price-per-share auction, tender offers well in excess of the USS offer of $125 per share may have been forthcoming. Of course, Mobil itself has offered $126 per share, conditional on the judicial removal of the options. Our task under the Williams Act is not to speculate about what price the Marathon shareholders might have been offered if the natural market forces existed in this tender offer contest, but rather to enforce the mandate of [the act] against manipulation of the market. The purpose of the Williams Act, protection of the target shareholders, requires that Mobil and any other interested bidder be permitted an equal opportunity to compete in the marketplace and persuade the Marathon shareholders to sell their shares to them.

The defendants argue that [the act] requires full disclosure and nothing more.

. . . It may be that the Marathon shareholders in this case have now been fully informed that their management granted USS the Yates Field option and the stock option. They may now understand fully how these options deter any tender offers higher than $125 per share. Yet, they have had no real alternative to accepting the USS offer, because Mobil's offer of $126 is conditional upon the validity of the options, and there is and could be no other comparable tender offer as long as the "lock-up" options remain in effect. The artificial ceiling on the price of their shares at $125 is manipulation to which they must submit whether it is disclosed to them or not, since in not tendering their shares to USS they risk being relegated to the "back end" of USS's takeover proposal and receiving only $90 per share.

In short, to find compliance with [the act] solely by the full disclosure of a manipulative device . . . would be to read the "manipulative acts and practices" language completely out of the Williams Act.

CASE QUESTIONS

1. What were the terms of the USS offer to shareholders? What were the terms of the Mobil offer? As a shareholder, which, if any, would you accept? Why?

2. Why does the court refer to the options as "lock-up" devices?

3. How does the court define "manipulation"? Do you agree with the court that the option agreement constituted a manipulation?

4. What if the board of directors voted itself a hefty salary increase and a lifetime contract with the company? Would this be a violation of the Williams Act? Explain.

5. What other courses of action were open to Marathon's board of directors to avoid the Mobil takeover?

CONTROL OF CORPORATE INSIDERS

Registration of a security under the Exchange Act also subjects certain corporate insiders to requirements and to liability for *short-swing profits*. Insiders, by definition, are directors, officers, and 10-percent owners of an issuer that has equity securities registered under the Exchange Act.

Because of their position, insiders within a corporation may acquire information that, when made public, will affect the value of the corporation's securities. Insiders familiar with the ultimate market impact of the information may trade to realize profits. For example, as a result of attending a board meeting, a corporate director may learn that the company has just made a valuable oil find. By purchasing that stock before the information becomes public, the director will realize profits.

The Exchange Act seeks to prevent such uses of inside information. Under the act an insider is liable for any profits made on the sale or purchase of equity securities within a six-month period. These short-swing profits are conclusively presumed to be a direct result of inside advantage. The fact that they did not result from inside information is no defense.

It is very unlikely that an insider will voluntarily surrender short-swing profits. However, the corporation can recover those profits by suing the insider. A shareholder can also sue on behalf of a corporation, but the government cannot sue to recover inside profits. To facilitate the enforcement by or on behalf of the corporation, directors, officers, and 10-percent owners are required to register with the SEC and file periodic reports disclosing their portfolio of corporate holdings. Any changes in ownership must be reported.

Director

A director of a corporation is a person who sits on its board of directors and participates in its affairs. The term director also applies to persons who perform similar functions, regardless of their assigned titles. Directors are liable for short-swing profits even if the purchase or sale by which the profits were realized occurred after they were no longer directors. One of the transactions must, however, occur while they are a director. The same holds true for corporate officers.

Officer

An officer of a corporation enjoys a position of responsibility and authority and normally has access to confidential information. Common titles of corporate officers are president, vice president, treasurer, and secretary. However, the title is inconclusive. Any person, regardless of title, who performs the functions of an officer is an insider. In contrast, a person whose position is merely honorary would not be considered an officer.

Ten-Percent Owner

A person who controls 10 percent of a corporation's shares presumably has access to nonpublic information that is vital to investment decision making. A 10-percent owner is liable for short-swing profits only if both the sale and purchase occur while the security holder owns at least 10 percent of the outstanding shares. A purchase that makes a security holder a 10-percent owner does not count.

Valuation of Profits

Short-swing profits are calculated by matching the lowest purchase price for a class of securities against the highest sale price. This yields the highest possible profit. Insiders may not offset their losses. Consider the following example and the calculation of short-swing profits.

On February 1 Insider purchased 200 shares of Megaton stock at $30 a share.

On March 1 Insider sold 200 shares of Megaton stock at $20 a share.

On April 1 Insider purchased 200 shares of Megaton stock at $40 a share.

On May 1 Insider sold 200 shares of Megaton stock at $50 a share.

Sold 200 shares at $50 a share	$10,000
Purchased 200 shares at $30 a share	− 6,000
Profit	4,000
Sold 200 shares at $20 a share	$ 4,000
Purchased 200 shares at $40 a share	− 8,000
Loss	$ (4,000)

Since losses are not taken into consideration, Insider is liable for $4,000 short-swing profits even though he broke even on the transactions.

FRAUDULENT ACTIVITIES

The Exchange Act includes various provisions that prohibit securities fraud. The act authorizes the SEC to enact rules and regulations to combat fraud in connection with the purchase or sale of securities. In connection with that authority the commission adopted Rule 10b–5, which prohibits fraud in connection with the purchase or sale of a security.

The rule has been invoked successfully against defendants charged with fraudulently inducing plaintiffs to sell corporate stock for less than its true value.[1] In the 1960s and '70s the rule was expanded to include liability for negligent conduct. As the next case indicates, that line of cases has since been reversed.

---

[1] *Kardon v. National Gypsum Co.,* 69 F. Supp. 512 (E.D.Pa. 1946).

Securities and Exchange Commission Rule 10b–5

It shall be unlawful for any person, directly or indirectly, by the use of any means or instrumentality of interstate commerce, or of the mails, or of any facility of any national securities exchange,

1. To employ any device, or scheme, or artifice to defraud,
2. To make any untrue statement of a material fact or to omit to state a material fact necessary in order to make the statements made, in the light of the circumstances under which they were made, not misleading, or
3. To engage in any act, practice, or course of business which operates or would operate as a fraud or deceit upon any person,

in connection with the purchase or sale of any security.

Ernst & Ernst v. Hochfelder

425 U.S. 185 (1976)

Ernst & Ernst (appellant), an accounting firm, was retained by First Securities Company of Chicago to audit its books on a regular basis. Ernst & Ernst conducted the audits and prepared the reports that First Securities was required to file with the SEC. Hochfelder and others (respondents) were customers of First Securities. They invested money in a fraudulent scheme contrived by the president of First Securities, Leston B. Nay, who owned 92 percent of its stock.

From 1942 through 1966 the respondents invested funds in "escrow" accounts, which Nay represented would earn high interest rates. No such accounts actually existed. Nay pocketed the funds for his own use. The escrow accounts did not appear on either the books of First Securities or on its periodic accountings to the respondents in connection with their other investments. They were not included in First Securities' filings with the commission or the Midwest Stock Exchange.

In 1968 Nay committed suicide. He left a note describing First Securities as bankrupt and revealed the escrow fraud. The respondents subsequently filed a complaint against Ernst & Ernst, charging that Nay's escrow scheme violated section 10(b) and commission Rule 10b–5, and that Ernst

& Ernst "aided and abetted" Nay's violations by failing to discover the fraud. The respondents contended that if Ernst & Ernst had used proper auditing procedures, it would have discovered Nay's mail rule—that only he could open mail addressed to him or to his attention, even if the mail arrived at First Securities in his absence. The respondents further contended that had Ernst & Ernst become aware of Nay's mail rule, it would have reported this irregular procedure to the commission and the stock exchange. This would have led to an investigation and an exposure of Nay's fraudulent scheme.

The district court granted Ernst & Ernst's motion for summary judgment and dismissed the action. The court of appeals reversed and remanded, reasoning that Ernst & Ernst had a duty to inquire into the adequacy of First Securities' internal control system and that the respondents were beneficiaries of that duty. The Supreme Court granted *certiorari* to resolve the question and reversed the court of appeals decision.

Justice Powell

The issue in this case is whether an action for civil damages may lie under §10(b) of the Securities Exchange Act of 1934 . . . and Securities and Exchange Commission Rule 10b–5 . . . in the absence of an allegation of intent to deceive, manipulate, or defraud on the part of the defendant.

*   *   *   *   *

Although §10(b) does not by its terms create an express civil remedy for its violation, and there is no indication that Congress or the Commission when adopting Rule 10b–5, contemplated such a remedy, the existence of a private cause of action for violations of the statute and the Rule is now well established. . . .

Section 10(b) makes unlawful the use or employment of "any manipulative or deceptive device or contrivance" in contravention of commission rules. The words "manipulative or deceptive" used in conjunction with "device or contrivance" strongly suggest that section 10(b) was intended to proscribe knowing or intentional misconduct. . . .

In its *amicus curiae** brief, however, the commission contends that nothing in the language "manipulative or deceptive device or contrivance" limits its operation to knowing or intentional practices. . . .

In addition to relying upon the commission's argument with respect to the operative language of the statute, respondents contend that since we are dealing with "remedial legislation," it must be construed " 'not technically and restrictively, but flexibly to effectuate its remedial purposes.' " They argue that the "remedial purposes" of the acts demand a construction of §10(b) that embraces negligence as a standard of liability. But in seeking to accomplish its broad remedial goals, Congress did not adopt uniformly a negligence standard even to express civil remedies. In some circumstances and with respect to certain classes of defendants, Congress did create express

---

* *Amicus curiae* is Latin for "friend of the court." It may be an individual or corporation that, because of strong interest in a case, petitions the court for permission to file a brief—Au.

liability predicated upon a failure to exercise reasonable care. . . . But in other situations good faith is an absolute defense. . . . And in still other circumstances Congress created express liability regardless of the defendant's fault.

* * * * *

Although the extensive legislative history of the 1934 Act is bereft of any explicit explanation of Congress' intent, we think the relevant portions of that history support our conclusion that §10(b) was addressed to practices that involve some element of scienter and cannot be read to impose liability for negligent conduct alone.

* * * * *

. . . The section was described rightly as a "catchall" clause to enable the commission "to deal with new manipulative [or cunning] devices." It is difficult to believe that any lawyer, legislative draftsman, or legislator would use these words if the intent was to create liability for merely negligent acts or omissions. Neither the legislative history nor the brief supporting respondents identify any usage or authority for construing "manipulative [or cunning] devices" to include negligence.

* * * * *

We have addressed, to this point, primarily the language and history of §10(b). The commission contends, however, that subsections (b) and (c) of Rule 10b–5 are cast in language which—if standing alone—could encompass both intentional and negligent behavior. These subsections respectively provide that it is unlawful "[t]o make any untrue statement of a material fact or to omit to state a material fact necessary

in order to make the statements made, in the light of the circumstances under which they were made, not misleading . . ." and "[t]o engage in any act, practice, or course of business which operates or would operate as a fraud or deceit upon any person. . . ." Viewed in isolation the language of subsection (b), and arguably that of subsection (c), could be read as proscribing respectively any type of material misstatement or omission, and any course of conduct, that has the effect of defrauding investors, whether the wrongdoing was intentional or not.

We note first that such a reading cannot be harmonized with the administrative history of the Rule, a history making clear that when the commission adopted the Rule it was intended to apply only to activities that involved scienter. More importantly, Rule 10b–5 was adopted pursuant to authority granted the commission under §10(b). The rulemaking power granted to an administrative agency charged with the administration of a federal statute is not the power to make law. Rather it is " 'the power to adopt regulations to carry into effect the will of Congress as expressed by the statute.' " . . . Thus, despite the broad view of the Rule advanced by the commission in this case, its scope cannot exceed the power granted the commission by Congress under §10(b). . . . When a statute speaks so specifically in terms of manipulation and deception, and of implementing devices and contrivances—the commonly understood terminology of intentional wrongdoing—and when its history reflects no more expansive intent, we are quite unwilling to extend the scope of the statute to negligent conduct.

CASE QUESTIONS

1. Do you think that the plain wording of Rule 10(b) is broad enough to encompass liability for negligent conduct? Explain.

2. How much weight did the Court attach to the legislative history of section 10(b)? Do you agree with the Court's rationale?

3. Is any other remedy available to the security holders who have been injured? Explain.

4. May accountants be grossly negligent or reckless and still avoid Rule 10b–5 liability? When does scienter exist?

5. What if, given facts similar to those in the case, the SEC had sought an injunction to prevent Ernst & Ernst from using "improper auditing procedures and disclosure principles in the preparation of First Securities reports to be filed with the SEC"? Would the result have been different? Discuss.

Inside Trading

Rule 10b–5 applies to fraud in connection with any sale or purchase of securities, which includes exchanges of stock and mergers. The rule has been invoked to impose liability on deceptive tender offerors and target companies. Rule 10b–5 has also been applied to the area of inside trading. In the landmark case of *SEC v. Texas Gulf Sulphur*, officers and employees of the company purchased stock after learning that exploratory drilling on the company's property gave evidence of a significant ore discovery.[2] They failed to disclose this information to the sellers of the stock and were found in violation of Rule 10b–5.

Originally the scope of insider liability for nondisclosure was confined to officers and directors of corporations who traded their securities on inside nonpublic information. Now it has evolved to encompass others who gain access to and trade on material nonpublic information without making disclosure. The concept is far broader than the class of insiders subject to the short-swing profit regulations previously discussed.

The expansion promotes the federal regulatory policy of ensuring that everyone has equal access to material information necessary for informed decision making. The broad application of 10b–5 manifests a concern for fairness in the marketplace. Investors will be less inclined to participate in market trading if they feel that others have a strategic advantage because of access to information generally unavailable. When this happens, the market is undermined.

In *Shapiro v. Merrill Lynch, Pierce, Fenner & Smith, Inc.* the stock brokerage firm, while preparing an offering of stock for Douglas Aircraft Company, learned from some Douglas officers, directors, and employees of unfavorable conditions that would affect Douglas's earnings.[3] The information was not yet public. Merrill Lynch disclosed the information to some of its customers. These customers sold their holdings in Douglas, or otherwise improved their positions, without disclosing the information to the purchasers. The court held that both Merrill Lynch, the "tipper," and the favored customers, the "tippees," were liable to the specific purchasers of the shares sold on the basis of Merrill Lynch's information. They were also liable to all those who purchased Douglas stock without

---

[2] 401 F.2d 833 (2d Cir. 1968).

[3] 495 F.2d 228 (2d Cir. 1974).

benefit of the material information in the defendants' hands. *Shapiro* sounds a warning not only to "nontrading tippers" but also to "trading tippees," who trade upon information they know or have reason to know is not public and was wrongfully obtained.

The following case involves a tippee who revealed nonpublic information about an insurance fraud scheme. It sets out the limits of tippee liability.

 **Dirks v. SEC**

103 Sup. Ct. 3255 (1983)

Raymond Dirks (petitioner) was an officer of a broker-dealer firm. Dirks received information from Ronald Secrist, a former officer of Equity Funding of America (Equity Funding). Secrist told Dirks that Equity Funding, a corporation that sold life insurance and mutual funds, was involved in fraudulent corporate activities. Secrist asked Dirks to verify the fraud and disclose it publicly.

Dirks investigated the allegations. He interviewed several officers and employees of the corporation. Although senior management denied any fraudulent practices, some employees confirmed Secrist's charges. In discussing the information with his clients, Dirks learned that some of those who held Equity Funding securities sold their holdings. Among them were five investment advisers who liquidated more than $16 million.

During the two-week period in which Dirks was conducting the investigation and spreading news of the fraud, the price of Equity Funding shares fell from $26 per share to $15 per share. The New York Stock Exchange halted trading of Equity Funding stock. The fraud was uncovered by state insurance authorities. The SEC (respondent) filed a complaint against Equity Funding. Shortly thereafter, *The Wall Street Journal* published a story about the Equity Funding fraud, based largely on Dirks's investigation.

The SEC investigated Dirks's role in the exposure of the fraud. An administrative law judge found that he violated Rule 10b–5 by repeating the fraud allegations to people who later sold their stock in Equity Funding. The SEC censored Dirks, and he sought review in the Court of Appeals for the District of Columbia, which found against him. The Supreme Court reversed.

Justice Powell

In the seminal case of *In re Cady, Roberts & Co.* . . . the SEC recognized that the com-

mon law in some jurisdictions imposes on "corporate 'insiders,' particularly officers, directors, or controlling stockholders" an "affirmative duty of disclosure . . . when dealing in securities." The SEC found that not only did breach of this common-law duty also establish the elements of a Rule 10b–5 violation but that individuals other than corporate insiders could be obligated either to disclose material nonpublic information before trading or to abstain from trading altogether. In *Chiarella,* we accepted the two elements set out in *Cady Roberts* for establishing a Rule 10b–5 violation: "(i) the existence of a relationship affording access to inside information intended to be available only for a corporate purpose, and (ii) the unfairness of allowing a corporate insider to take advantage of that information by trading without disclosure." . . . Such a duty arises . . . from the existence of a fiduciary relationship.

* * * * *

. . . Thus, an insider will be liable under Rule 10b–5 for inside trading only where he fails to disclose material nonpublic information before trading on it and thus makes "secret profits."

* * * * *

The SEC's position, as stated in its opinion in this case, is that a tippee "inherits" the *Cady, Roberts* obligation to shareholders whenever he receives inside information from an insider. . . .

* * * * *

Imposing a duty to disclose or abstain solely because a person knowingly receives material nonpublic information from an insider and trades on it could have an inhibiting influence on the role of market analysts, which the SEC itself recognizes is necessary to the preservation of a healthy market. It is commonplace for analysts to "ferret out and analyze information," and this often is done by meeting with and questioning corporate officers and others who are insiders.

And information that the analysts obtain normally may be the basis for judgments as to the market worth of a corporation's securities. The analyst's judgment in this respect is made available in market letters or otherwise to clients of the firm. It is the nature of this type of information and indeed of the markets themselves, that such information cannot be made simultaneously available to all of the corporation's stockholders or the public generally.

The conclusion that recipients of inside information do not invariably acquire a duty to disclose or abstain does not mean that such tippees always are free to trade on the information. The need for a ban on some tippee trading is clear. Not only are insiders forbidden by their fiduciary relationship from personally using undisclosed corporate information to their advantage, but they may not give such information to an outsider for the same improper purpose of exploiting the information for their personal gain. . . . Similarly, the transactions of those who knowingly participate with the fiduciary in such a breach are "as forbidden" as transactions "on behalf of the trustee himself." . . . Thus, the tippee's duty to disclose or abstain is derivative from that of the insider's duty. . . .

* * * * *

. . . [A] tippee assumes a fiduciary duty to the shareholders of a corporation not to trade on material nonpublic information only when the insider has breached his fiduciary duty to the shareholders by disclosing the information to the tippee and the tippee knows or should know that there has been a breach. . . .

In determining whether a tippee is under an obligation to disclose or abstain, it thus is necessary to determine whether the insider's "tip" constituted a breach of the insider's fiduciary duty. All disclosures of confidential corporate information are not inconsistent with the duty insiders owe to shareholders. . . . In some situations, the insider will act consistently with his fiduciary duty to shareholders, and yet release of the information may affect the market. For example, it may not be clear—either to the corporate insider or to the recipient analyst—whether the information will be viewed as material nonpublic information. Corporate officials may mistakenly think the information already has been disclosed or that it is not material enough to affect the market. Whether disclosure is a breach of duty therefore depends in large part on the purpose of the disclosure. . . . Thus, the test is whether the insider personally will benefit, directly or indirectly, from his disclosure. Absent some personal gain, there has been no breach of duty to stockholders. And absent a breach by the insider, there is no derivative breach. . . .

*   *   *   *   *

Determining whether an insider personally benefits from a particular disclosure, a question of fact, will not always be easy for courts. But it is essential, we think, to have a guiding principle for those whose daily activities must be limited and instructed by the SEC's inside-trading rules, and we believe that there must be a breach of the insider's fiduciary duty before the tippee inherits the duty to disclose or abstain. In contrast, the rule adopted by the SEC

in this case would have no limiting principle.

Under the inside-trading and tipping rules set forth above, we find that there was no actionable violation by Dirks. It is undisputed that Dirks himself was a stranger to Equity Funding, with no pre-existing fiduciary duty to its shareholders. He took no action, directly or indirectly, that induced the shareholders or officers of Equity Funding to repose trust or confidence in him. There was no expectation by Dirk's sources that he would keep their information in confidence. Nor did Dirks misappropriate or illegally obtain the information about Equity Funding. . . .

It is clear that neither Secrist nor the other Equity Funding employees violated their *Cady, Roberts* duty to the corporation's shareholders by providing information to Dirks. The tippers received no monetary or personal benefit for revealing Equity Funding's secrets, nor was their purpose to make a gift of valuable information to Dirks. As the facts of this case clearly indicate, the tippers were motivated by a desire to expose the fraud. In the absence of a breach of duty to shareholders by the insiders, there was no derivative breach by Dirks. . . .

We conclude that Dirks, in the circumstances of this case, had no duty to abstain from use of the inside information that he obtained.

CASE QUESTIONS

1. What is the *Cady, Roberts* rule?

2. When is a noninsider liable for violating Rule 10b–5?

3. What was the SEC's position? What problem did the court see with that position?

4. How do you determine whether an insider personally benefits from a particular disclosure?

5. Would it make any difference in this case if Dirks would have traded stock that he held in Equity Funding? Explain.

REMEDIES

The Exchange Act imposes liability on those who violate the act. It also imposes liability on everyone who controls a person who violates the act. A controlling person may avoid liability if he or she acted in good faith and did not induce the acts constituting the violation.

Willful violations of most provisions of the Exchange Act carry a penalty of up to $10,000 in fines and five years' imprisonment. Civil liabilities imposed under the Exchange Act are of two kinds. First, the Securities and Exchange Commission may enforce the act by taking administrative action or by instituting an action in a federal district court to compel compliance or enjoin violations. Second, purchasers or sellers of securities that have been injured as a result of an Exchange Act violation may bring suit in the federal courts. The complaint may demand relief in the form of an injunction to prevent or stop the prohibited conduct. The plaintiff may also seek damages for injury. These private civil remedies are predicated upon the antifraud provisions in the Exchange Act and SEC rules. The antifraud provisions may create an express or implied cause of action.

Several sections in the Securities Exchange Act provide for express civil remedies. We have already examined liability of an insider who acquires a short-swing profit. In addition, section 9 of the Exchange Act prohibits the manipulation of security prices. It provides an express remedy for sellers and purchasers against the manipulator. However, these remedies have short statutes of limitations, and plaintiffs invoking them find it difficult to prove that the violation caused the price change in the security. Consequently, express remedies are not often used by private parties.

Implied remedies do not have the same shortcomings as express remedies. The basis of an implied remedy is a finding that a legislative act which does not recognize an express right nonetheless implies a cause of action in favor of an injured party. A great majority of securities cases involving implied causes of actions are brought under Rule 10b–5.

The Uniform Securities Act, discussed in chapter 8, incorporates the wording of Rule 10b–5. Even states that have not adopted the act have a general antifraud provision authorizing criminal sanctions against violators and granting government officials the power to enjoin fraudulent activities. Violation of the state's antifraud provision may also be a basis for civil remedies by injured parties.

ALTERNATIVE APPROACHES

The SEC has simplified the securities registration process by coordinating the Securities Act and Exchange Act registration requirements. Some urge that it has not gone far enough. There have been proposals to eliminate the dual registration process altogether. One proposal would require company registration, as opposed to registration of securities. Companies subject to registration would be required to make annual, quarterly, and current reports similar to 10–K, 10–Q, and 8–K reports. Information concerning new public offerings of a registered company could be made on a current report.

Other critics of the current system would go all the way and eliminate mandated disclosures altogether. They maintain that the average investor does not rely on the disclosures and that the professional analyst demands more and different types of information than the present disclosure system affords. They advocate a market-motivated system, arguing that normal market forces would do a better job of regulating disclosure and would produce the type of information investors need. The information that the SEC requires is basically firm-oriented. However, surveys indicate that industry influences, market conditions, and other macroeconomic concerns are significant in determining the prices of securities. Consequently, investors need to look beyond the management and finances of the firm itself. Opponents of the present system further argue that mandated disclosure places an artificial restraint on the market by imposing costly registration on firms. This requirement, they argue, inhibits entry into the market and produces other anticompetitive side effects.

Finally, those who favor deregulation of the securities industry point to studies which indicate that the incidence of securities abuse has not decreased as a result of SEC-mandated disclosures. They believe that the antifraud provisions which impose civil and criminal penalties on wrongdoers are sufficient.

CHAPTER PROBLEMS

1. On May 23, 1972, Designcraft made a public offering of 300,000 shares of its common stock. The total outstanding common stock of Designcraft, including the 300,000 newly issued shares, was 817,500 shares. William Norton and Company, a broker-dealer in securities, was co-underwriter of the public offering, distributing 250,000 shares itself. The underwriting was made on a firm commitment basis requiring Norton to buy the shares from Designcraft and to resell them to the public, a process completed within a few days. At all material times Designcraft was registered pursuant to the Exchange Act. There was no relevant connection between Norton and Designcraft before the underwriting transaction took place. H. Perine, a stockholder of Designcraft, brought an action against Norton under the Exchange Act to recover the short-swing profits earned by Norton in its underwriting of the distribution. Is Norton liable for short-swing profits? Explain.

2. The Gladwins own voting stock in Medfield Corporation, a company that operates hospitals and other health facilities. In preparation for the annual shareholders meeting, Medfield sent shareholders an annual report and a proxy statement. A rival group known as the Medfield Shareholders Committee nominated its own slate of candidates in opposition to the management slate and solicited proxies.

At the annual meeting the management slate received 56 percent of the votes cast, while the slate endorsed by the Medfield Shareholders Committee received 44 percent. The Gladwins, who were aligned with the Medfield Shareholders Committee, alleged misstatements and material omissions in the Medfield Corporation proxy material in failure to disclose:

— A $2 million overpayment controversy with Blue Cross;
— A number of high-level management changes and the impending resignation of the company president;
— A 4.9 percent Medfield stock purchase by management nominees; and
— Its attempts to sell two of its nursing homes.

Do you think that the omissions are material? Why or why not? What remedies, if any, should be available to disappointed shareholders?

3. Elyria Corporation made a cash tender offer to purchase up to one million shares of ABC, Inc. for $30 a share. The offer provided that if less than one million shares were tendered within 30 days of the offer, Elyria would not be obligated to purchase any. It also gave Elyria the right to purchase all shares tendered in excess of one million shares. Assume that the market price was $20 a share at the time of the tender offer and that after the offer it increased to $25 a share. If you had 1,000 shares of ABC, Inc., what would you have done? Why?

4. Fred Lowenschuss is a shareholder of Great Atlantic & Pacific Tea Co., Inc. (A&P). He tendered A&P shares to Gulf & Western Industries, Inc. (G&W), in response to G&W's tender offer. The tender offer announced that G&W was willing to purchase up to 3,750,000 shares of A&P common stock (15 percent of its outstanding shares) at $20 per share. G&W held extensive investments in other food processors and distributors, and its acquisition of A&P stock would probably result in a violation of the antitrust laws. Furthermore, there was evidence to indicate that G&W intended to acquire a controlling position in A&P or at least to exercise influence over A&P's management and policies. Neither G&W's holdings nor its intentions regarding control over A&P were disclosed in the tender offer. Devise a strategy, which does not violate the Exchange Act, to prevent G&W from gaining control of A&P.

5. Cargill Incorporated announced an offer to purchase all the outstanding common stock of Missouri Portland Cement Company (MPC). MPC opposed the tender offer. In an attempt to muster shareholder support and defeat the takeover attempt, MPC made public statements explaining its reasons for opposing the offer. Cargill brought suit against MPC for its allegedly misleading and false statements. The parties agree that:

— MPC failed to disclose the seven-year employment contract for MPC's board chairman, approved by the company's directors within hours after they learned of the tender offer;
— MPC told its shareholders that their stock was worth much more than the $30 per share offered by Cargill, although MPC had made $30 the upper limit in authorizing repurchase of its stock on the market; and
— MPC advised its shareholders that an increase in the price of the stock during the term of the tender offer would not benefit those shareholders who had already tendered their shares, when the terms of the tender offer clearly stated otherwise.

Which, if any, of MPC's statements or omissions violate the Exchange Act? What relief will be granted to Cargill if it proves its contentions?

6. Alex Campbell, a financial columnist for the *Los Angeles Herald Examiner,* wrote a highly favorable analysis of American Systems, Inc. (ASI) based on interviews with ASI directors. These directors made material misrepresentations and omissions during the interview in the hope of inflating ASI stock prices. Just before the column was published, Campbell bought 5,000 shares from ASI at a substantial discount. The price of ASI stock rose swiftly after the column appeared, so Campbell sold 2,000 shares and recouped his entire investment.

Richard Zweig and Muriel Bruno merged their company with ASI in return for inflated ASI stock. They claim injury and allege that Campbell violated Rule 10b–5 by publishing his column without fully informing his readers of the fact that he bought ASI stock at a discount and intended to sell it at a profit after the column was published and the price rose. Is Campbell liable for the damages sustained by Zweig and Bruno? Explain.

7. Morgan Stanley & Co., Inc., and Kuhn Loeb & Co. are investment banking firms. They represent companies involved in mergers, acquisitions, tender offers, and takeovers. Courtois and Antoniu were employed by Morgan Stanley, but Antoniu later went to work for Kuhn Loeb. Through their employment, Antoniu and Courtois obtained confidential information about mergers and acquisitions entrusted to their employers by clients. They relayed this information to Newman, a securities manager in an over-the-counter trading firm. Newman passed the information to two others who, along with Newman, purchased stock in the target companies. They all reaped profits by selling the stock in these companies after the mergers and takeovers were announced. Has Newman violated the Exchange Act? Can this case be distinguished from *Dirks?*

8. Chiarella, a printer for Pandick Press, was responsible for printing five announcements of corporate takeover bids. The names of the target companies were omitted or replaced with false names. The real names were not sent to Chiarella until the night of the final printing. Despite these precautions, Chiarella was able to figure out the names of the target companies from other information in the documents. He immediately purchased stock in those companies and then (without informing the sellers of the forthcoming takeover bid) sold the shares after the takeover attempts were made public. As a result, he realized a $30,000 profit. Has Chiarella violated 10b–5? Explain.

9. Aaron was a managerial employee at E. L. Aaron & Co., a registered broker-dealer. He was responsible for supervising securities sales made by the firm's sales representatives. One security handled by the firm was Lawn-A-Mat Chemical & Equipment Corp. It sold lawn care franchises and supplied them with products and equipment.

Two sales representatives at E. L. Aaron & Co. made false and misleading statements about Lawn-A-Mat in an effort to sell its stock. They claimed that Lawn-A-Mat was manufacturing a new type of small car and tractor which would be marketed in six weeks. They also made unfounded optimistic projections about its financial position. The attorney for Lawn-A-Mat informed Aaron that his sales representatives were making false statements, but Aaron did nothing to stop them.

The Securities and Exchange Commission instituted an action against Aaron for violating Rule 10b–5. It based its claim on the fact that he knew or had reason to know that the employees were engaged in fraud but failed to take steps to prevent it. What is Aaron's argument in his defense?

10. Assume that two bills are pending in Congress. One would eliminate the dual registration process and cut down considerably on the required disclosures. The other bill would substantially deregulate the securities industry and place greater emphasis on antifraud administrative and private remedies. As a corporate manager in a large publicly held corporation, which bill do you favor? Why?

PART PROBLEMS

1. Unlimited, Inc., is the fastest growing department store chain in the United States. The store is designed to appeal to young urban professionals ("yuppies"). The company's stock is publicly traded on the National Stock Exchange. Unlimited has 500,000 outstanding shares of stock. Forty percent of the stock is owned by the company's officers and family members of the founder, Henry Waxman. Currently a share of Unlimited, Inc. is selling for $35.

It has long been known that Unlimited has been looking to purchase a company that has a large source of textiles. In January of this year Unlimited made a tender offer for the shares of U.S. Textiles. U.S. Textiles is one of the leading producers of textiles. It has 750 shareholders and 500,000 shares of outstanding stock currently selling over the counter for $21 a share. Unlimited is mainly interested in the long-term contracts that U.S. Textiles has with several European firms which would increase Limited's supply of raw textiles.

U.S. Textiles resists the takeover attempt. It issued a counter-takeover offer by bidding $26 a share for its outstanding shares. Also, it is seeking to tie up its long-term contracts by selling them to a firm on condition that Unlimited's tender offer is successful. It is also thinking about taking over Unlimited as a move to thwart the takeover.

The Unlimited board of directors met in February to determine how to proceed. At the meeting the board agreed to increase their tender offer to $30 a share. Thereafter, before the new tender offer was announced, one of the board members, Karl Lemon, was contacted by Fran Street, a stockbroker. Street was investigating the Limited and its current attempt to takeover U.S. Textiles. During the conversation Lemon admitted that a new tender offer would shortly be announced. He did not expose any further details. Street surmised that the tender offer would be increased. On this assumption she recommended to several of her customers that they buy U.S. Textiles stock. Several of those customers purchased additional shares of U.S. Textiles stock at $26/share.

a. Assume you are the chairman of the board of Unlimited. What strategies consistent with securities law would you suggest be implemented?

b. Assume you are the chairman of the board of U.S. Textiles. What additional strategies consistent with securities law would you suggest be implemented to avert the takeover?

c. What concerns do you expect the SEC will have? Explain

2. E. Turner Brite developed a scheme that he believed would either put him in the poorhouse or make him a South Sea retiree within two years. He started a company named Eternity Enterprises. The company sold "fountain of youth" packages. For $2,000 a purchaser received "three words" and a money-back guarantee to live 20 years (Bronze Plan). For $5,000 a purchaser received "two words" and a money-back guarantee to live 40 years (Silver Plan). For $10,000 a purchaser received "one word" and a money-back guarantee to live forever (Gold Plan). Eternity Enterprises marketed the "words" to persons who demonstrated a real knowledge of and interest in the spiritual. It sold:

— Bronze plans to 20 elderly members of an investment club and two salespersons in a stock brokerage firm.
— Silver plans to the widow of one of Brite's former business associates and to seven upper-echelon employees of an investment firm.
— Gold plans to 150 sophisticated investors and to an accountant, a lawyer, and three veterinarians.

Along with the words the purchasers received a handbook on how to use them and a script on how to organize "eternity youth-ins" to sell the plans to others. Portions of the handbook read:

> Always look energetic and alive; think young, talk young, dress young, act young, and expound on the virtues of the "words" and how they transformed your life. You are the living proof of the value of the "words." You are the product. Market yourself.

> Any deviation from the approved script will result in revocation of permission to sell the plans.

Eternity Enterprises provided all of the marketing materials used to sell the plans as well as the physical facilities for the youth-ins. A Bronze Plan purchaser could sell only Bronze plans; a Silver Plan purchaser could sell Silver and Bronze plans; and a Gold Plan purchaser could sell all three plans. For each sale the salesperson received 50 percent of the sales price.

There was no media advertising of the plans. Brite failed to file a registration statement covering the scheme with the SEC. The SEC sought an injunction against the further marketing of the scheme. In addition, 13 representatives of the estates of purchasers who died instituted a suit to rescind the transactions.

While those cases were pending, Brite developed plans to automate diamond cutting. He produced a working scale model of a mechanical diamond cutter, which he insured for $1,500,000. Brite incorporated Diamond Cutters International (DCI) in the State of Confusion, which had adopted the Uniform Securities Act. The corporation was approved by the secretary of the State of Confusion. In need of raising $20 million in capital to pursue the venture, DCI sold $20 million in stock. The corporation has 5,000 shareholders. It filed a registration statement under the Securities Act. DCI shares are traded over-the-counter.

James Malcolm, a sales representative of DCI, owned 1,500,000 shares of its stock. On April 1, 1985, he acquired 250,000 shares at $10 per share; on May 1, 1985, he acquired an additional 250,000 shares at $20 per share; on June 1, 1985, he sold 250,000 shares at $10/share; and on December 1, 1985, he sold the remaining shares at $50/share.

Of the 15,000,000 outstanding shares of DCI, the Brite faction controlled 41 percent while the Take Over Brite and Corporate Freedom groups, which sought control of the corporation, controlled 21 percent and 19 percent, respectively. In anticipation of an upcoming annual shareholders' meeting, all three groups sought proxies and filed proxy statements. The Brite faction omitted to mention that one of the persons whom it was supporting for a position on the board of directors had been charged with embezzling company funds, though the charges had been dismissed. In its proxy statement the Take Over Brite group failed to say that it intended to eliminate dividends for two years in order to improve the corporation's capital position. In fact, Bill Mellow, a shareholder, aware of that capital position and fearful of the consequences to the shareholders if the Take Over Brite group prevailed, gave notice to management of a proposal he desired to have included in its proxy statement. The proposal read, "Be it resolved that the present policy of issuing dividends annually will continue as long as there is a capital surplus." Management refused to include the proposal in its proxy materials.

At the shareholders' meeting the incumbents won by the following margin:

Brite Faction	51%
Take Over Brite	42
Corporate Freedom	7

The Take Over Brite and Corporate Freedom groups instituted suit and sought to have the election set aside. That action is pending.

Meanwhile, DCI has been threatened from the outside by Precious Jewels Hand Cutters, Inc. (PJ-HI), which has waged a campaign offering to purchase DCI stock at $40 per share, or $7 above the current market price. Of the 15,000,000 outstanding shares, it has acquired 637,500 shares thus far. In addition, PJ-HI is offering two shares of its stock in exchange for one share of DCI stock. As part of its campaign it has sought to undermine the Brite faction by exposing its "financial improprieties." DCI has retaliated by raising the DCI dividend and enlisting the Sway Mouth Universal Times (SMUT) advertising agency to aid it in its campaign. In reckless disregard of the truth, SMUT character-ized several PJ-HI officers and directors as "Marxist oriented" in their economic philoso-phy. Although PJ-HI has failed to file a registra-tion statement under the Williams Act, it has been delivering its prospectus to the sharehold-ers it has solicited. It has failed to inform them that its true motivation for the takeover is to demechanize DCI and return DCI to the tradi-tional hand diamond-cutter mold.

Brite has been in communication with Fran Bingham, PJ-HI's chief executive officer and chairman of the board. His discussions with her have convinced him that PJ-HI's takeover strategy will be successful. That strategy is to continue offering inflated prices to DCI share-holders, gradually increasing the offer to $75 per share over the next six months. Consequently, Brite has purchased several thousand shares of DCI stock at $60 per share, $5 above the current PJ-HI offer, in the hope of reselling them to PJ-HI for $75 per share in the future.

Discuss fully all of the relevant problems and resolutions available to Brite and DCI.

The effects of an antitrust violation are staggering. Many individuals and corporations have been either jailed or fined for violating the Sherman Act.

PART FOUR

ANTITRUST LAW

The American economy relies primarily on competition to regulate the provision of goods and services in the marketplace. Antitrust laws are designed to protect competition from the private accumulation of economic power. These laws are the principal means by which the government regulates conduct among competitors. The laws protecting competition are called "antitrust" laws because originally they were enacted in response to corporate misuse of the legal device known as a trust.

A *trust* is a legal arrangement through which property or other assets are secured for *beneficiaries*. Legal title and, usually, management responsibility are placed in a trustee. Trusts are most often established for benign purposes. An employer may establish a trust to provide retirement benefits for its employees. Parents may establish trusts to provide future financial support for their children.

In the late 19th century, however, trusts were used as covert devices to eliminate competition. Participating corporations pooled their stock, placing it under the control of trustees whom they selected. In return, they received trust certificates and were paid dividends. Since no corporate entity was involved, the participants projected a public image of independent companies competing with one another. In reality, these trustees made all crucial industry decisions: prices were fixed, supplies manipulated, and exclusive territories carved out. Thus, competition among member companies ceased, and outside competition was choked off. Disparities in the distribution of wealth widened markedly, and many blamed these disparities on the trusts that controlled petroleum, sugar, linseed oil, and whiskey. A number of states passed antitrust statutes designed to outlaw the trust device. But when the public learned that many trusts had received secret rebates from the railroads, Congress responded to citizen furor by enacting, in 1890, the Sherman Antitrust Act. In 1914, Congress enacted the Clayton Act and the Federal Trade Commission Act.

Although the trust device of the late 19th century is gone, the Sherman Act, Clayton Act, and Federal Trade Commission Act still function to protect the public from monopolistic control of the economy and to facilitate, but regulate, competition. The chapters in Part Four will explore these statutes in detail. At this point a brief overview of how these statutes are enforced, of the activities they regulate, and of the people they protect will orient the reader to the detailed discussions within the Part's chapters.

Whatever is not nailed down is mine. Whatever I can pry loose is not nailed down.

Collis P. Huntington,
pioneer railroad builder

Violations of the Sherman Act are both criminal and civil offenses, while violations of the Clayton and FTC acts are civil offenses. The Justice Department enforces civil provisions of both the Sherman and Clayton acts by seeking injunctive orders designed to remedy violations. Such orders may simply prohibit anticompetitive business practices or may require the defendant to take affirmative action, such as divesting itself of assets, divisions, or subsidiaries. Prior to filing a civil antitrust complaint, the Justice Department usually invites the prospective defendant to negotiate a consent decree. A *consent decree* is an order, agreed to by the parties, that prescribes or prohibits actions by the defendant. Until 1975, consent decree negotiations were often shrouded in secrecy. Since then, however, a 1974 amendment to the Clayton Act requires the government to publish all proposed consent decrees in the *Federal Register* at least 60 days before they became effective. The government must include a *competitive impact statement*, which summarizes the proceeding, the rationale for the remedy, and the remedies available to private parties damaged by the alleged violations. Summaries of these documents must appear in the newspapers published where the case is filed, and interested parties must be afforded an opportunity to comment on the proposed decree. After a hearing allowing interested persons to participate, the court must determine whether the proposed decree is in the public interest.

The Justice Department also enforces the Sherman Act's criminal provisions. As with all criminal proceedings, the government has the burden of proving the defendant guilty beyond a reasonable doubt, and the defendant is presumed innocent until proven guilty. Few criminal antitrust cases proceed to trial. Most terminate in bargained pleas of *nolo contendere*, in which the defendant does not admit guilt but chooses not to contest the pending charges.

Private individuals injured in their trade or business can sue alleged violators of the Sherman and Clayton acts and may recover treble damages, court costs and attorney's fees, and, in some cases, injunctive relief. Consumers are protected by the antitrust laws in two ways. First, under appropriate circumstances, they may sue the violators. Second, state attorneys general may bring actions on behalf of all injured individuals residing in their states.

A problem that has plagued the courts is which purchasers, if any, may recover damages from sellers of raw materials where antitrust violations have resulted in higher prices. The Supreme Court has held that the original purchaser may recover the full amount of the overcharge, all or part of which has been passed on.[1] Subsequent purchasers, however, may not recover.[2] This ruling has been criticized as particularly harsh on the ultimate purchaser, frequently a consumer, who has probably paid most of the overcharge.

I don't meet competition. I crush it.

Charles Revson

The Federal Trade Commission enforces section 5 of the Federal Trade Commission Act, which prohibits unfair methods of competition and unfair or deceptive trade practices. Unfair methods of competition include violations of the antitrust laws.

The FTC's jurisdiction over unfair methods of competition reaches conduct beyond that is specifically outlawed in the Sherman and Clayton acts. For example, although section 7 of the Clayton Act is limited to mergers of two or more corporations, the FTC may, pursuant to section 5, take action against a corporation acquiring businesses that are not incorporated. The FTC proceeds by administrative adjudication, utilizing the methods discussed in chapter 4.

The effects of an antitrust violation are staggering. Many individuals have been jailed and many more individuals and corporations have been

---

[1] *Hanover Shoe, Inc. v. United Shoe Machinery Corp.*, 329 U.S. 481 (1968).

[2] *Illinois Brick Co. v. Illinois,* 429 U.S. 1087 (1977).

fined for violating the Sherman Act. Private treble damage actions can produce judgments of hundreds of millions of dollars. The two largest money damage judgments in the history of the federal district courts involved private antitrust actions. In Part Four, chapter 10 considers restraints of trade; chapter 11 monopolization; chapter 12 mergers; and chapter 13 price discrimination. Finally, chapter 14 examines how antitrust laws have been used to regulate franchising.

CHAPTER 10

RESTRAINTS OF TRADE

At common law, certain agreements that restrained trade were unenforceable because they were against public policy. Courts took two approaches to restraints of trade. Under the first approach, a court would not enforce a restraint that was the primary agreement. However, the court would enforce a reasonable restraint that was ancillary to a broader agreement. Under the second approach, all reasonable restraints were enforced, whether they were primary or ancillary. In analyzing the reasonableness of restraints, the courts inquired into their purposes and effects. To be reasonable a restraint must have been justified by a legitimate business purpose and must not have had an anticompetitive effect.

The restraint of trade considered most often at common law was the *covenant not to compete*. A covenant not to compete is a promise by one person or company not to compete against another. It is usually part of a larger transaction. For example, assume that an individual buys a restaurant. Over the years, the restaurant probably developed a reputation for good food and service. That reputation is called *goodwill*. The buyer will probably pay for the restaurant's goodwill as well as its tangible assets. The purchase of goodwill is meaningless if the seller can establish a competing restaurant across the street, so the buyer will seek protection by obtaining the seller's promise not to compete.

Assume that the covenant not to compete prohibited the seller from establishing a restaurant in another state. The competing restaurant would pose no danger to the buyer's goodwill. In this case, the covenant would be broader than its legitimate business purpose. A similar result would arise if the covenant had bound the seller not to compete for five years. Within five years the buyer's efforts rather than the seller's name should account for the buyer's goodwill. Courts refused to enforce overbroad covenants not to compete and covenants that had no legitimate business purpose. Attempts to police restraints of trade under the common law were brought before courts only when one party sought to enforce them against another. Many of the most anticompetitive restraints, such as agreements fixing prices or allocating markets, were never challenged. The parties voluntarily adhered to them. In passing the Sherman and Clayton acts, Congress authorized the government and private parties to challenge these restraints.

This chapter considers the legality under the antitrust laws of agreements to restrain trade. It divides restraints into three primary categories: horizontal restraints, which are agreements among competitors; vertical restraints, which are agreements between customers and suppliers; and group boycotts, which are agreements not to deal with another party. All agreements are covered by section 1 of the Sherman Act. Certain vertical agreements also involve section 3 of the Clayton Act, which is discussed in the section dealing with vertical restraints.

SECTION 1 OF THE SHERMAN ACT

Sherman Act, Section 1
Every contract, combination in the form of trust or otherwise, or conspiracy, in restraint of trade or commerce among the several states, or with foreign nations, is declared to be illegal. . . .

Section 1 of the Sherman Act prohibits every contract, combination, and conspiracy that restrain trade in interstate or foreign commerce. The requirement that the restraint of trade involve interstate commerce is typical of federal regulatory legislation and is discussed in detail in chapter 3. The other two elements of a Sherman Act violation are: (1) a contract, combination, or conspiracy, and (2) an unreasonable restraint of trade.

Contract, Combination, or Conspiracy

A contract is an agreement between two or more parties to do things that they were previously not obligated to do. A conspiracy conjures up visions of clandestine meetings and elaborate plans. A combination seems less sinister than a conspiracy and less formal than a contract.

In antitrust legislation, however, "contract, combination, or conspiracy" is a term of art meaning joint or concerted action. Section 1 of the Sherman Act prohibits two or more entities from pooling their economic power to restrain trade. Unilateral action does not violate section 1 even though the identical action taken jointly would be illegal. The requirement of joint action will be discussed in relation to intraenterprise conspiracy and conscious parellelism.

Intraenterprise Conspiracy

An intraenterprise conspiracy occurs when two or more parts of the same enterprise agree to restrain trade. For example, a corporation may have many different divisions, each responsible for a different line of products. The divisions might compete with each other. However, the divisions are all part of the same corporation. There is only one legal entity, so there can be no conspiracy or agreement. Similarly, a corporation cannot conspire with its own officers or other employees when they are acting within the scope of their employment.

On the other hand, if a business organizes its different departments as separate subsidiaries, each subsidiary is a separate corporation and thus a separate legal entity. For many years the Supreme Court held that section one applied to conspiracies among a corporation and its subsidiaries. In recent years, lower courts have created exceptions to these rulings where the corporation and its subsidiaries operated as single wholly integrated enterprises. Finally, in late 1984, the Supreme Court reversed its prior rulings and held that a corporation cannot be found to have conspired with its wholly owned subsidiaries.[1] The Court reasoned:

> . . . [T]he very notion of an "agreement" in Sherman Act terms between a parent and a wholly owned subsidiary lacks meaning. A § 1 agreement may be found when "the conspirators had a unity of purpose or a common design and understanding, or a meeting of minds in an unlawful arrangement." But in reality a parent and a wholly owned subsidiary *always* have a "unity of purpose or a common design." They share a common purpose whether or not the parent keeps a tight rein over the subsidiary; the parent may assert full control at any moment if the subsidiary fails to act in the parent's best interests.

Conscious Parallelism

Conscious parallelism occurs when many competitors copy the actions of a market leader. When a few large producers dominate a highly concentrated market, the market is said to be *oligopolistic*. A change in the output of any one dominant firm will affect market conditions substantially, causing competitors to follow suit. Consciously parallel behavior usually affects price. Competitors copy the leader's announced increases or decreases.

When all or most competitors raise prices by similar amounts, the question is whether the price increases were arrived at unilaterally or by agreement. Where only consciously parallel behavior is shown, there is no section 1 violation because there is no agreement. However, circumstantial evidence may lead a jury to infer that what appears to be con-

---

[1] *Copperweld Corp. v. Independence Tube Corp.*, __ U.S. __, 52 U.S.L.W. 4821 (June 19, 1984).

sciously parallel behavior is actually the result of an agreement. This evidence may include meetings or other communications among competitors, parallel action that would benefit one competitor only if all others took the same action, and an overly complex series of consciously parallel steps.

Restraints of Trade—the Rule of Reason

Section 1 of the Sherman Act prohibits *"every* contract combination . . . or conspiracy that *restrains trade*. . . ."* The statute cannot be interpreted literally because virtually every contract restrains trade to a certain extent. For example, assume that a buyer intends to order 100 widgets and that several sellers are competing for that order. As soon as the buyer contracts with one seller, the others can no longer compete for the order. The contract has literally restrained trade. Thus, a literal interpretation of section 1 would result in declaring every contract to be illegal. This result was clearly not intended by Congress.

When Congress enacted the Sherman Act, it was aware of the common-law approach to restraints of trade. Therefore, courts have developed a rule of reason for interpreting section 1.

The Rule of Reason

Every agreement concerning trade, every regulation of trade restrains. To bind, to restrain, is of their very essence. The true test of legality is whether the restraint imposed is such as merely regulates and perhaps thereby promotes competition or whether it is such as may suppress or even destroy competition.

U.S. v. Chicago Board of Trade, 246 U.S. 231 (1918)

The rule of reason requires that a restraint be scrutinized for its purpose, effect, intent, and the power it confers upon the parties. To be reasonable, a restraint must be used for a procompetitive business purpose and not have an effect beyond that purpose. A restraint is unreasonable if the parties intended to suppress competition unlawfully, even though they could not or did not achieve that goal. A restraint is also unreasonable if it confers upon the parties the power to substitute their judgment for the judgment of the marketplace.

Per Se Violations

Per se unreasonable restraints are those whose effects on competition are so harmful that they cannot be justified. When such a restraint is involved, to find a violation of section 1 the court need only determine that the restraint exists. In this way, the court bypasses a rigorous inquiry into the restraint's reasonableness.

The per se rule serves a number of important functions. First, by declaring certain restraints per se illegal, the rule sets a standard of unreasonableness against which other restraints may be measured. This spares courts the necessity of performing complex economic analyses, for which they are ill-suited. Second, a standard of unreasonableness promotes the stability and predictability necessary for business planning.

It is tempting to label all restraints as requiring analysis under either the rule of reason or the per se rule. However, such a breakdown would be misleading because the per se rule is a specific application of the rule of reason. Restraints which at first may not appear to be per se unreasonable may, after preliminary analysis, prove identical with per se violations.

HORIZONTAL RESTRAINTS

Horizontal restraints involve agreements between two or more competitors to avoid competing with each other. When they occur among sellers of different brands they are said to suppress interbrand competition. When they occur among sellers of the same brand they are said to suppress intrabrand competition. The most common horizontal restraints are price fixes and divisions of territories, customers, or markets.

Price Fixing

The horizontal restraint first declared to be per se illegal was the price fix. In a free market economy, price is set by the interaction of supply and demand. When two or more competitors agree to fix the prices for their goods or services, they substitute their judgment for that of the marketplace. The Sherman Act is concerned with the power to manipulate prices as well as with the effect of artificially determined prices. Thus the reasonableness of the fixed price is irrelevant. A reasonably fixed price today may become an unreasonable price tomorrow. All price-fixing agreements are per se illegal.

Price-fixing arrangements are not limited to agreements which specify prices. Conspiracies to stabilize prices, set a floor under prices, or set a maximum level for prices are also per se illegal. Few restraints blatantly set forth an agreement to fix prices. Thus it is necessary to determine whether a seemingly innocuous restraint results in a price fix. If the parties to the restraint intend to set prices, then the restraint is per se illegal despite its appearance or its actual effect.

For example, a new-car dealers' association circulated a list of suggested retail prices that were higher than the manufacturer's sticker price. Their purpose was to set a starting point for use in bargaining with customers. Although most sales were made below the suggested prices, the use of the list was held to be an illegal price fix.[2]

---

[2] *Plymouth Dealers' Association v. United States* 279 F.2d 128 (9th Cir. 1960).

A particularly complex example of illegal price fixing occurred in the gasoline industry during the late 1920s and early 1930s. Most major oil companies had their own distribution facilities for entry into the retail market. But independent companies supplied 15 percent of retail gasoline, much of which was committed under long-term contracts. The uncommitted remainder of the independents' gasoline formed the spot market.

During the late 1920s and early 1930s more oil was being refined into gasoline than was demanded. Because the independents had little storage capacity, they were forced to sell their "distress oil" on the spot market. This glut on the market severely depressed prices.

The major oil companies responded with a buying program. Each "major," regardless of its needs, agreed to buy distress oil from a designated independent. Because the majors had plentiful storage capacity, they could keep the oil until a need for it developed.

Although it appeared that the majors were only seeking to purchase the gasoline on the spot market and were allowing the market to fix a price, the purpose of their buying program was to set a floor under prices and thereby to stabilize them. Purchases by the majors were timed to have maximum impact on stabilization of the spot market price. Stabilization, in turn, was compounded by pricing formulas in the long-term contracts which were based on the spot market price. The buying program was therefore held to be per se illegal.[3]

Not all business arrangements that affect prices are condemned as per se price fixes. Many legitimate business arrangements also have incidental effects on price. For example, a group of competing sellers may organize a buying cooperative to take advantage of bulk discounts. Such an arrangement may affect price, but its effects on price are incidental to its legitimate business purpose. Similarly, the use of joint selling agents by competitors may incidentally reduce price competition while achieving its legitimate purpose, economies of scale for the participants. The following decision illustrates the process by which a court determines whether an agreement is an illegal price fix.

Catalano, Inc. v. Target Sales, Inc.

446 U.S. 643 (1980)

Catalano and several other firms (petitioners) were beer retailers in the Fresno, California area. They sued Target and several others (respondents), who were beer wholesalers. Petitioners claimed that respondents agreed to sell beer only if payment were made at the time of or prior to delivery.

---

[3] *United States v. Socony-Vacuum Oil Co.,* 310 U.S. 150 (1940).

Before the alleged agreement, many wholesalers extended short-term, interest-free credit. The district court held that the alleged agreement to eliminate credit was not a per se violation of section 1 of the Sherman Act. The Ninth Circuit Court of Appeals affirmed. It believed that the agreement might increase competition by making it easier for new competitors to enter the market, and by making price more visible to purchasers. The Supreme Court reversed.

Per Curiam*

It has long been settled that an agreement to fix prices is unlawful *per se.* It is no excuse that the prices fixed are themselves reasonable. In *United States v. Socony–Vacuum Oil Co.,* we held that an agreement among competitors to engage in a program of buying surplus gasoline on the spot market in order to prevent prices from falling sharply was unlawful without any inquiry into the reasonableness of the program, even though there was no direct agreement on the actual prices to be maintained. In the course of the opinion, the Court made clear that

> "the machinery employed by a combination for price-fixing is immaterial.
> "Under the Sherman Act a combination formed for the purpose and with the effect of raising, depressing, fixing, pegging, or stabilizing the price of a commodity in interstate or foreign commerce is illegal *per se.*"

Thus, we have held agreements to be unlawful *per se* that had substantially less direct impact on price than the agreement alleged in this case. For example, in *Sugar Institute v. United States,* the Court held unlawful

an agreement to adhere to previously announced prices and terms of sale, even though advance price announcements are perfectly lawful and even though the particular prices and terms were not themselves fixed by private agreement. . . .

It is virtually self-evident that extending interest-free credit for a period of time is equivalent to giving a discount equal to the value of the use of the purchase price for that period of time. Thus, credit terms must be characterized as an inseparable part of the price. An agreement to terminate the practice of giving credit is thus tantamount to an agreement to eliminate discounts, and thus falls squarely within the traditional *per se* rule against price fixing. While it may be that the elimination of a practice of giving variable discounts will ultimately lead in a competitive market to corresponding decreases in the invoice price, that is surely not necessarily to be anticipated. It is more realistic to view an agreement to eliminate credit sales as extinguishing one form of competition among the sellers. In any event, when a particular concerted activity entails an obvious risk of anti-competitive impact with no apparent potentially redeeming value, the fact that a practice may turn out to be harmless in a particular set of circumstances will not prevent its being declared unlawful *per se.*

The majority of the panel of the Court of Appeals suggested, however, that a hori-

---

* *Per curiam* is Latin for "By the court." Used to distinguish an opinion of the entire court from an opinion written by a single judge. Sometimes used to denote a brief statement of the disposition of a case by a court not accompanied by any written opinion—Au.

zontal agreement to eliminate credit sales may remove a barrier to other sellers who may wish to enter the market. But in any case in which competitors are able to increase the price level or to curtail production by agreement, it could be argued that the agreement has the effect of making the market more attractive to potential new entrants. If that potential justifies horizontal agreements among competitors imposing one kind of voluntary restraint or another on their competitive freedom, it would seem to follow that the more successful an agreement is in raising the price level, the safer it is from antitrust attack. Nothing could be more inconsistent with our cases.

Nor can the informing function of the agreement, the increase price visibility, justify its restraint on the individual wholesaler's freedom to select his own prices and terms of sale. For, again, it is obvious that any industrywide agreement on prices will result in a more accurate understanding of the terms offered by all parties to the agreement. As the *Sugar Institute* case demonstrates, however, there is a plain distinction between the lawful right to publish prices and terms of sale, on the one hand, and an agreement among competitors limiting action with respect to the published prices, on the other.

Thus, under the reasoning of our cases, an agreement among competing wholesalers to refuse to sell unless the retailer makes payment in cash either in advance or upon delivery is "plainly anticompetitive." Since it is merely one form of price fixing, and since price-fixing agreements have been adjudged to lack any "redeeming virtue," it is conclusively presumed illegal without further examination under the rule of reason.

CASE QUESTIONS

1. Why does the Court conclude that a concerted denial of interest free credit is a price fix? Would it be relevant if prices decreased after all of the wholesalers eliminated interest-free credit?

2. What two justifications did the court of appeals rely on in concluding that the arrangement was not per se illegal? How did the Supreme Court respond to this?

3. Describe the restraint involved in the *Sugar Institute* case. Compare it to the restraint involved in *Catalano*.

4. A commodities exchange adopts a rule which provides that from the time the exchange closes at 4:00 P.M. until it reopens at 9:00 A.M. the next business day, no dealer shall sell commodities futures except at the last price quoted before the exchange closed. If the dealers agree to this rule, will they be engaging in price fixing? Explain.

Divisions of Territories, Customers, and Markets

When two or more competitors get together and agree to divide up territories or customers, they necessarily avoid competing with one another. Such arrangements are per se violations of section 1 even if the parties are free to set their own prices within their territories. Each competitor has eliminated the competitive forces within its territory that check its economic power.

Horizontal territorial or customer divisions are equally illegal, whether they occur among sellers of competing brands or among sellers of the same brand. An agreement between two Ford dealers to divide customers is as illegal as a comparable agreement between a Ford dealer and a Chevrolet dealer. The protection of intrabrand competition from horizontal restraints has a priority equal to the protection of interbrand competition. As the following case points out, a horizontal territorial division that restrains intrabrand competition cannot be justified even if it promotes interbrand competition.

 **United States v. Topco Associates, Inc.**

405 U.S. 596 (1972)

Topco was a membership association composed of 25 independent supermarket chains. Its members owned equal amounts of Topco stock, chose Topco's directors, and completely controlled Topco's operations. Topco marketed numerous groceries under the Topco brand name. Its members were each granted a territory in which it could sell Topco products. Members were prohibited from selling Topco products beyond their territories. Most of the territories granted members were exclusive; those that were not guaranteed to be exclusive were in practice exclusive. No member was permitted to expand into the territory of another member without that member's consent.

The government instituted a civil action to have Topco enjoined from enforcing the exclusivity agreements. The district court entered judgment for Topco, and the Supreme Court reversed.

Justice Marshall

While the Court has utilized the "rule of reason" in evaluating the legality of most restraints alleged to be violative of the Sherman Act, it has also developed the doctrine that certain business relationships are *per se* violations of the Act without regard to a consideration of reasonableness.

* * * * *

Antitrust laws in general, and the Sherman Act in particular, are the Magna Charta of free enterprise. They are as important to the preservation of economic freedom and our free enterprise system as the Bill of Rights is to the protection of our fundamental personal freedoms. And the freedom guaranteed each and every business, no matter how small, is the freedom to compete—to assert with vigor, imagination, devotion, and ingenuity whatever economic muscle it can muster. Implicit in such freedom is the notion that it cannot be foreclosed with respect to one sector of the economy because certain private citizens or groups believe that such foreclosure might promote greater competition in a more important sector of the economy.

The District Court determined that by limiting the freedom of its individual members to compete with each other, Topco was doing a greater good by fostering competition between members and other large supermarket chains. But, the fallacy in this is that Topco has no authority under the Sherman Act to determine the respective values of competition in various sectors of the economy. On the contrary, the Sherman Act gives to each Topco member and to each prospective member the right to ascertain for itself whether or not competition with other supermarket chains is more desirable than competition in the sale of Topco brand products. Without territorial restrictions, Topco members may indeed "[c]ut each other's throat." But we have never found this possibility sufficient to warrant condoning horizontal restraints of trade.

Chief Justice Burger (dissenting)

In joining in this cooperative endeavor, these small chains did not agree to the restraints here at issue in order to make it possible for them to exploit an already established line of products through non-competitive pricing. There was no such thing as a Topco line of products until this cooperative was formed. The restraints to which the cooperative's members have agreed deal only with the marketing of the products in the Topco line, and the only function of those restraints is to permit each member chain to establish and through its own local advertising and marketing efforts, [sic] a local consumer awareness of the trademarked family of products as that member's "private label" line. The goal sought

was the enhancement of the individual members' abilities to compete, albeit to a modest degree, with the large national chains which had been successfully marketing private label lines for several years. The sole reason for a cooperative endeavor was to make economically feasible such things as quality control, large quantity purchases at bulk prices, the development of attractively printed labels, and the ability to offer a number of different lines of trademarked products. All these things, of course, are feasible for the large national chains operating individually, but they are beyond the reach of the small proceeding alone. . . .

We can undoubtedly ease our task, but we should not abdicate that role by formulation of *per se* rules with no justification other than the enhancement of predictability and the reduction of judicial investigation. . . . [F]rom the general proposition that *per se* rules play a necessary role in antitrust law, it does not follow that the particular *per se* rule promulgated today is an appropriate one.

The District Court specifically found that the horizontal restraints involved here tend positively to promote competition in the supermarket field and to produce lower costs for the consumer. The Court seems implicitly to accept this determination, but says that the Sherman Act does not give Topco the authority to determine for itself "whether or not competition with other supermarket chains is more desirable than competition in the sale of Topco brand products." But the majority overlooks a further specific determination of the District Court, namely, that the invalidation of the restraints here at issue "would not increase competition in Topco private label brands." Indeed, the District Court seemed to believe that it would, on the contrary, lead to the likely demise of those brands in time. And the evidence before the District Court would appear to justify that conclusion.

There is no national demand for Topco brands, nor has there ever been any national advertising of those brands. It would be impracticable for Topco, with its limited financial resources, to convert itself into a national brand distributor in competition with distributors of existing national brands. Furthermore, without the right to grant exclusive licenses, it could not attract and hold new members as replacements for those of its present members who, following the pattern of the past, eventually grow sufficiently in size to be able to leave the cooperative organization and develop their own individual private label brands. Moreover, Topco's present members, once today's decision has had its full impact over the course of time, will have no more reason to promote Topco products through local advertising and merchandising efforts than they will have such reason to promote any other generally available brands.

CASE QUESTIONS

1. What is a private label? Why did offering private labels give the large national supermarkets a competitive edge over smaller regional chains? Is it possible for smaller chains to offer private labels without territorial divisions?

2. What effect did the restraint have on intrabrand competition?

3. What is the basis for the majority's holding that Topco's territorial divisions were per se illegal?

4. What is the basis for the Chief Justice's dissent?

5. If instead of assigning exclusive territories, Topco had assigned each member primary areas of responsibility and had required each member to advertise and otherwise develop the Topco name in its area, would the restraint have violated the Sherman Act?

VERTICAL RESTRAINTS

Vertical restraints are agreements between two or more parties at different levels of the distribution process. Typically they are agreements between manufacturer and distributor or retailer or between franchisor and franchisee. Vertical restraints frequently sacrifice some intrabrand competition to further interbrand competition. The most common vertical restraints are (1) resale price maintenance; (2) territorial, customer, and market restraints; (3) exclusive dealing arrangements; and (4) tying devices. The first two involve only the Sherman Act. The last two are also covered by section 3 of the Clayton Act.

Resale Price Maintenance

Resale price maintenance occurs when a manufacturer tries to control the retail price of its product. A manufacturer may wish to set a maximum retail price on its product as part of an aggressive campaign to take customers away from competitors. In other cases it may want to maintain a minimum price in order to give its goods an aura of high quality. If the manufacturer and retailer agree to minimum or maximum resale prices, the contract is a vertical price fix and per se violative of the Sherman Act. A number of states enacted fair trade laws that legalized resale price maintenance. These laws conflicted with the Sherman Act, and in the absence of a congressional intent to the contrary they would have been preempted. In 1937, however, Congress enacted the Miller-Tydings Amendment, which exempted from the Sherman Act resale price maintenance agreements sanctioned by state fair trade laws. This amendment was repealed in 1975. Consequently, all state fair trade laws are now preempted by the Sherman Act.

In determining whether a program of resale price maintenance violates the Sherman Act, the major issue is whether the required contract, combination, or conspiracy exists. A contract obligating a purchaser to resell at a given price clearly violates section 1. However, where only unilateral action by the initial seller exists, there is no violation. Thus, a manufacturer may lawfully maintain retail prices by suggesting retail prices and unilaterally terminating or refusing to deal with retailers that sell below the suggested prices.

Courts are quick to condemn resale price maintenance schemes whenever they find an agreement. If a manufacturer involves its distributors in policing such a scheme, a violation results. Similarly, if a manufacturer refuses to deal with a retailer because of the retailer's discount prices, but later reinstates the retailer, courts will infer an agreement fixing the resale price. The following case illustrates the judicial approach to resale price maintenance.

 **Monsanto Co. v. Spray-Rite Service Corp.**

104 S.Ct. 1464 (1984)

Spray-Rite (respondent) was a wholesale distributor of agricultural herbicide produced by Monsanto (petitioner). Monsanto terminated Spray-Rite's distributorship. Spray-Rite sued, claiming that it was terminated because it refused to participate in a conspiracy between Monsanto and other distributors to fix the price of herbicide. The district court jury found for Spray-Rite. The Seventh Circuit Court of Appeals affirmed, holding that the jury's verdict was supported by evidence that Spray-Rite was terminated shortly after other distributors complained to Monsanto that Spray-Rite was price cutting. The Supreme Court affirmed.

Justice Powell

This Court has drawn two important distinctions that are at the center of this and any other distributor-termination case. First, there is the basic distinction between concerted and independent action—a distinction not always clearly drawn by parties and courts. Section 1 of the Sherman Act requires that there be a "contract, combination . . . or conspiracy" between the manufacturer and other distributors in order to establish a violation. Independent action is not proscribed. A manufacturer of course generally has a right to deal, or refuse to deal, with whomever it likes, as long as it does so independently. *United States v. Colgate & Co.* Under *Colgate*, the manufacturer can announce its resale prices in advance and refuse to deal with those who fail to comply. And a distributor is free to acquiesce in the manufacturer's demand in order to avoid termination.

The second important distinction in distributor-termination cases is that between concerted action to set prices and concerted action on nonprice restrictions. The former have been *per se* illegal since the early years of national antitrust enforcement. The latter are judged under the rule of reason, which requires a weighing of the relevant circumstances of a case to decide whether a restrictive practice constitutes an unreasonable restraint on competition. See *Continental T.V., Inc. v. GTE Sylvania, Inc.*

While these distinctions in theory are reasonably clear, often they are difficult to apply in practice. . . . [T]he legality of arguably anticompetitive conduct should be judged primarily by its "market impact." But the economic effect of all of the conduct described above—unilateral and concerted vertical price-setting, agreements on price and nonprice restrictions—is, in many, but not all, cases similar or identical. And judged from a distance, the conduct of the parties in the various situations can be indistinguishable. For example, the fact that a manufacturer and its distributors are in constant communication about prices and marketing strategy does not alone show that the distributors are not making independent pricing decisions. A manufacturer and its distributors have legitimate reasons to exchange information about the prices and the reception of their products in the market. Moreover, it is precisely in cases in which the manufacturer attempts to further a particular marketing strategy by means of agreements on often costly nonprice restrictions that it will have the most interest in the distributors' resale prices. The manufacturer often will want to ensure that its distributors earn sufficient profit to pay for programs such as hiring and training additional salesmen or demonstrating the technical features of the product, and will want to see that "free-riders" do not interfere. Thus, the manufacturer's strongly felt concern about resale prices does not necessarily mean that it has done more than the *Colgate* doctrine allows.

Nevertheless, it is of considerable importance that independent action by the manufacturer, and concerted action on nonprice restrictions, be distinguished from price-fixing agreements, since under present law the latter are subject to *per se* treatment and treble damages. On a claim of concerted price-fixing, the antitrust plaintiff must present evidence sufficient to carry its burden of proving that there was such an agreement. If an inference of such an agreement may be drawn from highly ambiguous evidence, there is a considerable danger that the doctrines enunciated in *Sylvania* and *Colgate* will be seriously eroded.

The flaw in the evidentiary standard adopted by the Court of Appeals in this case is that it disregards this danger. Permitting an agreement to be inferred merely from the existence of complaints, or even from the fact that termination came about "in response to" complaints, could deter or penalize perfectly legitimate conduct. As Monsanto points out, complaints about price-cutters "are natural—and from the manufacturer's perspective, unavoidable—reactions by distributors to the activities of their rivals." Such complaints, particularly where the manufacturer has imposed a costly set of nonprice restrictions, "arise in the normal course of business and do not indicate illegal concerted action." Moreover, distributors are an important source of information for manufacturers. In order to assure an efficient distribution system, manufacturers and distributors constantly must coordinate their activities to assure that their product will reach the consumer persuasively and efficiently. To bar a manufacturer from acting solely because the information upon which it acts originated as a price complaint would create an irrational dislocation in the market. In sum, "[t]o permit the inference of concerted action on the basis of receiving complaints alone and thus to expose the defendant to treble damage liability would both inhibit management's exercise of independent business judgment and emasculate the terms of the statute."

Thus, something more than evidence of complaints is needed. There must be evidence that tends to exclude the possibility that the manufacturer and nonterminated distributors were acting independently. [T]he antitrust plaintiff should present direct or circumstantial evidence* that reasonably tends to prove that the manufacturer and others "had a conscious

---

* Circumstantial evidence is testimony not based on actual personal knowledge or observation of the facts in controversy, but of other facts from which inferences are drawn, showing indirectly the facts sought to be proved.—Au.

commitment to a common scheme designed to achieve an unlawful objective."

Applying this standard to the facts of this case, we believe that there was sufficient evidence for the jury reasonably to have concluded that Monsanto and some of its distributors were parties to an "agreement" or "conspiracy" to maintain resale prices and terminate price-cutters. In fact there was substantial *direct* evidence of agreements to maintain prices. There was testimony from a Monsanto district manager, for example, that Monsanto on at least two occasions in early 1969, about five months after Spray-Rite was terminated, approached price-cutting distributors and advised that if they did not maintain the suggested resale price, they would not receive adequate supplies of Monsanto's new corn herbicide. When one of the distributors did not assent, this information was referred to the Monsanto regional office, and it complained to the distributor's parent company. There was evidence that the parent instructed its subsidiary to comply, and the distributor informed Monsanto that it would charge the suggested price. Evidence of this kind plainly is relevant and persuasive as to a meeting of minds.

* * * * *

If, as the courts below reasonably could have found, there was evidence of an agreement with one or more distributors to maintain prices, the remaining question is whether the termination of Spray-Rite was part of or pursuant to that agreement. It would be reasonable to find that it was, since it is necessary for competing distributors contemplating compliance with suggested prices to know that those who do not comply will be terminated. Moreover, there is some circumstantial evidence of such a link. Following the termination, there was a meeting between Spray-Rite's president and a Monsanto official. There was testimony that the first thing the official mentioned was the many complaints Monsanto had received about Spray-Rite's prices. In addition, there was reliable testimony that Monsanto never discussed with Spray-Rite prior to the termination the distributorship criteria that were the alleged basis for the action. By contrast, a former Monsanto salesman for Spray-Rite's area testified that Monsanto representatives on several occasions . . . approached Spray-Rite, informed the distributor of complaints from other distributors—including one major and influential one—and requested that prices be maintained. Later that same year, Spray-Rite's president testified, Monsanto officials made explicit threats to terminate Spray-Rite unless it raised its prices.

We conclude that the Court of Appeals applied an incorrect standard to the evidence in this case. The correct standard is that there must be evidence that tends to exclude the possibility of independent action by the manufacturer and distributor. That is, there must be direct or circumstantial evidence that reasonably tends to prove that the manufacturer and others had a conscious commitment to a common scheme designed to achieve an unlawful objective. Under this standard, the evidence in this case created a jury issue as to whether Spray-Rite was terminated pursuant to a price-fixing conspiracy between Monsanto and its distributors.

CASE QUESTIONS

1. Is it possible for a manufacturer to lawfully maintain minimum resale prices? Explain.

2. What evidence did the court of appeals rely on in finding an illegal conspiracy? Why did the Supreme Court conclude that this evidence was insufficient to establish the conspiracy?

3. What evidence did the Supreme Court rely on in finding a conspiracy?

4. Why was it necessary to show that Spray-Rite's termination was linked to the price fix? What evidence established this?

Territorial, Customer, and Market Restraints

Manufacturers and franchisors frequently impose territorial restraints upon their distributors, retailers, or franchisees. These restraints may take the form of exclusive territories or customer divisions. Less restrictive restraints may also be used, such as assigning areas of primary responsibility or designating the location of a dealer or franchisee. Vertical territorial or customer restraints differ from horizontal restraints in that they are designed for the benefit of the manufacturer or the franchisor rather than for the benefit of the competing retailers, distributors, or franchisees.

Vertical territorial or customer divisions have received varied treatment from the Supreme Court. The issue was initially posed in *White*

Motor Co. v. United States.[4] White Motor, a truck manufacturer, granted its distributors and dealers exclusive territories but prohibited them from selling to government agencies without its permission. The district court held these restrictions to be per se violations of section 1. The Supreme Court reversed the district court's decision and remanded the case for trial and assessment of the reasonableness of the restrictions.

At trial the district court was required to consider White Motor's proffered justification for the restrictions. White Motor contended that it was a small manufacturer struggling for survival among giants. It claimed that the territorial restraints were necessary to induce competent dealers and distributors to make the capital investment involved in selling White Motor trucks and to insure that White Motor distributors and dealers would concentrate on competing with other brands instead of with one another. The customer restraints were justified, White Motor maintained, because they insured that large fleet accounts would not be lost due to incompetent handling by dealers or distributors.

In *White Motor* the Court's view was that its experience with vertical territorial restraints was not sufficient to declare them per se illegal. In *United States v. Arnold Schwinn & Co.,*[5] the court concluded that it had gained enough experience to do so. There the Court held that vertical territorial divisions were per se illegal if the manufacturer parted with ownership and control of the product. Where the manufacturer retained title to the product, however, exclusive territories were not per se unreasonable.

Many manufacturers found it impossible to change their distribution systems in a manner that would insure their retention of legal title to their products. These manufacturers resorted to assigning areas of primary responsibility and employing dealer location clauses. One such manufacturer was G.T.E. Sylvania, Inc.

Continental TV, Inc. v. GTE Sylvania, Inc.

433 U.S. 36 (1977)

Continental TV was a licensed dealer of GTE Sylvania products. Its license contained a dealer location clause prohibiting Continental from selling Sylvania products at locations other than the one specified. Continental violated the location clause by establishing a new store at another location

---

[4] 372 U.S. 253 (1963).

[5] 388 U.S. 350 (1967).

and transferring Sylvania products from the approved location to the new location. Sylvania canceled Continental's dealership, and Continental sued, contending that the dealer location clause violated section 1 of the Sherman Act. The lower courts held for Sylvania. The Supreme Court affirmed.

Justice Powell

We turn first to Continental's contention that Sylvania's restriction on retail locations is a *per se* violation of section one of the Sherman Act as interpreted in *Schwinn.* The restrictions at issue in *Schwinn* were part of the three-tier distribution system. . . .

* * * * *

In the present case, it is undisputed that title to the television sets passed from Sylvania to Continental. . . . [W]e are unable to find a principled basis for distinguishing *Schwinn* from the case now before us.

Both Schwinn and Sylvania sought to reduce but not to eliminate competition among their respective retailers through the adoption of a franchise system. . . . In intent and competitive impact, the retail-customer restriction in *Schwinn* is indistinguishable from the location restriction in the present case. In both cases the restrictions limited the freedom of the retailer to dispose of the purchased products as he desired. The fact that one restriction was addressed to territory and the other to customers is irrelevant to functional antitrust analysis and, indeed, to the language and broad thrust of the opinion in *Schwinn.*

* * * * *

Sylvania argues that if *Schwinn* cannot be distinguished, it should be reconsidered. Although *Schwinn* is supported by the principle of *stare decisis,* we are convinced that the need for clarification of the law in this area justifies reconsideration. *Schwinn* itself was an abrupt and largely unexplained departure from *White Motor Co. v. United States.* . . . Since its announcement, *Schwinn* has been the subject of continuing controversy and confusion. . . . The great weight of scholarly opinion has been critical of the decision, and a number of the federal courts confronted with analogous vertical restrictions have sought to limit its reach. In our view, the experience of the past 10 years should be brought to bear on this subject of considerable commercial importance.

* * * * *

The market impact of vertical restrictions is complex because of their potential for a simultaneous reduction of intrabrand competition and stimulation of interbrand competition. . . .

Vertical restrictions reduce intrabrand competition by limiting the number of sellers of a particular product competing for the business of a given group of buyers. Location restrictions have this effect because of practical constraints on the effective marketing area of retail outlets. Although intrabrand competition may be reduced, the ability of retailers to exploit the resulting market may be limited both by the ability of consumers to travel to other franchised locations and, perhaps more importantly, to purchase the competing products of other manufacturers. None of these key variables, however, is affected by the form of the transaction by which a manufacturer conveys his products to the retailers.

Vertical restrictions promote interbrand competition by allowing the manufacturer to achieve certain efficiencies in the distribution of his products. These "redeeming virtues" are implicit in every decision sustaining vertical restrictions under the rule of reason. Economists have identified a number of ways in which manufacturers can use such restrictions to compete more effectively against other manufacturers. For example, new manufacturers and manufacturers entering new markets can use the restrictions in order to induce competent and aggressive retailers to make the kind of investment of capital and labor that is often required in the distribution of products unknown to the consumer. Established manufacturers can use them to induce retailers to engage in promotional activities or to provide service and repair facilities necessary to the efficient marketing of their products. . . . The availability and quality of such services affect a manufacturer's goodwill and the competitiveness of his product. Because of market imperfections such as the so-called "free rider" effect, these services might not be provided by retailers in a purely competitive situation, despite the fact that each retailer's benefit would be greater if all provided the services than if none did.

Economists also have argued that manufacturers have an economic interest in maintaining as much intrabrand competition as is consistent with the efficient distribution of their products. . . .

* * * * *

We revert to the standard articulated in *White Motor*. . . . Accordingly, we conclude that the *per se* rule stated in *Schwinn* must be overruled. . . .

. . . When anticompetitive effects are shown to result from particular vertical restrictions they can be adequately policed under the rule of reason, the standard traditionally applied for the majority of anticompetitive practices challenged under section one of the Act.

CASE QUESTIONS

1. Why did the Court conclude that Sylvania's dealer location clause was indistinguishable from Schwinn's customer restrictions?

2. What factors led the Court to conclude that *Schwinn* should be overruled?

3. What justifications exist for the conclusion that vertical territorial restraints are reasonable?

4. What factors might lead a court to conclude that a vertical market allocation is unreasonable?

The Court's decision in *Sylvania* states that the per se rule is inapplicable to vertical territorial restraints. It further states that in assessing the reasonableness of vertical restraints, a court must compare their anticompetitive effects in the intrabrand market with their procompetitive effects in the interbrand market. This was precisely the comparison that the Court refused to make in *Topco*. Although *Topco* involved a horizontal rather than a vertical restraint, the Court's approach in *Sylvania* was very similar to that espoused in Chief Justice Burger's dissent in *Topco*. It is possible that *Topco* will be reexamined in light of *Sylvania*. Until that occurs, however, courts and businesses will have to distinguish vertical from horizontal restraints. This may be difficult where a manufacturer competes with its distributors or retailers. Territorial restraints in such situations will have both vertical and horizontal components. The manufacturer will have to establish that the restraints are intended to promote interbrand competiton, thereby enabling a court to conclude that they serve a vertical rather than a horizontal purpose.

Exclusive Dealing Contracts—Section 3 of the Clayton Act

Exclusive dealing agreements are contracts that obligate the buyer to purchase all of its requirements of a given commodity from the seller. Such arrangements may be made at the insistence of the seller or by mutual agreement. In the latter situation the buyer is assured of a constant supply, is protected against price increases, and avoids the costs of storage, while the seller reduces its selling expenses, is protected against market fluctuations, and is afforded a predictable market for its product.

Section 3 of the Clayton Act applies when a party conditions the sale or lease of goods or commodities upon the buyer's agreement not to deal in or use the goods of the seller's competitors. These conditions are illegal where they may tend to substantially lessen competition or tend to create a monopoly. Section 3 applies only to sales or leases of goods. It does not apply to services, trademark licenses, or extensions of credit. However, exclusive dealing requirements in transactions not involving goods may, if unreasonable, violate section 1 of the Sherman Act.

The Supreme Court has issued two significant decisions interpreting section 3 as applied to exclusive dealing arrangements. In the first case, *Standard Oil Co. of California v. United States,* Standard's exclusive dealing contracts with over 6,000 independent service stations, representing 16 percent of all outlets in seven western states, were challenged under section 3.[6] Standard was the leading refiner in the area, with 23 percent of the market, while its next six competitors together accounted for another 42 percent. Standard's exclusive sales contracts usually covered a period of one year, and such contracts were also employed by most other refiners. The market shares of all refiners had remained constant for a considerable period of time.

In determining what test should be applied to evaluate the legality of exclusive dealing contracts, the Court struggled with two conflicting concerns. On the one hand, the possible benefits of such agreements to buyers and sellers seemed to require a complex economic inquiry into each contract's economic usefulness and restrictive effects. Among the

---

[6] 337 U.S. 293 (1949).

subjects of that inquiry would be the reasonableness of the contract's duration in light of the industry, whether competition flourished despite the contract, and the seller's strength in the market. The Court viewed this inquiry as difficult at best. In *Standard Oil*, the refiners' market positions had remained constant and the exclusive dealing contracts were an industrywide practice. It was virtually impossible to determine whether this indicated that the exclusive dealing contracts had had no competitive impact or had enabled established refiners to maintain their positions by preventing entrants from gaining a foothold in the market. The Court, therefore, rejected the complicated economic inquiry and held that exclusive dealing arrangements would violate section 3 where "competition has been foreclosed in a substantial share of the line of commerce affected." In applying this test, the Court found that the Standard Oil contracts violated section 3.

The Supreme Court interpreted section 3 for the next and last time in *Tampa Electric Co. v. Nashville Coal Co.*[7] Tampa Electric contracted with Nashville Coal to supply all of Tampa's coal requirements for 20 years. The amount of commerce involved totaled $128 million. The lower courts found this substantial and held that the contract violated section 3. The Supreme Court, however, reversed.

The Court held that substantiality could not be measured in absolute quantities but must be considered in terms of the relevant market. It then engaged in an economic analysis similar to the type it had rejected in *Standard Oil*. It found the relevant market to include the entire Appalachian region and calculated the amount of commerce foreclosed by the contract as less than 1 percent of that market. The Court concluded that this was not substantial and consequently found no violation.

At first glance the rationales of *Tampa* and *Standard Oil* appear to conflict. The former employs rigorous economic analysis, while the latter rejects such analysis as impractical. The decisions can be reconciled, however, by comparing the facts of *Tampa* with those of *Standard Oil*. In *Tampa* the use of exclusive dealing contracts was not an industrywide practice and there were not a large number of outlets with substantial sales volumes. Tampa Electric and Nashville Coal had relatively equal bargaining power, and the agreement conferred substantial benefits on both parties. It therefore did not appear that the seller was coercing an interdependent buyer. Thus exclusive dealing arrangements are more likely to be found legal where they are not imposed by a dominant party on a weaker party and where they are not industrywide practices.

Tying Devices—Section 1 of the Sherman Act and Section 3 of the Clayton Act.

Tying devices, also known as tie-ins, occur when a party offers to provide one good or service only to those who agree to accept a good or service.

---

[7] 365 U.S. 320 (1961).

The desired good is called the tying product, and the one the buyer is forced to take is called the tied product.

All tie-ins are restraints of trade under section 1 of the Sherman Act. When the tying and tied products are tangible commodities, the tie-in is also covered by section 3 of the Clayton Act. There are three requirements for a tie-in.

First, a substantial amount of commerce must be affected. If the amount of commerce affected is insignificant, the impact of the tie-in on competition is trivial.

Second, two separate products or services must be involved. A situation in which two or more products must be sold together does not necessarily signal an illegal tie-in. If the two products are totally unrelated, the two-product requirement is satisfied, but some combinations of products are not tie-ins. For example, no tie-in exists even though it is impossible to purchase a new car without a spare tire. In determining if a particular arrangement is a valid package of goods or an illegal tie-in, the courts consider whether: (1) others in the field offer the products separately, (2) the number of pieces in each package varies considerably, (3) the purchaser is charged separately for each item, and (4) some of the items are available separately to other consumers.

Third, the defendant must have sufficient economic power in the tying product to enforce the tie-in. No tie-in exists, for example, if a supermarket refuses to sell eggs unless the customer also purchases bacon, if the customer can buy eggs separately at a store down the street. If, however, the supermarket is the only local source of eggs, it probably possesses sufficient economic power to enforce the tie.

When the above three requirements are met, the tie-in is a per se violation of the antitrust laws. It restrains competition in the product that the customer is forced to purchase. The customer purchases the tied product only because of the coercion applied. Price, quality, service, and other characteristics in which sellers usually compete become largely irrelevant. The following case illustrates the Supreme Court's approach to tie-ins.

 **Jefferson Parish Hospital District v. Hyde**

104 S.Ct. 1551 (1984)

Jefferson Parish Hospital District (petitioner) operated East Jefferson Hospital. The hospital agreed with Roux & Associates that Roux would provide all anesthesiology services needed by Jefferson patients. The hospital refused to allow any other anesthesiologists to provide these services to its patients. Hyde (respondent) sued, claiming that the hospital illegally tied anesthesiology services to other hospital services. The trial court found no violations, reasoning that the arrangement was justified because it resulted in improved patient care. The Fifth Circuit Court of Appeals reversed, holding that the arrangement was per se illegal. The Supreme Court reversed the Court of Appeals.

Justice Stevens

Certain types of contractual arrangements are deemed unreasonable as a matter of law. . . . It is far too late in the history of our antitrust jurisprudence to question the proposition that certain tying arrangements pose an unacceptable risk of stifling competition and therefore are unreasonable "per se." . . .

It is clear, however, that every refusal to sell two products separately cannot be said to restrain competition. If each of the products may be purchased separately in a competitive market, one seller's decision to sell the two in a single package imposes no unreasonable restraint on either market. . . . [T]he essential characteristic of an invalid tying arrangement lies in the seller's exploitation of its control over the tying product to force the buyer into the purchase of a tied product that the buyer either did not want at all, or might have preferred to purchase elsewhere on different terms. When such "forcing" is present, competition on the merits in the market for the tied item is restrained and the Sherman Act is violated.

* * * * *

Thus, the law draws a distinction between the exploitation of market power by merely enhancing the price of the tying product, on the one hand, and by attempting to impose restraints on competition in the market for a tied product, on the other. When the seller's power is just used to maximize its return in the tying product market, where presumably its product enjoys some justifiable advantage over its competitors, the competitive ideal of the Sherman Act is not necessarily compromised. But if that power is used to impair competition on the merits in another market, a potentially inferior product may be insulated from competitive pressures. . . . [T]o permit restraint of competition on the merits through tying arrangements would be . . . to condone "the existence of power that a free market would not tolerate."

. . . Of course, as a threshold matter there must be a substantial potential for impact on competition in order to justify per se condemnation. If only a single purchaser were "forced" with respect to the purchase of a tied item, the resultant impact on competition would not be sufficient to warrant the concern of antitrust law. It is for this reason that we have refused to condemn tying arrangements unless a substantial volume of commerce is foreclosed thereby. Similarly, when a purchaser is "forced" to buy a product he would not have otherwise bought even from another seller in the tied product market, there can be no adverse impact on competition because no portion of the market which would otherwise have been available to other sellers has been foreclosed.

Once this threshold is surmounted, per se prohibition is appropriate if anticompetitive forcing is likely. For example, if the government has granted the seller a patent or similar monopoly over a product, it is fair to presume that the inability to buy the product elsewhere gives the seller market power. . . .

The same strict rule is appropriate . . . [w]hen the seller's share of the market is high, or when the seller offers a unique product that competitors are not able to offer . . . When, however, the seller does not have either the degree or the kind of market power that enables him to force customers to purchase a second, unwanted product in order to obtain the tying product, an antitrust violation can be established only by evidence of an unreasonable restraint on competition in the relevant market.

The hospital has provided its patients with a package that includes the range of facilities and services required for a variety of surgical operations. . . . Petitioners argue that the package does not involve a tying arrangement at all—that they are merely providing a functionally integrated package of services. . . .

Our cases indicate, however, that the answer to the question whether one or two products are involved turns not on the functional relation between them, but rather on the character of the demand for the two items. . . .

Unquestionably, the anesthesiological component of the package offered by the hospital could be provided separately and could be selected either by the individual patient or by one of the patient's doctors if the hospital did not insist on including anesthesiological services in the package it offers to its customers. As a matter of actual practice, anesthesiological services are billed separately from the hospital services petitioners provide. . . . [C]onsumers differentiate between anesthesiological services and the other hospital services provided by petitioners.

* * * * *

The question remains whether this arrangement involves the use of market power to force patients to buy services they would not otherwise purchase. . . .

Seventy percent of the patients residing in Jefferson Parish enter hospitals other than East Jefferson. Thus, East Jefferson's "dominance" over persons residing in Jefferson Parish is far from overwhelming. . . . The Court of Appeals . . . recognized that East Jefferson's market share alone was insufficient as a basis to infer market power, and buttressed its conclusion by relying on "market imperfections" . . . the prevalence of third party payment for health care costs reduces price competition, and a lack of adequate information renders consumers unable to evaluate the quality of the medical care provided by competing hospitals. While these factors may generate "market power" in some abstract sense, they do not generate the kind of market power that justifies condemnation of tying.

Tying arrangements need only be condemned if they restrain competition on the merits by forcing purchases that would not otherwise be made. A lack of price or quality competition does not create this type of forcing. If consumers lack price consciousness, that fact will not force them to take an anesthesiologist whose services they do not want—their indifference to price will have no impact on their willingness or ability to go to another hospital where they can utilize the services of the anesthesiologist of their choice. Similarly, if consumers cannot evaluate the quality of anesthesiological services, if follows that they are indifferent between certified anesthesiologists even in the absence of a tying arrangement—such an arrangement cannot be said to have foreclosed a choice that would have otherwise been made "on the merits."

Thus, neither of the "market imperfections" relied upon by the Court of Appeals forces consumers to take anesthesiological services they would not select in the absence of a tie. It is safe to assume that every patient undergoing a surgical operation needs the services of an anesthesiologist; at least this record contains no evidence that the hospital "forced" any such services on unwilling patients. The record therefore does not provide a basis for applying the per se rule against tying to this arrangement.

Justice O'Connor *(with whom Chief Justice Burger, Justice Powell, and Justice Rehnquist join, concurring)*

*   *   *   *   *

The time has . . . come to abandon the "per se" label and refocus the inquiry on the adverse economic effects, and the potential economic benefits, that the tie may have. . . . This change will rationalize rather than abandon tie in doctrine as it is already applied.

*   *   *   *   *

Tying may be economically harmful primarily in the rare cases where power in the market for the tying product is used to create additional market power in the market for the tied product. . . . But such extension of market power is unlikely, or poses no threat of economic harm, unless the two markets in question and the nature of the two products tied satisfy three threshold criteria.

First, the seller must have power in the tying product market. Absent such power tying cannot conceivably have any adverse impact in the tied-product market, and can be only pro-competitive in the tying product market. . . .

Second, there must be a substantial threat that the tying seller will acquire market power in the tied-product market. No such threat exists if the tied-product market is occupied by many stable sellers who are not likely to be driven out by the tying, or if entry barriers in the tied product market are low. . . .

Third, there must be a coherent economic basis for treating the tying and tied products as distinct. . . . Unless it is to be illegal to sell cars with engines or cameras with lenses, this analysis must be guided by some limiting principle. For products to be treated as distinct, the tied product must, at a minimum, be one that some consumers might wish to purchase separately without also purchasing the tying product. When the tied product has no use other than in conjunction with the tying product, a seller of the tying product can acquire no additional market power by selling the two products together.

*   *   *   *   *

Application of these criteria to the case at hand is straightforward.

Although the issue is in doubt, we may assume that the Hospital does have market power in the provision of hospital services in this area. . . .

Second, in light of the Hospital's presumed market power, we may also assume that there is a substantial threat that East Jefferson will acquire market power over the provision of anesthesiological services in its market. By tying the sale of anesthesia to the sale of other hospital services the Hospital can drive out other sellers of those services who might otherwise operate in the local market. . . .

But the third threshold condition for giving closer scrutiny to a tying arrangement is not satisfied here: there is no sound economic reason for treating surgery and anesthesia as separate services. Patients are interested in purchasing anesthesia only in conjunction with hospital services, so the Hospital can acquire no additional market power by selling the two services together. . . .

Even if they are [separate services], the tying should not be considered a violation of §1 of the Sherman Act because tying here cannot increase the seller's already absolute power over the volume of production of the tied product, which is an inevitable consequence of the fact that very few patients will choose to undergo surgery without receiving anesthesia. . . . On the other side of the balance, the District Court found, and the Court of Appeals did not dispute, that the tie-in conferred significant benefits upon the hospital and the patients that it served.

The tie-in improves patient care and permits more efficient hospital operation in a number of ways. From the viewpoint of hospital management, the tie-in ensures 24 hour anesthesiology coverage, aids in standardization of procedures and efficient use of equipment, facilitates flexible scheduling of operations, and permits the hospital more effectively to monitor the quality of anesthesiological services. Further, the tying arrangement is advantageous to patients because, as the District Court found, the closed anesthesiology department places upon the hospital, rather than the individual patient, responsibility to select the physician who is to provide anesthesiological services. . . . Such an arrangement, that has little anti-competitive effect and achieves substantial benefits in the provision of care to patients, is hardly one that the antitrust law should condemn.

CASE QUESTIONS

1. Why wasn't this case brought under section 3 of the Clayton Act?

2. In Justice Stevens' view, why are tie-ins per se legal? Why does Justice O'Connor believe the per se approach should be abandoned?

3. In Justice Stevens' view were there two separate products? In Justice O'Connor's view? Explain.

4. Did the hospital have sufficient economic power to enforce the tie-in? Discuss the approaches of the Court of Appeals, Justice Stevens, and Justice O'Connor to this issue.

5. A hospital held a patent on a particular type of X-ray machine and would allow doctors to buy or rent it only if they agreed to refer all of their patients in need of hospitalization to that hospital. How would Justice Stevens analyze the legality of this arrangement? How would Justice O'Connor analyze it?

GROUP BOYCOTTS

An individual may refuse to deal with anyone without violating section 1 of the Sherman Act. Group boycotts, or concerted refusals to deal, however, are per se violations of the act.

The application of the per se rule to group boycotts arose from cases in which a group of firms at one level of the market coerced a group of firms at another level not to deal with competitors of the first group. For example, a group of retail lumber dealers circulated a black list to induce all retailers not to deal with wholesalers who also sold lumber at retail discount prices.[8] This practice was held illegal. Similarly, it was

---

[8] *Eastern States Retail Lumber Dealers Association v. United States,* 193 U.S. 38 (1904).

illegal for a group of automobile dealers to induce General Motors not to deal with competing discount outlets.[9]

The condemnation of group boycotts as per se illegal has serious consequences for self-regulated industries. Two Supreme Court decisions illustrate this point. In the first case, the Court found an illegal concerted refusal to deal where the defendant gas association refused to give its seal of approval to plaintiff's furnaces. Utility companies refused to supply gas to homes whose furnaces did not have the seal. The Court emphasized that there were no objective standards for determining when the seal would be withheld. Thus the charge that the seal was arbitrarily and capriciously withheld to induce a concerted refusal to deal was valid.[10]

In the second case, plaintiff, a stockbroker who was not a member of the New York Stock Exchange sued the exchange after it ordered its members to cut off his direct wire connection. Plaintiff needed the connection to trade in over-the-counter securities. The market for over-the-counter securities was established by traders through constant communication. The direct wire gave an individual instant information on the latest offers to buy and sell.

Despite plaintiff's efforts, the exchange refused to advise him of the reason for the cutoff or to give him an opportunity to protest. The Court acknowledged the exchange's power of self-regulation, but reaffirmed that the arbitrary exercise of such power constitutes a concerted refusal to deal. It would be impossible, the Court said, to check the exercise of such power unless the plaintiff were told the reasons for the cutoff and given an opportunity to contest them. The exchange's refusal to do this converted its self-regulation into a group boycott.[11]

Thus, self-regulating industries must apply objective standards to avoid liability for group boycotts. Before taking disciplinary action, a respondent must be given adequate notice of the charges and an opportunity to contest the action.

THE SHERMAN ACT IN ACTION: LIMITATIONS ON TRADE ASSOCIATION ACTIVITIES

Trade associations are organizations of competitors with common interests and business pursuits. Because section 1 of the Sherman Act has had a severe impact on many trade association activities, these groups are an excellent vehicle for observing the practical application of the antitrust laws. Several trade association activities are explored below.

Membership Qualifications

Trade associations often provide services that assist their members' businesses and thereby enhance their abilities to compete. Consequently, their

---

[9] *United States v. General Motors Corp.*, 384 U.S. 127 (1966).

[10] *Radiant Burners, Inc. v. Peoples Gas Light and Coke Co.*, 364 U.S. 656 (1961).

[11] *Silver v. New York Stock Exchange*, 373 U.S. 341 (1963).

membership criteria are subject to Sherman Act scrutiny under the rule of reason. Unreasonable restraints of trade result from membership requirements that are not related to the functioning of the service and from membership fees set so high that they raise barriers to entry.

An example of a trade association service is the multiple listing of houses maintained by most real estate associations. Each member broker lists houses for sale with the multiple listing service and has access to the houses listed by all other members. Thus, a member broker has the competitive advantage of access to the listings of many other brokers. Simply listing a seller's house enables a broker to make the house available for consideration by many buyers' brokers. Denial of admission to a real estate association results in denial of access to the multiple listing service. This makes it more difficult for a nonmember broker to compete for the business of buyers and sellers. But not all denials of membership are unlawful. The criteria upon which an exclusion rests must be analyzed.

Requirements that members approve applications of prospective members, that exclude part-time brokers from membership, or that freeze membership are unrelated to the functioning of the multiple listing service. Such requirements place nonmember competitors at a disadvantage and accordingly have been found to unreasonably restrain trade. On the other hand, objective membership requirements that ensure the high integrity and reliability of all users of the service have been found reasonable in light of each member's responsibility for the actions of other members.[12]

Statistical Reporting and Price Exchanges

Among the most important functions of American trade associations are the collection and dissemination of data providing a statistical profile of their industries. In an otherwise perfect market, greater access to information enhances competition. Data gathering activity, however, may also signal association members about pricing policies they have previously agreed upon. A trade association may lawfully gather and disseminate information on costs, volume of production, stocks on hand, and past transactions. Association members may meet and discuss such information, provided that no effort is made to reach any agreement on prices, units of production, or other restraints on competition. Data gathering schemes are viewed as price fixes, however, if they involve daily reporting, revealing the identities of participating companies and the information furnished by each, and audits to ensure accurate reporting.

The maintenance of the anonymity and confidentiality of reports is a critical factor in avoiding antitrust violations. For example, the manufacturers of corrugated containers agreed that each would, upon request, provide the others with its most recent price charged or quoted. The infor-

---

[12] For further discussion, see Miller and Shedd, "Do Antitrust Laws Apply to the Real Estate Brokerage Industry?" 17 *Am. Bus. L.J.* 313 (1979). Malin, "Real Estate Multiple Listing Services and the Sherman Act: A Response to Miller and Shedd," 18 *Am. Bus. L.J.* 77 (1980); Miller & Shedd, A Response to M. Malin's Response, 19 *Am. Bus. L.J.* 310 (1981).

mation exchanges were infrequent and irregular. The industry, however, involved a fungible product in which competition focused on price. Demand was inelastic, as buyers placed orders only for short-term needs. Low barriers to entry caused supply to exceed demand. Upon learning a competitor's price, a manufacturer tended to match it. Consequently, the Court found that the exchange of price information produced a uniformity of prices and resulted in an unreasonable restraint of trade.[13]

Product Standardization

Product standardization campaigns can have a procompetitive effect by eliminating consumer confusion and focusing consumer attention on price. Where products are standardized, however, prices frequently tend toward uniformity. The problem posed is whether that uniformity is a natural market response to standardization or whether standardization is a method of fixing prices. A few examples will illustrate the factors viewed by the courts and the FTC in determining the legality of a standardization program.

A trade association of crown bottle cap manufacturers standardized all aspects of the product, including decoration and color. Although there was no actual agreement to charge uniform prices, the members' prices were identical. A patent license for one type of cap required licensees to observe a minimum price. The association also promoted a freight equalization program under which the price charged did not depend upon the manufacturer's distance from the customer. The court affirmed the FTC's order that the association cease and desist all of these practices. The court recognized that the standardization program by itself was not illegal. However, it held that when combined with the other practices described above, the program revealed the association's overriding desire to present prospective customers with uniform products, prices, and terms of sale.[14]

In addition to facilitating price fixing, standardization may inhibit innovation. Generally the degree of standardization plays a leading role in determining whether a particular program unlawfully inhibits innovation. Standards that are recommended and are confined to legitimate aims such as improved safety will usually survive antitrust attack. However, where a program attempts to standardize color, design, size, or similar features, or where such a program imposes sanctions for deviations, the program may stifle innovation and violate the Sherman Act.

Codes of Ethics

Trade associations frequently promulgate ethical codes in an effort at industry self-regulation. Some code provisions, such as those fixing mini-

---

[13] *United States v. Container Corp.*, 393 U.S. 337 (1969).

[14] *Bond Crown & Cork Co. v. FTC*, 176 F.2d 974 (4th Cir. 1959).

mum fees, blatantly violate section 1. Others, such as those advising against fraudulent or deceptive advertising, are clearly reasonable. Code provisions between these extremes must be assessed under the rule of reason to determine whether they violate the Sherman Act. Code provisions must be justified as either procompetitive or as serving legitimate business purposes with no restraints or insubstantial restraints on competition.

Some codes of ethics are simply advisory in nature. Each association member must follow its own conscience in deciding whether it will comply. Many codes, however, contain sanctions for violations. The sanctions may range from reprimands to suspension or expulsion from the trade association. If a sanction is, in effect, a group boycott, it is a per se violation. Thus, an antitrust violation may result from the enforcement of a code provision that is otherwise lawful.

Activities Aimed at Customers or Suppliers

Some association activities dealing with customers and suppliers are per se illegal group boycotts under the Sherman Act. Sometimes boycott activity is blatant. For example, in an effort to combat style piracy, the members of an association of women's clothing designers agreed to boycott retailers that sold copies of their originals.[15] Similarly, the American Medical Association was found to have violated the Sherman Act by pressuring hospitals to boycott doctors who worked for a nonprofit health maintenance organization.[16]

Association activities not intended as group boycotts may lead individual members to boycott suppliers or customers or may imply that the concerted power of association members can coerce suppliers or customers into following association recommendations. Consequently, enforcement authorities view such activities cautiously, even where the activities may serve the interests of the association's members and the customers or suppliers.

Association activities that do not involve direct contact with customers or suppliers but are aimed at them do not violate the Sherman Act if they serve legitimate purposes and do not involve price fixing, boycotts, or other unreasonable restraints. The most common activity of this kind is credit reporting. Many companies are too small to carry out their own credit checks economically. These companies may band together through their trade association to achieve an economy of scale which enables them to establish a credit reporting service. Credit reporting generally does not violate section 1 unless it is accompanied by agreements to fix credit terms or to deny credit to particular customers.

Joint selling and buying activities may result in price fixing or may simply represent reasonable efforts to secure economies of scale. In the

---

[15] *Fashion Originators Guild v. FTC,* 312 U.S. 457 (1941).

[16] *American Medical Association v. United States,* 317 U.S. 519 (1943).

former case, section 1 of the Sherman Act has been violated, while in the latter case, as long as market forces continue to set prices, the restraints are reasonable.

ALTERNATIVE APPROACHES

The American approach to restraints of trade stands in marked contrast to the British approach as found in the British Restructive Trade Practices Act. The two approaches are compared in the following article.

A Comparison of the American Sherman Antitrust Act and the British Restrictive Trade Practices Act: The Trade Association Experience*

The Restrictive Trade Practices Act requires the registration of any restrictive business agreement related to the production or supply of goods. The following types of restrictive agreements must be registered: prices or recommended prices; terms or conditions of sale; quantities or descriptions of goods to be produced; processes of manufacture; persons or classes of persons with whom one will deal. . . .

Registration is administered by the Director General of Fair Trading. The director may, in his discretion, refer agreements for consideration by a Restrictive Practices Court, consisting of five nominated judges and up to ten lay members appointed on the basis of their knowledge in industry, commerce, or public affairs. The function of the court is to determine whether or not a particular agreement is consistent with the public interest. An agreement is conclusively presumed to be contrary to the public interest and will be voided unless at least one of eight justifications is applicable and unless the agreement itself is deemed reasonable when balanced against the detriment caused to the public or to persons not parties to the agreement. The eight justifications are that the agreement in question:

is reasonably necessary to protect the public from injury; provides the public specific and substantial benefits; is reasonably necessary to counteract restrictive practices undertaken by others; is reasonably necessary for the negotiation of fair terms with a preponderant buyer or seller; has a beneficial effect on unemployment; has a beneficial effect on the volume of earnings in exports; is reasonably necessary to maintain another agreement already found to be consistent with the public interest; or does not restrict or discourage competition to any material degree. If the court declares any provision of the agreement contrary to the public interest, that provision becomes void.

Several differences between the American and British statutes are immediately apparent. The Restrictive Trade Practices Act is narrower in scope than the Sherman Act because it specifically defines a limited number of types of agreements to which it applies, while the Sherman Act is essentially unrestrictive in language. Similarly, the Restrictive Trade Practices Act has no *per se* violations, and thus allows certain agreements prohibited by the Sherman Act. Finally, the British Act does not impose civil or criminal penalties on parties to restrictive agreements that are contrary to the public interest, as long as the parties register their agreements. Thus, the British apply

---

* Malin and Lawniczak, 59 *University of Detroit Journal of Urban Law* 198 (1982). Reprinted with permission.

their Act prospectively only; a British businessman is not liable for the past effects of his agreements in restraint of trade. On the other hand, the Sherman Act imposes substantial penalties for violations which can be imposed even against someone who acts in good faith ignorance that he is violating the law.

* * * * *

Under the Sherman Act, American courts use judicial and economic experience to declare certain classes of restraints *per se* unreasonable. The courts interpreting the Sherman Act then examine the purposes and effects of . . . activities to determine whether they sufficiently approximate the *per se* offenses or whether the intent of the participants is to achieve a result equivalent to a *per se* offense. The Restrictive Trade Practices Act, on the other hand, allows anticompetitive arrangements, which would be struck down without discussion in America, and affords the parties an opportunity to justify them.

The American approach has two advantages not present under the British scheme. First, the *per se* rules provide a specific yardstick by which to measure reasonableness of restraints. They thus are far easier to apply than the Restrictive Trade Practices justifications, since the only determination to be made is whether or not a specified result is intended or achieved. The British scheme, however, provides for efficient application of the economic justifications by providing for ten appointed members of the Restrictive Practices Court who are experts in industry, commerce, or public affairs.

Second, the Sherman Act's *per se* rules provide a consistent measure of predictability that is inherently absent from the Restrictive Trade Practices Act. For example, every informed American businessman must know that he cannot fix prices under any circumstances. The British scheme, however, minimizes this need for prior knowledge by providing no penalty until the specific agreement is condemned by the Restrictive Practices Court. On the other hand, restraints only receive official scrutiny under the Sherman Act when the government or a private party commences a law suit, and the consequences of liability may be disastrous. Registration of restrictive trade agreements brings the restraint under the immediate scrutiny of the British authorities, with consequences of violation minimal. Were penalties for entering illegal restrictive agreements comparable to those for violating the Sherman Act, the British system would require greater predictability. Thus, the American system emphasizes predictability and consistent treatment of classes of agreements to facilitate business planning and efficient judicial consideration, while the British system is willing to sacrifice such efficiencies for detailed economic analyses of individual agreements.

CHAPTER PROBLEMS

1. A group of gasoline station owners agree not to advertise the prices they charge for gasoline in any manner except by a small sign posted on the pump. Does this agreement violate section 1 of the Sherman Act? Why or why not?

2. Your corporation operates a national chain of discount department stores. You wish to induce independent food retailers to operate under the same roof and under the same name as your stores. You propose to license these retailers to use your company's name and to lease them space in your stores. You will limit the number and types of nonfood items they can sell and will require them to charge competitive prices on all goods they sell. If they sell any items that you also sell, you will require that they charge the same price as you charge. Will the proposal, if implemented, violate section 1 of the Sherman Act? Explain.

3. Semolina wheat is used in the manufacture of macaroni. Most macaroni manufacturers use almost 100 percent semolina. Due to unexpected severe weather the semolina harvest this year was poor. If all macaroni manufacturers continue to use 100 percent semolina, demand will far outstrip supply. Can the manufacturers agree to limit the semolina content of their macaroni without violating section 1 of the Sherman Act?

4. Sealy, Inc., manufactures box springs and mattresses. Its stock is owned by its licensees, and only licensees are eligible for seats on its board of directors. Licensees receive the right to manufacture and sell Sealy products. Sealy also provides licensees with national advertising, product development, sales training, and a means of central negotiations for selling to national retail organizations. Sealy specifies the location of each licensee's manufacturing plant and assigns each licensee an area in which it is primarily responsible for promoting Sealy products.

To deal with national retailers, Sealy developed a national accounts program. Sealy approached these retailers directly and negotiated agreements with them. Once an agreement was reached, each licensee was given the option to participate. If a licensee agreed to participate, it would supply Sealy products to the retailer's outlets in the licensee's area of primary responsibility at the prices set by Sealy and the retailer. Has Sealy violated any antitrust laws?

5. You are marketing director for a major oil company. For the past six months you have been considering requiring the retail gasoline stations that sell your brand to offer maintenance and repair services, with qualified mechanics on duty six days a week. Two months ago, one of your retailers ceased all maintenance and repair operations, converting to a "gas and

go" station. The retailer passed the savings on overhead on to its customers by lowering gasoline prices six cents per gallon. Your other retailers in the area have complained to you about this. Should you adopt your original plan?

6. Your company is entering the computer toys field. You wish to promote your toys as offering the highest quality for the lowest price. To this end you wish to set a maximum retail price and ensure that no one sells above it. How can you do this legally?

7. Coca-Cola Company manufactures and sells syrups and concentrates used in soft drink processing. It began operations around the turn of the century. At that time it produced no bottled soft drinks but licensed the Coca-Cola trademark in perpetuity to independent businesspersons who operated their own bottling and wholesaling operations with exclusive assigned territories.

Coca-Cola operates in the same way as it did when it began, with two exceptions:
a. It has repurchased the bottling rights for 27 of the territories and services those territories itself. Its territories account for 14 percent of the U.S. population.
b. It has introduced the soft drinks Tab, Sprite, Fresca, Fanta, and Mr. Pibb. These soft drinks are bottled and distributed in the same manner as Coke.

Coca-Cola's method of licensing bottlers in exclusive territories is an industrywide practice. The territories were originally parceled out at a time when manual equipment was used in bottling facilities and bottled soft drinks were delivered in horse-drawn wagons over dirt roads. Today bottlers use automated equipment and modern delivery trucks. There has been a vast increase in the production capacity of bottling plants. Most bottlers use this increased capacity to produce and distribute the soft drinks of competing manufacturers. Other bottlers have entered into agreements to supply neighboring bottlers' requirements for certain package sizes or have by consolidations combined their territories. Do Coca-Cola's exclusive territories violate the Sherman Act?

8. The publisher of the only morning newspaper in New Orleans also publishes one of the city's two evening newspapers. The publisher will only sell advertising in a package, which obligates the advertiser to place an ad in both newspapers. Has the publisher violated section 1 of the Sherman Act?

9. A trade association of china manufacturers conducted a cost accounting survey of its members. The study was conducted to enable members to bring their prices more nearly in line with costs. It was intended to replace an outdated study that had been conducted by a member of the association. The study's results were discussed at association meetings and unanimously adopted by members as their basis for determining price. There are over 1,700 sizes, shapes, and colors of china. China prices have never tended toward uniformity. Has the association violated the Sherman Act?

10. Compare and contrast the approaches of the American Sherman Act and the British Restructive Trade Practices Act.

CHAPTER 11

MONOPOLIES

The preceding chapter considered contracts, combinations, and conspiracies which restrain trade. It dealt with the legality of two or more entities pooling their economic power. Accumulations of economic power are not confined to combinations of entities. Frequently an individual entity is able to attain vast amounts of economic power. In these cases section 2 of the Sherman Act comes into play. Section 2 prohibits monopolization, attempts to monopolize, and conspiracies to monopolize. The way in which the law treats monopolies is the subject of this chapter.

MONOPOLIZATION

Courts have approached section 2's prohibition of monopolization by developing a rule of reason. Courts recognize that the underlying purpose of the antitrust laws is to promote competition. Literal interpretation of section 2 would not further this purpose. The Sherman Act is concerned with the accumulation of economic power. Therefore, in interpreting section 2, courts must evaluate the amount of economic power that a firm has and the way in which that power was obtained.

Literally, every producer is a monopolist of its own product. However, most producers do not have the economic power with which section 2 is concerned. Most producers have competitors who produce the same type of product. There may also be other products which can serve the same function. If a single producer raises its prices or reduces its quality, it will likely lose customers to these competitors. The firm therefore lacks the power that the Sherman Act is concerned with. Under these circumstances, a court would conclude that the firm does not have monopoly power.

Even if a firm accumulates monopoly power it does not necessarily violate section 2. The essence of competition is to attract business away from other competitors. The most successful competitors may become monopolists because of their successes. If section 2 was interpreted to condemn every monopolist, it would inhibit rather than promote competition. Thus, it applies only to monopolists who actively seek or maintain their monopolies.

Determining liability for offense of monopolizing under Section 2 is a three-step process:

— Determining the relevant market
— Assessing the defendant's power in that market
— Determining whether the defendant intended to monopolize

The Relevant Market

The relevant market provides a framework for assessing a firm's economic power. It may be defined as that segment of commerce in which a firm may, by becoming dominant, raise prices, exclude competitors, or generally operate independently of competitive forces. The relevant market must be defined in terms of product and geographic markets.

The Relevant Product Market

The relevant product market may be defined as the product or products for which a dominant firm can raise prices relatively independently of competitive forces. Courts usually focus on substitutability in determining whether to include particular products in the relevant market. This is because a firm which produces 100 percent of a product cannot raise prices if it faces competition from other products that can perform the same functions.

Courts use the economic concept of cross-elasticity of demand to measure whether one product is a substitute for another. *Demand* is defined as the amount of a particular good that consumers will buy in a given period of time. If the price charged for a good changes, the demand for that good may also change. *Elasticity of demand* measures the relationship between price changes and demand changes for a particular good. *Cross-elasticity of demand* measures the impact that a change in the price of one good has on the relationship between demand for that good and demand for a different good.

Economists define cross-elasticity of demand as the percentage change in the demand of one product divided by the percentage change in the price of another product. Thus, the cross-elasticity of demand for products *X* and *Y* would be defined as the ratio of change in the demand for *X* to the change in the price of *Y*. For example, consider butter and margarine. Assume that one week the price of margarine is $.60 per pound, and the price of butter is $1.00 per pound. Under these conditions, demand for each is 100. The following week the price of butter increases to $1.50 per pound. Demand for butter drops dramatically. This drop in demand indicates that butter is *price elastic;* that is, its demand is very sensitive to price changes. Consumers who bought butter at $1.00 but refused to buy it at $1.50 probably reacted in many different ways. Some reduced the amount of butter they used in their daily lives. Many probably substituted margarine. Assume that when the price of butter was increased to $1.50, demand for margarine increased to 125. In this case, a 50 percent increase in the price of butter produced a 25-percent increase in the demand for margarine. The cross-elasticity of demand between butter and margarine would be 25 percent divided by 50 percent, or ½.

If cross-elasticity of demand is negative, the products are complements; that is, as the price of Y decreases, demand for X increases. For example, cars and tires are complements; a decrease in the price of cars will probably cause an increase in the number of tires demanded. If cross-elasticity of demand is positive and high, the products are considered close substitutes. In the example in the preceding paragraph, a firm dominating the butter market cannot raise prices because customers will switch to margarine. Thus, the relevant product market should include both butter and margarine.

Economists find it difficult to calculate cross-elasticity of demand precisely. This is because conditions other than the demand for X and the price of Y rarely remain constant. Courts are even less able to measure cross-elasticity of demand. Because judges are usually not trained economists, they must almost always rely on the testimony of experts called by the parties. Expert opinions will differ, with each expert emphasizing the factors that support the position of the party for which the expert is testifying. A court must combine the economic testimony with common sense to arrive at a market definition.

The leading Supreme Court decision dealing with the method of determining relevant product market is *United States v. E. I. du Pont de Nemours & Co.*[1] The government charged Du Pont with monopolizing cellophane. The evidence showed that Du Pont produced 75 percent of the nation's cellophane and 20 percent of all flexible packaging materials. The Supreme Court affirmed the trial court's finding that the relevant market included all flexible packaging materials. The Court relied on evidence showing that cellophane accounted for only 7 percent of the wrappings for bakery products, 25 percent of the wrappings for candy, 32 percent for snacks, 35 percent for nuts, 32 percent for poultry, 27 percent for crackers and biscuits, 47 percent for fresh produce, 34 percent for frozen food, and 75–80 percent for cigarettes. Thus, only in the wrapping market for cigarettes was cellophane dominant. Other users were willing to employ substitutes for cellophane. Furthermore, the Court found that except for permeability to gases, cellophane's qualities were shared by many other wrapping materials. It found that at various points in time Du Pont had lost business to other materials, including substantial losses in meat packaging to Plio-

---

[1] 351 U.S. 377 (1950).

film and greased paper. Finally, the Court found that Du Pont had taken the prices of waxed paper, glassine, greaseproof paper, vegetable parchment, and similar materials into consideration when pricing cellophane. It had reduced its prices on several occasions and had succeeded in attracting customers away from other materials.

On the other hand, the Court has also affirmed trial court findings of very narrow relevant markets. In one case, the Court found a relevant market limited to championship boxing matches and rejected the defense contention that the market should encompass all prizefights. The Court relied on evidence that ticket prices, average revenues, payments for television rights, and Nielsen television ratings were substantially higher for championship fights than for other prize fights.[2]

Because measures of cross-elasticity alone may not provide an accurate gauge of economic power, such measures should not be the sole determinant of the relevant market.

For example, in *United States v. Aluminum Company of America* the government charged that Alcoa, the only domestic producer of virgin aluminum ingot, monopolized that market.[3] Alcoa sold its virgin ingot to aluminum fabricators which processed it into rolls and sheets. Alcoa also used some of the ingot itself to fabricate aluminum that it sold. The court included the aluminum fabricated by Alcoa in the relevant market because all ingot was used to fabricate intermediate or end products. Consequently, the court reasoned, all aluminum fabricated by Alcoa reduced the demand for ingot. If the court had excluded the aluminum fabricated by Alcoa, it would have effectively excluded from the market the ingot that Alcoa kept for itself.

The virgin ingot produced by Alcoa competed with secondary ingot recycled from scrap by many other companies. The prices of the two products were comparable, and many users of virgin ingot could just as easily use secondary ingot. Nevertheless, the court did not include secondary ingot in the relevant market. It reasoned that because Alcoa was the sole domestic supplier of virgin intgot and could predict what portion of the virgin would be recycled as secondary, Alcoa could control the amount of the secondary with which it would have to compete. Consequently, including the secondary ingot in the relevant market would distort the true picture of Alcoa's economic power.

Other instances in which substitutability alone has not been used to determine the relevant market are those in which the alleged monopolist offers a cluster of goods or services. Consider a soft drink manufacturer that makes cola. That manufacturer may diversify into other flavors, but it may also make such items as glass and party trays bearing its trademark. It may use these items as premiums or special offers to attract customers to its soft drinks. Although different, its products are related because they

---

[2] *International Boxing Club of New York, Inc., v. United States* 358 U.S. 242 (1959).

[3] 148 F.2d 416 (2d Cir. 1945).

can be used by the same customer and can be marketed by the same methods.

Courts have taken a practical approach in deciding whether to group such clusters in a single market. The particular facts and circumstances of each case are considered, with the views of consumers and producers given most emphasis. Where all producers tend to offer the same cluster of products or where consumers tend to view the cluster as a whole, the entire product line is likely to be included in the relevant market.

Substitutability may also be approached from the producer's viewpoint. Price increases in one product may cause producers of other products to enter the market. The factors to be considered include whether producers employ similar technologies and whether they could surmount the barriers to entry into the market. Where producers are substitutable, their potential competition checks the ability of a firm already in the market to raise prices. The interplay of economic concepts, legal standards, and common sense is illustrated in the following decision.

 **Telex Corp. v. International Business Machines Corp.**

510 F.2d 894 (10th Cir. 1975)

Telex (plaintiff) sued IBM (defendant), alleging that IBM monopolized peripheral data processing devices. The trial court held that the relevant market was peripheral devices plug compatible with IBM central processing units (CPUs). It entered judgment for Telex. The Tenth Circuit Court of Appeals reversed.

The data processing equipment industry consisted of central processing units and peripheral devices which could be connected to the central processing unit. Peripheral devices included information storage components such as magnetic tape drives, magnetic disc drives, magnetic drums, and magnetic strip files; terminal devices such as printers; memory units; and specialized storage units. Peripheral devices were said to be plug compatible with the central processing units that they fitted.

Per Curiam

The threshold issue is whether the court erred in its findings as to the scope and extent of the relevant product market for determination whether there existed power to control prices or to exclude competition, that is, whether there was monopoly power. [T]he court determined that the relevant product market was limited to peripheral devices plug compatible with IBM central processing units together with particular product submarkets; magnetic tape products, direct access storage products, memory products, impact printer products and communication controllers, all of which were plug compatible with an IBM CPU. IBM had sought a determination that the relevant product market consisted of electronic data processing systems together with the products which are part of such systems or at least that the relevant product market should consist of all peripheral products and not be limited to those currently attached to IBM systems.

The trial court's initial approach to the problem was restricted to consideration of whether the market "may be realistically subdivided in the time frame 1969–1972 to focus on and encompass only those parts of current product lines which are respectively attached to IBM systems rather than all those products which actually have similar uses in connection with other systems." The court recognized that inasmuch as every manufacturer, originally at least, has 100 percent of its own product, including the peripherals, the likelihood of finding monopolization in this area increases as the circumscribing products market is more circumscribed.

The trial court also recognized that the cost of adaptation of peripherals to the CPUs of other systems is roughly the same with respect to every system, that is, the cost of the interface, the attachment which allows the use of peripherals manufactured by one system to be used on another central processing unit is generally about the same. But these practical interchange possibilities did not deter the court in reaching a conclusion that the products markets was practically restricted. A factor which influenced the trial court was the commitment of Telex to supplying peripherals plug compatible with IBM systems. The court appeared to disregard the interchangeability aspect of the peripherals manufactured by compa-

nies other than IBM, giving emphasis to the fact that Telex, for example, had not chosen to manufacture such peripheral products of the kind and character manufactured by companies other than IBM. The trial court did, however, recognize the presence of interchangeability of use and the presence of cross-elasticity of demand. The court thought, however, that the presence of these factors were [*sic*] not sufficiently immediate.

We recognize that market definition is generally treated as a matter of fact and that findings on this subject are not to be overturned unless clearly erroneous. Our question is, therefore, whether it was clearly erroneous for the court to exclude peripheral products of systems other than IBM such as Honeywell, Univac, Burroughs, Control Data Corp. and others, together with peripheral products plug compatible with the system and, indeed, whether the systems themselves manufactured by the companies are to be taken into account. It is significant, of course, that peripheral products constitute a large percentage of the entire data processing system, somewhere between 50 and 75 percent.

Inasmuch as IBM's share of the data processing industry as a whole is insufficient to justify any inference or conclusion of market power in IBM, the exclusion from the defined market of those products which are not plug compatible with IBM central processing units has a significant impact on the court's decision that IBM possessed monopoly power.

* * * * *

In dealing with the issue whether peripheral products non-compatible with IBM systems ought to be considered, the court said in Finding 47 that as a practical matter there is no direct competition between IBM peripherals and the peripherals of other systems manufacturers. However, this finding is out of harmony with other findings which the court made. See, for example, Finding 38, wherein the court said that "It cannot be gainsaid that indirectly at least and to some degree the peripheral products attached to non-IBM systems necessarily compete with and constrain IBM's power with respect to peripherals attached to IBM systems." The court also stated in Finding 38 that:

> . . . [S]uppliers of peripherals plug compatible with non-IBM systems could in various instances shift to the production of IBM plug compatible peripherals, and vice versa, should the economic rewards in the realities of the market become sufficiently attractive and if predatory practices of others did not dissuade them. In the absence of defense tactics on the part of manufacturers of CPU's, the cost of developing an interface for a peripheral device would generally be about the same regardless of the system to which it would be attached, and such cost has not constituted a substantial portion of the development cost of the peripheral device.

*   *   *   *   *

[A Telex senior vice president testified] that the engineering costs of developing interfaces was [sic] minimal and that he had advocated modifying interfaces so that Telex products could be used with systems other than IBM. Another example of ease of interface design is shown by the fact that following RCA's decision to abandon the computer systems business and turn it over to Univac, Telex recognized a marketing opportunity and it began marketing its 6420 tape unit, the plug compatible equivalent of IBM's 3420 Aspen tape unit, as a plug compatible unit with RCA CPUs. . . .

Still another exhibit in the record recognizing the practicability of interface change on peripheral equipment is a February 4, 1972, memorandum of R. M. Wheeler, Chairman of the Board of Telex,

requesting a letter for his signature which could be sent to systems manufacturers. This letter was to be sent to systems manufacturers. It offered to sell peripheral equipment plug compatible with the central processing units of the manufacturers. Specific reference was made to the 6420 tape unit, among others, which would normally be compatible to IBM's central processing unit. The Wheeler letter stated that Telex would be willing to interface their equipment at no cost to the purchaser.

Manufacturers of peripherals were not limited to those which were plug compatible with IBM CPUs. The manufacturers were free to adapt their products through interface changes to plug into non-IBM systems. It also followed that systems manufacturers could modify interfaces so that their own peripheral products could plug into IBM CPUs. Factually, then, there existed peripheral products of other CPU manufacturers which were competitive with IBM peripherals and unquestionably other IBM peripherals were capable of having their interfaces modified so that their peripheral products would plug into non-IBM's CPU.

The fact that Telex had substantially devoted itself to the manufacture of peripheral products which were used in IBM CPUs and which competed with IBM peripheral products cannot control in determining product market since the legal standard is whether the product is reasonably interchangeable.

This standard was laid down by the Supreme Court in the famous case of *United States v. E. I. du Pont de Nemours & Co.* The Supreme Court determined that if one product may substitute for another in the market it is "reasonably interchangeable." On this the Court stated:

> [W]here there are market alternatives that buyers may readily use for their purposes,

illegal monopoly does not exist merely because the product said to be monopolized differs from others. If it were not so, only physically identical products would be a part of the market.

One evidence of cross-elasticity is the responsiveness of sales of one product to price changes of another. But a finding of actual fungibility is not necessary to a conclusion that products have potential substitutability. . . .

It seems clear that reasonable interchangeability is proven in the case at bar and hence the market should include not only peripheral products plug compatible with IBM CPUs, but all peripheral products, those compatible not only with IBM CPUs but those compatible with non-IBM systems. This is wholly justifiable because the record shows that these products, although not fungible,* are fully interchangeable and may be interchanged with minimal financial outlay, and so cross-elasticity exists within the meaning of the DuPont decision.

---

* Fungible goods or products are those of which each particle is identical with every other particle, such as grain and oil—Au.

CASE QUESTIONS

1. How did the trial court define the relevant market? How did it justify this definition? How did the court of appeals define the relevant market? What evidence did it point to in support of its definition?

2. Did the court of appeals examine substitutability from the producer's view or the consumer's view?

3. Why were all peripheral data service devices clustered in a single market and the central processing units excluded from the market?

4. Do you agree with the court of appeals that a product should be included in the relevant market where it is shown to be potentially substitutable although not actually fungible?

The Relevant Geographic Market

Questions concerning the relevant geographic market arise less frequently than those involving the relevant product market. When these questions do occur they can be very troubling. A restaurant located in the downtown section of a central city may draw its customers from all parts of the city and its suburbs. The restaurant competes for patrons with similar establishments in the far eastern suburbs and the far western suburbs. The restaurants of the eastern suburbs, however, probably do not compete at all with their counterparts in the western suburbs.

The courts have taken a practical approach to defining the relevant geographic market. The most important factors are the views and actions of consumers and producers. Do producers regard particular cities or regions as separate markets, or do they plan, sell, advertise, and operate nationally? Over what distances do most consumers travel to comparison-shop? The answers to these questions will depend on the size of the purchase and the needs of the consumer. For example, an individual living in a suburb of a large city may not be willing to travel more than a mile to find a Laudromat. That same individual will probably shop in the city and neighboring suburbs when buying a washer and dryer, while the Laudromat may shop regionally for the best buy on its fleet of washers and dryers. The manufacturers of the washers and dryers probably shop nationally for materials and component parts.

Factors in addition to producer and consumer actions which are frequently considered include transportation costs, availability of distribution networks, and legal restrictions such as licensing requirements and zoning laws. Sometimes a national geographic market may be useful for assessing monopoly power but must yield to more refined definitions when a remedy is being devised. For example, a national market may be used to assess monopoly power where most competitors operate nationally, use national price lists, and are affected by other national factors, even though the service is essentially local. In such a case, however, the national market must be refined into regional submarkets in order to devise a remedy.

Assessing Power in the Relevant Market

To be a monopolist under section 2, a firm must have monopoly power in its relevant market. Monopoly power is defined as the ability to raise prices and exclude competitors independently of market forces. Absolute independence is impossible to achieve, for there will always be poor substitutes that will compete effectively when the price of the monopolist's product is raised sufficiently. Thus, only relative ability to raise prices is required.

The starting point for determining market power is to determine the alleged monopolist's market share, expressed as a percentage of production, units sold, or revenue. This is frequently the end point as well. The court in *Alcoa* inferred from Alcoa's 90 percent share of the market that Alcoa had monopoly power. The court indicated that a two-thirds share of the market would be a questionable case and that a one-third share would clearly not amount to monopoly power. Although other opinions have used slightly different figures, it is clear that a firm possessing a market share between 85 percent and 100 percent is deemed conclusively to have monopoly power, while a firm whose share is less than 50 percent will be found to lack such power. When a firm controls between 50 percent and 85 percent of the market, factors beyond percentage share of the market must be considered. These factors include the structure of the market, barriers to entry into the market, and the strength of the alleged monopolist's competitors. Conduct inconsistent with a competitive marketplace, such as the imposition of one-sided contract terms upon customers or suppliers, is further evidence of monopoly power. Prices charged or profits made, however, are generally not relevant to the determination. The Sherman Act is concerned with the existence and acquisition of monopoly power, not with how it is exercised.

Intent to Monopolize

The mere existence of monopoly power does not violate section 2 of the Sherman Act. It is not illegal per se to be too big. The alleged monopolist must have acted with the intent to monopolize. Even when there is no specific intent behind a firm's actions, courts will examine the reasonably foreseeable consequences of those actions. If monopoly power is a reasonably foreseeable consequence, courts find that the firm intended to monopolize. This standard is known as *general intent.*

Many actions have, as their reasonably foreseeable consequences, the conferral of monopoly power. These actions are not limited to predatory, immoral, or unfair practices. They encompass actions which, in the absence of monopoly power, would generally be regarded as good business practices. For example, Alcoa was found to have monopolized aluminum ingot because it anticipated increases in demand and expanded production to meet those increases before other companies were able to enter the market.

When a firm achieves monopoly power without intending to, it is said to be a passive beneficiary of monopoly, or monopoly is said to have been thrust upon it. Such legal monopolies exist when the government confers a monopoly upon a firm, as in the case of public utilities and patents. In some cases a market is so small that only one firm can efficiently and profitably serve it. For example, a movie theater owner in a town whose population will support only one movie theater is the passive beneficiary of a monopoly. In other cases, changes in taste may drive out all but one producer, or a producer may develop a new product or technology and be the only firm in the market until other producers enter it. Finally, the alleged monopolist may have achieved its position as a result of a superior product or superior business acumen. In these instances, where as a result of superior skill, foresight, and industry one firm is the sole survivor of a group of active competitors, that firm is not viewed as a monopolist.

The line between a firm that has engaged in practices whose natural and foreseeable consequences are monopoly power and a firm that has achieved monopoly power as a result of superior skill is often a fine one. The policy which enables courts, attorneys, and businesses to draw that line recognizes that monopolies may be tolerated in order to preserve competitive incentives. The following decision illustrates the difference.

 **United States v. United Shoe Machinery Corp.**

110 F. Supp. 205 (D. Mass. 1953)

The United States (plaintiff) sued United Shoe Machinery Corporation (defendant), charging that it monopolized the market for shoe machinery. Judgment for the United States.

United Shoe Machinery Corporation was formed by the merger of several smaller companies. It supplied over 75 percent of the demand for shoe machines. It was the only manufacturer offering a full line of shoe machines and the only manufacturer of shoe machines with an extensive research and development operation. It leased machines under 10-year leases and provided maintenance and repair service free of additional charge. It refused to sell its machines. It required lessees to operate its machines at full capacity whenever possible.

Wyzanski, District Judge

On the foregoing facts, the issue of law is whether defendant in its shoe machinery business has violated that provision of §2 of the Sherman Act. . . .

* * * * *

. . . The facts show that (1) defendant has, and exercises, such overwhelming strength in the shoe machinery market that it controls that market, (2) this strength excludes some potential, and limits some actual competition, and (3) this strength is not attributable solely to defendant's ability, economies of scale, research, natural advantages, and adaptation to inevitable economic laws.

In estimating defendant's strength, this Court gives some weight to the 75 plus percentage of the shoe machinery market which United serves. But the Court considers other factors as well. In the relatively static shoe machinery market where there are no sudden changes in the style of machines or in the volume of demand, United has a network of long-term, complicated leases with over 90 percent of the shoe factories. These leases assure closer and more frequent contacts between United and its customers than would exist if United were a seller and its customers were buyers. Beyond this general quality, these leases are so drawn and so applied as to strengthen United's power to exclude competitors. Moreover, United offers a long line of ma-

chine types, while no competitor offers more than a short line. Since in some parts of its line United faces no important competition, United has the power to discriminate, by wide differentials and over long periods of time, in the rate of return it procures from different machine types. Furthermore, being by far the largest company in the field, with by far the largest resources in dollars, in patents, in facilities, and in knowledge, United has a marked capacity to attract offers of inventions, inventors' services, and shoe machinery businesses. And, finally, there is no substantial substitute competition from a vigorous second-hand market in shoe machinery.

To combat United's market control, a competitor must be prepared with knowledge of shoemaking, engineering skill, capacity to invent around patents, and financial resources sufficient to bear the expense of long developmental and experimental processes. The competitor must be prepared for consumers' resistance founded in their long-term, satisfactory relations with United, and on the cost to them of surrendering United's leases. Also, the competitor must be prepared to give, or point to the source of, repair and other services, and to the source of supplies for machine parts, expendable parts, and the like. Indeed, perhaps a competitor who aims at any large-scale success must also be prepared to lease his machines. These considerations would all affect *potential* competition, and have not been without their effect on *actual* competition.

Not only does the evidence show United has control of the market, but also the evidence does not show that the control is due entirely to excusable causes. The three principal sources of United's power have been the original constitution of the company, the superiority of United's products and services, and the leasing system. The first two of these are plainly beyond reproach. The original constitution of United in 1899 was judicially approved. It is no longer open to question, and must be regarded as protected by the doctrine of *res judicata*,* which is the equivalent of a legal license. Likewise beyond criticism is the high quality of United's products, its understanding of the techniques of shoemaking and the needs of shoe manufacturers, its efficient design and improvement of machines, and its prompt and knowledgeable service. . . .

But United's control does not rest solely on its original constitution, its ability, its research, or its economies of scale. There are other barriers to competition, and these barriers were erected by United's own business policies. Much of United's market power is traceable to the magnetic ties inherent in its system of leasing, and not selling, its more important machines. The lease-only system of distributing complicated machines has many "partnership" aspects, and it has exclusionary features such as the 10-year term, the full capacity clause, the return charges, and the failure to segregate service charges from machine

charges. Moreover, the leasing system has aided United in maintaining a pricing system which discriminates between machine types.

*   *   *   *   *

In one sense, the leasing system and the miscellaneous activities just referred to (except United's purchases in the second-hand market) were natural and normal, for they were "honestly industrial." They are the sort of activities which would be engaged in by other honorable firms. And, to a large extent, the leasing practices conform to long-standing traditions in the shoe machinery business. Yet, they are not practices which can be properly described as the inevitable consequences of ability, natural forces, or law. They represent something more than the use of accessible resources, the process of invention and innovation, and the employment of those techniques of employment, financing, production, and distribution, which a competitive society must foster. They are contracts, arrangements, and policies which, instead of encouraging competition based on pure merit, further the dominance of a particular firm. In this sense, they are unnatural barriers; they unnecessarily exclude actual and potential competition; they restrict a free market. While the law allows many enterprises to use such practices, the Sherman Act is now construed by superior courts to forbid the continuance of effective market control based in part upon such practices. Those courts hold that market control is inherently evil and constitutes a violation of §2 unless economically inevitable, or specifically authorized and regulated by law.

*   *   *   *   *

So far, nothing in this opinion has been said of defendant's *intent* in regard to its power and practices in the shoe machinery market. . . . Defendant intended to

---

* *Res judicata* is Latin for "a matter adjudged." The *res judicata* doctrine referred to by the Court is that a final judgment rendered by a court of competent jurisdiction on the merits is conclusive of the rights of the parties and as to them, is an absolute bar to a later action involving the same claim.—Au.

engage in the leasing practices and pricing policies which maintained its market power. That is all the intent which the law requires when both the complaint and the judgment rest on a charge of "monopolizing," not merely "attempting to monopolize." Defendant, having willed the means, has willed the end.

CASE QUESTIONS

1. What factors led the court to conclude that United possessed monopoly power?

2. What three factors produced United's monopoly position? How did the court evaluate each of these?

3. What features of the leasing system created barriers to entry? How did they do this?

4. Did United intend to monopolize? Explain.

Monopoly power not otherwise unlawful may violate section 2 if it was improperly obtained or is improperly used or maintained. For example, a patent obtained by fraud is invalid, and the resulting monopoly violates section 2 of the Sherman Act. Similarly, a firm may enter and compete for a market which can only support one company, but it will violate section 2 if it uses predatory or unfair methods. Illustrative of this situation is *Union Leader Corp. v. Newspapers of New England, Inc.*[4] The controversy revolved around a battle between two newspapers for the business of Haverhill, Massachusetts, a town capable of supporting only one newspaper. When workers at the *Haverhill Gazette* went on strike, a rival publisher of other Massachusetts newspapers began publishing a paper in Haverhill. The rival continued publishing after the strike was settled. It made payments to members of the striking labor union to create the appearance that organized labor supported it. It also gave secret payments, discounts, and kickbacks to advertisers that refused to do business with the *Gazette*. The court held that Union Leader's use of these predatory tactics in competing for a natural monopoly violated section 2 of the Sherman Act. Interestingly, the *Gazette* fought back with kickbacks and discounts of its own. The court held that as long as the *Gazette* confined such tactics to those necessary to meet the competition, no violation of the Sherman Act would result from them.

A company that obtains its monopoly legally may still violate section 2 if it acts intentionally to maintain or extend its monopoly power. For example, in *United States v. Griffith*, a chain of movie theaters in Oklahoma, Texas, and New Mexico owned theaters in 85 towns.[5] Some of the towns were natural monopolies, that is, their populations were so

---

[4] 284 F.2d 582 (1st Cir. 1960), *certiorari denied*, 365 U.S. 833 (1961).

[5] 334 U.S. 100 (1948).

small that they could support only one theater. The Griffith chain used its legally attained monopoly position in these towns to extract from distributors exclusive rights to motion pictures in towns where it faced competition. The court held that this use of a natural monopoly violated section 2. It indicated that monopoly power in one market might not be used to foreclose competition, or even to gain a competitive advantage, in another market.

In some instances a firm with a lawfully acquired monopoly may be required not only to refrain from using its power to gain a competitive advantage in another market but also to give its competitors access to its monopoly. Illustrative is *United States v. Terminal Railroad Association*.[6] Because of its geography, St. Louis could accommodate only one railroad terminal. Several railroads combined to form the Terminal Railroad Association, which owned and operated the city's sole terminal. The association required the unanimous consent of its members to allow nonmember railroads access to the facility. The court held it violative of section 2 for the association to refuse proper and equal use of the terminal by nonmember companies. The following case raises similar issues of misuse of monopoly power.

MCI Communications Corp. v. American Telephone & Telegraph Co.

708 F.2d 1081 (7th Cir. 1983)

MCI (plaintiff) sued AT&T (defendant) for alleged violations of section 2 of the Sherman Act. A jury found for MCI and awarded $600 million in damages, which the trial judge trebled to $1.8 billion. The Court of Appeals for the Seventh Circuit affirmed in part and reversed in part.

Prior to 1969, AT&T had a lawful regulated monopoly over all telecommunication. In addition to regular local and long distance service, AT&T provided three types of private long distance service: point to point private lines which connected two locations directly; foreign exchange service (FX) which allowed users to make and receive calls with a distant city as though they were local calls; and common control switching arrangements (CCSA) which linked several distant locations via a private line.

In 1969, the Federal Communications Commission (FCC), which regulated long distance telephone service, granted MCI permission to provide private line long distance service between Chicago and St. Louis via micro-

---

[6] 284 U.S. 383 (1912).

wave transmissions. This prompted a flood of requests from other companies for similar permission. As a result, the FCC held a rulemaking proceeding and in 1971 issued a general decision approving, in principle, entry of competitors into the long distance telecommunications field. (This decision is referred to by the court as the Specialized Common Carriers decision.) The decision was ambiguous. MCI claimed that the decision allowed MCI to offer FX and CCSA service and required AT&T to allow MCI at a reasonable fee, to interconnect its service with AT&T's local distribution facilities, so that a person could access MCI's system via a local telephone call. AT&T maintained that the decision limited MCI to private point to point service and did not require local interconnections. AT&T refused to provide local interconnections for MCI's FX and CCSA services.

MCI sought an order from the FCC concerning FX and CCSA services and obtained a federal district court order that AT&T provide local interconnections. AT&T complied and appealed. On April 15, 1974, the Third Circuit Court of Appeals held that the district court should not have acted while the matter was pending before the FCC and vacated the order. Although the FCC indicated that its decision was imminent, AT&T immediately disconnected MCI's customers. Eight days later the FCC issued its decision and ordered AT&T to reconnect MCI.

In October 1974, MCI filed a tariff with the FCC seeking authority to provide regular long distance service over its microwave network. In 1976, the FCC ruled that MCI was not authorized to provide such service. MCI appealed, and in 1977, the D.C. Circuit Court of Appeals reversed the FCC's denial of MCI's authority to provide regular long distance service. This decision also confirmed AT&T's obligation to provide MCI with local interconnections. (This decision is referred to by the Court as the Execunet decision).

Cudahy, Circuit Judge

AT&T contends that the district court should have dismissed this suit on its motion because the FCC's regulatory control over AT&T's conduct renders AT&T immune from antitrust liability.

* * * * *

. . . [T]he Communications Act of 1934 does not expressly grant AT&T immunity from the antitrust laws for the conduct challenged in the instant case. . . . [R]egulated industries "are not *per se* exempt from the Sherman Act." Repeal of the antitrust laws by implication is not favored and not casually to be allowed. Only where there is a "plain repugnancy between the antitrust and regulatory provisions" will repeal be implied.

* * * * *

With respect to interconnections, we conclude . . . that the FCC's regulatory authority under the Communications Act does not preclude application of the Sherman Act. . . . Although the FCC has authority to compel interconnection . . . the initial decision whether to interconnect rests with the utility, and the record shows that the

FCC did not control or approve of AT&T's interconnection practices so closely that the FCC's approval could be inferred.

*   *   *   *   *

Whether in a regulated context or not, the broad outline of the offense of monopolization is well understood. Most recently, the Supreme Court has stated:

> The offense of monopoly under §2 of the Sherman Act has two elements: (1) the possession of monopoly power in the relevant market and (2) the willful acquisition or maintenance of that power as distinguished from growth or development as a consequence of a superior product, business acumen, or historic accident.

> . . . [T]he presence of a substantial degree of regulation, although not sufficient to confer antitrust immunity, may affect both the shape of "monopoly power" and the precise dimensions of the "willful acquisition or maintenance" of that power.

*   *   *   *   *

In the instant case, the district court properly instructed the jury that, in determining whether AT&T possessed monopoly power in the relevant market,

> you may consider the effect of the FCC's exercise of regulatory authority over prices and entry, including interconnection. Similarly, you may consider the effect of the exercise by state regulatory agencies of regulatory authority over prices and entry in connection with the provision of local services and facilities. That AT&T may have had the largest share or the entire share of the telephone business in certain areas would not be sufficient to establish that AT&T possessed monopoly power if in fact regulation by regulatory agencies prevented AT&T from having the power to restrict entry or control prices.

*   *   *   *   *

AT&T's status as a regulated public utility also bears on the second element of a monopolization offense: the willful acquisition or maintenance of monopoly power. . . . Some courts . . . have concluded that . . . if the ordinary business conduct of a dominant firm leads to the acquisition or maintenance of monopoly power, that conduct is presumed to reflect the requisite willful monopolistic intent. Whatever merit this presumption may have in other contexts, we believe it is a particularly inappropriate means of identifying monopolistic conduct by a regulated utility or common carrier. For these industries, anticipating and meeting all reasonable demands for services is often an explicit statutory obligation.

*   *   *   *   *

The jury found that AT&T unlawfully refused to interconnect MCI with the local distribution facilities of Bell operating companies—an act which prevented MCI from offering FX and CCSA services to its customers. A monopolist's refusal to deal under these circumstances is governed by the so-called essential facilities doctrine. Such a refusal may be unlawful because a monopolist's control of an essential facility can extend monopoly power from one stage of production to another, and from one market into another. . . .

The case law sets forth four elements necessary to establish liability under the essential facilities doctrine: (1) control of the essential facility by a monopolist; (2) a competitor's inability practically or reasonably to duplicate the essential facility; (3) the denial of the use of the facility to a competitor; and (4) the feasibility of providing the facility.

*   *   *   *   *

AT&T had complete control over the local distribution facilities that MCI required. The interconnections were essential for MCI to offer FX and CCSA service. The facilities in question met the criteria of "essential facilities" in that MCI could not duplicate Bell's local facilities. . . .

Finally, the evidence supports the jury's determination that AT&T denied the essential facilities, the interconnections for FX and CCSA service, when they could have been feasibly provided. No legitimate business or technical reason was shown for AT&T's denial of the requested interconnections.

* * * * *

At trial, MCI contended that in denying interconnections, AT&T intended to prevent competition. AT&T argued that the Specialized Common Carriers decision was so vague that it gave no guidance on AT&T's obligation to interconnect or even on MCI's authority to provide FX and CCSA service. AT&T argued that it reasonably believed that MCI was not authorized to provide the services for which it sought interconnections, and that this good faith belief in the regulatory requirements was a complete defense to antitrust liability for the denial of interconnections.

* * * * *

AT&T asserted that the evidence was insufficient to sustain the Jury's finding that the FX and CCSA interconnection denials were made in bad faith. The first contention is that MCI never proved AT&T knew in 1973 and 1974 that the court would rule as it did in the 1977 Execunet decision. Therefore, says AT&T, its denial of interconnections was made in good faith. MCI argues, however, that AT&T made its interconnection decisions without reference to its understanding of the state of the law. For support, MCI introduced internal AT&T documents showing AT&T's expectation that a less limited interconnection policy

would be propounded in the near future and suggesting that AT&T's approach be one of "buying time" through "delaying tactics." One AT&T document noted Bell's adoption of policies designed to "limit flexibility of [the specialized carriers] and [their] ability to sell services utilizing our central office switching capacity." From this evidence, the jury could reasonably infer that AT&T's delays in permitting FX and CCSA interconnections were evidence of AT&T's improper intent "to limit competitive encroachments through devices such as restricting the use carriers may make of our facilities." AT&T's denial of interconnections must also be judged in context with its other actions. The evidence supports the inference that, regardless of whether it anticipated Execunet, AT&T intended to obstruct MCI's entry into the market and used the public interest standard in bad faith.

AT&T also urges that the evidence was insufficient to support the jury's rejection of AT&T's defense that it had in good faith interpreted the Specialized Common Carriers decision as limiting its duty to provide interconnections. The jury was entitled to credit the evidence showing that generally AT&T officials intended to impede competition regardless of the meaning of the 1971 decision. AT&T presented testimony of its officials and others familiar with the telecommunications industry. That evidence indicated that some persons familiar with the telecommunications industry viewed the FCC's use of the term "private lines" service in the Specialized Common Carriers opinion as vague enough to be read as limiting MCI to "point-to-point" private line service (an AT&T interpretation that would exclude FX and CCSA interconnections and limit required interconnections only to "tie lines" through local wire "links" that would not provide access to the public switched network). In response, however, MCI introduced evidence that AT&T always classified

FX and CCSA as "private line service," which was the principal descriptive term used in the 1971 order to describe the scope of service authorized; that the limiting term "point-to-point private line service" did not appear in the 1971 decision; and the "tie lines" could afford access to a switched network. The "tie line" point, which raised a fact issue, would sustain a jury conclusion that, even if MCI was limited to receiving tie line interconnections, there still was no basis for AT&T to conclude that access to the switched network was forbidden to MCI by the 1971 order.

* * * * *

In any event, regardless of whether AT&T reasonably believed that Specialized Common Carriers did not require interconnections, the jury was entitled to conclude, based on the evidence, that AT&T did not act in good faith when it purportedly determined that the public interest justified its denial of interconnections.

[Note: The remainder of the opinion reversed the judgment on the ground that damages were not properly calculated.]

CASE QUESTIONS

1. Describe the markets that MCI was attempting to serve. How did AT&T control entry into those markets?

2. Why did the court reject AT&T's claim of antitrust immunity? What impact did regulation have on the issues of possession of monopoly power and intent to monopolize?

3. What four elements are necessary for a case of monopolization under the essential facilities doctrine? How were these elements present in the instant case?

4. What was AT&T's defense? What evidence sustained the jury's rejection of that defense

5. Prior to January 1, 1984, local telephone companies and Western Electric Corp. were wholly owned subsidiaries of AT&T. Consumers could lease their telephones from their local phone companies, buy their phones from AT&T, or buy their phones from other sources such as retailers and discount stores. Although many companies manufactured telephones, AT&T purchased almost all of the phones it sold and almost all of the phones its local subsidiaries leased from Western Electric. Did this practice violate section 2 of the Sherman Act?

OLIGOPOLIES

Oligopolistic industries are industries dominated by a few large firms. Usually, none of the firms individually possesses sufficient market power to be a monopoly under section 2. Oligopolistic industries are usually marked by conscious parallelism and price leadership. However, as noted in chapter 5, consciously parallel action does not amount to a contract, combination, or conspiracy. Thus, oligopolistic markets are generally not subject to attack under section 1 of the Sherman Act.

Some individuals and authorities have suggested a theory of shared monopoly which would apply section 2 to oligopolies. Pursuant to this theory, where two or more companies act in an interdependent manner resulting in anticompetitive effects, the companies would be considered a single entity for section 2 purposes.

In 1972, the FTC filed complaints against the major cereal manufacturers and the major oil companies. The complaints charged that the companies acted interdependently to raise prices and to raise barriers to competition from new entrants in their respective markets. In 1981, the complaint against the oil companies was dismissed on procedural grounds,[7] while in 1982 the FTC dismissed the complaint against the cereal companies on the ground that the remedy sought was not appropriate.[8] Thus, today the shared monopoly concept remains only a theory yet to be tested in court.

ATTEMPTS TO MONOPOLIZE

Attempts to monopolize differ from monopolization. In an attempt to monopolize, the firm has not yet achieved monopoly power. The offense of attempted monopolization requires a specific intent. It also requires that the firm come dangerously close to monopolizing.

The requirement of a specific intent to monopolize necessitates an inquiry into the defendant's subjective state of mind. This inquiry may be less difficult where the defendant is a corporation rather than an individual, as intracompany memoranda and minutes of meetings will frequently be available as evidence. However, most evidence usually consists of inferring subjective intent from objective conduct. Thus, companies are often called upon to justify prior conduct in the guise of an inquiry into intent.

A complex factual issue arises when an effort is made to determine what point a company must reach to come dangerously close to monopoly. Closely aligned to this inquiry is whether the relevant market must be established to prove attempted monopolizing. The following case illustrates these issues.

William Inglis & Sons Baking Co. v. ITT Continental Baking Co.

668 F.2d 1014 (9th Cir. 1982)

Inglis (plaintiff) and ITT Continental (defendant) were wholesale bakeries selling bread to retail groceries and supermarkets. Inglis sued Continental

---

[7] See BNA—ATRR No. 1031 at A-28 (1981).

[8] See 42 BNA—ATRR 154 (1982).

for allegedly attempting to monopolize in violation of section 2 of the Sherman Act. A jury awarded Inglis $5,048,000, but the trial judge entered judgment for Continental, notwithstanding the jury's verdict. Inglis appealed and the court of appeals reversed the judgment for Continental and remanded the case for a new trial.

Both parties produced bread under private labels for specific retailers and under their own advertised labels of Wonder (Continental) and Sunbeam (Inglis). Inglis charged that because competition from private labels was hurting sales of the higher priced Wonder Bread, Continental pursued a strategy of predatorily pricing its private label bread to drive smaller producers such as Inglis from the market. The alleged goal was to achieve control over the private label market, raise private label prices, and thereby to reduce private label competition with Wonder.

Sneed, Circuit Judge

[T]he law of this circuit . . . recognizes three elements of an attempt claim under section 2 of the Sherman Act: (1) specific intent to control prices or destroy competition in some part of commerce; (2) predatory or anticompetitive conduct directed to accomplishing the unlawful purpose; and (3) a dangerous probability of success.

Each element interacts with others in significant and unexpected ways. The element of specific intent appears to have had its genesis in the distinctions—and similarities—between *monopolization* and *attempted monopolization*, both of which are proscribed in separate terms by section 2. . . . By analogy to the law of criminal attempt, the requirement of specific intent is used to confine the reach of an attempt to conduct threatening monopolization.

*   *   *   *   *

. . . [T]he existence of specific intent may be established not only by direct evidence of unlawful design, but by circumstantial evidence, principally of illegal conduct. Too heavy a reliance on circumstantial evidence incurs the risk of reducing almost to the point of extinction the existence of the requirement. The type of conduct that will

support the inference, therefore, must be carefully defined. This court has made it clear that the nature of such conduct varies with the conditions of the market and the characteristics of the defendant.

Thus, we consistently have held that the inference may be drawn from conduct that serves as the basis for a substantial claim of restraint of trade.

*   *   *   *   *

On the other hand, direct evidence of intent alone, without corroborating evidence of conduct, cannot sustain a claim of attempted monopolization. The necessity of corroborative conduct rests on the fact that direct evidence of intent alone can be ambiguous and misleading. The law of attempted monopolization must tread a narrow pathway between rules that would inhibit honest competition and those that would allow pernicious but subtle conduct to escape antitrust scrutiny. Direct evidence of intent to vanquish a rival in an honest competitive struggle cannot help to establish an antitrust violation. It also must be shown that the defendant sought victory through unfair or predatory means. Evidence of conduct is thus indispensable.

* * * * *

The third element, dangerous probability of success, like the first, also is rooted in the relationship between the separate offenses of monopolization and attempt to monopolize. Although this element is generally treated as separate and independent, it can be inferred from evidence indicating the existence of the other two. . . . That is, a dangerous probability of success may be inferred either (1) from direct evidence of specific intent plus proof of conduct directed to accomplishing the unlawful design, or (2) from evidence of conduct alone, provided the conduct is also the sort from which specific intent can be inferred.

. . . [T]he dangerous probability of success requirement is . . . a way of gauging more accurately the purpose of a defendant's actions. . . . Thus, if market conditions are such that a course of conduct described by the plaintiff would be unlikely to succeed in monopolizing the market, it is less likely that the defendant actually attempted to monopolize the market. Conversely, a firm with substantial market power may find it more rational to engage in a monopolistic course of conduct than would a smaller firm in a less concentrated market.

* * * * *

The conduct element of the attempt claim also is closely related to the other two elements. Thus, the first element, specific intent to control prices or exclude competition, may be inferred from certain types of conduct. The third element, dangerous probability of success, also is often dependent on proof of conduct. Finally, evidence of conduct is indispensable even when there is direct evidence of unlawful specific intent.

This interrelationship extends to the type and strength of proof required to establish each element. In the absence of direct and probative evidence of specific intent to monopolize, for example, a plaintiff must introduce evidence of conduct amounting to a substantial claim of restraint of trade or conduct clearly threatening to competition or clearly exclusionary. Direct evidence of intent, on the other hand, may permit reliance on a broader range of conduct, simply because the purpose of ambiguous conduct may be more clearly understood. But, in general, conduct that will support a claim of attempted monopolization must be such that its anticipated benefits were dependent upon its tendency to discipline or eliminate competition and thereby enhance the firm's long-term ability to reap the benefits of monopoly power. Such conduct is not true competition; it makes sense only because it eliminates competition. It does not enhance the quality or attractiveness of the product, reduce its cost, or alter the demand function that all competitors confront. Its purpose is to create a monopoly by means other than fair competition.

Inglis alleged in support of its section 2 claim that Continental set predatory prices for its private label bread with the purpose of eliminating weaker bread wholesalers.

* * * * *

Much of the dispute on appeal concerns the proper relationship between direct evidence of intent and evidence concerning the relationship between the cost and price of Continental's products.

* * * * *

One . . . economic test that has found favor in this and other circuits was developed by Professors Areeda and Turner. In their view a price should not be considered predatory if it equals or exceeds the marginal cost of producing the product. When a firm prices at marginal cost, they argue, only less efficient firms will suffer larger losses per unit of output at that price. Moreover, such pricing enables resources to be properly allocated because the price accurately "signals" to the consumer the true social cost of the product. Therefore, "pricing at marginal cost is the competitive and socially optimal result." In contrast, pricing below marginal cost should be conclusively presumed illegal. Recognizing that business records rarely reflect marginal costs of production, Areeda and Turner suggest the use of average variable cost as an evidentiary surrogate.*

*   *   *   *   *

Our approach to proof of intent through use of conduct is to focus on what a rational firm would have expected its prices to accomplish. . . . [A] price should be considered predatory if its anticipated benefits depended on its tendency to eliminate competition. If the justification for a price reduction did not depend upon this anticipated effect, then it does not support a claim of attempted monopolization, even if it had the actual effect of taking sales from competitors. We emphasize a defendant's rational expectations to avoid penalizing innocent miscalculations that result in anticipated profits being turned into losses, with damaging effects on competitors. Our focus does not require that plaintiffs in all cases come forward with evidence of the defendant's subjective state of mind. Predatory pricing may be proved by examining the relationship between the defendant's prices and costs. But such proof must tend to show that the anticipated benefits of the prices, at the time they were set, depended on their anticipated destructive effect upon competi-

tion and the consequent enhanced market position of the defendant.

In this case Continental has conceded that some of the prices challenged by Inglis were below average total cost. Taken alone this does not brand Continental's prices as predatory. Pricing below average total cost may be a legitimate means of minimizing losses, particularly when the firm is "temporarily" experiencing "excess capacity" in its productive facilities. When this is the case, the firm's average variable cost—the sum of those costs that vary with output divided by the total units of output—generally will be less than the firm's marginal cost—the variable cost associated with producing the last unit of output. Prices below the average total cost of production, but above the average variable cost, may represent a legitimate means of minimizing losses during the period of inadequate demand. Such a price will be sufficient to recover the variable costs of production and at least some portion of the firm's fixed costs—those costs that would remain even if the firm ceased production. To discontinue production under these circumstances would increase losses because even that portion of its total fixed costs would be lost. Pricing at this level, however, will not be rational over the long term because it will not justify renewal of investment at the previous level. . . .

Although pricing below average total cost in the short term may be legitimate, it is less likely that pricing below average variable cost will be. Such pricing, if sustained, will not permit the recovery of any portion of the firm's fixed costs. In addition, the firm, because it cannot recover all its variable costs, has out-of-pocket losses on each unit it sells. The economic case for discontinuance of production is strong.

Although pricing below average total cost and above average variable cost is not inherently predatory, it does not follow, however, that such prices are never preda-

---

* By evidentiary surrogate, the court means that average variable cost would serve as an adequate substitute for marginal cost. The terms variable cost, marginal cost, as well as total cost, are defined by the court later in the opinion—Au.

tory. Predation exists when the justification of these prices is based, not on their effectiveness in minimizing losses, but on their tendency to eliminate rivals and create a market structure enabling the seller to recoup his losses. This is the ultimate standard, and not rigid adherence to a particular cost-based rule, that must govern our analysis of alleged predatory pricing.

Guided by these principles, we hold that to establish predatory pricing a plaintiff must prove that the anticipated benefits of defendant's price depended on its tendency to discipline or eliminate competition and thereby enhance the firm's long-term ability to reap the benefits of monopoly power. If the defendant's prices were below average total cost but above average variable cost, the plaintiff bears the burden of showing defendant's pricing was predatory. If, however, the plaintiff proves that the defendant's prices were below average variable cost, the plaintiff has established a prima facie* case of predatory pricing and

---

* A prima facie case is one supported by sufficient evidence that it will prevail until contradicted and overcome by other evidence.—Au.

the burden shifts to the defendant to prove that the prices were justified without regard to any anticipated destructive effect they might have on competitors.

*   *   *   *   *

In this case the district court . . . concluded that Inglis' evidence concerning Continental's cost-price relationship was legally insufficient to establish predatory pricing. Although Inglis' expert testified that during the period examined in his study Continental's prices were below average variable cost, the district court concluded that because excess capacity existed in the relevant market, only proof of prices below marginal cost could establish predatory pricing. The district court erred. The jury reasonably could have concluded that prices below average variable cost were predatory. Even when excess capacity exists, pricing below average cost, to repeat, is sufficiently questionable to support the inference that the prices were designed to eliminate competition.

CASE QUESTIONS

1. What are the elements of an attempt to monopolize? How are they interdependent?

2. What is predatory pricing? How does proof of predatory pricing establish the elements of an attempt to monopolize?

3. What is the Areeda-Turner formula for predatory pricing? What is its rationale?

4. To what extent, if any, does the court adopt the Areeda-Turner formula?

5. Why did the district court enter judgment for Continental? Why did it err? Why was the case remanded for a new trial?

CONSPIRACIES TO MONOPOLIZE

Conspiracy to monopolize is a separate offense under section 2 of the Sherman Act. It requires proof that two or more entities conspired with the specific intent of monopolizing. Proving such conspiracy is no different from proving conspiracy under section 1 of the Sherman Act, while proving such intent is no different from proving intent in attempted monopolization cases.

ALTERNATIVE APPROACHES

At the beginning of this chapter it was emphasized that the Sherman Act prohibits monopolization rather than monopoly. A firm possessing monopoly power does not violate section 2 if it obtained that power as a result of superior skill or business acumen, government grant, or historical accident. A monopolist must actively seek, maintain, or expand monopoly power to violate section 2.

In June 1978, President Carter signed an Executive Order convening the National Commission for the Review of Antitrust Laws and Procedures. The commission issued its final report in 1979. It recommended, among other things, that Congress study the feasibility of amending section 2 to outlaw monopolies regardless of the monopolist's intent. The proposal would render illegal the acquisition and maintenance of "persistent monopoly power."

Proponents of the no-fault approach to monopoly argue that it would greatly reduce the costs of Sherman Act litigation. They suggest that in major monopolization cases, proof of the defendant's conduct consumes 30–45 percent of the time involved in the litigation. They further contend that the reasons for the defendant's monopoly position are not relevant to the evils section 2 was designed to remedy. Monopoly is undesirable because it misallocates resources, discourages innovation, and limits consumer choice. Even where a firm has achieved its monopoly power through superior performance, that power may survive long after the firm's original advantages have disappeared. Rivals may not challenge the firm because of their ineptness or their indifference to the market or because of barriers to entry. Thus proponents urge that the relevant inquiry would focus not on how the monopoly developed but on how to get rid of it. That is, the inquiry would focus on how the market could be made more competitive.

Opponents of the no-fault concept urge that its application would discourage entrepreneurs from competing aggressively. They contend that firms would be reluctant to undertake actions which might turn them into "monopolists" and subject them to dismemberment. They further argue that consideration of conduct is relevant to the evils the Sherman Act was designed to remedy. They hold that monopoly may be attributed to one of four factors: government grants, mergers, predatory actions, or superior efficiency. Mergers are governed by the Clayton Act. Government grants reflect a policy design that monopoly is desirable. It is therefore only predatory conduct that section 2 should be concerned with.

Opponents of the no-fault proposal also consider it unfair to break up a company that has achieved a dominant position in the market through positive conduct. They regard such a breakup as particularly unfair to the firm's investors, whom it would deprive of part of the returns to which they are entitled.

CHAPTER PROBLEMS

1. The chrysanthemum industry was internally specialized. Breeders created new varieties and sold them to propagators. The propagators distributed cuttings to growers, who sold them to retail florists. Yoder Brothers, Inc., a breeder and propagator, was charged with monopolizing. If the relevant market was chrysanthemums, Yoder had monopoly power, but if it was all ornamental flowers, Yoder did not have monopoly power. The ultimate consumer tended to accept any of several ornamental flowers. Market demand as the consumer level fluctuated with the prices of various ornamental flowers. Grower demand responded to consumer demand. Many growers handled a wide variety of ornamental flowers. However, factors such as greenhouse space and layout, watering systems, and use of lights made it inconvenient and somewhat costly for a grower to switch from one ornamental flower to another. Define the relevant market.

2. The Eastman Kodak Company is the world's largest manufacturer of film. Since 1952 its annual film sales have always exceeded 82 percent of the national volume and 88 percent of the national revenues. Kodak also produces instant-loading cameras designed for the mass market. Between 1954 and 1973 it never enjoyed less than 61 percent of the annual unit sales or less than 64 percent of the annual dollar volume, and in the peak year of 1964, Kodak cameras accounted for 90 percent of market revenues. Much of this success has been due to the firm's history of innovation.

In 1963 Kodak first marketed the 126 Instamatic instant-loading camera, and in 1972 it came out with the much smaller 110 Pocket Instamatic. These small, light cameras employ film packaged in cartridges that can simply be dropped in the back, thus obviating the need to load and position a roll of film manually. The introduction of these cameras triggered successive revolutions in the industry. Amateur still camera sales in the United States averaged 3.9 million units annually between 1954 and 1963, with little annual variation. In the first full year after Kodak's introduction of the 126, industry sales leaped 22 percent, and they took an even larger jump when the 110 came to market. Other camera manufacturers copied both of these cameras, but for several months after each was introduced, those who wished to buy one had to purchase a Kodak.

When Kodak introduced the 110 Instamatic it also introduced Kodacolor II film, which it marketed as a "remarkable new film" producing better pictures. Kodak made conscious decisions to introduce the new camera and film together, not to make the film available in the 126 format for 18 months, and not to provide its competitors with advance notice of the innovations. Kodak has also followed a consistent policy of refusing to make film available for formats other than those in which it makes cameras. Has Kodak violated section 2? Explain.

3. IBM, facing stiff competition from newcomers to the market for peripheral data processing devices, announced a series of price reductions designed to eliminate that competition. It also announced that it would lease peripheral devices for a fixed term of years instead of allowing customers to cancel leases on 30 days' notice. The fixed-term leases were for periods of up to two years, shorter in duration than those offered by IBM's competitors. If these changes allow IBM to capture a monopolist's share of the market, has IBM violated section 2 of the Sherman Act? Explain.

4. Plaza Theaters, Inc., owns all of the movie theaters in a city with a population of 50,000. A rival corporation from the other end of the state has announced plans to build a new theater that will compete with Plaza. Plaza warns the potential competitor: "If you open a theater here, Plaza will compete vigorously. It will go after all the first-run films and will offer them at the lowest possible prices. Plaza will make it impossible for you to survive in this town." If the rival cancels its plans to open the theater, has Plaza violated section 2? Explain.

5. The Otter Tail Power Company sold electric power to 465 communities in Minnesota and North and South Dakota. It functioned pursuant to municipally granted franchises of 10 to 20 years' duration. Several municipalities chose not to renew Otter Tail's franchises, deciding to replace the power company with municipally owned systems. Otter Tail responded by refusing to sell power at wholesale to the new municipal systems and by refusing to transport over its lines power which the municipal systems had purchased from other sources. Did Otter Tail violate section 2? Explain.

6. OAG, Inc. published the *Official Airlines Guide,* which became the primary reference for airlines and travel agents in booking passengers on flights. The guide listed both the direct and connecting flights of certified airlines but only the direct flights of commuter airlines. Thus, a person seeking passage between two cities that were not serviced by a direct flight could determine at a glance which certified airlines connected to which other certified airlines to complete the route. To determine how to complete a route by using a commuter airline, a person would have to consult a separate section of the guide to find what cities the commuter airlines provided direct service to and then turn to the certified airlines direct service station to find a connecting flight. This hampered the commuter airlines' ability to compete. Did OAG violate section 2? Explain.

7. Klearflax Linen Looms, Inc., was the sole domestic manufacturer of linen rugs. It sold rolls of linen rug material to distributors which would cut them into required sizes, finish them by binding the cut edges, and sell them to retail stores. Klearflax also cut and finished some rugs at its factory. For several years Klearflax was the sole bidder on federal government contracts to supply linen rugs. One year a Klearflax distributor also bid on the contract. The distributor's bid was lower, and it was awarded the contract. Klearflax then refused to supply the distributor with linen rug material. Did Klearflax violate section 2? Explain?

8. You are an executive vice president of DuPont, a major chemical company. One of your products is TiO_2, a white chemical pigment used in manufacturing paint. There is no substitute for TiO_2, and all producers compete nationwide. DuPont currently has 30 percent of the market.

There are two processes for producing TiO_2: the sulfate process and the chloride process. Either process can use rutile ore or ilmenite ore, but only DuPont possesses the technology to use ilmenite ore in the chloride process.

You have just received a staff report stating that recent shortages have inflated the price of rutile ore. These shortages are expected to worsen over the next 10 to 15 years. The cost of producing TiO_2 via the sulfate process has also increased substantially because of stricter pollution control regulations. Therefore, it is significantly cheaper to produce TiO_2 via the chloride process, using ilmenite ore. This cost advantage is expected to continue for at least the next 10 to 15 years. The report recommends that DuPont immediately expand its chloride process ilmenite facilities, announce its expansion plans, price its TiO_2 high enough to finance the expansion but below the prices charged by competitors using the sulfate process or rutile ore, and keep the chloride-ilmenite technology secret. It projects that DuPont's market share can increase to 42 percent in five years, 55 percent in ten years, and 68 percent in 13 years. Should you follow the recommendations? Discuss whether such a course of action might violate section 2 of the Sherman Act.

9. Describe the concept of shared monopoly. Should this concept be recognized under section 2 of the Sherman Act?

10. Discuss the arguments in favor of and against a no-fault monopoly law. What is your opinion on this issue?

CHAPTER 12

MERGERS

A merger combines two companies into one. Generally, this may be accomplished in any of three ways:

— Both companies are combined into a single new company.
— One company acquires the assets of the other.
— One company acquires the stock of the other.

Mergers can facilitate the flow of investment capital and channel business assets into areas of greater demand. They can replace ineffective managers with new leaders capable of revitalizing a failing company. However, mergers can also eliminate competitors, foreclose markets, and raise barriers to new entries into existing markets.

Between 1890 and 1914, anticompetitive mergers were attacked under the Sherman Act with infrequent success. In one case the Supreme Court held lawful a merger of sugar refiners which placed 98 percent of the nation's output of refined sugar in the hands of a single corporation.[1] In another case the Court held unlawful a combination of railroads which gave a single company control over all railroad routes to the West.[2]

In 1914, Congress responded to the ineffectiveness of the Sherman Act as a device for controlling mergers. It enacted the Clayton Act. Section 7 of that statute prohibited one corporation from acquiring the stock of another where the effect might be to lessen competition between them or to create a monopoly. The Clayton Act proved to be ineffective in blocking anticompetitive mergers. Companies were able to avoid it entirely by structuring their mergers as asset acquisitions rather than stock acquisitions. Furthermore, courts placed a strict interpretation on the anticompet-

---

[1] *United States v. E. C. Knight Co.,* 156 U.S. 1 (1895).
[2] *Northern Securities Co. v. United States,* 193 U.S. 197 (1904).

itive effect necessary to make a stock acquisition illegal. Thus, from 1914 to 1950 only 15 mergers were successfully attacked under section 7.

In 1950 the Celler-Kefauver Act amended section 7 of the Clayton Act, expanding it to encompass all mergers, regardless of their form. The amendment also prohibited mergers which might tend to lessen competition or tend to create a monopoly in any line of commerce in any section of the country. It applied regardless of whether the merging companies were direct competitors. Congress intended to make section 7 a preventative measure designed to nip anticompetitive conduct in the bud.

In 1976, Congress further amended the Clayton Act by requiring that large companies planning mergers notify the FTC of their intent at least 30 days before the merger. This advance notice allows the FTC and the Justice Department to attack anticompetitive mergers before they actually take place.

Today, any business considering a merger must evaluate its legality under section 7. That consideration involves a two-step process:

— Determining the relevant market
— Assessing the competitive effects

This chapter explores the principal issues posed by section 7. First, it discusses the two-step process for determining a merger's legality. Second, it applies the process to three types of mergers: horizontal, vertical, and conglomerate. Third, it considers defenses to section 7 liability. Fourth, it considers problems involved in remedying illegal mergers. Fifth, it discusses enforcement problems peculiar to section 7.

DETERMINING THE RELEVANT MARKET

Section 7 is concerned with the potential effects of mergers on competition. Firms compete in a marketplace, so the effects of a merger must be evaluated in the marketplace. The first step in evaluating a merger's legality is to define the relevant market.

Section 7 prohibits mergers that might tend to create a monopoly. Therefore, the relevant market determination focuses on markets capable of being monopolized. Courts consider the same factors used to determine relevant markets under section 2 of the Sherman Act. However, section 7 also prohibits mergers that may substantially lessen competition. It prohibits mergers that may foster anticompetitive practices such as other mergers or unreasonable restraints of trade. These practices can occur despite the presence of available substitutes. That is, these practices can occur in markets that are incapable of being monopolized. Therefore, a relevant market may have several submarkets. Section 7 is also concerned with protecting potential competition. This includes interindustry competition. A relevant market may thus be composed of two or more markets or submarkets.

The Product Market

In merger cases, courts take a very practical approach to defining relevant product markets. As with cases under section 2 of the Sherman Act, courts consider cross-elasticity of demand and other indicia of substitutability. However, they also consider such factors as:

a. Peculiar product characteristics
b. Unique production facilities
c. Distinct customers or prices
d. Sensitivity to price changes
e. Specialized vendors
f. Public or industry recognition

Judicial reliance on these factors indicates that a submarket can be viewed as an area subject to anticompetitive practices that fall short of monopolization. For example, a product may have many different uses, and demand for it may come from different types of buyers. Ninety percent of the buyers may have many available substitutes. These substitutes would be included within the relevant market. However, 10 percent may find it very difficult to substitute because they are dependent on the product's peculiar characteristics. They form a distinct group of customers. There may be distinct vendors who distribute the product to them. The price of the product may be somewhat sensitive to economic conditions affecting these distinct customers. Thus, the product itself would be a relevant submarket based on the remaining 10 percent of product demand.

The Geographic Market

The judicial approach to the geographic market in merger cases is equally practical. The geographic market must correspond to commercial realities and be economically significant. It, too, may include submarkets. For example, in *Brown Shoe Co. v. United States*,[3] the Supreme Court considered a merger of two national chains of shoe retailers. The Court approved the trial judge's definition of the relevant geographic markets as every city with a population exceeding 10,000 and its immediate contiguous suburbs. The Court recognized that different cities might produce different patterns of competition and that competition existed between smaller communities within standard metropolitan areas. Nevertheless, it found the trial court's definition workable because that definition included the most important competitors—downtown business districts and suburban shopping centers. The Court also approved the trial judge's method of analyzing the competitive effects in the geographic markets. The trial judge had analyzed the St. Louis market in detail, had made a statistical analysis

---

[3] 370 U.S. 294 (1961).

of market share in a representative sampling of cities, and had generalized to draw conclusions about all cities. The following case illustrates the judicial approach to relevant market in Clayton Act section 7 cases.

Jim Walter Corp. v. FTC

625 F.2d 676 (5th Cir. 1980)

Jim Walter Corp. (JWC appellant) appealed an order of the FTC (appellee) which found that its acquisition of Panacon Corp. violated section 7 of the Clayton Act and required that it divest itself of Panacon. JWC claimed that the FTC erred in finding the relevant market to be tar and asphalt roofing materials in the United States. The Fifth Circuit Court of Appeals vacated the order and remanded for further proceedings.

At the time of the acquisition, JWC owned Celotex, Corp., which manufactured and retailed construction materials, including tar and asphalt roofing products. Panacon manufactured and retailed similar products, including the Philip Carey line of tar and asphalt roofing materials. Most of Carey's sales occurred in a 26-state area.

Before the merger, Celotex accounted for 8.83 percent and Carey accounted for 8.79 percent of domestic sales of tar and asphalt roofing materials. They ranked fifth and sixth in the country. After the merger, the company was the country's second largest producer of these materials.

Tjolat, Circuit Judge

Section 7 prohibits acquisitions "where in any line of commerce *in any section of the country,* the effect of [the] acquisition may be substantially to lessen competition, or to tend to create a monopoly." Accordingly, "Determination of the relevant . . . geographic [market] is a necessary predicate to deciding whether a merger contravenes the Clayton Act." The FTC found that the relevant geographic market in this case was "the nation as a whole." . . .

Since Panacon marketed 93% of its roofing products in 26 states, JWC claims that the finding of a national market was incorrect as a matter of law.

* * * * *

[T]he relevant geographic market is the area of the country in which the acquired firm is a significant competitior. Such an approach recognizes that "it is the preservation of competition which is at stake, [and thus] the significant proportion of coverage is that within the area of effective competition."

We think that in surveying the boundaries of this area of effective competition in a particular case, the FTC may generally use either of two approaches. First, it may define the area by the points at which the acquired firm makes significant sales, the approach JWC argues it must take in every case. But second, the FTC may choose to define a relevant market by identifying the area in which the acquired firm's marketing activities have a perceptible competitive impact on the activities of other firms in the same area. As one court has observed:

> the geographic market for the purposes of determining the impact of a merger can include all areas where the trade in a product is affected by, and is not independent of, the trade in that product in other areas. . . .

This second approach is the one the FTC suggests is appropriate here.

We agree with the FTC, and that brings us to our second market issue, the evidentiary predicate needed under the second approach to support a finding that the entire United States is an area of effective competition for asphalt roofing products. Certainly the most compelling evidence that an area is competitively unified is statistical evidence of pricing interdependence, i.e., "if a change in price in one area has an effect on price in another area." But we think nonstatistical evidence can also be probative of a national market, if it tends to show that "regional markets are so interrelated that what happens in one has a direct effect in the others and none is so separate that the buyers and sellers are not concerned with prices and supply and demand in the others."

We now turn to whether there is substantial evidence to support the FTC's finding of a national market for tar and asphalt roofing products. . . .

[T]he FTC appears to have relied primarily on the causal observations of industry representatives and an economist, to the effect that large firms compete nationally. None of these individuals, however, was responding to questions relating to the legal standard for defining a geographic market. Other than this opinion testimony, which composes approximately three pages out of the 2,686 page transcript, the only evidence even slightly probative of a national market showed that some producers of asphalt roofing shipped some of their products beyond a 250 mile radius of their plants, that factors in addition to transportation costs affected the distance products could be shipped, and that more than half of all tar and asphalt sales were made in the 26-state region where Philip Carey was most active. We do not think, given the definition of geographic market outlined in this opinion, that this is substantial evidence of a national market.

Because of our holding that the FTC's national market finding is not supported by substantial evidence, we remand for reconsideration of the appropriate geographic market by which the merger of Panacon into Celotex must be judged.

In addition to the two issues we have discussed, JWC raises objections to the FTC's findings that the appropriate product market is limited to tar and asphalt roofing products and that the merger had anticompetitive effects. . . . Each of these issues would have to be reconsidered, however, if a regional market rather than national market were found. Therefore, we reserve our judgment on these questions, which JWC may raise after the FTC has reconsidered the case at the administrative level.

CASE QUESTIONS

1. What did JWC argue was the only possible relevent geographic market? Why did the court reject this argument?

2. How did the court define the relevant geographic market? Why

3. What evidence supported the finding of

a national market? Why was this insufficient to sustain the finding?

4. How did the FTC define the relevant product markets? What was JWC's objection to this definition? What information is needed to evaluate JWC's objection?

5. The publisher of the *Los Angeles Times*, the largest daily newspaper in southern California, acquired the largest local daily paper in San Bernardino County, which borders Los Angeles on the east. The *Times* provided detailed coverage of state, national, and international news, while the local newspaper focused on county news. The *Times* San Bernardino circulation was mostly in the western part of the county, while the local paper's circulation was mostly in the eastern part. Approximately 25 percent of their circulation overlapped. Define the relevant markets.

ASSESSING THE COMPETITIVE IMPACT

Once the relevant markets are defined, the section 7 inquiry focuses on whether the merger may tend to lessen competition or may tend to create a monopoly. The appropriate concern is the merger's potential anticompetitive effects. Congress intended section 7 to be a preventative measure. Therefore, even though a merger is not yet lessening competition it may violate section 7.

Each merger must be analyzed to predict its future impact on the relevant markets. Courts look at various factors in section 7 cases. These include the direct elimination of competition, foreclosure of a significant portion of the market from competitors, entrenchment of a dominant competitor, market trends, and postmerger evidence.

Elimination of Competition

Mergers may replace two vigorous competitors with one new firm. However, the elimination of competition need not be that direct for a section 7 violation to exist. Mergers may result in the elimination of potential competition as well.

If the acquiring company has considered entering the acquired company's market on its own, the merger has the effect of eliminating that potential competition. The loss of potential competition must be evaluated from the viewpoint of the potential entrant and of those already in the market. This requires assessing the likelihood that the potential entrant would enter the market independently were the merger not allowed and assessing the effect of that potential entry on the activities of those already in the market.

Sometimes a merger involves firms in different industries that serve similar functions. The merger may be unlawful if it reduces competition between the industries. For example, the Supreme Court held that a merger between the second leading producer of cans and the third leading producer of bottles violated section 7 because it lessened competition between the two types of containers.[4]

Market Foreclosure

A merger may foreclose competitors from a significant portion of the market. When a customer and supplier merge, competing suppliers may be foreclosed from the customer's business. Competing customers may also be hurt by the merger if the supplier produces a good whose demand exceeds its supply. Under these circumstances, the supplier might allocate the scarce good to the customer with whom it merged, to the detriment of the customer's competitors. The merger may make it difficult for companies operating at only one level to compete. Other customers and suppliers may feel the need to merge. Potential competitors may decide that they can no longer enter the market on only one level and may lose interest in entering the market.

Entrenchment of a Dominant Competitor

If a larger, wealthier firm acquires a smaller firm which is dominant in its market, the acquisition may have the effect of entrenching the smaller firm's position. This is particularly so if the larger firm could have entered the market on its own or by acquiring one of the weaker firms already in the market. The acquisition of a weak firm in the market is sometimes called a "toehold" entry into the market.

Potential for Reciprocity

Reciprocal dealing occurs when two companies agree to use each other's products. It gives each company an unfair advantage over its competitors. If company X produces a good whose market includes suppliers of company Y, a merger between X and Y may violate section 7 because suppliers of Y may purchase from X out of fear that they will lose Y as a customer.

FTC v. Consolidated Foods Co. illustrates the problem of reciprocity.[5] Consolidated, which owned food processing plants and a network of wholesale and retail food stores, acquired Gentry, Inc., a manufacturer of dehydrated onions and garlic. Because food processors which sold to Consolidated gave their onion and garlic business to Gentry for purposes of reciprocity, the Court held that the merger violated section 7.

Market Trends

Courts use market trends to place a merger in perspective. If a market is easy to enter and has attracted many new firms, a merger that directly

---

[4] *United States v. Continental Can Co.*, 378 U.S. 441 (1964).

[5] 380 U.S.C. 592 (1965).

eliminates a competitor may not be anticompetitive. On the other hand, a market that has become increasingly concentrated may be affected severely by a merger that reduces competition only slightly.

Using Postmerger Evidence

Many mergers are challenged after they occur. Several years may pass before the case comes to trial. During this period, the market will respond to the merger. Companies frequently try to show that the market remained competitive after the merger. This postmerger evidence, they argue, shows that the merger did not violate section 7. Courts view this type of evidence with extreme caution and are rarely swayed by it.

In rejecting postmerger evidence, courts have emphasized that section 7 requires an assessment of the probable effects of a merger rather than its actual effects. Thus, the fact that anticompetitive effects have not manifested themselves by the date of trial is no guarantee that such effects will not become apparent in the future. Furthermore, courts are reluctant even to imply that a merger did not adversely affect competition prior to trial because they find it impossible to deduce what would have happened had the merger not been consummated. Finally, courts are concerned that if they adopted a rule that considered postmerger evidence, the defendant would postpone aggressive or anticompetitive actions until after the trial.

On the other hand, postmerger evidence which indicates that a merger initially thought to lack anticompetitive effects has actually adversely affected competition may form the basis for attacking the merger several years later. The merged companies may not seek refuge in the statute of limitations, for it does not begin to run until the anticompetitive effects of the merger become apparent. Thus, a company that has acquired other companies must watch its behavior long after the acquisition to avoid possible section 7 attack.

APPLYING THE TWO STEP PROCESS

Analysis of a merger requires two steps: defining the relevant market and assessing the competitive impact. In applying the two step process, courts classify mergers as horizontal, vertical, or conglomerate. *Horizontal mergers* involve firms selling the same good or service at the same level of distribution. *Vertical mergers* involve firms at different levels of distribution—usually a supplier and a customer. *Conglomerate mergers* involve firms whose products or services are not directly related.

Horizontal Mergers

Horizontal mergers have the most consistent and immediate anticompetitive potential because they replace two competitors with a single, stronger firm. The effects of a horizontal merger are illustrated in Figure 12–1.

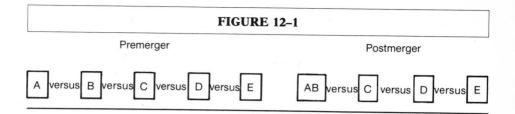

FIGURE 12–1

When the industry in which a horizontal merger occurs is concentrated and the merger results in a company with an "undue market share," a rebuttable presumption arises that the merger is illegal. The levels of concentration and market share necessary to trigger this presumption are not very great. They are particularly small where the industry has experienced a trend toward further concentration. Courts have reasoned that the Clayton Act is designed to stop anticompetitive practices in their incipiency and have feared that permitting even a small merger in an increasingly concentrated market will trigger further mergers or other anticompetitive activity.

For example, in *United States v. Von's Grocery Co.*[6] the government challenged the merger of Von's and Shopping Bag Food Stores, two supermarket chains in the Los Angeles metropolitan area. These chains ranked third and sixth, respectively, with 4.7 percent and 4.2 percent of the market. The top four firms had only 28.6 percent of the market, and there were thousands of competitors. Nevertheless, the Court held the merger presumptively illegal because the evidence showed a trend toward increased concentration. Specifically, the number of competitors had declined from 5,365 to 3,590 in a 13-year period.

Rebutting the Presumption of Illegality

Analysis of a horizontal merger begins with statistical evidence of market concentration and market share. It may also end at that point if there is no evidence to rebut the presumption of illegality.

A presumption of illegality cannot be rebutted by showing that the merger will have procompetitive effects in another market. For example, when the second and third largest commercial banks in Philadelphia merged, the Court refused to allow the banks to rebut the presumption of anticompetitive effects in metropolitan Philadelphia by showing that they could compete more effectively against banks from other major cities for national accounts.[7]

The rebuttal must focus on the characteristics and structure of the market concerned. It should emphasize characteristics which contradict the conclusion that a merger of two significant firms in a concentrated market is likely to trigger additional mergers, foreclose significant markets

---

[6] 384 U.S. 270 (1966).

[7] *United States v. Philadelphia National Bank,* 374 U.S. 321 (1963).

to competitors, or otherwise injure competition. The significance of the postmerger market share and concentration levels is lessened if barriers to entry are low and potential new competitors are strong and likely to enter. The presumption can be further rebutted with evidence of readily available substitutes for the defendant's product and consumers' willingness to switch to substitutes if prices vary slightly. In the following case, the Supreme Court found that a coal company had successfully rebutted the presumption.

United States v. General Dynamics Corp.

415 U.S. 486 (1974)

The government (appellant) sued General Dynamics (appellee), the successor to Material Service Corporation, a deep-mining coal producer, complaining that Material Service's acquisition of United Electric Coal Companies, a strip-mining coal producer, violated section 7 of the Clayton Act. The trial court entered judgment for General Dynamics, and the government appealed. The Supreme Court affirmed.

The government's case consisted of production statistics showing that in specified geographic markets the number of coal producers had been declining, that the markets for coal were concentrated, and that the acquisition substantially increased Material Service's market share. In finding that the merger would not substantially lessen competition, the trial court relied on evidence showing that United Electric's long-term reserves were almost depleted.

Justice Stewart

In prior decisions involving horizontal mergers between competitors, this Court has found prima facie violations of §7 of the Clayton Act from aggregate statistics of the sort relied on by the United States in this case. . . .

The effect of adopting this approach to a determination of a "substantial" lessening of competition is to allow the Government to rest its case on a showing of even small increases of market share or market concentration in those industries or markets where concentration is already great or has been recently increasing, since "if concentration is already great, the importance of preventing even slight increases in concentration and so preserving the possibility of eventual deconcentration is correspondingly great."

While the statistical showing proffered by the government in this case . . . would under this approach have sufficed to support a finding of "undue concentration" in the absence of other considerations, the question before us is whether the District Court was justified in finding that other pertinent factors affecting the coal industry and the business of the appellees mandated a conclusion that no substantial lessening of competition occurred or was threatened by the acquisition of United Electric. We are satisfied that the court's ultimate finding was not in error.

*   *   *   *   *

Much of the District Court's opinion was devoted to a description of the changes that have affected the coal industry since World War II. . . . First, it found that coal had become increasingly less able to compete with other sources of energy in many segments of the energy market. . . .

Second, the court found that to a growing extent since 1954, the electric utility industry has become the mainstay of coal consumption. . . .

Third, and most significantly, the court found that to an increasing degree, nearly all coal sold to utilities is transferred under long-term requirements contracts, under which coal producers promise to meet utilities' coal consumption requirements for a fixed period of time, and at predetermined prices. . . .

Because of these fundamental changes in the structure of the market for coal, the District Court was justified in viewing the statistics relied on by the Government as insufficient to sustain its case. Evidence of past production does not, as a matter of logic, necessarily give a proper picture of a company's future ability to compete. . . .

In the coal market, . . . statistical evidence of coal production was of considerably less significance. The bulk of the coal produced is delivered under long-term re-

quirements contracts, and such sales thus do not represent the exercise of competitive power but rather the obligation to fulfill previously negotiated contracts at a previously fixed price. The focus of competition in a given time frame is not on the disposition of coal already produced but on the procurement of new long-term supply contracts. . . . A more significant indicator of a company's power effectively to compete with other companies lies in the state of a company's uncommitted reserves of recoverable coal. . . .

The testimony and exhibits in the District Court revealed that United Electric's coal reserve prospects were "unpromising." . . . Many of the reserves held by United had already been depleted at the time of trial, forcing the closing of some of United's midwest mines. Even more significantly, the District Court found that of the 52,-033,304 tons of currently mineable reserves in Illinois, Indiana, and Kentucky controlled by United, only four million tons had not already been committed under long-term contracts. United was found to be facing the future with relatively depleted resources at its disposal, and with the vast majority of those resources already committed under contracts allowing no further adjustment in price. In addition, the District Court found that "United Electric has neither the possibility of acquiring more [reserves] nor the ability to develop deep coal reserves," and thus was not in a position to increase its reserves to replace those already depleted or committed.

. . . Irrespective of the company's size when viewed as a producer, its weakness as a competitor was properly analyzed by the District Court and fully substantiated that court's conclusion that its acquisition by Material Service would not "substantially . . . lessen competition. . . ."

CASE QUESTIONS

1. What was the basis for the government's case that the merger might substantially lessen competition?

2. Was the government's evidence suffi-

cient to raise a presumption that the merger was illegal?

3. What was the basis for rebutting the presumption?

Vertical Mergers

A vertical merger is a merger of firms that deal in the same product at different distribution levels. A widget manufacturer's acquisition of a retail widget chain would be a vertical merger. Vertical mergers may reflect a desire to realize economies in distribution, to ensure the availability of supplies, or to promote retail distribution of a manufacturer's product. Figure 12–2 illustrates a vertical merger.

FIGURE 12–2

Premerger   Postmerger

Vertical mergers are more difficult to evaluate than horizontal mergers because the same number of competitors remain in both the supplier and customer markets. A vertical merger may have anticompetitive effects on the markets of the supplier or the customer. The degree of market foreclosure is the starting point in analyzing any vertical merger. The larger the market that the merger forecloses to the competitor of one of the merging firms, the greater is the likelihood that the merger will be held illegal. The intent of the parties to the merger is another important consideration. The level of concentration in the merging firms' markets and trends toward increasing concentration in either market can also prompt a finding that the merger is illegal. The concern of courts is particularly acute where there is a trend toward vertical integration. Firms that merge vertically are frequently potential competitors in each other's markets. This is frequently a factor causing a court to invalidate a vertical merger. In the following case the court applied these factors in analyzing a vertical merger.

Fruehauf Corp. v. FTC

603 F.2d 345 (2d Cir. 1979)

Fruehauf Corp. (appellant) appealed a decision of the FTC (appellee) that Fruehauf's 1973 acquisition of Kelsey–Hayes Co. violated section 7 of the Clayton Act. The Court of Appeals for the Second Circuit reversed.

Fruehauf manufactured truck trailers for sale to trucking companies. Kelsey manufactured truck parts, including heavy duty wheels (HDW), which it sold to truck and trailer manufacturers. In 1973, Fruehauf accounted for 25 percent of the trailer sales in the United States; the top four firms accounted for 49 percent of the market and the top eight firms accounted for 64 percent. Kelsey was the fourth largest producer of HDWs, with 15 percent of the market. The top four firms controlled 65 percent to 71 percent, and the top eight controlled 93 percent to 95 percent. Fruehauf purchased an average of 5.8 percent of total HDW production.

Mansfield, Circuit Judge

A vertical merger, unlike a horizontal one, does not eliminate a competing buyer or seller from the market. It does not, therefore, automatically have an anticompetitive effect, or reduce competition. . . . [T]he competitive significance of a vertical merger results primarily from the degree, if any, to which it may increase barriers to entry into the market or reduce competition by (1) foreclosing competitors of the purchasing firm in the merger from access to a potential source of supply, or from access on competitive terms, (2) by foreclosing competitors of the selling firm (in this case other HDW or ASBD manufacturers) from access to the market or a substantial portion of it, or (3) by forcing actual or potential competitors to enter or continue in the market only on a vertically integrated basis because of advantages unrelated to economies attributable solely to integration. . . .

. . . Most important among the factors are the nature and economic purpose of the arrangement, the likelihood and size of any market foreclosure, the extent of concentration of sellers and buyers in the industry, the capital cost required to enter the market, the market share needed by a buyer or seller to achieve a profitable level of production (sometimes referred to as "scale economy"), the existence of a trend toward vertical concentration or oligopoly in the industry, and whether the merger will eliminate potential competition by one of the merging parties. To these factors may be added the degree of market power that would be possessed by the merged enterprise and the number and strength of competing suppliers and purchasers, which might indicate whether the merger would increase the risk that prices or terms would cease to be competitive.

* * * * *

The Truck Trailer Market

The Commission concluded that the merger violated §7 with respect to the truck trailer market solely on the theory that in the event of a shortage of HDWs Kelsey would give Fruehauf a substantial competitive advantage over other trailer manufacturers by diverting to Fruehauf wheels that would otherwise go to Kelsey's other customers, some of which are trailer manufacturers. This conclusion rests upon several assumptions, having no appreciable evidentiary support. One assumption is that Kelsey is a significant and substantial supplier of HDWs to Fruehauf's competitors. The record reveals that, on the contrary, trailer manufacturers have in the past purchased almost all of their HDWs from other suppliers, with Kelsey's sales of wheels to trailer manufacturers other than Fruehauf amounting to approximately $1.4 million per year out of total average annual HDW market sales amounting to $200 million per year during the three-year period prior to the merger. In the years 1970–72, sales to trailer manufacturers, including Fruehauf, accounted for only about 7 percent of Kelsey's HDW output. Thus Kelsey, while a large manufacturer of HDWs, has hardly been a substantial supplier of HDWs to trailer manufacturers.

The second unsupported assumption is that Kelsey would, in the event of an HDW shortage, divert to Fruehauf HDW sales that would otherwise be made to other customers. There is no evidence, and it is not alleged, that Fruehauf contemplated such a stratagem when it entered the merger with Kelsey. More important, there is no credible evidence that another shortage is reasonably foreseeable. Even if it were, the evidence that Kelsey would give priority to Fruehauf's needs is insubstantial. As to the likelihood of a shortage, the record indicates that the combined capacity of wheel producers was considerably expanded after the 1973–74 shortage and that, even when conservatively estimated, this capacity exceeds a liberal estimate of antici-

pated demand during the next five or ten years.

During past shortages Kelsey, like other wheel producers, has allocated its production pro rata* among its customers in accordance with their regular volume of purchases. . . . [A] spokesman from Trailmobile Corp., Fruehauf's largest competitor, testified that his company believed that the merger would not affect Kelsey's policy in favor of *pro rata* distribution in the event of a shortage . . . If Kelsey deprived its regular customers of a proportionate share of HDWs in times of shortage it would risk their retaliating by shifting to competing suppliers not only their purchases of HDWs but of other products presently bought from Kelsey, which could cause it greater economic harm. In addition, by granting priority to Fruehauf over other trailer manufacturers who purchase wheels from Kelsey, Kelsey would invite antitrust damage actions against it by these trailer firms. Under the circumstances, it appears highly unlikely that Kelsey would take such risks.

. . . Although neither of [the FTC's] assumptions is by any means beyond the realm of the possible, here they run counter to the actual evidence in the record. We cannot therefore say that they add up to a reasonable probability that the merger will substantially lessen competition. Accordingly, the finding of a §7 violation based upon the effect of the merger on the truck trailer market must be set aside as unsupported by substantial evidence.

* * * * *

The HDW Market

* * * * *

We accept at the outset the Commission's findings that the HDW market is significantly concentrated, based on evidence that

---

* *Pro rata* means proportionately.—Au.

the top four producers account for 65–71 percent of the market, the top eight for 93–95 percent, and Kelsey, the third largest producer, 15 percent. Moreover, the Commission's determination that barriers to entry into HDW production are substantial is supported by evidence that the initial capital outlay required to enter production at an efficient level is $10–$20 million.

* * * * *

The Commission further concluded that the amount of market foreclosure likely to result from the merger would range from "a weak 3.9" to a "strong 5.8" of the market production of HDWs . . . However, there is no evidence that competing purchasers of these products would be foreclosed from continuing to obtain all or part of their cast spoke needs from Kelsey or its competitiors at competitive prices. Nor was there proof that removal from the market of up to 5.8 percent of its HDW sales would preclude any existing competitor from continuing to operate economically or any potential competitor from entering the market.

* * * * *

The Commission further found that there had been periodic HDW shortages within the 12 years prior to the merger (i.e., in 1966, 1968–69, 1973–74) and that, although Fruehauf was not itself a potential competitor in the production of HDWs prior to the merger, it had engaged in certain pro-competitive activities, consisting of experiments with new types of fabricated aluminum and steel wheels and encouragement of one foundry, McConway and Torley, to produce cast spoke wheels.

* * * * *

With due respect for the Commission's expertise, we fail to find any logical basis in the evidence for this conclusion, even when the record is viewed most favorably to the Commission.

There is no evidence in the record that existing barriers to entry into the HDW market or the existing concentration of producers in it, both admittedly substantial, have been or would be increased by the merger. There is no reason to believe that the merger will adversely affect scale economies for HDW production, thereby increasing the cost of entry. Nor does the Commission suggest that as a result of the merger a firm could successfully enter the HDW or the trailer market only by simultaneously entering at both levels. As to the effect of the merger on the concentration of the HDW industry, since Fruehauf's principal supplier of spoke wheels has been Dayton-Walther, the largest producers of spokes and second largest wheel producer, any shifting of patronage from Dayton to Kelsey will tend to even out the market shares of the three largest sellers of HDWs, but not increase their aggregate market share. . . .

Moreover, there is no allegation that the merger of Fruehauf and Kelsey is part of an existing or prospective trend toward vertical integration. . . . There is no suggestion, much less evidence, that the merger was motivated by a desire to restrain competition. On the contrary, the evidence is undisputed that Kelsey, whose stock was selling substantially below book value, sought out Fruehauf in order to avoid takeover efforts on the part of others. Nor is there any evidence that the merger might impair competition by conferring upon one of the merging partners a "deep pocket" or financial clout not enjoyed by it rivals. It is true that some market foreclosure may ensue from the merger, but not one that deprives rivals from major channels of distribution, much less one that excludes them from the market altogether. Even if Fruehauf were to switch its purchase of its entire HDW wheel needs, amounting to 5.8 percent of the market, from others to Kelsey (which would require Kelsey to enter heavy duty disc production), there would merely be a realignment of existing market sales without any likelihood of a diminution in competition. . . .

According to the Commission, although it found that Fruehauf itself was not a potential entrant into the HDW market, Fruehauf had a pro-competitive effect on the market through its collaborative efforts to develop new types of heavy duty wheels and by virtue of its ability to draw new entrants into production of conventional wheels by offering to deliver its patronage.

In light of the record evidence, this theory is too ephemeral to sustain the Com-

mission's decision. Although Fruehauf did experiment in the development of new kinds of wheels and assisted one foundry in temporary production of HDWs, both adventures proved to be complete failures and there is no evidence that, if the merger were disapproved, Fruehauf would engage in similar activities. Moreover, the Commission has presented no evidence suggesting that Fruehauf was unique in its ability to elicit new competition, and there is no reason to believe that other firms patronizing the HDW market, particularly the automotive and trucking giants, will not encourage firms in the wings to enter that market, should they be dissatisfied with the quality of the existing competition.

CASE QUESTIONS

1. How does a vertical merger differ from a horizontal merger?

2. What factors are considered in evaluating the competitive effects of a vertical merger?

3. Describe the court's analysis of the com-

petitive effect of this merger on the trailer market.

4. Describe the court's analysis of the competitive effects of this merger on the HDW market.

Conglomerate Mergers

Conglomerate mergers pose the smallest immediate threat to competition. They do not combine two competitors into one, nor do they necessarily foreclose markets previously open to competitors. However, they may have other anticompetitive effects, particularly when they involve firms in similar or related industries. The following case presents a "product extension merger," which is often described as a form of conglomerate merger.

FTC v. Procter & Gamble Co.

386 U.S. 568 (1967)

The Federal Trade Commission (appellant) held that the acquisition by Procter & Gamble (appellee) of Clorox Chemical Company violated section

7 of the Clayton Act. At the time of the acquisition Clorox was the leading producer of household bleach, with 48.8 percent of the market. The top four firms accounted for 80 percent of the market, with the remaining 20 percent divided among 200 small producers. Clorox was the only company operating nationwide. Procter & Gamble (P&G) did not produce bleach, but it accounted for 54.4 percent of all packaged detergent sales. The top three firms controlled 80 percent of that market.

The FTC found that P&G's huge assets and advertising budget combined with Clorox's dominant position would dissuade potential entrants and that the merger eliminated P&G as a potential competitor. It also found that the merger gave P&G the potential to underprice Clorox so as to drive out competitors and to use its dominant position in household detergents so as to obtain preferred shelf space from retailers for Clorox. The FTC ordered divestiture. The Sixth Circuit Court of Appeals reversed the FTC, labeling its findings as speculation and relying on postmerger evidence that competitors had not been eliminated. The Supreme Court reversed the Sixth Circuit and instructed the circuit court to enforce the FTC's order.

Justice Douglas

Section 7 of the Clayton Act was intended to arrest the anticompetitive effects of market power in their incipiency. The core question is whether a merger may substantially lessen competition, and necessarily requires a prediction of the merger's impact on competition, present and future. This section can deal only with probabilities, not with certainties. And there is certainly no requirement that the anticompetitive power manifest itself in anticompetitive action before §7 can be called into play. . . .

All mergers are within the reach of §7, and all must be tested by the same standard, whether they are classified as horizontal, vertical, conglomerate or other. As noted by the Commission, this merger is neither horizontal, vertical, nor conglomerate. Since the products of the acquired company are complementary to those of the acquiring company and may be produced with similar facilities, marketed through the same channels and in the same manner, and advertised by the same media, the Com-

mission aptly called this acquisition a "product extension merger." . . .

*　*　*　*　*

The liquid bleach industry was already oligopolistic before the acquisition, and price competition was certainly not as vigorous as it would have been if the industry were competitive. Clorox enjoyed a dominant position nationally, and its position approached monopoly proportions in certain areas. The existence of some 200 fringe firms certainly does not belie that fact. Nor does the fact, relied upon by the court below, that, after the merger, producers other than Clorox "were selling more bleach for more money than ever before." In the same period, Clorox increased its share from 48.8% to 52%. The interjection of Procter into the market considerably changed the situation. There is every reason to assume that the smaller firms would become more cautious in competing due to their fear of retaliation by Procter. It is probable that

Procter would become the price leader and that oligopoly would become more rigid.

The acquisition may also have the tendency of raising the barriers to new entry. The major competitive weapon in the successful marketing of bleach is advertising. Clorox was limited in this area by its relatively small budget and its inability to obtain substantial discounts. By contrast, Procter's budget was much larger; and, although it would not devote its entire budget to advertising Clorox, it could divert a large portion to meet the short-term threat of a new entrant. Procter would be able to use its volume discounts to advantage in advertising Clorox. Thus, a new entrant would be much more reluctant to face the giant Procter than it would have been to face the smaller Clorox.

Possible economies cannot be used as a defense to illegality. Congress was aware that some mergers which lessen competition may also result in economies, but it struck the balance in favor of protecting competition.

The Commission also found that the acquisition of Clorox by Procter eliminated Procter as a potential competitor. . . . The evidence clearly showed that Procter was the most likely entrant. Procter had recently launched a new abrasive cleaner in an industry similar to the liquid bleach industry, and had wrested leadership from a brand that had enjoyed even a larger market share than had Clorox. Procter was engaged in a vigorous program of diversifying into product lines closely related to its basis products. Liquid bleach was a natural avenue of diversification since it is complementary to Procter's products, is sold to the same customers through the same channels, and is advertised and merchandised in the same manner. . . . Procter's management was experienced in producing and marketing goods similar to liquid bleach. Procter had considered the possibility of independently entering but decided against it because the acquisition of Clorox would enable Procter to capture a more commanding share of the market.

It is clear that the existence of Procter at the edge of the industry exerted considerable influence on the market. First, the market behavior of the liquid bleach industry was influenced by each firm's predictions of the market behavior of its competitors, actual and potential. Second, the barriers to entry by a firm of Procter's size and with its advantages were not significant. There is no indication that the barriers were so high that the price Procter would have to charge would be above the price that would maximize the profits of the existing firms. Third, the number of potential entrants was not so large that the elimination of one would be insignificant. Few firms would have the temerity to challenge a firm as solidly entrenched as Clorox. Fourth, Procter was found by the Commission to be the most likely entrant. These findings of the Commission were amply supported by the evidence.

CASE QUESTIONS

1. Is there a distinction between a conglomerate merger and a product extension merger?

2. What factors led the Court to conclude that the merger would have the probable effect of reducing competition?

3. Why did the Court discount the postmerger evidence.

4. How did the Court evaluate P&G as a potential competitor of Clorox?

5. If P&G had acquired one of the 200 small firms comprising the bottom 20 percent of the market, would the merger have violated section 7?

DEFENSES IN MERGER CASES

Most section 7 cases are defended by attacking the plantiff's definition of the relevant markets and its evidence of anticompetitive effects. There are also two affirmative defenses recognized under section 7: the failing company defense and the solely for investment defense. These defenses serve to legalize an otherwise illegal merger. The defendant bears the burden of proving them.

The Failing Company Defense

A merger that might otherwise violate section 7 is considered lawful if one of the companies is failing. For this defense to apply, the failing company must be about to die, with no reasonable hope of survival short of merger. The acquiring company must either be the only company interested in purchasing the failing company, or if other companies are interested, it must be the company that poses the least threat to competition. Finally, it must be shown that methods to save the failing company short of merger have been tried and have failed or that such methods would be futile.

The Solely for Investment Defense

Section 7 does not apply to corporations purchasing stock in other corporations "solely for investment and not using [the stock] by voting or otherwise to bring about, or in attempting to bring about, the substantial lessening of competition." This is known as the "solely for investment defense."

REMEDIES IN MERGER CASES

Most section 7 actions are brought by the government. Sometimes the government can obtain a preliminary injunction against the merger. To do so, it must show that it is likely to win the lawsuit and that allowing the merger to proceed will irreparably harm competition. Courts sometimes issue preliminary injunctions permitting mergers to occur, but requiring that the formerly independent companies continue to maintain their separate identities.

Where a merger is not enjoined, or has already taken place prior to the government's challenge, the court's task upon finding a violation is to unscramble the merger and restore market conditions to what they would have been had the merger not occurred. This is extremely difficult to do. The starting point is an order requiring the acquiring firm to divest itself of the acquired firm. However, such an order is often insufficient to restore preexisting competitive conditions. For example, assume that a family owns a small but aggressive and innovative competitor. The owners, wishing to retire, sell the company to the dominant firm in the market. If the acquisition is found to violate section 7, the dominant firm will be ordered to divest itself of the smaller firm. However, the owners who provided the smaller firm's aggressive, innovative method of operation will no longer be available to manage the business. It is very likely that the firm will be sold to another large corporation, albeit one which is not now competing in the market. This may have the ironic effect of raising additional barriers to new entries into the market. Even if not purchased by another large concern, the divested firm will probably face many of the start-up costs and recognition problems of a new entrant. The following case deals with a court's power to order relief beyond divestiture.

Ford Motor Co. v. United States

405 U.S. 562 (1972)

Ford (appellant) acquired the assets of Electric Autolite Company's Autolite Spark Plug division. The trial court held that the acquisition violated section 7 and ordered Ford to divest itself of the division. It also enjoined Ford from manufacturing spark plugs for ten years, ordered Ford to purchase at least one-half of its annual spark plug requirements from the divested firm for five years, and prohibited Ford from using its own trade names on spark plugs for five years. Ford appealed, and the Supreme Court affirmed.

Prior to the merger there were three major brands of spark plugs, of which two—Autolite and Champion—were independent. The third, AC, was owned by General Motors. Spark plug manufacturers sold their product to the auto companies at very low prices for use as original equipment (OE). They made their profits in the replacement market, known as the aftermarket. Mechanics servicing automobiles tended to replace OE plugs with plugs of the same brand. The trial court found that Ford's acquisition of Autolite eliminated Ford as a potential entrant into the spark plug market and foreclosed it as a purchaser of 10 percent of the industry's output. The Supreme Court affirmed the finding of violation and proceeded to consider the remedy.

Justice Douglas

The main controversy here has been over the nature and degree of the relief to be afforded.

* * * * *

The relief in an antitrust case must be "effective to redress the violations" and "to restore competition." The District Court is clothed with "large discretion" to fit the decree to the special needs of the individual case.

Complete divestiture is particularly appropriate where asset or stock acquisitions violate the antitrust laws.

Divestiture is a start toward restoring the pre-acquisition situation. Ford once again will then stand as a large industry customer at the edge of the market with a renewed interest in securing favorable terms for its substantial plug purchases. Since Ford will again be a purchaser, it is expected that the competitive pressures that existed among other spark plug producers to sell to Ford will be re-created. The divestiture should also eliminate the anticompetitive consequences in the *aftermarket* flowing from the second largest automobile manufacturer's entry through acquisition into the spark plug manufacturing business.

* * * * *

A word should be said about the other injunctive provisions. They are designed to give the divested plant an opportunity to establish its competitive position. The divested company needs time so it can obtain a foothold in the industry. The relief ordered should "cure the ill effects of the illegal conduct, and assure the public freedom from its continuance," and it necessarily must "fit the exigencies of the particular case." . . .

. . . The ancillary measures ordered by the District Court are designed to allow Autolite to re-establish itself in the OE and replacement markets and to maintain it as a viable competitor until such time as forces already at work within the marketplace weaken the OE tie. Thus Ford is prohibited for 10 years from manufacturing its own plugs. But in five years it can buy its plugs from any source and use its name on OE plugs.

* * * * *

The requirement that, for five years, Ford purchase at least half of its spark plug requirements from the divested company under the Autolite label is to give the divested enterprise an assured customer while it struggles to be re-established as an effective, independent competitor.

. . . Ford's own studies indicate that it would take five to eight years for it to develop a spark plug division internally. A major portion of this period would be devoted to the development of a viable position in the aftermarket. The five-year prohibition on the use of its own name and the 10-year limitation on its own manufacturing mesh neatly to allow Ford to establish itself in the *aftermarket* prior to becoming a manufacturer while, at the same time, giving Autolite the opportunity to re-establish itself by providing a market for its production. . . .

. . . Forces now at work in the marketplace may bring about a deconcentrated market structure and may weaken the onerous OE tie. The District Court concluded that the forces of competition must be nurtured to correct for Ford's illegal acquisition. We view its decree as a means to that end.

Chief Justice Burger *(concurring in part and dissenting in part)*

In addition to requiring divestiture of Autolite, the District Court made ancillary injunctive provisions that go far beyond any that have been cited to the Court. . . .

An understanding of the District Court's findings as to the spark plug market shows three reasons why it was in error in requiring Ford to support Autolite. First, the court did *not* find that the weakness of an independent Autolite's competitive position resulted from Ford's acquisition.

Rather, a reading of its findings makes apparent that the precariousness of Autolite's expected post-divestment position results from pre-existing forces in the market. Therefore, the drastic measures employed to strengthen Autolite's position at Ford's expense cannot be justified as a remedy for any wrong done by Ford. Second, the remedy will perpetuate for a time the very evils upon which the District Court based a finding of an antitrust violation. Third, the court's own findings indicate that the remedy is not likely to secure Autolite's competitive position beyond the termination of the restrictions. Therefore, there is no assurance that the judicial remedy will have the desired impact on long-run competition in the spark plug market.

* * * * *

The remedial provisions are unrelated to restoring the *status quo ante** with respect to the two violations found by the District Court, the ending of Ford's status as a potential entrant with a moderating influence on the market and the foreclosure of a significant part of the plug market. Indeed, the remedies may well be anticompetitive in both respects. First, the District Court's order actually undercuts the moderating influence of Ford's position on the edge of the market. It is the possibility that a company on the sidelines will enter a market through internal expansion that has a moderating influence on the market. By prohibiting Ford from entering the market through internal expansion, therefore, the remedy order wipes out, for the duration of the restriction, the pro-competitive influence Ford had on the market prior to its acquisition of Autolite. Second, the Court's order does not fully undo the foreclosure effect of the acquisition. Divestment alone

---

* *Status quo ante* is Latin for the existing state of things as they were before.—Au.

would return the parties to the *status quo ante*. Ford would then be free to deal with Autolite or another plug producer or to enter the market through internal expansion. Yet the Court has ordered Ford to buy at least half its requirements from Autolite for five years. Thus, the order itself forecloses part of Ford's need from the forces of competition.

* * * * *

The findings of the District Court indicate that Autolite's precarious position did not result from its acquisition by Ford. Prior to the acquisition both Champion and Autolite were in a continually precarious position in that their continued large share of the market was totally dependent on their positions as OE suppliers to auto manufacturers. The very factor that asssured that they faced no serious competition in the short run also assured that in the long run their own position was dependent on their relationship with a large auto manufacturer. Thus, the threat to Autolite posed by a simple divestiture is the same threat it had lived with between 1941 and 1961 as an independent entity: it might be left without any OE supply relationship with a major auto manufacturer, and therefore its market position based on this relationship might decline drastically.

* * * * *

In the final analysis it appears to me that the District Court, seeing the immediate precariousness of Autolite's position as a divested entitiy, designed remedies to support Autolite without contemplating whether it was equitable to restrict Ford's freedom of action for these purposes or whether there was any real chance of Autolite's eventual survival. I fear that this is a situation where the form of preserving competition has taken precedence over an understanding of the realities of the particular market. Therefore I dissent from today's affirmance of the District Court's harshly restrictive remedial provisions

---

CASE QUESTIONS

1. What relief in addition to divestiture did the district court order? Why was this relief justified?

2. What is the basis for Chief Justice Burger's dissent?

3. How would Justice Douglas answer the criticisms made by Chief Justice Burger?

4. If one company illegally acquires the stock of another company, can the court effectively remedy the acquisition by ordering the acquiring company to distribute the acquired stock to its shareholders?

ENFORCEMENT MATTERS

Section 7 violations, like all other Clayton Act violations, are civil offenses. Unlike Sherman Act violations, they are not crimes. Civil enforcement actions may be brought by private parties, the Justice Department, and the FTC.

Private section 7 actions are frequently used in tender offer battles. A tender offer is a publicly announced offer to purchase the stock of a target company's shareholders for a stated price contingent upon the offeror's obtaining sufficient shares to control the target company. Tender offers are discussed in detail in chapter 14.

The officers of a target company may seek to defeat a tender offer because they consider it bad for the company or because they fear they will lose their jobs if it succeeds. Officers of target companies have often challenged tender offers under section 7, contending that the resulting acquisition would reduce competition. This tactic has met with varying success.

The target company's management may also try to defeat the tender offer by merging with another company that is friendlier to the incumbent officers. When this occurs, the tender offeror may try to attack the merger under section 7.

FTC Premerger Notification

The Hart-Scott-Rodino Antitrust improvements Act of 1976 amended the Clayton Act to include a 30-day premerger notification program administered by the FTC. The purpose of the premerger notification is to allow the FTC and the Justice Department to enjoin mergers which they believe have anticompetitive effects. If the acquiring company has sales or assets of $100 million or more and the company to be acquired has sales or assets of $10 million or more, they must inform the FTC of the proposed merger 30 days before the merger is scheduled to take place. During the 30-day period the FTC may request additional data from the parties.

Justice Department Merger Guidelines

In 1968 the Justice Department issued guidelines, publicly stating its enforcement policy concerning mergers. The guidelines' purpose was to reduce uncertainty for merging businesses. The guidelines were substantially revised on June 14, 1982, and again on June 14, 1984. They now take a more permissive approach to mergers. In a statement accompanying the 1984 revision, the department characterized the guidelines: "The 1982 Guidelines recognized that most mergers do not threaten competition and that many are in fact procompetitive and benefit consumers." The 1984 revisions did not change this pro-merger philosophy.

The guidelines do not have the effect of law; the government is not bound by them and private parties need not even consider them before bringing suit. Nevertheless, they are useful for business planning in predicting the likely government response to a merger.

The guidelines define the relevant product and geographic markets as those in which "a hypothetical firm that was the only present and future seller . . . could raise price profitably." In some cases a general price increase can not be undertaken profitably, but increases to selected groups of buyers can be accomplished because those buyers are particularly dependent upon the hypothetical firm. In these cases, the guidelines consider the dependent buyers as a relevant submarket.

Within the relevant markets, the guidelines rely upon a formula known as the Herfindahl-Hirschman Index (HHI) to measure market concentration. The HHI is calculated by adding the squares of the individual market shares of all firms in the market. For example, in a pure monopoly, one firm has 100 percent of the market. The HHI equals 100^2 or 10,000. If two firms each control 50 percent, the HHI equals $50^2 + 50^2$ or 5,000. The smaller the HHI, the less concentrated the market. The guidelines classify markets as follows: unconcentrated = HHI below 1,000; moderately concentrated = HHI between 1,000 and 1,800; highly concentrated = HHI above 1,800.

In assessing market share, the guidelines recognize the impact of foreign competition. Foreign firms are assigned market shares in the same way as domestic firms. Foreign firms are not excluded from the market solely because their sales are subject to import quotas.

The guidelines discuss horizontal mergers, vertical mergers, and mergers reducing potential competition. Generally, the Justice Department is not likely to challenge horizontal mergers in unconcentrated markets; in moderately concentrated markets, the department is not likely to challenge horizontal mergers that increase the HHI by less than 100 points; in highly concentrated markets, the department is not likely to challenge horizontal mergers that increase the HHI by less than 50 points, and very likely to challenge those that increase the HHI by more than 100 points. Regardless of the HHI, if the leading company in a market has at least 35 percent and the next leading company's market share is less than half the leader's, the Justice Department is likely to challenge any horizontal merger between the leader and any firm having at least 1 percent of the market.

Changes in the HHI provide general guidance for evaluating a merger. The department considers additional factors in deciding whether to challenge a merger. These include the merging firm's financial condition and its ability to respond to market changes, such as the introduction of new technology. Another major factor considered is whether the merger increases efficiency. Improved efficiency can result from economies of scale, better integration of production facilities, plant specialization, and lower transportation costs.

Generally, the Justice Department will not challenge vertical mergers unless they are likely to facilitate collusion or raise barriers to entry in the relevant market. The department is not likely to challenge vertical mergers for facilitating collusion if the HHI is less than 1,800. It is not likely to challenge mergers for raising barriers to entry unless the merger creates conditions where new entrants to one market must also enter a second market, where the need to enter the second market makes entry into the first market more difficult and less likely, and where the market structure is highly concentrated (HHI of 1,800 or greater).

In deciding whether to challenge mergers that reduce potential competition, the department considers the ease of entry into the acquired firm's market, whether other firms similarly situated to the acquiring firm remain as potential entrants, the market share of the acquired firm, and market concentration. The department is not likely to challenge these mergers in markets when the HHI is below 1,800.

ALTERNATIVE APPROACHES

Merger activity has increased substantially in recent years. It is particularly high when firms with large cash surpluses see "bargains," firms whose stock is selling only slightly above or below the value of their assets. Some suggest that this is a shortsighted use of cash surpluses. They argue that for long-term economic growth firms must invest their cash in modernizing their operations.

Many scholars and policymakers view the trend toward large acquisitions with alarm. These mergers are often difficult to attack under section 7 because they are pure conglomerate mergers. The acquired company has been in a field totally unrelated to that of the acquiring company, so the merger does not lessen competition in any specific market.

Even large conglomerate mergers substantially increase the political power and influence of the acquiring firms. When firms merge, the number of political actors is reduced. Two formerly independent firms with potentially diverse views on political issues, candidates, and referenda are replaced by one united front. The large diversified firm further increases its political power by effecting economies of scale in lobbying and other political activities and by gaining access to the resources of the formerly independent firm for its own political interests. Thus, a car manufacturer that acquires a pharmaceutical company may use the latter's resources to lobby on issues affecting the auto industry. Prior to the merger, the pharmaceutical company would have had no concern with auto industry issues.

Mergers can also increase management's discretionary power, that is, management's power to make decisions with aims other than profit maximization. The exercise of this discretionary power in such areas as location of the enterprise, charitable contributions, and hiring and promotion policies can have substantial social impact. The concentration of these decisions in the hands of fewer corporate decision makers increases that impact. Finally, mergers can reduce organizational flexibility and diminish innovation.

Persons concerned with the increase in merger activity have proposed legislation to prohibit mergers where the resulting firm's sales or assets would exceed a certain level ($2 billion is a frequently cited figure) unless the acquiring firm simultaneously divests itself of a division whose size is comparable to that of the acquired firm.

Those who oppose this approach argue that its proponents exaggerate corporate political power. They contend that corporate political power is balanced by the power of other interest groups, such as labor unions and consumer organizations. Further, many Americans view the exercise of corporate political influence very skeptically, and this in turn reduces that influence.

These individuals also suggest that prohibiting mergers would be inefficient. They note that many firms become attractive acquisitions because of poor management. When a large conglomerate acquires such a firm, it is able to supply competent managers who restore the firm to a healthy business position. Mergers also promote efficiency by allowing the merged firms to combine research and development, advertising and marketing skills, and resources. Moreover, mergers achieve economies of scale in raising capital by reducing legal fees and underwriting costs.

Finally, these individuals are against prohibiting conglomerate mergers for philosophical reasons. They hold that the antitrust laws are intended to protect competition and thereby ensure the operation of a free market economy. They oppose government intervention that is not directed toward this goal. They view outright prohibitions of mergers as unrelated to the protection of competition.

CHAPTER PROBLEMS

1. General Motors Corporation, the nation's largest automobile manufacturer, decided to enter the snowmobile industry. It did this by creating a wholly owned subsidiary. The snowmobile market was previously characterized by low concentration and small firms. GM's subsidiary, backed by GM's massive advertising budget, offered its snowmobiles at an average price $50 below that of comparable models. In its first year of operation it gained 60 percent of the market. Did this violate section 7? Explain.

2. RSR Corporation acquired Quemetco, Inc. RSR produced secondary lead at smelting plants in Dallas, Texas and Newark, New Jersey. Quemetco produced secondary lead at plants in Seattle, Washington; Indianapolis, Indiana; and City of Industry, California. Quemetco was building a fourth plant in Walkill, New York. After the merger, RSR closed its Newark plant.

Secondary lead is recycled from scrap automobile batteries. It contains impurities and is generally used as hard or metallic lead. Primary lead is processed from lead ore. It is free of hardening impurities and is therefore used as soft lead. It can be hardened by adding metal, but the process is not economical. The principal users of primary and secondary leads are battery manufacturers. They use primary lead for battery oxides and secondary lead for posts and grids. Although secondary lead customarily sells for 10 percent less than primary, several commodities and metals exchanges do not distinguish between the two in quoting prices for trading in lead.

Secondary lead producers try to ship their products to customers located within a few hundred miles of their plants to minimize trucking costs. However, secondary lead producers are willing to ship over greater distances when shipment is justified by fluctuations in market conditions, prices, and trucking costs. Define the relevant market(s) for analyzing the legality of the merger.

3. Amax, Inc., and Copper Range Company merged. Prior to the merger Copper Range was the nation's seventh largest producer of copper, with 4.6 percent of the market. Amax mined copper pursuant to a joint venture with another company, and accounted for 1.4 percent of the market. All of Amax's reserves were obtained pursuant to joint ventures with other companies. Prior to the merger Amax announced its intention to expand its reserves and increase production. The copper industry was marked by high barriers to entry and high concentration, with the four largest companies holding 66 percent and the eight largest, 90 percent. Did the merger violate section 7? Explain.

4. Kennecott Copper Corporation, the largest copper producer in the country, accounting for 33 percent of the market, acquired Peabody Coal Company, the nation's largest coal producer, with 10 percent of the market. Due to dwindling copper reserves Kennecott liquidated some of its assets, thus obtaining a large amount of cash. It used this cash to buy Peabody. Kennecott made the purchase to diversify its operations in anticipation of the exhaustion of its copper reserves. Several years before the merger Kennecott had acquired a small coal company in order to supply its own needs for coal. The coal market was not highly concentrated, but it did have very high barriers to entry. Did the merger violate section 7? Explain.

5. Nestle S.A. of Switzerland, one of the world's largest producers of dairy products, chocolate, and instant and liquid drinks, is contemplating acquisition of Dietetic Snacks, Inc., a producer and retail outlet for health carob bars, carob-coated raisins, and other carob snacks. (Carob is made from the pod of a Mediterranean evergreen). The products contain honey but no sugar. Nestle produces 37 percent of the chocolate consumed in the United States, Hershey produces 27 percent, and Heath Bar produces 15 percent. The remaining chocolate is produced by 20 different firms. Dietetic Snacks, Inc. controls 40 percent of the retail market of carob snack products and produces 49 percent of the carob snack products sold in the U.S. Would the acquisition violate section 7? Explain.

6. Tenneco, Inc. is considering acquisition of Monroe Auto Equipment Co. Tenneco is a diversified company that manufacturers, among other things, automotive parts and is the nation's leading seller of exhaust system parts. Monroe is the number two manufacturer of automotive shock absorbers. Shock absorbers are sold to vehicle manufacturers for use as original equipment and to retail outlets and repair shops for use as replacement equipment. The replacement market is highly concentrated. Monroe and Gabriel, the market leader, together hold 77 percent of the market. The next two firms together account for 15 percent of the market. To operate at a minimum efficient scale, a manufacturer must annually produce 6 million shock absorbers, or roughly 10 percent of replacement market demand. This efficiency of scale, together with the need for technology and marketing skills, provide significant barriers to entry into the market.

Tenneco has wanted to enter the replacement shock absorber market for a long time. It views shock absorbers as complementary to the exhaust systems it already sells. It has considered acquiring two very small shock absorber manufacturers. Negotiations with one broke down because its management insisted that Tenneco purchase its stock at twice its market value. Negotiations with the second broke down when it demanded a selling price of 100 times earnings. There is one other small shock absorber manufacturer. Tenneco has decided not to pursue that company because the firm is in poor financial condition with outdated equipment and a mediocre reputation. Tenneco has also decided that start-up costs are too high to enter the market from scratch on its own.

Monroe recently approached Tenneco about a merger. Should Tenneco accept? Evaluate the legality of the proposal under section 7.

7. Widgets are an essential ingredient in the production of gizmos. The top seven widget firms control 90 percent of the market. The remaining 10 percent is divided among 25 small firms. Ace Gizmo Company is the leading manufacturer of gizmos, with 45 percent of the market. Ace accounts for 40 percent of the total domestic demand for widgets. Its needs have been supplied by a combination of large and small widget producers. Wonderful Widgets, Inc., is the 17th-largest widget manufacturer, with 0.3 percent of the market. Its sole customer has been Ace. Wonderful has run into cash flow difficulties and is unable to pay its bills as they come due. Creditors have threatened to file involuntary bankruptcy proceedings against it. Wonderful has proposed selling all its assets to Ace, paying its bills, and liquidating. Should Ace accept the deal?

8. CPS Industries, Inc., was the oldest and largest company in the gift wrap industry. Due to poor management it began suffering substantial losses. It was then acquired by Papercraft Corporation, the second largest company in the industry. Papercraft's management turned CPS around, restoring its profitability. The FTC found that the merger violated section 7 and ordered divestiture. It further ordered Papercraft not to deal with any parties which, during the two years before the merger, had been CPS customers. This prohibition was to last for three years. If Papercraft appeals the remedy, will it be successful?

9. ABC Gizmo Co. is the leading seller of gizmos in the country with 36 percent of the market. The next leading company has 12 percent. The next four firms have 10 percent each. Three other firms have 3 percent each, and two others have 1.5 percent each. Can ABC acquire any other firm in the market without fear that the Justice Department will challenge the merger? Explain.

10. Compare the arguments for and against prohibiting conglomerate mergers. What is your opinion on this issue?

CHAPTER 13

PRICE DISCRIMINATION

Antitrust activity in the early 1900s focused on the anticompetitive efforts of trusts and monopolies. But during this era price discrimination was also perceived as adversely affecting competition. Price discrimination occurs when a seller gives a more favorable price treatment to one buyer over another. Price discrimination was a familiar practice of large producers. They were in a position to remove competitors and dissuade potential entrants by selective territorial price discrimination. They achieved this result by lowering their prices in geographic areas where competition was heavy. Meanwhile, these large producers could offset their profit concession by maintaining higher prices in geographic markets where their position was secure.

In 1914 Congress enacted the Clayton Act. Section 2 of that act made it unlawful to "discriminate in price between different purchasers of commodities . . . where the effect of such discrimination may be *substantially to lessen competition* or tend to create a monopoly in any *line of commerce*" (emphasis added).

The act proved only partly successful in preventing price discrimination and its injurious effects. The phrase "line of commerce" was interpreted to confine the application of section 2 to a lessening of competition at the seller's level of distribution (primary-line injury). According to early judicial pronouncements, injury to competition at the buyer's level (secondary-line injury) was not encompassed by the statute.[1] Nonetheless, large purchasers were in a position to extract favorable discounts from their suppliers. This caused injury to competing purchasers that were not large enough to command such price concessions. In addition, judicial

---

[1] In 1929 *Van Camp & Sons Co. v. American Can Co.*, 278 U.S. 245 (1929), deviated from the traditional understanding of Clayton and extended its application to reach competitive injury at the buyer's level.

construction of section 2 was especially restrictive in its interpretation of "substantially to lessen competition." Only large firms were deemed within the scope of the language, as small firms rarely experienced sufficient injury to satisfy this statutory language.

Section 2 of the Clayton Act expressly exempted volume discounts. Congress believed that where volume discounts were offered, all sellers would realize an equal reduction of costs on volume sales and would supposedly be in an equal position to reduce their prices accordingly. However, under the act even a small variation in quantity justified a large price differential. Large chain stores, by avoiding the middle link in the normal distribution system, were able to extract larger discounts from the manufacturer than those obtained by smaller purchasers. By the 1920s, the large chain stores possessed a great advantage over the independent stores, which were forced to continue buying through the conventional distribution system in lesser volume than the chains. The larger the retail chain, the more leverage it possessed to extract additional discounts or other concessions from the manufacturer. Chain stores were increasing rapidly in number and were altering the complexion of the American retail market. By 1933 they accounted for 25 percent of the market. Independent groceries began to disappear, and wholesalers that customarily sold to these corner groceries were declining. To reverse this threatening trend, retail and wholesale grocers banded together in associations to increase their economic and political strength. The associations turned to Congress, which responded with the Robinson–Patman Act in 1936.

The Robinson–Patman Act is an amendment to the Clayton Act. It

---

TABLE 13–1
The Robinson–Patman Act

Section	Prohibition	Defenses
2(a)	Seller discrimination in price, in the sale of commodities of like grade and quality, in interstate commerce, causing competitive injury.	Meeting competition Cost justification Changing conditions
2(c)	Fictitious brokerage payments except for services actually performed.	None
2(d)	Payments on allowances by seller to buyers for promotional services except where available to all buyers on proportionally equal terms.	Meeting competition
2(e)	Seller furnishing promotional services except on proportionately equal terms to all buyers.	Meeting competition
2(f)	Buyer induced or knowing receipt of benefits of a violation of section 2(a).	Same as for section 2(a)

was designed to remove the shortcomings of the original Clayton Act in the area of price discrimination. It prohibits sellers from practicing price discrimination and buyers from inducing seller discrimination. It also prohibits price discrimination disguised as brokerage fees and requires that promotional allowances and services be available to all buyers on proportionally equal terms. The act's provisions are summarized in Table 13–1. Although the Robinson–Patman Act was aimed at abusive practices of large buyers and sellers, its prohibitions apply to all firms, regardless of size. This chapter explores these prohibitions.

SELLER DISCRIMINATION

Section 2(a) of the Robinson–Patman Act contains the statute's basic prohibition against price discrimination by sellers. For a violation of section 2(a) there must be a: *discrimination in price* in the *sale of commodities* of *like grade and quality* in *interstate commerce* resulting in *competitive injury*.

Discrimination in Price

Price discrimination is simply a difference in price. Price is computed on the basis of the purchaser's actual cost. The Robinson–Patman Act does not require that a seller provide lower prices to wholesalers than to retailers or consumers. A seller who charges the same price to all buyers regardless of their positions in the chain of distribution is not discriminating.

Some price differentials are indirect. Examples of indirect discrimination include variations in the terms of delivery, sales returns, cash discounts, and warehousing. Indirect discrimination also occurs when a seller gives a favored buyer a 30-day option to purchase a product at existing prices in a rising market. The Robinson–Patman Act equally prohibits indirect, as well as direct, price discrimination.

Two Sales

Price discrimination can occur only when there are at least two completed sales. A sale occurs only where there is an enforceable contract. For example, a sale to customer X for $6 and an offer to sell to customer Y for $5 is not illegal because only one sale has occurred. For the same reason, it does not violate the Robinson–Patman Act to sell to one party while refusing to sell to another. Simply quoting different prices to different buyers is lawful because no sales have been made.

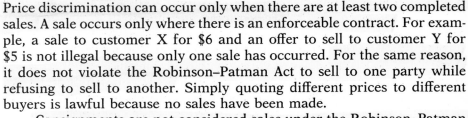

Consignments are not considered sales under the Robinson–Patman Act. A *consignment* occurs when one party delivers goods to a second in order to have the second party sell the goods. The party that delivers the goods is the *consignor,* while the party to which the goods are delivered is the *consignee.* What may be characterized as a consignment, however, may in reality be a sale. In a bona fide consignment the consignor retains title to the product until the ultimate sale to the consumer. If, title passes to the consignee, then the transaction is a sale.

Gifts are not considered sales under the act. However, one may not avoid the act by disguising a sale as a gift. For example, a supplier may not avoid the act by selling 100 tires to Tire, Inc. at $20 per tire while selling 50 tires to Tire, Inc.'s competitor, Whitewall, Inc. at the same price, coupling that sale with a gift of 50 tires to Whitewall, Inc.

Close in Time   Price discrimination occurs only when the two sales are reasonably close in time—a period determined by the circumstances surrounding the sale. In sales involving high-cost, low-volume products such as jet engines, two sales a year apart may be considered close in time. On the other hand, sales of smaller items traded in high volume with great fluctuations in supply and demand may not be considered close in time even though made within a few hours of each other.

Sales for future delivery may differ in price from sales for immediate delivery without running afoul of the act. For example, a seller, in January, may sell corn to be delivered to one buyer in March for a price that differs from the same seller's price to another buyer for immediate delivery. However, if a seller contracts with buyer 1 to deliver March futures corn for $3 per bushel and with buyer 2 to deliver March futures corn for $3.50 per bushel, a price discrimination exists.

Same Seller   The two sales must of course originate from the same seller before the Robinson–Patman Act applies. It is usually easy to tell whether this requirement has been met. The question becomes more difficult when a parent corporation and its subsidiary sell the same product at different prices to competing customers. The determining factor is often the degree of control exercised over the subsidiary by the parent corporation. The fact that the subsidiary is wholly owned and that the boards of the parent and the subsidiary have directors in common does not automatically result in a finding that they are the same seller for purposes of the Robinson–Patman Act. As long as the parent and the subsidiary are independent entities in their pricing and distribution policies, they will be deemed autonomous. In one reported case, the plaintiff operated a retail store that purchased its products from Philco Distributors, Inc., a wholly owned subsidiary of Philco, with common officers. Philco, the parent corporation, sold the same products for less to a competitor of the plaintiff. The plaintiff brought an action against Philco, alleging price discrimination. Since there was no evidence to show that Philco established prices for its subsidiary, the parent and the subsidiary were treated as two distinct sellers and no violation existed.[2]

---

[2] *Baim & Blank, Inc. v. Philco Distributors, Inc.,* 148 F. Supp. 541 (D.C.N.Y. 1957).

Commodities

The Robinson–Patman Act applies only to sales of commodities. *Commodities* are movable or tangible property. Intangibles such as services, leases, loans, mutual fund shares, and advertising are not commodities.

When a sale involves both commodities and services, the dominant nature of the transaction determines whether it falls within the act. For example, in one case a builder allegedly sold bricks at a discriminatory price in connection with a contract to construct public housing facilities. In the contract the price of the bricks was segregated from the price of the construction services and was a significant determinant of the total contract price. The court nevertheless found the whole contract to be an indivisible construction service contract.

Like Grade and Quality

Illegal price discrimination occurs only when the two products sold are of like grade and quantity. Thus, truck tires can be sold at a different price than bicycle tires. Goods, however, do not have to be of exactly the same grade and quality to fall under the jurisdiction of the Robinson–Putman Act. Slight differences in dimensions or quality will not exempt products from the act's prohibition. Juice containers that differ in size by only one-eighth inch are of like grade and quality since they are functionally similar in performance.

The role of customer preference as a factor in determining whether two products are of like grade and quality was examined by the Supreme Court in the following case.

FTC v. Borden Co.

383 U.S. 637 (1965)

The Borden Company (respondent) sells evaporated milk under the Borden name, a nationally recognized premium brand, and under private, nonpremium labels. The nonpremium brand milk is physically and chemically identical to the premium brand milk but is marketed to Borden's customers at a lower price than the premium brand. There is a distinct consumer preference for the premium brand. The FTC (petitioner) found that the two brands were of "like grade and quality" and held that the price differential was discrimination in violation of section 2(a) of the Robinson–Patman Act. The court of appeals reversed the commission's decision and found that the nonpremium brand was not of the same grade and quality as the premium brand. It based its decision on the fact that "decided consumer preference for one brand over another, reflected in the willingness to pay a higher price for the well-known brand, was . . . sufficient to differentiate chemically identical products and to place the price differential beyond the reach of section 2(a)." The Supreme Court rejected the rationale of the court of appeals and reversed and remanded the case.

Justice White

. . . The Commission's view is that labels do not differentiate products for the purpose of determining grade or quality, even though the one label may have more customer appeal and command a higher price in the marketplace from a substantial segment of the public. That this is the Commission's long-standing interpretation of the present Act, as well as §2 of the Clayton Act before its amendment by the Robinson–Patman Act, may be gathered from the Commission's decisions dating back to 1936. . . .

. . . Moreover, what legislative history there is concerning this question supports the Commission's construction of the statute rather than that of the Court of Appeals.

* * * * *

If two products, physically identical but differently branded, are to be deemed of different grade because the seller regularly and successfully markets some quantity of both at different prices, the seller could, as far as §2(a) is concerned, make either product available to some customers and deny it to others, however discriminatory this might be and however damaging to competition. Those who were offered only one of the two products would be barred from competing for those customers who want or might buy the other. The retailer who was permitted to buy and sell only the more expensive brand would have no chance to sell to those who always buy the cheaper product or to convince others, by experience or otherwise, of the fact which he and all other dealers already know—that the cheaper product is actually identical with that carrying the more expensive label.

* * * * *

Our holding neither ignores the economic realities of the marketplace nor denies that some labels will command a higher price than others, at least from some portion of the public. But it does mean that "the economic factors inherent in brand names and national advertising should not be considered in the jurisdictional inquiry under the statutory 'like grade and quality' test." And it does mean that transactions like those involved in this case may be examined by the Commission under §2(a). The Commission will determine, subject to judicial review, whether the differential under attack is discriminatory within the meaning of the Act, whether competition may be injured, and whether [the defendant has a statutory defense to the action]. . . .

CASE QUESTIONS

1. Did the Court "ignore the economic realities of the marketplace"? What are those realities?

2. What is the difference between "like grade" and "like quality"? Give an example of two products that are of like grade but not of like quality. Now give an example of two products that are of like quality but not of like grade.

3. Who is injured, if anyone, as a result of "private branding"? Why are consumers willing to pay more for the same product under a different label?

4. After a finding of "like grade and quality," does the inquiry end? Is Borden automatically guilty of a section 2(a) violation? Explain.

5. What if Borden produced only a small quantity of the private brand milk and the customer demand exceeded the supply? What effect might this have on competition?

Competitive Injury

A discrimination in price, by itself, does not violate the Robinson–Patman Act. The discrimination must cause competitive injury. As the following decision points out, even the price discrimination that the Supreme Court found in the *Borden* case was, upon further examination, found to be lawful.

Borden Co. v. F T C

381 F.2d 175 (5th Cir. 1967)

This is the same case as the case reprinted on page 419. Following the Supreme Court's decision, the case was remanded to the Fifth Circuit Court of Appeals. That court held that the sale of Borden brand milk and private label milk at different prices did not violate the Robinson–Patman Act.

Hutchinson, Circuit Judge

It is not disputed that a price discrimination, within the meaning of the statute, is present. However, we should point out that no overtones of business buccaneering are intended in the phrase "discriminate in price." In the context of Sec. 2(a), price discrimination means only a price difference, not an invidious price structure. Once the fact of a price difference is established, other provisions of the statute must be applied to determine whether the price difference is legal or illegal. This distinction is important to the instant case because although there is a price difference, Borden is not in any sense guilty of predatory behavior similar to that which may accompany territorial price wars. Borden did not subsidize below-cost or unrealistically low prices on its private label milk with profits received from sales of the Borden brand. Nor does this case involve any device similar to the conventional volume discount. All of Borden's customers, large and small alike, paid the price for the Borden brand milk or for the private label milk. . . . The complaint was issued solely because Borden marketed milk of like grade and quality under private labels at prices lower than under the Borden brand.

. . . Section 2(a) proscribes price discrimination whose effect "may be substantially to lessen competition . . . in any line of commerce or to [injure] competition with any person who either grants or knowingly received the benefit of such discrimination, or with customers of either of them." The statute seeks to protect against two types of injuries which may result from a seller's use of price differentials. First, it affords protection from a general injury to the [seller's competitors]. . . . Second, by prohibiting price differentials whose effect may be substantially to [injure] competition *with* a customer, the statute does safeguard individual customers of a seller, as distinguished from competition generally, from a more narrow type of injury.

* * * * *

Seven midwestern canners, competitors of Borden, testified in support of the complaint with respect to competitive injury to the primary line. . . . The competitors complained that portions of their sales had been lost to Borden during the period in question.

* * * * *

Although the testifying competitors did lose a significant number of sales to Borden, it is also true that they gained from other sources enough new sales to achieve an overall increase in absolute sales.

* * * * *

We conclude for two reasons that the record does not contain substantial evidence to support a finding that there may be a substantial injury to competition at the seller's level. The first is that we think it significant that the testifying competitors have experienced an increase in absolute sales volume and have bettered their market position in approximately the same proportion as has Borden.

The second reason is the absence of the necessary causal relationship between the difference in prices and the alleged competitive injury. The Commission's position is that the competing sellers may be hurt because Borden sells its private label milk cheaper than its Borden brand milk. But none of the evidence adduced by the testifying competitors relates to the price difference between the milks marketed by Borden; instead, it relates to the price difference between their own private label milk and Borden's private label milk. The competitors actually assert only that Borden was able to sell private label milk for a lower price than they could, and regarding that assertion, the price of Borden brand milk is immaterial in this case. In short, the evidence simply does not support the precise price discrimination alleged in the complaint.

* * * * *

It is easily understood why the private label milk is sold at all levels of distribution for substantially less than Borden brand milk. By increased advertising and promotional efforts over the years, Borden has created a decided consumer preference for milk bearing a Borden label. The label has come to represent a value in itself. Thus it was not surprising that the testifying wholesalers and retailers admitted that the private label milk was interesting to them only at a price $1.50 to $2.00 less per case than the Borden brand milk. This position reflects their knowledge that they would have had to sell the private label milk for a correspondingly lower price.

* * * * *

We are of the firm view that where a price differential between a premium and nonpremium brand reflects no more than a consumer preference for the premium brand, the price difference creates no competitive advantage to the recipient of the cheaper private brand product on which in-jury could be predicated. "[R]ather it represents merely a rough equivalent of the benefit by way of the seller's national advertising and promotion which the purchaser of the more expensive branded product enjoys." The record discloses no evidence tending to show that Borden's price differential exceeds the recognized consumer appeal of the Borden label. Nor has it been suggested that the prices are unreasonably high for Borden brand milk on the one hand, or unrealistically low for the private label milk on the other.

We conclude that there is not substantial evidence to support a finding that Borden has violated section 2(a). The price difference does not create a competitive advantage by which competition could be injured, and, furthermore, no customer has been favored over another.

CASE QUESTIONS

1. What type of competitive injuries does the Robinson–Patman Act protect against?

2. What type of competitive injuries were alleged in the *Borden* case?

3. Were competing sellers injured? Explain.

4. Were buyers injured? Explain.

5. Would the case have been decided differently if Borden had not made private label milk available to all buyers? Explain.

As the *Borden* decision points out, the Robinson–Patman Act protects competitive markets and specific competitors. The Act prohibits price discrimination which (1) may substantially lessen competition, (2) tend to create a monopoly, or (3) tend to injure, destroy, or prevent competition with any person granting or knowingly benefitting from the discrimination. The third type of injury is usually the easiest to prove. It is, therefore, the one most frequently invoked. Actual injury need not be shown; a probability of injury is sufficient to establish a violation. Injury can occur at various levels of the distribution process.

Primary-Line Injury

Primary-line injury (or injury at the seller's level) occurs when a seller suffers injury as a result of price discrimination by a competitor. This type of injury was alleged in the *Borden* case by Borden's competitors who had lost business to its private label. Primary-line injury normally occurs when a seller cuts prices to purchasers in one geographic area in an attempt to drive out a local competitor. The situation is demonstrated by the accompanying diagram:

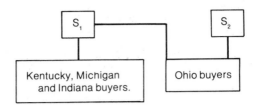

S_1 and S_2 are competitors in Ohio. If S_1 slashes its prices to Ohio buyers in an attempt to drive S_2 out of business, without a corresponding decrease in prices to its customers in Kentucky, Michigan, and Indiana, S_2 may suffer a primary-line injury. Before a violation of the act can occur, S_1's economic power must be sufficient to pose a probability of injury to S_2.

Secondary-Line Injury

Secondary-line injury (or injury at the buyer's level) occurs when a seller discriminates in price between two competing buyers. This injury is illustrated as follows:

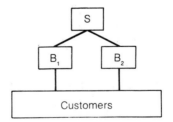

B_1 and B_2 are competing for the same customers. If S sells products at a lower price to B_1 than to B_2, then B_2 is at a competitive disadvantage and may suffer competitive injury. However, if the diagram appears as follows, no such competitive injury occurs:

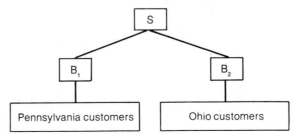

Here, since there is no competition at the buyer level, there can be no buyer-level injury based on price discrimination. In such a case, S may discriminate in price between B_1 and B_2 without violating the act. Should B_1 develop customers in Ohio, then S's more favorable treatment of B_1 may cause competitive injury to B_2 and thus violate the act.

Third-Line Injury

One of a seller's customers may operate at two levels of the distribution process while another customer may operate at only one level. The diagram in this instance appears as follows:

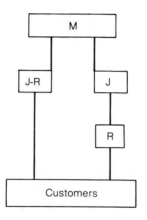

M (manufacturer) sells to J–R (jobber–retailer) and to J (jobber). Third-line injury can result in two ways. If M gives J–R a better price than it gives J, R may be injured in its ability to compete with J–R. If M gives J a better price than it gives J–R, J may be in a position to give R a price that enables R to undersell J–R. In both instances, competitive injury can occur at the third level of distribution. However, in the second case, where M prefers J over J–R, M will be liable only if it knows or should know that J will use its price advantage for anticompetitive purposes. This is because M cannot control the price that J charges R.

Fourth-Line Injury

Fourth-line injury is illustrated in *Standard Oil Co. v. Perkins*, where the plaintiff, Perkins, was an independent gasoline dealer in the wholesale and retail business.[3] Perkins received less favorable treatment than Standard Oil gave another wholesaler. The favored wholesaler sold to a firm that sold to retail outlets which competed with the plaintiff. The distribution diagram appears as follows:

---

[3] 395 U.S. 642 (1969).

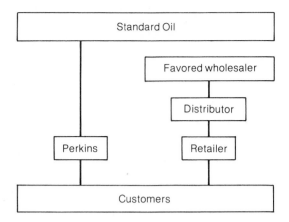

Perkins alleged and proved injury as a result of the discriminatory pricing. The Supreme Court upheld a jury verdict in favor of Perkins and put to rest the belief that the wording of the Robinson–Patman Act would not support a finding of competitive injury below the third-line level. As long as a causal relationship exists between the discrimination and the injury, the distribution level at which the injury occurs appears immaterial.

Commerce

Most federal regulatory statutes apply to all parties engaging in or affecting interstate commerce. As discussed in chapter 3, almost all activity affects interstate commerce. The Robinson–Patman Act is not as broad as most other federal statutes. For section 2(a) to apply, three conditions must be met.

First, a violator must be engaged in interstate commerce. Second, discriminatory practices must occur in the course of interstate commerce. Third, either of the purchases must be made in interstate commerce.

Generally, a company that sells its goods intrastate has failed to meet the first test that it be engaged in interstate commerce. However, if that firm resells goods it received from outside the state, it may be treated as a firm engaged in interstate commerce. Where, for example, gasoline is refined in Indiana and sold to a supplier in Michigan for temporary storage and ultimate resale in Michigan, the gasoline is deemed within the stream of interstate commerce. The subject of the resale satisfies the interstate commerce requirement. In certain cases a different result may be reached. If the product is substantially altered after it arrives in the state before resale, then the flow of interstate commerce ends. For example, if raw oil was shipped into Michigan from Indiana and then refined in Michigan before being sold within Michigan, the act of refining would destroy the interstate character of the oil. In this case the flow of interstate commerce has been interrupted by the intervening act of refinement. Similarly, goods shipped in from a foreign state may nonetheless come to rest intrastate, if incorporated into a finished product and resold intrastate.

A sale that is made in interstate commerce is necessarily made in the course of interstate commerce and thereby satisfies the second test if the sale involves price discrimination. For the third test to be met, one of the purchases must be made in interstate commerce. It does not matter whether the sale to the favored or unfavored customer is interstate, as long as at least one of the two transactions generates a discrimination across state lines. This requirement is met even if the objecting disfavored customer is a purely intrastate business as long as the other sale which is the subject of the complaint is interstate. For example, consider *Moore v. Mead's Fine Bread Company.*[4] The defendant was a New Mexico company engaged in the bread baking business in New Mexico. The company had a close marketing interrelationship with other corporations that did business in New Mexico and Texas. It also sold bread in Texas, which it serviced with a bread truck operating out of its New Mexico location. The plaintiff was engaged in a purely intrastate bakery business in New Mexico. Plaintiff alleged that the defendant cut prices to wholesalers in Texas but failed to do so in New Mexico, resulting in competitive injury. The court held that this was sufficient to satisfy the commerce requirements of the Robinson–Patman Act, since the defendant made discriminatory sales in interstate commerce.

Defenses

There are three basic defenses to an alleged price discrimination. They are cost justification, meeting competition, and changing market conditions.

Cost Justification

Section 2(a) of the Robinson–Patman Act provides a complete defense to a seller when price discrimination is justified by a difference in cost. The particular proviso affording the defense is satisfied as long as price differences are linked to "differences in the cost of manufacture, sale, or delivery resulting from the differing methods [used] or quantities" sold. A seller is not required to give a cost break to a buyer based on a cost saving, but it may do so as long as the cost saving is supported by a reliable cost study. If the seller gives a cost break to a particular buyer, the seller may not discriminate against other buyers. The cost saving must be equally available to them.

To sustain a cost justification defense, the seller must prove that a price difference is based on a cost difference. Cost differences in manufacturing or distribution can justify differences in price.

---

[4] 348 U.S. 115 (1954).

It is usually easier to justify price differences based on distribution costs than those based on manufacturing costs. Distribution costs include transportation, storage, advertising, accounting, management, clerical work, salaries, and customer services.

Although it is usually difficult to justify price differences based on manufacturing costs, there are two areas where manufacturing cost savings may be more readily proved. When a customer orders quantities well in advance, a supplier may justify charging that customer a lower price than the price charged a customer who orders for immediate needs during a rush season. A cost saving for the seller may occur in the form of cheaper off-season labor or elimination of overtime wages. Similarly, where a customer without storage facilities requires spot deliveries during the rush season for which the manufacturer must prepare and store, the manufacturer may be justified in charging that customer a higher price than the price charged another customer that orders in advance and handles the storage.

One type of price difference arises from a volume discount. Volume discounts are permitted if based on savings in sales personnel, travel, warehousing, or transportation.

Cost justification requires a cost study. A cost study is used to justify differences in the net prices charged to buyers. To arrive at the net price all discounts, rebates, and other reductions must be deducted from the selling price.

Cost justification would in most instances be impossible if not for the permissibility of placing customers in homogeneous groups in order to average the costs of selling to each group. The group classifications must be reasonable, and each group must have sufficient homogeneity so that the average costs for the whole group are fairly representative of the costs of dealing with each of its members. The cost study must be based on fair and consistent accounting procedures.

Meeting Competition

The meeting competition defense is rooted in section 2(b) of the Robinson–Patman Act, section 2(b) exonerates a seller that discriminates in price if the seller can show that the lower price "was made in good faith to meet an equally low price of a competitor." The seller has the burden of proving the defense.

The statute is very clear that a seller may discriminate only in order to meet competition. Beating competition is not allowed. This concept is more difficult to apply than it sounds. A price differentiation may not be justified where the seller of a premium product reduces its prices in a geographic area to the level charged by a competitor that is selling a nonpremium product. For example, Anheuser-Bush reduced the price of Budweiser beer in the St. Louis area from $2.93 per case to $2.35 per case in response to the price charged by three regional brewers that were selling their beer at $2.35 per case. Anheuser-Busch's meeting competition defense was rejected because the reduction was not necessary to hold its customers. The effect of the reduction was to beat competition rather than to meet it.[5]

Sellers must act in good faith when meeting competition. Their actions must be based on a reasonably prudent belief that responding by reducing prices is a competitive necessity. A seller that acts in good faith, though under an erroneous belief, is protected by the meeting competition defense. However, a seller has a duty to act with reasonable care in verifying competitive offers made to its prospective customers. When the competition is no longer a threat, the seller must cease discriminating in price.

Lowering prices to meet competition need not be aimed only at retaining old customers. Meeting competition may also have the effect of obtaining new customers. However, the seller must not act in bad faith and cross over from the permissible limits of meeting competition to the illegal area of driving out competition.

A seller may discriminate in price only to meet the competition posed by the sellers. A seller may not lower its price to assist its customer in meeting competition unless the reduction is made in response to competitive practices of the seller's competitor. The operation of the meeting competition defense is illustrated by the following case.

 **Falls City Industries, Inc. v. Vanco Beverages, Inc.**

460 U.S. 428 (1983)

Vanco Beverages (respondent) was a wholesale distributor of beer produced by Falls City Industries (petitioner). Vanco was the sole Falls City wholesaler in Vanderburgh County, Indiana. Vanderburgh County included the city of Evansville and some Evansville suburbs. Other Evansville suburbs were located in Henderson County, Kentucky. Dawson Springs, Inc. was the sole Falls City wholesaler in Henderson County.

Falls City's competitors raised wholesale prices in Indiana but not in Kentucky. Falls City followed suit. As a result, Dawson Springs was charged a lower price than Vanco. Dawson Springs passed the savings on to its retailers, who were able to charge lower prices than retailers in Indiana. Many consumers in the Evansville metropolitan area switched their purchases of Falls City beer from Indiana to Kentucky retailers.

Vanco sued Falls City alleging illegal price discrimination. Falls City claimed that its lower prices in Kentucky were necessary to meet competition there. The district court rejected this defense and awarded damages to Vanco. The Seventh Circuit Court of Appeals affirmed. The Supreme Court reversed.

---

[5] *F.T.C. v. Anheuser-Busch, Inc.,* 363 U.S. 536 (1960).

Justice Blackmun

On its face, §2(b) requires more than a showing of facts that would have led a reasonable person to believe that a lower price was available to the favored purchaser from a competitor. The showing required is that the "lower price . . . *was made* in good faith *to meet*" the competitor's low price. Thus, the defense requires that the seller offer the lower price in good faith *for the purpose* of meeting the competitor's price, that is, the lower price must actually have been a good faith response to that competing low price.

*   *   *   *   *

Almost 20 years ago, the FTC set forth the standard that governs the requirement of a "good faith response":

> "At the heart of Section 2(b) is the concept of 'good faith.' This is a flexible and pragmatic, not a technical or doctrinaire, concept. The standard of good faith is simply the standard of the prudent businessman responding fairly to what he reasonably believes is a situation of competitive necessity."

Whether this standard is met depends on " 'the facts and circumstances of the particular case, not abstract theories or remote conjectures.' "

*   *   *   *   *

Vanco . . . [argues] that the existence of industry-wide price discrimination within the single geographic retail market itself indicates "tacit or explicit collusion, or . . . market power" inconsistent with a good faith response. By its terms, however, the meeting-competition defense requires a seller to justify only its *lower* price. Thus, although the Sherman Act would provide a remedy if Falls City's higher Indiana price were set collusively, collusion is relevant to Vanco's Robinson–Patman Act claim only if it affects Falls City's lower Kentucky price. If Falls City set its lower price in good faith to meet an equally low price of a competitor, it did not violate the Robinson–Patman Act.

*   *   *   *   *

The Court of Appeals explicitly relied on two other factors in rejecting Falls City's meeting-competition defense: the price discrimination was created by raising rather than lowering prices, and Falls City raised its prices in order to increase its profits. Neither of these factors is controlling. Nothing in §2(b) requires a seller to *lower* its price in order to meet competition. On the contrary, §2(b) requires the defendant to show only that its "lower price . . . was made in good faith to meet an equally low price of a competitor." A seller is required to justify a price difference by showing that it reasonably believed that an equally low price was available to the purchaser and that it offered the lower price for that reason; the seller is not required to show that the difference resulted from subtraction rather than addition.

A different rule would not only be contrary to the language of the statute, but also might stifle the only kind of legitimate price competition reasonably available in particular industries. In a period of generally rising prices, vigorous price competition for a particular customer or customers may take the form of smaller price increases rather than price cuts. Thus, a price discrimination created by selective price increases can result from a good faith effort to meet a competitor's low price.

Nor is the good faith with which the lower price is offered impugned if the prices raised, like those kept lower, respond to competitors' prices and are set with the goal of increasing the seller's profits. . . .

Section 2(a) does not require a seller,

meeting in good faith a competitor's lower price to certain customers, to forego the profits that otherwise would be available in sales to its remaining customers. The very purpose of the defense is to permit a seller to treat different competitive situations differently. The prudent businessman responding fairly to what he believes in good faith is a situation of competitive necessity might well raise his prices to some customers to increase his profits, while meeting competitors' prices by keeping his prices to other customers low.

* * * * *

The Court of Appeals also . . . [ruled] that the meeting-competition defense " 'places emphasis on individual [competitive] situations, rather than upon a general system of competition,' " and "does not justify the maintenance of discriminatory pricing among classes of customers that results merely from the adoption of a competitor's discriminatory pricing structure." The Court of Appeals was apparently invoking the District Court's findings that Falls City set prices statewide rather than on a "customer to customer basis," and the District Court's conclusion that this practice disqualified Falls City from asserting the meeting-competition defense.

* * * * *

There is no evidence that Congress intended to limit the availability of §2(b) to customer-specific responses . . . Congress intended to allow reasonable pricing responses on an area-specific basis where competitive circumstances warrant them. The purpose of the amendment was to "restric[t] the proviso to price differentials occurring in actual competition." We conclude that Congress did not intend to bar territorial price differences that are in fact responses to competitive conditions.

Section 2(b) specifically allows a

"lower price . . . to any purchaser or purchasers" made in good faith to meet a competitor's equally low price. A single low price surely may be extended to numerous purchasers if the seller has a reasonable basis for believing that the competitor's lower price is available to them. Beyond the requirement that the lower price be reasonably calculated to "meet not beat" the competition, Congress intended to leave it a "question of fact . . . whether the way in which the competition was met lies within the latitude allowed." Once again, this inquiry is guided by the standard of the prudent businessman responding fairly to what he reasonably believes are the competitive necessities.

A seller may have good reason to believe that a competitor or competitors are charging lower prices throughout a particular region. In such circumstances, customer-by-customer negotiations would be unlikely to result in prices different from those set according to information relating to competitors' territorial prices. A customer-by-customer requirement might also make meaningful price competition unrealistically expensive for smaller firms such as Falls City, which was attempting to compete with larger national breweries in 13 separate States.

* * * * *

Of course, a seller must limit its lower price to that group of customers reasonably believed to have the lower price available to it from competitors. A response that is not reasonably tailored to the competitive situation as known to the buyer, or one that is based on inadequate verification, would not meet the standard of good faith. Similarly, the response may continue only as long as the competitive circumstances justifying it, as reasonably known by the seller, persist. One choosing to price on a territorial basis, rather than on a customer-by-customer basis, must show that this decision was a genuine, reasonable response to prevailing competitive circumstances. Unless the circumstances call into question the seller's good faith, this burden will be discharged by showing that a reasonable and prudent businessman would believe that the lower price he charged was generally available from his competitors throughout the territory and throughout the period in which he made the lower price available.

CASE QUESTIONS

1. Did Vanco and Dawson Springs compete with each other? Was there competitive injury caused by the different prices? Explain.

2. What argument did Vanco make against Fall City's meeting competition defense? Why did the Supreme Court reject the argument?

3. Why did the court of appeals reject the meeting competition defense? Why did the Supreme Court reject the court of appeals' analysis?

4. Explain the difference between meeting competition on a customer-by-customer basis and meeting competition on a market-by-market basis.

5. What information would an executive want to have before raising or lowering prices in response to market competition?

Changing Conditions

Sellers may reduce prices in response to changes in market conditions or in the marketability of their products. These changes are usually beyond the seller's control. Changing conditions include the threatened deterioration of perishable goods, the obsolescence of seasonal goods, distress sales under court process, and discontinuance of business in specified goods. The classic example of change in product marketability is provided by the automobile industry. Once automobile models for the new year become available, the old year's inventory becomes less marketable. In response, automobile manufacturers may reduce the prices of the old year's models without fear of Robinson–Patman liability.

BUYER DISCRIMINATION

Section 2(f) of the Robinson–Patman Act makes it unlawful to knowingly induce or receive a price discrimination in violation of section 2(a). This section was designed to reach the big purchasers that were in a position to extract large discriminatory price concessions from the seller. The following case represents the Supreme Court's interpretation of section 2(f).

Great Atlantic & Pacific Tea Co., Inc., v. FTC

440 U.S. 69 (1979)

The FTC (respondent) instituted a complaint against Great Atlantic & Pacific Tea Co., Inc. (A&P) (petitioner), which included a charge that A&P violated section 2((f) of the Robinson–Patman Act by knowingly inducing or receiving price discriminations from Borden. The FTC found that A&P knew or should have known that it was the beneficiary of unlawful price discrimination. A&P appealed the decision to the court of appeals, which affirmed the FTC. A&P sought review in the Supreme Court, which granted certiorari and reversed.

A&P was Borden's largest customer in the Chicago area. A&P wished to change from selling brand label milk to selling private label milk. It communicated this desire to Borden, which offered A&P a discount on private label milk. The offer would have saved A&P $410,000 per year. A&P then solicited offers from other dairies and received a more favorable bid from Bowman Dairy. It communicated this fact to Borden but refused to reveal the details of the Bowman bid. Borden, fearing the loss of A&P's business, responded with a new bid which would increase A&P's annual saving to $820,000. Borden stated that its new offer was designed to meet Bowman's bid. A&P accepted Borden's bid, knowing that it was better than Bowman's.

Justice Stewart

The petitioner . . . argues that it cannot be liable under §2(f) if Borden had a valid meeting competion defense. The respondent, on the other hand, argues that the petitioner may be liable even assuming that Borden had such a defense. The meeting competition defense, the respondent contends, must in these circumstances be judged from the point of view of the buyer. Since A&P knew for a fact that the Borden bid beat the Bowman bid, it was not entitled to assert the meeting competition defense even though Borden may have honestly believed that it was simply meeting competition. Recognition of a meeting competition defense for the buyer in this situation, the

respondent argues, would be contrary to the basic purpose of the Robinson–Patman Act to curtail abuses by large buyers

* * * * *

In a competitive market, uncertainty among sellers will cause them to compete for business by offering buyers lower prices. Because of the evils of collusive action the Court has held that the exchange of price information by competitors violates the Sherman Act. Under the view advanced by the respondent, however, a buyer, to avoid liability, must either refuse a seller's bid or at least inform him that his bid has beaten competition. Such a duty of affirmative disclosure would almost in-evitably frustrate competitive bidding and, by reducing uncertainty, lead to price matching and anticompetitive cooperation among sellers.

* * * * *

. . . Accordingly, we hold that a buyer who has done no more than accept the lower of two prices competitively offered does not violate §2(f) provided the seller has a meeting competition defense.

Because both the commission and the Court of Appeals proceeded on the assump-tion that a buyer who accepts the lower of two competitive bids can be liable under section 2(f) even if the seller has a meeting competition defense, there was not a spe-cific finding that Borden did in fact have such a defense. But it quite clearly did.

The test for determining when a seller has a valid meeting competition defense is whether a seller can "show the existence of facts which would lead a reasonable and prudent person to believe that the granting of a lower price would in fact meet the equally low price of a competitor.". . . "A good faith belief, rather than absolute cer-tainty, that a price concession is being of-fered to meet an equally low price offered by a competitor is sufficient to satisfy the Robinson–Patman's section 2(b) defense." Since good faith, rather than absolute cer-tainty, is the touchstone of the meeting com-petition defense, a seller can assert the de-fense even if it has unknowingly made a bid that in fact not only met but beat his competition.

Under the circumstances of this case, Borden did act reasonably and in good faith when it made its second bid. The petitioner, despite its longstanding relationship with Borden, was dissatisfied with Borden's first bid and solicited offers from other dair-ies. . . .

* * * * *

Thus Borden was informed by the peti-tioner that it was in danger of losing its A&P business in the Chicago area unless it came up with a better offer. . . . In light of Borden's established relationship with the petitioner, Borden could justifiably con-clude that A&P's statements were reliable and that it was necessary to make another bid offering substantial concessions to avoid losing its account with the petitioner.

Borden was unable to ascertain the de-tails of the Bowman bid. It requested more information about the bid from the peti-tioner, but this request was refused. It could not then attempt to verify the existence and terms of the competing offer from Bowman without risking Sherman Act liability. Faced with a substantial loss of business and unable to find out the precise details of the competing bid, Borden made another offer stating that it was doing so in order to meet competition. Under these circum-stances, the conclusion is virtually inesca-pable that in making that offer Borden acted in a reasonable and good faith effort to meet its competition, and therefore was entitled to a meeting competition defense.

Since Borden had a meeting competi-tion defense and thus could not be liable under §2(b), the petitioner who did no more than accept that offer cannot be liable under §2(f).

CASE QUESTIONS

1. Under a strict reading of section 2(f), is A&P guilty? Why did the administrative law judge, the commission, and the Second Circuit Court of Appeals all hold that A&P had violated section 2(f)?

2. Do you think that Borden's desire was to meet its competition or to beat it? Why?

3. Does the seller have any duty to make good faith attempts to ascertain its competitors before lowering the price of its goods? What if A&P had told Borden the competitor's price and then Borden and A&P had agreed on that exact price? Would there have been a Sherman Act violation? What dilemma is Borden faced with if A&P refuses to reveal the details of the Bowman bid?

4. How would A&P establish a defense to a section 2(f) violation based on cost justification?

5. Are we back where we started from with large buyers having the power to extract discriminatory price concessions from suppliers? Discuss.

BROKERAGE PAYMENTS

Section 2(c) prohibits making or receiving "brokerage payments" except when the payments are made for services actually performed. This section was intended to eliminate "dummy" brokerage fees that large buyer chains extracted from sellers. The results of this practice were price concessions and, in reality, unfair price discriminations for favored buyers. A seller may not give a brokerage fee to the buyer's broker since the buyer's broker does not render services to the seller. To do so would violate section 2(c).

Section 2(c) is self-containing and without reference to any other sections. As such, no cost justification, meeting competition, or changing market defenses appear to be available. A violation of section 2(c) may result from a single transaction. There is no need for two sales. No showing of competitive injury is needed. All that is required for a violation is a brokerage fee flowing from buyer to seller, or vice versa, without supportive services rendered. However, recent cases have been chipping away at the traditional approach, so that more and more of section 2(a) elements and the cost justification and meeting competition defenses are seeping into the case law.

PROMOTIONAL ALLOWANCES AND SERVICES

Price concessions are not the only way a seller may favor one customer over another. The Robinson–Patman Act also comprehends such forms of discrimination as promotional allowances, signs, displays, demonstrations, packaging, warehousing, return privileges, and a host of other merchandising services. These potential abuses are covered in sections 2(d) and 2(e). Section 2(d) requires that any payments or allowances by a seller to a buyer for promotional services be available on proportionally equal terms to competing customers. Section 2(e) requires that any services furnished by a seller to a buyer be made available on proportionally equal terms to all competing customers.

Only sellers can violate sections 2(d) and 2(e). However, buyers who induce sellers to violate sections 2(d) and 2(e) may be committing unfair trade practices and violating section 5 of the Federal Trade Commission Act.

The seller must inform customers of the availability of advertising allowances and promotional services. The terms should be openly communicated to all customers by the same media to avoid the suspicion of discriminatory conduct. However, a seller need only make the allowances and services available to competing customers. Whether two customers compete must be determined primarily on the basis of geography. It is unlikely that a California customer competes with a Florida customer. However, a Queens, New York, customer may compete with a Long Island, New York, customer. In close cases a resort to market analysis and conditions may be necessary to determine whether two customers actually compete. The seller may not formulate a promotional plan that benefits only some competing customers. Each competing customer must be able to take advantage of the seller's promotional plan even if this requires tailoring the plan to fit a specific competitor's needs.

The promotional allowances or services must be made available to competing customers on "proportionally equal terms." Proportionally equal terms may be computed as a percentage of the dollar volume of goods sold or of the quantity of goods purchased. If a seller makes available to each customer an advertising allowance equal to 2 percent of annual purchases, the proportionally equal terms requirement would be satisfied. However, if the 2 percent allowance would not apply until a specified quantity of products were purchased, the allowance might be violative of the requirement if only a few large buyers could benefit from it. The following case illustrates the operation of sections 2(d) and 2(e)

Bouldis v. U.S. Suzuki Motor Corp.

711 F.2d 1319 (6th Cir. 1983)

Pete Bouldis (plaintiff) owned Bold–Morr, Inc., a Suzuki (defendant) motorcycle dealership. The dealership ran into financial difficulties and applied for credit through the Suzuki Finance Program. Suzuki denied the application. Ultimately, because of its financial problems, the dealership went out of business.

Bold–Morr claimed that its problems were caused by the following Suzuki actions: (1) denial of credit; (2) conditioning of freight allowances on minimum purchase requirements that Bold–Morr could not meet; (3) discrimination in accepting returns of merchandise; and (4) Suzuki's co-op advertising program. Under the co-op advertising program, co-op funds were generated by the purchase of motorcycles. Specified dollar amounts, which varied from time to time and model to model, were credited to each dealer's co-op account, based on the number of motorcycles purchased by the dealer. The trial court granted summary judgment to Suzuki. The Sixth Circuit Court of Appeals affirmed.

Phillips, Circuit Judge

Bold–Morr contends that the district court erred in finding that Suzuki's practice of extending credit, granting freight allowances, services and return privileges did not violate §§2(d) and 2(e) of the Clayton Act, as amended.

Section 2(d) prohibits a seller from making payments to one customer for services or facilities furnished by the customer, unless such payments are available to all purchasers on an equally proportional basis. On the other hand, §2(e) prohibits the seller from furnishing services or facilities connected with the process and handling of commodities upon all terms not accorded to all purchasers on a proportionally equal basis.

The aim of both sections is to eliminate devices by which preferred buyers obtain discriminatory preferences under the guise of promotional allowances. However, it is important to note that the discriminatory practices made unlawful by §§2(d) and 2(e) must occur in connection with commodities obtained by the purchaser for *resale*.

Bold—Morr first claims that Suzuki's credit programs . . . violated §§2(d) and 2(e), as such programs were only available to certain favored customers. This claim is without merit because discriminatory practices in the extension of credit from the seller to the buyer are beyond the scope of either §2(d) or §2(e). . . . [T]he extension of credit is a practice incident to the original sale rather than to the subsequent resale of the product, and, therefore, outside the coverage of §§2(d) and 2(e).

Bold–Morr also argues that Suzuki's freight allowances (prepaid freight promotions), conditioned upon the purchase of a specific number of motorcycles, violated §§2(d) and 2(e). This claim also lacks merit, since freight allowances relate merely to the initial sale of the product and not its resale. Therefore, freight allowances fall outside the coverage of both §2(d) and §2(e).

It is also asserted that Suzuki violated §§2(d) and 2(e) by refusing to accept merchandise returns from Bold–Morr, while accepting returns from other dealers. . . .

It has been held that a seller who permits certain of its customers to return unsold goods for credit, while not extending the same privilege to other customers violates §2(e). However, it is also required that the return privilege be connected with the resale of the product to trigger the application of §2(e). In the present case, Bold–Morr's dealership was terminated by the time the repurchase option became effective, and, therefore, Bold–Morr no longer was engaged in the ongoing business of selling motorcycles. Clearly, this situation is unlike one where return privileges are denied to an ongoing and viable business enterprise. Accordingly, with the dealership terminated, the failure of Suzuki to exercise its repurchase option with respect to portions of Bold–Morr's Inventory, had no relation to the resale of the goods as required by §2(e).

The final claim under §§2(d) and 2(e) is that advertising monies, termed co-op funds, were made available to other dealers which were not practically available to Bold–Morr. There is no dispute that these advertising allowances fall within the scope of §2(d), and, thus, Suzuki was required to make the allowances available on proportionally equal terms to all of its customers.

Generally, to assure proportionality, the seller is free to devise any particular method, so long as the system utilized does not discriminate in favor of the large volume buyer. The Federal Trade Commission has stated that the best way to assure fairness in advertising allowances is to base the payments "on the dollar volume or on the quantity of goods purchased during a specified period."

The record shows that Suzuki based the allocation of co-op advertising funds according to the number of motorcycles purchased by a dealer. Under this plan, a certain dollar amount for each model purchased by the dealer would be credited to the dealer's co-op advertising fund. The record further demonstrates that Suzuki's promotional programs which offered allowances for advertising, involved modest requirements to assure that the co-op funds were available to all dealers on a proportionately equal basis. Therefore, since Suzuki allocated its advertising allowances pursuant to a plan acceptable to the Federal Trade Commission, we conclude that it was appropriate to grant summary judgment on this issue as well.

CASE QUESTIONS

1. Did the credit denials violate sections 2(d) or 2(e)? Explain.

2. Did the freight allowances violate sections 2(d) or 2(e)? Explain.

3. Did the refusal to take merchandise returns violate sections 2(d) or 2(e)? Explain.

4. Did the co-op advertising program violate sections 2(d) or 2(e)? Explain.

5. Could any of the above four practices have violated section 2(a)? Explain.

Cost justification and lack of competitive injury are not available defenses to a section 2(d) or section 2(e) violation. Nonetheless, they have been considered by courts in determining whether a promotional plan is discriminatory. The meeting competition defense is available in a proper section 2(d) or section 2(e) case. As with a section 2(a) price discrimination case, the seller must show that more favorable services or allowances are designed in good faith to meet, not beat, competition.

ALTERNATIVE APPROACHES

Although the Robinson–Patman Act was aimed at the discriminatory activities of large buyers and sellers, it applies to all businesses regardless of size. Thus, a small business may not adopt an aggressive pricing policy in an effort to beat large competitors if that policy discriminates among different customers.

In contrast to the American approach, the German price discrimination law applies only to cartels (i.e., competitors who fix prices), enterprises that engage in resale price maintenance (both of these are prohibited in the United States by the Sherman Act), and enterprises that dominate their markets or have relative market power. Market domination may result from a firm's market share, access to supply or sales markets, or barriers to market entry by new competitors. Relative market power exists when buyers or sellers are dependent on a firm because of the absence of sufficient and reasonable alternative suppliers or customers.

The German Approach to Price Discrimination and Other Forms of Business Discrimination*

A brief comparison of the German approach to the problem of business discrimination with the approach of the U.S. Robinson–Patman Act highlights some important differences between the two systems and may serve to place the German approach in perspective as an alternative means of dealing with the anticompetitive effects of discrimination. The first respect in which the two systems differ is in their "coverage"—*who* is subject to them. The German approach is selective. It applies the prohibition against discrimination only to a defined and limited group of enterprises which are viewed as being in a position to create substantial anticompetitive effects.

* * * * *

The Robinson-Patman Act, on the other hand, takes a blanket approach. Its provisions may apply to any enterprise which discriminates, regardless of its size or the likelihood that discrimination by such enterprise may be anticompetitive. The screening function, which in the German system is performed by subjecting only

certain enterprises to the discrimination provisions, is performed in the American system by requiring that discrimination is actionable only "where the effect of such discrimination may be substantially to lessen competition or tend to create a monopoly in any line of commerce. . . ."

An important benefit of the German selective approach is that it relieves most enterprises of the burden of compliance costs—i.e., the legal and administrative costs associated with complying with the law, including the costs of determining whether particular cases of discrimination may violate the law. Under the American system each time a party discriminates there is the possibility that this discrimination could lead to a lawsuit; under the German system most enterprises are not subject to the statute and therefore need not bear the costs of taking into consideration the legal rules and their potential ramifications. Such compliance costs are most burdensome for those who can least afford them. They hit hardest at small enterprises as to which price discrimination of an anticompetitive type is likely to be either impossible, justifiable, or simply a mistake.

Even with a selective approach, however, there remains a degree of uncertainty with respect to whether or not the rules ap-

* Gerber, "The German Approach to Price Discrimination and Other Forms of Business Discrimination," © Federal Legal Publications, Inc. 157 Chambers Street, New York, N.Y. 10007, *The Antitrust* Bulletin, 27:1982, pp. 241–273.

ply in a particular case. More importantly, there is a risk that selective provisions will not cover all situations in which protection is called for, thus leaving certain groups or types of enterprises subject to potentially significant discrimination.

The second major difference between the Robinson–Patman Act approach and the German approach lies in the scope of the discriminatory behavior subject to the discrimination rules. The Robinson–Patman Act deals only with discrimination involving effective prices, whereas the German system includes virtually all types of discrimination in business relationships, including refusals to deal and other types of cases which under American law are dealt with under principles unrelated to discrimination concepts.

The extraordinarily broad coverage of the German provisions calls for an effective means of limiting situations in which they might be applied, and therefore tends to favor a selective approach. Conversely, the fact that the Robinson–Patman Act applies only to price discrimination tends to reduce the impact of having a less efficient screening mechanism.

Finally, there are significant differences between the two systems with regard to the kinds of defenses which may be used to defeat a charge of discrimination. Under the Robinson–Patman Act, defenses are limited and clearly specified, focusing on cost differences and the need to meet competi-

tion. This means that costly accounting studies are often the basis of the defense, and it significantly limits the flexibility of the approach. The German system is, on the other hand, highly flexible in this regard. Any "material" justification may be proffered as a defense to a charge of discrimination.

One difficulty in making progress in legal thinking is that once a problem has been given a "solution," and that solution has stood the "test of time," thinking in the area tends to begin with the solution rather than with the problem. This could hardly be better exemplified than in the area of price discrimination. The Robinson–Patman Act of 1936 has become the accepted model. It has dominated thinking about price discrimination in the U.S.—and in much of the western world—for over four decades. Moreover, the dominance of this model has tended to lead to a "Robinson–Patman-Act-or-nothing" approach to the issue of price discrimination. This has distorted thinking on the question by limiting its range and by making progress on the practical level in the form of compromise solutions virtually impossible.

Breaking this impasse may call for the injection of new ideas and alternative approaches into discussions of the issues. In this article I have described an alternative approach which may be of value in that effort.

CHAPTER PROBLEMS

1. Mayer Paving & Asphalt Company was in the asphalt paving business in Skokie, Illinois. Material Service Corporation produced and distributed crushed limestone, sand, and other compounds used in the paving and construction business. It operated five quarries in Chicago and distributed its products to paving and construction contractors in Indiana and Illinois. Material Service charged Mayer Paving more for crushed stone than it charged Mayer Paving's competitors, all of which were located in Illinois. Mayer Paving complains that Material Service has violated section 2(a) of the Robinson–Patman Act. Does the court have jurisdiction to hear the case? Explain.

2. The *Bismarck Tribune* is a daily newspaper based in Bismarck, North Dakota. The *Morning Pioneer* is a daily newspaper based in Mandan, North Dakota, which is about seven miles from Bismarck. The two newspapers have a long history of coexistence, each serving its own market area without attempting to infringe the market of the other.

Recent developments have caused this amicable relationship to break down, and the *Tribune* is now waging an active campaign to capture the Mandan market. In its attempt to win the *Pioneer's* customers the *Tribune* has reduced the price of its newspaper delivered in Mandan below the Bismarck price.

The *Tribune* delivered in Mandan contains older news than the *Tribune* delivered in Bismarck. Also, the *Tribune* advertisements are valuable only to those persons who shop in Bismarck. The *Pioneer* has brought an action to prevent the *Tribune* from engaging in what the *Pioneer* considers illegal activity in violation of section 2(a) of the Robinson–Patman Act. What is the *Pioneer's* argument? What is the *Tribune's* counterargument? Has the *Tribune* violated section 2(a)? Explain.

3. The Folger Company, manufacturer of Folger's Coffee, is considering undertaking a major promotional campaign whereby it will give directly to consumers free samples, refunds, and coupons good for 50 cents off on a purchase of a two-pound can. Although Folger's coffee is sold nationwide, the company plans to limit its promotional campaign to the metropolitan Chicago area. Will this limitation violate section 2(a) of the Robinson–Patman Act? Explain.

4. Continental Baking Co. manufactures white bread which markets under the label Wonder Bread. Continental sold Wonder Bread to supermarket chains and independent groceries. Many independents have formed a buying cooperative. Continental has agreed to sell the cooperative private label bread at 20 percent below the price it charges for Wonder Bread. Members of the cooperative will market it as Tender Crust Bread. The private label bread is identical to Wonder Bread except for its brand name. The cooperative has also agreed that its members

will give Wonder Bread preferred shelf space over competing brands. Has Continental violated the Robinson–Patman Act? Why or why not?

5. Sun Oil Company (Sun), a major integrated refiner and distributor of petroleum products, markets a single grade of gasoline under the trade name Sunoco in 18 states. Gilbert McLean is the lessee-operator of a Sunoco gas station in Jacksonville, Florida. He operates in a sales territory which includes eight other Sun stations.

Initially all Sun stations within McLean's territory received gasoline from Sun at the same price and obtained the same profit upon resale to the public. Four months after McLean began business, the Super Test Oil Company opened a Super Test gas station diagonally across the street from McLean and began selling its gasoline at a price far below the price at which McLean and the other Sun stations within his territory sold their gasoline. After suffering dramatic losses due to the competition of the Super Test station, McLean appealed to Sun and was granted a price reduction. This reduction was not extended to any other Sun dealers within McLean's territory.

As a result of the reduction in price McLean was able to compete with the Super Test station. McLean also succeeded in luring customers away from the other Sun stations within his sales territory. The FTC brought action against Sun, alleging a violation of the Clayton Act. What action on Sun's part would the FTC find objectionable? Can Sun justify its policy? Would the situation be different if Sun could prove that the Super Test station's supplier was offering Super Test at a reduced price? Explain.

6. Morton Salt Company manufactures and sells different brands of table salt to wholesalers and larger retail grocery chains. Its finest brand, Blue Label, is sold on a "standard quantity discount system." Blue Label purchasers pay a delivered price based on the quantities bought:

	Per case
Less than carload purchases	$1.60
Carload purchases	1.50
5,000-case purchases in any consecutive 12 months	1.40
50,000-case purchases in any consecutive 12 months	1.35

Only five companies operating large chains of retail stores have been able to buy Blue Label at $1.35 per case. Because of the discount these companies command, they are able to sell Blue Label at retail cheaper than the wholesaler purchasers can sell it to independently operated retail stores. Many of those independently operated stores compete directly with the retail outlets of the five large chains. The FTC seeks to enjoin Morton from sales of salt under this discount system. Identify and discuss the key issues.

7. Kroger Company operates a chain of more than 1,400 retail grocery stores located in 19 states. Its sales exceed $2 billion a year. The competitors of Kroger's Charleston Division include national and regional chains and independent supermarkets.

Beatrice Foods, a large U.S. dairy company, has $569 million in annual sales. Beatrice supplies Kroger's Charleston Division.

Kroger decided to sell private label brands in order to become more competitive. It invited companies to submit bids for bottling Kroger-label milk for its Charleston Division. Broughton submitted the first bid. Beatrice officials then met with a Kroger representative in the hope of making a successful bid for bottling Kroger's private brand milk. When a Beatrice official said that his company would offer a 15 percent discount, the Kroger representative replied, "Well, forget it—I've already got one at 20 percent off the list price." Actually, Kroger had not received any bid lower than the Beatrice offer. Beatrice then offered to meet the 20 percent discount, and Kroger accepted the offer. Is Beatrice in violation of the Robinson–Patman Act? Why or why not? Is Kroger in violation of the act? Why or why not?

8. S. J. Greene Company wholesaled frozen and prepared seafood products. E. J. Kozin Company took over a seafood business that was in competition with Greene. Bernard Kane, Greene's sales manager and the son-in-law of Greene's president, left Greene to become a director and officer of Kozin as well as its principal shareholder. Thereafter Kane persuaded Greene officials to purchase substantial quantities of seafood from Kozin. In return he received $19,780 in sales commissions from Kozin. Greene went bankrupt, and the trustee in bankruptcy brought a treble-damage action against the Kozin Company and Kane, alleging a violation of section 2(c) of the Robinson–Patman Act. Decide the case.

9. Purdy, a seller of mobile homes, sued Champion, a manufacturer and distributor of mobile homes, alleging that it had been denied its proportionate share of promotional services in relation to its competitors, in violation of section 2(e). Champion granted Purdy the exclusive right to purchase and resell "Tamarack" mobile homes within a prescribed area. It also marketed two other substantially identical mobile homes to other dealers within the same area, without making those homes available to Purdy. Decide the case.

10. Compare and contrast the German and American approaches to price discrimination.

CHAPTER 14

FRANCHISING

To the average person, franchising means fast-food chains along major streets. Franchising, however, includes a much broader segment of the marketplace. Franchises cover real estate brokerages, accounting and bookkeeping services, computer software, temporary help and other employment services, car rentals, building supplies, and many other areas. Virtually anything that has a marketing plan and can be packaged into something salable can be franchised. Two marketing and management experts have described the franchise relationship as follows:

> The basis of franchising is a contract, or franchise, by which a franchisor in return for a consideration, and the assumption of certain responsibilities by the franchisee, grants to the franchisee the right to use a trademark or copyright. Commonly, the brand or trademark applies to the system according to which business under that franchise is to be conducted as well as to the product or service which is the subject of the franchise.[1]

Franchising has expanded tremendously in recent years. It enables franchisors to establish national distribution networks with minimal capital outlays. It also allows small local concerns to affiliate with nationally known operations.

The relationship between the franchisor and its franchisees is usually governed by contracts. These contracts may violate section 5 of the Federal Trade Commission Act, the Sherman Act, or section 3 of the Clayton Act. This chapter explores the impact of these antitrust laws on various aspects of the franchisor–franchisee relationship.

---

[1] Jones and Hamacher, "Franchising," in *Marketing Manager's Handbook* 765 (Britt ed. 1978).

ATTRACTING POTENTIAL FRANCHISEES—THE FTC FRANCHISE RULE

As was seen in the introduction to Part IV, the Federal Trade Commission enforces section 5 of the FTC Act. Section 5 prohibits unfair methods of competition and unfair or deceptive trade practices. Section 5 includes, but is broader than, the Sherman and Clayton acts. To implement section 5, the FTC issues trade regulation rules setting basic standards of lawful business conduct. In response to widespread abuses by franchisors, the FTC has promulgated a rule governing the offering of franchises. The rule requires that all franchisors subject to it provide a prospective franchisee with a document containing specific disclosures.

The Rule's Coverage

The FTC rule is designed to cover all franchise systems, including retail business distribution rights for trademarked products, and vending machine route programs. It defines franchises as contractual relationships of either of two types.

The first type of franchise encompasses what marketing experts have traditionally called a franchise—a marketing system centered on uniform standards and a trademark or trade name. Type I has three requirements:

1. The franchisee must operate under the franchisor's commercial symbol and distribute goods or services that are either identified by the franchisor's symbol or required to meet the franchisor's quality standards. A Coca-Cola bottler is covered because, although the bottler may operate under its own name, it distributes soft drinks identified by the franchisor's trademarks such as Coca-Cola, Tab, and Sprite. A franchisee operating a Century 21 real estate brokerage franchise is also covered because, although it does not distribute any trademarked items, it is required to meet the franchisor's quality standards and operates under the Century 21 trademark.

   A McDonald's franchisee would meet both alternatives of this requirement. It offers food for sale under such commercial symbols as Big Mac and Egg McMuffin. It must meet the franchisor's standards governing the quality of food served, and it operates under the McDonald's name using commercial symbols such as golden arches.

2. The franchisor exercises significant control over the franchisee's methods of operation or gives the franchisee significant assistance in its operation. Areas of significant control or assistance include the franchisee's business organization, promotional activities, management, or marketing plan.

3. The franchisee is obligated to pay a fee of at least $500 to the franchisor within six months after starting business.

The second type involves business opportunities such as middle-level distributorships and vending machine supply contracts, even when they are not centered on specific trademarks or subject to uniform standards. Type II also has three requirements:

1. The franchisee offers, sells, or distributes goods, commodities, or services that are supplied either by the franchisor or by another party with whom the franchisee is required to deal.
2. The franchisor secures for the franchisee retail outlets, accounts, or sites for vending machines, rack displays, or similar sales displays.
3. The franchisee is obligated to pay a fee of at least $500 to the franchisor within six months after starting business.

Both types of franchises are covered only if the franchisee is required to pay the franchisor $500 or more within six months after starting business. This is because the rule is aimed at the prerule practices of some franchisors who received large franchise fees after making unrealistic or even fraudulent promises.

A franchisor is not subject to the rule if the total of all required franchise payments in the first six months is less than $500. The $500 limit includes not only payments made for the right to have a franchise but also payments for tools, equipment, promotional material, and other noninventory goods and services provided by the franchisor. However, it does not include franchisee payments for inventory, optional franchisee payments, and franchisee payments required after the six months.

Payments for Inventory

The typical retail franchisee is required to establish an initial inventory. For example, new automobile dealerships are required to purchase an initial inventory of vehicles, parts, and accessories. Inventory purchases are not considered required payment if they are made in quantities a reasonable entrepreneur would require and at fair wholesale prices. However, where inventory requirements are unreasonable in price or quantity, the FTC may view them as required payments.

Optional Payments

Franchisees frequently purchase noninventory goods or services from the franchisor. To avoid inclusion of these purchases within the $500 limit, franchisors can allow their franchisees to obtain these goods and services from alternative sources. If the franchisee chooses to obtain them from the franchisor anyway, the franchisee's payments to the franchisor are considered optional. The franchisee's option to purchase from alternative sources must be realistic in light of the industry and community.

The FTC has indicated that it is particularly suspicious of real estate purchases and leases where the franchisor has considerable incentive to require the franchisee to use franchisor-owned property that would otherwise be vacant. For example, the FTC considers service station leases to be required payments even though the franchisee has the option of leasing a station from other sources, purchasing an existing station, or constructing a new station. Traffic patterns, traffic access, and zoning restrictions give existing leases a comparative advantage over other alternatives, while the initial capital required and uncertainties in financing make the purchase or construction of a new station a dubious possibility for new franchisees.[2]

Payment Required after the First Six Months

The FTC's franchise rule assumes that in six months the franchisee will become sufficiently familiar with the franchisor to be able to make informed judgments about the relationship. Thus, payments to be made after the first six months are not counted in determining the rule's applicability. A franchisor can avoid the rule's operation by accepting a promissory note payable later than six months from the start of business. For the note to be effective the franchisor must not be able to discount it and thus destroy the franchisee's ability to assert legal defenses in the collection process.

Required Disclosure

All franchisors covered by the FTC rule must furnish a disclosure document to prospective franchisees. The rule does not provide for prior review of the document by the FTC. The cover of the document must contain the following statement in boldface 12-point type:

INFORMATION FOR PROSPECTIVE FRANCHISEES REQUIRED BY FEDERAL TRADE COMMISSION

*   *   *   *   *

To protect you, we've required your franchisor to give you this information. *We haven't checked it, and don't know if it's correct.* It should help you make up your mind. Study it carefully. While it includes some information about your contract, don't rely on it alone to understand your contract. Read all of your contract carefully. Buying a franchise is a complicated investment. Take your time to decide. If possible, show your contract and this information to an advisor, like a lawyer or an accountant. If you find anything you think may be wrong or anything important that's been left

---

[2] FTC Franchise Advisory Opinions Nos. 17 and 18 to Sinclair Marketing, Inc., and Marathon Oil Co. (Oct. 1, 1979, and Oct. 5, 1979).

out, you should let us know about it. It may be against the law.

There may also be laws on franchising in your state. Ask your state agencies about them.

Federal Trade Commission
Washington, D.C. 20580

The document must then set forth the franchisor's name and address and the names of its officers and directors. It must give the following information about its officers and directors:

— Their business experience
— Their felony convictions, if any, for fraud, embezzlement, fraudulent conversion, misappropriation of property, or restraint of trade
— All of their involvements in civil or administrative agency litigation concerning fraud, dishonesty, or the franchise relationship
— Any bankruptcy proceedings in which they have been involved
— Describe the franchise, including its trademarks, format, the market for its good or services, and its expected competition
— Disclose the requirements of franchisees, including required payments, obligations to purchase goods from the franchisor, and personal participation in operating the franchise
— Disclose the restrictions on franchise territories, customers, or site selection
— Describe the financing and training made available by the franchisor

Finally, the document must provide information on the grounds for terminating the franchise or denying its renewal, statistics on the number of franchisees terminated in the past year, and balance sheets and income statements for the last three years. The financial statements need not be certified, but they must be prepared in accordance with generally accepted accounting and auditing procedures.

Earning Predictions

If the franchisor suggests the franchisee may achieve a specific level of potential sales, income, or profit, there must be a reasonable basis for the representations. The material supporting the predictions must be made available to prospective franchisees and the FTC. The predictions must be made in a separate document containing all bases and assumptions, the number and percentage of franchise outlets known to have at least equaled the predicted record, and the dates on which that record was attained. The document must also contain the following statement in bold-face 12-point type.

CAUTION

These figures are only estimates of what we think you may earn. There is no assurance you'll do as well. If you rely upon our figures, you must accept the risk of not doing so well.

Instead of predicting what prospective franchisees will earn, some franchisors advise them of the sales, income, or profits of existing outlets. That way, franchisors lead the prospects to infer that they will do as well. These statements must also be given in a separate document that contains the following in boldface 12-point type.

CAUTION

Some outlets have (sold) (earned) this amount. There is no assurance you'll do as well. If you reply upon our figures, you must accept the risk of not doing so well.

All such earnings statements must have cover sheets with the following in boldface 12-point type:

INFORMATION FOR PROSPECTIVE FRANCHISEES ABOUT FRANCHISE (SALES) (INCOME) (PROFIT) REQUIRED BY THE FEDERAL TRADE COMMISSION

To protect you, we've required the franchisor to give you this information. *We haven't checked it and don't know if it's correct.* Study these facts and figures carefully. If possible, show them to someone who can advise you, like a lawyer or an accountant. Then take your time and think it over.

If you find anything you think may be wrong or anything important that's been left out, let us know about it. It may be against the law.

There may also be laws on franchising in your state. Ask your state agencies about them.

**Federal Trade Commission
Washington, D.C.**

Violations of the Rule

Franchisors who violate the FTC rule are subject to civil fines of up to $10,000. The FTC may also bring actions for damages on behalf of franchisees in federal district court. The FTC's formidable enforcement powers are illustrated by its first enforcement action under the rule. H. N. Singer, Inc., promised investors in Hot Box Products frozen pizza distributorships "$100,000 per Year and More." Singer also promised to secure retail accounts such as bowling alleys and bars in advance. There was no reasonable basis for the earnings claim. Furthermore, the promised accounts never materialized.

The FTC brought an administrative enforcement action against Singer. It also obtained a preliminary injunction in federal district court prohibiting Singer from disposing of any of its property without court approval. The order also prohibited banks, savings and loan associations, and brokerage houses from allowing Singer to make withdrawals from its accounts. The Ninth Circuit Court of Appeals upheld the order.[3]

SELECTING FRANCHISEES—GROUP BOYCOTT ISSUES

Generally a franchisor may choose to accept or decline an application for a franchise. The franchisor's rejection of an applicant is usually a lawful unilateral refusal to deal. Franchisors, like all other businesses, have the right to choose the parties with whom they will deal. However, if the franchisor consults other franchisees before rejecting an applicant, a court may infer the existence of a group boycott. Group boycotts are per se violations of section 1 of the Sherman Act. The issue of franchisor–franchisee consultation is considered in the following case.

 **Borger v. Yamaha International Corp.**

625 F.2d 390 (2d Cir. 1980)

Yamaha (appellant) imports audio products such as amplifiers, turntables, speakers and tape decks into the United States. It distributes its products through franchised retailers.

Borger (appellee) operated hardware and appliance stores in Manhattan. Borger applied for a Yamaha franchise, and preliminary discussions were favorable. However, before proceeding further, Yamaha consulted

---

[3] *FTC v. H. N. Singer, Inc.*, 668 F.2d 1107 (9th Cir. 1982).

with its two existing Manhattan franchisees: Harmony and Harvey. The two franchisees did not consult with each other. However, they each expressed concern to Yamaha that there was a shortage of Yamaha products and that granting a third franchise would make it more difficult for them to obtain the quantity of Yamaha products they needed. Yamaha then rejected Borger's application.

Borger sued Yamaha, claiming that Yamaha's action was the result of a group boycott. The trial court held that Yamaha's rejection of Borger was not per se illegal. However, the jury found Yamaha's action to have unreasonably restrained trade. The trial court awarded Borger $454,158 in damages and $125,000 in attorney fees. The Second Circuit Court of Appeals reversed.

Van Graafeiland, Circuit Judge

Because the court had instructed the jury that there was no evidence to support a finding of horizontal combination or contract, the question for the jury was whether Yamaha had entered into a vertical combination with one or both of the dealers with whom it consulted prior to rejecting Borger's application.

* * * * *

The trial court charged that before the jury could find the existence of a combination or contract, it had to find that one or both of the dealers canvassed by Yamaha requested that a dealership not be granted to Borger's and that Yamaha, either expressly or impliedly, agreed with one or both not to take on Borger's as a dealer. . . .

So far as it went, this was a correct statement of the law. The question is whether it went far enough. Where, as here, the evidence of a vertical combination is largely inferential, it is important that a jury understand how such an agreement comes into being. In fairness to Yamaha, the jury should have been instructed that it was not improper for Yamaha to consult with its dealers and that those consultations, standing alone, would not establish the existence

of a combination or agreement under the Sherman Act.

Finding no evidence of horizontal combination, group boycott, nor "anything like price fixing," the trial court concluded correctly that the rule of reason standard applied. . . . The Court instructed the jury in part that "[i]f Borger's was in all respects qualified to be a Yamaha dealer and the sole purpose of Yamaha was to protect Harmony or Harvey, or both, from competition, that would be an unreasonable purpose and that would render any agreement of the kind we are talking about an unreasonable restraint of trade within the doctrine of the Sherman Act." That instruction is similar to the one held erroneous in *Oreck Corp. v. Whirlpool Corp.* and is equally erroneous.

In *Oreck*, plaintiff, a distributor of vacuum cleaners, alleged that Whirlpool had refused to renew its distributorship agreement at the behest of Sears, Roebuck & Co., which distributed Whirlpool cleaners under the Kenmore label. Oreck's termination left Sears as the sole distributor of Whirlpool cleaners in the United States and Canada, and Oreck contended that the reason for the termination was Sears's desire to end competition from Oreck. The trial court in that case instructed the jury to find the defendant liable if it found an agreement between Whirlpool and Sears for the purpose of excluding Oreck from the market for vacuum cleaners generally or Whirlpool cleaners in particular. [T]his Court reversed. . . .

Oreck followed *Continental T.V. Inc. v. GTE Sylvania Inc.,* which held that vertical restrictions aimed at intrabrand competition do not necessarily have an adverse effect on interbrand competition, described by the Court as the "primary concern of antitrust law." In the instant case, the jury was instructed to find Yamaha liable solely on the basis of a purpose to restrict intrabrand competition, without any finding of either a purpose or effect related to interbrand competition. This was a reversible error.

Although the district court found no evidence of "anything like price fixing," . . . he charged, nonetheless, that if Yamaha's sole purpose was to protect the dealers from price competition or discounting, this would be an unreasonable and unlawful purpose. It is undisputed that Borger's had decided in 1975 to move out of the discounting business, and the very reason it sought a Yamaha franchise for its new store was to secure a limited distribution line which did not require cut-rate discounting. There is no evidence that Yamaha exerted any pressure upon Borger's to reach this already made decision. This is hardly the stuff upon which an illegal price-maintenance finding can be based.

CASE QUESTIONS

1. What is a horizontal group boycott? Was it present in this case? Explain.

2. What is a vertical group boycott? Was it present in this case? Explain.

3. Are horizontal and vertical group boycotts treated in the same manner under the Sherman Act? Explain.

4. How did the trial court instruct the jury concerning the reasonableness of the restraint? Why was this erroneous?

5. Would the result have been different if Yamaha had rejected Borger because the existing franchisees complained that they feared Borger would undercut their prices? Why or why not?

CONTROLLING FRANCHISEE INVENTORY— EXCLUSIVE DEALING PROBLEMS

Exclusive dealing contracts obligate the franchisee to deal only in products of the franchisor. These contracts may be useful for both parties. The contracts assure the franchisee of a steady supply of goods meeting the franchisor's quality control standards. They also assure the franchisor of uniformity throughout the franchise. These advantages, however, do not necessarily insulate a franchisor-franchisee exclusive dealing contract from antitrust attack.

Exclusive dealing contracts that tend to substantially lessen competition or create a monopoly violate section 3 of the Clayton Act. Even where the contract does not have an immediate anticompetitive effect, It may violate section 5 of the FTC Act. For example, in *FTC v. Brown Shoe Co.*, Brown, the second largest shoe manufacturer in the country, entered into franchise agreements with 650 independent retailers. Brown agreed to provide franchisees with services that it did not make available to other retailers. The services included architectural plans, costly merchandising records, assistance from a Brown field representative, and the right to participate in group insurance at rates lower than would have been available to the franchisees individually. In return, each franchisee promised to "[c]oncentrate my business within the grades and price lines of shoes representing Brown Shoe Company Franchises of the Brown Division and will have no lines conflicting with Brown Division Brands of the Brown Shoe Company."

The FTC found that the franchise program "effectively foreclosed Brown's competitors from selling to a substantial number of retail shoe dealers." The commission did not find that the franchise program tended to substantially lessen competition. However, the commission held that the program was an unfair method of competition and violated section 5 of the FTC Act.

The Supreme Court agreed. It emphasized Brown's size and stated that the franchise program "obviously conflicts with the central policy of. . . . §3 of the Clayton Act." It concluded that the FTC could thwart anticompetitive restraints before they developed into full-blown Clayton Act violations.[4]

Courts and the FTC have generally permitted franchisors to require franchisees to stock a representative cross section of the franchisor's products in quantities sufficient to meet demand. This requirement serves the franchisor's legitimate interest in marketing its products without unduly restricting franchisee choice. Thus, a Chevrolet dealer can be required to keep a reasonable quantity of General Motors replacement parts on hand. This enables GM to advertise that its parts are available from the local Chevrolet dealer while allowing the dealer to offer competing brands.

CONTROLLING FRANCHISEE QUALITY—TYING PROBLEMS

As discussed in chapter 10, tie-ins may violate section 3 of the Clayton Act and section 1 of the Sherman Act. Franchisors cannot tie together in packages goods that are not generally sold together unless they also make the goods available separately.

Most tie-in liability for franchisors arises under section 1 of the Sherman Act. At one time many franchisors required their franchisees to pur-

---

[4] 384 U.S. 316 (1966).

chase certain goods only from them. This requirement assured the franchisor of a market for its products and of a uniform quality at all outlets. The franchisor's goodwill hinges on this uniformity. The reputation associated with the trademark is the heart of the franchisor's marketing scheme. If a local outlet is substandard, the negative repercussions will be felt by all franchisees.

Although such purchasing requirements were the subject of several previous challenges, the most significant development in the law was the decision of the Ninth Circuit Court of Appeals in *Siegel v. Chicken Delight, Inc.*[5] The franchisees of Chicken Delight, a fast-food franchisor, paid no franchise fees or royalties but were required to purchase their cookers, fryers, packaging supplies, and coating mixes from it. The prices charged by Chicken Delight for these items were higher than those charged for comparable items by other potential suppliers. Siegel, a disenchanted franchisee, sued, alleging that the items were illegally tied to the license to use the Chicken Delight trademark.

A trademark license is not a tangible commodity. Consequently, section 3 of the Clayton Act did not apply. Siegel therefore alleged that Chicken Delight's purchasing requirement was per se unreasonable in violation of section 1 of the Sherman Act. A per se illegal tie-in under section 1 must meet three conditions: two distinct products, sufficient power in the tying product to enforce the tie-in, and a substantial amount of commerce affected.

It was agreed that the amount of commerce affected was substantial. The court then considered whether there were two separate products. It held that the trademark license was a separate product, distinct from the items allegedly tied to it. Finally, the court considered Chicken Delight's economic power. It compared the trademark to a good protected by patent or copyright. It reasoned that because trademark protection conferred a legal monopoly to determine who might use the mark, sufficient economic power to enforce the tie would be presumed as a matter of law. The court rejected Chicken Delight's contention that the tie-in was necessary for quality control. It noted that by providing specifications, the franchisor could maintain uniform quality without severely restraining competition.

The *Chicken Delight* case raised numerous questions of antitrust policy which have not been definitively resolved by the Supreme Court or Congress. Should a trademark license be considered a tying product separate from the items that the franchisee is required to purchase? Would the answer be the same if Chicken Delight merely requires its franchisees to purchase their chicken from it as it would be if Chicken Delight extended the requirement to paper plates and napkins? In the following case, the Ninth Circuit elaborated on its *Chicken Delight* decision.

---

[5] 448 F.2d 43 (9th Cir. 1971).

Krehl v. Baskin–Robbins Ice Cream Co.

664 F.2d 1348 (9th Cir. 1982)

Krehl and other franchises (appellants) sued Baskin–Robbins (appellee, referred to as BRICO) for allegedly violating section 1 of the Sherman Act. BRICO required all franchisees to sell only Baskin–Robbins ice cream products, which they were required to purchase from BRICO or a BRICO-licensed area franchisor. The franchisees claimed this requirement was an illegal tie-in and a per se violation of section 1 of the Sherman Act. The trial court disagreed and entered judgment for BRICO. The Ninth Circuit Court of Appeals affirmed.

Ely, Circuit Judge

It is well settled that there can be no unlawful tying arrangement absent proof that there are, in fact, two separate products, the sale of one (i.e., the tying product) being conditioned upon the purchase of the other (i.e., the tied product). Franchisees argue that Baskin–Robbins' policy of conditioning the grant of a franchise upon the purchase of ice cream exclusively from Baskin–Robbins constitutes an unlawful tying arrangement. According to franchisees, the tying product is the Baskin–Robbins trademark and the tied product is the ice cream they are compelled to purchase.

*   *   *   *   *

In support of their tie-in claim, franchisees rely heavily on *Siegel v. Chicken Delight, Inc.*. They contend that *Chicken Delight* established, as a matter of law, that a trademark is invariably a separate item whenever the product it represents is distributed through a franchise system. A careful reading of *Chicken Delight*, however, precludes such an interpretation and discloses that it stands only for the unremarkable proposition that, under certain circumstances, a trademark may be sufficiently unrelated to the alleged tied product to warrant treatment as a separate item.

In *Chicken Delight*, we were confronted with a situation where the franchisor conditioned the grant of a franchise on the purchase of a catalogue of miscellaneous items used in the franchised business. These products were neither manufactured by the franchisor nor were they of a special design uniquely suited to the franchised business. Rather, they were commonplace paper products and packaging goods, readily available in the competitive market place. In evaluating this arrangement, we stated that, "in determining whether the [trademark] . . . and the remaining . . . items . . . are to be regarded as distinct items . . . consideration must be given to the function of trademarks." Because the function of the trademark in *Chicken Delight* was merely to identify a distinctive business format, we found the nexus between the trademark and the tied products to be sufficiently remote to warrant treating them as separate products.

A determination of whether a trademark may appropriately be regarded as a separate product requires an inquiry into the relationship between the trademark and the products allegedly tied to its sale. In evaluating this relationship, consideration must be given to the type of franchising system involved. In *Chicken Delight,* we distinguished between two kinds of franchising systems: 1) the business format system and 2) the distribution system. A business format franchise system is usually created merely to conduct business under a common trade name. The franchise outlet itself is generally responsible for the production and preparation of the system's end product. The franchisor merely provides the trademark and, in some cases, supplies used in operating the franchised outlet and producing the system's products. Under such a system, there is generally only a remote connection between the trademark and the products the franchisees are compelled to purchase. This is true because consumers have no reason to associate with the trademark, those component goods used either in the operation of the franchised store or in the manufacture of the end product. "Under such a type of franchise, the trademark simply reflects the goodwill and quality standards of the enterprise it identifies. As long as . . . franchisees [live] up to those quality standards . . . neither the protection afforded the trademark by law nor the value of the trademark . . . depends upon the source of the components."

Where, as in *Chicken Delight,* the tied products are commonplace articles, the franchisor can easily maintain its quality standards through other means less intrusive upon the competition. Accordingly, the coerced purchase of these items amounts to little more than an effort to impede competition on the merits in the market for the tied products.

Where a distribution type system, such as that employed by Baskin–Robbins, is involved, significantly different considerations are presented. Under the distribution type system, the franchised outlets serve merely as conduits through which the trademarked goods of the franchisor flow to the ultimate consumer. These goods are generally manufactured by the franchisor or, as in the present case, by its licensees according to detailed specifications. In this context, the trademark serves a different function. Instead of identifying a business format, the trademark in a distribution franchise system serves merely as a representation of the end product marketed by the system. "It is to the system and the *end product* that the public looks with the confidence that the established goodwill has created." Consequently, sale of substandard products under the mark would dissipate this goodwill and reduce the value of the trademark. The desirability of the trademark is therefore utterly dependent upon the perceived quality of the product it represents. Because the prohibition of tying arrangements is designed to strike solely at the use of a dominant *desired* product to compel the purchase of a second *undesired* commodity, the tie-in doctrine can have no application where the trademark serves only to identify the alleged tied product. The desirability of the trademark and the quality of the product it represents are so inextricably interrelated in the mind of the consumer as to preclude any finding that the trademark is a separate item for tie-in purposes.

In the case at bar, the District Court found that the Baskin–Robbins trademark merely served to identify the ice cream products distributed by the franchise system. Based on our review of the record, we cannot say that this finding is clearly erroneous. Accordingly, we conclude that the District Court did not err in ruling that the Baskin–Robbins trademark lacked sufficient independent existence apart from the ice cream products allegedly tied to its sale to justify a finding of an unlawful tying arrangement.

CASE QUESTIONS

1. Describe the differences between a business format system and a distribution system of franchising.

2. How did this case differ from *Chicken Delight*?

3. If BRICO had required all of its franchisees to buy their napkins and plastic utensils from BRICO, would the result have been different? Why or why not?

4. If BRICO had obtained its ice cream from another manufacturer and had prohibited its franchisees from dealing directly with the other manufacturer, would the result have been different? Why or why not?

If the franchise trademark license is found to be a separate product from goods the franchisee is required to purchase, the inquiry does not end. For a tie-in to exist, the franchisor must have sufficient economic power in the trademark to enforce the tie.

Some courts, including the Ninth Circuit, view the trademark as analogous to the patent or copyright because it also confers a legal monopoly. Without the consent of the franchisor, the franchisee may not use the trademark or operate the franchise. According to this view, in all instances the franchisee will be forced to buy the required items from the franchisor.

Other courts believe the trademark is different from the patent and copyright. Patents and copyrights protect the product itself, guaranteeing that it is unique. The trademark, in contrast, only protects the symbol affixed to the product. The legally unique name, these courts reason, does not by itself justify a presumption of economic power. These courts require a showing that the franchisor has the power to raise prices or impose burdensome terms on an appreciable number of franchisees. It is usually not difficult to make such a showing. Most franchisees enter the franchise relationship because of their desire to benefit from the success and goodwill associated with the franchise name. Thus the practical effect of the two views on the presumption of economic power is more apparent than real.

The courts and the FTC have recognized that a tie-in may be necessary where the franchisor lacks less restrictive means to effectuate its quality control program. For example, a tie-in may be justified where specifications would be so detailed and cumbersome that they cannot be practicably supplied. This justification is most likely to be accepted for products whose technology has been developed recently or is changing rapidly. As the technology develops further, however, the franchisor will have to require the franchisee to follow specifications.

A second justification that has been accepted for franchise tie-ins is that specifications are impossible because the quality control is subjective. For example, the FTC allowed a restaurant franchisor to tie its coffee to the franchise license because it was impossible to specify a formula for the appropriate blend of coffee beans. The blend depended upon the quality of the different types of beans and the appropriate blend could only be obtained by tasting the coffee.[6]

Although franchisors are prohibited from requiring their franchisees to purchase items from them, they are not prohibited from supplying their franchisees with items pursuant to voluntary contracts. The franchisee may not voluntarily agree to purchase from the franchisor and later attempt to avoid the agreement by alleging a tie-in. In these circumstances courts require franchisees to prove that the franchisor coerced them into purchasing supplies from it.

Franchisors frequently seek to avoid tie-in liability by using specifications or authorized suppliers. Unreasonable specifications, however, may result in franchisor liability under section 1 of the Sherman Act, for they are not justified by quality control considerations. If specifications are reasonably related to quality control, the franchisor will not be liable even if it should turn out that only the franchisor is capable of meeting them in a manner sufficiently efficient to supply the franchisees. There is no requirement that other suppliers be available. What is required is that other suppliers be given an opportunity to compete for the franchisees' business.

If the franchisor wishes, it may require its franchisees to purchase only from authorized suppliers. However, if the franchisor or a company affiliated with it is one of the authorized suppliers, it must be careful to avoid pressuring its franchisees to buy from it. Courts tend to uphold franchisor-authorized supplier plans where the franchisor sets forth reasonable objective criteria which authorized suppliers must meet and is willing to authorize any supplier able to meet those criteria. The number of authorized suppliers is another relevant factor. The following case presents one major fast-food franchisor's plans for authorized suppliers.

Kentucky Fried Chicken Corp. v. Diversified Container Corp.

549 F.2d 368 (5th Cir. 1977)

Kentucky Fried Chicken Corporation, a franchisor of fast-food restaurants, included in its franchise agreements a clause requiring its franchisees to purchase all of their napkins, towelettes, plastic eating utensils, and carryout chicken boxes from either Kentucky Fried or an approved supplier. Nine independent suppliers received Kentucky Fried's approval. No

---

[6] Chock Full o' Nuts, [1973–1976 Transfer Binder] Trade Reg. Rep. [CCH] ¶20,441.

supplier that requested approval had ever been turned down. The approved suppliers were required to affix the Kentucky Fried "finger lickin' good" trademark to all materials. Diversified never sought Kentucky Fried's approval, but began producing boxes, napkins, towelettes, and utensils with Kentucky Fried's trademark affixed to them.

Kentucky Fried sued Diversified for trademark infringement. Diversified filed a counterclaim alleging that the franchise agreements were illegal tie-ins in violation of section 1 of the Sherman Act. The district court rendered judgment in favor of Kentucky Fried, and Diversified appealed. Only the portion of the opinion dealing with the antitrust issue is reproduced.

Goldberg, Circuit Judge

This case presents us with something mundane, something novel, and something bizarre. The mundane includes commercial law issues now well delimited by precedent. The novel aspects of the case center on intriguing and difficult interrelationships between trademark and antitrust concepts. And the bizarre element is the facially implausible—some might say unappetizing—contention that the man whose chicken is "finger-lickin' good" has unclean hands.

* * * * *

Container's antitrust counterclaim forces us to confront three conclusions: (1) that Kentucky Fried's conduct constitutes a tie-in and thus a *per se* antitrust violation, (2) that if Kentucky Fried's approved source requirement is not a tie it should nonetheless be held to constitute a new category of *per se* offense, and (3) that in any event Kentucky Fried's arrangement contravenes the rule of reason. We reject each contention of the triad.

Container's primary contention is that Kentucky Fried has established a tying arrangement in violation of §1 of the Sherman Act. . . .

* * * * *

A plaintiff must show that the challenged arrangement is in fact a tie; that two separate products are involved and that, in addition to complying with the literal terms of the imprecise definition, the seller's behavior follows the general pattern found unacceptable in the earlier tying cases. To measure an arrangement against that general pattern we must take into account the principal evil of tie-ins: they may foreclose the tying party's competitors from a segment of the tied product market, and they may deprive the tie's victims, of the advantages of shopping around.

The problem in the case at bar is to determine whether Kentucky Fried's arrangement is in fact a tie—i.e., whether its behavior follows the general pattern found unacceptable in earlier tying cases. We begin with an analysis of tying in the context of franchise operations. The issue has taken on considerable significance in recent years; franchising has increased while tying structures have grown tighter.

In the commonly recurring situation, the tying product is the franchise itself, and

CONTROLLING FRANCHISEE QUALITY

the tied products may be such things as the equipment the franchisees will use to conduct the business, the ingredients of the goods that the franchisee will ultimately sell to consumers, or the supplies the franchisee will distribute to the public in connection with the main product. [A] franchisor who requires franchisees to use trademarked supplies does not escape the impact of tying principles to any extent. The franchisor's right to prevent others from selling supplies bearing its trademarks must yield to the antitrust laws' command to open the tied market to competitors.

*   *   *   *   *

Despite this relatively low threshold for invoking the *per se* doctrine, however, the franchisor retains a potentially significant defense—one designed to accommodate the franchisor's interests in the franchisee's performance. The franchisor is free to demonstrate that the tie constitutes a necessary device for controlling the quality of the end product sold to the consuming public. Product protection through tying can have a legal legitimacy. As part of this defense, however, the franchisor must establish that the tie constitutes the method of maintaining quality that imposes the least burden on commerce. . . .

With this background we turn to Container's claim that Kentucky Fried's arrangement constitutes a tie. . . .

The difference between this arrangement and a traditional tie is readily apparent. Here the franchise agreement does not require franchisees to take the "tied" product (supplies) from Kentucky Fried; they can take their entire requirements from other sources.

*   *   *   *   *

We conclude that this arrangement simply does not constitute a tie. A monolithic tie may bring down the wrath of *per se* guilt, but not every use of string tangles with the antitrust laws. . . .

That the arrangement is not a tie does not, of course, prevent *per se* treatment; tying is not the only *per se* antitrust violation. . . . We are not prepared to say, however, that approved-source requirements are so universally devoid of redeeming virtue that they warrant *per se* treatment. [T]ies themselves are not as completely objectionable in the franchise context as in the contexts in which tying law originally developed. Moreover, franchise arrangements may sometimes create better competitive markets than would otherwise exist. A system under which an independent franchisee's choices are somewhat restricted may nevertheless prove superior to a system in which retail outlets are owned by the national firm. If, for example, Kentucky Fried had chosen not to franchise local outlets but rather to own them outright, the antitrust laws would leave it relatively free to supply the individual stores solely through the national office. Competition at the national level for Kentucky Fried's supplies business would continue, just as competition to sell Kentucky Fried the supplies it will in turn sell to franchisees is currently unencumbered. But competition at the local level would be as nonexistent under a system of national ownership rather than franchising. We can safely assume, however, that for the most part the application of tying principles to franchise operations will not affect a business's decision whether to engage in franchising.

When we turn from tying to approved-source requirements, however, the situation is somewhat different. We must encourage business ingenuity so long as it is not competitively stifling. We deal here not with tie-ins, whose adverse effects and lack of redeeming virtue are by now quite familiar, but instead with approved-source requirements. When we become more familiar with large-scale franchising and with approved-source requirements, we may discern that the latter are wholly unnecessary to the former. It will be time enough, however, to declare such requirements to be *per se* violations when that day arrives.

*   *   *   *   *

Our conclusion is that Kentucky Fried has not committed a *per se* antitrust violation: it has not established a de facto tie through coercive tactics, and its approved-source provision is not a *per se* violation. Container's attack on Kentucky Fried's arrangement is not yet exhausted, however, for the rule of reason remains. An antitrust claimant who unsuccessfully seeks to establish a *per se* violation may nonetheless prevail by showing that its adversary's conduct unreasonably restrains competition. The burden of proving unreasonable effects rests with the antitrust plaintiff.

In the case at bar Container has failed to carry this burden. First, Container has not demonstrated that Kentucky Fried's arrangement adversely affects competition. Indeed, container has presented no evidence at all of the actual competitive effect of Kentucky Fried's system. Antitrust claims need not be established by euclidean proof, but they cannot be merely fantasized. For all that appears in this record, competition among suppliers of the franchisees is as open and vigorous as it would be under a system in which Kentucky Fried exerted no control at all over franchisees. Kentucky Fried has excluded not a single supplier from the market; it has narrowed the negotiations between franchisees and their suppliers in not a single respect. The approved-source provision is hardly a boon to competition, but on this record we can only conclude that this approved-source requirement is as innocuous as any could be. Unless we were willing to condemn all ap-

proved-source requirements, we could not condemn this one. We have refused, however, to make such provisions *per se* violations, and Container's failure to adduce evidence of this provision's adverse impact therefore defeats its claim.

*   *   *   *   *

Here, Kentucky Fried seeks to justify its approved-source requirement as a device for controlling quality. Kentucky Fried's argument possesses a substantial measure of intuitive appeal. A customer dissatisfied with one Kentucky Fried outlet is unlikely to limit his or her adverse reaction to the particular outlet; instead, the adverse reaction will likely be directed to all Kentucky Fried stores. The quality of a franchisee's product thus undoubtedly affects Kentucky Fried's reputation and its future success. Moreover, this phenomenon is not limited to the quality of the chicken itself. Finger-lickin' good chicken alone does not a satisfied customer make. Kentucky Fried has a legitimate interest in whether cartons are so thin that the grease leaks through or heat readily escapes, in whether the packet of utensils given a carry-out customer contains everything it should and in whether the towelette contains a liquid that will adequately perform the Herculean task of removing Augean refuse from the customer's face and hands.

We therefore conclude that Container has not prevailed on its rule-of-reason contention, both because it has failed to demonstrate adverse competitive impacts and because it has failed to show that Kentucky Fried's system is not a reasonable method for achieving quality control. The district court correctly held for Kentucky Fried with respect to Container's antitrust counterclaim. This knot was not conceived as a loophole in our antitrust statutes.

CASE QUESTIONS

1. How did Kentucky Fried's program differ from a tie-in?

2. What policy considerations led the court to reject Container's argument that approved-source requirements be condemned as per se illegal?

3. What factors led the court to conclude that Kentucky Fried's approved-source requirement did not unreasonably restrain trade?

4. Assume that Kentucky Fried decided not to approve more than 15 independent suppliers. It justified this limitation on the ground that it would be too costly for Kentucky Fried to inspect more than 15 operations to insure that they were complying with its requirements. If Container were rejected as an approved supplier solely on the ground that it would be the 16th such supplier could it successfully sue Kentucky Fried? Explain.

5. Would it be reasonable to impose an approved-supplier requirement for goods and services the public does not receive directly, such as the services provided by bookkeeping or employment agencies? Explain.

COVENANTS NOT TO COMPETE

Many franchisors try to ensure loyalty by prohibiting franchisees from operating competing enterprises. Franchisee covenants not to compete, like all other contract provisions, violate the Sherman Act if they unreasonably restrain trade. The purpose and effect of these covenants are the most important factors to be considered. The typical franchisor may have several legitimate business purposes to justify a franchisee's covenant not to compete.

Where a covenant not to compete is restricted to the area immediately surrounding the city or town of the franchisee's business, the covenant may be justified on the ground that it insures that the franchisee's primary efforts will be devoted to the franchised outlet. The covenant also protects the franchisor against the possibility that the franchisee will use the franchisor's good name to attract customers and then divert those customers to a competing business.

Characteristics of a franchisor's operation may justify more extensive covenants not to compete. For example, Holiday Inns' standard franchise agreement bound its franchisees to avoid operating non-Holiday Inns motels anywhere. The court found this provision by itself to be reasonable because it protected the integrity of the franchisor's Holidex system of nationwide reservations. Were franchisees permitted to operate competing motels even in cities where they did not own Holiday Inns franchises, they could be expected to refer guests to their competing motels rather than to the Holiday Inns in those cities.

Franchise covenants not to compete also insure that information, training, and other services provided by the franchisor will not be used by a franchisee in competition with the franchise. In many cases these covenants may also facilitate exchanges of information and ideas among franchisees.

Even where these or other justifications are present, however, the covenant not to compete may, when combined with other restrictive arrangements, unreasonably restrain trade. For example, although the Holiday Inns' covenant discussed above was justified and reasonable by itself, it was combined with a franchisor policy that singled out specific towns in which all outlets were to be franchisor owned. The court held that this combination amounted to a horizontal territorial division and was consequently per se illegal.[7]

FRANCHISOR–FRANCHISEE COMPETITION

Many franchisors choose, as Holiday Inns did, to own and operate some outlets themselves. In such instances the franchisor stands in both a vertical and horizontal relationship with the franchisees. Dual distribution systems are not in themselves illegal. They do, however, invite legal troubles if the franchisor gives its own outlets treatment more favorable than that afforded its franchisees.

Much of the law on the antitrust implications of dual distribution systems has come from cases involving automobile dealerships. This is due in part to the dealer enterprise plans used by the major automobile manufacturers to finance new dealers. Originally these manufacturers retailed only through independent dealers. In order to penetrate the market further, the manufacturers established the dealer enterprise plans, which enabled dealers to begin operations without large amounts of capital. Under the plans the dealer owns 25 percent of the dealership's common stock, with the manufacturer owning the remaining 75 percent. The manufacturer controls the dealership's board of directors, while the dealer serves as the president and general manager. The dealer uses the dealership's profits to purchase the manufacturer's stock, gradually buying the manufacturer out.

Chrysler Corporation, finding the dealer enterprise plan insufficient, began a dealer contract program. Under this plan Chrysler advanced all of the initial capital and owned all of the stock. The dealer then used the dealership's profits to purchase the stock. When the dealer had purchased 25 percent of the stock, the dealership converted to the dealer enterprise plan.

Under both plans the dealership had several advantages which independent dealerships lack. First, initial capital costs were eliminated. Second, the manufacturer provided operating loss subsidies which enabled the dealer to operate out of a larger, more attractive showroom and to spend more money on advertising. Finally, the manufacturer provided free services to key managerial employees. the following case is one of

---

[7] *American Motors Inns, Inc. v. Holiday Inns, Inc.,* 521 F.2d 1230 (3d Cir. 1975).

several brought by independent dealers alleging that these subsidies violated the Sherman Act.

 **Coleman Motor Co. v. Chrysler Corp.**

525 F.2d 1338 (3d Cir. 1975)

Coleman Motor Co. (plaintiff-appellee), an independent Dodge dealership, brought a private antitrust action against Chrysler Motors Corporation (defendant-appellant). Coleman charged that Chrysler discriminated between its factory and independent dealers "with the intent to destroy independent Dodge dealerships. . . ." A jury found in favor of Coleman. The Third Circuit Court of Appeals remanded the case to the district court for a new trial.

Rosenn, Circuit Judge

It is undisputed that Chrysler financially subsidized factory dealerships. It provided the initial capital for these businesses, thereby eliminating cost of capital. Chrysler also provided significant operating loss subsidies. These funds enabled the factory dealerships to spend significantly greater amounts of money than could Coleman on larger, more attractive showrooms and on advertising.

Chrysler contends that the advertising campaign was intended to increase overall sales of Dodge vehicles in Allegheny County. It is fair to state this increase could have been achieved by spreading advertising loss subsidies over all dealers, both independent and factory. Subsidization of Boulevard Dodge's advertising losses in substantial sums cannot be justified over an eight-year period on the basis that Boulevard Dodge was a new entrant in the Dodge retail market in need of assistance in order to survive—in its first year of operation,

Boulevard Dodge had cornered 39 percent of the Dodge market.

It is also noteworthy that when plaintiff went out of business, one of its close competitors, Boulevard Dodge, decreased its advertising expenditures. . . .

There was some testimony that defendants discriminated in favor of the factory dealerships and against the private dealerships in the release of new automobiles. In 1962, when defendants for the first time marketed a full size car which had wide public acceptance, all the Dodge dealers advertised in advance about the release of the car, but only the factory dealership at Boulevard Dodge received immediate delivery of the car.

There was also evidence that Chrysler paid the salaries of key managerial employees of factory dealerships at various times; that Chrysler paid the salaries of accountants and the two Chrysler board members of factory dealerships; and that Chrysler provided free furniture, tools, and equipment to the factory dealership at Cloverleaf Dodge.

When plaintiff lost its used car lot to the redevelopment authority, it arranged to move to a new location four blocks away. Plaintiff's franchise agreement required it to seek permission from Chrysler, which was refused.

Vernon Staley, former president of Boulevard Dodge, testified that he informed Chrysler's regional manager Harris after several months of operation of his concern for the amount of losses his company was sustaining. Staley stated that Harris told him not to worry: "Just roll those cars out. We will make our money at the front end, and, if you can get this somewhere close to a breakeven we will be satisfied." Staley further testified that when Harris was attempting to engage him for the Dodge franchise, Harris indicated that Chrysler intended to reduce the number of Dodge dealers in Allegheny County from 16 to 11, under their new marketing program.

* * * * *

From this evidence, the jury could reasonably have concluded that defendant combined and conspired with managers of factory dealerships. . . . Although the evidence is weak, the jury could have found further that Chrysler's actions were unfairly competitive and that their effect was to force plaintiff out of business. . . .

Plaintiff's expert, Dr. Rubin E. Slesinger, professor of Economics at Pittsburgh, testified that large infusions of funds to factory dealers, as subsidies to offset losses, and the expenditure for advertising of two to four times the amount spent by independent dealers, and other preferential treatment of factory dealers, would tend to monopolize the Dodge market in Allegheny County. The plain implication of his testimony is that factory dealers would take sales away from independent dealers by these practices.

The jury may also have determined that Chrysler deliberately took advantage of Coleman's financial situation. Plaintiff was in breach of its Direct Dealer Agreement because it had not met its minimum sales requirement between 1962 and 1969, except in 1963. Consequently, Chrysler had the right under the agreement to terminate plaintiff's franchise. Chrysler apparently chose to let plaintiff remain in existence and contribute to overall sales of Dodge vehicles. While plaintiff was losing money, Chrysler was subsiding factory dealer losses. When plaintiff went out of business, Boulevard Dodge lowered its advertising expenses and, after 1971, operated at a profit. Thus, the jury could have concluded that Chrysler had accomplished its purposes of increasing Dodge sales and consolidating retail sales in the hands of several strong Chrysler-controlled dealerships.

The question thus posed is whether the above findings are sufficient to establish an unreasonable restraint of trade under section one of the Sherman Act. The problem is one of restraint *vel non* in intrabrand competition.

* * * * *

While Chrysler's ability to cease doing business with franchisees may generally be restricted only by contractual provisions, the means it chose to accomplish this end here have an anticompetitive effect. If Chrysler had simply ceased doing business with Coleman, Coleman might have been able to seek a franchise from another manufacturer and become an interbrand competitor. However, the continuation of predatory practices for a number of years in the face of Coleman's substantial losses could have so severely damaged Coleman's financial ability that he could not reenter the market as an interbrand competitor. A combination of distributors, which through unfair practices eliminates a competitor and leaves it in such a condition that it lacks the ability to continue business as an inter-brand competitor, has an adverse effect on the marketplace.

CASE QUESTIONS

1. What actions taken by Chrysler allowed the jury to infer a conspiracy to unreasonably restrain trade?

2. Does the case hold that all dealer enterprise plans are illegal? That all subsidies to dealer enterprise dealerships are illegal?

3. Would Chrysler have been liable if it had simply terminated Coleman's dealership in order to benefit Boulevard?

Subsequent court decisions have held that automobile manufacturers may subsidize dealer enterprise and dealer contract dealerships when the purpose of such subsidies is market penetration. This is so, even if the subsidies force independent dealers out of business. However, where the manufacturer's intent is predatory, or where the subsidies effect vertical integration, such subsidies will violate the Sherman Act.

Dealer enterprise and dealer contract dealerships differ from other franchisor-owned outlets. The primary purpose of these dealerships is to finance the initial business costs of future independent dealers. The ultimate goal is for the dealers to independently own and operate the outlets. The more typical franchisor-owned outlet is not designed to be turned over to an independent franchisee. Thus the intent of market penetration is not as easily established in the typical franchise cases as in the cases involving the auto dealer plans. In the typical franchise cases, where more favorable terms are provided to company-owned outlets, a court may infer that the franchisor's motivation is vertical integration.

CUSTOMER AND TERRITORIAL RESTRAINTS

If a franchisor assigns exclusive customers or territories to its franchisees, the restraints are usually considered to be vertical. As seen in chapter 10, vertical territorial restraints are analyzed under the rule of reason.

The restraints must be justified as reasonable or they will violate the Sherman Act. The restraints may be necessary to attract qualified franchisees, to avoid free rider effects where franchisees are expected to provide customer services or expend money on developing a local market, to facilitate quality control, or for similar purposes. The more established the franchisor, the less severe will be the problems posed by free rider effects and the more difficult it will be to justify territorial restraints.

If the franchisor competes with its franchisees, territorial and customer restraints may be either vertical or horizontal. The characterization may be crucial to the restraint's legality. As seen in chapter 10, horizontal divisions of customers or territories are per se unlawful. In the following case, the court considered how to characterize these restraints.

Krehl v. Baskin–Robbins Ice Cream Co.

664 F.2d 1348 (9th Cir. 1982)

This is the same case excerpted on page 454. Baskin–Robbins (appellee, referred to as BRICO) operated under a three-tiered distribution system. BRICO divided the country into six exclusive territories. In each of five territories BRICO licensed independent area franchisors to select franchisees and supply them with ice cream products. In the sixth territory BRICO served as area franchisor.

Krehl and other franchisees (appellants) claimed that BRICO's division of exclusive territories for area franchisors was a per se violation of section 1 of the Sherman Act. The trial court entered judgment for BRICO. The Ninth Circuit Court of Appeals affirmed.

Ely, Circuit Judge

Franchisees contend that the "dual distribution" system used by Baskin–Robbins constitutes an unlawful horizontal market allocation. This contention is premised on BRICO's dual role as both trademark licensor and area franchisor. According to franchisees, BRICO's practice of licensing exclusive territories to other area franchisors while retaining certain areas for itself constitutes a market allocation among competitors. Franchisees further argue that any "dual distribution" system is, in and of itself, a *per se* violation of the antitrust laws. We address the former contention first.

The hallmark of a horizontal market allocation is collusion among competitors

to confer upon each a monopoly in a specific area.

* * * * *

BRICO is neither owned nor controlled by the area franchisors. Unlike the situation in *Topco* . . . , the area franchisors have no voice over BRICO's decisions regarding grants of additional territories. Indeed, the District Court found that at all times the allocation of territory was dictated unilaterally by BRICO. "When a manufacturer acts on its own, *in pursuing its own market strategy*, it is seeking to compete with other manufacturers by imposing what may be defended as reasonable vertical restraints." Accordingly, the District Court concluded that the territorial restrictions imposed by BRICO are vertical in nature and therefore not *per se* illegal.

. . . Because the findings on this issue are not clearly erroneous, we decline to overturn the District Court's determination that franchisees failed to establish their horizontal market allocation claim.

Franchisees also urge us to extend the rule of *per se* illegality to encompass dual distribution systems such as that practiced by Baskin–Robbins.

Neither the Supreme Court nor this court has yet squarely ruled whether dual distribution systems fall within the rule of *per se* illegality.

* * * * *

The test for determining whether the rule of *per se* illegality should be extended to a business practice not heretofore afforded *per se* treatment is "whether the practice facially appears to be one that would always or almost always tend to restrict competition and decrease output . . . or instead one designed to 'increase economic efficiency and render markets more, rather than less, competitive.' " Applying this test to the system at issue here, we conclude that application of the rule of *per se* illegality would be both inappropriate and anti-competitive.

It is evident that were BRICO to abandon its area franchisor responsibilities, the system here would be identical to that involved in *GTE Sylvania*. We do not believe that BRICO's decision to retain these responsibilities in certain areas has any significant effect on competition. Regardless of BRICO's decision, there would still be fourteen areas, each exclusively served by a single manufacturer-franchisor. Only the identity of the franchisor in a given area is affected by BRICO's decision to retain

area franchisor responsibilities in certain territories. . . .

Franchisees have failed to establish here any significant, adverse impact upon either interbrand or intrabrand competition. Regarding intrabrand competition, the District Court found that franchisees failed to show that any area franchisor is capable of servicing the area of another on a sustained basis. Nor did franchisees establish the feasibility of a more extensive licensing program for the manufacture of Baskin–Robbins ice cream products.

Franchisees similarly failed to establish any adverse effect upon interbrand competition. Indeed, it appears that the distribution system at issue here may have actually fostered interbrand competition. Through the exclusive licensing of independent manufacturers, BRICO was able to expand into new grographic markets and promote the wider availability of its products. This expansion allowed BRICO to grow from a small manufacturer serving only local markets into a vigorous competitor with outlets throughout the world.

Moreover, moderate economic thought indicates that the invalidation of a distribution system, absent a showing of anti-competitive effect, may actually retard competition. "Competition is promoted when manufacturers are given wide latitude in establishing their method of distribution and in choosing particular distributors. Judicial deference to the manufacturer's business judgment is grounded in large part on the assumption that the manufacturer's interest in minimum distribution costs will benefit the customer."

Accordingly, we conclude that, in the absence of proof of anti-competitive purpose or effect, dual distribution systems must be evaluated under the traditional rule of reason standard.

CASE QUESTIONS

1. Explain how Baskin–Robbins' dual distribution system operated. Why did it appear to have both horizontal and vertical elements to it?

2. Did the court treat the territorial divisions as horizontal or vertical? Why?

3. Why did the court reject the franchisee's claim that all dual distribution systems are per se illegal?

4. How did the court view the reasonableness of the BRICO system?

PROMOTIONAL CAMPAIGNS—PRICE-FIXING PROBLEMS

As has been seen throughout this section, vertical arrangements such as exclusive territories have received more lenient treatment by courts than have similar arrangements agreed to horizontally. The major exception is price fixing. Vertical price fixing remains illegal per se. In controlling advertising, a franchisor has considerably more leeway where nonprice advertising is involved.

Advertising or promotional requirements that may result in price fixing violate the Sherman Act. Franchisors may run promotional discount programs or similar programs but may not require franchisees to participate. Franchisors have generally recognized this, and their giveaways or discount promotions usually read "at participating dealers." Similarly, a franchisor may suggest prices that a franchisee should charge but cannot legally require the franchisee to charge those prices.

Where the franchisor suggests prices or involvement in promotions it may use persuasion but not coercion to get franchisee adherence to the suggestions. The line between persuasion and coercion is sometimes difficult to draw. Offering incentives for participation on a nondiscriminatory basis is not coercion. Thus, a franchisor that wishes its franchisees to offer trading stamps may also offer to split the cost of those stamps with each participating franchisee.

A significant case is *Hanson v. Shell Oil Co.*[8] Hanson, a Shell franchisee, alleged that Shell was coercing him and other franchisees into lowering prices. Shell maintained a dealer assistance program under which a dealer faced with stiff price competition could request reductions in Shell's wholesale gasoline prices. When Shell granted such requests, it extended the reductions to all Shell dealers in the area. Shell owned and operated two retail outlets in Tucson, Arizona. When it granted dealer assistance requests in Tucson, it frequently also lowered prices at its two retail outlets. Hanson contended that this was an effort by Shell to coerce its franchisees into lowering their retail prices. The court, however, held that these activi-

---

[8] 541 F.2d 1352 (8th Cir. 1976).

ties were persuasion rather than coercion. The court was persuaded by Shell's history of providing dealer assistance regardless of whether the dealer actually lowered prices. The franchisor's strong interest in maintaining the image of the franchise will generally justify reasonable franchisor restrictions on the advertising and promotions of individual franchisees.

The line between reasonable restrictions and franchisor price fixing is often difficult to draw. For example, in *Levine v. McDonald's Corp.*, a franchisee attacked McDonald's policy of prohibiting franchisees from using discount coupons to promote their products.[9] McDonald's allowed franchisees to set their own prices. It also allowed franchisees to give away items, such as free french fries with purchase of a Big Mac. It simply required that franchisees adhere to those prices that they set. McDonald's concern was that coupon discounting conveyed an impression of a cheapened product. The court held that McDonald's was not fixing resale prices but was simply controlling its franchisees' promotional and marketing plans.

TERMINATION OF THE FRANCHISE RELATIONSHIP

A franchisee may choose to terminate the franchise relationship and sell the business to another party. The franchisor's strong interest in protecting its reputation will usually justify a requirement of franchisor approval prior to sale or transfer of the operation. However, the franchisor cannot unreasonably withhold approval.

If the franchisor terminates the relationship or refuses to renew a franchise agreement which has expired, the termination will not violate the antitrust laws unless it has an anticompetitive motivation. Franchisor refusals to renew are usually protected as unilateral refusals to deal. Where a franchisor terminates one franchisee and replaces it with another, there is usually no anticompetitive effect.

Although termination without predatory intent does not violate the Sherman Act, as a practical matter termination often invites antitrust litigation. Most antitrust franchise litigation has resulted from franchisee terminations. A frequent reflex reaction by franchisees to termination is to scrutinize all franchisor policies for antitrust violations. The franchisees then allege that they were terminated because they objected to the violations.

ALTERNATIVE APPROACHES

This chapter has explored the application of various provisions of the antitrust laws to franchising. Many of the alternative approaches explored

---

[9] 1983–1 Trade Cas. (CCH) para. 65,270 (D. Ariz. 1982).

in the four preceeding chapters might be applied to franchising. For example, chapter five discussed the British Restrictive Trade Practices Act. The British law does not categorize restraints as per se illegal. Instead, it requires that certain restrictive agreements be registered and that they be justified if challenged. Application of this approach to franchising would require franchisors to justify the need for and effects of tie-ins, territorial restraints, pricing and promotional campaigns and similar policies regardless of whether they are classified as per se restraints.

Similarly, the German approach to price discrimination, discussed in chapter seven, might be applied to franchising. This approach would cover franchisor discrimination in all terms against franchisees who are dependent upon them. It would also cover franchisor refusals to deal with and terminations of franchisees. In all instances franchisors would be required to justify their actions.

These alternative approaches should be evaluated in the context of two potentially conflicting trends in American regulation of franchising. One concern expressed by many courts and regulatory agencies is to protect the franchisee. Many franchisees are first-time investors attracted to franchises by the prospect of owning their own businesses. Many have lost their life's savings to promises of profits that never materialized. Those who succeed may still find themselves at the mercy of the franchisor who retains the power to terminate their franchises. Regulations such as the FTC's franchise rule and court decisions such as *Chicken Delight* seek to protect franchisees from fraudulent practices and allow them considerable freedom to act.

A second and potentially conflicting concern is to allow the franchisor sufficient control to insure uniform quality and appearance. Franchisors that are unable to retain sufficient control over their franchisees' operations may vertically integrate, thereby reducing competition. Some have suggested that overregulation could destroy the benefits derived from franchising. This second concern is reflected in court decisions such as *GTE Sylvania* and *Baskin–Robbins*. One thing is certain. As franchising continues to expand, it will become increasingly difficult to strike the proper balance between the two concerns.

CHAPTER PROBLEMS

1. A franchisor of hardware stores wishes to use a table that shows potential franchisees what the investor's gross profits will be if a particular number of items are sold in a given period of time from certain retail locations. What liability, if any, might result from the use of the chart? What must it do to avoid liability?

2. A manufacturer and retailer of radios and other electronic consumer goods entered into an agreement with an individual to manage one of its stores. The manufacturer supplied the inventory, determined the merchandising policies, and retained title to the goods. The manufacturer set the prices for all goods sold. The individual received a percentage of the store's profits and controlled day-to-day managerial decisions, including hiring and firing. The manufacturer never gave the individual a disclosure statement. Has it violated the FTC or Sherman acts? Explain.

3. A franchisor of temporary help agencies restricts the location and territories of its franchisees. It also requires its franchisees to comply with the franchisor's operating manual and to attend annual training sessions. The manual and training sessions cost $1,000. What antitrust and FTC problems might this franchisor face?

4. An automobile manufacturer requires its dealers to obtain replacement parts from the manufacturer when performing warranty work on cars. The dealer is paid by the manufacturer for doing the warranty repairs. Does this exclusive dealing requirement violate section 3 of the Clayton Act? Explain.

5. McDonald's principal business is franchising limited-menu fast-food restaurants. McDonald's develops new restaurants according to master plans that use demographic data to evaluate potential sites. The most favorable sites are selected, and development of an area is planned three years ahead. The land is acquired, the building is constructed, and a franchisee is approved. The franchisee pays a franchise fee and a periodic royalty and is required to lease the real estate from McDonald's at a rental of 8½ percent of gross sales. The franchise and lease both run for 20 years, and termination of one terminates the other. Neither is available separately. Does McDonald's compulsory lease violate the Sherman or Clayton acts? Explain.

6. An oil company has numerous retail franchisees who sell gasoline and maintain and service cars. The franchisor has been losing money because its volume of sales has been low. It has decided to change its method of retailing by eliminating maintenance and service operations and restricting overall operations to retail sales of gasoline. The reduced overhead expenses will be passed on to the consumer in the form of price reductions. If the franchisor terminates all of its franchisees for this purpose, will it violate the Sherman Act? Explain.

7. Would your answer to question 6 differ if the franchisor terminates franchisees who do not agree to convert to gasoline only? Explain.

8. Weight Watchers International is a franchisor of weight reducing facilities. It requires its franchisees to charge each member a registration fee upon enrollment, a fee for each class attended, and a missed class fee or a new registration fee if a member stops attending and later seeks to rejoin. Each franchisee is free to determine the amount of these fees and to offer discounts. Franchisees, however, may not offer prepayment plans under which a member could receive a discount by paying for a number of meetings in advance. Do these restrictions violate the Sherman Act? Explain.

9. Nissan–Japan manufactures Datsun automobiles. Nissan–U.S.A., a wholly-owned subsidiary of Nissan–Japan, distributes and markets Datsuns in the U.S. Nissan–U.S.A. licenses Datsun franchises. Each time a franchisee buys a new Datsun car for resale, it must pay Nissan–U.S.A. a fee that is contributed to a cooperative advertising fund. Nissan–U.S.A. contributes an identical amount to the fund. Nissan–U.S.A. controls the fund and uses it to reimburse franchisees for advertising expenditures. To be reimbursed, the franchisee must advertise new Datsuns, name the manufacturer's suggested retail price or not state any price, and avoid stating or implying that one Datsun dealer is in a better position to sell a new car than another dealer. Franchisees may use other advertisements but must do so at their own expense. Does the cooperative advertising plan violate the Sherman Act? Explain.

10. A franchisor's basic franchise agreement contains a resale price-fixing clause. The franchisor has never enforced the clause, and most franchisees openly ignore it. One of the most aggressive franchisees has been cutting prices severely and misrepresenting the product in its advertising. The franchisee has been assigned to handle several potentially major accounts, and has neglected them. Can the franchisor terminate the franchisee without incurring antitrust liability? Explain.

PART PROBLEMS

1. You are an executive with a major automobile manufacturer. The manufacturer sells its vehicles at wholesale to its dealers around the country. The manufacturer also sells vehicles directly to large fleet buyers—mostly rental car companies. The rental car companies use the cars for one to three years and then sell them as used cars to consumers. The rental car companies purchase in large volume and consequently have much greater bargaining power than individual dealers. They are able to obtain prices averaging 20 percent below the wholesale price to dealers.

The manufacturer relies on dealers to handle paper work and delivery of cars to the fleet buyers. The dealers are paid a processing fee for this service. Under the dealer's standard agreement, each dealer is obligated to process the fleet transactions upon the manufacturer's request. In practice many dealers refuse to handle these transactions and the manufacturer does not enforce the obligation. Instead the manufacturer places the transactions with those dealers willing to handle them.

There is intense retail competition among dealers. Although the manufacturer sets a "sticker" retail price for each vehicle, very few vehicles are sold at that price. A large number of dealers compete by offering deep discounts. These dealers make very little money on each car and depend on a high volume of sales to make a profit. Many of these dealers have refused to process fleet sales because the processing fee does not allow them to make a profit.

Recently, many of the high volume-low mark up dealers have complained about the fleet sales. Their complaints are twofold. First, they claim that the processing fee is too low. Second, they claim that because of the price break, the fleet buyers are able to sell their used cars below the prices charged by dealers for comparable used cars. They have asked the manufacturer to charge the fleet buyers the same price as it charges the dealers and pass the increase along to the dealers in the form of a higher processing fee.

Several other dealers who do not discount very deeply have also complained that many deep discounters do not handle their fair share of fleet accounts. They have asked the manufacturer to either uniformly enforce the obligation to process fleet accounts or to reward those dealers that process the accounts with favored treatment in filling their orders, etc.

The rash of complaints has led to your assignment. Evaluate the company's distribution system for dealers and fleet accounts. Consider the legality of the current system and the legality of agreeing to the demands of either group of complaining dealers.

2. Huge Ungainly Grasping Enterprises Ltd. (HUGE) is a large conglomerate that owns, among other corporations, Big Buns, Inc., the second largest supplier of buns, pastries, and condiments to fast-food franchisees. Big Buns currently covers 30 percent of the bun and pastry market and 18 percent of the condiment market. The leading firms in these two markets have shares of 45 percent and 25 percent, respectively. The leading bun and pastry supplier also has 13 percent of the condiment market, ranking fourth behind a condiment supplier that has 16 percent. The leading condiment firm also ranks third in buns and pastries, with 20 percent of the market. The remainder of the buns and pastries and condiments markets are occupied by franchisors that supply their franchisees.

HUGE would like to enter the fast-food restaurant business. Another HUGE subsidiary owns a large number of small parcels of real estate that are notable locations for fast-food enterprises. The parcels are currently vacant. The fast-food restaurant business is highly competitive, with the top 10 firms dividing 98 percent of the market as follows:

Firm	Percent of Market Share
1	35
2	25
3	10
4	9
5	7
6	4
7	3
8	2
9	2
10	1

HUGE is considering acquiring firm seven or starting a new fast-food franchise. Whichever approach it takes, HUGE will seek new franchisees and require them to lease its currently vacant land parcels and operate from those locations. It will also offer a 20 percent discount to all franchisees who buy their buns and condiments from Big Buns and a 30 percent discount to those who enter into three-year requirements contracts with Big Buns. As president of Big Buns, you must react to the proposal.

*B*usinesses and workers . . . attempting to deal
with each other on a day-to-day basis, must do so
in a workplace dominated by government regulation.

PART FIVE

LABOR LAW

Between the Civil War and World War I, the United States was transformed
from a nation of farmers and individual merchants and artisans into a
nation of urban wage earners and capitalists. Urbanization transformed
the nature of the employment relationship. Due to a dramatic increase
in capital investment, the personal employer-employee relationship that
had existed in smaller enterprises gave way to an impersonal worker-
management relationship. The workers previously employed by individuals became a part of large impersonal organizations. Employers dealt
with these workers as groups rather than as individuals. An adversarial
relationship developed between employers and workers.

Urbanization also made possible greater social intercourse and that,
inevitably, led to a movement for social reforms. Improved communications and an influx of immigrants, who threatened the economic security
of skilled craftsmen, strengthened skilled workers' awareness of the need
for solidarity. Labor organizations, such as the Knights of Labor and the
American Federation of Labor, were formed.

Initially the law was unresponsive to changing social conditions and
the emergence of an organized labor movement. Although Congress enacted the Railway Labor Act in 1926 providing for collective bargaining
in the railroad industry, no other major labor law legislation was passed
prior to the Great Depression of 1929. The Depression stimulated a major
wave of labor legislation led by the New Deal administration of Franklin
D. Roosevelt.

The unifying themes of these statutes were the recognition of employee rights, assurance of more humane working conditions, and prevention of another depression. The National Labor Relations Act, also known as the Wagner Act, declared an official government policy of promoting collective bargaining and guaranteed employees the right to organize and bargain collectively. It was expected that collective bargaining would foster industrial peace and raise worker living standards, thereby stimulating demand for consumer goods and avoiding another depression. The Fair Labor Standards Act (FLSA) was also designed to improve worker living standards and stimulate employment. The act set minimum wages, established maximum hours, and banned oppressive child labor. Congress passed the Social Security Act to provide retirement benefits to maintain

---

. . . More and more workers are demanding a voice in the work place. They're demanding a democratization of the system . . . .

Douglas Fraser, former
United Auto Workers President

---

workers' living standards in their nonworking years. States were encouraged to establish unemployment insurance systems that would keep recessions from turning into depressions by maintaining the living standards and purchasing power of the unemployed.

During the 1940s and 1950s, Congress amended the National Labor Relations Act and changed the government's policy from promoting labor unions and collective bargaining to regulating labor-management relations. During the 1960s, a new wave of labor law legislation hit the country. The Civil Rights movement resulted in enactment of the Equal Pay Act of 1963, prohibiting sex discrimination in compensation; Title VII of the 1964 Civil Rights Act, prohibiting employment discrimination based on race, sex, religion, and national origin; and the Age Discrimination in Employment Act (ADEA) of 1967. The liberal social reform movement continued into the 1970s with enactment of the Occupational Safety and Health Act (OSHA) of 1970, the Employee Retirement Income Security Act (ERISA) of 1974, and expansions of Title VII in 1972 and the ADEA in 1978.

Today, many American businesses are facing new competition and aging facilities. Because of these changing economic conditions, many representatives of business and labor believe that the adversarial relationship between workers and employers must yield to a more cooperative one. Former United Auto Workers President Douglas Fraser states that workers are "demanding a democratization of the system, and the companies are catching on. . . . They're beginning to give the workers a bigger role because it's in their self-interest to do it."[1]

Chrysler Corporation Industrial Relations Vice President Thomas Miner has expressed similar thoughts from management's perspective when he recognizes that the "adversity which has plagued Chrysler has brought about a closer working relationship between the Union and Management. . . . The result has been that the historical "We-Them" is gradu-

---

*T*he hope for the future of American industry [depends] . . . on how successful labor and management are in changing the collective bargaining process from one based on conflict to one based on cooperation.

Thomas Miner, Chrysler Corportion
Industrial Relations Vice President

---

ally being replaced by a joint approach to problem solving." Regardless of this new-found cooperation, Miner says that labor and management "are not home yet by a wide margin, but are on the way to change."[2]

Businesses and workers attempting to develop more cooperative approaches, or simply attempting to deal with each other on a day-to-day basis, must do so in a workplace dominated by government regulation. The next three chapters consider that regulation in detail. Chapter 15 discusses labor-management relations under the National Labor Relations Act. Chapter 16 explores the protections afforded workers by OSHA, ERISA, workers' compensation, social security, unemployment insurance, and the FLSA. Chapter 17 covers the myriad laws relating to discrimination in employment.

---

[1] Fraser, "Worker Participation in Corporate Government: The UAW-Chrysler Experience," 58 *Chicago Kent L. Rev.*, 949, 959, (1982).

[2] Miner, "Concession Bargaining," 59 *Chicago Kent L. Rev.*, 981, 996 (1963).

CHAPTER 15

LABOR–MANAGEMENT RELATIONS

The interests of businesses and their workers frequently conflict. Workers want higher wages and better working conditions, but these demands can lower corporate profits. Businesses sometimes wish to change their operating methods in ways that threaten workers' job security. Most individual workers have little bargaining power when dealing with their employers. Consequently, they often group together in labor unions to deal collectively with employers. Employers frequently resist unionization because it tends to reduce their power over their workers. Both unions and employers have appealed to government to support their efforts.

The early government approach emphasized employer rights. This was consistent with a general government policy of promoting business expansion and industrialization. Courts held that labor unions or other combinations of workers were illegal criminal conspiracies because they sought improper goals and used improper means to achieve their goals. For example, in the *Philadelphia Cordwainers* case of 1806, several cordwainers (shoemakers) were convicted of conspiracy after striking for higher pay. The trial judge instructed the jury that "a combination of workers to raise wages may be considered in a twofold point of view: one is to benefit themselves, the other is to injure those who do not join their society. The rule of law condemns both."

During the eighteenth and early nineteenth centuries, almost all workers were disqualified from voting because they did not own property. In the 1820s and 1830s states began to abolish property requirements for voting. By 1880, increased numbers of workers had become voters, and criminal prosecutions of trade unionists had become politically unpopular with prosecutors. Employers turned to the civil courts to combat unions through injunctions. An *injunction* is a court order commanding someone to do something or to refrain from doing something. Disobedience of an injunction is punishable by fine or imprisonment for contempt of court. The use of injunctions as antilabor weapons was so prevalent that American labor law was frequently characterized as "law by injunction."

Organized labor's political power was finally felt in 1932, when Congress passed the Norris–LaGuardia Act. The statute prohibitied federal court injunctions in labor disputes as long as the dispute did not involve violence that local law enforcement agencies were incapable of handling. Many states enacted similar legislation. The practical effect of these enactments was to permit unions to exert effective economic power against employers. However, it did not obligate employers to negotiate with unions.

Most employers refused to deal with unions unless they were forced to do so. Because the government would not force employers to recognize and bargain with unions, many unions resorted to strikes and violence to gain recognition.

Congress responded to the anarchy in labor management relations in 1935 by passing the Wagner Act, also known as the National Labor Relations Act (NLRA). The statute established an administrative procedure through which unions could compel employers to recognize them. It created the National Labor Relations Board (NLRB), an agency composed of experts in labor management relations, to administer that procedure. The NLRA prohibited certain types of employer conduct, designated "unfair labor practices," and gave the NLRB power to enforce its prohibitions. The statute placed no restrictions on union conduct.

Following World War II, union membership grew significantly. National strikes took place in several industries at times of peak consumer demand. But public reaction to the strikes led to an amendment of the NLRA in 1947. The amendment became known as the Taft–Hartley Act or the Labor–Management Relations Act.

The Taft–Hartley Act added union unfair labor practices to the NLRA's list of unlawful activities. It also recognized that collective bargaining did not always resolve disputes and therefore made available the alternative processes of mediation and "cooling-off" injunctions. The act created the Federal Mediation and Conciliation Service to assist in collective bargaining. It also gave the federal government power to intervene in strikes that threatened the national welfare and to seek an 80-day injunction from a federal court to serve as a cooling-off period.

Senate investigations into union corruption resulted in passage of the Labor–Management Reporting and Disclosure Act of 1959, usually referred to as the Landrum-Griffin Act. The statute extended federal regulation into internal union affairs, establishing a "bill of rights for union members." It also added several union unfair labor practices. In 1974 Congress enacted the health care amendments to the NLRA. These brought private health care facilities under the act.

This piecemeal legislative response to particular labor relations problems has placed the government in the position of neutral regulator of union-management relations. This chapter explores that regulation at the different stages of the union-employer relationship. Before doing so, however, it is necessary to understand the NLRB's structure and the scope of the NLRA's coverage.

An Overview of the National Labor Relations Act

The heart of the NLRA is section 7, which provides:

> Employees shall have the right to self-organization, to form, join, or assist labor organizations, to bargain collectively through representatives of their own choosing, and to engage in other concerted activities for the purpose of collective bargaining or other mutual aid or protection, and shall also have the right to refrain from any or all of such activities except to the extent that such right may be affected by an agreement requiring membership in a labor organization as a condition of employment as authorized in section 8(a)(3).

Most unfair labor practices are designed to safeguard employee section 7 rights. Therefore, a frequent threshhold issue is whether the employee's conduct is covered by section 7. It is important to realize that employee activity need not involve a formal labor union to qualify for section 7 protection. For example, if a group of employees walk off the job to protest unsafe working conditions, they are protected under section 7. However, the activity must be *concerted*. Action by a single employee usually is not protected.

Section 8 sets forth the NLRA's prohibitions in the form of unfair labor practices. Section 8(a) establishes five employer unfair labor practices. Section 8(b) establishes seven union unfair labor practices. They are summarized in Tables 15–1 and 15–2.

TABLE 15–1 Unfair Labor Practices/Employer	
Employer	*NLRA Section*
Interfere, restrain, coerce employee exercise of §7 rights	8 (a)(1)
Dominate, interfere, support labor organization	8 (a)(2)
Discriminate to encourage or discourage union membership	8(a)(3)
Retaliate against employees who file charges or testify under the act	8 (a)(4)
Refuse to bargain in good faith	8 (a)(5)

TABLE 15–2 Unfair Labor Practices/Union	
Union	*NLRA Section*
Restrain or coerce employee exercise of §7 rights or employer choice of bargaining representative	8 (b)(1)
Force employer to discriminate to encourage or discourage union membership	8 (b)(2)
Refuse to bargain in good faith	8 (b)(3)
Engage in secondary boycotts or picket in a work assignment dispute	8 (b)(4)
Require excessive dues on a union shop	8 (b)(5)
Require employer to pay for services not performed or not to be performed (featherbedding)	8 (b)(6)
Picket for recognition under certain circumstances	8 (b)(7)

Section 9 establishes procedures whereby elections may be held to enable employees to choose to have a union represent them or to discontinue an incumbent union's representation. When a majority of employees voting in an NLRB-conducted election choose to have a union represent them, the union is *certified* as their *exclusive bargaining representative*.

THE NATIONAL LABOR RELATIONS BOARD

The NLRA is administered and enforced by the National Labor Relations Board (NLRB), an independent regulatory agency. The NLRB has two principal functions:

— To prevent and remedy unfair labor practices,
— To conduct secret ballot elections in which employees decide whether unions will represent them in collective bargaining.

Board Organization

The NLRB is made up of the board, the general counsel, and regional offices.

The Board   The board consists of five members who serve staggered five-year terms. Each member is appointed by the president with Senate approval. The board decides unfair labor practices cases and representation cases (cases involving the certification of a union as the bargaining representative of an employer's workforce). Its adjudicatory functions have been delegated to administrative law judges (ALJs) located in the regional offices. An ALJ holds judicial hearings at the regional offices and makes recommendations to the board.

The General Counsel

To guarantee the separation of enforcement and adjudicatory functions, the NLRA established the office of general counsel to serve as the agency's enforcement arm. The general counsel is appointed by the president with Senate approval for a four-year term. While centered in Washington, D.C., the general counsel maintains staff at the regional offices to investigate charges of unfair labor practices, to decide whether to issue complaints, and, if a complaint is issued, to prosecute the complaint before the board.

The Regional Offices

The regional offices, located in major cities throughout the country, are under the general supervision of the general counsel. Each office is under the direction of a regional director, who is assisted by a regional attorney. The staff consists of field executives, who conduct investigations of charges and direct or administer representation elections; and attorneys, who prosecute complaints before administrative law judges.

Board Procedure

The NLRB can act only when it is formally requested to do so by employers, unions, or employees. Two types of requests may be filed with the NLRB: representation petitions and unfair labor practice charges. Each is filed in the appropriate regional office.

Representation Cases

A union may file a representation petition if it can show that at least 30 percent of the employees desire that union's representation. A union usually shows this with cards signed by the employees authorizing the union to represent them. These cards are called *union authorization cards*.

If a union demands that an employer recognize it, the employer may file a representation petition. Employees who are currently represented by a union may file representation petitions to decertify that union. Decertification petitions must be supported by at least 30 percent of the employees.

When a petition is filed, the regional staff investigates it to determine whether the board has jurisdiction. The regional office notifies the other parties involved of the petition. Those parties may consent to an election or object to the petition. When objections are filed, a hearing is conducted before a hearing officer. The hearing transcript is then transferred to the regional director, who rules on the objections.

If the regional director finds that a question of representation exists, he or she directs an election by secret ballot. The election results may be challenged. The regional director rules on the objections and either orders a new election or certifies the results. If a union receives a majority of the votes cast, it is certified; if no union gets a majority, that result is certified. A certified union is entitled to recognition from the employer as the exclusive bargaining agent for the employees in the unit. However, decisions of the regional director may be appealed to the board.

Unfair Labor Practice Cases

Unfair labor practice charges may be filed by employees, unions, or employers. A charge must be filed within six months following the alleged unfair labor practice. The party filing the charge is called the *charging party*. The party who allegedly committed unfair labor practices is called the *respondent*.

The regional office investigates the charge, whereupon the regional director determines whether to formally charge the respondent union or employer with having committed an unfair labor practice. If the regional director declines to file a formal charge, the charging party may appeal to the general counsel. The general counsel's decision is not subject to judicial review.

Once formal charges are filed, the regional office attempts to settle the case. If settlement is unsuccessful, the case proceeds to a trial-type hearing before an ALJ. The ALJ issues a recommended ruling, which the parties may appeal to the board. If the board finds that the respondent committed unfair labor practices, it orders the respondent to cease and desist those practices and to take appropriate affirmative measures to remedy the damage that has been caused.

NLRB orders are not self-enforcing. If the respondent refuses to comply, the board must petition the U.S. Court of Appeals to order compliance. The general counsel represents the board in court. The respondent may also petition the court to overturn the board's decision. If the court enforces the board's order, the respondent must comply or face contempt of court charges. Further review may be sought in the Supreme Court by *certiorari*.

COVERAGE OF THE NLRA

Congress extended the NLRA's coverage to the full limit of its constitutional powers under the commerce clause. These powers are discussed in detail in Chapter 3. However, Congress specifically excluded certain classes of employers and employees and gave the NLRB discretion to further limit its jurisdiction.

Excluded Employers

The NLRA does not cover the railroad and airline industries, which are subject to the Railway Labor Act. It also excludes government entities and wholly owned government corporations. The statute does cover the U.S. Postal Service.

The NLRB may decline to assert jurisdiction over employers where the effect on commerce of labor disputes in which those employers may become involved "is not sufficiently substantial to warrant the exercise of its jurisdiction." The board has adopted certain requirements for exercising its jurisdiction, called *jurisdictional standards*. These standards are based on the yearly amount of business done by an enterprise or on the yearly amount of its sales or purchases. They are stated in terms of total dollar volume of business and are different for different kinds of enterprises. An enterprise that exceeds the total annual dollar volume of business listed in the standard is covered by the NLRA.

Excluded Employees

Certain classes of employees are not covered by the NLRA and thus are not within the board's jurisdiction. The act specifically excludes the following types of employees from its provisions: agricultural laborers, domestic servants, employees of a parent or spouse, government employees, employees of railroads and airlines, independent contractors, and supervisors.

Independent contractor status generally depends upon the degree of supervision and the right to control the process. In an employment relationship, the employer controls the end to be achieved and the means used by the employee to achieve that end. In an independent contractor relationship, the party receiving the service may specify the end to be achieved, but the means are controlled by independent contractor.

Whether an individual is a supervisor depends on his or her authority over employees and not merely on his or her job title. The NLRA defines a supervisor as

> any individual having authority, in the interest of the employer, to hire, transfer, suspend, lay off, recall, promote, discharge, assign, reward, or discipline other employees, or responsibly to direct them, or to adjust their grievances, or effectively to recommend such action, if in connection with the foregoing the exercise of such authority is not of a merely routine or clerical nature, but requires the use of independent judgment.

In addition, the board has excluded managerial employees, who are defined as those who formulate and effectuate management policy by expressing and making operative their employer's decisions and as those who have discretion in performing their jobs which is independent of their employer's established policy. Supervisors and managers are excluded from the act to assure their single-minded loyalty to the employer by not involving them in a conflict of interest between the employer and their union representative. The following case shows the Supreme Court's present approach to these exclusions.

NLRB v. Yeshiva University

444 U.S. 672 (1980)

Full-time faculty at Yeshiva University (appellee), a private institution, petitioned the NLRB (appellant) to conduct an election to determine whether a majority of the faculty wished to be represented by a labor union. Yeshiva claimed that its faculty were managerial employees. The NLRB concluded that they were professional employees and conducted the election. Yeshiva appealed to the Second Circuit Court of Appeals, which reversed, holding faculty to be managers. The NLRB petitioned the Supreme Court for review. The Court affirmed the Second Circuit.

Yeshiva's faculty participated in university-wide governance through representatives on elected committees. The university was divided into relatively autonomous schools, whose faculty met to decide matters of institutional and professional concern. They determined curriculum, grading systems, admission standards, academic calendars, course schedules, hiring, promotion, tenure, and sabbatical leaves. All faculty decisions were in the form of recommendations to the central administration, but these recommendations were usually followed.

Justice Powell

Yeshiva does not contend that its faculty are not professionals under the statute. But professionals, like other employees, may be exempted from coverage under the Act's exclusion for "supervisors" who use independent judgment in overseeing other employees in the interest of the employer, or under the judicially implied exclusion for "managerial employees" who are involved in developing and enforcing employer policy. Both exemptions grow out of the same concern: that an employer is entitled to the undivided loyalty of its representatives. . . .

Managerial employees are defined as those who "formulate and effectuate management policies by expressing and making operative the decisions of their employer." These employees are "much higher in the managerial structure" than those explicitly

mentioned by Congress, which "regarded [them] as so clearly outside the Act that no specific exclusionary provision was thought necessary." . . . Managerial employees must exercise discretion within or even independently of established employer policy and must be aligned with management. . . . Although the Board has established no firm criteria for determining when an employee is so aligned, normally an employee may be excluded as managerial only if he represents management interests by taking or recommending discretionary actions that effectively control or implement employer policy.

The Board . . . contends that the managerial exclusion cannot be applied in a straightforward fashion to professional employees because those employees often appear to be exercising managerial authority when they are merely performing routine job duties. The status of such employees, in the Board's view, must be determined by reference to the "alignment with management criterion." The Board argues that the Yeshiva faculty are not aligned with management because they are expected to exercise "independent professional judgment" while participating in academic governance, and because they are neither "expected to conform to management policies [nor] judged according to their effectiveness in carrying out those policies." Because of this independence, the Board contends there is no danger of divided loyalty and no need for the managerial exclusion. In its view, union pressure cannot divert the faculty from adhering to the interests of the university, because the university itself expects its faculty to pursue professional values rather than institutional interests. . . .

The controlling consideration in this case is that the faculty of Yeshiva University exercise authority which in any other context unquestionably would be managerial. Their authority in academic matters is absolute. They decide what courses will be offered, when they will be scheduled, and to whom they will be taught. They debate and determine teaching methods, grading policies, and matriculation standards. They effectively decide which students will be admitted, retained, and graduated. On occasion their views have determined the size of the student body, the tuition to be charged, and the location of a school. When one considers the function of a university, it is difficult to imagine decisions more managerial than these. To the extent the industrial analogy applies, the faculty determines within each school the product to be produced, the terms upon which it will be offered, and the customers who will be served. . . .

*   *   *   *   *

In arguing that a faculty member exercising independent judgment acts primarily in his own interest and therefore does not represent the interest of his employer, the Board assumes that the professional interests of the faculty and the interests of the institution are distinct, separable entities with which a faculty member could not simultaneously be aligned. The Court of Appeals found no justification for this distinction, and we perceive none. In fact, the faculty's professional interests—as applied to governance at a university like Yeshiva—cannot be separated from those of the institution.

The problem of divided loyalty is particularly acute for a university like Yeshiva, which depends on the professional judgment of its faculty to formulate and apply crucial policies constrained only by necessarily general institutional goals. The University requires faculty participation in governance because professional expertise is indispensable to the formulation and implementation of academic policy. It may appear, as the Board contends, that the professor performing governance functions is less "accountable" for departures from institutional policy than a middle-level industrial manager whose discretion is more confined. Moreover, traditional systems of collegiality and tenure insulate the professor from some of the sanctions applied to an industrial manager who fails to adhere to company policy. But the analogy of the university to industry need not, and indeed cannot, be complete. It is clear that Yeshiva and like universities must rely on their faculties to participate in the making and implementation of their policies. The large measure of independence enjoyed by faculty members can only increase the danger that divided loyalty will lead to those harms that the Board traditionally has sought to prevent.

We certainly are not suggesting an application of the managerial exclusion that would sweep all professionals outside the Act in derogation of Congress' expressed intent to protect them. The Board has recognized that employees whose decisionmaking is limited to the routine discharge of professional duties in projects to which they have been assigned cannot be excluded from coverage even if union membership arguably may involve some divided loyalty.

Only if an employee's activities fall outside the scope of the duties routinely performed by similarly situated professionals will he be found aligned with management. We think these decisions accurately capture the intent of Congress, and that they provide an appropriate starting point for analysis in cases involving professionals alleged to be managerial.

CASE QUESTIONS

1. What was the "independent professional judgment" test that the NLRB used in determining the managerial status of the Yeshiva faculty? Why did the Court reject this approach? What standard did the Court fashion in determining whether university faculty members were professional or managerial employees? When will a professional employee not be excluded from the NLRA's protections as a managerial employee?

2. How does the exclusion for managers differ from the exclusion for supervisors?

3. If the Yeshiva faculty are exempt from the NLRA, what Yeshiva employees are protected by the act?

4. Could the associates of a major CPA firm organize a union under the NLRA's protections? What facts would be helpful in deciding this?

EMPLOYER RESPONSES TO UNION ORGANIZING

When a group of employees feel that their working conditions are inadequate, they may seek to have a union represent them in bargaining with their employer. They usually begin by approaching an existing union, which will send a union organizer to talk with the employees who wish to unionize. The organizer will attempt to convince these employees of the advantages of becoming a local of the union. If they are convinced, they will form an organizing committee of employees to work with the union organizer to convince the rest of the workforce of the need to unionize.

Although most organizing efforts are initiated at the local level, national union organizing campaigns sometimes occur. These campaigns usually take place when a unionized company establishes a new plant whose employees are not organized. The union representing the rest of the company's plants may send organizers to the new plant to bring its employees into the organization. Sometimes national organizing campaigns start when a union targets a particular employer for unionization. This frequently occurs when a nonunion employer exists in a predominantly unionized industry.

An employer, upon learning of the organizing campaign, may instinctively react. The employer may call employees into the personnel office and interrogate them about the union, fire the union activists, forbid employees from discussing the union on company property, or grant new benefits with the hope that the employees will reject the union. These reactions may constitute unfair labor practices. These unfair labor practices can occur at any time, but they most commonly arise during union organizing campaigns.

Employer Interference, Restraint, or Coercion

Section 8(a)(1) of the NLRA prohibits employer interference, restraint, or coercion of employees exercising their section 7 rights. All other employer unfair labor practices also violate 8(a)(1). Additionally, there are several 8(a)(1) violations that do not violate other provisions of the act. The NLRA does not prohibit employer activities that tend to obstruct organizational efforts but do not amount to interference, restraint, or coercion. Section 8(c) provides that the mere "expressing of any views, argument or opinion . . . shall not constitute an unfair labor practice . . . if such expression contains no threat of reprisal or force, or promise of benefit." Section 8(c) is known as the *employer free speech* provision. The act attempts to balance the self-organizational rights of employees with the property rights of their employer.

**No
Solicitation
Rules**

The self-organizational rights of employees come into conflict with the property rights of their employer when organizing activity is attempted on company property. Employers frequently have rules forbidding solicitation and the distribution of literature. Employers are permitted to have rules prohibiting the distribution of literature or solicitation during an employee's work time or in work areas if the rules apply to everyone, not just to union supporters. However, any absolute ban on employee solicitation, such as a rule forbidding the distribution of literature in nonwork areas (e.g., lunchrooms and parking lots) or during an employee's nonwork hours, is an unfair labor practice. Although employees may thus use company property for organizational purposes within certain limits, nonemployee organizers may use the employer's property only when there is no other practical method of reaching the employees. Furthermore, the employer may prohibit solicitation for purposes not related to labor organizing. The following case deals with the limits of employees' rights to solicit.

Eastex, Inc. v. NLRB

437 U.S. 556 (1978)

Eastex (petitioner) prohibited its employees from distributing on its property literature opposing a proposal to incorporate the Texas right-to-work law (which prohibited union shop agreements.*) into the state constitution and protesting a presidential veto of a minimum wage increase. The NLRB (respondent) held that Eastex violated section 8(a)(1). The court of appeals and the Supreme Court affirmed.

Justice Powell

Section 7 provides that "[e]mployees shall have the right . . . to engage in . . . concerted activites for the purpose of collective bargaining or other mutual aid or protection. . . ." Petitioner contends that the activity here is not within the "mutual aid or protection" language because it does not relate to a "specific dispute" between employees and their own employer "over an issue which the employer has the right or power to affect." . . . Petitioner rejects the idea that §7 might protect any activity that could be characterized as "political," and suggests that the discharge of an employee who engages in any such activity would not violate the Act.

We believe that petitioner misconceives the reach of the "mutual aid or protection" clause. The "employees" who may engage in concerted activities for "mutual aid or protection" are defined by §2(3) of the Act, to "include any employee, and shall not be limited to the employees of a particular employer, unless the Act explicitly states otherwise. . . ." This definition was in-

tended to protect employees when they engage in otherwise proper concerted activities in support of employees of employers other than their own. . . .

We also find no warrant for petitioner's view that employees lose their protection under the "mutual aid or protection" clause when they seek to improve terms and conditions of employment or otherwise improve their lot as employees through channels outside the immediate employee-employer relationship. The 74th Congress knew well enough that labor's cause often is advanced on fronts other than collective bargaining and grievance settlement within the immediate employment context. It recognized this fact by choosing, as the language of §7 makes clear, to protect concerted activities for the somewhat broader purpose of "mutual aid or protection" as well as for the narrower purposes of "self-organization" and "collective bargaining." . . .

It is true, of course, that some concerted activity bears a less immediate relationship to employees' interests as employees than other such activity. We may assume that at some point the relationship becomes so attenuated that an activity cannot fairly be deemed to come within the

---

* A union shop agreement requires employees to join the union at some specified time after hire, usually 30 days, in order to continue working for the employer.—Au.

"mutual aid or protection" clause. It is neither necessary nor appropriate, however, for us to attempt to delineate precisely the boundaries of the "mutual aid or protection" clause. That task is for the Board to perform in the first instance as it considers the wide variety of cases that come before it. . . .

The Board determined that distribution of the second section, urging employees to write their legislators to oppose incorporation of the state "right-to-work" statute into a revised state constitution, was protected because union security is "central to the union concept of strength through solidarity" and "a mandatory subject of bargaining in other than right-to-work states." The newsletter warned that incorporation could affect employees adversely "by weakening Unions and improving the edge business has at the bargaining table." . . . We cannot say that the Board erred in holding that this section of the newsletter bears such a relation to employees' interests as to come within the guarantee of the "mutual aid or protection" clause. . . .

The Board held that distribution of the third section, criticizing a presidential veto of an increase in the federal minimum wage and urging employees to register to vote to "defeat our enemies and elect our friends," was protected despite the fact that petitioner's employees were paid more than the vetoed minimum wage. It reasoned that the "minimum wage inevitably influences wage levels derived from collective bargaining, even those far above the minimum," and that "concern by [petitioner's] employees for the plight of other employees might gain support for them at some future time when they might have a dispute with their employer." We think that the Board acted within the range of its discretion in so holding. . . .

In sum, we hold that distribution of both the second and the third sections of the newsletter is protected under the "mutual aid or protection" clause of §7.

The question that remains is whether the Board erred in holding that petitioner's employees may distribute the newsletter in nonworking areas of petitioner's property during nonworking time. . . .

*   *   *   *   *

Petitioner contends that the Board must distinguish among distributions of protected matter by employees on an employer's property on the basis of the content of each distribution. . . .

We hold that the Board was not required to adopt this view in the case at hand. . . . Here, petitioner's employees are "already rightfully on the employer's property," so that in the context of this case it is the "employer's management interests rather than [its] property interests" that primarily are implicated. As already noted, petitioner made no attempt to show that its management interests would be prejudiced in any way by the exercise of §7 rights proposed by its employees here. Even if the mere distribution by employees of material protected by §7 can be said to intrude on petitioner's property rights in any meaningful sense, the degree of intrusion does not vary with the content of the material. Petitioner's only cognizable property right in this respect is in preventing employees from bringing literature onto its property and distributing it there—not in choosing which distributions protected by §7 it wishes to suppress.

On the other side of the balance, it may be argued that the employees' interest in distributing literature that deals with matters affecting them as employees, but not with self-organization or collective bargaining, is so removed from the central concerns of the Act as to justify application of a different rule. Although such an argument may have force in some circumstances, the

Board to date generally has chosen not to engage in such refinement of its rules regarding the distribution of literature by employees during nonworking time in nonworking areas of their employers' property. We are not prepared to say in this case that the Board erred in the view it took.

It is apparent that the complexity of the Board's rules and the difficulty of the Board's task might be compounded greatly if it were required to distinguish not only between literature that is within and without the protection of §7, but also among subcategories of literature within that protection. . . .

. . . This is a new area for the Board and the courts which has not yet received mature consideration. . . . For this reason, we confine our holding to the facts of this case.

CASE QUESTIONS

1. How did the literature in this case differ from the literature in union organizing campaigns? Was this difference significant? Explain.

2. Does the Court hold that an employer may never prohibit the distribution of political literature by its employees on its property? Explain.

3. If the NLRB had resolved the issues in Eastex's favor and the union had appealed, would the Court have reversed the NLRB? Explain.

4. Could Eastex prohibit nonemployees from distributing the same literature on its property? Explain.

Speeches to the Employees

Although employers may within limits have no-solicitation/no-distribution rules for employees and outsiders, they may wish to violate their own rules by using company property and time to address employees and distribute antiunion literature. In determining whether such employer efforts constitute employer free speech under section 8(c) or an unfair labor practice under section 8(a)(1), the board considers the enormous economic power employers have over their employees. Thus, the employer may not make any statement threatening union supporters or promising benefits to those who do not support the union. An employer's predictions of adverse economic consequences following unionization are considered coercive unless they are based on objective facts over which the employer has no control.

Although an employer has a captive audience when addressing employees on company property and time, the employer need not offer the union an equal opportunity to respond, so long as the employer's speech is not coercive. However, the board forbids even noncoercive speeches to captive audiences during the 24-hour period before a representation election. This election eve rule does not ban speeches where attendance is voluntary and on the employee's own time.

**Granting
Benefits
to the
Employees**

A natural reaction by an employer to a union organizing drive is to find out why the employees are unhappy and remedy the situation. For example, if the workers believe they are underpaid, the employer might raise their wages. In the following case the Supreme Court considered whether such conduct constitutes an unfair labor practice.

NLRB v. Exchange Parts Co.

375 U.S. 405 (1964)

The Exchange Parts Company (respondent) was the subject of an organizing drive by the International Brotherhood of Boilermakers. The Boilermakers petitioned the NLRB to hold a representation election. After the drive began, Exchange Parts' vice president announced to the employees that they would have an additional holiday, that there would be a new system of computing overtime during holiday weeks, which would increase wages for those weeks, and a new vacation schedule which would enable employees to sandwich their vacation time between weekends. The NLRB found that these improvements in wages and benefits were intended to influence the representation election and held that respondent had violated section 8(a)(1). The court of appeals agreed that the new overtime and vacation procedures were intended to influence the election but held that they did not violate section 8(a)(1), because they were put into effect unconditionally and permanently. The Supreme Court agreed with the NLRB and reversed the court of appeals.

Justice Harlan

The broad purpose of §8(a)(1) is to establish "the right of employees to organize for mutual aid without employer interference." We have no doubt that it prohibits not only intrusive threats and promises but also conduct immediately favorable to employees which is undertaken with the express purpose of impinging upon their freedom of choice for or against unionization and is reasonably calculated to have that effect . . . The danger inherent in well-timed increases in benefits is the suggestion of a fist

inside the velvet glove. Employees are not likely to miss the inference that the source of benefits now conferred is also the source from which future benefits must flow and which may dry up if it is not obliged. The danger may diminish if, as in this case, the benefits are conferred permanently and unconditionally. But the absence of conditions or threats pertaining to the particular benefits conferred would be of controlling significance only if it could be presumed that no question of additional benefits or renegotiation of existing benefits would arise in the future; and, of course, no such presumption is tenable.

* * * * *

We cannot agree with the Court of Appeals that enforcement of the Board's order will have the "ironic" result of "discourag-ing benefits for labor." . . . The beneficence of an employer is likely to be ephemeral if prompted by a threat of unionization which is subsequently removed. Insulating the right of collective organization from calculated good will of this sort deprives employees of little that has lasting value.

CASE QUESTIONS

1. What is the Court's rationale for holding that a conferral of benefits with an intent to influence an election violates section 8(a)(1)?

2. What factors might establish that the employer's intent in conferring benefits was to influence the election?

3. Under what circumstances might an em-ployer confer benefits even though an election is pending without violating section 8(a)(1)?

4. If an employer plans to give a wage increase but, upon learning of a union organizing drive, decides to withhold it, has the employer violated section 8(a)(1)?

Interrogation and Polling

Sometimes an employer will want to gauge the union's strength by interro-gating employees. An employer's questioning of employees will be evalu-ated by the NLRB in the context of the whole campaign. Isolated interroga-tions are generally not regarded as sufficiently coercive to set aside an election, but, depending on the closeness of the election, may constitute illegal interference. If an employer desires to determine how many em-ployees support the union, a secret poll of the employees may be con-ducted, provided the employer observes the following safeguards:

— The poll's purpose is to test the validity of a union's claim of majority support
— The purpose is communicated to the employees
— Assurances against reprisals are given
— The employer has neither committed prior unfair labor practices nor created a coercive atmosphere

Company Unions

Before enactment of the NLRA, many employers fought independent unions by organizing company unions, which they dominated and re-quired all employees to join. Section 8(a)(2) of the NLRA was designed to outlaw company unions.

Section 8(a)(2) prohibits employer domination, interference, and financial or other support of a labor organization. An employer violates section 8(a)(2) by taking an active part in organizing a union or committee to represent its employees, bringing pressure upon employees to join a particular union, or playing favorites with one of two or more competing unions. An employer who voluntarily recognizes a union that is not supported by a majority of the employees violates section 8(a)(2) even if the employer in good faith believes that the union has majority support.

If a union is employer-dominated, the NLRB will order it *disestablished,* meaning that the union will be barred from ever representing the employees. If a union is unlawfully supported or interfered with, the NLRB will order it *decertified,* meaning that the union will be barred from representing employees until it has been certified in an NLRB election.

The prohibition of employer domination, interference, or support goes beyond unions and encompasses labor organizations. The NLRA defines a *labor organization* as any organization or plan "in which employees participate and which exists for the purpose, in whole or in part, of dealing with employers concerning grievances, labor disputes, wages, rates of pay, hours of employment, or conditions of work." In the landmark case of *NLRB v. Cabot Carbon Co.,*[1] the Supreme Court held that an in-plant employee committee system was a labor organization. The employer had prepared committee bylaws which were then adopted by majority vote of the employees. According to the bylaws, the committees were created to provide procedures for: considering ideas and problems of mutual interest to employees and management; establishing a fixed term for committee membership; providing for regular elections of employees to the committees; and handling grievances at nonunion plants. The Court indicated that section 8(a)(2) did not prohibit such committees, but that section 8(a)(2) required that they be free of employer domination and interference.

Today many employers are experimenting with employee quality circles and other participative management programs. Such programs may potentially violate section 8(a)(2). To avoid violations, they either must be free from employer domination or interference, or they must not deal with the employer concerning grievances or working conditions.

Employer Discrimination Based on Union Membership

Selection 8(a)(3) forbids employers to discriminate against employees for the purpose of encouraging or discouraging membership in any labor organization. For example, employers cannot demote or discharge an employee for urging coworkers to join or organize a union. The principal issue in cases brought under this section is employer motivation. The employer may discipline a union activist for poor job performance or

---

[1] 360 U.S. 203 (1959).

misconduct. On the other hand, even where an employee is guilty of misconduct, discipline may not be imposed if the employer's real motivation is the employee's union activities.

Illegal employer discrimination is not limited to dealings with individual employees. Employers may not relocate or close part of their operations simply because the employees have selected a union. However, they can relocate or change operations for economic reasons and can go out of business altogether regardless of motive.

THE REPRESENTATION PROCESS

As previously discussed, a union may petition the NLRB to hold a representation election if the petition is supported by 30 percent of the employees. Usually, unions do not file representation petitions immediately upon attaining 30 percent support. They try to gain majority support because they cannot represent the employees without it.

When a majority of the employees have signed authorization cards, the union will usually advise the employer of this fact and demand recognition. The employer may respond by filing a representation petition with the NLRB. The employer and union might also agree to have an independent third party check the authorization cards against the payroll list to verify the union's claim of majority support. If the claim is verified, the employer must recognize the union.

An employer can simply ignore the union's demand for recognition. The union must then file a representation petition and go through an election to force the employer to recognize it.

Appropriate Bargaining Units

For purposes of collective bargaining, employees are grouped into bargaining units. When a union files a representation petition, it must designate the bargaining unit in which it seeks to represent employees. The employer may challenge that unit as inappropriate for collective bargaining. The NLRB uses the following factors to resolve such challenges:

— Similarity in wages, hours and working conditions
— Similarity in work performed
— Similarity in skills and training
— Contact among employees
— Geographic proximity
— Common supervision
— Bargaining history
— Employee desires
— Extent of union organization

The board does not determine whether the union has chosen the most appropriate bargaining unit. An employer challenging the union's choice must show that it is inappropriate, not simply that a different unit would be more appropriate.

Protection of Laboratory Conditions

Before the election, the union and the employer wage a campaign to win the workers over to their positions. This campaign is regulated by the board. The board has stated that such elections must be conducted under laboratory conditions; that is, the election proceedings must be conducted under conditions that make it possible to determine the uninhibited wishes of the employees.

Actions that would otherwise be legal may destroy laboratory conditions. For example, employers normally may hold captive audience meetings of employees on company time. However, to protect laboratory conditions, such meetings are prohibited within 24 hours before the election. Similarly, an employer normally need not furnish a union with a list of employees' names and addresses. However, when an election is ordered, the employer must provide such a list to the NLRB regional director for use by the union.

The board's policy regarding misrepresentations in election campaign propaganda wavered in recent years. In the 1962 case of *Hollywood Ceramics* it ruled that an election will be set aside if substantial misstatements are made and the opponent does not have time to respond.[2] In 1977, it reversed the *Hollywood Ceramics* doctrine in the case of *Shopping Kart Food Market, Inc.* It held that elections would no longer be set aside solely because of misleading campaign statements.[3] However, it maintained this position for only one year. In *General Knit of California,* the board overruled *Shopping Kart* and readopted its prior standard of reviewing allegations of election campaign misrepresentations.[4] In 1982, in *Midland National Life Insurance Co.,*[5] the board again reversed itself and returned to its position in *Shopping Kart.*

The controversy centers over regulatory philosophy. Proponents of the *Hollywood Ceramics* doctrine argue that employees require protection from misrepresentations. Opponents contend that employees are sophisticated enough to assess the validity of campaign propaganda, that regulation of speech should be kept to a minimum, and that the *Hollywood Ceramics* approach encourages frivolous challenges to elections interposed only for delay.

Laboratory conditions may also be violated by emotional appeals. For example, appeals to racial prejudice may result in the setting aside of an election.

If the losing party feels that the board's campaign rules have been

---

[2] 140 NLRB 221 (1962).

[3] 228 NLRB 1311 (1977).

[4] 239 NLRB 619 (1978).

[5] 263 NLRB 24 (1982).

violated, it may file obligations with the board, setting forth the violations. If the objections are valid, the board sets aside the election and orders a new one.

Unfair labor practices automatically destroy laboratory conditions. An aggrieved employer, union, or employee may file unfair labor practice charges. If the NLRB finds that a union committed unfair labor practices during an election, it will set aside any union victory in the election, order the union to cease and desist its illegal activity, and order other affirmative relief. If the NLRB finds that an employer committed unfair labor practices during an election, it will set aside any union defeat, order the employer to cease and desist its illegal conduct, and order other affirmative relief. If it finds employer interference with employee choice so serious that a fair election cannot be conducted, it may order the employer to bargain with the union even when the union has lost the election. This is known as a board *bargaining order*.

NEGOTIATION OF THE COLLECTIVE BARGAINING AGREEMENT

Once the union has been certified, the employer must recognize and bargain with it as the exclusive representative of the employees. The employer may not negotiate individual contracts with individual employees. The certification binds all members of the bargaining unit to the act's policy of majority rule. The union must fairly represent all of the employees in the bargaining unit, and both the union and the employer must bargain in good faith.

Because a newly elected union needs time to establish itself and implement its programs, it is permitted a "reasonable period" to achieve its promised goals through collective bargaining. The board interprets a "reasonable period" as one calendar year from the certification date. Thus, the union is presumed to represent a majority of the employees for one year, and an employer cannot refuse to bargain during that time. This is true even if the employees no longer want the union as their representative. The rationale for not permitting the employees to switch representatives for one year is that to permit such switches to occur so easily would contradict the NLRA goal of promoting industrial stability.

After a year, there remains a continuing presumption that the union has majority status. The employer may rebut this presumption and refuse to continue bargaining with the union if the employer has objective evidence that a majority of the employees do not wish to be represented by the union.

The Duty to Bargain in Good Faith

Section 8(d) defines the type of collective bargaining that is required as follows:

[T]he performance of the mutual obligation of the employer and the representative of the employees to meet at reasonable times and confer in good faith with respect to wages, hours, and other terms and conditions of employment . . . [B]ut such obligations does not compel either party to agree to a proposal or require the making of a concession.

Collective bargaining usually begins with the union making a request for a meeting of the parties. It is common practice for the union to request in writing, shortly after certification, that the employer meet with it for the purpose of negotiating a contract. Section 8(d) requires that the meeting be "at reasonable times" for both parties. The act contains no precise requirements regarding the time and place of negotiations, but a reasonableness standard is used. Excessive delays are not allowed.

Under the act, it is an unfair labor practice for either party to refuse to bargain in good faith. The board uses two standards to assess the bargaining faith of parties: the totality of the circumstances approach and the per se violations approach. Some practices are viewed as evidencing bad faith but are considered in light of other practices to see whether the total circumstances add up to bad faith bargaining. The act does not require the parties to reach an agreement, but it prohibits bad faith bargaining designed to avoid a contract.

Some practices are so inconsistent with good faith bargaining, that they are per se violations. These include:

— Refusing to bargain at all
— Insisting on an illegal provision in the contract
— Refusing to execute a written contract
— For an employer, unilaterally changing some aspect of wages, hours and working conditions during negotiations without consulting the union
— For an employer, refusing to negotiate because the employees are out on a lawful strike
— For either party, refusing to supply the other with relevant information.

A party's duty to provide the other side with information is determined by balancing the information's relevance against the interests served by keeping it secret. For example, generally an employer need not let the union see its books. Although this information is relevant to bargaining, its proprietary nature should be protected. However, if an employer raises its financial health during negotiations, the books take on a heightened relevance and must be disclosed.

Subjects of Bargaining

There are three categories of bargaining subjects; mandatory subjects, permissive subjects, and prohibited subjects. If either party makes a proposal on a mandatory subject during negotiations, the other party cannot refuse to bargain on the proposal. Section 8(d) requires bargaining on "wages, hours, and other terms and conditions of employment," but the NLRA does not define what subjects can be classified as falling under these headings. However, by its decisions the board has developed what may be described as an exhaustive list of mandatory subjects. These include retirement benefits, vacations, rest periods, and work assignments.

Permissive subjects are those that either party may refuse to bargain on without committing an unfair labor practice. Among permissive subjects are corporate organization, the size of the supervisory force, and the location of plants.

Neither the board nor the courts will enforce agreements on prohibited subjects. Illustrations of prohibited subjects are: provisions for a closed shop (requiring that the employer hire only union members) and hot cargo clauses (stating that workers will not be required to handle goods of a nonunion employer). While the classifications seem fairly straightforward, the following case reveals the complexity of these classifications.

First National Maintenance Corp. v. NLRB

452 U.S. 666 (1981)

First National Maintenance Corp. (petitioner) provided maintenance services to commercial establishments. Petitioner's employees were represented by the National Union of Hospital and Health Care Employees. One of the petitioner's customers was Greenpark Care Center nursing home. Greenpark and First National had a stormy relationship for some time. After a dispute over petitioner's fee, petitioner decided to terminate its contract with Greenpark and discharge its employees who had been assigned to the Greenpark work. Petitioner refused to bargain with the union over the decision to terminate the Greenpark contract.

The NLRB (respondent) held that petitioner had a duty to bargain over the decision to terminate the Greenpark contract and found petitioner guilty of violating section 8(a)(5). The court of appeals enforced the NLRB's order. The Supreme Court reversed.

Justice Blackmun

A fundamental aim of the National Labor Relations Act is the establishment and maintenance of industrial peace to preserve the flow of interstate commerce. Central to achievement of this purpose is the promotion of collective bargaining as a method of defusing and channeling conflict between labor and management. .

Although parties are free to bargain about any legal subject, Congress has limited the mandate or duty to bargain to matters of "wages, hours, and other terms and conditions of employment." A unilateral change as to a subject within this category violates the statutory duty to bargain and is subject to the Board's remedial order. Conversely, both employer and union may bargain to impasse over these matters and use the economic weapons at their disposal to attempt to secure their respective aims. Congress deliberately left the words "wages, hours, and other terms and conditions of employment" without further definition, for it did not intend to deprive the Board of the power further to define those terms in light of specific industrial practice.

Nonetheless, in establishing what issues must be submitted to the process of bargaining, Congress had no expectation that the elected union representative would become an equal partner in the running of the business enterprise in which the union's members are employed. Despite the deliberate openendedness of the statutory language, there is an undeniable limit to the subjects about which bargaining must take place.

* * * * *

Some management decisions, such as choice of advertising and promotion, product type and design, and financing arrangements, have only an indirect and attenuated impact on the employment relationship. Other management decisions, such as the order of succession of layoffs and recalls, production quotas, and work rules, are almost exclusively "an aspect of the relationship" between employer and employee. The present case concerns a third type of management decision, one that had a direct impact on employment, since jobs were inexorably eliminated by the termination, but had as its focus only the economic profitability of the contract with Greenpark, a concern under these facts wholly apart from the employment relationship. This decision, involving a change in the scope and direction of the enterprise, is akin to the decision whether to be in business at all, "not in [itself] primarily about conditions of employment, though the effect of the decision may be necessarily to terminate employment.' '. . . At the same time, this decision touches on a matter of central and pressing concern to the union and its member employees: the possibility of continued employment and the retention of the employees' very jobs . . .

Petitioner contends it had no duty to bargain about its decision to terminate its operations at Greenpark. This contention requires that we determine whether the decision itself could be considered part of petitioner's retained freedom to manage its affairs unrelated to employment. The aim of labeling a matter a mandatory subject of bargaining, rather than simply permitting, but not requiring, bargaining, is to "promote the fundamental purpose of the Act by bringing a problem of vital concern to labor and management within the framework established by Congress as most conducive to industrial peace." . . . The concept of mandatory bargaining is premised on the belief that collective discussions backed by the parties' economic weapons will result in decisions that are better for both management and labor and for society as a whole. This will be true, however, only if the subject proposed for discussion is amenable to resolution through the bargaining process. Management must be free from the constraints of the bargaining process to the extent essential for the running of a profitable business. It also must have some degree of certainty beforehand as to when it may proceed to reach decisions without fear of later evaluations labeling its conduct an unfair labor practice. Congress did not explicitly state what issues of mutual concern to union and management it intended to exclude from mandatory bargaining. Nonetheless, in view of an employer's need for unencumbered decisionmaking, bargaining over management decisions that have a substantial impact on the continued availability of employment should be required only if the benefit, for labor-management relations and the collective-bargaining process, outweighs the burden placed on the conduct of business.

* * * * *

Both union and management regard control of the decision to shut down an operation with the utmost seriousness. As has been noted, however, the Act is not intended to serve either party's individual interest, but to foster in a neutral manner a system in which the conflict between these interests may be resolved. It seems particularly important, therefore, to consider whether requiring bargaining over this sort of decision will advance the neutral purposes of the Act.

A union's interest in participating in the decision to close a particular facility or part of an employer's operations springs from its legitimate concern over job security. The union's practical purpose in participating, however, will be largely uniform: it will seek to delay or halt the closing. No doubt it will be impelled, in seeking these ends, to offer concessions, information, and alternatives that might be helpful to management or forestall or prevent the termination of jobs. It is unlikely, however, that requiring bargaining over the decision itself, as well as its effects, will augment this flow of information and suggestions. There is no dispute that the union must be given

a significant opportunity to bargain about these matters of job security as part of the "effects" bargaining mandated by §8(a)(5). And, under §8(a)(5), bargaining over the effects of a decision must be conducted in a meaningful manner and at a meaningful time, and the Board may impose sanctions to insure its adequacy. A union, by pursuing such bargaining rights, may achieve valuable concessions from an employer engaged in a partial closing. It also may secure in contract negotiations provisions implementing rights to notice, information, and fair bargaining.

* * * * *

Management's interest in whether it should discuss a decision of this kind is much more complex and varies with the particular circumstances. If labor costs are an important factor in a failing operation and the decision to close, management will have an incentive to confer voluntarily with the union to seek concessions that may make continuing the business profitable. At other times, management may have a great need for speed, flexibility, and secrecy in meeting business opportunities and exigencies. It may face significant tax or securities consequences that hinge on confidentiality, the timing of a plant closing, or a reorganization of the corporate structure. The publicity incident to the normal process of bargaining may injure the possibility of a successful transition or increase the economic damage to business. The employer also may have no feasible alternative to the closing, and even good-faith bargaining over it may both be futile and cause the employer additional loss.

There is an important difference, also, between permitted bargaining and mandated bargaining. Labeling this type of decision mandatory could afford a union a powerful tool for achieving delay, a power that might be used to thwart management's intentions in a manner unrelated to any feasible solution the union might propose.

* * * * *

We conclude that the harm likely to be done to an employer's need to operate freely in deciding whether to shut down part of its business purely for economic reasons outweighs the incremental benefit that might be gained through the union's participation in making the decision, and we hold that the decision itself is *not* part of §8(d)'s "terms and conditions," over which Congress has mandated bargaining.

CASE QUESTIONS

1. What factors led the Court to conclude that a decision to terminate part of a business is not a mandatory subject of bargaining?

2. What is the difference between decision bargaining and effects bargaining? Can there be meaningful effects bargaining without decision bargaining?

3. Is an employer prohibited from bargaining over its decision to close part of the business?

4. A company that employs five janitors decides that the work could be done less expensively if it fires the janitors and hires an outside contractor to perform janitorial services. Must the company bargain with the janitors' union about the decision?

ADMINISTERING THE COLLECTIVE BARGAINING AGREEMENT

Although many issues affecting employment may be resolved in the collective bargaining contract, controversies will continue to arise after the parties have entered into the contract. The parties are obligated to bargain in good faith over contract interpretation. The settlement of contract interpretation disputes is often left to an arbitrator.

Arbitration

Arbitration is a process in which the parties submit issues for decision by a mutually agreed upon third party. It differs from mediation, a process in which the third party attempts to persuade the parties to reach an agreement. Most collective contracts contain an arbitration clause, providing for certain grievance and arbitration procedures to resolve contract interpretation disputes. The clause generally outlines a grievance procedure, and it establishes a method for choosing an arbitrator if the issue cannot be resolved in the early stages of the grievance procedure.

The arbitrator's authority is based on the contract's arbitration clause.

Most contracts contain broad arbitration clauses, authorizing the arbitrator to decide all disputes regarding the interpretation and application of the contract. If a controversy arises over whether a dispute is arbitrable or whether it must be decided by a court. The presumption is that the dispute is arbitrable. If the parties do not wish to have disputes decided by arbitration, they must explicitly withdraw arbitration from their contract.

Usually, in exchange for a grievance and arbitration procedure, unions agree not to strike for the duration of the collective bargaining agreement. If the union strikes in breach of a no-strike clause and the underlying dispute is arbitrable, a federal district court can enjoin the strike and order the parties to arbitration.

The arbitrator's authority is confined to deciding disputes under the contract. That is, the arbitrator must use the contract as the governing document in deciding disputes involving the contract's application. Where contract interpretation is the issue, the arbitrator uses "the law of the shop," examining past practices of the parties to give meaning to the contract's terms.

Judicial Deferral to an Arbitrator's Award

In three cases decided on the same day, the Supreme Court established a policy favoring judicial deferral to arbitration awards. These cases involved the United Steelworkers and collectively are called the Steelworkers Trilogy. The Supreme Court held that the merits of an arbitration award are irrelevant when a federal court is asked to enforce it. If a claim comes within an arbitration clause, the court must order the matter to be resolved by arbitration. Once the arbitrator makes an award, judicial review is limited to whether the award was within the authority conferred upon the arbitrator by the collective contract. The Court's decision to defer to the arbitrator on the merits of the case rests on the recognition that arbitration is part of a system of industrial self-government, in which the parties select an arbitrator who has special expertise that courts generally lack.

STRIKES, BOYCOTTS, AND PICKETING

Although the national labor policy promotes industrial peace through collective bargaining, occasionally bargaining efforts fail to produce agreement and the parties resort to their economic weapons. The economic weapon of labor is the strike. Employer economic weapons include lockouts and hiring strike replacements.

The NLRA specifically guarantees employees the right to strike. Nevertheless, certain job actions are not protected. Violent conduct is not protected; neither are slowdowns, partial strikes, refusals to work overtime, or similar actions. Sometimes the line between protected and unprotected conduct is difficult to draw, as the following case illustrates.

NLRB v. Local 1229, International Brotherhood of Electrical Workers

346 U.S. 464 (1953)

Local 1229 of the International Brotherhood of Electrical Workers (respondent) was at an impasse in bargaining with Jefferson Standard Broadcasting Co., which operated radio station WBT in Charlotte, North Carolina. Although the Brotherhood did not strike, it did picket the station. After about six weeks, several picketers began distributing handbills which read:

> ### IS CHARLOTTE A SECOND-CLASS CITY?
>
> You might think so from the kind of television programs being presented by the Jefferson Standard Broadcasting Co. over WBTV. Have you seen one of their television programs lately? Did you know that all the programs presented over WBTV are on film and may be from one day to five years old. There are no local programs presented by WBTV. You cannot receive the local baseball games, football games or other local events because WBTV does not have the proper equipment to make these pickups. Cities like New York, Boston, Philadelphia, Washington receive such programs nightly. Why doesn't the Jefferson Standard Broadcasting Company purchase the needed equipment to bring you the same type of programs enjoyed by other leading American cities? Could it be that they consider Charlotte a second-class community and only entitled to the pictures now being presented to them?
> —WBT Technicians

The company responded by discharging the employees. The NLRB (petitioner) held that the employees' action was unprotected and that the employer did not commit an unfair labor practice when it discharged the employees. The court of appeals remanded the case to the NLRB to determine whether the employees' conduct was unlawful. The Supreme Court reversed the court of appeals.

Justice Burton

In its essence, the issue is simple. It is whether these employees, whose contracts of employment had expired, were discharged "for cause." They were discharged solely because, at a critical time in the initiation of the company's television service, they sponsored or distributed 5,000 handbills making a sharp, public, disparaging attack upon the quality of the company's product and its businesslike policies, in a manner reasonably calculated to harm the company's reputation and reduce its income. The attack was made by them expressly as "WBT Technicians." It continued ten days without indication of abatement. The Board found that —

"It [the handbill] occasioned widespread comment in the community, and caused Respondent to apprehend a loss of advertising revenue due to dissatisfaction with its television broadcasting service.

"In short, the employees in this case deliberately undertook to alienate their employer's customers by impugning the technical quality of his product. As the Trial Examiner found, they did not misrepresent, at least willfully, the facts they cited to support their disparaging report. And their ultimate purpose—to extract a concession from the employer with respect to the terms of their employment—was lawful. That purpose, however, was undisclosed; the employees purported to speak as experts, in the interest of consumers and the public at large. They did not indicate that they sought to secure any benefit for themselves *as employees*, by casting discredit upon their employer."

*   *   *   *   *

There is no more elemental cause for discharge of an employee than disloyalty to his employer. It is equally elemental that the Taft-Hartley Act seeks to strengthen, rather than to weaken, that cooperation, continuity of service and cordial contractual relation between employer and employee that is born of loyalty to their common enterprise.

Congress, while safeguarding, in §7, the right of employees to engage in "concerted activities for the purpose of collective bargaining or other mutual aid or protection," did not weaken the underlying contractual bonds and loyalties of employer and employee.

*   *   *   *   *

In the instant case the Board found that the company's discharge of the nine offenders resulted from the sponsoring and distributing the "Second-Class City" handbills of August 24–September 3, issued in their name as the "WBT TECHNICIANS." Assuming that there had been no pending labor controversy, the conduct of the "WBT TECHNICIANS" from August 24 through September 3 unquestionably would have provided adequate cause for their disciplinary discharge. . . . Their attack related itself to no labor practice of the company. It made no reference to wages, hours or working conditions. The policies attacked were those of finance and public relations for which management, not technicians, must be responsible. The attack asked for no public sympathy or support. It was a continuing attack, initiated while off duty, upon the very interests which the attackers were being paid to conserve and develop. Nothing could be further from the purpose of the Act than to require an employer to finance such activities. Nothing would contribute less to the Act's declared purpose of promoting industrial peace and stability.

The fortuity of the coexistence of a labor dispute affords these technicians no substantial defense. While they were also union men and leaders in the labor controversy, they took pains to separate those categories. In contrast to their claims on the picket line as to the labor controversy, their handbill of August 24 omitted all reference to it. The handbill diverted attention from the labor controversy. It attacked public policies of the company which had no discernible relation to that controversy. The only connection between the handbill and the labor controversy was an ultimate and undisclosed purpose or motive on the part of some of the sponsors that, by the hoped-for financial pressure, the attack might extract from the company some future concession. A disclosure of that motive might have lost more public support for the employees than it would have gained, for it would have given the handbill more the character of coercion than of collective bargaining. Referring to the attack, the Board said "In our judgment, these tactics, in the circumstances of this case, were hardly less 'indefensible' than acts of physical sabotage." In any event, the findings of the Board effectively separate the attack from the labor controversy and treat it solely as one made by the company's technical experts upon the quality of the company's product. As such, it was as adequate a cause for the discharge of its sponsors as if the labor controversy had not been pending.

CASE QUESTIONS

1. How did the handbilling in this case differ from a conventional strike? Is not a strike an act of disloyalty? Why is a strike protected when the handbilling is not?

2. Could the union have changed the handbill in any way to make it protected? Explain.

3. Does the union's handbilling amount to a breach of its duty to bargain in good faith? Explain.

4. The employees of Intercity Bus Co. are on strike. They distribute handbills that alert consumers to the strike, state that the buses are not being operated by dependable union bus drivers, and that the union cannot vouch for the safety of the company's operation. Can the employer fire the strikers? Why or why not?

Illegal Job Actions

Some economic weapons that unions employ, in addition to being unprotected, are also unfair labor practices. These include secondary boycotts, work assignment disputes, and picketing for recognition.

Secondary Boycotts

Section 8 (b)(4) prohibits secondary boycotts. A *secondary boycott* exerts union pressure on a party with whom it has no dispute to cease dealing with a party with whom the union has a dispute. Secondary boycotts must be distinguished from lawful *primary activity*. For example, if the union has a dispute with XYZ Co. and goes on strike, the activity is primary and lawful, even though XYZ's customers find their supplies interrupted and take their business to XYZ's competitors. However, if the union pickets XYZ's customers to force them to cease doing business with XYZ, the activity is secondary and unlawful.

It is sometimes difficult to distinguish primary from secondary activity, particularly if two companies are located at the same site. Generally, the picketing will be considered primary where four conditions are met:

— The picketing is limited to times when the primary employer is present

— The primary employer is engaged in its normal business at the site
— The picketing is restricted to places reasonably close to the primary employer
— The picket signs clearly disclose that the dispute is with the primary employer

A corrolary to the common site situation is the "reserved gate rule." If an employer reserves a plant entrance for the exclusive use of outside contractors, a union on strike against the employer may not picket that entrance.

A *hot cargo agreement* is a form of secondary boycott and is therefore illegal. A hot cargo agreement provides that the employer will not deal with nonunion employers or that the employees need not handle nonunion goods.

Work Assignment Disputes

In a work assignment dispute, an employer is caught between conflicting claims of two unions. For example, assume that a contractor employs sheet metal workers represented by the Sheet Metal Workers Union and carpenters represented by the Carpenters Union. The company accepts a job to install a heating system that requires attaching metal duct work to wooden supports. If the employer assigns the work to its sheet metal workers, the carpenters will strike. If it assigns the work to its carpenters the sheet metal workers will strike.

Section 8(b)(4) prohibits strikes and similar conduct to coerce the assignment of work to a particular group of employees. If such coercion is applied, the employer may file a charge with the NLRB. The NLRB must affirmatively resolve the work assignment dispute.

Recognition Picketing

A union that is not certified to represent a company's employees might picket the employer to recognize it or to force the employees to choose it as their representative.

Section 8(b)(7) bans such recognitional or organizational picketing where: (1) another union has already been recognized by the employer as the employees' representative and the board will not conduct an election because of an existing contract with the other union; (2) the employees voted in a valid board representation election within the preceding 12 months; or (3) the union pickets for more than 30 days without filing a petition for a representation election.

A union's informational picketing is protected. Informational picketing is picketing for the purpose of truthfully advising the public that an employer does not employ union members or have a contract with a labor organization. The protection given to informational picketing is lost where it induces individuals employed by others to refuse to pick up or deliver goods or perform other services.

Employer Responses to Strikes

If a strike or job action is illegal or unprotected, the employer may discharge the strikers. Protected strikes are of two types: *economic strikes*, which involve collective bargaining issues, and *unfair labor practice strikes*, which are caused or prolonged by an employer's unfair labor practices.

An employer can permanently replace economic strikers, and it need not fire the replacements when the strikers are ready to return to work. However, an employer cannot fire the strikers. Even those who have been replaced remain employees and must be recalled if positions open up for them. Unfair labor practice strikers may not be permanently replaced.

The legality of other employer actions depends on whether they are legitimate economic weapons or are inherently destructive of employee rights. For example, an employer may lock out, but it may not grant superseniority to replacements. Superseniority would guarantee replacements preferred treatment over strikers as long as they remain with the employer. The effects of superseniority remain long after the strike has ended and are necessarily destructive of employee rights.

ALTERNATIVE APPROACHES

The adversarial model of labor relations in the United States differs from the labor practices of other capitalist countries, most notably the countries of Western Europe. In most Western European countries cooperation, not conflict, is the thrust of labor relations policy. While there are many examples of labor relations systems based on cooperation, perhaps the most striking is the concept of codetermination.

Codetermination is sometimes called "industrial democracy" or "participatory management." Under codetermination, workers share in management decision making by participating on corporate boards of directors and plant works councils. Employee representatives may have voting seats on corporate boards. They may consult corporate boards and participate in formulating corporate policy. Employee representatives may also sit on works councils, which are plant-level committees consisting of management and labor representatives who implement policy. A works council may decide such matters as plant production schedules and employee discipline cases. The objective of codetermination is to instill a spirit of cooperation into labor-management relations, from the top levels of policy making to implementation on the shop floor.

The existence of codetermination on the Continent and its absence in the United States suggest either that labor–management relations in the two areas are developing in different directions, or that they are at different stages of development. The existence abroad of alternative forms of labor relations may spur American management to experiment with such forms. Whether the NLRA can accommodate these alternative approaches remains to be seen.

CHAPTER PROBLEMS

1. Grossinger's, Inc. is a resort hotel. Its employees, primarily waiters, waitresses, kitchen workers, lifeguards, and camp counselors, live in housing provided by Grossinger's. They eat all of their meals on the grounds. They are allowed to use the hotel's recreational facilities on their time off. Consequently, many rarely leave the premises. The Hotel and Restaurant Workers Union is trying to organize Grossinger's employees. Can Grossinger's prohibit the union from distributing its literature on Grossinger property? Why or why not?

2. Consolidated Conglomerates, Inc. is a major conglomerate that wholly owns or has controlling interest in 45 different companies, one of which is Ace Widget Co. The Widget Workers Union began an organizing drive at Ace on January 2. On February 1, the union filed a representation petition with the NLRB. Consolidated administers a health insurance plan that covers all employees of Consolidated and its subsidiaries. On January 15, Consolidated decided to amend the plan, effective February 15, to provide dental benefits. The officials in charge of the plan were unaware of the organizing drive at Ace.

A representation election is scheduled at Ace for March 15. Should Ace delay implementing the dental benefits until after March 15? What are the risks of implementing the plan at Ace on February 15? What are the risks of delaying implementation?

3. General Foods Corp. has established a job-enrichment program under which 30 employees are divided into four teams. The teams act by consensus and make job assignments to individual team members, assign job rotations, and schedule overtime among team members. They also interview job applicants.

General Foods has also retained a consultant to hold periodic meetings with team members and first line supervisors in an effort to improve communications and build trust. At these meetings complaints about the company and job conditions may be aired. Is General Foods in danger of violating section 8(a)(2)? Explain.

4. Wallace Widget Work's workforce is 57 percent white and 43 percent black. Wallace has never discriminated on the basis of race in hiring or layoffs. There have been some recent layoffs in which employees with the least seniority were let go. About half of these employees were black and half white. During an election campaign the International Widget Workers distributed leaflets which stated, among other things: "If all blacks don't vote together in a group and the union loses the election, all blacks will be fired. Wallace is already using the slow period as an excuse to fire blacks." About a week before the election Wallace placed in each employee's pay envelope a leaflet entitled "The Truth about Layoffs" which provided a breakdown by race of all employees laid off. The union won the election. Will the NLRB set it aside?

5. Lucy's Lounge employs 75 waiters, waitresses, bartenders, and kitchen workers who are represented by the Hotel and Restaurant Employees Union. The union is on strike over Lucy's failure to agree to a new collective bargaining agreement. Can Lucy appeal to the employees to return to work? If so, how should the appeal be worded? If a majority of the employees return, must Lucy continue to bargain with the union?

6. The United Automobile, Aerospace, and Agricultural Implement Workers, Local 588, represents the employees of an automobile parts stamping plant operated by the Ford Motor Company. For many years Ford has provided in-plant food services to the employees. These services, which include both cafeterias and vending machines, are managed by ARA Services, Inc., under a contract with Ford whereby ARA provides the food services in exchange for reimbursement of costs and a 9 percent surcharge on receipts. Over the years, Ford and the union have negotiated about food services. Their local contract has included provisions covering the staffing of service lines, the restocking and repair of vending machines, and menu variety. Ford, however, has always refused to bargain about the prices of food items. Ford notified the union that cafeteria and vending machine prices would be increased by unspecified amounts. The union requested bargaining over prices and services and asked for information regarding Ford's involvement in food services. These requests were refused by Ford. The union filed an unfair labor practice charge with the NLRB. Will the union succeed in obtaining an NLRB order to bargain on the union requests? Explain.

7. During the course of collective bargaining, the employer objected to the union's demands for a wage increase, claiming that "anything over 1 percent will make us unprofitable and anything over 3 percent will bankrupt us." The union has demanded that it be permitted to audit the employer's books to verify the claim. Must the employer agree? Why or why not?

8. Safeco Title Insurance Company does business with several title companies that derive over 90 percent of their gross income from the sale of Safeco insurance policies. When contract negotiations between Safeco and the Retail Store Employees Union Local 1001, the bargaining representative of certain Safeco employees, reached an impasse, the employees went on strike. The union picketed each of the title companies, urging customers to support the strike by canceling their Safeco policies. Safeco and one of the title companies filed complaints with the NLRB charging that the union had engaged in an unfair labor practice. Will the board order the union to cease and desist picketing? Explain.

9. Due to a dispute over wages, High Tech Industries was struck by a union representing 75 of its employees. High Tech continued operating during the strike and further automated its operations. The strike was long and bitter. By the time it ended, High Tech had eliminated 35 of the 75 jobs. High Tech recalled 40 of the 75 employees. Of the remaining 35, 15 did not seek to return to their jobs, 15 were not recalled because they had assaulted supervisors and others who had crossed the union's picket lines, and 5 were not recalled because they were the union officers who led the strike. Did High Tech violate the NLRA? Why or why not?

10. What economic, political, and social differences may account for the differences between American and Western European labor relations policies?

CHAPTER 16

LABOR STANDARDS AND EMPLOYEE SAFETY

During the first century of U.S. history, employment practices were established and regulated by the individuals involved. There was little need for governmental intervention, for employment relationships then were relatively simple. As the U.S. economy expanded and became more complex, employment relationships became more impersonal and the need for regulation emerged. The industrial revolution drastically altered traditional work conditions and employment practices.

The common law did not quickly adapt to these changing conditions. Most employment relationships were for indefinite periods of time. Courts generally held that these relationships were terminable at the will of either party. The result was that employers were able to exercise absolute authority over their employees. In response to this situation, Congress and state legislatures sought to enact legislation aimed at protecting the rights of workers.

Early attempts to regulate employment practices were frustrated by successful constitutional challenges. Legislation was deemed to infringe upon the freedom to contract as guaranteed by Article 1, Section 10, of the Constitution and by the due process clauses of the fifth and fourteenth amendments. Gradually, however, judicial interpretation began to view contractual freedom as a limited right that Congress and the states could regulate. These constitutional considerations are discussed in detail in chapter three.

With their regulatory powers firmly established, Congress and state legislatures moved to enact much-needed social legislation designed to provide minimum labor standards and safety for the American worker. Recently, courts have begun to reevaluate the validity of the traditional common-law rule that employment contracts are terminable at will. As a result, today's manager must be prepared to deal with a complex maze of statutory, administrative, and judicial regulation of the basic terms and conditions of employment. This chapter explores these fundamental regulations.

THE EVOLVING COMMON LAW OF EMPLOYMENT

The employment relationship is based on a contract. The employee agrees to perform services for the employer, who agrees to compensate the employee. Most employees are hired for an indefinite period of time. Frequently nothing is said about how or why the contract may be terminated.

The Employment-at-Will Rule

The traditional common-law rule is that the employment contract of indefinite duration is terminable at the will of either party. In other words, the employee is free to quit and the employer is free to fire at any time, for any reason, or for no reason at all. This employment-at-will rule developed when the prevailing economic philosophy was laissez-faire. It has persisted because of a view that there must be mutuality of obligation on the part of both parties to a contract. Forcing an individual to continue working for an employer when the employee no longer wishes to do so, would be tantamount to imposing an involuntary servitude, prohibited by the Thirteenth Amendment to the Constitution. Thus, if an employee is free to quit at any time, the concept of mutuality suggests that the employer should be free to fire at any time.

Erosion of the At-Will Rule

The traditional common-law view is being gradually eroded. Courts in most jurisdictions still agree that an employer has the power to discharge an employee at will. A growing number, however, have held that when an employer exercises that power in a manner that contravenes public policy, the employee may sue in tort for *abusive discharge.* These jurisdictions disagree over the circumstances under which a discharge violates public policy.

Under the most restrictive view of the tort, public policy violations occur only when the discharge is in retaliation for the employee's exercise of a statutory right or refusal to violate a statutory prohibition. A more liberal approach requires a statutory declaration of public policy but finds it violated whenever the discharge conflicts with the statutory policy. The most liberal approach allows the judiciary to define public policy independently of the legislature. The following example illustrates these conflicting approaches.

Ace Chemical Company manufactured a pesticide that was shown to cause cancer. As a result, Congress prohibited sale of the chemical in the United States after January 1. In February, Ace sold the pesticide to a number of American farmers and to agriculture supply wholesalers in Mexico. Ace fired Arnold because he refused to back-date the American sales to make it appear that they occurred before January 1. Ace fired Betty when she protested to Ace's board of directors that the chemical was being sold illegally in the U.S. The company fired Carol when she refused to sell the pesticide to customers in Mexico.

Arnold was fired for refusing to aid and abet Ace's violation of the statute banning domestic sales of the pesticide after January 1. He may recover for abusive discharge under all three views of the tort. Betty was not ordered to violate the statute, nor did she have a statutory right to complain to the board of directors. Thus, under the most restrictive view, she may not recover. She may recover under the other two views because she was attempting to prevent a violation of the statute. Carol's activity, however, did not involve the statute. It was legal to sell the pesticide in Mexico. She may recover only under the third, most liberal, approach, and only if the court decides that her discharge contravened its notions of public policy.

Although most erosion of the common law at-will rule has occurred in tort, a few jurisdictions have begun a more fundamental reexamination of the employment contract. Some of these jurisdictions imply a promise to deal in good faith. For example, suppose a sales representative is fired just prior to making enough sales to earn a substantial bonus. If this was done to prevent the sales representative from qualifying for the bonus, the employer will have breached its promise to deal in good faith. The employee can recover for breach of contract.

Other jurisdictions have held that employer promises of job security are enforceable. These jurisdictions have enforced promises found in employers' statements at the time of hire and in their personnel handbooks. One of the leading authorities in this area is the Supreme Court of Michigan, which reconsidered the employment contract in the following case.

 **Toussaint v. Blue Cross & Blue Shield of Michigan**

408 Mich. 579, 292 N.W.2d 880 (1980)

This case involved the consolidated appeals of *Toussaint v. Blue Cross* and *Ebling v. Masco Corp.* Toussaint was fired after five years in a management position with Blue Cross. At the time he was hired, he inquired about job security and was told he would be with the company as long as he was doing his job. He was also given a personnel policy manual which provided that employees who completed their probationary periods would be terminated only for just cause. He sued, claiming his discharge was not for just cause, and the jury returned a verdict of $72,835.52 in his favor. The Michigan Court of Appeals reversed; the Michigan Supreme Court reversed the Court of Appeals and reinstated the verdict.

Ebling was fired after two years in a management position with Masco. Before he was hired he negotiated with Masco and was told he would not be discharged if he was doing his job. Ebling sued, claiming his discharge was not for cause, and the jury returned a verdict of $300,000 in his favor. The Michigan Court of Appeals affirmed, as did the Michigan Supreme Court.

Justice Levin

Masco and Blue Cross contend:

(1) It is settled Michigan law that employment contracts for an indefinite term are terminable at the will of either party unless the employee has furnished consideration* to his employer other than his services. A promise by an employer to discharge only for an obviously determinable cause represents such a departure from firmly established doctrines of contract formation and the normal expectations accompanying an indefinite employment relationship that it should require separate and distinct consideration in order to be enforceable.

(2) Where a definite term of employment is specified, each party has furnished consideration by limiting his right to terminate the relationship at will, but where one party (the employer) obligates himself to continue the relationship as long as the other desires and the other (the employee) reserves the right to terminate at will, there is no mutuality of obligation and so the agreement must fail for lack of consideration.

* * * * *

So explained, the "rule" for which the employers contend appears to be a principle

of substantive contract law rather than a rule of construction.

The enforceability of a contract depends, however, on consideration and not mutuality of obligation. The proper inquiry is whether the employee has given consideration for the employer's promise of employment.

The "rule" is useful, however, as a rule of construction. Because the parties began with complete freedom, the court will presume that they intended to obligate themselves to a relationship at will.

* * * * *

We see no reason why an employment contract which does not have a definite term—the term is "indefinite"—cannot legally provide job security. When a prospective employee inquires about job security and the employer agrees that the employee shall be employed as long as he does the job, a fair construction is that the employer has agrees to give up his right to discharge at will without assigning cause and may discharge only for cause (good or just cause). The result is that the employee, if discharged without good or just cause, may maintain an action for wrongful discharge. Suppose the contracts here were written, not oral, and had provided in so many words that the employment was to continue for the life of the employee who could not

---

* Consideration is something exchanged in return for an enforceable promise. It is one of the elements of a contract usually required by a court.—Au.

be discharged, except for cause. . . . To construe such an agreement as terminable at the will of the employer would be tantamount to saying, as did the Court of Appeals in *Toussaint,* that a contract of indefinite duration *"cannot* be made other than terminable at will by a provision that states an employee will not be discharged except for cause.". . .

Where the employment is for a definite term—a year, five years, ten years—it is implied, if not expressed, that the employee can be discharged only for good cause and collective bargaining agreements often provide that discharge shall only be for good or just cause. There is, thus, no public policy against providing job security or prohibiting an employer from agreeing not to discharge except for good or just cause. That being the case, we can see no reason why such a provision in a contract having no definite term of employment with a single employee should necessarily be unenforceable and regarded, in effect, as against public policy and beyond the power of the employer to contract.

*   *   *   *   *

Toussaint's testimony was sufficient to create a question of fact for the jury whether there was a mutual understanding that it was company policy not to discharge an employee "as long as [he] did [his] job," and that this policy, expressed in documents (which said "for just cause only"), assertedly handed to Toussaint when he was hired, would apply to him as to other Blue Cross employees.

We do not, however, rest our conclusion that the jury could properly find that the Blue Cross policy manual created contractual rights solely on Toussaint's testimony concerning his conversation with the executive who interviewed and hired him.

While an employer need not establish personnel policies or practices, where an employer chooses to establish such policies and practices and makes them known to his employees, the employment relationship is presumably enhanced. The employer secures an orderly, cooperative and loyal workforce, and the employee the peace of mind associated with job security and the conviction that he will be treated fairly. No pre-employment negotiations need take place and the parties' minds need not meet on the subject; nor does it matter that the employee knows nothing of the particulars of the employer's policies and practices or that the employer may change them unilaterally. It is enough that the employer chooses, presumably in its own interest, to create an environment in which the employee believes that, whatever the personnel policies and practices, they are established and official at any given time, purport to be fair, and are applied consistently and uniformly to each employee. The employer has then created a situation "instinct with an obligation."

*   *   *   *   *

If there is in effect a policy to dismiss for cause only, the employer may not depart from that policy at whim simply because he was under no obligation to institute the policy in the first place. Having announced the policy, presumably with a view to obtaining the benefit of improved employee attitudes and behavior and improved quality of the work force, the employer may not treat its promise as illusory.

Justice Ryan *(dissenting in Toussaint)*

The only direct evidence in the record bearing on the plaintiff's claim that the Supervisory Manual and the Guidelines constituted the written portion of his employment contract is Mr. Toussaint's testimony that the documents were handed to him on the day he was hired, and his testimony that he "felt" he had an employment contract and that three portions of the manual described in his complaint were "part of it."

Nowhere, either in the manual or the Guidelines pamphlet, is there to be found any reference to Mr. Toussaint, by name or otherwise, to his specific duties, job description or the compensation to be paid him. The documents contain no reference to a contract of employment of any kind. Neither document is signed by the plaintiff or any representative of the defendant, nor is a place provided for such signatures.

Repeatedly throughout the manual notebook there appears the declaration that the document is a statement of company policy on the subjects addressed. Pages of the manual are regularly added and deleted by company officials unilaterally, under the supervision of the Blue Cross Personnel Department, without notice to any employee.

The record bears no evidence that during Mr. Toussaint's several pre-employment interviews any reference was made either to the manual or guidelines, or even to the subject of a written employment contract. Mr. Toussaint did not learn of the existence of the manual and guidelines until they were handed to him *after* he was hired on May 1, 1967. That is in keeping with the testimony of defendant's witnesses that the manual is given to supervisory level employees as an aid in supervising persons in their charge and not as declarative of the contract terms of an employee's hire.

*   *   *   *   *

We have no doubt that circumstances could exist in which an employer's written policies, including those of the defendant, might be incorporated by reference, expressly or impliedly, into an otherwise oral employment contract and thus become a declaration of the employment agreement. This, however, is not such a case. Here the record is wholly devoid of evidence, direct or circumstantial, to justify the conclusion that the parties agreed that the manual or the Guidelines, or either of them, would become the plaintiff's contract of employment.

Defendant's 250-page manual of personnel policies cannot become its employment contract with some or all of its employees by reason of the company's inadvertence and inattention, or by accident. Neither can defendant be chargeable with incorporating by reference some or all of the terms of its manual into an oral employment agreement with plaintiff simply because a copy of the manual was handed to the plaintiff after he was hired or because the policy manual speaks in general terms to many of the same subjects with which a contract of employment would be concerned, such as sick benefits, vacation time, hours of work and similar provisions.

*   *   *   *   *

Employment contracts, like other binding agreements, are the product of informed understanding and mutual assent as to the subject matter. . . .

CASE QUESTIONS

1. What does Justice Levin mean when he characterizes the at-will rule as a rule of construction rather than a rule of law? Why is this significant?

2. Is it significant to Justice Levin that Toussaint was given a copy of the personnel manual? To Justice Ryan? Explain.

3. Is it significant to Justice Levin that the

manual was handed to Toussaint after he was formally hired? Is it significant to Justice Ryan? Explain.

4. Does *Toussaint* require just cause whenever an employee is to be discharged? Explain.

5. If Blue Cross required Toussaint to sign a statement acknowledging that he was terminable at will, would the outcome have been different? Why or why not?

WORKERS' COMPENSATION

Workers' compensation statutes were the first legislative reaction to the common law's failure to respond to the changing employment environment. Enacted at the state level, these statutes protect workers and their families from the risks of employment-related injury, disease, or death. This section discusses the common-law background and origin of workers' compensation statutes. It also examines the scope of coverage and benefits of current statutes and some of the more common issues that arise in determining whether coverage should be afforded in a particular case.

Common-Law Background

At common law, an employee injured in the course of employment could sue the employer whose negligence caused the injury. Negligence is the failure to exercise ordinary care in such a way as to injure another person whom it is one's duty to protect against harm. Ordinary care is the degree of care a reasonable person would exercise under the circumstances. The reasonable person is a mythical figure who serves as the legal standard against which one's actions or nonactions are measured. An employer whose conduct falls short of that expected from a reasonable person has breached the standard of ordinary care. If that breach results in injury to an employee, the employer may be liable. Negligence is discussed at greater length in chapters 1 and 5.

At common law, the employer's liability was usually defeated by three legal defenses:

— The fellow servant doctrine
— Assumption of the risk
— Contributory negligence

The Fellow Servant Doctrine

Under the fellow servant doctrine, an employer is not liable to an employee who is injured as a result of a coemployee's negligence. The defense first emerged in 1827 in the English case of *Priestley v. Fowler*[1] but was quickly imported into the United States. The first state court to adopt the doctrine reasoned that an implied contract between the employer and the employee

---

[1] (1837) M&W 1, 150 Reprint 1030.

relieved the former of liability. Because a laissez-faire economic philosophy prevailed and courts desired to spur industrial enterprise, the fellow servant doctrine was soon extended throughout the states.

Assumption of the Risk

Another prong of the *Priestley* decision was the observation that "the servant is not bound to risk his safety in the service of his master and may, if he thinks fit, decline any service in which he reasonably apprehends injury to himself." Accordingly, an employee is charged with assuming the risk of injury that a particular job entails. If in the face of the normal dangers of a job, the employee continues to work, that employee may not recover for injury. This doctrine was also imported into the United States.

Contributory Negligence

Just as the common law recognized an employer's responsibility to exercise reasonable care to protect employees from injury, it also recognized that employees were obligated to exercise reasonable care for their self-protection. Thus, employees could not recover for injuries to which their own negligence contributed. If, for example, the employer negligently failed to warn an employee of a dangerous crevice in a mine, the employer was not held liable if the employee fell into the crevice while negligently ignoring the obvious danger. The contributory negligence defense was a complete bar to recovery by the employee. This was true even when the employee's negligence was slight compared to that of the employer.

In 1903 the Federal Employers' Liability Act (FELA) was enacted. It was a pivotal event in the development of a workers' compensation employee protection system. FELA covered employees of common carriers engaged in interstate or foreign commerce. It provided that:

— Contributory negligence would reduce damages but would not completely bar recovery.
— Neither contributory negligence nor assumption of the risk would apply in the event of employer safety statute violations.
— A railroad employer was liable for the negligence of all officers and agents causing injury to employees.

In 1902 Maryland enacted the first state workers' compensation statute. It applied only to miners. Montana followed suit in 1909. By 1920 only eight states were without some type of workers' compensation law. By 1949 every state had some such law to cover specified employees. Although these laws vary from state to state, they possess some common features.

Coverage

The objective of workers' compensation laws is to provide assistance to employees or their dependents when the employees are injured or killed on the job. Fault is immaterial. Injured employees are entitled to benefits whether or not they were negligent and whether or not their employer was free from fault. In most states, an injured employee cannot sue an employer for damages beyond the benefits allowed by the compensation statute unless the employer has not complied with the compensation law. The injured employee can still sue third parties who cause injury, such as negligent coemployees or manufacturers of defective machines. However, the employer or the state workers' compensation insurance fund is usually indemnified from the recovery up to the amount of workers' compensation benefits that it paid to the injured employee.

Employees are covered. Independent contractors are not. The basic distinction between an employee and an independent contractor turns on the degree of the employer's control over the worker. An employer controls the method and manner with which employees perform the work. If the employer does not retain control of these details but is merely interested in its ultimate results, the worker is an independent contractor. For example, a salesperson who sells magazines door to door on a solely commission basis is usually considered an independent contractor. Here the employer does not normally dictate the details of the work, such as its hours and methods. However, a magazine salesperson would probably be considered an employee if attendance at sales meetings, canvass of a specified area, and specified working hours were required. Often the distinction between an employee and an independent contractor is subtle, turning on particular facts of the contractual relationship.

Many states mandate that an employer provide coverage for its employees. In other states, coverage is discretionary and an employer may elect to opt out. In almost all of the elective jurisdictions, both employer and employee have the right to reject coverage, but acceptance is presumed in the absence of express rejection. Normally some workers, such as agricultural and casual employees, are excluded from workers' compensation statutes.

Benefits

Although compensation benefits vary from state to state, they normally include payment for hospital and medical expenses, including artificial limbs and rehabilitation services. They also include compensation for lost wages. The amounts vary from one-half to two-thirds of the employee's average weekly wage. Some states require that an employee be out of work for a specified period of time, such as a week, before qualifying for lost income benefits. Lost income benefits may be divided into four categories:

— Temporary total disability
— Temporary partial disability
— Permanent partial disability
— Permanent total disability

Temporary total disability is present when an injury prevents an employee from returning to work for a specific time. Temporary partial disability occurs when an employee is forced by injury to return to a lower-paying job for a specific time. For example, a textile mill threader whose threading finger and thumb are injured on the job might be able to return to lower-paying work. Here the wage impairment disability benefits are designated temporary partial. These benefits are computed on the basis of diminution in wages.

Permanent partial disability prevents an individual from performing his or her current job but does not bar the employee from all forms of gainful employment. Many states have statutory guidelines that translate the percentage of permanent partial disability into a monetary award.

A permanently and totally disabled employee is one who will never again be able to do any type of work. Some state statutes presume permanent total disability when an employee loses any two limbs or eyes. In the absence of such a presumption, the employee must show that the injury in fact caused permanent incapacity to work.

In addition to these four forms of loss-of-income disability, many states provide for a loss-of-member compensation according to a statutory schedule for losses. For example, in Ohio the loss of a thumb is compensated by 60 weeks of benefits to the injured employee in a weekly amount equal to two-thirds of the employee's average weekly wage. Most states also pay death awards to the employee's dependents or survivors.

Administration

Workers' compensation systems are usually administered by an agency referred to as an industrial commission or a workers' compensation bureau. The system used for the administration of compensation claims in Ohio is typical. There administrative control over the program is exercised by the Bureau of Workers Compensation. The bureau has two primary administrative functions: adjudication of claims and control of the general business management of the workers' compensation system.

A typical claim process begins when an injured employee applies to the bureau for benefits. When the application is received, it is checked for completeness and correctness, numbered, indexed, and docketed, so that it is ready for adjudication by a claims examiner. If the employer verifies the facts contained in the claim, the claim is certified and the employer waives the right to a formal hearing. Eight-five percent of all claims are certified, and almost all of those are allowed by the claims examiners.

Claims examiners determine the proper payment of benefits in all certified claims. The remaining claims are sent for investigation to the district office nearest the claimant's residence. About 66 percent of these are accepted and processed without a formal hearing. Thus, only 5 percent of all claims are contested.

Contested claims are heard by a district hearing officer. The hearing is informal, and rules of evidence and procedure are relaxed. Legal representation is optional. When the decison is rendered, either party may file for a reconsideration hearing, which is routinely conducted in the central office by members of the administrator's staff. If dissatisfied with the outcome of this hearing, a party can appeal to the regional board. The administrator, represented by the attorney general, becomes a party at this stage. A pretrial conference is held, followed by a hearing at which a decision is rendered. The regional board's decision can be appealed to the Industrial Commission, which may hear the case or decline to hear it and thus affirm the regional board decision. At this point, a dissatisfied party may seek further review in the court of common pleas, the trial court of general jurisdiction. Once the validity of an employee's claim is finally established, the employer must satisfy the award.

Funding

State workers' compensation statutes generally use one of three accepted methods for funding compensation benefits: private insurance, self-insurance, and payment into a state fund. The amount paid by the employer is determined by various factors, including the type of industry and prior accident experience. Most states have official rating systems for determining the premiums necessary to pay all accepted claims. Rate determination is an administrative function and differs among the states. Many states have a merit rating system whereby an employer with a history of fewer injuries receives a premium concession.

Compensable Injuries

Injuries that arise out of the employment and happen in the course of the employment are normally compensable under workers' compensation acts. Determining whether an injury arose out of the employment often requires an examination of the relationship between the injury and the job. Is the risk or hazard that resulted in injury peculiar to the type of work the employee performed? If so, then the injury arose out of the employment. For example, a bulldozer operator who is injured when the bulldozer overturns on an embankment has obviously sustained injury as a result of a risk peculiar to the job. But if a bulldozer operator is struck and killed by a low-flying plane, there is a serious question of whether the death arose out of the employment. The risks created by the plane appear to be no greater to the bulldozer operator than to the public at large. They are not peculiar to the job. However, many states grant recovery in such a case, reasoning that but for the particular employment the injury would not have occurred.

A serious question of compensability occurs when, for example, an employee suffers an epileptic seizure while working and as a result falls to the floor and sustains a head injury. Most courts would probably deny recovery because the employee's preexisting epileptic condition was a contributory cause of the injury and was personal to the employee. The courts that deny recovery hold that the injury does not arise out of the employment because there is no causal connection between the epileptic attack and the job. More liberal courts allow recovery in these circumstances. They reason that the injury was caused by the impact with which the employee's head struck the floor and that this contact is a risk or hazard incident to the employment.

In addition to arising out of the employment, an injury must have occurred in the course of the employment. Here courts examine the time, location, and circumstances of the accident in relationship to the employment.

Courts have exhibited a liberal tendency in awarding compensation on a finding that an accident both arose out of and was in the course of employment. For example, the Supreme Court of New Jersey upheld a workers' compensation award to an employee who was robbed and shot during his lunch break as he was returning to his place of employment after purchasing a soda and sandwich "to go."[2]

Going and Coming Rule

The most familiar and troublesome employment problems are those that involve the going and coming rule. Under this rule, employees with a fixed time and place of employment are not generally compensated for injuries sustained on the way to and from the workplace. They are not deemed to be within the course of employment. The converse of the going and coming rule is that employees usually recover for injuries if they have arrived on the job or have not yet departed from it. It is not always easy to discern when an employee has actually arrived at or departed from work. In *Lee v. Cady* an employee on his way to work, in the act of reaching for the door handle of his place of work, slipped on an icy public sidewalk and was injured.[3] Even though the employee had actually crossed the employer's boundary, recovery was denied because the employee was still "subject to the common risks" of the street.

Most courts apply the *premises rule* as a criterion for determining whether an employee may recover under the going and coming rule. Under the premises rule, an employee injured while on the employer's premises may recover even though going to or coming from the work site.

It is generally agreed that carrying work-related items while going to and from work does not automatically negate the going and coming rule. An accountant carrying papers to work on at home in the evening would not normally be protected if injury resulted from a slip on the icy steps leading to his or her home. Normally an accountant could remain at the office to do the work; it is taken home only for the accountant's

---

[2] *Wyatt v. Metropolitan Maintenance Co.*, 74 N.J. 167, 376 A.2d 1222 (1977).
[3] 294 Mich. 460, 293 N.W. 718 (1940).

convenience. However, protection is afforded if on the way home an employee performs a service to an employer. For example, where an employee mails work-related letters on the way home, most courts permit recovery for injuries incurred on the way to the mailbox.

Employees whose work entails travel away from the employer's premises do not fit easily under the going and coming rule. Most jurisdictions find such employees to be continuously within the course of employment during a trip, except where a distinct deviation from the course of employment occurs. Issues involved in the going and coming rule are explored in the following case.

Robinson v. Industrial Commission

449 N.E. 2d 106 (Ill. 1983)

Mrs. Robinson (petitioner) appealed the Industrial Commission's denial of compensation for the death of Mr. Robinson, her husband (decedent). The Illinois Supreme Court reversed.

Mr. Robinson was a marketing director for a real estate developer (respondent). His job involved traveling between his office and real estate development sites. On December 23, 1976, Mr. Robinson left his office to visit the Red Haw development and to take his son Christmas shopping. He apparently planned to take the most direct route to accomplish both tasks; go first to his home to pick up his son, then to Red Haw, and then to the shopping mall. This was not the most direct route between his office and Red Haw. Mr. Robinson was killed in a traffic accident between his office and home.

Justice Goldenhersh

This court has on many occasions been required to consider the question whether accidental injuries sustained by an employee while away from his place of employment are compensable. In *Ace Pest Control, Inc. v. Industrial Com.* the court said:

"The Workmen's Compensation Act was not intended to insure employees against all accidental injuries but only those which arise out of acts which the employee is instructed to perform by his employer; acts which he has a common law or statutory duty to perform while performing duties for his employer; or acts which the employee might be reasonably expected to perform incident to his assigned duties."

* * * * *

In *Ace Pest Control* a termite control operator was killed by a passing automobile while assisting a stranded motorist. In holding that his death arose out of and in the course of his employment the court said that the activities in which he was engaged at the time of his death "were such as might have been reasonably expected or foreseen by his employer." . . .

The testimony shows that the least circuitous route to follow in accomplishing decedent's objective of picking up his son, visiting the houses at Red Haw and then taking his son to a shopping mall was to go first to his home, then to Red Haw and then to the mall. . . . [D]ecedent's supervisor testified that his action in stopping to pick up his son on the way to the job site did not violate any of respondents' rules. . . . [T]he extent of the deviation which resulted from his first going to his home rather than directly to Red Haw. . . . appears to be insubstantial. Had the accident occurred while the decedent was en route from his office directly to Red Haw there would be no question of compensability, and recovery should not be denied because he performed the reasonable and foreseeable act of stopping on the way to pick up his son.

*   *   *   *   *

We hold that the decision of the Industrial Commission is contrary to the manifest weight of the evidence. . . . The judgment is therefore reversed . . . and the cause is remanded to the Industrial Commission with directions to award workmen's compensation in the appropriate amount.

Justice Moran (dissenting)

I disagree with the majority's conclusion that because decedent's trip to his home to pick up his son was reasonable it therefore arose out of and in the course of his employment. The mere fact that one is an outside employee does not *ipso facto** bring all of his reasonable activities within the course of employment. "Employees whose work entails travel away from the employer's premises are held in the majority of jurisdiction [*sic*] to be within the course of their employment continuously during the trip, except when a distinct departure on a personal errand is shown."

Picking up his son to go Christmas shopping was not in the course of the decedent's business; rather, it was part of his own personal affairs. "When an employee deviates from his business route by taking a side-trip that is clearly identifiable as such, he is unquestionably beyond the course of his employment while going away from the business route and toward the personal objective. . . ."

The evidence showed . . . decedent had turned off the closest, direct route to Red Haw and headed toward his home. As such, dependent was on a personal side-trip at the time of his accident and was therefore not in the course of his employment. For this reason, I would affirm the denial of compensation.

---

* By the mere fact itself.—Au.

CASE QUESTIONS

1. What standard does Justice Goldenhersh apply to the decedent's conduct? What standard does Justice Moran apply?

2. Is it significant that the employer's rules permitted decedent to pick up his son on the way to Red Haw? Why?

3. Assume that decedent's home had been located on the most direct route between his office and Red Haw. What effect would this have had on the case?

4. How would Justice Moran reconcile his dissent in this case with the result in the *Ace Pest Control* case?

Horseplay

Engaging in horseplay may remove an employee from the course of employment category. However, the innocent victim of horseplay is not automatically outside the course of employment and will normally be compensated. For example, in *Burns v. Merritt Engineering Co.* a coemployee offered the injured party a drink from a bottle purported to contain gin.[4] It actually contained carbon tetrachloride, and the worker became violently ill and disabled after drinking the contents. Despite a rule in the employment contract that forbade drinking alcohol on company property, the court determined that the injury occurred in the course of employment and was compensable.

In determining whether a participant should be compensated for injury in horseplay cases, courts consider the extent of the deviation from employment, the seriousness of the deviation, and whether some horseplay is normally expected in the course of the employment involved. Some states permit recovery even to instigators of horseplay.

Occupational Disease

All states provide coverage for occupational diseases, though compensation in this area has lagged behind compensation for occupational accidents. Generally coverage is granted for any disease arising out of exposure to harmful conditions of employment when those conditions are present in a greater degree than exists in employment generally. Lung and skin disorders, allergies, and hearing loss have been the subject of compensation awards for occupational diseases. Some courts have even gone so far as to compensate the aggravating effect of "compensationitis," a psychological disorder which causes symptoms of an injury to continue past the normal recovery period.

Mental Injury

In recent years courts have been faced with an increased number of cases in which employees seek recovery for mental injury. Three distinct categories of cases have emerged. The first involves cases in which a physical injury sustained at work results in mental illness or injury. A worker who receives an electric shock while working on an electric wire may, in addition to incurring physical harm, experience psychic injury such as a phobic reaction to electric wires or a hysterical paralysis. Here courts have had little difficulty in compensating the full injury, including the mental portion. The second category involves cases in which a mental impact or mental stimulus encountered on the job results in distinct physical injury. For example, fright due to a sudden noise or an electric flash may result in a cerebral hemorrhage or heart failure. Compensation is generally awarded in such cases. Other cases in this category involve physical injuries which result, not from a single traumatic episode, but from the cumulative effect of mental pressure over a period of time. An employee may sustain a heart attack because of years of on-the-job mental

---

[4] 303 N.Y. 131, 96 N.E.2d 739 (1951).

strain. In most jurisdictions, workers' compensation coverage in such cases turns on the connection between the work and the injury. If the strain or exertion caused by employment contributed to the injury, it will be compensable regardless of other contributing factors. The third category is the most troublesome. It involves mental injury absent physical impact. The jurisdictions split regarding the compensability of such injuries.

FAIR LABOR STANDARDS

In 1938 Congress enacted the Fair Labor Standards Act (FLSA) in an attempt to combat the devastating effects of the Great Depression. Congress intended to stimulate and stabilize the economy. Toward that end, the FSLA regulates minimum wages, maximum hours, and child labor practices. In addition, the act provides for the administrative apparatus necessary to ensure compliance and enforcement.

Wage and Hour Laws

The most important provisions of the FLSA are concerned with the regulation of wages and hours. Initially the act stipulated a minimum wage of 25 cents per hour and a maximum standard workweek of 44 hours. Any employee who fell under the act's coverage was guaranteed a wage of not less than the minimum wage for every hour worked up to 44 hours per week. For every hour over 44, a wage of not less than 1½ times the worker's regular wage was to be paid. Since their enactment in 1938, the wage and hour provisions have been amended many times. As of January 1, 1981, the minimum wage under the FLSA was $3.35 per hour and the standard workweek was 40 hours.

Effect on Employment Relations

The primary effect of the FLSA's wage and hour provisions has been to establish certain standards by which employment practices are measured. The act does not regulate the method, means, or system by which wages or other compensation is paid.

Factors Determining Coverage

As originally enacted, the FLSA covered only employees who were personally "engaged in commerce or in the production of goods for commerce." However, in 1961, Congress extended the act's coverage by adding the category of *enterprise coverage.* Under this category the act covers *all* the employees of a firm that engages in commerce. Thus, the employer's activities, not those of the individual employee, are determinative.

Exemptions

Application of the act's standards to certain groups of employees and employers engaged in interstate commerce would be impracticable, inequitable, or impossible. To meet the needs of these groups, Congress has explicitly exempted various occupations from some or all of the FLSA's provisions.

The occupations exempt from coverage have not remained constant since the enactment of the FLSA. Congress has gradually removed exemptions and broadened coverage. Exemptions from some or all of the act's provisions are now granted to workers employed in certain phases of agriculture, commercial fishing operations, casual domestic service, certain retail service positions, outside salespersons, and child actors.

The most common exemptions that managers must deal with are those governing executive, administrative, and professional personnel. An executive employee manages an enterprise, department or subdivision and directs the work of two or more employees. The executive must receive a salary of at least $250 per week, or receive $155 per week and have the authority to hire, fire or promote and spend less than 20 percent of the workweek (40 percent in retail or service jobs) on nonexempt work. An administrative employee is one who performs nonmanual work of a general managerial, business or administrative nature. An administrative employee must receive a salary of at least $250 per week or at least $155 per week if the employee regularly assists an executive or performs other general supervisory assignments requiring special training and if the employee spends less than 20 percent of the workweek (40 percent in retail and service jobs) on nonexempt work.

A professional employee performs work that requires advance knowledge in a field of science or learning and the consistent exercise of discretion and judgment. The employee must receive a salary of at least $250 per week or at least $170 per week if the employee's work is predominantly intellectual and varied so that it cannot be standardized in relation to a given period of time, and if the employee spends less than 20 percent of the workweek on nonexempt work.

On January 13, 1981, the Labor Department issued revised regulations, effective February 13, 1983, increasing the minimum salaries for white collar exemptions. Under these revisions, the minimums would have risen to $345 per week or $250 per week with additional restrictions. However, on January 29, 1981, President Reagan issued a memorandum directing federal agencies to postpone the effective dates of certain regulations. Accordingly, increases in the minimum salaries were postponed indefinitely.

To qualify for the white collar exemptions, employees must be paid on a salary basis. Hourly employees do not qualify. The salary must be paid regardless of the number of hours worked in a given week as long as the employee is ready, willing, and able to work. The minimum amount must be paid free and clear of the value of lodging, meals, or other facilities provided by the employer and of unreimbursed expenses that the employer requires the employee to incur.

Minimum Wage Computation

The FLSA allows employers to pay apprentices, handicapped workers, and students wages below the applicable minimum hourly rate, provided that permission is granted by the secretary of labor. FLSA permits employers to pay employees who regularly receive more than $20 per month in tips as little as one half of the minimum wage. To do this, the employer credits the employee's tips against wages to be paid. The credit may account for up to 50 percent of the minimum wage. Employers must inform these employees of this FLSA's provision.

Employers are also permitted to deduct from wages the reasonable cost of board, lodging, or other facilities furnished to employees, even if it results in a cash wage below the statutory minimum. The facilities provided must be for the benefit of the employees rather than for the convenience of the employer. For example, an employer may apply the reasonable cost of the meals it regularly provides waiters and waitresses toward their wages. Other deductions, however, may result in violations, as occurred in the following case.

Mayhue's Super Liquor Stores, Inc. v. Hodgson

464 F.2d 1196 (5th Cir. 1972)

Mayhue's operated a chain of retail liquor stores. It required its cashiers to sign agreements that they would voluntarily repay cash register shortages. Mayhue's sued for a declaratory judgment that the repayments did not violate the FLSA's minimum wage provisions. Hodgson, the secretary of labor, counterclaimed that Mayhue's was violating the act. The district court entered judgment for Mayhue's. The Fifth Circuit Court of Appeals reversed.

Roney, Judge

The controlling provision of the agreement provides:

> "It is understood that the employee is responsible for any money entrusted to him. Any shortages that occur through misappropriation, theft, or otherwise, shall be voluntarily repaid by the employee to the employer. In executing this contract at the time of employment, it is understood by both parties that the employee is the sole and only person using or entering into the safe, cash deposit box, or sole operator of a cash register.

> The employee agrees to voluntarily repay said missing funds to the employer within a reasonable period of time. The employer shall not deduct said shortages from the paycheck of the employee. It is understood that said shortages are considered to be a valid debt owed to the employer.

> *   *   *   *   *

> Said debt repayment is, for all purposes, unconnected with payroll procedures and are not to be considered as payroll deductions."

In holding that this agreement in no way violates the provisions of the Fair Labor Standards Act, the district court said that a contrary holding

> "would amount to a 'judicial invitation' to such employees to steal. Certainly the Act is not intended to prevent an employer from protecting his property, including assets in the form of cash. Such losses, however, should not be deducted from the employees pay whether wages are being paid in cash or by check. The agreement being approved by the court contemplates 'voluntary' repayment by employees. Any contrary action by the employer would, in the court's opinion, violate the provisions of the Act."

The "judicial invitation" to steal argument is not persuasive. There is no evidence that Mayhue's shortages were the result of theft on the part of the cashiers or were in any way different from the usual losses which are to be expected where cashier employees handle a large number of transactions. The agreement required repayment regardless of the reason for the shortages. If the agreement required only repayment of money that the employee himself took or misappropriated it obviously would not collide with the Act. As a matter of law the employee would owe such amounts to the employer, and as a matter of fact, the repayment of moneys taken in excess of the money paid to the employee in wages would not reduce the amount of his wages. This case is distinguishable from the situation where an employee has taken some money, has had the use of it, and is required to return it. In such a case there would be no violation of the Act because the employer has taken more than the amount of his wage and the return could in no way reduce his wage below the minimum.

The "voluntary-involuntary" dichotomy is meaningless for two reasons. First, if the intent of the parties were to make repayment purely voluntary on the part of the employee, an agreement would not be necessary. The agreement would be pointless. Yet the employer requires the execution of the agreement as a condition of employment. Second, the provision in the agreement that the "shortages are considered to be a valid debt owed to the employer" obviously controls the matter and expresses the intent of the parties. It overrides any argument that the repayments are voluntary on the part of the employee.

With the employee's financial picture burdened with the "valid debt" of the shortages, he is receiving less for his services than the wage that is paid to him. Whether he pays the "valid debt" out of his wages or other resources, his effective rate of pay is reduced by the amount of such debts. When it is reduced below the required minimum wage, the law is violated.

* * * * *

We agree with the Secretary that this agreement tended to shift part of the employer's business expense to the employees and was illegal to the extent that it reduced an employee's wage below the statutory minimum. This amounts to nothing more than an agreement to waive the minimum wage requirements of the Fair Labor Standards Act. Such an agreement is invalid.

CASE QUESTIONS

1. What reasons, other than theft, could account for cash box shortages? Why can the employer not hold the employees accountable for these shortages?

2. How does the court distinguish theft from other shortages? Why is the distinction significant for FLSA purposes?

3. Assume that Mayhue's noticed that a particular cashier was short $25 every night for three weeks. The store manager confronted the cashier about the shortages. Despite the cashier's claims of innocence, the manager threatened to file a criminal complaint if the cashier did not make up the shortages. They agreed that the cashier would repay $15 per week. Assuming that the cashier's weekly wage exceeded the statutory minimum by $20, did the agreement violate the FLSA?

4. A restaurant pays its dishwashers the statutory minimum wage. May the restaurant deduct from their wages the cost of replacing dishes that they break? Explain.

Determination of Overtime Compensation

The calculation of overtime wages can be complicated. One source of difficulty is the fact that there are two formulas. Applicable law treats employees engaged entirely in private business differently from those engaged in selling goods or services to the government.

The FLSA governs minimum wage and overtime standards for private employment. A parallel law, the Walsh-Healey Act, governs minimum wage and overtime standards for all employees on all government contracts exceeding $10,000 in value. As previously stated, the FLSA requires that at least 1½ times the regular wage be paid for each hour worked over 40 hours per workweek. The Walsh-Healey Act, by contrast, sets a series of minimum wages for each occupation, based on comparable wages in private industry for similar jobs. The Walsh-Healey Act requires that 1½ times the regular wage be paid for every hour worked *over 8 hours per workday* as well as every hour worked over 40 hours per workweek. Thus employers on government contracts may be required to pay overtime even though their employees are not on the job more than 40 hours a week. The distinction between the two laws can cause considerable confusion to employers, especially to those that engage simultaneously in providing goods and services to both the government and the private sector. Each employee's activity determines which regulatory act applies. However, unless separate employment records are kept, there is a presumption that everyone in a plant with a government contract is working on it.

Another source of difficulty in calculating overtime wages arises whenever compensation other than the employee's regular wage is paid. An employee's regular wage is the basis for computation of overtime payments. However, the regular wage may include some forms of nonstandard compensation, such as an incentive bonus or a profit-sharing plan. If such a nonstandard form of compensation is paid, it must be included in the employee's regular wage for purposes of overtime computation. This provision can cause a good deal of confusion. Fortunately for employers, many forms of nonstandard payments are statutorily excluded from the provision. The excluded payment forms include Christmas bonuses, reimbursements for expenses, and completely discretionary bonuses.

However, nondiscretionary awards objectively based on performance are not excluded and must be taken into account in overtime wage computation.

Child Labor Laws

In addition to governing minimum wage and maximum hour standards, the FLSA regulates the use of child labor in private employment. Generally, the child labor provisions of the FLSA prohibit the shipment in interstate commerce of any goods produced in an establishment where any oppressive child labor has been employed. In addition, the FLSA empowers the secretary of labor or representatives to conduct investigations of all child labor practices and to require proof of age for all employees.

Child labor laws were designed to encourage school attendance and to eliminate specific abuses such as wage exploitation and child labor in industrial manufacturing plants. Nevertheless, the laws apply uniformly to all child labor practices, whether or not they are exploitative or oppressive.

The particular practices that constitute "oppressive child labor" are determined by the secretary of labor and vary according to type of occupation. The child labor provisions of the FLSA do not apply to employees over 17 years of age. Employment of minors 16 or 17 years old in industries declared by the secretary of labor to be hazardous is restricted but not prohibited. Hazardous industries include coal mining, logging, roofing, explosive work, and excavation. Employment of 16- and 17-year-olds is not restricted in nonhazardous occupations. Children 14 and 15 years old may be employed only in certain approved jobs. These approved jobs are primarily in retail, food, and gasoline service establishments and in school-supported or administered work experience and career exploration programs. Subject to explicit exceptions, employment of children 13 years old or younger is prohibited.

Administration and Enforcement

To ensure compliance and provide for enforcement of the FLSA's regulations, Congress established an elaborate new bureaucratic agency.

The Wage and Hour Division

The agency created to oversee enforcement of the FLSA is the Wage and Hour Division of the Employment Standards Administration, which is part of the Department of Labor. The Wage and Hour Division is headed by an administrator who is appointed by the president with the advice and approval of the Senate. The administrator is charged with promulgating rules and regulations pertaining to the act's interpretation and enforcement, employment regulations and restrictions, and the record-keeping and notice-posting requirements of employers. The administrator and his or her representatives are empowered to conduct investigations into alleged violations and to initiate inspections of employers' premises and employment records. If the administrator or the secretary of labor feels that such action is warranted, suit may be brought under the direction and control of the attorney general to restrain violations of the act. Though the powers of the Wage and Hour Division's administrator are broad, his or her actions are always subject to review by the courts and by Congress.

Judicial Proceedings   Injured employees and the secretary of labor may sue an employer who violates the wage and hour law. They can collect unpaid minimum wages, overtime compensation, and liquidated damages (a sum equal to twice the amount of unpaid compensation). In addition, the secretary may seek an injunction restraining an employer from failing to pay the required minimum or overtime wage or violating any other provision of the FLSA.

Both federal and state courts have jurisdiction to hear suits concerning violations of the FLSA's provisions. In addition to civil suits, criminal proceedings may be brought against employers who willfully violate the act. As used by the courts, willfulness does not require evil intent. It is instead defined as a deliberate or purposeful failure to comply. Mere mistake or oversight is not enough to constitute willful violation.

UNEMPLOYMENT COMPENSATION

In 1933, at the height of the Great Depression, 25 percent of the American workforce was unemployed. The vast majority of these 13 million workers had little or no outside income with which to support themselves and their families. The resulting hardship so severely suffered by so many gave great impetus to the creation of governmental unemployment compensation plans, a form of social insurance taken for granted today.

The Federal Law and its Coverage

Congress could not constitutionally force the states to adopt unemployment compensation plans. It could, however, use the federal taxing power to pressure state legislatures into complying with congressional wishes. Through the use of a tax offset procedure, Congress accomplished its goal. Though only Wisconsin had an unemployment insurance (UI) plan in 1935, by 1937 all the states and several territories had established such plans.

Under the tax offset procedure, a federal unemployment tax was imposed on all covered employers. If, however, the employers made contributions to a federally approved state UI system, they could be relieved of paying to the federal government an amount equal to their state contributions, up to 90 percent of the federal tax. Thus, enacting an approved state UI plan provided benefits for the state's unemployed without putting in-state employers at a competitive disadvantage. If a state did not enact an approved plan, employers in the state would pay the same amount anyway, but unemployed workers would receive no benefits. In addition, federal provisions allowed state plans to collect less from employers with good unemployment records than from employers with poor unemployment records. This gave employers an incentive to maintain a stable work force. Given the choices provided by the tax offset procedure, it is easy to see why all the states quickly adopted UI systems.

Though the basic structure of the federal UI system has remained the same since 1935, Congress has expanded the system's coverage by taxing a greater number of employers and by bringing new categories of workers within the system. For example, beginning in 1956 the federal unemployment tax was assessed on all employers of four or more employees in at least 20 different weeks of the year, as opposed to only those with eight or more employees, as originally enacted. In 1970 coverage was extended further to include employers of at least one employee who works a minimum of 20 weeks of the year and employers who had a quarterly payroll of at least $1,500.

In 1955 Congress extended coverage to employees of the federal government, and in 1958 unemployed ex-servicemen were included. A 1960 amendment added employees working in commercial and industrial activities of nonprofit organizations, and a 1970 law extended coverage to workers in the charitable, educational, and scientific areas of such organizations.

As initially enacted, the federal unemployment tax applied to an employer's entire payroll. However, this generated more funds than were needed. At present, the federal unemployment tax applies to the first $6,000 of each employee's annual wages.

Congress has varied the net federal percentage in accordance with revenue needs. While the tax offset percentage has remained at 2.7 percent of total taxable wages since 1938, the net federal portion of taxable wages has varied. Employers are currently subject to a federal unemployment tax rate of at least 3.4 percent (states may adopt higher tax rates) of the first $6,000 of each employee's annual wages. Of this amount, 0.7 percent must go to the federal government, and, ignoring experience-rating rebates, 2.7 percent to an approved state UI plan.

State Unemployment Insurance Programs

Though no two state systems are identical, certain generalizations can be made about state benefit plans. Most states set a maximum duration for the payment of benefits. However, both the federal government and the state can extend the duration of benefit payments if economic conditions warrant such action. Published economic indicators, such as the national unemployment level, sometimes trigger extension of the payment duration when a predetermined level has been reached.

The amount of unemployment compensation received weekly is generally some percentage of average base period earnings. To determine a given benefit percentage of a worker's full-time earnings, most states compute the weekly benefit by using the worker's average earnings during the highest one or two quarters, thus reflecting most closely the worker's full-employment earning levels.

Eligibility

Eligibility for state unemployment benefits is usually based on having earned at least a specified, average minimum income during a base period, which is usually 52 weeks. The required minimum earnings range from $300 to $1,000. The minimum earnings requirement is designed to ensure that benefits go to workers newly unemployed and not to people who have not recently been gainfully employed.

To be eligible for benefits, unemployed workers must be available for work and actively looking for work. Unemployed workers may be disqualified from receiving benefits if they refuse to accept suitable employment, although they need not accept work drastically different from their former jobs. Disqualification may also result from voluntarily quitting employment without good cause, discharge for serious misconduct, or loss of employment due to a labor dispute. In such instances, the employer's characterization of the circumstances surrounding employment terminations are subject to challenge by the employee. Such a challenge was made in the following case.

Everett Lumber Co. v. Industrial Commission

565 P.2d 967 (Colo. App. 1977)

Everett Lumber Co. (appellant-employer) fired two employees for refusing to take polygraph (lie-detector) tests. The tests were being administered as part of the employer's investigation of a series of thefts. The employees initially consented to the tests but refused to sign waiver forms and told the polygraph operator that they would not answer certain questions. Under these circumstances the operator refused to administer the tests.

The Industrial Commission of Colorado awarded unemployment benefits to the employees, and the employer appealed. The Colorado Court of Appeals affirmed.

Berman, Judge

The employer . . . argues that having previously obtained the consent of its employees to the taking of the polygraph test, it could not be held responsible for their subsequent refusal to take the test or for the terminations because of such refusals.

We need not decide whether prior consent to take such a test and subsequent refusal would operate to bar an award of benefits in an appropriate case, for here, more was required of the employees than merely taking the test.

Before the testing agency would administer the polygraph test it required each employee to sign a certain waiver form. . . . (T)hese forms would have had the effect of waiving the signing-employees' Fifth Amendment rights against self-incrimination.

Although both employees testified that they had given their written consent to taking a polygraph test, there was no evidence that they had also consented to waiving their Fifth Amendment rights in connection with the taking of such a test. Nor did the employer allege that any waiver of such rights had occurred either through the em-ployees' execution of the consent form or otherwise.

The question thus presented is whether these employees, who, in the course of a theft investigation, refused to waive the protections afforded by the Fifth Amendment, are precluded from receiving an award of unemployment compensation benefits because of that refusal. We hold that invoking the protection of the Fifth Amendment, or refusing to waive its protections, may not be used as the basis for denying these claimants unemployment compensation benefits.

Here, the test would not be administered by the testing agency unless the particular employee signed the waiver form, and it follows that the employer, by requiring its employees to submit to the demands of the testing agency or be discharged, must be deemed basically responsible for the terminations. Accordingly, full awards of benefits were warranted in the instant cases.

CASE QUESTIONS

1. Was the employer arguing that the employees were discharged for misconduct? Explain.

2. Was the employer arguing that the employees voluntarily quit their jobs? Explain.

3. Had the employees not been asked to sign the waiver forms but still refused to take the lie detector tests, would the result have been different? Why or why not?

4. An employee who was sensitive to cigarette smoke complained to the employer that many coworkers were smoking and asked the employer to bar smoking in all working areas. When the employer refused, the employee quit. Can the employee collect unemployment compensation? Why or why not?

5. A sales manager was warned several times about low productivity. Despite the warnings, the manager's sales did not increase and the manager was fired. Is the manager eligible for unemployment compensation? Why or why not?

Experience-Rating Provisions   Experience-rating provisions allow an employer whose workforce has historically experienced low unemployment to pay less tax than an employer whose workforce experiences recurrent high unemployment. Depending upon the particular experience-rating method used, an employer with a good record can substantially reduce the tax (in some states, no tax at all is required of employers with the best rating), while an employer with a bad rating may have to pay the entire tax. In any case, the net federal tax must be paid. It is only the contribution to the state plan that can be reduced.

An obvious effect of the experience-rating provisions is that employers have an incentive to keep unemployment to a minimum. It is financially advantageous for employers to keep their former employees off the unemployment rolls. If an employer can prove that the employee quit or was dismissed with cause, unemployment benefits will be denied and the employer's experience rating maintained.

A less obvious and somewhat detrimental effect of the experience-rating provisions is that the aggregate taxes which the business sector must pay are highest when unemployment is high and lowest when unemployment is low. Thus, employers bear a greater tax burden during economic downturns, which are almost always accompanied by high unemployment.

SOCIAL SECURITY

The Social Security Act of 1935 created a federal social insurance system designed to prevent the severe financial hardship that many elderly persons suffer upon retirement. Under the system, employees are compelled to pay a certain percentage of their annual income to the government during their entire working lifetime. Upon attaining retirement age, the contributors become eligible to receive various benefit payments from the general social security fund.

Old-Age, Survivors, and Disability Insurance

In common usage, when people refer to social security, they are talking about Old-age, Survivors, and Disability Insurance (OASDI). The OASDI program is a compulsory retirement plan. All except a very few working Americans contribute to, and are covered by, OASDI. Persons not covered by OASDI are generally protected by similar plans, such as those created by the Railroad Retirement Act.

Payment of Social Security Taxes

Taxes paid into the social security fund are governed by the provisions of the Federal Insurance Contributions Act (FICA). The collection of these taxes is handled by the Internal Revenue Service in much the same way as the collection of income taxes. Social security taxes on employees are withheld on a pay-as-you-go basis. In addition, each employer is required to contribute a matching amount to the social security fund.

The social security tax rate applies only to the wage base—that is, to all gross income earned up to a statutory maximum. The tax rate is the same for all employees regardless of income. Taxes are withheld from employee paychecks, with employers contributing an equivalent amount for each employee. Self-employed individuals are subject to FICA tax at a different rate. Both the wage base and the tax rate have increased over the years and have risen rapidly since 1978.

Benefit Provisions of OASDI

Unlike the public programs of old-age social insurance which exist in some countries, OASDI is not based on the principle of universal coverage, that is, coverage of the entire population. Rather, coverage is conditioned upon having substantially participated in the active workforce, though the minimum requirements for eligibility are not stringent. Coverage for employed persons is compulsory and immediate. Thus, the OASDI system can be viewed as a device by which currently employed persons are forced by law to contribute to the maintenance of retired and disabled workers. Financial need is not generally a condition of eligibility for benefits under OASDI.

Eligibility Conditions

Eligibility is based on the number of quarters of coverage an individual has been credited with during employment. One quarter of credit is earned for each calendar quarter in which at least $50 in income was earned ($100 for self-employed individuals).

There are three categories of insured status. Fully insured status grants eligibility for all types of old-age and survivor benefits. In most cases, for an individual to achieve fully insured status his or her quarters of coverage must equal or exceed the number of years elapsing after 1950 or since the attainment of age 21. Currently insured status yields eligibility for some survivor benefits. It is achieved by having at least six quarters of coverage in the 13-quarter period ending with death, disability, or the attainment of age 62. Disability status gives eligibility for disability benefits and is usually achieved by having at least 20 quarters of coverage in the 40 quarters preceding disablement. (There are special provisions for young disabled workers who have been in the labor force for less than 20 quarters.) An individual's insured status is used to determine his or her benefits and beneficiary category.

Benefit Formulas

Benefit amounts are calculated from a complicated formula that is modified from year to year to account for cost-of-living increases. As mentioned, the benefit formulas are heavily weighted in favor of lower-income contributors. Thus, the benefits for those on the bottom of the wage scale are likely to be greater than their actual average monthly wage, while the benefits for upper-income contributors are certainly less than their average monthly wage.

Recipient Earnings Test

The earnings test is generally used to screen out individuals who are still gainfully employed. Benefits are not paid to retirees or survivors who are still engaged in substantial employment. Benefit payments are adjusted downward for every dollar the beneficiary earns over a statutory minimum. However, as the adjustment is less than 100 percent of earnings above the minimum, there is still some incentive to remain employed past the attainment of retirement age. Moreover, the earnings test is not applicable to beneficiaries older than 70.

Disability Benefits

Eligible workers may receive disability benefits under OASDI. In addition to having attained insured status, a beneficiary must be incapable of any substantial gainful activity due to a medically determinable physical or mental impairment. The impairment must be expected either to prove fatal or to last for at least 12 months. Mere inability to continue doing one's job does not necessarily qualify a worker for Social Security disability payments. If an individual has remedial capacity to do other jobs that exist in significant numbers in the national economy, that person is not entitled to benefits—even if there are few or no vacancies for those jobs. Social Security Administration regulations list a number of severe impairments that are automatically considered disabling. Other impairments are assessed individually. Age, education, and previous work experience are considered.

Social Security disability benefits should not be confused with workers' compensation benefits. Although they may overlap in some cases, there are several significant differences. These are highlighted in Table 16–1.

TABLE 16–1
Differences between Workers' Compensation and Social Security Disability

Workers' Compensation	Social Security
Coverage immediately upon employment.	Coverage upon attaining insured status.
Injury must arise out of and occur in the course of employment.	Impairment need not be work-related.
Benefits available for temporary and partial as well as permanent and total disabilities.	Disability must be total and last at least 12 months.
Benefits cover medical expenses and rehabilitation services as well as lost earning capacity.	Benefits only replace lost earning capacity.

Medicare

In addition to the OASDI system, the Social Security Act governs an extensive health and medical care insurance program for old and disabled persons. Enacted in 1965, the program is officially entitled Health Insurance for the Aged and Disabled, though it is more commonly referred to as medicare.

Medicare coverage consists of two distinct insurance plans. The first, Hospital Insurance (HI), provides hospital and related benefits to all persons who are at least 65 years old and are entitled to receive OASDI or Railroad Retirement benefits. The second medicare plan is Supplementary Medical Insurance (SMI), which covers all persons over age 65 and all disabled persons covered by HI. This plan provides benefits for physicians' services and related medical services. SMI coverage is provided only on a voluntary basis. Unlike HI and OASDI benefits, which are provided as a matter of entitlement once eligibility is established, SMI coverage must be elected by its beneficiaries, who pay a premium in partial financial support of the plan. If an eligible person elects SMI, the federal government will pay an amount at least equal to the person's premium. SMI closely resembles private health insurance plans, but the coverage is partly subsidized by the government.

PRIVATE PENSION PLANS

Private pension plans were introduced over a century ago, but they have become important to retirement planning only in the last 50 years. In the early twentieth century, pension benefits were viewed as gratuitous rewards from grateful employers to faithful employees. Benefit payments were largely discretionary, and few employers assumed any legal obligation to make them. Many early pension plans stated specifically that no employee rights were created thereunder and that the employer could terminate the plans or reduce their benefits at any time. Gradually, however, the pension movement gained acceptance. By the end of World War II, the private pension plan had become a significant means of combating financial hardship in old age.

Until recently, private pension plans were subject only to provisions of the Internal Revenue Code, which had limited regulatory objectives, and to a few scattered, rather specific federal laws. Before 1974 there was no all-inclusive body of law to control the formation and operation of pension plans. The diversity of the practices and pension provisions which developed during this period ultimately served as the catalyst in the movement toward a uniform, regulatory law.

The Employee Retirement Income Security Act

In 1974 Congress passed a comprehensive and complex new law designed to effect sweeping reforms in private pension plans. Officially entitled the Employee Retirement Income Security Act, the law is more commonly known by its acronym, ERISA. Several hundred pages in length, ERISA ambitiously attempts to bring uniformity to pension planning by outlining acceptable and unacceptable practices for a wide range of employee benefit plans. Its major requirements are explored below.

Reporting and Disclosure

All employee benefit plans covered by ERISA are subject to its reporting and disclosure requirements. The plan administrator must file with the Labor Department a description of the plan, a summary plan description, a statement of any material modifications to the plan, annual reports including certified financial statements, and terminal and supplementary reports if the plan is to be terminated. Upon request, the plan administrator must also supply copies of any documents relating to the plan and any other information necessary to carry out the purposes of the act.

Plan administrators must automatically provide plan participants with a summary plan description, a summary of material modifications, periodic updated summary plan descriptions that incorporate these modifications, and annual report summaries. Upon request, the plan administrator must make available for inspection and provide at reasonable charge, copies of the following: the plan description, the latest updated summary description, the latest annual report, terminal reports, and the documents establishing the plan. Additionally, the administrator must furnish any plan participant or beneficiary upon request a statement of total benefits accrued and of nonforfeitable pension benefits accrued, or the date on which such benefits will vest.

Fiduciary Duties

Most benefit plans covered by ERISA are subject to its imposition of fiduciary responsibility on those who have discretionary authority over plan management, administration, or handling of assets and on all paid investment advisers. ERISA requires that these individuals:

— Act solely in the interest of the plan participants and beneficiaries
— Act with the skill and care of a prudent person qualified to act in such matters
— Diversity plan assets to minimize the risk of large losses

ERISA also specifically prohibits certain transaction, such as conflicting interests, generally those involving dealings between the plan and its fiduciaries.

Participation, Vesting, and Funding

Pension plans are subject to minimum ERISA standards for participation, vesting, and funding. Employee participation may not be delayed beyond the date on which the employee attains age 25 and has rendered one year of service. One year of service is defined as a 12-month period in which the employee works at least 1,000 hours. If an employee immediately becomes 100 percent vested, participation may be delayed until age

25 and completion of three years of service. Employers must affirmatively select one of three vesting schedules:

— 100 percent vesting after 10 years of service.
— 25 percent vesting after 5 years of service, 5 percent additional vesting for each year thereafter until 10 years of service, and 10 percent additional vesting for each year thereafter. This produces 100 percent vesting after 15 years.
— When the sum of an employee's age and years of service totals 45, and the employee has at least 5 years of service, the employee is credited with 50 percent vesting and receives an additional 10 percent vesting for each year thereafter. Participants with 10 years of service must be 50 percent vested regardless of age and vest an additional 10 percent each year thereafter.

Defined benefit plans—those that provide specific retirement benefits based on age and length of service—are subject to ERISA's fundings requirements. These plans must be funded in an orderly way to ensure that money will be available to pay benefits. Pension credits for current service are funded as employees earn them. Pension credits for past service that have not yet been funded and compensation for experience losses and changes in actuarial assumption are funded over a specified period ranging from 15 to 30 years.

The participation, vesting, and funding requirements are reinforced by a provision of ERISA which states that, with a few narrow exceptions, "an employee's right to his normal retirement benefit is nonforfeitable upon the attainment of normal retirement age." The meaning of this provision was at issue in the following case.

Alessi v. Raybestos—Manhattan, Inc.

451 U.S. 504 (1981)

Alessi (petitioner, referred to in the Court's opinion as retiree) was a retired employee of Raybestos-Manhattan, Inc. (respondent) receiving benefits under its pension plan. After retirement, Alessi received a workers' compensation award. His retirement benefits were reduced by the amount of the award, pursuant to a requirement stated in the pension plan. Alessi sued, and a federal district court held that the reduction was an illegal forfeiture prohibited by ERISA. The Third Circuit Court of Appeals reversed. The Supreme Court affirmed the court of appeals.

Justice Marshall

Retirees rely on [the] sweeping assurance that pension rights become nonforfeitable in claiming that offsetting those benefits with workers' compensation awards violates ERISA. Retirees argue first that no vested benefits may be forfeited except as expressly provided. Second, retirees assert that offsets based on workers' compensation fall into none of those express exceptions. Both claims are correct. . .

Despite this facial accuracy, retirees' argument overlooks a threshold issue: what defines the content of the benefit that, once vested, cannot be forfeited? ERISA leaves this question largely to the private parties creating the plan. . . . [T]he statutory definition of "nonforfeitable" assures that an employee's claim to the protected benefit is legally enforceable, but it does not guarantee a particular amount or a method for calculating the benefit.

* * * * *

It is particularly pertinent for our purposes that Congress did not prohibit "integration," a calculation practice under which benefit levels are determined by combining pension funds with other income streams available to the retired employees. Through integration, each income stream contributes for calculation purposes to the total benefit pool to be distributed to all the retired employees, even if the nonpension funds are available only to a subgroup of the employees. The pension funds are thus integrated with the funds from other income maintenance programs, such as Social Security, and the pension benefit level is determined on the basis of the entire pool of funds. Under this practice, an individual employee's eligibility for Social Security would advantage all participants in his private pension plan, for the addition of his anticipated Social Security payments to the

total benefit pool would permit a higher average pension payout for each participant. The employees as a group profit from that higher pension level, although an individual employee may reach that level by a combination of payments from the pension fund and payments from the other income maintenance source. In addition, integration allows the employer to attain the selected pension level by drawing on the other resources, which, like Social Security, also depend on employer contributions.

Following its extensive study of private pension plans before the adoption of ERISA, Congress expressly preserved the option of pension fund integration with benefits available under both the Social Security Act, and the Railroad Retirement Act of 1974. Congress was well aware that pooling of nonpension retirement benefits and pension funds would limit the total income maintenance payments received by individual employees and reduce the cost of pension plans to employers.

* * * * *

Congress forbade any reductions in pension payments based on increases in Social Security or Railroad Retirement benefits authorized after ERISA took effect.

In setting this limitation on integration with Social Security and Railroad Retirement benefits, Congress acknowledged and accepted the practice, rather than prohibiting it. Moreover, in permitting integration at least with these federal benefits, Congress did not find it necessary to add an exemption for this purpose to its stringent nonforfeiture protections. Under these circumstances, we are unpersuaded by retirees' claim that the nonforfeiture provisions by their own force prohibit any offset of pension benefits by workers' compensation awards. Such offsets work much like the integration of pension benefits with Social Security or Railroad Retirement payments. The individual employee remains entitled to the established pension level, but the payments received from the pension fund are reduced by the amount received through workers' compensation. . . .

Nonetheless, ERISA does not mention integration with workers' compensation, and the legislative history is equally silent on this point. An argument could be advanced that Congress approved integration of pension funds only with the federal benefits expressly mentioned in the Act. A current regulation issued by the Internal Revenue Service, however, goes further, and permits integration with other benefits provided by federal or state law. We now must consider whether this regulation is itself consistent with ERISA.

. . . The Regulation interprets the section of the Internal Revenue Code which replicates for IRS purposes ERISA's nonforfeiture provision. The Regulation plainly encompasses awards under state workers' compensation laws. In addition, in Revenue Rulings issued prior to ERISA, the IRS expressly had approved reductions in pension benefits corresponding to workers' compensation awards.

Retirees contend that the Treasury Regulation and IRS rulings to this effect contravene ERISA. . . .

[R]etirees claim that workers' compensation provides payments for work-related injuries, while Social Security and Railroad Retirement supply payments solely for wages lost due to retirement. Because of this distinction, retirees conclude that integration of pension funds with workers' compensation awards lacks the rationale behind integration of pension funds

with Social Security and Railroad Retirement. Retirees' claim presumes that ERISA permits integration with Social Security or Railroad Retirement only where there is an identity between the purposes of pension payments and the purposes of the other integrated benefits. But not even the funds that the Congress clearly has approved for integration purposes share the identity of purpose ascribed to them by petitioners. Both the Social Security and Railroad Retirement Acts provide payments for disability as well as for wages lost due to retirement, and ERISA permits pension integration without distinguishing these different kinds of benefits.

Furthermore, when it enacted ERISA, Congress knew of the IRS rulings permitting integration and left them in effect. . . . The IRS rulings base their allowance of pension payment integration on three factors: the employer must contribute to the other benefit funds, these other funds must be designed for general public use, and the benefits they supply must correspond to benefits available under the pension plan. The IRS employed these considerations in approving integration with workers' compensation benefits . . .

Without speaking directly of its own rationale, Congress embraced such IRS rulings. Congress thereby permitted integration along the lines already approved by the IRS, which had specifically allowed pension benefit offsets based on workers' compensation. Our judicial function is not to second-guess the policy decisions of the legislature, no matter how appealing we may find contrary rationales.

CASE QUESTIONS

1. How does the Court distinguish between the forfeiture of a pension benefit and the

method of calculating the amount of the benefit? Why does it conclude that the offset of workers' compensation benefits does not constitute a forfeiture?

2. What is the significance of ERISA's express authorization of the integration of pension benefits with Social Security and Railroad Retirement benefits?

3. Explain the significance of the IRS rulings issued prior to enactment of ERISA.

4. Would the following pension offsets violate ERISA: Compensatory damages recovered in a personal injury lawsuit? Unemployment insurance benefits? Disability benefits received under a private disability insurance policy? Explain.

5. A pension plan provides that all employees become fully vested after 7 years of service. However, if between 7 and 10 years of service, an employee goes to work for a competitor, the employee forfeits all benefits. After 10 years of service, the forfeiture does not apply. Does this violate ERISA? Explain.

Termination

ERISA establishes the Pension Benefit Guaranty Corporation (PBGC) within the Department of Labor. All defined benefit pension plans that qualify for favorable tax treatment must pay for termination insurance provided by the PBGC. Premiums are based on the number of plan participants. Plan administrators must notify the PBGC of plan terminations. The PBGC guarantees to beneficiaries of terminated plans payment of nonforfeitable vested benefits. Employers that contribute to or otherwise maintain such plans may be liable to the PBGC to the extent that the plan's assets are insufficient to meet its guaranteed benefits. However, an employer is not liable to the PBGC if it paid contingent liability insurance premiums for each of the five plan years immediately preceding plan termination.

Pension Plans

A multiemployer pension plan is established pursuant to a collective bargaining agreement between several employers and a labor union. Special rules govern when one of the employers withdraws from the multiemployer plan. The withdrawing employer is liable to the plan for its share of the plan's unfunded vested benefits. The methods used to determine withdrawal liability are extremely complicated. The liability can run into millions of dollars.

OCCUPATIONAL SAFETY AND HEALTH PROTECTION

Until recently, the federal government's provision for safety protection extended to only very limited classes of workers. These included railroad employees, coal miners, maritime workers, and workers under certain federal construction and service contracts. The states were left with the responsibility of assuring safe working conditions for the bulk of the labor force. In the 1950s and 1960s, with the advent of atomic energy, laser beams, microwave equipment, and other technological innovations, concern about industrial health reached new heights. Death, disability, and disease resulting from on-the-job conditions reached epidemic levels. Each year about 14,000 workers died, 2¼ million were disabled, and 400,000 contracted occupational diseases. During this period, some 25 million workers, including those who sustained nonserious injuries, suffered from industrial accidents. Every 20 minutes a new potentially lethal chemical was introduced into the industrial environment. The prospects for a healthy future for the American worker were dim.

Yet even in the late 1960s the states were not ensuring adequate protection for the labor force. Eight states made no provision for health or safety, and the remaining states averaged less than 35 inspectors to enforce health and safety standards. In the wake of these somber conditions and of pressure from various labor-oriented groups, Congress passed the Occupational Safety and Health Act (OSH Act) in 1970. The act marked a new era in safety and health protection for about 60 million members of the workforce.

Coverage

Congress passed the OSH Act under its constitutional authority to regulate interstate commerce. Any employer that is "engaged in a business affecting commerce" and has at least one employee is covered by the act, unless specifically exempted. Virtually any effect on interstate commerce is sufficient to bring a business within the "affecting commerce" provision.

Exempted from the OSH Act are employers that are regulated under other occupational safety acts. These acts include the Coal Mine Safety Act, Railway Safety Act, and Nuclear Regulatory Act, all of which involve extrahazardous industries. Also excluded from OSH Act compliance are employers of domestic household employees and religious organizations whose employees are engaged in religious activities.

Administration

The secretary of labor administers the OSH Act. The act established three federal administrative agencies: the Occupational Safety and Health Administration, the National Institute of Occupational Safety and Health, and the Occupational Safety and Health Review Commission. The Occupational Safety and Health Administration (OSHA), which is within the Department of Labor, is charged with conducting inspections and enforcing compliance with the OSH Act. OSHA is also responsible for formulating and enacting safety and health standards and is assisted by the National Institute of Occupational Safety and Health (NIOSH) toward those ends. NIOSH, which is housed in the Department of Health and Human Services, makes safety standard recommendations to the secretary of labor based on its research into occupational diseases and health-related problems in the workplace. NIOSH is also responsible for developing programs designed to educate and train employers and employees to recognize and avoid unsafe working conditions. Finally, the Occupational Safety and Health Review Commission (OSHRC) is an independent agency created by the act, whose duties are to hear appeals from OSHA citations, abatement period determinations, and proposed penalties. OSHRC has three members who are appointed by the president for staggered six-year terms.

Duties

The OSH Act imposes upon employers a general duty to provide a place of employment free from "recognized hazards causing or likely to cause death or serious physical harm to employees" and a duty to comply with all OSHA health and safety standards. Employees must also comply with all OSHA rules.

The General Duty

A hazard must meet four criteria to trigger the general duty under the OSH Act. If these criteria are met, the employer has an absolute duty to remove the hazard:

— The hazard must be from a condition arising from employment.
— The condition must be generally recognized in the industry as a hazard about which the employer knows or should know. For example, although carbon monoxide fumes cannot be perceived by the senses, an employer in a chemical processing industry should detect the hazard with monitoring devices. In addition, NIOSH has published a list of over 64,000 toxic substances. Because the list places employers on notice, each substance is considered a recognized hazard.
— There must be a causal connection between the condition and the likelihood of serious physical harm. Since the recognized hazard must cause or be likely to cause death or serious physical harm, its effects must be substantial. Recognized hazards are those that result in temporary disablement requiring hospitalization. Hazards that result in dizziness or minor abrasions are not recognized hazards.
— The hazard must be preventable in the course of business.

Specific Safety Standards

The OSH Act further requires employers to comply with specific occupational safety and health standards promulgated under the act. The standards are outlined in a readily available OSHA publication. They cover specific conditions, methods, operations, and processes. Many of these standards have been derived from NIOSH recommendations, safety requirements imposed under other federal statutes, industry standards prepared by employer groups, and proposals from citizen interest groups. These standards must be reasonably necessary or appropriate to provide safe and healthful employment.

The statute requires that standards dealing with toxic substances or harmful physical agents adequately assure, to the extent feasible, that no employee will suffer material physical impairments despite regular exposure to the hazard throughout the employee's working life. In *American Textile Manufacturers Institute (ATMI) v. Donovan*,[5] the Supreme Court interpreted this language to require that OSHA promulgate standards that reduce or eliminate risks to the maximum extent that is economically and technologically feasible. The court rejected ATMI's position that OSHA can promulgate standards only when the threat to health outweighs the costs of correcting the hazard.

The act also requires workers to comply with OSHA rules, but it does not specifically impose penalties upon employees in violation. The secretary of labor is empowered to seek an injunction in federal district court prohibiting "any conditions or practices . . . which are such that a danger exists which could reasonably be expected to cause death or serious physical harm." The secretary may seek an injunction against an employee whose activities are creating a safety hazard. In addition, an employer may discipline an employee who breaches an OSHA standard.

Variance

Any employer may request a temporary or permanent variance from an OSHA standard. An employer that needs additional time to comply with a standard will request a temporary variance. A temporary variance will be granted only if the employer can show that all the necessary steps will be taken to protect the employees until compliance has been attained. Employees are entitled to a hearing to contest the variance. If the temporary variance is granted, it may not continue any longer than necessary to permit the employer time to effect compliance with the standard. A permanent variance may be granted to an employer only if it is shown that under the variance the employer will provide an environment as safe as would have been obtained if the standard were followed.

Other Excuses for Noncompliance

Isolated incidents of employer noncompliance may be excused. The isolated incident defense has been successfully raised in cases where the alleged violation resulted exclusively from an employee's misconduct that was in breach of the employer's express safety rules. For this defense to be successful the employer must have provided an adequate safety and training program for the employees, must have actually enforced the safety rules, and must have been ignorant of the employees' noncompliance.

In rare cases the hazard involved in complying with an OSHA safety standard is greater than the hazard involved in compliance. In such cases

---

[5] 452 U.S. 490 (1982).

compliance is excused. Similarly, if the nature of the physical plant or of the work in process make it impossible to comply with a standard, compliance may be excused. For example, if expert engineering opinion confirms that the noise in a plant cannot be reduced to the level prescribed by the OSHA standard, this defense would be available. This, of course, would not excuse the employer from requiring that employees wear earplugs to reduce the harmful effects of the noise. If compliance renders the performance of the work impossible or unfeasible, then the employer's defense is apt to be sustained. For example, if guardrails required by an OSHA standard damage the work in process and prevent further work, strict compliance is excused.

Record-Keeping, Notification, and Posting Requirements

Employers are required to file reports as prescribed by the secretary of labor. Only recordable incidents need be reported. Such incidents include occupational injuries or illnesses which result in fatalities, lost workdays, job transfers, job termination, medical treatment other than first aid, loss of consciousness, and restriction of work or motion.

The employer must maintain a detailed log of all recordable incidents and enter each incident in the log no later than six work days after learning of it. In addition, each establishment must complete an annual summary of all injuries and illnesses within one month after the close of the calendar year. The summary is a numerical breakdown of injuries and illnesses in various prescribed categories. The log and the summary must be available for OSHA inspection. An employer with fewer than 11 employees is exempt from the above record keeping.

Within 48 hours of any fatality or any accident that results in the hospitalization of more than four employees, an employer must notify OSHA of the incident by telephone or telegraph. The notification must include an account of the circumstances surrounding the incident, the extent of the injuries, and the number of fatalities.

Employers are required to post information telling employees of their protections and obligations under the OSH Act and applicable standards. The information must be posted conspicuously in close proximity to the employees' place of work.

Enforcement, Inspection, and Procedure

In order to enforce the OSH Act's safety requirements OSHA officials are authorized to inspect work premises. However, there are far too few compliance officers to cover all the workplaces. As a result, inspection priorities are generally assigned as follows:

1. Investigation of safety hazards where workers may be killed or seriously injured if corrective action is not taken immediately

2. Catastrophe or fatality investigation
3. Complaints investigation
4. Target industry inspection emphasizing high-hazard industries and operations
5. General random inspection

In most instances, advance notice of inspection is prohibited. A person who gives unauthorized advance notice of an OSHA inspection to an employer is subject to fines and/or imprisonment. Where advance notice is permitted, usually not more than 24 hours' notice may be given.

An inspection begins when a compliance officer presents his or her official credentials to the employer and requests permission to inspect the premises. The employer or a designated representative is entitled to accompany the officer during the walkaround, and a representative authorized by the employees may also be present. At the termination of the walkaround, there is a closing conference between the officer and the employer or the designated representative to "informally advise [the employer] of any apparent safety or health violations disclosed by the inspection."

Employees or their representatives may request an inspection of their employer's premises if they believe a violation of a safety or health standard exists which threatens physical harm. The complaint should be in writing. Under most circumstances the identity of employees who have requested inspections will be protected. An inspection will be conducted if the secretary determines that there are reasonable grounds for believing that a condition exists which violates the act. After it has been decided that an inspection should be made, the employer will be provided with a copy of the complaint with the employee's name deleted.

As discussed in chapter 3, inspections may not occur unless the employer consents or the inspector obtains a warrant. In practice, over 95 percent of employers have consented. To obtain a warrant, OSHA must demonstrate a reasonable basis for selecting the workplace in question for inspection. Employee complaints, high accident rates, a history of employer noncompliance with the OSH Act, a large number of employees in a large business place, and the passage of a long interval since the last inspection may all be neutral criteria that constitute the necessary reasonable basis for obtaining an administrative search warrant.

In cases where a hazard presents imminent danger of death or serious physical harm, OSHA may seek injunctions in the federal district court, requiring that the hazard be abated. The OSH Act defines "imminent danger" as a condition "which could be reasonably expected to cause death or serious physical harm immediately or before the imminence of such danger can be eliminated through the enforcement procedures otherwise provided by this Act."

Upon a finding by the secretary or an authorized representative that an OSH Act violation exists, the secretary must issue a written citation to the employer with reasonable promptness. The citation must (1) contain a detailed description of the violation, (2) state which standard has been violated, and (3) provide a reasonable time for abatement of the violation. An employer may receive a citation at the worksite immediately following an inspection or by mail within six months of the inspection. Unless contested, the citation becomes final 15 work days after it is served.

An employer wishing to contest a citation files a notice of contest with OSHRC. A trial-type hearing is held before an administrative law judge (ALJ) who issues recommended findings and conclusions. The parties may file exceptions to the ALJ's opinion with OSHRC. OSHRC's decision may be appealed to the U.S. Court of Appeals, with further review in the Supreme Court by certiorari.

Penalties

The OSH Act authorizes the secretary of labor to issue penalties for safety violations. In assessing a penalty the compliance officer will consider the severity of the condition, the size of the business, and the employer's good faith and previous safety record. Violations may result in fines, imprisonment, or both. The gravity of violations are graduated as follows.

De Minimis Violation

This violation is deemed to have no direct or immediate relationship to job safety. The employer may be notified of the violation, but no citation will be issued and no penalty imposed. Failure to provide a receptacle for disposal of used paper cups has been held to be *de minimis.*

Nonserious Violation

This violation relates to job safety, but it presents no substantial probability of death or serious harm. The compliance officer is authorized to level a penalty of up to $1,000 for a nonserious violation. Failure to comply with a standard requiring that instructional charts be posted on machinery has been held to be a nonserious violation, because their presence is only a warning and their absence does not create a substantial probability of death or serious harm.

Serious Violation

A serious violation exists when an employer knows or should know of a hazard that is likely to result in death or serious injury. A penalty of up to $1,000 is mandatory for such a violation.

Willful or Repeated Violation

When a willful violation results in the death of a worker, a penalty of up to $10,000 and/or up to six months in jail is mandatory. A second offense exposes an employer to a fine of up to $20,000 and one year imprisonment.

Employer Retaliation

The OSH Act forbids discharge or any other discrimination against an employee who exercises rights under the act. An employee who believes that he or she has been discriminated against may within 30 days thereafter lodge a complaint with the secretary of labor. The secretary is required to conduct an investigation, and if it is determined that a violation has occurred, appropriate relief may be sought in a U.S. district court. Such relief may include reinstating the employee to a former position with back pay. In the following case the secretary sought appropriate relief under the OSH Act, on behalf of two employees who were suspended when they refused to work under conditions that posed an imminent threat to their safety.

Whirlpool Corp. v. Marshall

445 U.S. 1 (1980)

Secretary of Labor Marshall (respondent) filed suit against Whirlpool (petitioner), alleging that Whirlpool's act of reprimanding and suspending two employees for refusing to work under what they believed were unsafe conditions violated a regulation promulgated under the Occupational Safety and Health Act. The secretary sought to have Whirlpool ordered to expunge the reprimands from the employees' personnel files and to compensate the employees for the time they lost as a result of the disciplinary suspensions. The district court denied the requested relief, holding that the secretary's regulation was inconsistent with the act. The court of appeals reversed. The U.S. Supreme Court affirmed the judgment of the court of appeals.

Justice Stewart

The petitioner company maintains a manufacturing plant in Marion, Ohio, for production of household appliances. Overhead conveyors transport appliance components throughout the plant. To protect employees from objects that occasionally fall from these conveyors, the petitioner has installed a horizontal wire mesh guard screen approximately 20 feet above the plant floor. This mesh screen is welded to angle-iron frames suspended from the building's structural steel skeleton.

Maintenance employees of the petitioner spend several hours each week re-

moving objects from the screen, replacing paper spread on the screen to catch grease drippings from the material on the conveyors, and performing occasional maintenance work on the conveyors themselves. To perform these duties, maintenance employees usually are able to stand on the iron frames, but sometimes find it necessary to step onto the steel mesh screen itself.

In 1973 the company began to install heavier wire in the screen because its safety had been drawn into question.

On June 28, 1974, a maintenance employee fell to his death through the guard screen in an area where the newer, stronger mesh had not yet been installed. Following this incident, the petitioner effectuated some repairs and issued an order strictly forbidding maintenance employees from stepping on either the screens or the angle-iron supporting structure. An alternative but somewhat more cumbersome and less satisfactory method was developed for removing objects from the screen. This procedure required employees to stand on power-raised mobile platforms and use hooks to recover the material.

On July 7, 1974, petitioner's maintenance employees, Virgil Deemer and Thomas Cornwell, met with the plant maintenance superintendent to voice their concern about the safety of the screen. The superintendent disagreed with their view, but permitted the two men to inspect the screen with their foreman and to point out dangerous areas needing repair. Unsatisfied with the petitioner's response to the results of this inspection, Deemer and Cornwell met on July 9 with the plant safety director. At that meeting, they requested the name, address, and telephone number of a representative of the local office of the Occupational Safety and Health Administration (OSHA). Although the safety director told the men that they "had better stop and think about what [they] were doing," he furnished the men with the information they requested. Later that same day, Deemer contacted an official of the regional OSHA office and discussed the guard screen.

The next day, Deemer and Cornwell reported for the night shift at 10:45 P.M. Their foreman, after himself walking on some of the angle-iron frames, directed the two men to perform their usual maintenance duties on a section of the old screen. Claiming that the screen was unsafe, they refused to carry out this directive. The foreman then sent them to the personnel office, where they were ordered to punch out without working or being paid for the remaining six hours of the shift. The two men subsequently received written reprimands, which were placed in their employment files.

* * * * *

. . . The Secretary is obviously correct when he acknowledges in his regulation that, "as a general matter, there is no right afforded by the Act which would entitle employees to walk off the job because of potential unsafe conditions at the workplace." By providing for prompt notice to the employer of an inspector's intention to seek an injunction against an imminently dangerous condition, the legislation obviously contemplates that the employer will normally respond by voluntarily and speedily eliminating the danger. And in the few instances where this does not occur, the legislative provisions authorizing prompt judicial action are designed to give employees full protection in most situations from the risk of injury or death resulting from an imminently dangerous condition at the worksite.

As this case illustrates, however, circumstances may sometimes exist in which the employee justifiably believes that the express statutory arrangement does not sufficiently protect him from death or serious injury. Such circumstances will probably not often occur, but such a situation may arise when (1) the employee is ordered by his employer to work under conditions that the employee reasonably believes pose an imminent risk of death or serious bodily injury, and (2) the employee has reason to believe that there is not sufficient time or opportunity either to seek effective redress from his employer or to apprise OSHA of the danger.

Nothing in the Act suggests that those few employees who have to face this dilemma must rely exclusively on the remedies expressly set forth in the Act at the risk of their own safety. But nothing in the Act explicitly provides otherwise. Against this background of legislative silence, the Secretary has exercised his rulemaking power . . . and has determined that, when an employee in good faith finds himself in such a predicament, he may refuse to expose himself to the dangerous condition, without being subjected to "subsequent discrimination" by the employer.

The question before us is whether this interpretative regulation constitutes a permissible gloss on the Act by the Secretary. . . . Our inquiry is informed by an awareness that the regulation is entitled to deference unless it can be said not to be a reasoned and supportable interpretation of the Act.

The regulation clearly conforms to the fundamental objective of the Act—to prevent occupational deaths and serious injuries. The Act, in its preamble, declares that its purpose and policy is "to assure so far as possible every working man and woman in the Nation safe and healthful working conditions and to preserve our human resources. . . ."

To accomplish this basic purpose, the legislation's remedial orientation is prophylactic in nature. The Act does not wait for an employee to die or become injured. It authorizes the promulgation of health and safety standards and the issuance of citations in the hope that these will act to prevent deaths or injuries from ever occurring. It would seem anomalous to construe an Act so directed and constructed as prohibiting an employee, with no other reasonable alternative, the freedom to withdraw from a workplace environment that he reasonably believes is highly dangerous.

Moreover, the Secretary's regulation can be viewed as an appropriate aid to the full effectuation of the Act's "general duty" clause. That clause provides that "[e]ach employer . . . shall furnish to each of his employees employment and a place of employment which are free from recognized hazards that are causing or are likely to cause death or serious physical harm to his employees.". . . Since OSHA inspectors cannot be present around the clock in every workplace, the Secretary's regulation ensures that employees will in all circumstances enjoy the rights afforded them by the "general duty" clause.

The regulation thus on its face appears to further the overriding purpose of the Act, and rationally to complement its remedial scheme. . . . [T]he Secretary's regulation must, therefore, be upheld, particularly when it is remembered that safety legislation is to be liberally construed to effectuate the congressional purpose.

CASE QUESTIONS

1. Under what authority did the secretary promulgate the regulation relied upon by the two employees? Is the regulation derived from any express provisions of the act? Is it implied? How?

2. Aside from the secretary's regulation, what else did Whirlpool violate?

3. What conditions must be present to justify an employee's refusal to work?

4. Will this decision result in many employees walking off their jobs and consequently increase work stoppages? What should management do to ensure that this does not happen?

5. As a result of *Whirlpool*, could a firefighter refuse to enter a burning building because of the unsafe conditions and successfully seek the protection of the secretary's regulation? Explain.

ALTERNATIVE APPROACHES

Regulation of terms and conditions of employment in the United States has been characterized by a piecemeal setting of minimum standards. The FLSA sets minimum standards for wages and hours; the OSH Act sets minimum safety standards; and a patchwork of social legislation sets minimum insurance standards to establish economic security for the retired, disabled, unemployed, and injured. All such pieces of legislation were responses to problems in the workplace and share common goals of eliminating those problems. Other, perhaps more direct approaches may be considered.

For example, in the area of workplace safety, current legislation merely requires the avoidance of recognized deadly hazards and observance of minimum regulatory standards. Other countries have taken different regulatory approaches. For example, West Germany has enacted OSH Act-type legislation. However, in West Germany, the general duty of safety requires that state of technology equipment be maintained in certain facilities. Employers must evaluate the status of technological advances and incorporate them on an ongoing basis. Moreover, West Germany requires that environmental engineers, industrial doctors, and safety personnel be engaged in certain facilities to constantly monitor the safety situation and report to the employer and employees as to the conditions. The goals of these laws are not only to ensure safety for the workers, but to encourage interaction among workers and employers and to promote employer capital investment in safety development.

Another approach might be to tax employers according to their levels of occupational injuries. Such an approach might provide an incentive for employers to improve working conditions beyond the minimum standards required by law.

The workplace has become increasingly regulated. Employers complain of the burdens of compliance, paperwork, and defense costs even when they are in the right. Employees complain of inadequate protection. Consideration of alternative approaches under these circumstances may be worthwhile.

CHAPTER PROBLEMS

1. International Sales, Inc. induced Jane Jones to leave her position as marketing vice president of Domestic Service Co. and assume a similar position with International. Jane's agreement with International provided for a base salary of $120,000 per year, payable at $10,000 per month. Her salary could be increased or decreased monthly according to a complicated formula. Jane was paid $16,000 in each of two months. She believed International misapplied the formula and should have paid her $18,500 each month. When she complained, International recomputed the formula and determined that Jane should have received only

$14,500 in each of the two months. It demanded that she repay $3,000. Jane reiterated her position that she was underpaid. When discussions aimed at settling the dispute proved fruitless, International threatened to withhold the $3,000 from Jane's next paycheck. Jane responded that if any money was withheld from her paycheck, she would sue. International responded by firing Jane. If Jane sues for breach of contract and abusive discharge, what is the likely result?

2. Vincent Martin was employed as a laborer by the Bonclarken Assembly. During his lunch hour he went swimming in a lake on the assembly's grounds, which he had permission to do. The lake had a swimming area enclosed by a rope, and within the swimming area a smaller section was enclosed by a chain. When Vincent entered the lake, the lifeguard had left to eat lunch. When the lifeguard left, he removed some buoys from the water and locked them up. No sign said that the pool was closed. This sign was posted by the lake entrance at a place where Vincent could have read it:

LAKE REGULATIONS

MONDAY–SATURDAY: Swimming and boating under supervision of lifeguard until 4:30 P.M.
MONDAY–SATURDAY: Swimming *only* 5:00 P.M.–7:00 P.M. AT YOUR OWN RISK.
SUNDAY ONLY: Lake open from 2:00 P.M.–5:00 P.M. under supervision of lifeguard.

SWIMMING TEST BY LIFEGUARD
REQUIRED FOR SWIMMING
BEYOND CHAINED AREA

Vincent drowned in the lake. He was within the rope area outside the chain when he drowned. His parents filed a claim to recover death benefits under the state workers' compensation statute. Bonclarken Assembly contended that the accident which caused Vincent's death was not one "arising out of and in the course of" his employment. Who is right? Suppose that Vincent had been struck and killed by a meteorite while swimming in the lake under the same

circumstances. Would the parents have been entitled to death benefits? Suppose that the parents had sued Bonclarken Assembly for negligence. What common-law defenses would have been available to the employer? On what factual basis?

3. Two workmen were on a scaffold when the supporting cables broke. One fell to his death, but the other landed safely on the roof of an adjacent building. Thereafter he was unable to work in high places and suffered from a nervous disorder evidenced by temporary paralysis, troubled sleep, nightmares, eyelid tremors, and other symptoms. He filed a workers' compensation claim for loss of wages as well as medical and psychiatric expenses. Should he recover? Is he eligible for Social Security disability payments?

4. Makeshift Muffler, Inc., is in the business of replacing and repairing automobile mufflers. It has 20 employees. Wally Worker is employed as a welder for Makeshift. He was specially trained by Makeshift in the procedures and safety precautions applicable to installing replacement mufflers on cars. One rule of which he was aware involved a prohibition against installing a muffler on any car which had heavily congealed oil or grease or which had any leaks. Wally disregarded this rule, and as a result a car caught fire, causing extensive injury to Wally. Assuming that Makeshift has workers' compensation (insurance pursuant to a state workers' compensation statute), what are Wally's rights and Makeshift's liability? Explain. Assuming the same facts except that Makeshift has no workers' compensation insurance, which is in violation of state law, what are the legal implications to Makeshift and to Wally? Explain.

5. You are the personnel manager for a large corporation. One of its divisions employs 10,000 hourly workers who are represented by a union and 2,500 professional, administrative, and managerial employees who are not unionized. The union has threatened to strike over an impasse in collective bargaining negotiations. You plan to keep operating during the strike by using many of your professional, administrative, and managerial employees to do rank and file work. Most of them will work 50–60 hours per week and many will spend 50–75 percent of their time doing rank and file work. Must you pay them time and a half for the hours they work in excess of 40 per week? Explain.

6. Our Place is a restaurant at which waiters and waitresses average $7.50 per hour in tips. They are paid no wage, but are told that if their tips do not at least equal the statutory minimum wage, they will receive the difference between their tips and the minimum wage. Is this practice legal? Why or why not?

7. A plumber residing in the Detroit, Michigan area was laid off due to lack of work. The plumber was unable to find work in the Detroit area, but found a job in Cincinnati, Ohio, 270 miles away. He lived in Cincinnati during the week, returning home on the weekend. After one month, he found that he was having transportation problems and that the weekend commuting was straining his family life and himself. He quit the Cincinnati job and applied for unemployment compensation in Detroit. Is he eligible? Explain.

8. All employees of the Grumman Corporation participate in the company pension plan. The plan's three trustees are also officers of Grumman. The LTV Corporation recently announced a tender offer of $45 per share for up to 70 percent of Grumman stock, conditioned on obtaining at least 50.01 percent of all shares. Prior to the announcement, the stock had been selling at $25 a share.

The Grumman board of directors passed a resolution to fight the LTV takeover attempt. The pension plan currently owns 525,000 shares of Grumman stock. It has the opportunity to purchase an additional 1,258,000 shares at an average price of $37 a share. The plan administrator has asked the trustees to decide whether to purchase additional Grumman stock, to tender the existing 525,000 shares to LTV, or to do nothing. What should the trustees do? Explain.

9. Old Bridge Chemical, Inc. (Old Bridge) was charged with a serious OSHA violation for failing to abide by a safety standard and for failing to adequately train employees who were engaged in the rescue of other employees from a railroad tank car. An employee had been assigned to collect chemical samples from the bottom of a railroad tank car. He passed out after being manually lowered through a hatch at the top of the car. A second employee jumped in to rescue the first and was also overcome by fumes. A third employee, who was lowered into the tank in an attempt to rescue the second, also succumbed to fumes. The employees had never been instructed in the hazards of confined entry space and emergency rescue procedures. The employer had admonished its employees not to enter the tank without authorization.

An OSHA standard requires that employers provide rescuers with air respirators. Old Bridge failed to do this on the ground that air respirators were not needed since the chemical in the tank did not form a vapor, dust, or fumes. Was Old Bridge in violation? Explain. Would the result be different if the employees received safety instruction procedures but ignored them? What if the employees were provided with air respirators but refused to use them? What should employers do to ensure employee compliance with health and safety instructions?

10. Select one of the employment regulation areas discussed in this chapter. What are the objectives of the law in the area you selected? Are the objectives being met? Explain. How would you improve the law that governs the area you selected?

CHAPTER 17

EQUAL EMPLOYMENT OPPORTUNITY

During the Reconstruction Period, Congress passed several civil rights acts to protect the newly freed slaves. These acts were soon forgotten as segregation and discrimination became widespread within America's social institutions. Although many Americans worked against segregation in the late nineteenth and early twentieth centuries, it was not until the 1950s that the civil rights movement began to gain momentum. The movement achieved its most significant legislative victory with the passage of the Civil Rights Act of 1964. The statute is a comprehensive assault on discriminatory practices in America. Title VII of the Civil Rights Act prohibits discrimination in employment on the basis of race, color, religion, national origin, or sex. It is the broadest federal statute regulating employment practices. Today it is one of six major sources of federal equal employment regulation. These regulations weave a tangled legal web that can snare today's employers. Each of these equal employment opportunity laws is discussed in this chapter. They are:

1. *Title VII of the Civil Rights Act of 1964* prohibits employment based on race, color, religion, national origin, and sex. The Equal Employment Opportunity Commission (EEOC) enforces its provisions.

2. *The Equal Pay Act of 1963*, which predated Title VII, prohibits pay differentials based on sex. Until 1979 the Department of Labor (DOL) enforced this act. Currently the EEOC is vested with enforcement responsibility. The Equal Pay Act was enacted as an amendment to the Fair Labor Standards Act (FLSA), discussed in chapter 16. Its coverage is similar to the basic FLSA coverage.

3. *The Age Discrimination in Employment Act of 1967* (ADEA) outlaws discrimination against individuals between the ages of 40

1TLE VII OF THE CIVIL RIGHTS ACT OF 1964 557

and 70. As with the Equal Pay Act, enforcement of the ADEA has been transferred from the DOL to the EEOC.

4. Sections 503 and 504 of the *Vocational Rehabilitation Act of 1973* prohibit federal contractors from discriminating against handicapped persons. Federal contractors are firms that do business with the federal government. These businesses are also required to take affirmative action in hiring qualified handicapped persons. The DOL enforces this legislation.

5. *The Civil Rights Act of 1866* applies to racial discrimination in private employment and entitles workers to sue directly in federal courts.

6. *Executive orders* have been issued banning employment discrimination by federal contractors and requiring affirmative action to hire minorities and women. The Office of Federal Contract Compliance Programs (OFCCP) administers the executive order program.

In addition to the federal laws discussed in this chapter, most states have enacted laws prohibiting discrimination on the basis of race, color, religion, national origin, sex, age, and physical disability. Many of these laws reach beyond comparable federal legislation.

TITLE VII OF THE CIVIL RIGHTS ACT OF 1964

Title VII of the Civil Rights Act of 1964 covers employers that have 15 or more employees, unions that deal with covered employees or operate hiring halls, and employment agencies that service covered employers. Title VII prohibits employer discrimination on the basis of race, color, religion, national origin, or sex with regard to hiring; firing; compensation; and terms, conditions, or privileges of employment. Employers also cannot limit, segregate, or classify employees on any of these five bases in any way that tends to deprive any individual of employment, apprenticeship, or training program opportunities, or adversely affects his or her employment status. Unions and employment agencies are prohibited from similar discrimination with regard to their membership criteria or their referral activity. Liability under Title VII may result from:

— Disparate treatment of an individual based on race, sex, religion, or national origin
— Disparate impact of an employment practice on a race, sex, religion, or nationality
— Pattern or practice of discrimination

Title VII does not require an employer to hire, promote, or retain anyone. It simply prohibits an employer from using race, sex, religion, or national origin as a basis for an employment decision. Anyone attacking an employment decision has the burden of proving that it was based on one of these characteristics.

Disparate Treatment

Disparate treatment results when an employer, union, or employment agency treats one employee less favorably than another because of race, sex, religion, or national origin. Thus, disparate treatment is intentional discrimination. In a disparate treatment case the focus is on the defendant's motive.

When a disparate treatment case is tried in court, the plaintiff must prove that the defendant's motive was discriminatory. Initially, the plaintiff must present evidence that would lead a reasonable person to conclude that the defendant discriminated. When this is accomplished, the plaintiff is said to have established a *prima facie* case.

The plaintiff may establish a prima facie case of disparate treatment with direct evidence of discriminatory motive. For example, the administrator of a union hiring hall may have stated in the presence of witnesses, "We don't refer blacks to those jobs"; or an employer may have sent a rejection letter to a female applicant stating, "You are certainly well qualified, but this is a man's job."

Usually, direct evidence of discriminatory motive is not available. It is impossible to read a defendant's mind to discover motive. Motive therefore must be inferred from a defendant's conduct under the circumstances. A plaintiff may raise an inference of discrimination and thereby establish a prima facie case of disparate treatment by showing that he or she: belonged to a protected class (i.e., racial minority, nationality, sex, religion); applied and was qualified for a job for which the employer was seeking applicants; was rejected despite his or her suitability for the job, after which the position remained open and the employer continued seeking applicants with the plaintiff's qualifications. This approach requires complainants to establish on a comparative basis that they have been denied an employment opportunity which they are qualified to fill. Similar comparisons may establish a prima facie case of disparate treatment with regard to matters other than initial hire.

When a prima facie case of disparate treatment has been established, the defendant must provide a legitimate nondiscriminatory explanation for the disparate treatment. The defendant is not required to prove that it did not discriminate, nor must it prove the factual validity of the proffered explanation.

Once the defendant provides an explanation, the plaintiff must prove that the explanation is really a pretext for discrimination. To do so, the plaintiff may attempt to show that the defendant's rationale lacks credibility, that the rationale was not uniformly applied, or that statistics indicate a general practice of discrimination by the defendant. The ultimate issue is a factual one: Is the defendant's apparently valid reason a cover-up for discrimination?

Disparate Impact

Employment discrimination is not limited to overt acts of discrimination. Today discrimination is often covert and unintentional. Title VII litigation typically results from the use of what at first glance appear to be neutral and objective job criteria. Closer examination, however, may reveal that applying a facially neutral job criterion adversely affects the employment opportunities of a disproportionate number of women or minorities. For example, consider an employer that requires security guards to be at least six feet tall. Initially the requirement appears nondiscriminatory. However, if scrutinized, it may prove to have an adverse impact upon women, Latinos, and Orientals. Because their average height is less than six feet, these groups may be systematically excluded from consideration for the security guard jobs.

In cases challenging the use of neutral criteria, courts require the plaintiff to prove that a criterion disproportionately affects the employment opportunities of a protected group, classified by race, color, religion, sex, or national origin. Once the disparate impact is shown, the defendant must establish that the criterion is job-related or required by a business necessity. Therefore, the employer that requires security guards to be at least six feet tall will have to show that protection of the property requires not just a tall, strong person, but persons at least six feet tall. If this is done, the plaintiff must establish the availability of a less discriminatory alternative that would also meet the employer's needs.

It is important to realize that employers are not generally required to justify their employment criteria. The requirement applies only when the criteria have a disparate impact on women or minorities. Measuring that impact can sometimes be problematic. For example, assume that an employer advertises 10 openings for security guards. One hundred people apply: 60 males and 40 females. The employer immediately rejects all applicants who are not at least six feet tall and interviews the rest. Of the women, 36 are rejected and 4 are interviewed. Of the men, 40 are rejected and 20 are interviewed.

It appears that the height requirement has a disparate impact on women because it disqualifies 90 percent of the female applicants and only 66⅔ of the men. However, assume that after the interviews the employer hires all 4 women and 6 of the 20 men. The employer might be truly impressed by the women, or it might be deliberately trying to avoid a claim of disparate impact. At the bottom line, the employer has hired 4 of 40 female applicants and 6 of 60 male applicants, or 10 percent of each group. In the following case, the Supreme Court considered whether disparate impact should be judged solely by the bottom line or also according to the components of the hiring procedure.

Connecticut v. Teal

457 U.S. 440 (1982)

Teal and three other black employees (respondents) of the State of Connecticut (petitioner) sought promotion to permanent supervisory positions. The first step of the promotion selection process required candidates to score at least a 65 on a written test. Respondents failed the test; 54.17 percent of black applicants and 79.54 percent of white applicants passed the test. Those who passed the test were evaluated on the basis of past job performance, recommendations, and seniority. When the process was completed, 22.9 percent of the black applicants and 13.5 percent of the white applicants were promoted.

Respondents sued, claiming that the test had a disparate impact on blacks. The district court dismissed respondents' action because the overall selection procedure lacked any disparate impact and actually treated blacks more favorably than whites. The Second Circuit Court of Appeals reversed. The Supreme Court affirmed the Second Circuit.

Justice Brennan

To establish a prima facie case of discrimination, a plaintiff must show that the facially neutral employment practice had a significantly discriminatory impact. If that showing is made, the employer must then demonstrate that "any given requirement [has] a manifest relationship to the employment in question," in order to avoid a finding of discrimination. Even in such a case, however, the plaintiff may prevail, if he shows that employer was using the practice as a mere pretext for discrimination.

* * * * *

Petitioners' examination, which barred promotion and had a discriminatory impact on black employees, clearly falls within the literal language of §703(a)(2). . . . The statute speaks, not in terms of jobs and promotions, but in terms of limitations and classifications that would deprive any individual of employment opportunities. A disparate impact claim reflects the language of §703(a)(2) and Congress' basic objectives in enacting that statute: "to achieve equality of employment opportunities and remove barriers that have operated in the past to favor an identifiable group of white employees over other employees." When an employer uses a non-job-related barrier in order to deny a minority or woman applicant employment or promotion, and that barrier has a significant adverse effect on minorities or women, then the applicant has been deprived of an employment opportunity "because of . . . race, color, religion, sex, or national origin." In other words, §703(a)(2) prohibits discriminatory "artificial, arbitrary, and unnecessary barriers to employment," that "limit". . . or classify . . . applicants for employment . . . in any way which would deprive or tend to deprive any individual of employment opportunities.". . . The examination given to respondents in this case surely created such a barrier.

* * * * *

In short, the District Court's dismissal of respondents' claim cannot be supported on the basis that respondents failed to establish a prima facie case of employment discrimination under the terms of §703(a)(2). The suggestion that disparate impact should be measured only at the bottom line ignores the fact that Title VII guarantees these individual respondents the opportunity to compete equally with white workers on the basis of job-related criteria. Title VII strives to achieve equality of opportunity by rooting out "artificial, arbitrary and unnecessary" employer-created barriers to professional development that have a discriminatory impact upon individuals. Therefore, respondents' rights under §703(a)(2) have been violated, unless petitioners can demonstrate that the examination given was not an artificial, arbitrary, or unnecessary barrier, because it measured skills related to effective performance in the role of Welfare Eligibility Supervisor.

Having determined that the respondents' claim comes within the terms of Title VII, we must address the suggestion of petitioners . . . that we recognize an exception, either in the nature of an additional burden on plaintiffs seeking to establish a prima facie case or in the nature of an affirmative defense, for cases in which an employer has compensated for a discriminatory pass-fail barrier by hiring or promoting a sufficient number of black employees to reach a non-discriminatory "bottom line." We reject this suggestion, which is in essence nothing more than a request that we redefine the protections guaranteed by Title VII.

Section 703(a)(2) prohibits practices that would deprive or tend to deprive "any individual of employment opportunities." The principal focus of the statute is the protection of the individual employee, rather than the protection of the minority group as a whole. . . .

In suggesting that the "bottom line" may be a defense to a claim of discrimination against an individual employee, petitioners . . . appear to confuse unlawful discrimination with discriminatory intent. The Court has stated that a nondiscriminatory "bottom line" and an employer's good faith efforts to achieve a nondiscriminatory work force, might in some cases assist an employer in rebutting the inference that particular action had been intentionally discriminatory. . . . But resolution of the factual question of intent is not what is at issue in this case. Rather, petitioners seek simply to justify discrimination against respondents, on the basis of their favorable treatment of other members of respondents' racial group. Under Title VII . . . [i]t is clear that Congress never intended to give an employer license to discriminate against some employees on the basis of race or sex merely because he favorably treats other members of the employees' group.

In sum, petitioners' nondiscriminatory "bottom line" is no answer, under the terms of Title VII, to respondents' prima facie claim of employment discrimination.

CASE QUESTIONS

1. What is the rationale for the disparate impact theory of Title VII liability? Why is an employer not required to show that a practice is job-related or compelled by business necessity if the practice does not disproportionately impact a protected group?

2. Is the Court's rejection of the "bottom line" defense consistent with the disparate impact rationale? Explain.

3. Does the Court treat the disparate impact case as similar to or different from the disparate treatment case? Evaluate the Court's approach.

4. If Connecticut had not set a specific passing score on the test, but had considered test performance as a factor in the promotion decision, would the result have been different? Explain.

5. May a job applicant who fails a test attack specific questions asked on the test even though the test as a whole does not have a disparate impact? Why or why not?

Disparate impact liability applies regardless of intent to discriminate. Disparate treatment liability applies only where there is intentional discrimination. Both may be present in the same case. For example, assume that Susan Jones applies to Ace Sporting Goods for a job as a salesperson and is rejected. Ace claims that it rejected her because it only hires people who were varsity athletes in high school or college for its sales staff. If Susan sues Ace, it may have to defend against claims of disparate treatment and disparate impact.

Assume Susan shows that she applied for the job, that she had seven years' sporting good sales experience, and that two days after rejecting her Ace hired Ted Jones, a male with similar qualifications. She has established a prima facie case of disparate treatment. Ace may then come forward and explain that Susan was not hired because she did not play varsity sports in school. The judge may believe this explanation and hold that Ace is not liable for disparate treatment. However, if Susan then shows that Ace has never hired a woman for the position but has hired several men who never played varsity sports, the judge may conclude that Ace's explanation is a pretext for sex discrimination. Ace would be liable for disparate treatment.

Even if the judge believes Ace's explanation, the company could still be liable for disparate impact. There are fewer opportunities for women to play varsity sports than for men, so Susan may be able to show that this job requirement has a disparate impact on women. Ace would then have to show that the job requirement is a business necessity.

Pattern or Practice of Discrimination

In a pattern or practice case the plaintiff attempts to demonstrate that the defendant's general policy has been to treat minorities less favorably than other employees. The pattern or practice case contrasts with the disparate treatment case, which involves a specific instance of discrimination. In pattern or practice discrimination a policy of discrimination must be proved by circumstantial evidence. Employers rarely say "Blacks [or other minorities] need not apply."

The strongest circumstantial evidence of a policy of discrimination is provided by a statistical comparison between the percentage of minorities in the employer's workforce and the percentage of minorities in the relevant labor market. Where the percentage of a minority group in the employer's workforce is two or three standard deviations less than what would be expected from random hiring, a strong inference is raised that the employer discriminated against members of the minority group.

Standard deviation is a statistical measurement used to determine the probability that a particular result occurred by chance. It may be illustrated by the following example.

Assume that an employer has 1,000 qualified applicants for 100 openings and that 500 applicants are black and 500 are white. If the employer hires randomly, one would expect 50 blacks and 50 whites to be hired. Fifty is said to be the *expected value*. If the employer hires 47 blacks, it is still very likely that the selection is random. If only 10 blacks are hired, one may suspect discrimination. If no blacks are hired, it is almost certain that the employer discriminated. One cannot be absolutely certain because it is possible to randomly select 100 whites. Nevertheless, the greater the deviation from the expected value, the less likely it is that the result occurred by chance.

If the frequency of all possible random outcomes is plotted on a graph, the result is a bell curve, as illustrated below:

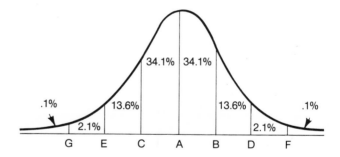

Point *A* is the expected value. Points *B* and *C* are equal distances away from point *A*. We expect to find 68 percent of all results between points *B* and *C;* 34 percent between *A* and *B;* and 34 percent between *A* and *C*. Points *D* and *E* are equidistant from points *B* and *C* respectively. Between points *D* and *E*, we expect to find 96 percent of all results. The distance between each point and its closest neighboring point is one standard deviation. Thus, when the minority or sexual composition of an employer's workforce is two to three standard deviations less than the expected value, we are 96 percent to 99.8 percent sure that the hiring did not occur randomly. Under these circumstances, a court will infer that the employer has a general policy of discrimination.

The statistical inference may be strengthened with direct evidence of specific instances of disparate treatment or direct evidence of a policy of discrimination. Such evidence may consist of statements made by officials or supervisors of the employer.

The employer faced with a pattern or practice charge may attempt to rebut the inference in several ways. The employer may argue that the statistical comparison is not valid because the plaintiff failed to select the appropriate relevant labor market. The appropriate relevant labor market depends upon the skill required for the job. If the job requires little specialized skill, general population figures would provide an appropriate basis of comparison. If the job is highly specialized, the relevant labor market must be restricted to those who are qualified. For example, the workforce of an employer charged with discriminating in hiring messengers may be compared to the general population, whereas the workforce of an employer charged with discriminating in hiring certified public accountants must be compared to CPAs generally.

The employer's location may also influence the composition of the relevant labor market. Commuting patterns in a given metropolitan area may be significant in determining the relevant labor market of an employer located in the central city or in a suburb.

Besides attacking the validity of the statistical comparison, the defendant may also attack its probative value. For example, the employer might show that its workforce has experienced little turnover and little expansion since the effective date of Title VII. The employer might also offer nondiscriminatory explanations for statistical disparities.

Finally, the employer may rebut the evidence offered by the plaintiff to corroborate the statistical evidence. It may offer nondiscriminatory explanations for individual cases of disparate treatment. It may also attack the credibility of those testifying to statements made by supervisors or company officials and may show that the people who made the statements were not in positions to know about or influence hiring policy.

When a pattern or practice of discrimination has been established, it is presumed that all minority applicants who were refused employment are entitled to relief. Each individual is not required to establish a prima facie case of disparate treatment. The employer has to show that a specific individual's rejection was due to reasons other than race, sex, religion, or national origin. Even persons who did not apply for positions may be entitled to relief. If they can establish that they would have applied but were deterred from doing so because of the employer's policy of discrimination, they will have the same presumption as the rejected applicants.

Exceptions

The above prohibitions against employment discrimination are subject to three major exceptions:

— Bona fide occupational qualifications
— Professionally developed ability tests
— Bona fide seniority systems

The Bona Fide Occupational Qualification

The bona fide occupational qualification, or bfoq, is a statutory exception to employment practices that might otherwise violate Title VII. This exception allows an employer to discriminate in its hiring where religion, national origin, or sex is a "bona fide occupational qualification" reasonably necessary to the normal operation of a particular business or operation. The exception excuses sexual, religious, and national origin discrimination in some hiring situations, but it can never excuse racial discrimination.

To establish a bfoq the employer must show that employees of a given sex, religion, or national origin are a business necessity because any other groups would "undermine the essence of" the business operation. This may be done by showing that certain qualifications possessed by persons of a given sex, religion, or national origin are essential to the employer's business and that it is impracticable to find members of the excluded class who possess these qualifications.

The bfoq is interpreted narrowly, and the employer bears a heavy burden of proof. Thus, an employer hiring tour guides to lead a trip to Spain cannot restrict its hiring to persons of Spanish origin. Although Spanish-speaking employees are essential, it is relatively easy for the employer to test the fluency of non-Spanish applicants. Similarly, an airline may not restrict its hiring to female flight attendants. Even if the airline can establish that women are generally far better able than men to provide courteous service and set anxious passengers at ease and that it is impracticable to test such abilities in advance of hire, the qualification is not a business necessity. Courtesy, or the lack of it, does not seriously affect the airline's ability to transport passengers safely. In both instances, it is convenient for the employer to hire people of a particular sex or national origin, but the requirement is not necessary to the business.

Professionally Developed Ability Tests

Title VII permits the use of any "professionally developed ability test," provided that the test is not designed or used to discriminate. In *Griggs v. Duke Power Co.* the Supreme Court held that Title VII prohibits an employer from requiring that applicants have a high school education or attain a minimum score on a standardized general intelligence test as a condition of employment when (1) both requirements operate to disqualify black applicants at a substantially higher rate than white applicants and (2) neither requirement is shown to be significantly related to successful job performance.[1]

In *Albemarle Paper Co. v. Moody* the Court further required that any employment test adversely affecting minorities be validated.[2] The EEOC has issued guidelines detailing the validation processes that it approves for establishing the job relatedness of any selection procedure which has an adverse impact on a protected group. Under the guidelines

---

[1] 401 U.S. 424 (1971).
[2] 422 U.S. 405 (1975).

a test is considered discriminatory if it results in a selection rate for one race, sex, religion, or national origin which is less than four-fifths of the selection rate for another. The burden is then on the user of the test to validate the test by one of three methods.

Criterion validity establishes a statistical relationship between performance on the test and an objective indicator of job performance. Content validity establishes that the test representatively samples a function of the job. A typing test for a typist is content valid. Construct validity establishes that the test indicates a psychological trait required for the job. A test indicating leadership ability is construct valid for a police commander.

Seniority Systems

Section 703(h) permits an employer to apply different standards of employment pursuant to a bona fide seniority system provided that the system is not the result of an intention to discriminate. Seniority is the cornerstone of many collective bargaining agreements. From organized labor's perspective, a seniority system provides employment security to workers because it eliminates favoritism and gives senior workers preference in any promotion or layoff. From the employer's perspective, a seniority system is justified because it adds to the safety and efficiency of the employer's place of business. The theory is that a more experienced worker will be safer and more efficient than a less experienced worker. What constitutes a bona fide seniority system is the subject of the following case.

 **Teamsters v. United States**

431 U.S. 324 (1977)

The United States (respondent) alleged that the Teamsters Union and T.I.M.E.–D.C., Inc. (petitioners), engaged in a pattern or practice of discrimination against blacks and Spanish in the hiring, assignment, transfer, and promotion of line (i.e., intercity) truck drivers. The government further alleged that the petitioners' seniority system locked in the effects of this discrimination and was therefore not bona fide. The lower courts granted relief. The Supreme Court reversed.

The seniority system maintained separate seniority lists for line drivers. An individual who transferred to another job with the company was not credited with seniority accumulated in the previous job for purposes of layoffs, promotions, and bidding for assignments. The government established that petitioners discriminated against blacks and Spanish both before and after the effective date of Title VII.

Justice Rehnquist

Because the company discriminated both before and after the enactment of Title VII, the seniority system is said to have operated to perpetuate the effects of both pre- and post-Act discrimination. Post-Act discriminatees, however, may obtain full "make whole" relief, including retroactive seniority . . . without attacking the legality of the seniority system as applied to them. . . . [R]etroactive seniority may be awarded as relief from an employer's discriminatory hiring and assignment policies even if the seniority system agreement itself makes no provision for such relief. . . .

What remains for review is the judgment that the seniority system unlawfully perpetuated the effects of *pre-Act* discrimination. . . .

The primary purpose of Title VII was "to assure equality of employment opportunities and to eliminate those discriminatory practices and devices which have fostered racially stratified job environments to the disadvantage of minority citizens." To achieve this purpose, Congress "proscribe[d] not only overt discrimination but also practices that are fair in form, but discriminatory in operation.". . .

One kind of practice "fair in form, but discriminatory in operation" is that which perpetuates the effects of prior discrimination. . . .

Where, because of the employer's prior intentional discrimination, the line drivers with the longest tenure are without exception white, the advantages of the seniority system flow disproportionately to them and away from Negro and Spanish-surnamed employees who might by now have enjoyed those advantages had not the employer discriminated before the passage of the Act. This disproportionate distribution of advantages does in a very real sense

"operate to 'freeze' the status quo of prior discriminatory employment practices." But both the literal terms of §703(h) and the legislative history of Title VII demonstrate that Congress considered this very effect of many seniority systems and extended a measure of immunity to them.

Throughout the initial consideration of H.R. 7152, later enacted as the Civil Rights Act of 1964, critics of the bill charged that it would destroy existing seniority rights. The consistent response of Title VII's congressional proponents and of the Justice Department was that seniority rights would not be affected, even where the employer had discriminated prior to the Act. . . .

. . . Section 703(h) was enacted as part of the Mansfield-Dirksen compromise substitute bill that cleared the way for the passage of Title VII. The drafters of the compromise bill stated that one of its principal goals was to resolve the ambiguities in the House-passed version. As the debates indicate, one of those ambiguities concerned Title VII's impact on existing collectively bargained seniority rights. It is apparent that §703(h) was drafted with an eye toward meeting the earlier criticism on this issue with an explicit provision embodying the understanding and assurances of the Act's proponents, namely, that Title VII would not outlaw such differences in treatments among employees as flowed from a bona fide seniority system that allowed for full exercise of seniority accumulated before the effective date of the Act. . . .

In sum, the unmistakable purpose of §703(h) was to make clear that the routine application of a bona fide* seniority system would not be unlawful under Title VII. As the legislative history shows, this was the

---

* Bona fide means actual, genuine.—Au.

intended result even where the employer's pre-Act discrimination resulted in whites having greater existing seniority rights than Negroes. . . . Accordingly, we hold that an otherwise neutral legitimate seniority system does not become unlawful under Title VII simply because it may perpetuate pre-Act discrimination. . . .

*   *   *   *   *

The seniority system in this litigation is entirely bona fide. It applies equally to all races and ethnic groups. To the extent that it "locks" employees into non-line-driver jobs, it does so for all. The city drivers and servicemen who are discouraged from

transferring to line-driver jobs are not all Negroes or Spanish-surnamed Americans; to the contrary, the overwhelming majority are white. The placing of line drivers in a separate bargaining unit from other employees is rational, in accord with the industry practice, and consistent with National Labor Relation Board precedents. It is conceded that the seniority system did not have its genesis in racial discrimination, and that it was negotiated and has been maintained free from any illegal purpose. In these circumstances, the single fact that the system extends no retroactive seniority to pre-Act discriminatees does not make it unlawful.

CASE QUESTIONS

1. Why doesn't the perpetuation of postact discrimination defeat the bona fides of the seniority system?

2. Why doesn't the perpetuation of preact discrimination defeat the bona fides of the seniority system?

3. What factors did the Court consider in holding this seniority system to be bona fide?

4. Would the result have been different if the seniority system had been put into effect after the effective date of Title VII? Explain.

5. Would the result have been different if the seniority system had been unilaterally implemented by the employer rather than negotiated with a labor union? Explain.

Title VII's prohibitions and exceptions are involved generally in assessing allegations that an employment policy discriminates on the basis of race, sex, religion, or national origin. Each category of discrimination has also produced a unique set of issues. These issues are considered below.

Race

The staggering problem of unequal job opportunities for minority races was finally addressed by Title VII's ban on racial discrimination in employment. Congress realized that conscious or unconscious discrimination by employers was the cause of the disproportionate number of minorities found in low-paying jobs and among the unemployed. Although Title VII was clearly aimed at improving economic opportunities for minorities, its language broadly prohibits all racial discrimination in employment.

Inevitably, courts have been called on to determine whether Title VII also covers discrimination against whites.

"Reverse Discrimination" and Affirmative Action

In *McDonald v. Santa Fe Train Transportation Co.*, the Supreme Court held that Title VII applied to racial discrimination in employment directed against whites[3] In *Santa Fe,* several white employees were discharged for misappropriating their employer's property, but their black accomplice was not dismissed. The Court stated that "Title VII . . . prohibits the discharge of 'any individual' because of such 'individual's race.' . . . Its terms are not limited to discrimination against members of any particular race."[4] *Santa Fe* left open the issue of the legality of voluntary affirmative action programs. That issue was addressed in the following case.

United Steelworkers v. Weber

443 U.S. 193 (1979)

Kaiser and the United Steelworkers of America (petitioners) entered into a collective bargaining agreement which established training programs to teach unskilled production workers the skills necessary to become craft workers. The program reserved 50 percent of the openings for black employees. This aspect of the program was to continue until the percentage of blacks in the craft workforce approximated the percentage of blacks in the local labor force. Before the program began, Kaiser hired only experienced craft workers, almost all of whom were white.

Weber (respondent) brought a class action alleging that junior black employees were accepted into the program ahead of more senior whites. The trial court held that this violated Title VII, and the Fifth Circuit Court of Appeals affirmed. The Supreme Court reversed.

Justice Brennan

The only question before us is the narrow statutory issue of whether Title VII *forbids* private employers and unions from voluntarily agreeing upon bona fide affirmative action plans that accord racial preference in the manner and for the purpose provided in the Kaiser-USWA plan. That question was expressly left open in *McDonald v. Santa Fe Trail Trans. Co.*

Respondent argues that Congress intended in Title VII to prohibit all race-conscious affirmative action plans. Respondent's argument rests upon a literal interpretation of §§703(a) and (d) of the Act. Those sections make it unlawful to "dis-

[3] 427 U.S. 273 (1976).

[4] Id. at 278–79.

criminate . . . because of . . . race" in hiring and in the selection of apprentices for training programs. Since, the argument runs, *McDonald v. Santa Fe Trail Trans. Co., supra,* settled that Title VII forbids discrimination against whites as well as blacks, and since the Kaiser-USWA affirmative action plan operates to discriminate against white employees solely because they are white, it follows that the Kaiser-USWA plan violates Title VII.

Respondent's argument is not without force. But it overlooks the significance of the fact that the Kaiser-USWA plan is an affirmative action plan voluntarily adopted by private parties to eliminate traditional patterns of racial segregation. In this context respondent's reliance upon a literal construction of §§703(a) and (d) and upon *McDonald* is misplaced. It is a "familiar rule, that a thing may be within the letter of the statute and yet not within the statute, because not within its spirit, nor within the intention of its makers." The prohibition against racial discrimination in §§703(a) and (d) of Title VII must therefore be read against the background of the legislative history of Title VII and the historical context from which the Act arose. Examination of those sources makes clear that an interpretation of the sections that forbade all race-conscious affirmative action would "bring about an end completely at variance with the purpose of the statute" and must be rejected.

Congress' primary concern in enacting the prohibition against racial discrimination in Title VII of the Civil Rights Act of 1964 was with "the plight of the Negro in our economy." Before 1964, blacks were largely relegated to "unskilled and semi-skilled jobs."

It plainly appears from the House Report accompanying the Civil Rights Act that Congress did not intend wholly to prohibit private and voluntary affirmative action efforts as one method of solving this problem. The report provides:

> No bill can or should lay claim to eliminating all of the causes and consequences of racial and other types of discrimination against minorities. There is reason to believe, however, that national leadership provided by the enactment of Federal legislation dealing with the most troublesome problems will create an atmosphere conducive to voluntary or local resolution of other forms of discrimination.

Given this legislative history, we cannot agree with respondent that Congress intended to prohibit the private sector from taking effective steps to accomplish the goal that Congress designed Title VII to achieve. The very statutory words intended as a spur or catalyst to cause "employers and unions to self-examine and to self-evaluate their employment practices and to endeavor to eliminate, so far as possible, the last vestiges of an unfortunate and ignominious page in this country's history," cannot be interpreted as an absolute prohibition against all private, voluntary, race-conscious affirmative action efforts to hasten the elimination of such vestiges. It would be ironic indeed if a law triggered by a Nation's concern over centuries of racial injustice and intended to improve the lot of those who had "been excluded from the American dream for so long," constituted the first legislative prohibition of all voluntary, private, race-conscious efforts to abolish traditional patterns of racial segregation and hierarchy.

Our conclusion is further reinforced by examination of the language and legislative history of §703(j) of Title VII. . . . The section provides that nothing contained in Title VII "shall be interpreted to *require* any employer . . . to grant preferential treatment . . . to any group because of the race . . . of such . . . group on account of" a *de facto* racial imbalance in the employer's work force. The section does *not* state that "nothing in Title VII shall be interpreted to *permit*" voluntary affirmative efforts to correct racial imbalances. The natural inference is that Congress chose not to forbid all voluntary race-conscious affirmative action.

The reasons for this choice are evident from the legislative record. Title VII could not have been enacted into law without substantial support from legislators in both Houses who traditionally resisted federal regulations of private business. Those legislators demanded as a price for their support that "management prerogatives and union freedoms . . . be left undisturbed to the greatest extent possible." Section 703(j) was proposed by Senator Dirksen to allay any fears that the Act might be interpreted in such a way as to upset this compromise. The section was designed to prevent §703 of Title VII from being interpreted in such a way as to lead to undue "Federal Government interference with private businesses because of some Federal employee's ideas about racial balance or imbalance." Clearly, a prohibition against all voluntary, race-conscious, affirmative action efforts would disserve these ends. Such a prohibition would augment the powers of the Federal Government and diminish traditional management prerogatives while at the same time impeding attainment of the ultimate statutory goals. In view of this legislative history and in view of Congress' desire to avoid undue federal regulation of private businesses, use of the word "require" rather than the phrase "require or permit" in § 703(j) fortifies the conclusion that Congress did not intend to limit traditional business freedom to such a degree as to prohibit all voluntary, race-conscious affirmative action.

We therefore hold that Title VII's prohibition in §§703(a) and (d) against racial discrimination does not condemn all private, voluntary, race-conscious affirmative action plans.

CASE QUESTIONS

1. Describe the history of and motivation for the affirmative action plan. Did the plan deprive Weber of an employment opportunity? Did the racial quota deprive Weber of an employment opportunity?

2. What is the basis for the Court's conclusion that the Kaiser affirmative action plan did not violate Title VII?

3. Can *Weber* be reconciled with *McDonald v. Santa Fe Trail Transportation Co.?*

4. What is the line of demarcation between permissible and impermissible affirmative action plans?

5. Did Weber allege disparate treatment or disparate impact? Can a white successfully allege a case of disparate impact? Why or why not?

Sex

Sexual discrimination in employment is not a new phenomenon. The concepts of "men's work" and "women's work" have been ingrained in society since civilization began. Today sex roles in our society are being altered. Yet the notion of gender-based jobs remains a threat to the freedom to work regardless of sex.

Many of the problems peculiar to sex discrimination result from industry practice, stereotyped social roles, and erroneous beliefs. For example, many employers that would not think of asking a man whether he has young children will not hire a woman who has young children. This and other discriminatory attitudes are discussed below.

Sex-Plus Discrimination

Sex-plus discrimination denotes the imposition of a constraint or requirement on members of one sex but not on members of the other sex. For example, if an employer hires men regardless of their educational background but hires only women with at least high school diplomas, the employer is practicing sex-plus discrimination. Although the employer hires both men and women, it requires a plus factor for women.

Another example of sex-plus discrimination is a requirement that female employees be single while males may be married or single. This policy once prevailed in the airline industry, where female flight attendants (stewardesses) were generally required to be single, while male attendants (stewards) could be married. EEOC guidelines now prohibit this policy, and courts agree.

Women have been subjected to a number of discriminatory employment policies resulting from their status as mothers. In *Phillips v. Martin Marietta Corp.* an employer's refusal to hire women with preschool-age children was considered.[5] This hiring practice did not appear to discriminate against women because 70–75 percent of the job applicants were women and 75–80 percent of those hired for the position were women. Hence no question of bias against women as such was presented. The Court ruled, however, that since men with preschool-age children were hired but women were not, the practice violated Title VII.

Pregnancy

Only women can become pregnant but not all women choose to do so. Is discrimination on the basis of pregnancy a discrimination on the basis of sex—and therefore illegal disparate treatment—or is it discrimination on the basis of a medical condition and therefore facially neutral? In 1976 in *General Electric Co. v. Gilbert,* the Supreme Court held that the exclusion of pregnancy benefits from an employer's medical insurance plan did not violate Title VII.[6] The Court reasoned that the exclusion did not discriminate between females and males, but rather between pregnant females and nonpregnant females and males.

Two years later, Congress passed the Pregnancy Discrimination Act, amending Title VII to overrule the *Gilbert* interpretation. The terms "because of sex or on the basis of sex," as used in Title VII, were modified to include "because of or on the basis of pregnancy, childbirth, or related medical conditions." The act further provides that:

---

[5] 400 U.S. 542 (1971).

[6] 429 U.S. 125 (1976).

> [W]omen affected by pregnancy, childbirth, or related medical conditions shall be treated the same for all employment-related purposes, including the receipt of benefits under fringe benefit programs, as other persons not so affected but similar in their ability or inability to work.

The act raised many new issues of interpretation. In *Newport News Shipbuilding Co. v. EEOC,* the Supreme Court held that an employer may not exclude pregnancy coverage from the medical insurance it provides for employees' spouses.[7] The court concluded that such an exclusion discriminated against male employees.

Pregnancy discrimination most frequently involves pregnancy-related exclusions from fringe benefit plans. Sometimes, however, it also involves different work rules for pregnant, or even for fertile nonpregnant, employees. This occurred in the following case.

Wright v. Olin Corp.

697 F.2d 1172 (4th Cir. 1982)

Theresa Wright (plaintiff or claimant) sued Olin Corporation (defendant), claiming that Olin's "fetal vulnerability program" violated Title VII. The district court held that there was no violation because Olin was motivated only by medical and humane reasons. Wright appealed, and the Fourth Circuit Court of Appeals reversed and remanded.

Under the fetal vulnerability program, Olin divided its jobs into three categories: unrestricted, controlled, and restricted. The classification of a job was based on the degree of contact with toxic substances, primarily lead, known or thought to pose health risks to a pregnant woman or her fetus. Unrestricted jobs had no contact with toxic substances and were open to all women. Controlled jobs required very limited contact with toxic substances and were generally closed to pregnant women. Restricted jobs involved contact with and exposure to toxic substances and were closed to all fertile women. All jobs were open to all men.

Phillips, Circuit Judge

Olin contends that the proper analytical framework is that developed for assessing claims of disparate treatment and . . .

[that] the purpose of the program sufficed as a . . . "legitimate nondiscriminatory reason" to rebut any *prima facie* case of sex discrimination established by proof of the program's existence and intended operation. . . .

---

[7] 103 S. Ct. 2622 (1983).

On the other hand, claimants contend that the undisputed evidence of the programs' intended operation, with its manifestly adverse effect upon the employment opportunities of women only, established a *prima facie* case of overt, intentional discrimination. . . . A *prima facie* case of this kind may only be overcome by establishment of the narrow, statutory b.f.o.q. defense specially provided. . . .

Alternatively, claimants contend that if the fetal vulnerability program is construed as a "facially neutral" policy based upon the potential for pregnancy, mere proof of its existence and implementation established a *prima facie* case of disparate impact. . . . Such a *prima facie* case may only be overcome by establishment of the judicially developed business necessity defense.

* * * * *

[The inferential] disparate treatment proof scheme is . . . wholly inappropriate for resolving the legal and factual theories of claim and defense centered on the fetal vulnerability program. Turning to the overt sex-discrimination/b.f.o.q. theory of claim and defense and the disparate impact/business necessity theory, we conclude that the latter is best suited for a principled application of Title VII doctrine to the fetal vulnerability program.

The factual claim and defense actually advanced here by the parties find their closest parallel in the paradigmatic fact pattern out of which this theory of claim and defense evolved. That pattern involves "employment practices that are facially neutral in their treatment of different groups but that in fact fall more harshly on one group than another and cannot be justified by business necessity."

While the "facial neutrality" of Olin's fetal vulnerability program might be suspect to logical dispute, the dispute would involve mere semantic quibbling having no relevance to the underlying substantive principle that gave rise to this theory. That principle, one of profound importance in the evolution of Title VII doctrine, has as its critical feature the consequences of employment policies rather than the "neutrality" with which the policies happen to be formally expressed. Its essence is that disproportionate consequences of an employment practice, even if unintended or indeed benignly motivated, may, like intentional invidiously discriminatory employer actions, constitute violations of Title VII.

* * * * *

We therefore hold . . . that the evidence of the existence and operation of the fetal vulnerability program established as a matter of law a *prima facie* case of Title VII violation.

* * * * *

It remains to adapt the business necessity defense—in both its substantive and procedural aspects—to the unique circumstances presented by this employment practice.

* * * * *

[T]he Supreme Court has . . . put it that the necessity runs to "safe and efficient job performance."

But the question of *whose* safety may properly be considered a matter of "business necessity" remains an open one. The logical possibilities include women workers themselves, customers . . . of the business, and others . . . legitimately exposed under the circumstances of the particular business to any of its workplace hazards.

Though the safety of women workers themselves might be thought the most obvious subject of necessity—hence legally justifiable—restrictions on their employment opportunities, the opposite of course has been held. [T]he general view when these defenses have been raised by employers has been that they must be rejected because "it is the purpose of Title VII to allow the individual woman to make [the] choice for herself."

The same overriding consideration does not, of course, apply to the safety of others than the women workers themselves. And when that other is a customer required by the very nature of the business to be exposed to certain hazards related to its operation by employees, then the "safety and efficiency" of the operation is in effect an indivisible concern rather than two distinct ones. In such cases, the safety of the customer has been recognized to be of such overriding business necessity that the legal defense should in appropriate circumstances be available.

For the purposes of our analysis, the legitimacy of an employer's purpose to protect by discriminatory means the safety of the unborn children of workers would appear to lie conceptually somewhere between a purpose to protect the safety of workers themselves and a purpose to protect that of customers exposed in the normal course to workplace hazards.

*   *   *   *   *

[W]e believe the safety of unborn children is more appropriately analogized to the safety of personal service customers of the business. The business necessity to provide for customer safety is obviously one of more "overriding" importance than is the necessity to provide for business "visitor" safety. But we cannot believe that Congress meant by Title VII absolutely to deprive employers of the right to provide any protection for licensees and invitees legitimately and necessarily upon their premises by any policy having a disparate impact upon certain workers. Especially do we think it unlikely that Congress could have intended

such a consequence—given the business imperatives of good labor relations—when the "visitors" protected are members, or potential members, of workers' families.

On this basis we hold that under appropriate circumstances an employer may, as a matter of business necessity, impose otherwise impermissible restrictions on employment opportunity that are reasonably required to protect the health of unborn children of women workers against hazards of the workplace.

Having determined that the business necessity defense may under appropriate circumstances be an available one in the instant case, we turn now to the problem of how—substantively and procedurally—the defense, as adapted to the program here in issue, may be established in proof. The following principles, drawn from developed business necessity doctrine, we hold to be controlling.

1. The burden of persuasion is upon the employer to prove that significant risks of harm to the unborn children of women workers from their exposure during pregnancy to toxic hazards in the workplace make necessary, for the safety of the unborn children, that fertile women workers, though not men workers, be appropriately restricted from exposure to those hazards and that its program of restriction is effective for the purpose.

2. This burden may not be carried by proof alone that the employer subjectively and in good faith believed its program to be necessary and effective for the purpose. Irrespective of the employer's subjective belief and motivation, the significance of the risk, the extent of its confinement to the unborn children of women as opposed to men workers, and the effectiveness of the actual program for the intended purposes must be established by independent, objective evidence.

3. . . . [T]he essentially scientific nature of the dispositive issues requires that findings

and conclusions establishing the defense be supported by the opinion evidence of qualified experts in the relevant scientific fields.

4. To establish the requisite degree and cast of the risk of harm, it is not necessary to prove the existence of a general consensus on the points within the qualified scientific community. It suffices to show that within that community there is so considerable a body of opinion that significant risk exists, and that it is substantially confined to women workers, than an informed employer could not responsibly fail to act on the assumption that this opinion might be the accurate one.

5. Proof of the requisite degree and cast of the risk of harm and of effectiveness of the challenged program to avoid it establishes the business necessity defense *prima facie*.

6. This *prima facie* defense may, however, be rebutted by proof that there are "acceptable alternative policies or practices which would better accomplish the business purpose . . . of protecting against the risk of harm or accomplish it equally well with a lesser differential . . . impact between women and men workers."

7. Such rebutting evidence to the *prima facie* defense, if accepted, may have either of two effects, both resulting in employer liability, but with possibly different remedial consequences.

By showing an "acceptable alternative" that would accomplish the protective purpose "equally well with lesser differential impact," the evidence would at least negate *prima facie* proof of the business necessity of the specific program by having demonstrated an "unnecessary" degree of overkill in it.

While this would require a finding of liability, any resulting remedial decree should only vindicate, in both prospective and monetary relief aspects, the claimant's rights as they would exist under the "acceptable alternative" policy.

But it is possible that the "rebuttal" evidence might suffice, either alone or in conjunction with other evidence, to carry the claimant's retained burden of persuasion that behind the proved but *prima facie* justified disparate impact of the program there lay in fact a discriminatory intent; that the program in effect involved "disparate treatment." This would result from proof that in view of the demonstrated degree of overkill in the challenged program, the purpose advanced for it had now been revealed to be all along a mere "pretext."

Upon such a determination, with liability now established for a disparate treatment violation, any resulting remedial decree should of course vindicate claimant's rights wholly freed of any restrictive policy.

CASE QUESTIONS

1. Does the court view this case as involving disparate treatment or disparate impact? Why?

2. Would the court's business necessity analysis also apply to a bfoq defense? Explain.

3. In light of this decision, must an employer make a detailed scientific inquiry into the effects of toxic substances on fetuses of pregnant employees before implementing a fetal protection program? Explain.

4. Can an employer legally exclude non-pregnant fertile women from jobs having contact with toxic substances? Explain.

5. An employer's study reveals that certain jobs involve exposure to a toxic substance that could harm a fetus. Exposure can result from direct contact with the substance or from direct contact with another person who was exposed to the substance in the preceding eight hours. What type of safety rule can the employer legally implement? Explain.

Sexual Harassment

Sexual harassment does not per se violate Title VII. Sexual harassment that is discriminatory can violate Title VII. For example, an employee who is required to have sexual relations with a supervisor to secure, maintain, or advance in employment is subjected to conditions that are not imposed upon employees of the opposite sex. An employee who is promoted as a reward for having relations with a supervisor is given an opportunity which employees of the opposite sex do not have. Even where submission to sexual advances is not used as a basis for employment decisions, the existence of sexual harassment in the workplace may create a hostile, intimidating, or offensive atmosphere. An employee who quits because of that atmosphere may file a Title VII claim alleging that the quit amounted to a "constructive discharge." The following guidelines represent the EEOC's position on sexual harassment.

EEOC Guidelines on Sexual Harassment

29 C.F.R. §1604.11

(a) Harassment on the basis of sex is a violation of . . . Title VII. Unwelcome sexual advances, requests for sexual favors, and other verbal or physical conduct of a sexual nature constitute sexual harassment when (1) submission to such conduct is made either explicitly or implicitly a term or condition of an individual's employment, (2) submission to or rejection of such conduct by an individual is used as the basis for employment decisions affecting such individual, or (3) such conduct has the purpose or effect of unreasonably interfering with an individual's work performance or creating an intimidating, hostile, or offensive working environment.

(b) In determining whether alleged conduct constitutes sexual harassment, the Commission will look at the record as a whole and the totality of the circumstances. . . .

(c) Applying general Title VII principles, an employer . . . is responsible for its acts and those of its agents and supervisory employees with respect to sexual harassment regardless of whether the specific acts complained of were authorized or even forbidden by the employer and regardless of whether the employer knew or should have known of their occurrence. . . .

(d) With respect to conduct between fellow employees, an employer is responsible for acts of sexual harassment in the workplace where the employer . . . knows or should have known of the conduct, unless it can show that it took immediate and appropriate corrective action.

(e) An employer may also be responsible for the acts of

nonemployees, with respect to sexual harassment of employees in the workplace, where the employer . . . knows or should have known of the conduct and fails to take immediate and appropriate corrective action. In reviewing these cases the Commission will consider the extent of the employer's control and any other legal responsibility which the employer may have with respect to the conduct of such non-employees.

(f) Prevention is the best tool for the elimination of sexual harassment. An employer should take all steps necessary to prevent sexual harassment from occurring, such as affirmatively raising the subject, expressing strong disapproval, developing appropriate sanctions, informing employees of their right to raise and how to raise the issue of harassment under Title VII, and developing methods to sensitize all concerned.

(g) Other related practices: Where employment opportunities or benefits are granted because of an individual's submission to the employer's requests for sexual favors, the employer may be held liable for unlawful sexual discrimination against other persons who were qualified for but denied that employment opportunity or benefit.

Source: 29 Code of Federal Regulations, Sec. 1604.11

Pensions and Life Insurance

It is an established fact that as a class, women live longer than men. Consequently, it has been an established practice of insurance and annuity companies to classify life expectancy tables by sex. Thus, women have historically received lower annual pension benefits and greater life insurance benefits than similarly situated men.

However, the use of sex-based actuarial tables to determine pension and life insurance benefits violates Title VII. Title VII protects individuals from sex discrimination. Employees must be treated as individuals rather than as members of a class of men or women. Distinctions in benefits must be based on individual characteristics rather than sex.

Religion

The term religion encompasses traditional religions such as Judaism, Catholicism, Protestantism, and Islam, but is far broader. It includes all moral or ethical beliefs that are sincerely held with the strength of traditional religious views. Atheism and agnosticism are considered religions for Title VII purposes.

The Duty to Accommodate Religion

Title VII requires an employer to make reasonable accommodations to employees' religious beliefs and practices unless accommodation would work an undue hardship on the business. The most frequent charges of religious discrimination dealt with by courts and the EEOC involve not raw prejudice, but instances in which an employer's work rule, innocent in intent, conflicts with an employee's religious belief. Such conditions trigger the employer's duty to accommodate the employee's religious beliefs. The nature of that duty is the subject of the following case.

Trans World Airlines, Inc. v. Hardison

432 U.S. 63 (1977)

Hardison (respondent), a Sabbatarian, was employed by Trans World Airlines (petitioner) as a clerk in TWA's maintenance and overhaul base in Kansas City. The base was required to operate 24 hours per day, 365 days per year. Under the applicable collective bargaining agreement, employees received shift assignments according to seniority, with the most senior employees receiving first choice. Hardison advised the employer of his religious convictions, which prevented Saturday work. TWA agreed that the union steward would seek a job swap or change of days off for Hardison and that Hardison would have his religious holidays off whenever possible if he agreed to work traditional holidays when asked. Hardison was initially employed in one building on the late night shift, where he had sufficient seniority to avoid working on his Sabbath. He then transferred to another building and the day shift, where he was second from the bottom of the seniority list. When a fellow employee went on vacation, Hardison was asked to work Saturdays. He refused. TWA asked the union to seek a change of work assignments, but the union refused to waive the seniority provision. When Hardison failed to report for work on Saturdays he was fired.

Hardison brought suit, alleging that TWA's failure to accommodate his religious beliefs violated Title VII. The district court entered judgment for TWA, but the Eighth Circuit Court of Appeals reversed. The Supreme Court reversed the court of appeals.

Justice White

The emphasis of both the language and the legislative history of [Title VII] is on eliminating discrimination in employment; similarly situated employees are not to be treated differently solely because they differ with respect to race, color, religion, sex, or national origin.

The prohibition against religious discrimination soon raised the question of whether it was impermissible under §703(a) (1) to discharge or refuse to hire a person who for religious reasons refused to work during the employer's normal workweek. In 1966 an EEOC guideline dealing with this problem declared that an employer had an obligation under the statute "to accommodate to the reasonable religious needs of employees . . . where such accommodations can be made without serious inconvenience to the conduct of the business."

In 1967 the EEOC amended its guidelines to require employers "to make reasonable accommodations to the religious needs of employees and prospective employees where such accommodations can be made without undue hardship on the conduct of the employer's business.". . .

This question—the extent of the required accommodation—remained unsettled when this Court, in *Dewey v. Reynolds Metals Co.*, affirmed by an equally divided Court the Sixth Circuit's decision. The discharge of an employee who for religious reasons had refused to work on Sundays was there held by the Court of Appeals not to be an unlawful employment practice because the manner in which the employer allocated Sunday work assignments was discriminatory in neither its purpose nor effect; and consistent with the 1967 EEOC guidelines, the employer had made a reasonable accommodation of the employee's beliefs by giving him the opportunity to secure a replacement for his Sunday work.

In part "to resolve by legislation" some of the issues raised in *Dewey,* Congress included the following definition of religion in its 1972 amendments to Title VII:

> The term "religion" includes all aspects of religious observance and practice as well as belief, unless an employer demonstrates that he is unable to reasonably accommodate to an employee's or prospective employee's religious observance or practice without undue hardship on the conduct of the employer's business.

* * * * *

. . . [T]he employer's statutory obligation to make reasonable accommodation for the religious observances of its employees, short of incurring an undue hardship, is clear, but the reach of that obligation has never been spelled out by Congress or by EEOC guidelines. With this in mind, we turn to a consideration of whether TWA has met its obligation under Title VII to accommodate the religious observances of its employees.

* * * * *

. . . In summarizing its more detailed findings, the District Court observed:

> TWA established as a matter of fact that it did take appropriate action to accommodate as required by Title VII. It held several meetings with plaintiff at which it attempted to find a solution to plaintiff's problems. It did accommodate plaintiff's observance of his special religious holidays. It authorized the union steward to search for someone who would swap shifts, which apparently was normal procedure.

It is also true that TWA itself attempted without success to find Hardison another job. The District Court's view was that TWA had done all that could reasonably be expected within the bounds of the seniority system.

* * * * *

We are convinced . . . that TWA itself cannot be faulted for having failed to work out a shift or job swap for Hardison. Both the union and TWA had agreed to the seniority system; the union was unwilling to entertain a variance over the objections of men senior to Hardison; and for TWA to have arranged unilaterally for a swap would have amounted to a breach of the collective-bargaining agreement.

. . . Collective bargaining aimed at effecting workable and enforceable agreements between management and labor, lies at the core of our national labor policy, and seniority provisions are universally included in these contracts. Without a clear and express indication from Congress, we cannot agree with Hardison and the EEOC that an agreed-upon seniority system must give way when necessary to accommodate religious observances. . . .

Any employer who, like TWA, conducts an around-the-clock operation is presented with the choice of allocating work schedules either in accordance with the preferences of its employees or by involuntary assignment. Insofar as the varying shift preferences of its employees complement each other, TWA could meet its need through voluntary work scheduling. . . .

Whenever there are not enough employees who choose to work a particular shift, however, some employees must be assigned to that shift even though it is not their first choice. Such was evidently the case with regard to Saturday work. . . .

*   *   *   *   *

. . . Allocating the burdens of weekend work was a matter for collective bargaining. In considering criteria to govern this allocation, TWA and the union had two alternatives: adopt a neutral system, such as seniority, a lottery, or rotating shifts; or allocate days off in accordance with the religious needs of its employees. TWA would have had to adopt the latter in order to assure Hardison and others like him of getting the days off necessary for strict observance of their religion, but it could have done so only at the expense of others who had strong, but perhaps nonreligious, reasons for not working on weekends. There were no volunteers to relieve Hardison on Saturdays, and to give Hardison Saturdays off, TWA would have had to deprive another employee of his shift preference at least in part because he did not adhere to a religion that observed the Saturday Sabbath.

Title VII does not contemplate such unequal treatment. . . . It would be anomalous to conclude that by "reasonable accommodation" Congress meant that the employer must deny the shift and job preference of some employees, as well as deprive them of their contractual rights, in order to accommodate or prefer the religious needs of others, and we conclude that

Title VII does not require an employer to go that far.

*   *   *   *   *

The Court of Appeals also suggested that TWA could have permitted Hardison to work a four-day week if necessary in order to avoid working on his Sabbath. Recognizing that this might have left TWA shorthanded on the one shift each week that Hardison did not work, the court still concluded that TWA would suffer no undue hardship if it were required to replace Hardison either with supervisory personnel or with qualified personnel from other departments. Alternatively, the Court of Appeals suggested that TWA could have replaced Hardison on his Saturday shift with other available employees through the payment of premium wages. Both of these alternatives would involve costs to TWA, either in the form of lost efficiency in other jobs or higher wages.

To require TWA to bear more than a *de minimis** cost in order to give Hardison Saturdays off is an undue hardship. Like abandonment of the seniority system, to require TWA to bear additional costs when no such costs are incurred to give other employees the days off that they want would involve unequal treatment of employees on the basis of their religion. By suggesting that TWA should incur certain costs in order to give Hardison Saturdays off the Court of Appeals would in effect require TWA to finance an additional Saturday off and then to choose the employee who will enjoy it on the basis of his religious beliefs. While incurring extra costs to secure a replacement for Hardison might remove the necessity of compelling another employee to work involuntarily in Hardison's place, it would not change the fact that the privilege of having Saturdays off would be allocated according to religious beliefs.

---

* De minimus means a minimal or very small amount.—Au.

CASE QUESTIONS

1. What efforts did TWA make to accommodate Hardison's religious beliefs?

2. How did the Court define undue hardship? What reasoning supports this definition?

3. What amount do you think TWA would have had to spend annually to accommodate Hardison's religious beliefs? What does this amount suggest about the de minimis standard?

4. Brown is an assembly line worker for General Motors Corporation (GM). GM operates six days per week, with all employees given Sunday off. The employees bid by seniority for their second day off. Brown, a Sabbatarian with low seniority, is required to work Saturdays. GM employes "extraboard men" who are on call to work in case of unscheduled absences. Must GM accommodate Brown's religious beliefs?

National Origin

National origin refers to the country from which an individual or the individual's ancestors came. It also includes persons with characteristics generally identified with particular national groups. EEOC guidelines interpret Title VII's protections to prohibit discrimination based on:

— Marriage or association with persons of a particular national origin.
— Membership in a lawful organization identified with or seeking to promote the interests of a given nationality or ethnic group.
— Attendance at a school or church commonly utilized by persons of a particular national origin.
— A surname indicative of a particular national origin.

Alienage

Although Title VII prohibits national origin discrimination, it does not forbid discrimination on the basis of American citizenship. This does not mean that aliens have no Title VII rights. They are entitled to the same protection from discrimination on the basis of national origin as citizens. Thus, Mexican citizens residing in the United States cannot claim illegal national origin discrimination against employers who require American citizenship for a job, but they can press a claim against an employer who refuses to hire persons of Mexican ancestry.

Proficiency in English

EEOC guidelines suggest that it is illegal to require English language proficiency or to use tests written in English when English language skill is not a job requirement. Some courts have taken a narrower view, suggesting that an employer is not required to translate otherwise valid tests for every job applicant whose native tongue is not English.

Title VII Administration and Enforcement

The Equal Employment Opportunity Commission administers Title VII. Its principal methods of enforcement are the voluntary compliance efforts of conciliation and mediation. If these efforts fail, the commission is authorized to initiate litigation in a federal district court on behalf of aggrieved persons.

Filing the Charge

EEOC involvement is triggered when an aggrieved person—the charging party—files a written charge in one of the commission's regional offices, claiming to have been the victim of unlawful discrimination. The timing and procedure for filing the charge varies depending on the state in which the alleged discrimination occurred. If the state has a statute covering the discrimination charged and an administrative agency empowered to enforce the statute, the charging party must first file a complaint with the state agency. A charge may be filed with the EEOC only after the state agency has terminated proceedings or 60 days have passed, whichever occurs first. Charges received by the EEOC before this date are held in abeyance and formally filed when state jurisdiction lapses. Charges must be filed with the EEOC within 300 days following the alleged discriminatory act.

In states that do not have antidiscrimination statutes and enforcement agencies, charges may be filed immediately with the EEOC. Charges must be filed within 180 days following the discriminatory act.

EEOC Investigation

The EEOC sends a notice of the charge to the respondent. Its investigation may take a variety of forms. Interrogatories (written questions) may be sent to the respondent, or the respondent's plant may be visited. Interrogatories are usually sent along with the notice of the charge. Plant visits are usually made only after the employer has been sent a copy of the notice. Upon presenting proper identification, an EEOC investigator may examine the respondent's records and ask questions of employees. The EEOC has the power to subpoena any relevant documents.

Determination of Reasonable Cause

The EEOC's investigation culminates in a determination of whether there is reasonable cause to believe that a Title VII violation occurred. If the commission finds no reasonable cause, the charge is dismissed and the charging party is advised of his or her right to sue the respondent in federal district court within 90 days. The EEOC's dismissal of the charge does not prohibit the charging party from suing. If there is a finding of reasonable cause, the EEOC issues a determination letter notifying the respondent that it seeks to eliminate the alleged unlawful practice by an informal method of conciliation.

The Conciliation Process

Parties to the conciliation process, which is a confidential proceeding, are the charging party and the respondent. In practice, however, the charging party is rarely present at the conciliation conference. His or her interests are represented by an EEOC representative. The commission may also send its attorney to the conference, in anticipation of a court proceeding.

The conciliation process results in either the execution of a conciliation agreement or an impasse in the negotiations. The conciliation agreement, which is binding, must be signed by the parties and approved by the EEOC director of the region in which the charge has been filed. The agreement may bar most civil actions the charging party could bring against the respondent based on the complaint.

If conciliation fails, one of two things may happen: the EEOC regional office may refer the case to one of its litigation centers for possible direct action against the respondent, or it may notify the charging party that conciliation has been fruitless and that the charging party has a right to sue in federal court within 90 days. If the party elects to sue, the court may, at its discretion, appoint counsel. Successful litigants may be awarded costs and attorney's fees.

Records

Title VII requires all covered employers, unions, and employment agencies to make and keep records relevant to determining whether unlawful discriminatory practices have been or are being committed. The commission's regulations require employers to keep all personnel records for six months. These include records relating to job application, hiring, promotion, demotion, transfer, layoff, pay rates, and selection for apprenticeship and training programs. In addition, if a discrimination charge has been filed or a lawsuit brought, the commission requires that all records relevant to the charge be preserved until the final disposition of the case.

Reporting Requirements

The EEOC mandates that employers, unions, and employment agencies audit their minority population annually. All employers covered by Title VII that have 100 or more employees and government contracts of $50,000 or more must file Employer Information Report Form EEO-1, which details the composition of the employer's workforce.

Posting Requirement

The EEOC requires that employers, unions, and employment agencies post a prescribed notice summarizing pertinent provisions of Title VII. The notice is available in both English and Spanish. It must be conspicuously posted where employment notices are customarily displayed. Willful violation of this requirement is punishable by a fine of up to $100 for each offense.

Retaliation

Employers and other persons may not retaliate against individuals for participating in Title VII enforcement proceedings or for opposing discriminatory practices. Individuals have an absolute right to participate in Title VII enforcement proceedings. This includes the right to file charges and testify. No one may retaliate against individuals exercising this right, even if the charges are false and maliciously filed.

Individuals have a more limited right to oppose illegal employment discrimination apart from participating in enforcement proceedings. For example, they may complain to higher officials within a company that a subordinate official is discriminatory. Individuals exercising this right need not be absolutely certain that the offending practices are illegal, but they must have a reasonable good faith belief that they are. Their opposition activity must be lawful and reasonable under the circumstances.

THE EQUAL PAY ACT OF 1963

The Equal Pay Act, a short amendment to the Fair Labor Standards Act of 1938 (the wage and hour law that provides for federal minimum wage and overtime pay), requires the payment of equal wages for equal work between the sexes. Until 1979 it was enforced by the Wage and Hour Division of the Department of Labor. Enforcement responsibility was then transferred to the EEOC.

Equal Pay for Equal Work

The Equal Pay Act prohibits differences in pay between the sexes for employees who are performing work that requires "equal skill, effort, and responsibility" and is "performed under similar working conditions." If even one worker is paid at a higher rate than members of the opposite sex who are doing equal work, a violation of the act may be found.

The term "equal" does not require that the work of men and women employees be identical, but only that it be substantially equal, to justify equal pay. Thus, small differences in job descriptions will not make jobs so unequal as to justify a higher pay scale for one sex.

In writing the Equal Pay Act, Congress referred to equality of "skill," "effort," and "responsibility" exercised "under similar working conditions" because these are the criteria by which industry evaluates jobs for classification purposes. For example, in *Corning Glass v. Brennan* the Supreme Court considered whether the differences between the day and night shifts were sufficient to justify paying male night shift employees more than female day-shift employees.[8] The Court rejected the employer's argument that different shifts constituted different working conditions, noting that in the glass industry working conditions did not usually refer to the time of day during which work was performed.

Exceptions

There are several exceptions to the equal work-equal pay standard:

— Bona fide seniority and merit systems
— Earnings based on quantity or quality of output
— Factors other than sex

---

[8] 417 U.S. 188 (1974).

Pay differentials based on seniority or on performance evaluations are justified provided that the policy is uniformly applied. Systems in which employees are paid according to an individual production piece rate are immunized from liability by the quantity or quality of output exception.

Exceptions for factors other than sex immunize other legitimate bases for wage disparities. For example, although a shift differential results in unequal pay for equal work under similar conditions, the inequity may be justified because it arises from a factor other than sex.

Sexual discrimination does not exist where a wage disparity arises out of a bona fide management training program that rotates employees of one sex through all departments, thereby requiring them to work temporarily with members of the opposite sex who receive a lower rate than the trainees. However, training programs that are available only to employees of one sex are scrutinized to determine whether they are, in fact, bona fide exceptions. If the programs are informal, do not regularly result in promotion to the position being trained for, and appear to be geared more to the employer's needs than to actual training, they are not likely to survive scrutiny.

Comparable Worth

For many years women were discriminated against and excluded from high-paying jobs. They were forced to take clerical and service positions where they were paid considerably less than men who occupied positions that were closed to women. For example, consider a business that employs truck drivers and secretaries. Most likely the truck drivers are predominantly male and the secretaries are predominantly female. The truck drivers are probably paid considerably more than the secretaries. The secretaries, believing that they are worth as much as the truck drivers, may claim that the wage difference is discriminatory.

Paying male truck drivers more than female secretaries does not violate the Equal Pay Act. This is because the two jobs do not involve equal skill, effort, and responsibility and similar working conditions. However, the wage disparity may violate Title VII.

Many employers conduct their own job evaluations. Recently, a few courts have held that a firm violates Title VII if it pays less for predominantly female jobs that the firm's own evaluation system shows to be of comparable value to higher-paying predominantly male jobs. This area of the law is in its early stages of development.

THE AGE DISCRIMINATION IN EMPLOYMENT ACT

During the congressional debates over Title VII of the 1964 Civil Rights Act, amendments were proposed to prohibit age discrimination. These amendments were rejected, but the secretary of labor was directed to investigate and report on the problem. The secretary's study found that although age discrimination was widespread, it was based more on misconceptions about the abilities of older workers than on malicious prejudice. The secretary's report resulted in enactment of the Age Discrimination in Employment Act (ADEA) in 1967. The ADEA was substantially amended in 1978.

The ADEA covers employers that have 20 or more employees, unions that have 25 or more members or who operate hiring halls, and employment agencies that serve at least one covered employer. The ADEA protects employees between the ages of 40 and 70.

ADEA's Prohibitions and Requirements

ADEA's prohibitions generally parallel those contained in Title VII. Employers are prohibited from discriminating against persons between the ages of 40 and 70 in hiring, compensation, or other conditions of employment. Any segregation or classification of employees is unlawful if it is based on age. ADEA also bans retaliatory action against individuals who participate in proceedings or oppose policies prohibited by the act.

Employers must maintain a conspicuously posted notice explaining the act's provisions. Record-keeping requirements have also been imposed on all covered entities to effectuate the administration of the act. If there has been discrimination in the payment of wages, a reduction in the higher wage rate will not cure the violation. The older employee earning the lower rate must be brought up to the higher rate.

Courts have adapted the Title VII liability theories of disparate impact and disparate treatment, pattern, or practice to the ADEA. Cases brought under Title VII have involved all aspects of the employment process, including refusals to hire, refusals to promote, terminations, and disparities in wages and fringe benefits. However, more than 90 percent of the cases brought under the ADEA have involved terminations. This is particularly true during economic recessions, when many companies lay off or terminate large numbers of workers. The following case arose out of a recession-induced termination.

 **Coburn v. Pan American World Airways**

711 F.2d 339 (D.C. Cir. 1983)

Coburn (appellant) was 43 years old and had worked for Pan Am (appellee) for 17 years when he was terminated from his job as reservations supervisor in Pan Am's Washington, D.C. central ticket office. Coburn's termination resulted from a reduction in force (rif) caused by Pan Am's financial difficulties. The rif called for termination of two managers in Pan Am's eastern central region, including one from the Washington office. Pan Am terminated Coburn when an evaluation by his superiors found him to be the least productive employee within his peer group.

Coburn sued, claiming that his discharge violated the ADEA. A jury returned a verdict for Coburn, but the district court granted Pan Am judgment notwithstanding the jury's verdict. The D.C. Court of Appeals affirmed.

McNichols, Circuit Judge

The standard for awarding a judgment [notwithstanding the jury's verdict] is the same as that applied when ruling on a motion for a directed verdict . . . [T]he motion should not be granted unless the evidence, together with all the inferences that can reasonably be drawn therefrom is so one-sided that reasonable men could not disagree on the verdict.

*　*　*　*　*

We thus face the question whether reasonable persons could have concluded on the basis of the evidence at trial that Pan Am discriminated against Coburn on the basis of his age.

*　*　*　*　*

To make out a prima facie case "a plaintiff must demonstrate facts sufficient to create a reasonable inference that age discrimination was 'a determining factor' in the employment decision." . . . An inference of discrimination is created if the plaintiff shows that he (1) belongs to the statutorily protected age group (40–70), (2) was qualified for the position, (3) was terminated, and (4) was disadvantaged in favor of a younger person.

*　*　*　*　*

Once a prima facie case has been established, the employer has the burden of producing evidence tending to show that the applicant was denied employment for a legitimate, nondiscriminatory reason. If the employer does so, and if his evidence is credible, the plaintiff must show by a preponderance of the evidence that the employer's asserted legitimate reason is merely pretextual.

*　*　*　*　*

This analysis is easily adaptable from a failure to hire situation to the context of this case, an allegedly discriminatory discharge. The issue before us is whether reasonable jurors could have decided on the basis of the evidence at trial that Peter Coburn's age was a determining factor in Pan Am's decision to fire him.

The District Court . . . ruled that Coburn failed to prove a prima facie case because none of the evidence at trial would support an inference of discrimination, and for a jury to so infer would be a result of "impermissible conjecture and surmise." The District Court further ruled that even assuming plaintiff proved a prima facie case, the evidence was insufficient to support a jury finding that defendant's reasons for terminating Coburn were a pretext for discrimination. According to the District Court, the record was devoid of any evidence that Coburn's age was a determining factor in Pan Am's decision to fire him. Because we believe Coburn failed to carry his burden of proving discriminatory motive, we affirm the trial court's judgment.

* * * * *

We rule initially, contrary to the district court, that Coburn created a reasonable inference of discrimination by making out a prima facie case under the ADEA. Coburn was (1) 43 years old, (2) acknowledged by all to be qualified as a Reservations Supervisor, and (3) was fired while (4) younger persons were retained and others later promoted. The evidence produced at trial was clearly sufficient to support a jury finding of a prima facie case.

* * * * *

Pan Am urges us to require an ADEA plaintiff to prove something extra to make out a prima facie case in a reduction-in-force situation. Pan Am's rationale is that with a reduction-in-force the discharged employee will virtually always be qualified. Thus, anyone in the protected age group will presumptively have a cause of action under the ADEA. They therefore argue that direct evidence of discrimination should be required to make out a prima facie showing in a reduction-in-force case. . . . We believe the exigencies of a reduction-in-force can best be analyzed at the stage where the employer puts on evidence of a nondiscriminatory reason for the firing. In this manner the employee always retains the burden of proving discrimination while the employer's situation is analyzed on a case-by-case basis.

In the face of Coburn's prima facie showing we now turn to the question of Pan Am's articulated nondiscriminatory reason for firing Coburn. Pan Am's evidence demonstrated a company in serious financial straits seeking to cut costs in an attempt to survive. The reduction-in-force was instituted to reduce what Pan Am viewed as a surplus of management personnel. The guidelines called for termination of the "least productive" employee in a designated peer group. Pan Am, using a numerical ranking system, evaluated its Reservations Supervisors on the basis of qualifications, abilities, productivity, and length of service. Additional credit was given to employees over 40 years of age. Coburn was terminated when he was evaluated the least productive. We find that Pan Am carried its burden of proffering a legitimate, nondiscriminatory reason for terminating Coburn by instituting a written policy, following it to the letter, and making an employment decision based on its results. The procedure satisfied Pan Am's statutory burden.

Coburn then was required to show by a preponderance of the evidence that Pan Am's asserted reason was pretextual. . . .

Coburn first notes that both employees terminated in the Eastern Central Region of Pan Am's organizational structure were over 40. This is pure coincidence. The oldest employee, age 51, in Coburn's Washington Reservations and Ticket Office was retained. The other two managers retained in Washington were close to Coburn in age, though slightly younger. No other evidence was offered to show that Pan Am terminated a disproportionate number of older employees. On this record no pattern of age discrimination could reasonably be inferred.

Coburn finds suspicious Pan Am's attempt to induce managers aged 55–65 to retire early. Early retirement is a common corporate practice utilized to prevent individual hardship. It is a humane practice well accepted by both employers and employees, and is purely voluntary. The evidence showed that Pan Am was justified in attempting to reduce its costs, and voluntary retirement was clearly a fair attempt to do so. It supports not a hint of age discrimination.

Coburn takes issue with the composition of his peer group. He complains because two younger women who were employed as Trainers were not included with his category of Reservations Supervisors. However, the evidence makes it clear the two positions were distinct and not properly combinable under established Pan Am policies. Coburn also relies on the fact that these two female employees were later made Reservations Supervisors to show discrimination. However, these employees were only promoted after implementation of a merger between Pan Am and another airline. The merger resulted in less need for trainers and an increased volume of sales, an increase creating a new need for more Reservations Supervisors. That these trainers were promoted does not indicate an age discriminatory animus on Pan Am's part.

Coburn attempts to demonstrate inconsistencies between prior Pan Am evaluations and the reduction-in-force evaluation. He claims he was the highest rated supervisor in February 1980, yet rated lowest for purposes of the reduction-in-force in August, just six months later. The short answer to this contention is that it is not supported by the evidence. All four Reservations Su-

pervisors were rated "good" in February and given substantially similar ratings on more specific categories. The reduction-in-force criteria were specifically designed to determine the "least productive" employee. Coburn was fired only after ranking lowest overall after being rated in four distinct aspects of his job, and after being given extra credit for being over 40 years old. While Coburn disputed his rating in several regards, he produced no evidence that age was the reason he was rated low. Therefore, evidence of Pan Am's motive in the peer group analysis is "one sided" against the jury's verdict. We must conclude that under any view of the case, the evidence concerning age discrimination and the reasonable inferences to be drawn therefrom simply do not support a finding that peer group analysis was manipulated to Coburn's disadvantage because of his age.

* * * * *

Coburn draws a compelling picture of a long-time loyal employee who may have been treated less than fairly. But the record is devoid of any evidence that age was a "determining factor" in Pan Am's decision to terminate him.

CASE QUESTIONS

1. How was Coburn able to establish a prima facie case of age discrimination? How did Pan Am rebut the prima facie case?

2. What evidence did Coburn produce to show pretext? Why was it insufficient?

3. Explain Pan Am's argument for treating reductions-in-force prima facie cases differently

than other cases and discuss the court's rejection of that argument.

4. Why do you think the jury found for Coburn?

5. If Pan Am's evaluation procedures had been less formal and less uniform, would the case have been decided differently? Explain.

Exceptions

The ADEA contains bfoq and bona fide seniority system exceptions that parallel those contained in Title VII. It also excepts employment decisions based on reasonable factors other than age and discharges for cause. These two exceptions are essentially denials of, rather than justifications for, age discrimination. They have been interpreted as codifying the employer's burden of rebutting a prima facie case of disparate treatment with legitimate, nondiscriminatory reasons for its actions.

The ADEA excepts bona fide employee benefit plans that are not subterfuges to avoid the act. This exception enables an employer to provide lower levels of fringe benefits to older employees where the costs of those benefits increase as employees age. For example, an employer may reduce the amount of life insurance it provides employees as they get older, provided that the reductions are cost-justified.

Finally, the ADEA allows employers to require certain highly paid executives to retire at age 65. These executives must have been employed in executive positions at least two years before retirement and must be entitled to an annual nonforfeitable retirement benefit of at least $27,000.

ADEA Administration and Enforcement

The ADEA was originally administered by the Department of Labor. In 1979 this function was transferred to the EEOC.

Enforcement of the ADEA is very similar to enforcement of Title VII. Persons must file charges with the EEOC within 300 days in states that have similar age discrimination statutes and enforcement agencies, and within 180 days in other states. Unlike Title VII charges, ADEA charges may be filed with the EEOC at the same time or even before charges are filed with the appropriate state agency. Also, unlike Title VII, a party need not wait for the EEOC to complete its investigation and conciliation processes before filing suit in federal district court. Suit may be filed any time after 60 days following the filing of the EEOC charge. Suit must be filed within two years of the discriminatory act for nonwillful violations and within three years for willful violations.

THE REHABILITATION ACT OF 1973

Sections 503 and 504 of the Vocational Rehabilitation Act of 1973 prohibit discrimination against handicapped persons by federal contractors and require federal contractors to take affirmative action in hiring qualified handicapped persons. A qualified handicapped person is anyone who has (or had a record or history of) a physical or mental impairment that substantially limits one or more of life's major activities. This includes such diverse impairments as blindness, diabetes, epilepsy, heart disease, and alcoholism.

The law applies to any job that, with "reasonable accommodation" for his or her handicap, a worker can perform at the minimum level of productivity expected of a normal person in that job. However, sections 503 and 504 do not require employers to hire persons unqualified to do the job.

The Labor Department enforces this legislation. The department has issued regulations forbidding discrimination against handicapped persons and requiring employers having federal contracts for more than $2,500 to take affirmative action to hire the handicapped. The regulations provide that such a contractor "must attempt to make a reasonable accommodation to the physical and mental limitations of an employee or applicant" unless the contractor can establish that this would impose undue hardship on the conduct of the contractor's business. The regulations provide for consideration of business necessity, financial expense and cost, and resultant personnel problems in determining the extent of a contractor's accommodation responsibilities. Contractors that are in noncompliance may be liable for breach of contract and may be barred from entering into future federal contracts.

THE CIVIL RIGHTS ACT OF 1866

The Thirteenth Amendment to the Constitution prohibits slavery and involuntary servitude. It also empowers Congress to legislate enforcement of its prohibitions.

The Civil Rights Act of 1866 (42 U.S.C. section 1981) sought to implement the Thirteenth Amendment and to eliminate the incidence of servitude. The act provides that all persons in the United States "shall have the same right . . . to make and enforce contracts . . . and to the full and equal benefit of all laws . . . as is enjoyed by white citizens."

In 1975 the Supreme Court held in *Johnson v. Railway Express Agency, Inc.*, that section 1981 provided a federal remedy against racial discrimination in employment.[9] Although the phrase "as is enjoyed by white citizens" seemed to limit the act's application to racial discrimination directed against nonwhites, the Supreme Court in *McDonald v. Santa Fe Trail Transportation Co.* relied upon the act's language and legislative history. The Court concluded that section 1981 also applied to racial discrimination in employment against white persons. Sex discrimination has been excluded from the act's coverage. Courts have applied section 1981 to discrimination against aliens. Thus, although an alien has no remedy under Title VII, he or she can sue in federal court under section 1981. Courts are divided over whether section 1981 covers national origin discrimination.

Section 1981 applies only to racial discrimination, whereas Title VII includes other forms of discrimination. Title VII provides assistance in investigation, conciliation, and counsel, which are unavailable under section 1981. In litigation under section 1981, employers do not have available the bfoq defense that is available under Title VII in cases of national origin discrimination. Under Title VII a back pay award is limited to two years of unpaid wages, whereas section 1981 does not restrict the plaintiff's remedy.

---

[9] 421 U.S. 454 (1975).

THE EXECUTIVE ORDER PROGRAM

Various executive orders not only ban discrimination in employment by federal contractors but also require that federal contractors undertake affirmative action plans. The Office of Federal Contract Compliance Programs (OFCCP) of the Labor Department administers the executive order program.

The concept of affirmative action originated through a series of executive orders. The most important of these, Executive Order 11246, requires that government contractors take affirmative action to insure that their employees are hired and promoted on a nondiscriminatory basis.

Executive Order 11246 requires that all government contracts include a clause which states the contractor's agreement not to discriminate on the basis of race, creed, color, or national origin (a later executive order added sex as a category). The clause also states the contractor's agreement to take affirmative action to insure that no discrimination occurs. Thus, under the executive order program the duties of nondiscrimination and affirmative action are conditions included in every federal contract. Contractors wishing to do business with the federal government must agree to these terms or take their business elsewhere. Executive Order 11246 provides that contracts may be canceled or suspended in part and that contractors may be declared ineligible for further government contracts.

Revised Order No. 4

To supplement the affirmative action programs required of all government contractors, the OFCCP issued Revised Order No. 4. This is used as a guide in developing and judging the affirmative action programs of contractors outside the construction industry. It states that a covered contractor will be in noncompliance with Executive Order 11246 unless it has developed an acceptable affirmative action plan by using the standards and guidelines set forth in the revised order. Revised Order No. 4 requires that an affirmative action plan with realistic goals and timetables be prepared by each employer with 50 or more employees and a contract or sub contract of $50,000 or more. It offers a comprehensive statement of the steps required to develop and implement such a plan. First, the employer must perform a utilization analysis, including evaluation of the size of the minority and female population and labor force in the area, the requisite skills among minorities and women in the area, and the available training programs and facilities. Having completed this analysis, the employer must identify the deficiencies in its workforce. It must then establish attainable goals for correcting and eliminating those deficiencies and a timetable for achieving the goals. The employer must develop methods for implementing the plan that will achieve the goals. Such methods include wide internal and external dissemination of the employer's policy, making a high-level official responsible for implementation, utilizing minority and female sources to seek personnel, and utilizing minority and female employees as recruiters.

An employer is not in violation of its plan if it fails to meet its goals, provided the employer has made good faith efforts to do so. This is the principal difference between goals and quotas. If a contractor is required by law to meet the goals, they become quotas.

ALTERNATIVE APPROACHES

Civil rights laws prohibit the use of particular characteristics as the basis for employment decisions. Some persons contend that the civil rights laws have gone beyond ensuring equal opportunity for minorities, women, older workers, and the handicapped and have resulted in members of these groups receiving more favorable treatment than white males. They suggest that employers are less likely to reject or terminate members of the protected classes than members of the majority because they fear potential civil rights liability.

Others contend that our civil rights laws have not gone far enough. They point out that minority unemployment rates have generally doubled white unemployment rates. They cite that there are still very few minorities and women in upper-level positions.

An alternative to prohibiting employment actions based on particular characteristics is to require that employment actions be based on specified factors. For example, many have proposed that employers be prohibited from discharging employees except for just cause. Employers could also be required to base hiring, promotion, and compensation decisions only on objectively validated criteria. Such affirmative requirements would represent a major change from the basic approach of American labor law. They might also impose new major cost burdens on employers. In evaluating these alternatives, their costs should be balanced against the likelihood that they might protect all workers and provide for true equal employment opportunity.

CHAPTER PROBLEMS

1. An insurance company has found that black people are more likely to buy insurance if approached by a black agent, while white people are more receptive to a white agent. The company plans to assign its black agents to offices in predominantly black neighborhoods and its white agents to offices in predominantly white neighborhoods. Is the practice legal? Why or why not?

2. An employer requires all of its entry-

level managers to complete a six-month training program. The employer gives a test to all applicants for entry-level management positions. The passing rate is 75 percent for whites and 45 percent for blacks. The test measures several skills that are needed to succeed in the training program but are not necessarily needed to perform the entry-level managerial jobs. Are the tests legal?

3. A state requires prison guards to be at

least 5 feet 2 inches tall and to weigh at least 120 pounds. Although an equal percentage of the male and female job applicants meet these qualifications, statistics compiled by the Census Bureau show that nationally 41 percent of the female population does not meet the height requirement, as compared to 1 percent of the male population. Does the requirement violate Title VII?

4. A restaurant hires only female waitresses and cashiers. It features "businessmen's lunches" and "stag dinners." All waitresses and cashiers work topless. Is the restaurant violating Title VII?

5. An employer requires that its director of Latin American marketing be male. The position involves extensive travel to Latin America to deal with present and potential customers. Business meetings are often held in hotel rooms. Many Latin American customers would find conducting business with a woman in a hotel room offensive to their cultural customs and mores. They generally prefer to do business with men and would probably switch to a competitor if the employer's Latin American marketing director was female. Does the employer's refusal to consider females for the position violate Title VII? Why or why not?

6. An employer obtains all of its employees from the union-run hiring hall. The agreement between the employer and the union provides for job referrals based on seniority. Employees are classified as permanent or temporary, with permanent employees given preference over temporaries. To be classified permanent, an employee must work at least 45 weeks in a year. Before Title VII became effective, the employer refused to hire blacks. After 1965 the employer dropped its whites-only policy, but because black employees lack seniority, few of them have been able to accumulate the 45 work weeks needed to become permanent employees. Does this violate Title VII?

7. Prior to 1975 an employer refused to hire blacks or women. After 1965 the employer dropped this policy but failed to attract many qualified black or female employees except at the low levels. Consequently, the employer and the union agreed to implement an affirmative

action program designed to eliminate a perceived racial imbalance in the employer's work force. The program called for a special apprenticeship program, with the graduates guaranteed employment. Preference for entry to the program was given to current low-level employees according to seniority. Seventy-five percent of the slots were reserved for blacks. When the program began, there were 20 slots. Ten whites and 30 blacks applied. Five of the whites were male, and five were female. All of the blacks were male. The white males had worked for the employer since 1963. Because they had far greater seniority than the white females they received the five white slots in the program. The 15 black slots went to 15 black males, 10 of whom had less seniority than the 5 white females. Has Title VII been violated?

8. An employer was found to have violated Title VII by discriminating against blacks. As part of the remedy the employer was required to hire at least 10 blacks for its next 20 openings. The employer did so and completed the hiring two years ago. The employer recently lost two major customers and must now lay off 25 workers. A collective bargaining agreement with the employees' union requires layoffs to be made by seniority. Can the employer adhere to the seniority provision even though all 10 blacks will be laid off? Why or why not?

9. An employer pays its secretaries an average of $2 per hour less than it pays its manual laborers. Although both jobs are open to both sexes, all of the employer's manual laborers are male while all of its secretaries are female. Is the employer violating either Title VII or the Equal Pay Act?

10. Your company has decided to close an absolete plant. The plant employs 15 supervisors. The company has room to transfer 12 to other plants, but must lay off 3. The ages of the three oldest supervisors are 61, 60, and 58. These supervisors are eligible for early retirement, whereas the remaining 12 are not. They have been with the company longest and therefore receive the highest salaries. If you force them to take early retirement, you will save a substantial sum in salaries and retirement contributions and benefits. If you do so, will you violate ADEA?

PART PROBLEMS

1. You are the vice president in charge of labor relations for Ace Building Company (ABC). ABC is nonunion. Prior to 1965 ABC refused to hire blacks. After 1965 it dropped its whites-only policy, but few blacks sought jobs with ABC. By 1975 only 17 of its 200 employees were black despite the fact that 25 percent of the general population in the surrounding area and 18 percent of all members of building trades unions were black. In 1975 ABC began an affirmative action program under which it actively recruited black workers. Today ABC employs 220 workers, 37 are black.

Last week several ABC employees were excavating a pit. I. M. Eager, a black hired under the affirmative action program, was operating a front-end loader up and down ramps leading into the pit. In violation of company rules several other employees were riding the running board of the front-end loader. On one occasion H. E. Macho, the site foreman, was riding the running board when the front-end loader skidded off the ramp. Both Eager and Macho jumped. Eager landed clear of the front-end loader but hurt his back. He will miss work for six weeks. Macho was killed when the front-end loader landed on top of him. Eager has filed a complaint with OSHA.

Work has fallen off in the past year, and ABC will have to lay off 20 employees shortly. Rumors of layoffs have been circulating among the employees. The day after the front-end loader accident, Willie White, a white employee, began distributing a leaflet during the lunch break. The leaflet charged that ABC had become "a black man's operation," that this had caused the death of a white foreman, and that ABC planned to lay off white workers. It urged employees to join the White Workers Union and secure "white rights" through collective bargaining. Osbourn Black, a black employee, objected to the leaflet distribution. White punched Black in the face, breaking his jaw.

ABC's president has called a meeting of all vice presidents to discuss the company's deteriorating employee relations. In preparation for the meeting, consider these questions:

1. Are Eager, Black, and the widow Macho entitled to workers' compensation benefits?
2. What can OSHA be expected to do?
3. Can ABC fire Eager?
4. Can ABC fire White? Black?
5. Can ABC lay off 20 employees according to seniority even though that will result in layoff of 20 blacks?
6. Can ABC lay off the 20 least senior white employees?
7. Can ABC prohibit White and his supporters from soliciting for their union on company property?

2. The Gregarious Gizmo Company (GGC) is a major manufacturer of gizmos. Employees who work on the assembly line are represented by Local 1 of the Gizmo Employees International Union. The collective bargaining agreement is silent concerning whether employees are permitted to smoke while on duty. The past practice has been to allow smoking.

Recently two groups of employees have written letters to the president of GGC complaining about a petition signed by 10 percent of the line employees who claimed that their health was being harmed because they were being forced to inhale the fumes of cigarette smoke. A second group submitted a petition signed by all the female line employees (about 20 percent of all the line employees) who claimed that inhaling the fumes from cigarette smokers endangers the life of a fetus and urged that cigarette smoking be banned in light of the fact that 10 line employees were pregnant.

The president of GGC has read much of the available literature on the effects of smoking on nonsmokers and is concerned about the threat of smoking to the health of nonsmokers and to the fetuses of pregnant employees. Prepare a report for the president that considers the following:

1. Can we ban smoking without discussing it with the union?
2. Can we discuss the question of a smoking ban with representatives of the two petitioning groups?

3. If we do not ban smoking, can we expect trouble from OSHA?
4. If we do not ban smoking, can we require all pregnant employees to take maternity leave as soon as we learn of their pregnancy?

Management planning and policy implementation today must take into account the environment facing the firm.

PART SIX

SOCIAL ENVIRONMENT OF BUSINESS

Business does not operate in a vacuum. Rather, it is one of society's major institutions. It is an important part of the social fabric, helping to shape a nation's legal, political, and economic environment.

Responding to this social environment is a primary concern for today's manager. Only a short-sighted manager would adopt the thinking of Cornelius Vanderbilt, who said, "The public be damned, I work for my shareholders." Management planning and policy implementation today must take into account the environment facing the firm. Careful attention must be given to ever-changing social conditions. Business must either anticipate or acquiesce to changes in its environment. The success of a particular strategy often depends on how wisely management responds to this challenge. In nature, the existence of a species depends on its ability to adapt to and interact with its environment. Similarly, the success or even the existence of a business depends upon its compatibility with its environment.

In the 1960s, two movements developed, each dramatizing the need for corporate responsiveness to the external world. The environmental movement addressed corporate responsiveness to the natural environment. The movement toward recognizing a corporate social responsibility addressed corporate social performance. Both movements are continuing today. Each illustrates a fundamental fact of modern management: that the consequences of corporate conduct extend beyond shareholders, employees, and consumers. For example, a factory smokestack in Ohio can cause acid rain in Vermont. And a decision to relocate a factory from the traditionally industrial Northeast to the Sunbelt states in the nation's Southwest can affect population demographics, shift political power, and alter local economies.

According to recent polls, concern for the nation's natural environment continues to rank high on the priority list of most Americans—alongside concern for crime and national defense. This concern for protecting America's environmental heritage may be viewed as part of an environmental movement that emerged by mid-century. By then, the industrialization of America had become complete. War and prosperity spurred industrialization, carving new inroads into America's natural resources. A population of roughly 200 million, bigger cities, and bigger industry made pollution of the air and water a national problem.

In 1962, Rachael Carson drew attention to the environmental threat posed by pesticides in her book, *Silent Spring*. Her prophecy of a silent spring resulting from the death of robbins and other insect-eating birds that had been deprived of sufficient food as a result of pesticide use dramatized the threat to humans who stand at the end of the food chain. Carson awakened in Americans an awareness of the place of humans in the ecological system.

Environmental criticism was often directed at America's business, which released industrial chemicals into the nation's rivers and air and mass marketed products, such as laundry detergents and aerosol sprays, that further added to the nation's pollution problem. By 1965, the *New York Times* editorialized that "If man refuses to follow wise conservation practices in controlling his economic affairs, the ultimate victim may not be natural beauty or birds and fish, but man himself."

---

*F*ew trends could so thoroughly undermine the very foundation of our free society as the acceptance by corporate officials of a social responsibility other than to make as much money for their stockholders as possible. This is a fundamentally subversive doctrine.

Milton Friedman, Economist

In 1969, Congress responded to the public interest in the environment by enacting the Environmental Policy Act, which expressly recognized "that each person should enjoy a healthful environment." Congress later enacted other, more specific legislation directed toward this goal. Today, several environmental laws are in place, each aimed at protecting an area of the nation's environment. Among them are the Clean Air Act, the Clean

Water Act, and the Toxic Substances Control Act. These laws and others are discussed in chapter 18.

At the same time Americans were awakening to the threat of environmental pollution, a public debate was occurring over business ethics and corporate social responsibility. In the early 1960s, the public was shocked when 20 indictments charged 29 electrical equipment manufacturers and 45 corporate executives with criminal violations of the antitrust laws. The prosecutions resulted in pleas of guilty and no contest. Seven corporate officials went to jail.

*M*ere *money-making cannot be regarded as the legitimate end . . . since with the conduct of business human happiness or misery is inextricably interwoven.*

Louis Brandeis,
former Supreme Court Justice

Ten years later, congressional investigating committees discovered numerous illegal corporate domestic campaign contributions and uncovered the common corporate practice of bribing foreign government officials. This led to passage of federal lobbying legislation (discussed in Chapter 2) and the federal Foreign Corrupt Practices Act (also discussed in Chapter 2). More importantly, however, these developments directed public attention to the topics of business ethics and corporate social responsibility and also led to calls for the teaching of ethics in the nation's business schools. The topics of business ethics and corporate social responsibility are discussed in Chapter 19.

CHAPTER 18

ENVIRONMENTAL LAW

Statistical evidence, substantiated by dramatic events, made American legislators of the 1960s and 1970s acutely aware of the nation's dependence upon a protected environment. Evidence that emissions of sulfur dioxide increased from 22 million to 33 million tons annually between 1940 and 1970, for example, was punctuated by reports of deaths in Los Angeles caused by photochemically activated smog. Acid rain from fossil fuel combustion in the northeastern United States destroyed 200 lakes in the New York Adirondack Mountains alone; the fish in those lakes had been killed, and the aquatic vegetation had dwindled severely. Floating wastes in the Great Lakes around Ohio self-ignited.

During the 1970s, state and federal legislators responded to these hazards and other problems by enacting laws to protect the environment. Common-law environmental protections still served to settle some individual disputes, but broader environmental policy concerns had to be addressed by statutes. This chapter explains the nature and limitations of common-law environmental protections; discusses national environmental policy; describes federal and state programs for pollution control, land use, and resource management; and concludes with a discussion of alternative approaches to environmental protection.

Business decisions must include consideration of environmental law. For example, when a company decides to build a factory, its management has to determine if permits are needed from environmental agencies. Obtaining these permits usually takes a great deal of time, which can affect the construction schedule. Certain technology may need to be installed in the factory before a permit will be issued. This will require that the factory's plans incorporate environmental protection technology and that the cost of this technology be considered.

Environmental protection is expensive. Billions of dollars are spent on regulation. Although the burden of protecting the nation's environment is initially placed on industry, the costs are ultimately passed on to consumers in the form of higher prices. Nevertheless, public opinion polls report that Americans still place a high priority on protecting the environment. Managers must continue to consider environmental issues when making decisions.

COMMON-LAW PROTECTIONS

Under common law, landholders can use a range of responses to keep their land free of encumbrances, their water free of obstructions, and their air free of debris. Depending upon the interests they have at stake, landholders can sue under the tort theories of trespass, nuisance, negligence, or strict liability.

Trespass

A trespass is an unlawful interference with another's property. The trespass action protects landholders' interests in the exclusive possession of their properties. A person who physically intrudes onto another's property commits a trespass. However, the intruder need not physically set foot on the property to be liable. An intruder may be held liable for setting events in motion that cause the intrusion. For example, someone who sends pollutants upon a neighbor's land commits a trespass.

Early common law viewed every unauthorized and direct intrusion as a trespass unless the intruder had permission or was privileged to enter the land. The present prevailing view finds liability only in the case of intentional intrusion, negligent intrusion, or intrusion resulting from an "abnormally dangerous activity." A trespass may be committed by a single act or by a continuing presence on the land.

Single Trespass

A single trespass is a momentary intrusion. For example, if a worker begins a construction project on lot 1 but drives a truck across lot 2 to bring in supplies, the owner of lot 2 can sue the worker for trespass. The worker's liability to the owner includes the costs of repairing any damage done to the owner's sod. If the worker does not damage the sod or even leave tracks across lot 2, the worker will still be liable for nominal damages. In many cases this amounts to only $1.

Continuing Trespass

A continuing trespass is an intrusion that persists for a protracted time. It may be committed by the continued presence of a structure or other thing put on the land by an intruder. For example, if in excavating the foundation for a house on lot 1, a worker dumps dirt and trees on lot 2, the owner of lot 2 can sue for trespass. Trespass in this case, however, is not a simple, completed act. The presence of dirt and trees on lot 2 makes this a continuing trespass.

The common law did not settle on a simple remedy for continuing trespass. Some courts allowed landholders to maintain successive actions, recovering periodically as long as the offending objects remained. Other courts, dissatisfied with the inconvenience this caused landholders, allowed them to dispose of these matters in a single action. By awarding in a single suit all damages, past and prospective, these courts made recovery more convenient. Still, damages were often speculative and trespasses were sometimes terminated long after judgments.

Continuing trespasses were further complicated where the offending objects were particles set onto the owner's lot by a factory on a neighboring lot. Historically, the trespass action depended upon proving a direct physical invasion of the land as clear as a worker's dumping debris from a wheelbarrow. The invasion of land by particles smaller than the eye could see was an insufficient ground for finding a trespass because invasion was impossible to prove. This limitation was a significant drawback to the use of trespass actions to fight fine dusts emanating from factories, which, slowly but surely, might cover the ground as effectively as debris from a wheelbarrow. Today, the test of a trespass does not rest on proving a direct invasion, but whether the invasion interferes with the right to the exclusive possession of property.

Nuisance

A nuisance is a substantial and unreasonable interference with the use and enjoyment of an interest in land. A cause of action for nuisance thus protects landholders' interests in the use and enjoyment of their properties. In environmental litigation, nuisance includes interferences in the form of smoke, odor, noise, and vibration. The interference may be intentional, or it may be the result of negligence or "abnormally dangerous" conduct.

Trespass and Nuisance Distinguished

A trespass is an invasion of the right to exclusive possession of land, as by entry upon it. A nuisance is an interference with the interest in the private use and enjoyment of land and does not require direct interference with possession. For example, the flooding of another's land constitutes a trespass because it interferes with the landholder's interest in possession. In contrast, a noxious odor spewing from a nearby factory smokestack might constitute a nuisance to the neighboring owners' use and enjoyment of their property. The principal difference in theories is that the tort of trespass covers all tangible invasions, however slight, of another's property. Nuisance requires proof of substantial and unreasonable interference with use and enjoyment of the property.

The two torts often overlap, and plantiffs sue for both nuisance and trespass. For example, repeated and prolonged flooding of land might interfere with the use and enjoyment of that land as well as with the owner's interest in possession.

Balancing Test

In determining whether a nuisance exists, the courts balance various factors—a practice referred to as "balancing the equities." All landholders' rights to use and enjoy their properties are necessarily subject to the rights of other landholders to do the same, so the courts weigh the utility of the conduct of one landholder against the gravity of the harm caused to another. Generally, if harm outweighs utility, the courts deem the conduct a nuisance. Other relevant considerations are the existence of practical means to avoid causing the harm and the location of the properties.

Gravity of Harm

The gravity of the harm that one landholder's conduct causes another depends upon several factors. The greater the extent and duration of the harm, the more likely it is to be considered grave. Occasional puffs of smoke from factory chimneys, for example, are not as grave as clouds of smoke that are always present. The greater the physical damage caused by the harm, the graver its character. Fumes carrying chemicals that destroy lung tissue, for instance, are graver than clouds carrying dust that makes people sneeze.

Harm will not be considered grave if complaining landholders can avoid it by taking simple precautions. Thus, landholders may reasonably be expected to close their windows to keep out occasional noise.

The gravity of harm may also vary with the use complaining landholders make of their own properties. Runoff water from another's land, for example, is a more serious problem if the land is used for a residence than it is if the land is used to graze cattle.

Utility of Conduct

Although certain conduct causes harm, it may also have social utility or value. Thus, landholders may sometimes have to tolerate moderate blasting noise, airplane vibrations, or refinery smells as unavoidable side effects of industrial progress.

Means to Prevent Harm

If landholders have reasonably practical means to avoid harming their neighbors, they may be liable for nuisance even if the harm of their conduct is shown to be slight and its social utility great. Thus, if adding coolants could reduce the temperature of power plant effluents discharged into fishing waters, failure to do so would make power plant owners responsible for depleting fishers' catches. However, if incorporating coolants into the discharge process at the power plant entailed redesign and reconstruction of portions of the plant, the owners would probably not be required to undertake those projects.

Property Locations

Whether parties have legitimate claims or defenses to nuisance actions may depend upon where their properties are located. Courts recognize that friction among landholders has been reduced in areas divided into residential, industrial, and agricultural districts. Therefore, they are not likely to act on complaints about noise from a homeowner who has built on property in the middle of a business district. Neither are they likely to heed pleas from a sawmill owner to allow expanded operations in a residential district.

Remedies

Courts have broad powers to remedy nuisances. They can order defendants to relocate their factories, to compensate plaintiffs for their losses, or to buy out plaintiffs. Courts also have the power to order polluters to install the best pollution control technology. Where technological accommodation is impossible or too expensive, courts can order operational changes, such as limiting a noisy blasting operation to daytime hours.

However, courts have been reluctant to use their full remedial powers. They factor general community concerns in with the special interests of the parties. They also consider the impact on local community growth and employment, especially when requested to order the closing of a factory. Faced with these community concerns and with substantial corporate investments in the community, courts have limited the application of injunctions, as shown in the following case.

Boomer *v.* Atlantic Cement Company

257 N.E. 2d 870 (N.Y. 1970)

Atlantic operates a cement company near Albany, New York, Boomer and other neighboring landowners sought an injunction against Atlantic to stop dirt, smoke, and vibrations emanating from the plant that were injuring their property. The trial court found that these conditions were a nuisance. It did not grant an injunction because techniques to eliminate annoying by-products of cementmaking were unlikely to be developed by any research that Atlantic could undertake within a short period and because the plant represented an investment in the community of more than $45 million and had 300 employees. Rather, it allowed temporary damages to compensate for harm done to the properties of Boomer and others and granted the landowners the right to sue for damages suffered in the future. An intermediate appellate court affirmed. The landowners then appealed to the highest state court, which reversed the lower courts and granted permanent damages.

Bergan, Judge

The public concern with air pollution arising from many sources in industry and in transportation is currently accorded ever wider recognition accompanied by a growing sense of responsibility in State and Federal Governments to control it. Cement plants are obvious sources of air pollution in the neighborhoods where they operate.

* * * * *

It seems apparent that the amelioration of air pollution will depend on technical research in great depth; on a carefully balanced consideration of the economic impact of close regulation; and of the actual effect on public health. It is likely to require massive public expenditure and to demand more than any local community can accomplish and to depend on regional and interstate controls.

A court should not try to do this on its own as a by product of private litigation and it seems manifest that the judicial establishment is neither equipped in the limited nature of any judgment it can pronounce nor prepared to lay down and implement an effective policy for the elimination of air pollution. This is an area beyond the circumference of one private lawsuit. It is a direct responsibility for government and should not thus be undertaken as an incident to solving a dispute between property owners and a single cement plant, one of many, in the Hudson River valley.

* * * * *

The ground for the denial of injunction, not withstanding the finding both that there is a nuisance and that plaintiffs have been damaged substantially, is the large disparity in economic consequences of the nuisance and of the injunction. This theory cannot, however, be sustained without overruling a doctrine which has been consistently reaffirmed in several leading cases in this court and which has never been disavowed here, namely that where a nuisance has been found and where there has been any substantial damage shown by the party complaining an injunction will be granted.

* * * * *

Although the court at Special Term and the Appellate Division held that injunction should be denied, it was found that plaintiffs had been damaged in various specific amounts up to the time of the trial and damages to the respective plantiffs were awarded for those amounts. The effect of this was, injunction having been denied, plaintiffs could maintain successive actions

at law for damages thereafter as further damage was incurred.

The court at Special Term also found the amount of permanent damage attributable to each plaintiff, for the guidance of the parties in the event both sides stipulated to the payment and acceptance of such permanent damage as a settlement of all the controversies among the parties. The total of permanent damages to all plaintiffs thus found was $185,000. This basis of adjustment has not resulted in any stipulation by the parties.

This result at Special Term and at the Appellate Divison is a departure from a rule that has become settled; but to follow the rule literally in these cases would be to close down the plant at once. This court is fully agreed to avoid that immediately drastic remedy; the difference in view is how best to avoid it.

One alternative is to grant the injunction but postpone its effect to a specified future date to give opportunity for technical advances to permit defendant to eliminate the nuisance; another is to grant the injunction conditioned on the payment of permanent damages to plaintiffs which would compensate them for the total economic loss to their property present and future caused by defendant's operations. For reasons which will be developed the court chooses the latter alternative.

If the injunction were to be granted unless within a short period—e.g., 18 months—the nuisance be abated by improved methods, there would be no assurance that any significant technical improvement would occur.

The parties could settle this private litigation at any time if defendant paid enough money and the imminent threat of closing the plant would build up the pressure on defendant. If there were no improved techniques found, there would inevitably be applications to the court at Special Term for extensions of time to perform on showing of good faith efforts to find such techniques.

Moreover, techniques to eliminate dust and other annoying by-products of cement making are unlikely to be developed by any research the defendant can undertake within any short period, but will depend on the total resources of the cement industry nationwide and throughout the world. The problem is universal wherever cement is made.

For obvious reasons the rate of the research is beyond control of defendant. If at the end of 18 months the whole industry has not found a technical solution a court would be hard put to close down this one cement plant if due regard is given to equitable principles.

On the other hand, to grant the injunction unless defendant pays plaintiffs such permanent damages as may be fixed by the court seems to do justice between the contending parties. All of the attributions of economic loss to the properties on which plaintiffs' complaints are based will have been redressed.

* * * * *

The present cases and the remedy here proposed are in a number of other respects rather similar to *Northern Indiana Public Service Co. v. W. J. & M. S. Vesey,* decided by the Supreme Court of Indiana. The gases, odors, ammonia and smoke from the Northern Indiana company's gas plant damaged the nearby Vesey greenhouse operation. An injunction and damages were sought, but an injunction was denied and the relief granted was limited to permanent damages "present, past, and future."

Denial of injunction was grounded on a public interest in the operation of the gas plant and on the court's conclusion "that less injury would be occasioned by requiring the appellant (Public Service) to pay the appellee (Vesey) all damages suffered by it

. . . than by enjoying the operation of the gas plant; and that the maintenance and operation of the gas plant should not be enjoined."

The Indiana Supreme Court opinion continued: "When the trial court refused injunctive relief to the appellee upon the ground of public interest in the continuance of the gas plant, it properly retained jurisdiction of the case and awarded full compensation to the appellee. This is upon the general equitable principle that equity will give full relief in one action and prevent a multiplicity of suits."

It was held that in this type of continuing and recurrent nuisance permanent damages were appropriate. *See, also, City of Amarillo v. Ware,* where recurring overflows from a system of storm sewers were treated as the kind of nuisance for which permanent depreciation of value of affected property would be recoverable.

* * * * *

Thus it seems fair to both sides to grant permanent damages to plaintiffs which will terminate this private litigation. The theory of damage is the "servitude on land" of plaintiffs imposed by defendant's nuisance. *See United States v. Causby,* where the term "servitude" addressed to the land was used by Justic Douglas relating to the effect of airplane noise on property near an airport.

The judgment, by allowance of permanent damages imposing a servitude on land, which is the basis of the actions, would preclude future recovery by plaintiffs or their grantees.

Jasen, Judge *(dissenting)*

I see grave dangers in overruling our long-established rule of granting an injunction where a nuisance results in substantial continuing damage. In permitting the injunction to become inoperative upon the payment of permanent damages, the majority is, in effect, licensing a continuing wrong. It is the same as saying to the cement company, you may continue to do harm to your neighbors so long as you pay a fee for it. Furthermore, once such permanent damages are assessed and paid, the incentive to alleviate the wrong would be eliminated, thereby continuing air pollution of the area without abatement.

It is true that some courts have sanctioned the remedy here proposed by the majority in a number of cases, but none of the authorities relied upon by the majority are analogous to the situation before us. In those cases, the courts, in denying an injunction and awarding money damages, grounded their decision on a showing that the use to which the property was intended to be put was primarily for the public benefit. Here, on the other hand, it is clearly established that the cement company is creating a continuing air pollution nuisance primarily for its own private interest with no public benefit.

* * * * *

I would enjoin the defendant cement company from continuing the discharge of dust particles upon its neighbors' properties unless, within 18 months, the cement company abated this nuisance.

It is not my intention to cause the removal of the cement plant from the Albany area, but to recognize the urgency of the problem stemming from this stationary source of air pollution, and to allow the company a specified period of time to develop a means to alleviate this nuisance.

I am aware that the trial court found that the most modern dust control devices available have been installed in defendant's plant, but, I submit, this does not mean that better and more effective dust control devices could not be developed within the time allowed to abate the pollution.

Moreover, I believe it is incumbent upon the defendant to develop such devices, since the cement company, at the time the plant commenced production (1962), was well aware of the plaintiffs' presence in the area, as well as the probable consequences of its contemplated operation. Yet, it still chose to build and operate the plant at this site.

In a day when there is a growing concern for clean air, highly developed industry should not expect acquiescence by the courts, but should, instead, plan its operations to eliminate contamination of our air and damage to its neighbors.

CASE QUESTIONS

1. Before this case was decided, what was the prevailing New York rule on issuing injunctions against nuisances? Why did the majority say they had to change this rule?

2. Both the majority and the dissent would issue an injunction in the future if certain conditions were not met. How do the conditions imposed by the majority and the dissent differ?

3. How do the majority and the dissent differ in their views of how far the courts should go in establishing broad pollution control policies?

4. A pulp mill that invested $1 million in a small community discharges its pulp into a stream that flows by a local farmer's land. The farmer finds that he can no longer irrigate his crops with water from the stream without severely stunting their growth. How would the majority and dissent of the court in *Boomer* decide the farmer's complaint for an injunction?

Private versus Public Nuisance

Nuisance law is often inadequate in controlling widespread pollution, partly because of the common-law distinction between private and public nuisances. At common law, a public nuisance was one that damaged many people. However, only certain persons, such as the local prosecutor, could sue to abate a public nuisance. A private individual could not bring suit to abate a nuisance unless he or she could show "special" damage, distinct from and more severe than that inflicted on the general public. This problem has been alleviated in many states by constitutional or statutory provisions that allow private citizens to sue to abate public nuisances.

Negligence

Negligence is unintentional conduct that nevertheless creates an unreasonable risk of harm. For example, a cropdusting pilot who fails to curtail pesticide spray while making a turn over neighboring property is negligent.[1] All persons have a legal duty to prevent unreasonably great risks of harm to others whenever they act. Breaching that duty renders a person liable for damages caused to another.

Foreseeability of Consequences

Liability for negligence is limited to foreseeable consequences of someone's conduct. Businesses may not be liable for negligence if the risks of harmful consequences from their actions are so remote that society would not find it necessary to burden human actions with precautions against them.

For example, the risk of a flash flood causing barrels to roll off the grounds of a chemical manufacturer and crush a farmer's nearby corn plants is probably too remote to require the plant to tie down all the barrels on its property. However, if the risk of harm is appreciable and the possible consequences are serious, courts are more likely to find negligence. For example, consider the chemical manufacturer who transports highly toxic and flammable chemicals in barrels on flatbed trucks without tying the barrels down. It is foreseeable that a barrel might fall off a truck, and the resulting injury to persons and property nearby is likely to be serious. If a barrel falls off a truck, explodes, and damages nearby property, a court would probably require the manufacturer to pay for the damage.

Burden of Taking Precautions

The burden that taking adequate precautions would pose to businesses is considered by courts in determining whether they have been negligent. Tying barrels down to keep them from rolling away may be required, whereas building a structure to house them may be considered an unduly expensive alternative. An enterprise that serves the public interest may be allowed to run greater risks if costly precautions would otherwise prohibit its operation. The probability and the extent of the harm to a com-

---

[1] *Hammon Ranch Corp. v. Dodson*, 199 Ark. 846, 136 S.W.2d 484 (1940).

plainer's interests are thus weighed against the social utility of the actor's conduct. Both parties' interests are finally judged by their social value.

Reasonable Conduct

Courts will impose liability for negligence only where the actor's conduct is unreasonable. Businesses are thus held to the standard of what a reasonable and prudent person would do under the same or similar circumstances. For example, if a manufacturer uses the latest technology to prevent the discharge of pollutants from its plant, it would not be liable to property holders damaged by any escaping pollutants.

Negligence Per Se

When enacting statutes or regulations, legislatures and agencies sometimes weigh the risk of harm resulting from certain conduct and the conduct's social utility. For example, a statute may prohibit the transportation of toxic chemicals through city downtown areas, or an agency regulation may provide that toxic waste dumps separate chemical wastes which, if mixed, result in toxic pollution. If violations result in injury to someone intended to be protected by the statute or regulation, the violator would be negligent per se. The concept of negligence per se means that the mere violation of a statute or regulation in a manner that causes injury to those intended for protection is, by itself, negligence.

Strict Liability

Strict liability is liability imposed without regard to a person's intent or negligence. It has been applied in the environmental context to abnormally dangerous activities. Thus, individuals or companies engaged in hazardous activities such as oil drilling will be strictly liable for any injuries arising from those activities. It does not matter that the offender did not intend to cause injury or was exercising all reasonable care.

The theory of strict liability serves to reimburse victims harmed by abnormally dangerous activities that are carried on voluntarily. It treats the risk of injury as a cost of engaging in the activity. Under strict liability, those engaged in abnormally dangerous activity must always pay for the damage they cause. Under negligence, the victim would not be compensated if reasonable care were undertaken in the performance of such dangerous activity. Negligence theory offers no redress to the victims of dangerous yet reasonable activity; strict liability does.

Abnormally dangerous activities involve a serious risk of harm to people, land, or property. That risk cannot be eliminated even if the actor exercises great care. Businesses engaged in abnormally dangerous activities bear responsibility for the injuries they cause despite any precautions taken to prevent them.

Activities are usually dangerous because they are out of place in their locality. Blasting operations and the storage of large quantities of explosives or flammable gases are abnormally dangerous when conducted in cities. Such activities pose serious threats to human life and the integrity of property. The *Restatement of Torts, Second,* Section 520 (discussed in the following case) lists the factors that are pertinent in determining whether an activity is abnormally dangerous.

Cities Service Company v. Florida

312 S.2d 799 (Fla. App. 1975)

On December 3, 1971, a dam burst at a phosphate mine operated by Cities Service Company in Polk County, Florida. Approximately one billion gallons of phosphate slime retained in a settling pond escaped into Whidden Creek. The slimes reached the Peace River, killing countless fish and inflicting other damage.

The State of Florida filed suit against Cities Service Company seeking injunctive relief and damages. The trial court granted summary judgment in favor of the state. Cities Service Company appealed to the Second District Court of Appeals in Florida, which affirmed the trial court judgment.

Grimes, Judge

The determination of this appeal necessarily requires the consideration of the doctrine of strict liability for the hazardous use of one's land which was first announced in *Rylands v. Fletcher.* In that case the defendants, who were millowners, had constructed a reservoir upon their land. The water broke through into the shaft of an abandoned coal mine and flooded along connecting passages into the adjoining mine of the plaintiff. When the case reached the Exchequer Chamber, Justice Blackburn said:

> "We think that the true rule of law is that the person who for his own purposes brings on his land and collects and keeps there anything likely to do mischief if it escapes, must keep it at his peril, and if he does not do so he is prima facie answerable for all the damage which is the natural consequences of its escape."

This statement was limited in the House of Lords to the extent that Lord Cairns said that the principle applied only to a "non-natural" use of the defendant's land as distinguished from "any purpose for which it might in the ordinary course of the enjoyment of land be used."

Since that time there have been countless decisions both in England and America construing the application of this doctrine. However, the pendulum has now decidedly swung toward its acceptance. [B]y 1971 the doctrine had been approved in principle by thirty jurisdictions with only seven states still rejecting the principle.

* * * * *

In early days it was important to encourage persons to use their land by whatever means were available for the purpose of commercial and industrial development.

In a frontier society there was little likelihood that a dangerous use of land could cause damage to one's neighbor. Today our life has become more complex. Many areas are overcrowded, and even the non-negligent use of one's land can cause extensive damages to a neighbor's property. Though there are still many hazardous activities which are socially desirable, it now seems reasonable that they pay their own way. It is too much to ask an innocent neighbor to bear the burden thrust upon him as a consequence of an abnormal use of the land next door. The doctrine of *Ryland v. Fletcher* should be applied in Florida.

There remains, however, the serious question of whether the impounding of phosphate slime by Cities Service in connection with its mining operations is a non-natural use of the land. In opposition to the State's motion, Cities Service filed an affidavit* of the manger of the plant where the dam break occurred. The affidavit points out that the property is peculiarly suitable for the mining of phosphate and that the central Florida area of which Polk County is the hub is the largest producer of phosphate rock in Florida. It further appears that Florida produced over 80% of the nation's marketable phosphate rock and one-third of the world production thereof in 1973. The affidavit goes on to explain that the storing of phosphate slimes in diked settling ponds is an essential part of the traditional method of mining phosphate rock. Hence, Cities Service argues that its mining operations were a natural and intended use of this particular land.

* * * * *

The American Law Institute has considered this question in §520 of the Restatement of the Law of Torts.

---

* An affidavit is a statement that is signed and whose truthfulness is sworn to before an official, usually a notary public.—Au.

* * * * *

In §520, the following factors are said to be pertinent in determining whether an activity is abnormally dangerous:

"(a) Whether the activity involves a high degree of risk of some harm to the person, land or chattels of others; (b) Whether the harm which may result from it is likely to be great; (c) Whether the risk cannot be eliminated by the exercise of reasonable care; (d) Whether the activity is not a matter of common usage; (e) Whether the activity is inappropriate to the place where it is carried on; and (f) The value of the activity to the community."

* * * * *

Some or all of the factors enumerated above recur in most of the cases involving the determination of whether a particular use in natural or non-natural. As applied to the instant case, the first four weigh in favor of the State while the last two favor Cities Service. As in many cases, there is much to be said for both sides.

In the final analysis, we are impressed by the magnitude of the activity and the attendant risk of enormous damage. The impounding of billions of gallons of phosphatic slimes behind earthen walls which are subject to breaking even with the exercise of the best of care strikes us as being both "ultrahazardous" and "abnormally dangerous," as the case may be.

This is not clear water which is being impounded. Here, Cities Service introduced water into its mining operation which when combined with phosphatic wastes produced a phosphatic slime which had a high potential for damage to the environment. If a break occurred, it was to be expected that extensive damage would be visited upon property many miles away. In this case, the damage, in fact, extended almost to the mouth of the Peace River, which is far beyond the phosphate mining area described in the Cities Service affidavit. We conclude that the Cities Service slime reservoir constituted a non-natural use of the land such as to invoke the doctrine of strict liability.

CASE QUESTIONS

1. The *Cities Service* court held that "value to the community," by itself did not determine the outcome of the case. How would a Texas court apply this factor in a case based on strict liability for an accident arising out of the operation of an oil or gas well? Explain.

2. A propulsion company conducted a test firing of a solid fuel rocket motor on its 9,100-acre premises. Although the test was conducted in a remote and underdeveloped area, a ranch was damaged by the blast. How would the *Cities Service* court apply strict liability? Explain.

3. In considering the six factors in the *Restatement of Torts*, Section 520, which did the *Cities Service* court conclude favored the state?

4. What is the effect of the *Cities Service* court's determination that as a matter of law the maintenance of a slime reservoir by a phosphate company is a nonnatural use of the land? Explain.

NATIONAL ENVIRONMENTAL POLICY

Federal environmental legislation before the 1970s was designed to fund research projects and assist states in pollution control and resource management. During the 1970s Congress took a more aggressive part in setting and enforcing standards for assuring environmental quality. Declaring a national environmental policy was its first major step in this direction.

The National Environmental Policy Act (NEPA) establishes the nation's environmental policy, sets goals, and provides means for carrying out the policy. With NEPA, Congress declared a national policy of supporting harmony between man and the environment. The goal of NEPA is to ensure that environmental information is made available to government officials and the public before decisions are reached or actions are taken. NEPA policies are carried out by means of (1) the Council on Environmental Quality (CEQ) and (2) the environmental impact statement (EIS), a document disclosing the environmental effects of a major federal action.

Council on Environmental Quality (CEQ)

Congress created the Council on Environmental Quality (CEQ) to monitor and report annually on the status and condition of the nation's resources. The council also reviews programs affecting the conservation and utilization of natural resources and proposes legislation to remedy their deficiencies. The CEQ has issued guidelines describing the contents of the EIS and the procedures to be used in preparing the statement.

The CEQ consists of three members appointed by the president with the advice and consent of the Senate. One of the members is designated by the president as the chairman. The CEQ is located within the Executive Office of the President.

Environmental Impact Statement (EIS)

NEPA requires that agencies undertaking "major federal actions significantly affecting the quality of the human environment" must prepare a statement detailing the environmental impact of the proposed action and any alternative actions. Copies of the EIS are to be distributed to federal agencies, state and local agencies, the president, the CEQ, and the public.

The CEQ guidelines describe the purpose of an EIS as follows:

> The primary purpose of an environmental impact statement is to serve as an action-forcing device to insure that the policies and goals of NEPA are infused into the ongoing programs and actions of the federal government. It shall provide full and fair discussion of significant environmental impacts and shall inform decision-makers and the public of the reasonable alternatives which would avoid or minimize adverse impacts or enhance the quality of the human environment. . . . An environmental impact statement is more than a disclosure document. It shall be used by federal officials in conjunction with other relevant material to plan actions.

Activities Requiring an EIS

An agency must prepare an EIS whenever it plans or engages in *major federal actions significantly affecting the quality of the human environment.* As NEPA has been interpreted, activities wholly undertaken by federal agencies are not the only federal actions subject to EIS preparation. Activities also require an EIS if they are supported by federal funding assistance or by federal entitlement for land use. Private enterprise thus may be consulted on information for EIS preparation when it carries on business under federal contracts, grants, subsidies, or loans. Private companies may also become involved where they need federal leases, permits, licenses, or certificates to operate.

Though many federal actions consist solely of granting private enterprise papers of entitlement to operate, these activities are generally considered to be major. Major federal action occurs in the licensing of electric, nuclear, or hydraulic power plant operations. It also occurs in Bureau of Indian Affairs approval of leases permitting commercial development of Indian lands. Authorizing the development of highways and the abandonment of railways are also major federal actions, unless it concerns small, insignificant stretches in relationship to large-scale ongoing projects. Whether major federal actions significantly affect the human environment depends upon the types of impacts those actions have.

Consultation

NEPA requires the federal agency preparing an EIS to consult with other agencies having jurisdiction or special expertise on the environmental impacts involved. This is to be done before the EIS is issued.

The CEQ guidelines require agencies to "scope," or search for related activities, early in the planning or decision-making stages. Where many agencies are involved in conducting or funding actions, the guidelines suggest that they pool their resources and prepare one EIS, designating a single "lead" agency to assume supervisory responsibility. All of the agencies involved contribute their expertise to the preparation of the EIS, and the statement is completed before any agency takes major or irreversible actions.

A federal agency may seek industry input in preparing an EIS, particularly when seeking information on the feasibility of developing technology. Although businesses may assist in preparing the EIS, it is unlawful for a federal agency to rely on a private concern to write the EIS.

EIS Contents   NEPA requires that every EIS include the following items:

1. The environmental impact of the proposed action
2. Any adverse environmental effects that would be unavoidable if the proposed action were taken
3. The relationship between local short-term uses of the environment and the maintenance or enhancement of long-term productivity
4. Irreversible commitments of resources that would be involved if the proposed action were taken
5. Alternatives to the proposed action

In the following case, the Supreme Court addresses the question of which "environmental impacts" or "environmental effects" of proposed federal action (items 1 and 2 listed above) must be discussed in an EIS.

Metropolitan Edison Co. v. People Against Nuclear Energy

103 S. Ct. Rptr. 1556 (1983)

Metropolitan Edison Company (petitioner) owns two licensed nuclear plants at Three Mile Island near Harrisburg, Pennsylvania. On a day when one plant (TMI–1) was shut down for refueling, the other plant (TMI–2) suffered a serious accident that damaged the reactor and caused widespread concern. The Nuclear Regulatory Commission (NRC) ordered Metropolitan to keep TMI–1 shut down until it determined whether the plant could be operated safely. The NRC invited interested parties to submit legal briefs on whether psychological harm or other direct effects of the accident or of renewed operation of TMI–1 should be considered.

People Against Nuclear Energy (PANE) (respondent), an association of residents from the Harrisburg area who were opposed to further operation of either TMI reactor, submitted such a brief. After reviewing the briefs, the NRC decided not to include a discussion of the psychological effects in the EIS. PANE filed a petition for review in the court of appeals, contending that NEPA required the NRC to consider psychological effects. The Court of Appeals for the District of Columbia Circuit held that the NRC failed to consider whether the risk or an accident at TMI–1 might harm the psychological health and community well-being of residents around Three Mile Island. The Supreme Court reversed.

Justice Rehnquist

All the parties agree that effects on human health can be cognizable under NEPA, and that human health may include psychological health. The Court of Appeals thought these propositions were enough to complete a syllogism that disposes of the case: NEPA requires agencies to consider effects on health. An effect on psychological health is an effect on health. Therefore, NEPA requires agencies to consider the effects on psychological health asserted by PANE.

PANE, using similar reasoning, contends that because the psychological health damage to its members would be caused by a change in the environment (renewed operation of TMI–1), NEPA requires the NRC to consider that damage. Although these arguments are appealing at first glance, we believe they skip over an essential step in the analysis. They do not consider the closeness of the relationship between the change in the environment and the "effect" at issue.

Section 102(c) of NEPA, directs all federal agencies to

"include in every recommendation or report on proposals for legislation and other major Federal actions significantly affecting the quality of the human environment, a detailed statement by the responsible official on—

(i) the environmental impact of the proposed action,[and]

(ii) any adverse environmental effects which cannot be avoided should the proposal be implemented . . ."

To paraphase the statutory language in light of the facts of this case, where an agency significantly affects the quality of the human environment, the agency must evaluate the "environmental impact" and any unavoidable adverse environmental effects of its proposal. The theme of § 102 is sounded by the adjective "environmental": NEPA does not require the agency to assess every impact or effect of its proposed action, but only the impact or effect on the environment. If we were to seize the word "environmental" out of its context and give it the broadest possible definition, the words "adverse environmental effects" might embrace virtually any consequence of a governmental action that someone thought "adverse." But we think the context of the statute shows that Congress was talking about the physical environment—the world around us, so to speak. NEPA was designed to promote human welfare by alerting governmental actors to the effect of their proposed actions on the physical environment.

* * * * *

Thus, although NEPA states its goals in sweeping terms of human health and welfare, these goals are ends that Congress has chosen to pursue by means of protecting the physical environment.

To determine whether § 102 requires consideration of a particular effect, we must look at the relationship between that effect and the change in the physical environment caused by the major federal action at issue.

*   *   *   *   *

Some effects that are "caused by" a change in the physical environment in the sense of "but for" causation, will nonetheless not fall within § 102 because the causal chain is too attenuated. For example, residents of the Harrisburg area have relatives in other parts of the country. Renewed operation of TMI–1 may well cause psychological health problems for these people. They may suffer "anxiety, tension and fear, a sense of helplessness," and accompanying physical disorders, because of the risk that their relatives may be harmed in a nuclear accident. However, this harm is simply too remote from the physical environment to justify requiring the NRC to evaluate the psychological health damage to these people that may be caused by renewed operation of TMI–1.

Our understanding of the congressional concerns that led to the enactment of NEPA suggests that the terms "environmental effect" and "environmental impact" in § 102 be read to include a requirement of a reasonably close causal relationship between a change in the physical environment and the effect at issue. The issue before us, then, is how to give content to this requirement. This is a question of first impression of this Court.

The federal action that affects the environment in this case is permitting renewed operation of TMI–1. The direct effects on the environment of this action include re-lease of low-level radiation, increased fog in the Harrisburg area (caused by operation of the plant's cooling towers), and the release of warm water into the Susquehanna River. The NRC has considered each of these effects in its EIS. . . . Another effect of renewed operation is a risk of a nuclear accident. The NRC has also considered this effect.

PANE argues that the psychological health damage it alleges "will flow directly from the risk of [a nuclear] accident." But a risk of an accident is not an effect on the physical world. In a causal chain from renewed operation of TMI–1 to psychological health damage, the element of risk and its perception by PANE's members are necessary middle links. We believe that the element of risk lengthens the causal chain beyond the reach of NEPA.

Risk is a pervasive element of modern life; to say more would belabor the obvious. Many of the risks we face are generated by modern technology, which brings both the possibility of major accidents and opportunities for tremendous achievements. Medical experts apparently agree that risk can generate stress in human beings, which in turn may rise to the level of serious health damage. For this reason among many others, the question whether the gains from any technological advance are worth its attendant risks may be an important public policy issue. Nonetheless, it is quite different from the question whether the same gains are worth a given level of alteration of our physical environment or depletion of our natural resources. The latter question rather than the former is the central concern of NEPA.

Time and resources are simply too limited for us to believe that Congress intended to extend NEPA as far as the Court of Appeals has taken it. The scope of the agency's inquiries must remain manageable if NE-PA's goal of "ensur[ing] a fully informed and well considered decision," is to be accomplished.

If contentions of psychological health damage caused by risk were cognizable under NEPA, agencies would, at the very least, be obliged to expend considerable resources developing psychiatric expertise that is not otherwise relevant to their congressionally assigned functions. The available resources may be spread so thin that agencies are unable adequately to pursue protection of the physical environment and natural resources.

*   *   *   *   *

If a harm does not have a sufficiently close connection to the physical environment, NEPA does not apply.

*   *   *   *   *

For these reasons, we hold that the NRC need not consider PANE's contentions.

CASE QUESTIONS

1. Why did the Supreme Court support the NRC's reading of NEPA rather than that of the court of appeals?

2. How did the Supreme Court determine whether § 102 of NEPA requires an agency to consider a particular effect in preparing an EIS?

3. Suppose that the Department of Health and Human Services were to implement extremely stringent requirements for hospitals and nursing homes receiving federal funds. Many perfectly adequate hospitals and homes might be forced out of existence. The remaining facilities might be so limited or expensive that many ill people would be unable to afford medical care and would suffer severe health damage. Would NEPA require the department to prepare an EIS evaluating that damage? Explain.

POLLUTION CONTROL MEASURES

Antipollution measures are designed to eliminate or control the diffusion of waste particles through the air, water, and land. In the 1970s, legislatures enacted major antipollution measures in response to decades of studies showing that waste particles in natural resources had devasting effects on public health.

Environmental Protection Agency (EPA)

Congress created the Environmental Protection Agency (EPA) to oversee many of the federal pollution control programs, and states formed similar agencies. Figure 18–1 shows the organization of the EPA. The EPA and the CEQ are complementary agencies. The CEQ is concerned with all aspects of environmental quality: wildlife preservation, land use, pollution, and the effects of population growth on the environment. The EPA, on the other hand, has a narrower scope. It is charged with protecting the environment by abating pollution.

FIGURE 18–1
Environmental Protection Agency

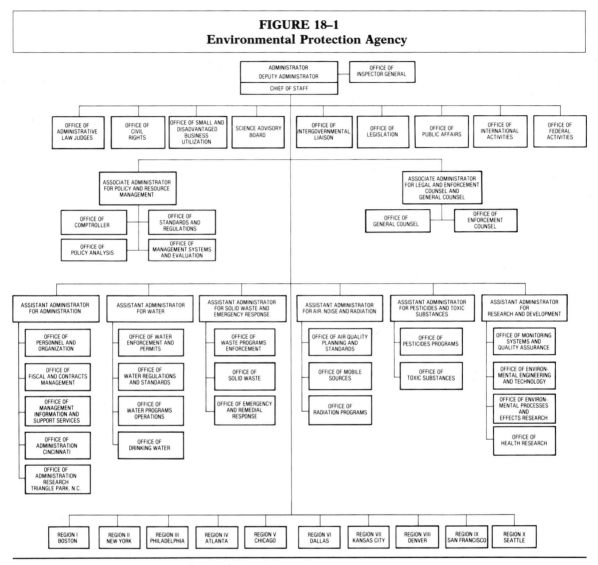

Source: *U.S. Government Manual 1983–1984.*

The EPA was created in 1970 to consolidate federal environmental pollution responsibilities. Its primary function is to establish and enforce standards, conduct research on pollution effects, monitor and analyze the environment, advise the CEQ of new policies to protect the environment from pollution, and assist state and local pollution control programs. Table 18–1 summarizes the major activities of the EPA that are discussed in this chapter.

> ### TABLE 18–1
> ### Major EPA Activities
>
> *Water*
>
> Develops and enforces water quality criteria and effluent limitations
>
> Issues permits for point source discharges
>
> Administers cleanup of hazardous substances
>
> *Air*
>
> Develops national ambient air quality standards
>
> Develops emission standards for new stationary sources
>
> Monitors enforcement of state implementation plans
>
> *Solid Waste*
>
> Develops hazardous waste standards and regulations
>
> Identifies solid waste generators and monitors them
>
> Issues manifests to waste transports
>
> Issues permits to waste storage, treatment, or disposal facilities
>
> *Superfund*
>
> Administers federal cleanup of toxic substance spills
>
> *Toxic Substances*
>
> Issues rules and orders relating to the use of toxic substances
>
> *Pesticides*
>
> Monitors state certification of pesticide applicators
>
> Issues rules relating to the use and labeling of pesticides
>
> Establishes tolerance levels for pesticides in food

Clean Water Act (CWA)

Congress enacted the Clean Water Act (CWA) and two stated goals. It sought to make the nation's water safe for swimming and fishing by 1984, and it sought to eliminate the discharge of all pollutants into navigable waters by 1985. To accomplish these goals, Congress authorized the EPA to establish *water quality criteria* regulating the concentrations of pollutants that are permissible in a body of water, and *effluent limitations* regulating the amount of pollutants that are discharged from a particular source. To enforce these water and quality criteria and effluent limitations, the Clean Water Act relies on a permit system, called the *National Pollutant Discharge Elimination System (NPDES)*. Companies must obtain permits to discharge pollutants into the water. Although the Clean Water Act is administered by the EPA, the agency delegates enforcement to any state that requests such authority and agrees to meet EPA specifications.

National Permit System

The Clean Water Act makes it illegal to discharge any pollutant without an NPDES permit. Permits can only be granted by the EPA or authorized state agencies. Although the EPA delegates this authority to the states, it retains authority to veto a state permit or to step in and take enforcement action if a state fails to do so.

The permit specifies each pollutant that can be discharged and sets average and maximum daily limits on each. Permit holders are required to monitor their discharges and to report the amount and nature of waste components. Polluters who discharge without a permit or violate permit conditions may be fined up to $10,000 per day of violation. Willful or grossly negligent violations are punishable by fines of $25,000 per day and up to one year in prision for the first offense, and twice that for later offenses.

Permits are needed only for discharges from *point sources.* A point source is defined as any discernible and confined conveyance, such as a pipe, ditch, well, or canal. Nonpoint sources of water pollution include such things as overflows from irrigated agriculture, runoffs from mining activities, and runoffs from construction sites. Although the EPA sets effluent limitations and issues permits on point source discharges, it can only issue informative guidelines for identifying and evaluating nonpoint sources of water pollution.

New Source Performance Standards

The treatment of pollution discharges requiring a permit depends upon the source of the discharges. If the source is a new plant, the plant must meet New Source Performance Standards set by the EPA. Food processing, paper and paperboard manufacturing, and petroleum processing are just a few of the industries for which the EPA has already developed such standards. For industries not covered, the EPA will develop standards in the course of considering a permit application for the process involved.

Performance Standards for Existing Sources

Plants already in operation when the statute was passed had to meet other EPA standards. By 1977, existing plants had to discharge in accordance with standards based on the best practicable control technology then available (BPT). By 1987, all plants will have to comply with standards based on the best available technology economically achievable in their categories (BAT).

Publicly Owned Treatment Works

Discharges into publicly owned sewage treatment works, though also point-source discharges, require no permit. Still, industrial users must meet certain pretreatment standards before they make their discharges. They must treat wastes to remove pollutants before discharging them into the system. Pretreatment standards are designed to assure that the pollutants in industrial discharges are compatible with the treatment process used by the sewage treatment works. Sewage treatment works that are receiving federal grants must charge industrial users for their treatment services.

Hazardous Substances

The Clean Water Act forbids the discharge of hazardous substances in harmful quantities. Dischargers must report any leaking, spilling, pumping, or dumping and are liable for cleanup costs. The EPA may clean up the spill, or authorize another agency to clean it up, and assess the discharger for the costs. The discharger is not liable if the spill results from (1) an act of God, (2) an act of war, (3) the negligence of the federal government, or (4) an act or omission of a third party.

Enforcement   The Clean Water Act authorizes the EPA administrator to bring a civil action to obtain an injunction or a civil penalty against any permit violator. The administrator may also cause criminal proceedings to be instituted. The administrator may provide emergency assistance and recover the cost of providing such assistance from the owner or operator of the source of the discharge. The statute also provides for citizen suits. Any citizen having standing may bring a civil action on his or her own behalf against a violator.

Clean Air Act (CAA)

Congress passed the Clean Air Act (CAA) in response to mounting evidence that airborne particulates could cause disease and death. The act encourages states to control local sources of harmful airborne particles, classified as carbon monoxide, particulates, sulfur oxides, hydrocarbons, and nitrogen oxides.

National Ambient* Air Quality Standards (NAAQS)   Congress required the EPA to determine concentrations of various particles that would be consistent with human health. In 1971, the EPA set standards for common pollutants such as dust, carbon monoxide, and ozone.

State Implementation Plans (SIP)   Once the EPA set the National Ambient Air Quality Standards, states were responsible for controlling and cleaning up areas that did not comply with them. States had to detail the measures they would use to achieve the standards and submit their plans to the EPA. The EPA could withhold federal funds, prohibit the construction of new air pollution sources, or intercede with its own measures if a state's implementation plan was inadequate.

All SIPs must include *emission limitations* and measures that will be taken to uphold air standards. Emission limitations are specific rules that operators of pollutant sources must follow to reduce emissions.

Many states developed programs to control effluents from mobile sources of pollution. Automobile inspection and monitoring curbed the production of carbon monoxide and reduced the smog generated by the breakdown of hydrocarbons. Airborne leads diminished with reductions in gasoline lead content.

The problems caused by stationary sources of pollution were more intractable. States developed some methods for reducing local industrial pollution, including the installation of filters and brushes in plant smokestacks. Tall smokestacks were a less satisfactory solution. While they decreased local pollution, they created regional problems. In fact, particles released into higher strata of air have contributed to the international

---

* The term "ambient" refers to atmospheric air, as opposed to air inside of buildings.

problem of acid rain. This occurs when drops of moisture mix with residues of high-sulfur coals burned in power plants and smelting operations.

Nonattainment Areas

Many state regions, including virtually all urban areas, failed to meet the NAAQS by 1977, the act's first deadline. These regions are called *nonattainment areas*. As a result, in 1977, Congress amended the Clean Air Act to provide that SIPs require owners or operators in a nonattainment area to obtain a permit for the construction or modification of any major stationary pollutant source.

States may issue a permit for construction or modification of a major source only if four conditions are met:

1. The increased emissions from the proposed source must not exceed the allowances for growth identified in the SIP, or alternatively, the applicant must obtain sufficient reductions in emission in the nonattainment area to offset the increased emissions from the proposed source. This latter alternative is known as the *emissions offset policy*. In other words, the operator of the new pollution source has to install improvements or cut production in its own plant or in the plant of another operator.
2. The proposed source must comply with the *lowest achievable emission rate*.
3. The applicant must demonstrate that all other major sources in the state under its control are in compliance or are on a schedule for compliance with applicable emissions limitations.
4. The state must be carrying out the applicable implementation plan for the nonattainment area in which the proposed source is to be located. If the nonattainment area lacks an EPA-approved SIP, a "construction moratorium" prevails, and no major stationary source that would emit the nonattainment pollutants can be constructed or modified in the area.

Prevention of Significant Deterioration

In the 1977 CAA amendments, Congress dictated the special protection of areas whose air quality is higher than that designated by the national standards. Congress accordingly made the EPA responsible for monitoring the prevention of significant deterioration (PSD) in the air quality of these areas. States must now submit PSD programs for EPA review as part of their revised state implementation plans for meeting required air quality standards.

The preconstruction review program is the EPA's major mechanism for monitoring the potential for deterioration in clean air areas. A new or modified source of pollution with the potential to emit a designated tonnage of pollutants must submit to a review before it is granted a construction permit. Part of the review is a check to see whether the best available control technology has been applied for each pollutant regulated by the act.

**The Bubble
Concept**

EPA regulations treat all pollution-emitting devices within an existing plant as a "stationary source" of air pollution. This allows a company to install or modify such devices without meeting stringent permit conditions as long as the alteration does not increase total plant emissions. This has been likened to putting a bubble over the plant and allowing adjustments within so long as the net effect is no change. In 1984, the Supreme Court upheld the EPA's bubble concept regulations as a permissible interpretation of the Clean Air Act.[3] Industry favors the bubble concept and would like to see it implemented across multiple facilities, towns, and even greater areas.

Enforcement

The EPA administrator is authorized to require owners who control emission sources to maintain records, make reports, install and maintain monitoring equipment, sample emissions, and provide other necessary information. Anyone who knowingly tampers with any monitoring device or falsifies reports may be fined up to $10,000 and/or imprisoned up to six months. The EPA administrator may issue an order to anyone violating a SIP or national emission standard for hazardous air pollutants. The order states the violation and sets a time for compliance. If the violator fails to comply with the order , the administrator may bring a civil action in federal district court for an injunction and recover a civil penalty of up to $25,000 per day of violation. The administrator can seek injunctions to enforce emission standards for new motor vehicles and can enjoin the construction of a major emitting facility that does not conform to PSD requirements. The Clean Air Act also authorizes citizen suits.

Solid Waste Disposal

To help states and local governments develop resource recovery and solid waste disposal programs, Congress enacted the Solid Waste Disposal Act (SWDA) in 1965 and amended it in 1970. States and municipalities addressed waste disposal problems in various ways. Certain states granted tax breaks to companies recycling waste materials. Other states enacted "bottle bills," which were essentially designed to encourage the use of recoverable containers. Many municipalities began to provide sanitary landfills for waste disposal.

In 1976 Congress led the states to address the special problems of hazardous waste sites by passing the Resource Conservation and Recovery Act (RCRA). Under the RCRA, handlers of hazardous wastes are required to conform with specified standards. Handlers include those who generate, transport, treat, or store hazardous wastes. Hazardous wastes are wastes that contribute significantly to a serious, irreversible illness or pose a hazard to human health when improperly managed. According to EPA

---

[3] *Chevron U.S.A., Inc. v. Natural Resources Defense Council*, 52 L.W. 4845 (1984).

regulations, hazardous wastes are characterized by ignitability, corrosivity, reactivity, and toxicity.

Generators and Transporters

Generators and transporters of wastes with these characteristics must notify the EPA of the location and general description of their activities. They must also specify what wastes they are handling. The EPA issues identification numbers to each handler.

Generators of waste must keep records on their hazardous wastes. If waste generators transport the wastes off site, they must package and label the wastes and ship the packages with a manifest. The manifest identifies the persons originating, carrying, and receiving the wastes and states the nature and quantity of the wastes. If a generator does not receive a signed copy of the manifest from the intended receiver within 45 days of the time it transports its wastes, it must report to the EPA regional administrator. In any event, generators must report to the regional administrator yearly.

Transporters must comply with the terms of the manifests they receive from generators and must keep a copy of each manifest. If waste discharge occurs during carriage, transporters must take appropriate immediate action to protect human health and the environment. They may have to clean up the discharge or notify authorities, depending upon what action is officially approved for them.

Owners or Operators

Owners or operators of a hazardous waste treatment, storage, or disposal facility (TSDF) have to apply for permits allowing them to dispose of their hazardous wastes. Permits will not be issued unless certain performance standards are met. Owners or operators of TSDFs must obtain an identification number from the EPA. In running their facilities, they must analyze representative samples of waste before storing or treating them. They must also provide training for personnel and inspect facilities to discover malfunctions. Where discharges occur, they must take necessary remedial action.

EPA employees are authorized to enter facilities at reasonable times. They may inspect and obtain samples, and they may copy records. If violations of the hazardous waste provisions are not corrected, violators may ultimately be liable for a civil penalty of $25,000 per day. Knowingly making a false statement in required documents is a crime punishable by fines and by imprisonment for up to one year.

Superfund Legislation

"Superfund," formally known as the Comprehensive Environmental Response, Compensation and Liability Act of 1980, was enacted to deal with the uncontrolled releases of hazardous wastes, such as the one that occurred at Times Beach, Missouri. Superfund establishes a federal response mechanism for the immediate cleanup of contamination resulting from the release of hazardous substances. Superfund contains three major provisions:

1. It authorizes the president to require the cleanup of releases of hazardous substances according to a presidentially implemented "national contingency plan."
2. It makes owners and operators of facilities releasing hazardous substances liable to the government for cleanup costs and for destruction of government-owned natural resources.
3. It establishes a fund (financed partly by taxes on the production of toxic chemicals) to be used for payment of "response costs," which include the expenses of carrying out the national contingency plan and the government's costs of restoring natural resources that have been injured by toxic chemicals.

Notice Requirement

Persons in charge of a vessel or a facility that has released a hazardous substance must notify the National Response Center immediately. Notice must also be provided to potentially injured parties by publication in local newspapers. Failure to comply with these notice requirements subjects the person in charge to a fine of up to $10,000 per day of violation and/or to imprisonment of up to one year.

Obligations of Industry

Owners and operators of facilities that have released hazardous substances may be ordered to take cleanup action. Those who comply are liable only for the response costs and damage to government-owned natural resources. Although the statute makes owners and operators strictly liable for cleanup costs, the act contains certain liability limitations. Liability is not imposed where the release results from an act of God, an act of war, or the act or omission of a third party. Furthermore, the statute limits liability for cleanup costs to $5 million for cargo vessels and $50 million for all other facilities. These liability limits are lost if an owner or operator refuses to take remedial action as directed by the government. In that case, the owner or operator may be liable for three times the cost incurred by the Superfund.

Victims' Compensation Proposal

Superfund does not provide for liability for injuries to private individuals. However, the statute does not supersede any state or common-law remedies available to private individuals.

A 1982 report to Congress recommended amending Superfund to allow for victim compensation and private suits to compensate victims of exposure to hazardous wastes. The report called for creation of a compensation system that would operate under federal law but be managed by the states through federal grants-in-aid to the states from Superfund taxes on toxic chemical production. Under the proposal, victims of hazardous waste exposure would be entitled to full recovery for medical expenses, recovery of two-thirds of lost earnings, and death benefits for survivors. Injured persons would have the choice of applying to the fund for compensation or suing in federal court for damages that are recoverable in such tort claims.

If an injured person chose to sue in federal court, the report recommended applying a standard of strict liability. Injured persons could apply for immediate short-term relief from Superfund and then sue in federal court. However, the amount of any compensation benefits received from the fund would be subtracted from the court award and repaid to the fund.

Currently, only California and Minnesota have enacted compensation statutes for the victims of hazardous substances. Critics of the victims' compensation proposal believe that existing common-law rules represent an optimal balance of the equities. They also question the cost of financing the system through taxes on toxic chemicals.

Toxic Substances Control Act (TSCA)

Congress passed this act in 1976 to regulate hazardous chemical substances and mixtures. Manufacturers, processors, and distributors were initially required to make reports to the EPA so that it could compile an inventory of all chemical substances and mixtures handled in the United States.

After the inventory was published, all persons seeking to manufacture any new substance or to process a present substance for a significant new use had to notify the EPA of their intention.

Congress gave the EPA administrator the power to make rules necessary to protect personal health and the environment against unreasonable risks posed by all substances and mixtures. The administrator must apply the least burdensome rule that will be effective, but the possible rules range from requiring notice of the unreasonable risk of injury to entirely prohibiting the manufacture of the substance or mixture. Intermediate options include limiting its scope of distribution or its concentration for certain uses. The EPA may also mandate that adequate warnings or instructions be given or that continuous testing and record keeping be done. TSCA also established an Interagency Testing Committee. The committee's function is to inform the administrator of substances and mixtures that should be tested immediately in order to propose rules.

The administrator may issue rules upon review of a premanufacturing notice. If the information the proposed manufacturer has given is sufficient for the administrator to evaluate the risk of harm posed by the substance to be manufactured, the administrator may propose an order to prohibit its manufacture. The administrator would then go to court only if the manufacturer or processor filed an objection to the proposed order. Where threatened with the imminent production of a substance hazardous to the public, however, the administrator may directly seek an injunction in a U.S. district court to stop the manufacturing process.

Federal Environmental Pesticide Control Act (FEPCA)

Pesticides are not covered by the Toxic Substances Control Act. Since 1947 they have been regulated by the Federal Insecticide, Fungicide, and Rodenticide Act (FIFRA). That act provides that pesticides in interstate shipments be adequately labeled and unadulterated. The Federal Environmental Pesticide Control Act, passed in 1972, extended the control of FIFRA to interstate manufacturing and actual misuse of pesticides.

Pesticides are classified for general or restricted use. Restricted pesticides may be applied only by persons certified to use them. States certify pesticide applicators under the approval of the EPA.

The use of any registered pesticide in a way inconsistent with its labeling instructions is prohibited. Knowing violations of FEPCA's provisions by farmers or private applicators may lead to $1,000 in fines or 30 days in jail. More severe penalties apply to commercial applicators, dealers, or distributors who purposely violate the law. Pesticide manufacturing plants must register with the EPA. The plants must report annually on types and amounts of pesticides produced and sold. EPA agents may inspect the plants and take samples.

When a pesticide violates FEPCA provisions, the EPA administrator may issue an order to stop its sale or use. Pesticides violating the law may also be seized.

LAND USE AND RESOURCE MANAGEMENT

Energy demands in the highly industrialized United States prompted strip mining, wetlands filling, and other activities that destroyed virgin lands and spoiled scenic places. Animals displaced by these activities rarely survived. In the 1970s federal and state legislators passed laws to allow development to continue in critical areas such as virgin lands and scenic places while minimizing environmental damage. Critical areas include parks, forests, tidelands, wetlands, and continental shelves.

Approximately one-third of the land area in the United States is owned by the federal government, which preserves part of its critical areas for natural beauty and develops part of them through permits granted to private industry. The U.S. government regulates both federal and state lands when licensing nuclear power plants. Federal regulations cover both nuclear power plant operations and the nuclear by-products that pose waste shortage problems for the entire country.

Nuclear Power Development

Congress passed the Atomic Energy Act of 1946 in the belief that the government would monopolize the development of nuclear power. In the early 1950s, however, Congress concluded that development might proceed more rapidly if competitive pressures of the private sector were brought to bear on researching and applying nuclear power. Thus, in the Atomic

Energy Act of 1954, Congress created the Atomic Energy Commission to oversee the private construction, ownership, and operation of commercial nuclear power reactors.

Experimenting under the 1954 act, private industry discovered that prospects for profit making in atomic energy development were uncertain, while risks of operations were substantial. The most significant risk of operation was catastrophic nuclear accident. Although such a disaster was considered remote, the potential liability overwhelmed the pooled resources of industry and private insurance companies.

Concerned that the private sector would have to withdraw from the nuclear power field, Congress passed in 1957 the Price-Anderson Act. Under this act, the nuclear power industry would have to buy the maximum available amount of privately underwritten public liability insurance; then, if damages from a nuclear disaster exceeded the amount of insurance available, the act provided that the federal government would indemnify the licensee by up to $500 million. Since $60 million of private insurance was available in 1957, this effectively put a ceiling on the liability for a single nuclear disaster at $560 million.

A 1966 amendment to the act essentially required that those indemnified under the act waive all legal defenses in the event of a substantial nuclear accident. This insured a common, strict liability standard for nuclear accidents in all jurisdictions, rather than a patchwork quilt of liability standards that might be created under varying state laws.

A 1975 amendment to the act provided that those owning nuclear reactors would have to contribute $2–$5 million toward the cost of compensating victims in the event of a nuclear disaster. The intended effect of this deferred premium provision was to reduce the federal government's contribution to the liability pool. While Congress extended the act's coverage to 1987, it also provided that if damages exceeding the $560 million ceiling of liability occurred in any nuclear accident, Congress itself would review the incident and take whatever action was deemed necessary and appropriate to protect the public from the consequences of such a disaster.

The Price-Anderson Act and its $560 million limitation on liability for nuclear incidents was challenged in the 1970s. The case that follows details the Supreme Court's position on why the act is constitutional.

 ### Duke Power Co. v. Carolina Environmental Study Group, Inc.

438 U.S. 59 (1978)

In 1973 the Carolina Environmental Study Group, the Catawba Central Labor Union, and 40 individuals who lived within close proximity of planned nuclear power plants in North and South Carolina (appellees) sued Duke Power Company (appellant), the investor-owned public utility that was constructing them. The district court found: (1) that the operations of the plants had "immediate" adverse effects upon the appellees, including thermal pollution of local lakes and emissions of nonnatural radiation into the local environment, and (2) that there was a "substantial likelihood" that Duke would not be able to complete construction and maintain operation of the plants "but for" the protection provided by the act. Thus, the district court held that the appellees had standing to challenge the act's constitutionality. The appellees chose to attack the provisions for a $560 million liability ceiling for nuclear incidents. The district court later agreed with the appellees that these provisions violated the constitutional mandate that neither human life nor property should be taken without due process of law because: (1) the $560 million amount was not rationally related to the potential losses; (2) the act tended to encourage irresponsibility in matters of safety and environmental protection; and (3) the act's protections did not provide a quid pro quo (a satisfactory exchange) for state law provisions that the act superseded. Duke Power Company appealed to the Supreme Court, which disagreed with the district court's holding.

Chief Justice Burger

A

Our due process analysis properly begins with a discussion of the appropriate standard of review. Appellants, portraying the liability-limitation provision as a legislative balancing of economic interests, urge that the Price-Anderson Act be accorded the traditional presumption of constitutionality generally accorded economic regulations and that it be upheld absent proof of arbitrariness or irrationality on the part of Congress. Appellees, however, urge a more elevated standard of review on the ground that the interests jeopardized by the Price-Anderson Act "are far more important than those in the economic due process and business-oriented cases" where the traditional rationality standard has been invoked. An intermediate standard like that applied in cases such as *Craig v. Boren* (equal protection challenge to statute requiring that males be older than females in order to purchase beer) or *United States Trust Co. of New York v. New Jersey* (Contract Clause challenge to repeal of statutory covenant providing security for bondholders) is thus recommended for our use here.

As we read the Act and its legislative history, it is clear that Congress' purpose was to remove the economic impediments in order to stimulate the private development of electric energy by nuclear power while simultaneously providing the public compensation in the event of a catastrophic nuclear incident. The liability-limitation provision thus emerges as a classic example of an economic regulation—a legislative effort to structure and accommodate "the burdens and benefits of economic life." "It is by now well established that [such] legislative Acts . . . come to the Court with a presumption of constitutionality, and that the burden is on one complaining of a due process violation to establish that the legislature has acted in an arbitrary and irrational way." That the accommodation struck may have profound and far-reaching consequences, contrary to appellees' suggestion, provides all the more reason for this Court to defer to the congressional judgment unless it is demonstrably arbitrary or irrational.

B

When examined in light of this standard of review, the Price-Anderson Act, in our view, passes constitutional muster. The record before us fully supports the need for the imposition of a statutory limit on liability to encourage private industry participation and hence bears a rational relationship to Congress' concern for stimulating the involvement of private enterprise in the production of electric energy through the use of atomic power; nor do we understand appellees or the District Court to be of a different view. Rather their challenge is to the alleged arbitrariness of the *particular figure* of $560 million, which is the statutory ceiling on liability. The District Court aptly summarized its position:

> The amount of recovery is not rationally related to the potential losses. Abundant evidence in the record shows that although major catastrophe in any particular place is not certain and may not be extremely likely, nevertheless, in the territory where these plants are located, damage to life and property for this and future generations could well be many, many times the limit which the law places on liability.

Assuming, *arguendo,** that the $560 million fund would not insure full recovery in all conceivable circumstances—and the hard truth is that no one can ever know— it does not by any means follow that the liability limitation is therefore irrational

and violative of due process. The legislative history clearly indicates that the $560 million figure was not arrived at on the supposition that it alone would necessarily be sufficient to guarantee full compensation in the event of a nuclear incident. Instead, it was conceived of as a "starting point" or a working hypothesis. The reasonableness of the statute's assumed ceiling on liability was predicated on two corollary considerations—expert appraisals of the exceedingly small risk of a nuclear incident involving claims in excess of $560 million, and the recognition that in the event of such an incident, Congress would likely enact extraordinary relief provisions to provide additional relief, in accord with prior practice.

* * * * *

Given our conclusion that, in general, limiting liability is an acceptable method for Congress to utilize in encouraging the private development of electric energy by atomic power, candor requires acknowledgment that whatever ceiling figure is selected will, of necessity, be arbitrary in the sense that any choice of a figure based on imponderables like those at issue here can always be so characterized. This is not, however, the kind of arbitrariness which flaws otherwise constitutional action. When appraised in terms of both the extremely remote possibility of an accident where liability would exceed the limitation and Congress' now statutory commitment to "take whatever action is deemed necessary and appropriate to protect the public from the consequences of" any such disaster, we hold the congressional decision to fix a $560 million ceiling, at this stage in the private development and production of electric energy by nuclear power, to be within permissible limits and not violative of due process.

This District Court's further conclusion that the Price-Anderson Act "tends to encourage irresponsibility . . . on the part

---

* *Arguendo* means for the purpose of argument.—Au.

of builders and owners" of the nuclear power plants simply cannot withstand careful scrutiny. We recently outlined the multitude of detailed steps involved in the review of any application for a license to construct or to operate a nuclear power plant; nothing in the liability-limitation provision undermines or alters in any respect the rigor and integrity of that process. Moreover, in the event of a nuclear accident the utility itself would suffer perhaps the largest damages. While obviously not to be compared with the loss of human life and injury to health, the risk of financial loss and possible bankruptcy to the utility is in itself no small incentive to avoid the kind of irresponsible and cavalier conduct implicitly attributed to licensees by the District Court.

The remaining due process objection to the liability-limitation provision is that it fails to provide those injured by a nuclear accident with a satisfactory *quid pro quo*** for the common-law rights of recovery which the Act abrogates. Initially, it is not at all clear that the Due Process Clause in fact requires that a legislatively enacted compensation scheme either duplicate the recovery at common law or provide a reasonable substitute remedy. However, we need not resolve this question here since the Price-Anderson Act does, in our view, provide a reasonably just substitute for the common-law or state tort law remedies it replaces.

The legislative history of the liability-limitation provisions and the accompanying compensation mechanism reflects Congress' determination that reliance on state tort law remedies and state-court procedures was an unsatisfactory approach to assuring public compensation for nuclear accidents, while at the same time providing the necessary incentives for private devel-

opment of nuclear-produced energy. The remarks of Chairman Anders of the NRC before the Joint Committee on Atomic Energy during the 1975 hearings on the need for renewal of the Price-Anderson Act are illustrative of this concern and of the expectation that the Act would provide a more efficient and certain vehicle for assuring compensation in the unlikely event of a nuclear incident:

> The primary defect of this alternative [nonrenewal of the Act], however, is its failure to afford the public either a secure source of funds or a firm basis for legal liability with respect to new plants. While in theory no legal limit would be placed on liability, as a practical matter the public would be less assured of obtaining compensation than under Price-Anderson. Establishing liability would depend in each case on state tort law and procedures, and these might or might not provide for no-fault liability, let alone the multiple other protections now embodied in Price-Anderson. The present assurance of prompt and equitable compensation under a pre-structured and nationally applicable protective system would give way to uncertainties, variations and potentially lengthy delays in recovery. It should be emphasized, moreover, that it is collecting a judgment, not filing a lawsuit, that counts. Even if defenses are waived under state law, a defendant with theoretically "unlimited" liability may be unable to pay a judgment once obtained. When the defendant's assets are exhausted by earlier judgments, subsequent claimants would be left with uncollectable awards. The prospect of inequitable distribution would produce a race to the courthouse door in contrast to the present system of assured orderly and equitable compensation.

Appellees, like the District Court, differ with this appraisal on several grounds. They argue, that recovery under the Act would not be greater than without it, that the

---

** *Quid pro quo* as used here means exchange.— Au.

waiver of defenses required by the Act is an idle gesture since those involved in the development of nuclear energy would likely be held strictly liable under common-law principles; that the claim-administration procedure under the Act delays rather than expedites individual recovery; and finally that recovery of even limited compensation is uncertain since the liability ceiling does not vary with the number of persons injured or amount of property damaged. The extension of short state statutes of limitations and the provision of omnibus coverage do not save the Act, in their view, since such provisions could equally well be included in a fairer plan which would assure greater compensation.

We disagree. We view the congressional *assurance* of a $560 million fund for recovery, accompanied by an express statutory commitment, to "take whatever action is deemed necessary and appropriate to protect the public from the consequences of" a nuclear accident, to be a fair and reasonable substitute for the uncertain recovery of damages of this magnitude from a utility or component manufacturer, whose resources might well be exhausted at an early stage. The record in this case raises serious questions about the ability of a utility or component manufacturer to satisfy a judgment approaching $560 million—the amount guaranteed under the Price-Anderson Act. Nor are we persuaded that the mandatory waiver of defenses required by the Act is of no benefit to potential claimants. Since there has never been, to our knowledge, a case arising out of a nuclear incident like those covered by the Price-Anderson Act, any discussion of the standard of liability that state courts will apply is necessarily speculative. At the minimum, the statutorily mandated waiver of defenses establishes at the threshold the right of injured parties to compensation without proof of fault and eliminates the burden of delay and uncer-

tainty which would follow from the need to litigate the question of liability after an accident. Further, even if strict liability were routinely applied, the common-law doctrine is subject to exceptions for acts of God or of third parties—two of the very factors which appellees emphasized in the District Court in the course of arguing that the risks of a nuclear accident are greater than generally admitted. All of these considerations belie the suggestion that the Act leaves the potential victims of a nuclear disaster in a more disadvantageous position than they would be in if left to their common-law remedies—not known in modern times for either their speed or economy.

Appellees' remaining objections can be briefly treated. The claim-administration procedures under the Act provide that in the event of an accident with potential liability exceeding the $560 million ceiling, no more than 15% of the limit can be distributed pending court approval of a plan of distribution taking into account the need to assure compensation for "possible latent injury claims which may not be discovered until a later time." Although some delay might follow from compliance with this statutory procedure, we doubt that it would approach that resulting from routine litigation of the large number of claims caused by a catastrophic accident. Moreover, the statutory scheme insures the equitable distribution of benefits to all who suffer injury—both immediate and latent; under the common-law route, the proverbial race to the courthouse would instead determine who had "first crack" at the diminishing resources of the tortfeasor, and fairness could well be sacrificed in the process. The remaining contention that recovery is uncertain because of the aggregate rather than individualized nature of the liability ceiling is but a thinly disguised version of the contention that the $560 million figure is inadequate, which we have already rejected.

* * * * *

. . . The Price-Anderson Act not only provides a reasonable, prompt, and equitable mechanism for compensating victims of a catastrophic nuclear incident, it also guarantees a level of net compensation generally exceeding that recoverable in private litigation. Moreover, the Act contains an explicit congressional commitment to take further action to aid victims of a nuclear accident in the event that the $560 million ceiling on liability is exceeded. This panoply of remedies and guarantees is at the least a reasonably just substitute for the common-law rights replaced by the Price-Anderson Act. Nothing more is required by the Due Process Clause.

CASE QUESTIONS

1. In the Court's opinion, the $560 million limit on liability is not irrational or violative of due process. Why not?

2. What incentive does the Court believe that utilities have for avoiding irresponsibility in building and operating nuclear power plants?

3. Why does the Court think that Price–Anderson provides a reasonably just substitute for the common-law or state-law remedies it replaces?

4. Do you agree with the Congressional policy decision, embodied in the Price–Anderson Act, to put a ceiling on liability for a single nuclear disaster at $560? Explain.

Under the Atomic Energy Act the full responsibility for nuclear power development in the United States was initially with the Atomic Energy Commission (AEC). The Energy Reorganization Act of 1974 divided the AEC's former jurisdiction between two new agencies whose duties to conduct research on and develop nuclear power would not conflict with their duties to protect the public health and safety. The Nuclear Regulatory Commission (NRC) assumed the licensing and regulatory activities of the AEC with respect to the siting and operation of nuclear power plants; the Energy Research and Development Agency (ERDA) took control over all major federal research and development programs, including nuclear weapons testing.

Nuclear Plant Licensing Procedure

The Nuclear Regulatory Commission inherited its basic framework for the licensing of nuclear power plants from the AEC. The AEC followed a two-stage licensing process for nuclear power plants, the first authorizing the plant to be built, the second authorizing it to operate.

Persons seeking to build a nuclear power plant must apply for a construction permit. A major portion of the application is devoted to a Preliminary Safety Analysis Report. The report must include the following:

— A description of the proposed site
— The plant's unusual design features

— The equipment for controlling normal emissions of radioactive materials

— The procedures for coping with emergencies, possible accidents, and their potential consequences

— The applicant's technical and financial qualifications

— And the provisions for off-site shipment of waste

Two reviews of the Preliminary Safety Analysis Report take place after it has been prepared. The NRC reviews the application and contacts the applicant, questioning the applicant until it is satisfied enough to conclude in a safety evaluation report why the facility can be safely constructed and operated.

Concurrently with the NRC staff review, the 15-member Advisory Committee on Reactor Safeguards (ACRS) holds hearings and reviews the applications as it exchanges documents with the applicant and other experts. ACRS reports discuss health and safety issues surrounding the facility.

If the NRC and the ACRS agree that a construction permit can be issued, the three-member Atomic Safety and Licensing Board conducts a hearing. Notice must be given at least 30 days before the hearing; time must be allowed for interventions by persons interested in the proceedings.

If a construction permit is issued, the initial application to build is carried over to the operational licensing stage. The application is adjusted by new facts that emerge during the course of construction; at the end, the preliminary safety analysis report becomes the final analysis report. Unless good cause can be shown as to why an operating license should not be issued, the license is awarded when the facility has been completed.

NRC Criteria for Plant Siting

The suitability of an applicant's site is determined by comparing the design and operating characteristics of the proposed reactor with the physical characteristics of the site. The human environment of the site is also considered, with particular regard for population density in the surrounding area. Otherwise unacceptable sites can become acceptable if compensating engineering safeguards are included in reactor designs. Special design concerns include withstanding vibrations from earthquakes and high winds from tornadoes. High waters from floods require special precautions also, since significant quantities of radioactive effluents might accidentally flow into nearby streams or rivers or find access to underground water tables.

A hypothetical accident releasing fission products from the reactor core is the basis used for determining whether a site is suitable in relation to the population distribution in the surrounding area. The site must permit room for three zones based on radiation dosages acceptable for persons residing in the vicinity of the plant should such an accident occur. The applicant must provide for an exclusion zone over which it can exercise power to exclude or remove personnel and property. Surrounding the exclusion zone must be a low population zone from which residents can be readily evacuated. Population centers must be at least $1\frac{1}{3}$ times as far away from the low population zone's outer boundary as that outer boundary is from the nuclear reactor. The Supreme Court has affirmed the NRC's position that the distance to the population center is based on the distance to a population concentration rather than to the political boundaries of the population center.

Management of High-Level Radioactive Waste

It was concern with the mounting accumulation of nuclear waste that caused Congress to enact the Nuclear Waste Policy Act of 1982. This act establishes a national plan for the disposal of highly radioactive nuclear waste. The statute sets into motion a process for locating and constructing two permanent repositories (storage facilities) for high-level nuclear waste and provides for the temporary storage of spent nuclear fuel until permanent repositories are built.

Permanent Repositories

Construction on the first permanent repository for high-level nuclear waste is to begin by January 1, 1989, and, for the second, by January 1, 1992. The Department of Energy (DOE) is to undertake studies and recommend to the president the location of each repository. The statute forbids placing the repository in a highly populated area or adjacent to a one-square-mile area with a population of 1,000 or more. The repository is to be used for the storage of either spent fuel or the high-level radioactive waste that results from reprocessing.

Temporary Spent Fuel Storage

The Nuclear Waste Policy Act also authorizes the DOE to provide up to 1,900 metric tons of storage capacity for the temporary storage of spent fuel from civilian nuclear reactors. This away-from-the reactor storage is to be available only for waste from utilities that have filled the storage space at the reactor site and cannot provide adequate additional storage at the site. Temporary storage costs are paid with fees collected from utilities using the storage facility.

State Veto

A state may veto a federal decision to place a nuclear waste repository holding 300 tons or more of spent fuel within its borders. This veto will stand unless it is overruled by Congress within 90 days.

Fees

The Nuclear Waste Policy Act establishes a Nuclear Waste Fund, composed of fees levied on utilities, to pay for the costs of constructing and operating permanent repositories.

Wildlife Preservation

The Endangered Species Act of 1973 protects many species from activities that would harm them or their habitats. The act makes it a federal offense to buy, sell, possess, export, or import any species listed by the Interior Department as endangered or threatened, or any product made from such a species. Federal agencies must ensure that their projects do not jeopardize a listed species or adversely affect its habitat. Agencies must obtain a permit by consulting with the Interior Department for land-based species or the Commerce Department for marine species.

Under the act, a $78 million dam project near Knoxville, Tennessee was halted to save the habitat of a three-inch fish called the snail darter. Although the project was nearing completion, the Supreme Court ruled that it be halted because Congress had made saving endangered species one of the highest federal priorities.[3] Congress later allowed the project to proceed, finding that the fish could be transported to new habitats.

The snail darter case illustrated an industry criticism of the statute. Although a proposed federal project can be exempted from the act when no feasible alternative is available, industry critics claimed that this process was cumbersome and time-consuming. In 1982, Congress amended the act and addressed this criticism by streamlining the exemption process and by removing the threat of criminal penalties or project shutdown for industries that kill threatened species incidentally in the course of their activities.

ALTERNATIVE APPROACHES

The United States carries out most of its environmental protection programs through direct regulation. This is true nationally for the control of air and water pollution, pesticides, and radiation. Under this approach, the government sets standards of behavior or maximum allowable amounts of discharge for particulant pollutants and industries, and it uses administrative and judicial means to enforce these standards. This approach has yielded important gains in the fight against environmental harm, yet critics of direct regulation claim that it is costly and cumbersome. They suggest a decentralized market-oriented approach to solving environmental problems.

A market imperfection referred to by economists as the problem of externalties currently keeps the market system from allocating resources in a way that is efficient and responsive to society's demand for environmental preservation. In an ideal market system, commodity prices reflect the full costs of resources expended in production. In reality, not all costs and benefits of resource use are internal to the bargaining parties. Some decisions may be privately profitable (such as discharging factory waste into a stream) even if they are not socially profitable. Market solutions will not produce an efficient allocation of resources if social costs

---

[3] *TVA v. Hill,* 437 U.S. 153 (1978).

(called external costs) and benefits are not taken into account. Economists say that external costs must be "internalized"—added to private costs—to restore market efficiency. Producers can solve externality problems by internalizing all the consequences of their actions, which then sets private costs and benefits equal to social costs and benefits.

Economists maintain that direct environmental regulation is costly and that government regulation should be limited to correcting market failure. They argue that a properly functioning market will more efficiently provide an optimal level of environmental protection.

The two approaches most frequently suggested by economists as alternatives to direct regulation of the environment are: (1) the creation of a market in pollution rights, and (2) the use of charges or taxes to create economic incentives to improve the environment.

Permit Trading

Current federal efforts to control pollution rely heavily on the use of source-specific standards (such as effluent limitations under the Clean Water Act) set by a central agency (the EPA). Critics contend that this command-and-control approach to regulation is wasteful. Many economists advocate the creation of a market in transferable property rights, known as transferable discharge permits (TDP). Under a TDP policy, rights to discharge pollutants, once issued by a government agency in the form of a permit, may be transferred among users as property rights. Working examples of transferable permits currently exist in other areas of regulation. Liquor licenses, taxicab medallions, and land development rights are transferable in some states and localities.

The basic model of an emissions market envisions the government's role as defining a market area and establishing a limit on aggregate emissions. Licenses that define allowable emissions in terms of pollutant concentrations would be issued, and potential emitters would buy the "right to pollute" from existing polluters. Firms with high marginal abatement costs would buy away emissions from firms with low abatement costs. For each market, the aggregate level of emissions would be produced efficiently. The government's role would be to define the market area appropriately and choose an aggregate level of emissions that equate marginal cost to marginal damage.

To a certain extent, TDP is currently embodied in the Clean Air Act's "bubble concept." The bubble allows a transfer of emission reduction credits between emissions units within a facility. Bubbles, however, do not involve transfers between firms.

In 1981, Wisconsin became the first state to include the option of permit trading into its administrative code regulating the discharge of wastewater into its rivers. The Wisconsin statute forms the basis for the operation of a market in one type of permit, biochemical oxygen demand

(BOD) effluent permits. The rule specifies an allocation of allowable effluent levels for individual dischargers that is intended to maintain a target level of dissolved oxygen (DO) under a variety of water flow and temperature conditions. In addition, the rule allows the permits to be traded among the dischargers in quantities that preserve the DO target. Permits can be traded with the approval of the Wisconsin Department of Natural Resources, which scrutinizes each proposed trade for consistency with the preservation of desired dissolved oxygen levels.

Charges

Another approach to internalizing external costs is to tax environmentally harmful conduct. By raising the costs of continuing that conduct, the charge persuades the offender to adopt more environmentally acceptable means of achieving its goals. In other words, the obligation to pay for environmental harm provides an incentive not to cause that harm. Advocates of the charge system argue that it is a cost-effective means of achieving environmental goals because each source decides how much to control pollution on the basis of its own costs. Thus, sources whose costs of control are high will control less; those with low costs will control more.

East Germany was one of the first countries to apply the charge concept to environmental protection. As part of the "new economic policy" initiated in 1963 to promote decentralized decision making at the enterprise level, a system of "economic levies" was introduced whereby the environmental costs of an enterprise's activities are charged directly to that enterprise. A "land-use charge" was enacted in 1967, a "water-use charge" in 1969, a "waste-use charge" in 1970, and a "dust-and-gas-emission charge" in 1973. The latter two charges, which were imposed on a trial basis in three of the most heavily polluted counties in 1969, are prorated according to the amount of specified pollutants emitted into the water or atmosphere by each enterprise. An interesting feature of East German legislation is that these charges are treated as economic penalties. According to the Industrial Price Calculation Decree of 1972, they may not be budgeted or passed on to consumers by way of price adjustments. The revenues generated by the penalties are kept in the region where they are paid and are used for pollution control planning, environmental improvement, and victims' compensation.

In the United States, the charge concept is employed in the Superfund's tax on toxic chemicals and in the Nuclear Waste Policy Act's charges on users of radioactive waste storage facilities. A few states, notably Oregon, Vermont, Michigan, and Maine, have enacted "bottle bills." Consumers purchasing reusable containers pay a deposit that is refunded when the empty bottles or cans are returned to retail outlets. Thus, the person who adds soft drink or beer cans to the solid waste stream pays a charge, and the person who picks up and returns them is paid a bounty.

CHAPTER PROBLEMS

1. Bigdome Manufacturing, Inc., without Smith's consent or other privilege to do so, erects on its own land a dam that backs up water on Smith's land. What legal remedies are available to Smith? Explain.

2. Dustin company allows its employees to spray-paint company cars on its back lot. The spray occasionally drifts to Mrs. Perkins' garage, leaving specks of blue, yellow, and brown on the walls and door. If Mrs. Perkins sues to make the Dustin Company stop authorizing this activity, what is the court likely to decide? Why?

3. In 1952, Estelle Lowe leased 135 acres of land that she owned in Gibson County, Indiana to the Ashland Oil & Refining Co. for oil and gas exploration. Ashland drilled a well along the western edge of the property, offsetting a well that had been drilled on the adjacent property, which Ashland also leased. The well on the Lowe property ceased operating by 1956 and was plugged that year by Ashland. In September 1955, before the well was plugged, Ashland commenced waterflood operations, which involved injecting salt water at high pressure into the oil strata to force the remaining oil from the "cypress" oil sands into the well on the adjacent property. The operation was authorized and approved by the Oil and Gas Division of the Indiana Department of Conservation. In 1958 and again in 1959, long after the well on Lowe's land was plugged, crude oil was found seeping out on Lowe's land at ground level around that well. In July 1963, crude oil leaked into and contaminated the nearby fresh water well that supplied Lowe's domestic water. The Ashland waterflood caused salt water and oil to seep from the cypress sands under the adjacent property into the well on the Lowe property. If Lowe sues Ashland to recover for the damage resulting from the waterflood operation, will Ashland be held liable? Explain.

4. In November 1974 the secretary of defense announced 111 actions involving realignment of units and closures of Army bases. One of these actions affected the Lexington-Bluegrass Army Depot (LBAD) in Lexington, Kentucky. The action was to eliminate 18 military jobs and

2,630 civilian jobs in the Lexington area, with personnel transferred to depots in California and Pennsylvania. The Army prepared an environmental assessment which concluded that because there would be no significant effect on the human environment, a formal environmental impact statement was not required. A nongovernmental research institution studied the possible socioeconomic impact of the action and concluded that the Lexington area would suffer only minimal short-term unemployment as a result of the partial closure. In August 1975, four Kentucky congressmen, two U.S. senators, two county judges, the city of Richmond, the Lexington-Fayette Urban County Government, the Greater Lexington Chamber of Commerce, three property and business owners in the vicinity of LBAD, and four civilian employees of LBAD all sued to block the proposed action. They claimed that an environmental impact statement is required before action by the Army can be undertaken. Is an environmental impact statement required? Explain.

5. On November 20, 1975, Marathon Pipe Line Co. was notified by local police that a pipeline it owned had ruptured and was discharging crude oil into the Kaskaskia River in southern Illinois. The company immediately took steps to contain the spill and reported the occurrence to the Environmental Protection Agency. In all, 19,992 gallons of crude oil were discharged from the pipeline and 10,920 gallons were recovered or burned, so that approximately 9,072 gallons escaped downriver. Subsequent investigation by the company revealed that a bulldozer had struck the four-inch buried pipe in June or July of 1975 while digging an irrigation ditch for the owners of the land. The bulldozer operator reported the damage to the landowners, but since they thought that the pipeline was no longer in use, neither ever reported the damage to Marathon. The location of the pipeline was a matter of public record, the easement having been duly recorded with the local recorder's office, and the pipeline was marked in accordance with all federal regulations. What liability does Marathon Pipe Line Co. have to neighboring property owners on whose land the oil spilled? Explain. What is Marathon's liability to property owners located downriver from the spill with regard to property damage? Explain. If the Environmental Protection Agency cleans up the 9,072 gallons that Marathon was unable to recover or burn, what recourse does the EPA have against Marathon? Explain.

6. Ohio has been found to produce twice as much sulfur dioxide as all the New England states combined. The EPA administrator attempted to implement a plan to clean up Ohio's air when Ohio could not produce a satisfactory state implementation plan to achieve national clean air standards. The administrator found that the EPA was without sufficient money or political power to control the local situation effectively. By what authority could the administrator provide a plan for Ohio? What alternative actions could the administrator have taken, and how effective were those actions likely to be?

7. Donegal's Power Company is planning to build a nuclear power plant along the Pacific Ocean. Donegal's scientists have determined that earthquake activity is not significant in the area in which they want to build, but that tremors in the region may produce vibrations sufficient to cause occasional flooding. Will Donegal's be able to build its plant in the place the scientists have chosen?

8. The core of Nuclear Power Plant XIII has melted down, releasing radioactive wastes, water, and air at 50 times acceptable levels as far as 20 miles away. The countryside for 10 miles is thoroughly poisoned, and vegetation for 15 miles has become wilted or diseased. Increased levels of cancer have been detected among populations formerly located near the plant. Losses by farmers in land, livestock, and private residences have already been estimated at $500 million. If the farmers sue immediately, will victims of radiation poisoning or cancer suing later have to split the remaining $60 million available under Price-Anderson's liability limit? Explain.

9. The design of Commons Nuclear Power Plant proves to be faulty. Water used in cooling the power plant becomes contaminated and seeps into water holes used by grazing animals in nearby low-population zones. How much of its own money would the utility company have to pay out to livestock owners? What is the company's maximum responsibility?

10. Compare and contrast the advantages and disadvantages of environmental protection through: (1) direct regulation, as is currently undertaken in the United States; (2) an emissions market approach, such as is provided with regard to wastewater pollution in Wisconsin; and (3) a charge system, as is provided by East German environmental law. Which method of environmental protection do you prefer? Explain.

CHAPTER 19

BUSINESS ETHICS AND CORPORATE SOCIAL RESPONSIBILITY

In the 1970s Americans followed news of scandal on Wall Street and in Washington. On Wall Street, one of the nation's largest financial services corporations, The Equity Funding Corporation of America, was exposed as a gigantic fraud. In Washington, Congress, the Supreme Court, and the White House wrestled with the political scandal stemming from the bugging and burglary of the Democratic National Committee headquarters at the posh Watergate condominium complex.

In 1973, The Equity Funding Corporation of America purported to have assets of one billion dollars. Its record growth for over a decade exceeded that of any other major diversified financial company in the U.S. However, despite its spectacular "record," the compnay was a billion-dollar bubble. It did not earn a penny of profit; in fact, it lost money. Through the systematic efforts of many employees, phony earnings statements were used to inflate the value of the company's stock.

One scheme involved computer fraud. Phony insurance policies were reported on the company's computers as having been sold. These same nonexistent policies were later sold to other insurance companies. When the bubble finally burst (a fired employee named Ron Secrist blew the whistle), the company's chief executive officer, its chief accountant, and its chief actuary were convicted and imprisoned. In all, 22 people pled guilty to various crimes. The company was plunged into bankruptcy. Lawsuits were brought by stockholders, state insurance commissions, prosecutors, and the Securities and Exchange Commission.

At the same time, the nation was preoccupied with Watergate. This scandal led to the only resignation of an American president and the conviction of several high government officials. These included the attorney general of the United States, the secretary of commerce, the president's counsel, and the president's two top domestic advisors. Investigation into the burglary led to the discovery of illegal corporate contributions to domestic political campaigns. Further inquiry revealed that bribing foreign government officials was a common business practice.

The Equity Funding fraud scandal and the prevalence of large-scale illegal corporate political activity were two of the most spectacular business scandals. Unfortunately, similar practices are also common on a smaller scale. Activities that are not illegal but are arguably unethical take place daily.

This chapter explores problems that fall under the general headings of business ethics and corporate social responsibility. These subjects are vitally important to today's business manager.

Executive misconduct threatens the very existence of an organization, as the Equity Funding scandal demonstrates. More importantly, public outcry against unethical business activities threatens the free enterprise system itself. When the public loses confidence in the ability of market forces to prevent corporate misbehavior, it often demands increased government regulation. For example, disclosure of corporate bribes to foreign officials led to passage of the Foreign Corrupt Practices Act.

Finally, business decisions have an enormous impact on people's lives and on the social climate of the country. Corporate executives and citizens agree that business should make a positive contribution to the general moral climate of the community. Failure to answer the challenge of corporate social responsibility exposes business to public hostility. The "public be damned" attitude of the nineteenth century industrial barons led to restrictive changes in the antitrust laws.

Strategies that address corporate social concerns may also pay off in the marketplace. Johnson & Johnson, for example, developed a corporate credo spelling out the company's responsibilities to its customers, its employees, the communities where it operates, and its shareholders—in that order. It then examined its own behavior in light of the credo in weeks of meetings and discussions with corporate executives. The first institutional test of its policy was the nationwide Tylenol recall in 1982, following the deaths of seven Chicago-area residents who took capsules contaminated with cyanide. The company emerged from the incident with its reputation if not its earnings, intact. Shortly after the recall, the *New York Times* quoted company chairman James Burke as saying, "It showed that the credo works. The Tylenol recall isn't going to pay our bills for the next year or two, but in the long run it will be worth it in values."[1]

BUSINESS ETHICS

Managers frequently face decisions that present ethical dilemmas. A particular course of conduct may prove financially lucrative but may also conflict with personal standards of morality. Certain situations may present

---

[1] Lewin, "Business Ethics' New Appeal," *The New York Times*, Dec. 11, 1983, p. 4F.

ethically unappealing alternatives which compel the decision maker to choose the lesser of two evils. The following paragraphs discuss issues of business ethics. Much of the material consists of readings. This is the authors' way of avoiding sermonizing about truth with a capital *T*.

Defining Business Ethics

Like other fundamental concepts, such as truth and love, the term *ethics* seems to defy definition. Yet some attempt to grasp its meaning must be made before exploring ethical problems in the business arena. The following essay works toward a definition of ethics. It suggests that corporate or organizational ethics may differ from individual ethics.

Ethics in the Corporate Policy Process: An Introduction*

What is Ethics?

Ethics is reflection on the moral meaning of action. Ethics does not reveal suddenly a new reality of right and wrong totally invisible to us before. Ethics does not offer a single, absolute right way of behavior. Rather, much like economics or political science, ethics assists us to see more clearly and understand with greater precision what we were already aware of but saw only dimly or inadequately. Ethics is the process by which individuals, social groups, and societies evaluate their actions from the perspective of moral principles and values. This evaluation may be on the basis of traditional convictions, of ideals sought, of goals desired, of moral laws to be obeyed, of an improved quality of relations among humans and with the environment. When we speak of "ethics" and ethical reflection, we mean the activity of applying these various yardsticks to the actions of persons and groups.

For some, morality may mean utilizing only a single yardstick by which to measure and evaluate action. One such set of criteria is the Ten Commandments. Another is the Golden Rule. Persons are taught some form of morality in their home and immediate childhood community. Similar guides may be discovered in other major religions—Hindu, Buddhist, Muslim, and in the philosophical traditions—Kantian, utilitarian, hedonist, and others.

For most of us in this society, ethics includes more than a single set of ideals or moral principles. We feel the pull of divergent loyalties and desires within ourselves as individuals. In an even more complex way, the actions of organizations are based on many different interests, values, and convictions. Ethics works within this diversity and develops criteria to evaluate and guide actions related to specific situations.

In our pluralistic world of complex so-

* C. McCoy et al., 2–4 (1975). Reprinted with permission of the Center for Ethics and Social Policy, Graduate Theological Union, Berkeley, California.

cial organizations, ethical issues arise in situations where persons from differing perspectives meet and share in shaping policy. Rigid moral judgments based on one individual's views are inadequate. Ethical issues arise also because groups affected by policy are not represented in policy making. Ethics applicable to corporations or other social organizations must take account of diverse perspectives and seek for criteria inclusive of divergent interests, goals, and beliefs.

Corporate Ethics

Corporate ethics is concerned not with individual, private behavior, but with the moral meaning of organizational action and purpose. Corporate ethics evaluates and guides the actions, policies, and decision-making processes of social groups. In *Moral Man and Immoral Society,* Reinhold Niebuhr insists that "a sharp distinction must be drawn between the moral and social behavior of individuals and of social groups." He attacks a naive confidence in the moral capabilities of human collectives and demonstrates that power, rather than goodwill or reasonableness alone, is necessary in overcoming social injustice.

Individual ethics remains important for the ethics of an organization. Decisions made by individuals have a significant bearing on organizational decisions and policy. One person's errors or dishonesty can destroy the reputation of an entire group. And a single individual's moral courage at a crucial juncture may stem a wave of disastrous decisions or enlarge the visions of the group's responsibility and action.

Yet corporate ethics is more than the sum of the ethics of individuals within the group. No matter how important individual actions may be, an organization involves more than the collection of actions and views of the individuals who participate in it. An organization has an existence of its own: its own history and traditions, its own rules and ways of operating derived from its constituting character and its customs, its own patterns of informal understandings, its own particular network of influence and factions within it, its own relations to other organizations, its own particular place in a nexus of social and cultural functions. An individual thinks and acts differently in family relationships, in recreational activities, in professional/vocational groups, in each different group, he or she takes on the social patterns, expectations, and responsibilities which belong to each distinctive organization and group relation. Writing of President Truman's decision to drop the atomic bomb on Japan in 1945, Robert Batchelder comments on the power of organizational process:

> Social institutions appear to take on an independence and a power of their own which defy the attempts of individual men to control them. General Groves has said of President Truman's decision to use the bomb: "Truman did not so much say yes as not say no. It would indeed have taken a lot of nerve to say no at that time."

Though the president has great power, it is exercised within an organizational policy process even more powerful.

It is more important to develop discussion of organizational ethics among those people primarily responsible for shaping policy. Persons as individuals frequently exhibit greater awareness of the ethical implications of policy when apart from the policy-making process than when operating within that process. In organizational situations caution, prudence, and "group think" may triumph over innovation and individual awareness. Discussions of corporate ethics must therefore occur with the processes of organizational interaction, raise the consciousness of the policy-making group, and seek change, not only of individual perception, but also of the organization's policy process.

Corporate ethics may focus on particular aspects of organizational action: on its adherence to law and organizational standards, on purposes, priorities, and consequences, or on relationships; on the overall shape of policy, on the processes by which policy is formulated, or on issues of legitimacy. A comprehensive corporate ethic will integrate the widest possible spectrum of organization for analysis and evaluation.

Ethical Dilemmas in Business Affairs

The typical corporate official does not identify with criminals or unethical people. Most corporate officials who have engaged in questionable business practices would say that they did so for the benefit of the corporation. It is difficult to turn down a $50 million—$5 million profit—contract with a foreign government simply because in order to obtain the contract an official of that government has to be hired as a consultant for a fee of $200,000. The corporate reflex is to take action designed to maximize earnings. It is not difficult to lose sight of basic values in doing so. Unethical corporate activity is more often a result of failures to consider ethical consequences than of conscious decisions to act improperly.

In 1983, the Gallup Organization conducted a survey for the *Wall Street Journal* to find out how Americans would handle specific situations involving ethical issues. The following article reports the results of that survey. Read the article and consider how you would have responded to the dilemmas that were posed. Following the article are several ethical dilemmas that were included in a similar questionnaire given to *Harvard Business Review* readers. Consider how you would respond to the questions and how the average executive would answer them.

 **Ethics in America***

It's the sort of dilemma companies encounter all the time.

An employer finds that the candidate who is by far the best qualified for a job really earned only $18,000 a year in his last job, and not the $28,000 he claimed. Should the employer hire the candidate anyway, or should he choose someone else even though that person will be considerably less qualified?

In a Gallup Organization poll conducted for the *Wall Street Journal*, general citizens overwhelmingly back the lenient approach: Some 63 percent surveyed recommended hiring the able but errant applicant, and only 27 percent say the employer should choose somebody else. But among the executives polled, 52 percent would choose somebody else, and only 47 percent would hire the applicant with a false claim.

* * * * *

Sometimes Gallup threw in complications. For instance, in the case of the candidate who lied about his previous salary, it asked half the members of its sample what they would do if the real salary were $25,000, only $3,000 less than the amount claimed. . . .

The general public reacts about the same as when the real salary was $18,000. Some 68 percent would hire the candidate and 22 percent wouldn't. But to executives, the amount involved matters. When the discrepancy between claimed salary and real salary was only $3,000 per year, 60 percent of the executives would hire the candidate and only 38 percent wouldn't.

To obtain this data, Gallup this summer polled a representative national general-public sample of 1,558 adults and a sample of 396 middle-level big-company executives. It interviewed the general citizens in person and mailed confidential questionnaires to the executives. The polling organization figures there is a sampling error of up to 3 percent in the general-public poll and up to 5 percent in the smaller executive poll.

Here is how the people Gallup surveyed say they would handle the dilemmas:

Family versus Ethics

Jim, a 56-year-old manager with children in college, discovers that the owners of his company are cheating the government out of several thousand dollars a year

in taxes. Jim is the only employee who would be in a position to know this. Should Jim report the owners to the Internal Revenue Service at the risk of endangering his own livelihood, or disregard the discovery in order to protect his family's livelihood?

More often than not, both executives and general citizens say family responsibilities should take precedence. Roughly half—49 percent of the public and 52 percent of the executives—think Jim should disregard his discovery in order to protect his family. About 34 percent of both the executives and the public think he should report the owners.

The money involved "isn't worth the loss of a job," says a manufacturing executive in his 50s. "Hundreds of thousands could make a difference." A company controller urges disregarding the cheating and adds: "The IRS has auditors to catch this kind of thing."

A financial executive says that to disregard the cheating "is not my real answer, but the chances of a 56-year-old 'whistleblower' finding employment in this society might be difficult." Some executives suggest options that weren't offered in the question: resign or look for another job.

The Roundabout Raise

When Joe asks for a raise, his boss praises his work but says the company's rigid budget won't allow any further merit raises for the time being. Instead, the boss suggests that the company "won't look too closely at your expense accounts for a while." Should Joe take this as authorization to pad his expense account on grounds that he is simply getting the same money he deserves through a different route, or not take this roundabout "raise"?

Though the public took a permissive approach to some of the other dilemmas, it decisively rejected the roundabout raise—and the executives rejected it even more overwhelmingly. Some sixty-five percent of the general citizens and 91 percent of the executives say Joe should turn down the circuitous raise. Only 25 percent of the public and 7 percent of the executives think he should "take this as authorization to pad his expense account."

The Faked Degree

Bill has done a sound job for over a year. Bill's boss learns that he got the job by claiming to have a college degree, although he actually never graduated. Should his boss dismiss him for submitting a fraudulent resume or overlook the false claim since Bill has otherwise proven to be conscientious and honorable, and making an issue of the degree might ruin Bill's career?

More executives recommended dismissing Bill (50 percent) than suggest overlooking the claim (43 percent). The general public decisively recommends (66 percent to 22 percent) overlooking the false claim rather than dismissing Bill.

Within the general public, however, 33 percent of those with professional occupations recommend dismissal. Gallup points out that academic credentials might be particularly important to people in these occupations.

In an otherwise identical question asked of a subsample, Bill didn't merely fail to graduate—he never attended college at all. But the distinction didn't seem to matter. Both subsamples gave similar answers to the question.

Sneaking Phone Calls

Helen discovers that a fellow employee regularly makes about $100 a month worth of personal long-distance telephone calls from an office telephone. Should Helen report the employee to the company or disregard the calls on the grounds that many people make personal calls at the office?

In an otherwise identical question asked of part of the sample, Gallup has the employee making only $10 a month worth of personal long-distance calls instead of $100.

The difference matters, especially to executives. When the employee is sneaking $100 a month worth of calls, 64 percent of the public and 76 percent of the executives think that Helen should report him. Some 26 percent of the public and 19 percent of the managers favor disregarding the calls.

But when the amount involved is $10 a month, only 47 percent of the public and 48 percent of the executives favor reporting the employee. About 38 percent of the public and 47 percent of the executives favor disregarding the calls.

Put another way, when $100 a month is involved, the executives are tougher than the public. But when the figure is only $10 a month, the executives are more inclined than the public to disregard the calls.

Cover-up Temptation

Bill discovers that the chemical plant he manages is creating slightly more water pollution in a nearby lake than is legally permitted. Revealing the problem will bring considerable unfavorable publicity to the plant, hurt the lakeside town's resort business and create a scare in the community. Solving the problem will cost the company well over $100,000. It is unlikely that the outsiders will discover the problem. The violation poses no danger whatever to people. At most, it will endanger a small number of fish. Should Bill reveal the problem despite the cost to his company, or consider the problem as little more than a technicality and disregard it?

The respondent can find all sorts of rationales for letting Bill disregard the pollution problem. Yet general citizens and executives alike took a tough line. Some 63 percent of the general public and 70 percent of the executives say Bill should reveal the problem and spend the money. Only 25 percent of the general citizens and 24 percent of the executives think he should disregard it as a technicality.

This is the only ethical-dilemma question in which young people are "significantly more likely to take the stricter ethical option" than their elders, observes Andres Kohut, president of the Gallup Organiza-

tion. "There are great environmental concerns among the young," he adds.

Those who worry about the ethics of young America may find at least a little welcome news in the reaction to this question. For all the permissiveness the young reveal throughout the survey, they appear quite capable of developing a stricter ethical standard on some issues than their elders. "Ethics follow values," Mr. Kohut observes.

QUESTIONS*

1. An executive earning $30,000 a year has been padding his expense account by about $1,500 a year. I think that this is: *(a)* acceptable if other executives in the company do the same thing, *(b)* unacceptable regardless of the circumstances, *(c)* acceptable if the executive's superior knows about it and says nothing.

2. Imagine that you are the president of a company in a highly competitive industry. You learn that a competitor has made an important scientific discovery which will give him an advantage that will substantially reduce, but not eliminate, the profits of your company for about a year. If there were some hope of hiring one of the competitor's employees who knew the details of the discovery, would you try to hire him? I *(a)* probably would hire him, *(b)* probably would not hire him.

3. The minister of a foreign nation where extraordinary payments to lubricate the decision-making machinery are common asks you as a company marketing director for a $200,000 consulting fee. In return, he promises special assistance in obtaining a $100 million contract which should produce at least $5 million in profit for your company. What would you do? *(a)* pay the fee, feeling it was ethical in the moral climate of the foreign nation; *(b)* pay the fee,

feeling it was unethical but necessary to ensure the sale; *(c)* refuse to pay, even if the sale is thereby lost.

4. At a board meeting of High Fly Insurance Company (HFI), a new board member learns that HFI is the "officially approved" insurer of the Private Pilots Benevolent Association (PPBA), which has 200,000 members. On joining PPBA, members automatically subscribe to HFI's accident insurance dues assessment. In return, HFI pays PPBA a fee tied to the value of business PPBA members generate and gets use of the PPBA mailing list, which it uses to sell aircraft liability policies (its major source of revenues). PPBA's president sits on HFI's board of directors, and the two companies are both located in the same office building. In this situation, the average new director *who is a recently promoted HFI employee: (a)* would do nothing; *(b)* would privately and delicately raise the issue with the chairman of the board; *(c)* would express opposition in a directors' meeting, but would go along with whatever position the board chose to take; *(d)* would express vigorous opposition and resign if corrective action were not taken. Using the same choices, what would the average new *outside* director do in this situation?

---

* Reprinted by permission of the Harvard Business Review. Excerpts from "Is the Ethics of Business Changing?" by Steven N. Brenner and Earl A. Molander (January/February 1977). Copyright © 1977 by the President and Fellows of Harvard College; all rights reserved.

Whose Ethics? Corporate Ethics or Individual Ethics?

Business executives are sometimes forced to choose between their personal or professional ethics and the ethics of their employer. Loyalty to the employer is usually reinforced by the legal doctrine of employment-at-will, discussed in Chapter 16. This doctrine provides that employees whose working relationships are of indefinite duration are considered employees-at-will. This means that the employment can be terminated by either party for any reason, unless a statute or contract provides otherwise. The effect of the doctrine is to permit employers to discharge workers who refuse to comply with the employer's requirements. Some states have recognized an exception to the employment-at-will rule where the discharge is wrongful or abusive. Wrongful or abusive discharges are those that violate public policy.

In the following case, the employee confronted the choice of complying with her interpretation of her professional oath and the demands of management.

Pierce v. Ortho Pharmaceutical Corp.

417 A.2d 505 (N.J. 1980)

Dr. Grace Pierce (plaintiff) was Director of Medical Research for Ortho Pharmaceutical Corp. (defendant). She supervised the development of therapeutic drugs and established procedures for testing their safety, effectiveness, and marketability. One drug being developed was loperamide, a liquid for treating diarrhea in infants and elderly persons. Because Ortho's loperamide formula contained 44 times the amount of saccharin permitted in soft drinks by the Food and Drug Administration, the research team for the project, which included Dr. Pierce, agreed unanimously that it was unsuitable for therapeutic use. In response to management pressure, all but Dr. Pierce agreed to proceed with testing of the formula. As the team's only medical doctor, she maintained her opposition on ethical grounds, basing her refusal to work upon the Hippocratic Oath. She urged the development of an alternative formula containing less saccharin. As a result, Dr. Pierce was removed from the loperamide project staff and severely criticized by her supervisor. She then resigned her position and filed suit. She claimed that her resignation under the circumstances was a "constructive discharge"; that is, a forced resignation. As such, she argued that the discharge was wrongful. The trial court granted summary judgment for Ortho. The court of appeals reversed. The New Jersey Supreme Court reversed the appellate court and reinstated the trial court decision.

Justice Pollock

This case presents the question whether an employee at will has a cause of action against her employer to recover damages for the termination of her employment following her refusal to continue a project she viewed as medically unethical.

* * * * *

We hold that an employee has a cause of action for wrongful discharge when the discharge is contrary to a clear mandate of public policy. The sources of public policy include legislation; administrative rules, regulations or decisions; and judicial decisions. In certain instances, a professional code of ethics may contain an expression of public policy. However, not all such sources express a clear mandate of public policy. For example, a code of ethics designed to serve only the interests of a profession or an administrative regulation concerned with technical matters probably would not be sufficient. Absent legislation, the judiciary must define the cause of action in case-by-case determinations. An employer's right to discharge an employee at will carries a correlative duty not to discharge an employee who declines to perform an act that would require a violation of a clear mandate of public policy. However, unless an employee at will identifies a specific expression of public policy, he may be discharged with or without cause.

* * * * *

We now turn to the question whether Dr. Pierce was discharged for reasons contrary to a clear mandate of public policy.

* * * * *

Dr. Pierce argues that by continuing to perform research on loperamide she would have been forced to violate professional medical ethics expressed in the Hippocratic oath. She cites the part of the oath that reads: "I will prescribe regimen for the good of my patients according to my ability and my judgment and never do harm to anyone." Clearly, the general language of the oath does not prohibit specifically research that does not involve tests on humans and that cannot lead to such tests without governmental approval.

* * * * *

Viewing the matter most favorably to Dr. Pierce, the controversy at Ortho involved a difference in medical opinions.

* * * * *

Dr. Pierce contends, in effect, that Ortho should have stopped research on loperamide because of her opinion about the controversial nature of the drug.

Dr. Pierce espouses a doctrine that would lead to disorder in drug research. Under her theory, a professional employee could predetermine the propriety of a research project even if the research did not involve a violation of a clear mandate of public policy. Chaos would result if a single doctor engaged in research were allowed to determine, according to his or her individual conscience, whether a project should continue. An employee does not have a right to continued employment when he or she refuses to conduct research simply because it would contravene his or her personal morals. An employee at will who refuses to work for an employer in answer to a call of conscience should recognize that other employees and their employer might heed a different call. However, nothing in this opinion should be construed to restrict the right of an employee at will to refuse to work on a project that he or she believes in unethical. In sum, an employer may discharge an employee who refuses to work unless the refusal is based on a clear mandate of public policy.

*   *   *   *   *

Under these circumstances, we conclude that the Hippocratic oath does not contain a clear mandate of public policy that prevented Dr. Pierce from continuing her research on loperamide. To hold otherwise would seriously impair the ability of drug manufacturers to develop new drugs according to their best judgment.

Justice Pashman *(dissenting)*

I agree with the majority's ruling that a professional employee may not be discharged for refusing to violate a clearly recognized legal or ethical obligation imposed on members of his profession. However, the majority's application of this principle defies logical explanation.

*   *   *   *   *

The majority's analysis recognizes that the ethical goals of professional conduct are of inestimable social value. By maintaining informed standards of conduct, licensed professions bring to the problems of their public responsibilities the same expertise that marks their calling. The integrity of codes of professional conduct that result from this regulation deserves judicial protection from undue economic pressure. Employers are a potential source of this pressure, for they can provide or withhold—until today, at their whim—job security and the means of enhancing a professional's reputation. Thus, I completely agree with the majority's ruling that "an employee has a cause of action for wrongful discharge when the discharge is contrary to a clear mandate of public policy" as expressed in a "professional code of ethics."

The Court pronounces this rule for the first time today. One would think that it would therefore afford plaintiff an opportunity to seek relief within the confines of this newly announced cause of action.

*   *   *   *   *

The majority denies plaintiff this opportunity. I do not understand why.

[The majority] appears to believe that Dr. Pierce had the power to determine whether defendant's proposed development program would continue at all. This is not the case, nor is plaintiff claiming the right to halt defendant's developmental efforts. . . . Plaintiff claims only the right to her professional autonomy. She contends that she may not be discharged for expressing her view that the clinical program is unethical or for refusing to continue her participation in the project. She has done nothing else to impede continued development of defendant's proposal; moreover, it is undisputed that defendant was able to continue its program by reassigning personnel. Thus, the majority's view that granting doctors a right to be free from abusive discharges would confer on any one of them complete veto power over desirable drug development is ill-conceived.

CASE QUESTIONS

1. Which opinion, the majority's or the dissent's, do you find more persuasive? Explain.

2. Should the code of ethics of a private association be considered an expression of public policy? Explain.

3. Should companies create informal internal procedures to resolve ethical dilemmas for their employees? If so, what form could such procedures take?

4. Suppose that Dr. Pierce had taken her ethical reservation to the local medical association. Could Ortho discharge her for disloyalty? Explain.

Changes in the employment-at-will doctrine may have consequences with regard to organizational behavior. Employers may not be able to demand the single-minded loyalty of their employees when doing so conflicts with an employee's loyalty to his or her profession. Consider the following article.

 **Manager's Journal: Multiple Loyalties***

"It is not the lofty sails but the unseen wind that moves the ship," wrote W. Mac-Neile Dixon. His observation explains a major change that is taking place in the corporate world. Management textbooks and training programs focus on the "sails" of management-marketing, control, finance, and the rest. Important as these functions are, they are not the "unseen wind" that moves many corporations in a fresh direction. That force is a new attitude toward authority, and it results from the dramatic growth of professional and technical employees.

Numbers don't tell the story but, like a wind speed indicator, they suggest rapidity and direction. Between 1950 and 1975, according to the U.S. Bureau of Census, the number of managers and administrators in the United States increased by about one-third (from 6.4 million to 8.6 million); the number of salesworkers increased by almost one-half (from 3.8 million to 5.5 million); and the number of clerical workers doubled (from 7.6 million to 15.2 million). The number of professional and technical employees, however, almost *tripled* (from 4.5 million to 12.8 million) during that period.

Professionals bring to the corporation not one but multiple loyalties. Traditionally, management has demanded the exclusive allegiance of an employee. As the U.S. Supreme Court put it in 1953, in a decision that is becoming as outmoded as the manual typewriter, "There is no more important cause for discharge of an employee than disloyalty to the employer." The professional takes a different view. He (or she) says he must share his loyalty to the company with loyalty to society and his profession.

Dr. Frank von Hippel of Princeton University points to the code of the National Society of Professional Engineers, which states that the engineer "will use his knowledge and skill for the advancement of human welfare." When this duty brings the engineer into conflict with the demands of an employer, the code instructs him to "regard his duty to the public welfare as paramount."

When Marvin Murray, an engineer employed by Microform Data Systems in California, alleged that a new computer console developed by the company failed to meet the state safety codes, he voiced his objections even though management did not want to hear them. He was fired. He went to court and last year was awarded damages by the Superior Court in Santa Clara.

Although Mr. Murray fared better than do most dissidents in court, his willingness to challenge management typifies a growing tendency in the ranks of engineers and scientists. One result is to reduce the unilateral character of management decisions. Another is to reduce the speed and ease of decision making.

Professionals are more interested in effectiveness than in efficiency. They prefer to see an employer corporation doing the right thing inefficiently than the almost right or wrong thing efficiently.

In 1972 three engineers who had worked on the development of the San Francisco Bay Area Rapid Transit System lost their jobs when, after plans had been approved and the work had got under way, they disclosed information about safety defects in the braking system to members of the BART Board of Directors. No executive steeped in the traditional management culture would question management's decision in this case. On the other hand, professionals would.

In fact, among professionals there is a growing conviction that actions of the sort taken by the BART engineers are not only permissible but obligatory. In 1975, an ad hoc committee of the American Association for the Advancement of Science reported on the changing requirements of scientific freedom and responsibility. The committee concluded that more than a right is involved in the release of facts that are in the public interest, regardless of timing. Experts possessing such information *should* release it, the committee stated, "even though they might prefer to remain silent."

This philosophy is incompatible with the textbook philosophy of management control, with its corollaries of secrecy and obedience once the organization commits itself to a course. It destroys the notion of competition and the pursuit of profit as a "game" with rules that must be honored by all participants. Whatever its positive implications for the public interest, it means that, at least in the short run, corporations sometimes will find it harder to meet budgeted costs and deadlines.

Professionals reject the notion of total commitment to the enterprise. They consider after-hours activities as strictly their own affair. Louis V. McIntire, a veteran chemist employed by Du Pont Co. in Orange, Texas, was fired after writing (with his wife) a novel satirizing corporate management. Soon after publication of the novel, Du Pont fired him.

Mr. McIntire claims the discharge was in retaliation for his book and is suing his former employer in federal district court. (Du Pont declines to comment on the reasons for his dismissal.) While the discharge meets with approval among many traditional managers, many of Mr. McIntire's colleagues in the American Chemical Society have expressed support for him. (The society's weekly magazine, incidentally, frequently cites employers for "unprofessional dismissal.")

"Where it is a duty to worship the sun," said Viscount Morley, "it is pretty sure to be a crime to examine the laws of heat." For the traditional manager, the corporation is the sun, and there is such a duty. But for the professional there is no sun to worship, unless possibly it be the scientific method.

QUESTIONS

1. David Ewing's article focuses on the multiple loyalties of professionals working for corporations and the impact these loyalties have on corporate managerial decision making. What effects does Ewing see from such multiple loyalties? Did the New Jersey Supreme Court recognize these effects in *Pierce v. Ortho*? Should only professional engineers and scientists maintain such multiple loyalties? Should the concept of the "professional executive" or "professional manager" be applied so as to foster such multiple loyalties in managers? Are managers professionals? What distinguishes managers from other recognized professionals, such as physicians and attorneys?

2. Do you favor a legally implied "discharge for cause" standard for professionals but not for others within the corporate organization? Do you favor such a standard for discharge for all corporate employees regardless of status? How would you define a "discharge for good cause"? Explain. Give examples of discharges for cause.

3. If the law were to protect all employees against unjust discharge, to what remedies should the wrongfully discharged employee be entitled? Should he or she be entitled to reinstatement to the job in addition to damages? Should damages be reduced by any earnings from subsequent employment? Explain.

Institutionalizing Ethics

Many trade and professional associations employ ethical codes as a means of self-regulation. These industry codes are frequently suggested as an alternative to government regulation. In fact, many trade and professional association codes of ethics are developed in cooperation with government. Violations may result in government sanctions. For example, a lawyer may be disbarred for violating the bar association's Code of Professional Responsibility. However, most business managers are not regulated by an industrywide code of ethics in the same way that other professionals are. Hence, many individual companies have developed their own ethical standards.

In 1978, researchers at Southern Methodist University launched a study of a representative sample of U.S. corporations. Its 1980 report analyzed the ethical policy statements of 174 corporations. It found that most statements were brief, with almost half running five pages or less. Almost all were concerned with internal standards regulating the day-to-day operations of a corporation, its officers, and its employees (such as the use of the company name by employees). The second most common topic was compliance with U.S. laws. Most of the corporations had statements regarding their relationships to customers, suppliers, and foreign governments and societies. Fewer of them had statements concerning relationships to U.S. society and employees. Over half the corporations had statements on specific issues such as bribes, gifts and payments to or from government officials, customers, and suppliers.[2]

The policy statement of the Cummins Engine Company of Columbus, Indiana is more detailed than most. It contains both a general statement of the company's ethical standards and directives regarding specific practices such as questionable payments, financial representations, and supplier selection. The document is too long to be reproduced in its entirety. The following excerpt contains the Company's general statement of ethical standards and outlines the procedures followed by the Company in applying its standards.

 **Cummins Engine Company Practice***

Subject: Ethical Standards

There is much discussion in many circles today about ethical standards in U.S. corporations. The following discussion and policies elaborate on our traditional policy in order to provide personal guidance and to establish procedures for problem resolution. This practice is corporate in scope.

Practice

A. For Cummins, ethics rests on a fundamental belief in people's diginity and decency. Our most basic ethical standard is to show respect for those whose lives we affect and to treat them as we would expect them to treat us if our positions were reversed. This kind of respect implies that we must:

1. Obey the law.

* Cummins Engine Company. Reprinted with permission.

2. Be honest—present the facts fairly and accurately.

3. Be fair—give everyone appropriate consideration.

4. Be concerned—care about how Cummins' actions affect others and try to make those effects as beneficial as possible.

5. Be courageous—treat others with respect even when it means losing business. (It seldom does. Over the long haul, people trust and respect this kind of behavior and wish more of our institutions embodied it.)

B. The reason for such behavior is that, in the long run, nothing else works. If economies and societies do not operate in this way, the whole machinery begins to collapse. No corporation can long survive in situations where employees, creditors and communities don't trust each other. Since a corporation lives by

[2] Foundation of the Southwestern Graduate School of Banking, *A Study of Corporate Ethical Policy Statements 6–7*, (Dallas: Southern Methodist University, 1980).

society's consent, it must plan on earning and keeping that consent for the duration. Successes we have today—in securing sales, completing negotiations, obtaining credit, enlisting employee loyalties—are in major part made possible by the fact that others have learned to expect that Cummins will deal with them fairly. What we do today will maintain or undermine that legacy.

C. Our aim is that Cummins—its individual members, each of its distributors, and their people—all be known worldwide as trustworthy in all respects. "In all respects" is important. We can't operate by one set of standards internally and by another set externally. We can't say one thing and do another. Our ethical standards shouldn't tolerate split behavior.

D. On numerous occasions the Company has reiterated its commitment to fundamental ethical standards. There are, however, reasons for more specific statements:

  1. As we grow larger, we have to set down in writing those standards which have informally guided our action in the past.
  2. Not only do we have to make these statements formal and written, but they must be expressed in policy statements to ensure that all management employees have easy access to them.
  3. Finally, general statements are important for setting the tone and character of a company, but specific policies are required in addition to make the intent of the general principles clear to each person.

E. Accordingly, all employees are expected to understand and subscribe to the following general standards of corporate behavior.

1. Cummins Engine Company, Inc. competes on a straight commercial basis; if something more is required, the Company is not interested.
2. Cummins employees do nothing in search of business that they should not reveal willingly and publicly to *any* other member of the Cummins family or to *any* government official in any land.
3. Cummins neither practices nor condones any activity that will not stand the most rigorous public ethical examination.
4. If an employee has *any* doubt about the appropriateness or morality of *any* act, it should not be done. If an employee believes that there is a conflict between what his or her supervisors expect and what corporate ethical standards require, the employee should raise the issue with the Corporate Responsibility Department. The Company is prepared to help any employee resolve a moral dilemma and to ensure that no employee is put at a career disadvantage because of his or her *willingness* to raise a question about a corporate practice or *unwillingness* to pursue a course of action which seems inappropriate or morally dubious.

Responsibility

A. In order to administer these general standards the following corporate-wide processes have been developed and agreed upon by the various Groups of the Company. Ethical practices adopted will be published in the Cummins Practice Manual, circulated annually to all exempt employees, and updated as needed. During the second quarter of each year each Group, Division, and Department head should review these practices with his or her staff and should consider whether revisions or additions are appropriate. Revisions and/or additions to these practices will take effect when approved by each Group head and the President, and signed by the Chairman. Corporate Responsibility will continue to coordinate this process. Corporate Auditing will be responsible for auditing compliance with these practices and will keep such records and make such reports as are required by the various practices.

B. Each Group, Division, and Department head is responsible for ensuring that employees within his or her area, including new employees, fully understand and comply with these practices. Each Group, Division, and Department head is also responsible for dealing with cases of non-compliance. North American Divisional Vice Presidents should review these practices with all Distributor Principals in their territories during the second quarter of each year to make sure that Cummins Distributors understand the standards under which Cummins operates. Heads of International Areas or Regional Managers should review these practices with all Distributor Principals in their territories at contract review time.

C. All employees of the Company are responsible for following the provisions of this practice.

Counsel

The Chairman should be consulted for any advice needed concerning this practice.

The author of the following article advocates a change in corporate structure to factor ethical considerations into corporate policy making at the highest level of management, the board of directors.

 **Institutionalizing Ethics on Corporate Boards***

Will Codes Help Ethical Behavior?

Many professional associations have not found ethics so subjective or so fuzzy that they were afraid to set up their own ethical standards. The American Institute of Certified Public Accountants describes its code of professional ethics "as a voluntary assumption of self-discipline above and beyond the requirements of the law." It further states that in general usage the word ethics means "the philosophy of human conduct, with emphasis on right and wrong, which are moral questions." The AICPA then cites many examples and applications of ethics in the accounting and auditing professions.

The American Psychological Association drew up its ethical code for psychologists from practical problem cases drawn from professional-client relationships.

---

* Purcell, 36 *Review of Social Economy* 41 (1978). Reprinted with permission of the publisher.

The American Bar Association (1971) has a detailed code and canons. Of course, we know that Watergate brought the legal profession into serious self-questioning and subjected it to public skepticism; yet it is also true that some Watergate lawyers have been disbarred.

Especially, it is not easy to draw up an ethical code for doing international business among countries with very different values and customs. Yet the Organization for Economic Cooperation and Development (OECD) has recently drawn up such a code. Time will tell how much it helps.

It is important to stress, however, that ethical codes are not a panacea, even when they can be enforced on association members, something not too common. Though they often merely relate the profession to individual clients rather than to the collective public, codes nonetheless can help clarify ethical thinking and encourage ethical behavior.

* * * * *

Ethics versus the Law

Some people say ethical motivation and profit motivation are incompatible. Therefore: "forget about ethics and social responsibility, just talk about the law." Laws are necessary, of course. The Civil Rights Act of 1964, to take one example, was absolutely essential. But there is a danger in all this. Some years ago, Douglass Brown's presidential address for the Industrial Relations Research Association (1971) warned that excessive legalism was harming industrial relations.

We now find the field of equal employment opportunity going this same route of legalism and litigiousness. We cannot have laws, government agencies, lawyers and courts involved in every management decision. The country would soon be bogged down by a legal bureaucracy and could ultimately produce a contempt for law. We

may be seeing something of this now in the medical malpractice mess.

Furthermore, many management decisions involve social issues about which no laws provide guidance and probably no viable laws can be written. What then? Social awareness and conscience can be the only guides.

* * * * *

The Need for Corporate Ethics Specialists

. . . Is it not time to appoint a small number of directors and also perhaps officers to be the corporations' ethical "devil's advocates" or better yet, their ethical "angel's advocates"?

We should institutionalize ethical expertise at the board of directors and top management levels, perhaps focusing on one director but with responsibilities shared by a committee of the board. These director/ethical advocates need not be philosophers in the field of ethics, but they should keep up to date on the extensive literature of ethics as applied to business. A number of companies such as General Mills and General Electric already have public responsibility committees. Could not such committees also take on an explicitly ethical function? According to Fred T. Allen (1975) of Pitney Bowes: "A moral dimension should be added to the board's criteria for judging a CEO (chief executive officer) and his principal subordinates.

About 28 large companies now have on their boards of directors committees that are explicitly designated as ethics committees: [Among them are] the Norton Company of Massachusetts, the world's largest manufacturer of abrasives, and the Consolidated Natural Gas Company, Headquartered in Pittsburgh.

The director/ethical advocates proposed here might also include corporate officers, perhaps the general counsel, as suggested by William Gossett, former President of the American Bar Association and Vice-President of Ford Motor Company. Such an appointment admittedly would be controversial. One top management team of a major corporation warns: "Any officer with marketing, financial, legal, staff or whatever responsibilities can scarcely be expected to step back in complete objectivity and to perform the role you envisage."

They may be right. But a firm could well have ethical advocates on its board if not among its officers. However, there is no neat formula here. Much depends on the top management personalities of a given company, their management styles, the structure of the corporation and related characteristics.

A principal function of the ethics committee would be to identify generic questions of an ethical nature that should be asked routinely along with the usual legal, financial and marketing questions. For example, a strategic planner might ask, "If we take certain actions, what would our market share be and will we run afoul of antitrust laws? What would our discounted cash flow be?"

The ethics advocates might want to know how a given decision will affect the rights of employees versus the rights of the corporation. Or will an action help or hurt the long-run general welfare of the cities or countries (South Africa, for instance) where our plants are located? Or, how shall the firm balance the public's right to know about minority hiring with the company's right to keep competitive information confidential? Or will a new product help or hurt the environment, the conservation of energy, the quality of life or the safety of consumers?

The corporate ethics advocates would need to be socially sensitive enough to phrase such questions in generic terms but still keep them sufficiently practical and thus manageable for specific top management decisions. . . . They might help develop an ethical code for their company and encourage ethics seminars for top, middle and lower managers in their mid-careers, when their experience will lead them to see more clearly the ethical implications of their decisions. They might encourage the study of ethical principles and cases in schools of business administration, some of which could perhaps help them and their industry with the ethical problems that they face.

If the committee is entirely composed of corporate officers, its secretary will need to be a strong and able manager who has the backing of the chief executive officer. The CEO will be a prime force in the success or failure of the ethical advocacy idea. But a board committee is better.

The committee and its secretary should expect to encounter strong resistance. They will have to win over operating managers—no small assignment when ethical considerations compete with immediate profits or personal power. Their policies may have to persuade managers, not by talking ethics, but by focusing on long-range business problems. (For example, an inner-city plant may have to hire and promote minorities if it is going to have any work force at all. Furthermore, if it makes a consumer product, the inner-city could provide an important market.) But at times the ethics committee should also appeal to a sense of ethics, because operating managers may turn out to be more receptive than one might expect. In any case, the problems of the ethics advocates may be only a little more difficult or different from the problems of any other corporate officers, such as the equal employment director, who has to deal with managers in the field. At the start, at least, the main function of the ethics committee will be to ask questions rather than to impose answers.

QUESTIONS

1. Do you favor ethical codes for industry? If so, would you prefer a code dealing with general precepts or one delineating specific practices? Would you expect an ethical code to help executives *(a)* raise the ethical level of their industry, *(b)* define the limits of acceptable conduct, or *(c)* refuse unethical requests? Or do you think that such a code is incapable of changing executive conduct in these areas? Do you feel that people would violate the code whenever they thought they could avoid detection?

2. How should ethical codes be enforced? Would such a code be easy to enforce? Should the code be enforced *(a)* at the company level, *(b)* by a combined group of industry executives and members of the community, *(c)* at the industry level by either a trade association or a group of industry executives, or *(d)* by a government agency? What are some advantages and disadvantages of each of the above forms of enforcement?

3. What are the merits and demerits of the ethical advocacy idea proposed by Purcell? Would Purcell's proposal amount to mere tokenism? Would the proposal remove ethical issues from consideration by shifting them onto specialists—convert what is everybody's business into the business of a few specialists? On the other hand, would not the institutionalization of corporate ethics specialists be just as desirable as the institutionalization of corporate functional experts in other areas, such as law, finance, marketing, public relations and research?

CORPORATE SOCIAL RESPONSIBILITY

It has become fashionable in recent years to speak of the social responsibility of the corporation as an institution. Concerns relating to social responsibility are frequently intertwined with concerns about individual ethics. For example, assume that a company manufactures a food additive that is known to cause cancer. The Food and Drug Administration prohibits the sale of the substance in the United States, but it is legal in Mexico. Should the company continue to manufacture the substance and distribute it in Mexico? Your answer to this question will depend upon your view of the role of the corporation in society and upon your personal values. Your personal ethics will influence how you view the social responsibility of corporations.

Some experts assert that a corporation's sole responsibility is to maximize earnings, provided the corporation abides by the law. They argue that the corporation cannot be separated from the shareholders who own it. All nonprofit activities in which the corporation engages and all opportunities for profit which the corporation forgoes diminish corporate profits that would otherwise accrue to the shareholders in the form of dividends or increases in the value of their shares. Thus, the use of corporate resources for any activity other than profit maximization may be viewed as forcing the shareholder to subsidize the ideals of corporate management.

Historically, the corporation has not been regarded as a profit maximizer. Initially each corporation received a charter from the legislature and the charter frequently included such privileges as government-guaranteed monopolies. It was granted on the theory that the corporation was designed to serve a specific public purpose, such as the operation of a canal or a turnpike. Thus, the corporation's function was to meet a mixture of public and private needs.

During the late nineteenth century the corporation came to be viewed as an institution operated solely for the benefit of its shareholders. Profit maximization came to be seen as its only function. This change in attitude coincided with a period of major industrial expansion and economic development spearheaded by corporations. Consequently, corporations devoted exclusively to profit maximization were seen as consistent with the national interest.

The law's treatment of corporate activity reflects changing perceptions of the role of the corporation. The earliest U.S. corporations were chartered by special legislative action. Then, beginning in 1795, state statutes began to provide for general incorporation without special legislative charter. The first such statutes limited general incorporation procedures to enterprises serving a public purpose. In 1795 North Carolina provided such procedures for companies digging canals. In 1799 Massachusetts established similar procedures for companies operating aqueducts.

In 1837 Connecticut became the first state to adopt procedures permitting incorporation for any lawful purpose. Other states were slow to follow. New York did not adopt such procedures until 1866. However, the drive for economic development during the latter half of the nineteenth century furnished the necessary incentive for wide-scale reform of the incorporation process. By 1900 almost all jurisdictions prohibited incorporation by legislative charter and provided general incorporation procedures.

Thus, the method of establishing corporations changed to reflect society's changed perceptions of their role. With the corporation serving exclusively private purposes, there was no need for legislatures to consider each incorporation individually.

The profit maximization view of corporate purpose also influenced the development of the law controlling managerial discretion. The most famous case involved a dispute between the Dodge brothers and Henry Ford.

The Ford Motor Company was organized in 1903 with a capital stock of $150,000. By 1916 its surplus of assets over liabilities and capital stock totaled almost $112 million. Ford paid dividends of 5 percent per month to its shareholders. It also paid special dividends which had totaled $41 million through 1915. In 1916 Henry Ford announced that the company would cease paying special dividends indefinitely and would use its profits to expand its plant, produce more cars, and lower its prices. The declared ambition of Henry Ford was "to spread the benefits of this industrial system to the greatest possible number, to help them build up their lives and their homes."

The Dodge brothers were shareholders in Ford. They sued to prohibit the expansion and compel the further declaration of special dividends. The trial court granted the relief requested. The Michigan Supreme Court vacated the trial court's order enjoining the expansion, on the ground that the expansion was in the best interest of the company. The Supreme Court, however, affirmed the trial court's order that $19 million in dividends be paid, explaining:

> A business corporation is organized and carried on primarily for the profit of the stockholders. The powers of the directors are to be employed for that end. The discretion of directors is to be exercised on the choice of means to attain that end, and does not extend to a change in the end itself, to the reduction of profits, or to the non-distribution of profits among stockholders in order to devote them to other purposes.[3]

The *Ford* decision did not serve as a complete bar to nonprofit corporate activities. Such activities were not set aside where they were reasonable and in the best interests of the corporation. For example, a corporation's contribution to a charity could be justified as improving its image and thereby promoting goodwill. Similarly, numerous corporate grants to educational institutions have been justified as designed to insure a sufficient supply of trained employees.

Constrained by the profit maximization view of corporate purpose, courts and corporate managers grasped for farfetched justifications for upholding corporate nonprofit activities as valid exercises of business judgment. A particularly interesting case is *Shlensky v. Wrigley,* in which shareholders challenged the decision made by the Chicago Cubs management not to install lights in Wrigley Field.[4] Philip K. Wrigley, the president and majority shareholder of the club, considered baseball to be a day game and believed that night games ruined its flavor. He also expressed concern that night baseball would contribute to the decay of the surrounding neighborhood. The court accepted the "decay of neighborhood" argument. It upheld the decision of the Chicago Cubs management on the ground that neighborhood decay could result in reduced attendance.

In recent decades many business relationships have been depersonalized by such developments as automation, mass production, and large-scale methods of distribution. Consequently, many people now believe that the corporation must serve not only the interests of its shareholders but also the well-being of employees, consumers, suppliers, creditors, and the community. This view is shared by many modern managers. The Committee for Economic Development has aptly summarized it:

> The modern professional manager . . . regards himself, not as an owner disposing of personal property as he sees fit, but as a trustee balancing the interests of many diverse participants and constituents

---

[3] *Dodge v. Ford Motor Co.,* 204 Mich. 459, 170 N.W. 668 (1919).
[4] 96 Ill. App. 2d 173, 237 N.E. 2d 776 (1968).

in the enterprise, whose interests sometimes conflict with those of others. The chief executive of a large corporation has the problem of reconciling the demands of employees for more wages and improved benefit plans, customers for lower prices and greater values, vendors for higher prices, government for more taxes, stockholders for higher dividends and greater capital appreciation—all within a framework that will be constructive and acceptable to society.[5]

The law has also changed to accommodate the changing view of the role of the corporation in society. The modern view is that corporate nonprofit activity is justified for reasons of public policy. The New Jersey Supreme Court expressed the underlying rationale as follows:

> When the wealth of the nation was primarily in the hands of individuals, they discharged their responsibilities as citizens by donating freely for charitable purposes. With the transfer of most of the wealth to corporate hands and the imposition of heavy burdens of individual taxation, they have been unable to keep pace with increased philanthropic needs. They have therefore, with justification, turned to corporations to assume the modern obligations of good citizenship in the same manner as humans do.[6]

Many states have amended their corporation statutes to authorize nonprofit activities. In these states such activities of management are shielded from shareholder attack unless the activities are arbitrary or in bad faith.

Corporate Social Responsibility and the Individual Employee

The discussion so far has focused on the corporation's responsibility to society. However, the corporation's conception of its social responsibility is formulated and implemented by individuals. Hence, it is helpful to consider the question of corporate social responsibility from the perspective of the individual employee. What responsibility does an employee have with regard to the corporation's conduct?

In the following case, *United States v. Park*, the responsibility of the individual employee is presented. In *Park*, the employee is the company's chief executive officer. The case illustrates the evolving criminal liability of corporate executives. The *Park* decision reflects a serious current philosophical and legal debate regarding the accountability (and liability) of individuals for the actions they take or do not take while serving in positions of authority.

---

[5] Committee for Economic Development, *Social Responsibilities of Business Corporations* 22 (1971).

[6] *A. P. Smith Mfg. Co. v. Barlow.* 13 N.J. 148, 98 A.2d 581 (1953).

United States v. Park

421 U.S. 658 (1975)

The United States (government) brought a criminal action against Acme Markets, Inc. (Acme) and John Park (respondent). The government charged them with the unsanitary storage of food in Acme's Baltimore warehouse in violation of the Federal Food, Drug, and Cosmetics Act. Acme pleaded guilty, but Park contested the charge.

Park was Acme's chief executive officer. The Food and Drug Administration (FDA) advised him by letter of rodent infestation at the warehouse. According to trial testimony, Park functioned by delegating "normal operating duties," including sanitation, but retained "certain things, which [were] the big, broad, principles of the operation of the company." Park testified that although all of Acme's employees were in a sense under his general direction, the company had an "organizational structure for responsibilities for certain functions" according to which different phases of its operation were assigned to individuals who, in turn, had staff and departments under them. Park testified that he identified those responsible for sanitation and was assured that the Baltimore division vice president "was investigating the situation immediately and would be taking corrective action and would be preparing a summary of the corrective action to reply to the letter." The jury found Park guilty and fined him $250. The court of appeals reversed. That court viewed the government as arguing that "the conviction may be predicated solely upon a showing that . . . Park was the president of the offending corporation." Then the court stated that as "a general proposition, some act of commission or omission is an essential element of every crime." The Supreme Court reversed the court of appeals decision.

Chief Justice Burger

The rule that corporate employees who have "a responsible share in the furtherance of the transaction which the statute outlaws" are subject to the criminal provisions of the Act was not formulated in a vacuum. . . . Cases under the Federal Food and Drugs Act of 1906 reflected the view both that knowledge or intent were not required to be proved in prosecutions under its criminal provisions, and that responsible corporate agents could be subjected to the liability thereby imposed. . . . Moreover, the principle had been recognized that a corporate agent, through whose act, default, or omission the corporation committed a crime, was himself guilty individually of that crime. The principle had been applied whether or not the crime required "consciousness of wrongdoing," and it had been applied not only to those corporate agents who themselves committed the criminal act, but also to those who by virtue of their managerial positions or other similar relation to the actor could be deemed responsible for its commission.

In the latter class of cases, the liability of managerial officers did not depend on their knowledge of, or personal participation in, the act made criminal by the statute. Rather, where the statute under which they were prosecuted dispensed with "consciousness of wrongdoing," an omission or failure to act was deemed a sufficient basis for a responsible corporate agent's liability. It was enough in such cases that by virtue of the relationship he bore to the corporation, the agent had the power to have prevented the act complained of. . . .

The rationale of the interpretation given the Act . . . , as holding criminally accountable the persons whose failure to exercise the authority and supervisory responsibility reposed in them by the business organization resulted in the violation complained of, has been confirmed in our . . . cases. Thus, the Court has reaffirmed the proposition that "the public interest in the purity of its food is so great as to warrant the imposition of the highest standard of care on distributors." . . . In order to make "distributors of food the strictest censors of their merchandise," . . . the Act punishes "neglect where the law requires care, or inaction where it imposes a duty." "The accused, if he does not will the violation, usually is in a position to prevent it with no more care than society might reasonably expect and no more exertion than it might reasonably exact from one who assumed his responsibilities." Similarly, . . . the Courts of Appeals have recognized that those corporate agents vested with the responsibility, and power commensurate with that responsibility, to devise whatever measures are necessary to ensure compliance with the Act bear a "responsible rela-

tionship" to, or have a "responsible share" in, violations.

Thus . . . the cases . . . reveal that in providing sanctions which reach and touch the individuals who execute the corporate mission—and this is by no means necessarily confined to a single corporate agent or employee—the Act imposes not only a positive duty to seek out and remedy violations when they occur but also, and primarily, a duty to implement measures that will insure that violations will not occur. The requirements of foresight and vigilance imposed on responsible corporate agents are beyond question demanding, and perhaps onerous, but they are no more stringent than the public has a right to expect of those who voluntarily assume positions of authority in business enterprises whose services and products affect the health and well-being of the public that supports them. . . .

The Act does not . . . make criminal liability turn on "awareness of some wrongdoing" or "conscious fraud." The duty imposed by Congress on responsible corporate agents is, we emphasize, one that requires the highest standard of foresight and vigilance, but the Act, in its criminal aspect, does not require that which is objectively impossible. The theory upon which responsible corporate agents are held criminally accountable for "causing" violations of the Act permits a claim that a defendant was "powerless" to prevent or correct the violation to "be raised defensively at a trial on the merits." If such a claim is made, the defendant has the burden of coming forward with evidence, but this does not alter the Government's ultimate burden of proving beyond a reasonable doubt the defendant's guilt, including his power, in light of the duty imposed by the Act, to prevent or correct the prohibited condition. Congress has seen fit to enforce the accountability of responsible corporate agents dealing with products which may affect the health of consumers by penal sanctions cast in rigorous terms, and the obligation of the courts is to give them effect so long as they do not violate the Constitution.

We cannot agree with the Court of Appeals that . . . the Government had the burden of establishing "wrongful action." . . . The concept of a "responsible relationship" to, or a "responsible share" in, a violation of the Act indeed imports some measure of blameworthiness; but it is equally clear that the Government establishes a prima facie case when it introduces evidence sufficient to warrant a finding . . . that the defendant had, by reason of his position in the corporation, responsibility and authority either to prevent in the first instance,

or promptly to correct, the violation complained of, and that he failed to do so. The failure thus to fulfill the duty imposed by the interaction of the corporate agent's authority and the statute furnishes a sufficient causal link. The considerations which prompted the imposition of this duty, and the scope of the duty provide the measure of culpability.

* * * * *

We are satisifed that the Act imposes the highest standard of care and permits conviction of responsible corporate officials who, in light of this standard of care, have the power to prevent or correct violations of its provisions.

CASE QUESTIONS

1. Was Park found guilty simply because he was the chief executive officer of Acme? Explain.

2. What actions did Park take to alleviate the problem at the Baltimore warehouse? What should he have done? What are the lessons and implications of the *Park* decision for organizational communication structures and decision-making processes?

3. You are a buyer employed by Acme. On two visits to the Baltimore warehouse you notice the presence of rat infestation. You advise the vice president for the Baltimore division of the problem. The vice president does nothing. Are you legally or ethically obligated to advise the president?

ALTERNATIVE APPROACHES

Corporate social responsibility advocates have offered a variety of proposals to encourage socially responsible corporate performance. Reform proposals have called for the federal chartering of large corporations, changes in corporate governance, and corporate disclosure to assure greater accountability.

Federal Chartering of Corporations

In the 1970s, advocates of corporate social responsibility, led by Ralph Nader, urged that corporate charters be dispensed by the federal government as distinct from state corporate charters to tighten the government's grip on corporate actions.[7] Several bills were introduced in Congress to this effect, but none was passed into law. Although cries for federal chartering of corporations have subsided, the following article points out that the demand often resurfaces at times of public dissatisfaction with business.

A Case for Federal Chartering of Corporations*

Early Efforts at Federal Chartering

Serious discussion of federal chartering seems to occur whenever public concern mounts about the concentration of corporate economic and political power. In the past, the result of the agitation has been the adoption of reform legislation dealing with the particular problem, rather than any more comprehensive remedy.

In the 1880s agitation for federal incorporation was a factor leading to the adoption of the Sherman Anti-Trust Act. The enactment of that measure did not quiet the debate for long. Demands for federal incorporation resumed in the early 1900s as part of various muckraking crusades. Theodore Roosevelt became a major spokesmen for federal incorporation, calling for federal chartering in a 1905 message to Congress:

> Experience has shown conclusively that it is useless to try to get any adequate regulation and supervision of the great corporations by state action. Such regulation and supervision can only be effectively exercised by a sovereign whose jurisdiction is co-extensive with the field of work of corporations—that is, by the National government.

During the period from 1903 to 1914, twenty bills were introduced in Congress

proposing increased federal regulation in the form of federal licensing or federal incorporation. Although none of this legislation became law, many other corporate reform measures were adopted during the period. Then, the interest in federal incorporation subsided with the advent of World War I and did not reappear as a significant movement until the 1930s.

The Depression rekindled thoughts of corporate reform. Senator Joseph O'Mahoney sponsored the cause for federal chartering, and his subcommittee held extensive hearings in 1937 and 1938 on a bill to establish a federal incorporation law. The coming of another war dispelled these efforts, but the period produced extensive reform legislation, including all the federal securities laws.

Current Advocates of Federal Chartering

The contemporary advocates of federal incorporation again perceive a need to regulate the vast power exercised by the managers of large corporations. To some, management's power is seen as a threat to the stockholders of the corporation which has not been constrained by the rituals of corporate democracy. Others see corporate power exercised by management even more threatening because of its potential impact on society as a whole.

In the vanguard of the modern reformers urging federal corporation law is Ralph

---

* Schwartz, 31 *The Business Lawyer* 1125, 1126–28 (1976). Reprinted by permission.

---

[7] R. Nader & M. Green, *Constitutionalizing the Corporation: The Case for Federal Chartering of Giant Corporations* (1976).

Nader. Mr. Nader urges establishment of a Federal Chartering Agency to which major corporations engaged in interstate commerce would be required to apply for a charter. That charter would provide for increased corporate democracy and increased personal liability for managements. It would set forth strict antitrust requirements and elaborate disclosure standards regarding the economic, social, and environmental impacts of the corporation.

Other suggestions for reform emphasize varying specifics that might be covered by a new statute. Joel Henning, for instance, would attempt to confine industrial concentration by limiting corporations to a stated percentage of the relevant market, and Professor John Flynn has suggested wider employee ownership and participation, largely for the purpose of achieving a redistribution of wealth. Professor Willard Mueller emphasizes substantially increased public disclosure of corporate affairs. Professor John Kenneth Galbraith favors restructure of the governance of corporations by replacing the board of directors with a public board of auditors. Morton Mintz and Jerry Cohen favor federal chartering in order to achieve a broad range of public goals.

Another critical tack has been pursued by Lewis Gilbert, who endorsed federal chartering as long ago as 1937 when he testified before the O'Mahoney Committee. Now, as then, Mr. Gilbert advocates strengthening the democratic process within the corporation in order to bolster the position of stockholders. . . .

All the critics share a conviction that federal legislation and the elimination of charter mongering is essential to the achievement of their goals. For various reasons, they see corporate power and management power as threatening to a democratic society. They believe that our existing system of allowing a market place for corporation law, in which the managers alone do the shopping, contributes to this threat. I share many of these perceptions about the nature of the corporations and its impact. Along with the benefits that much of our society has enjoyed from corporate activity, those corporate activities also create or exacerbate a wide range of society's problems. I believe that for the protection of both investors and the broader community, a federal law of corporations, preempting much of state law, is part of the answer.

Changes in Corporate Governance

As noted in the previous article, some of the reform proposals associated with the federal chartering of corporations have involved changes in the governance structure of the corporation. Critics of corporate performance have called for appointing outsiders to corporate boards of directors, filling board seats from constituent groups (employees, women, consumers, and minorities, along with stockholders), and equipping boards with private staffs that are beyond management's control. Most of these proposals have focused on reforming the board of directors. However, the concept of changing corporate governance systems goes even further in the following reading.

Where The Law Ends*

The corporation, like any modern complex organization and, indeed, like the entire social order viewed as a whole, is built upon an elaborate network of institutional roles, or offices. This division of functions—into legislators, prosecutors, judges, juries, in the broader social system; into directors, chief executive officers, vice-presidents, project managers, in the corporate world—involves specifying such matters as who is to develop and evaluate what data, what sorts of things are to be considered by whom, and who has the authority (preliminarily and finally) to make what classes of decision.

In some measure, the aim of such systems is to provide predictability and stability of organizational performance in the face of constant changeover of personnel. If the system is working well, it has purely procedural virtues—that those with a problem will know where it should be taken for redress. But it is important to remember that such vital "procedural" matters as which threshold questions will pass into the decisional system, and how each of them will be defined—matters inseparable from how the organizational roles are established—have an obvious influence on outcome: what the organization's final decision will be. Thus, it should not surprise us that, at least in the public arena, one of the important ways in which we influence the direction of our society is through structural and procedural changes in the government. Consider the Environmental Protection Act† for a contemporary example of policy being implemented through the design of decisional procedures. That is to say,

the act does not legislate particular substantive outcomes—for example, that all pollution into Lake Erie must stop at once, or that companies engaged in timber cutting over and above some defined amount shall be subject to a fine. Contemplating environmental problems where no such clear-cut legislative remedies now seem advisable, the act proceeds more cautiously, and perhaps more sophisticatedly: It seeks to affect decisions by shaping the structure of the decision process itself. Section 202 creates a Council on Environmental Quality; it places the Council in the Executive Office of the President; it provides for three members to be appointed by the President with the advice and consent of the Senate; Section 204 specifies the "duty and function" of the Council as:

1. to assist and advise the President in the preparation of the Environmental Quality Report . . . ;
2. to gather timely and authoritative information concerning the conditions and trends in the quality of the environment . . . , to analyze and interpret such information . . . , and to compile and submit to the President studies relating to such conditions and trends;
3. to review and appraise the various programs and activities of the Federal Government in the light of the policy set forth in . . . this Act for the purpose of determining the extent to which such programs and activities are contributing to the achievement of such policy, and to make recommendations to the President with respect thereto;
4. to develop and recommend to the President national policies to foster and promote the improvement of environmental quality . . . ;
5. to conduct investigations, studies, surveys, research, and analyses relating to ecological systems and environmental quality;

---

* C. Stone, *Where the Law Ends* 122–124 (1975). Reprinted by permission.

† This statute is discussed further in Chapter 18.—Au.

6. to document and define changes in the natural environment . . . ; and to accumulate necessary data and other information for a continuing analysis of these changes or trends and an interpretation of their underlying causes;
7. to report at least once each year to the President on the state and condition of the environment; and
8. to make and furnish such studies, reports thereon, and recommendations with respect to matters of policy, and legislation as the President may request.

The act operates, in other words, not by saying—at least in the first instance—that this or that can or cannot be done, but by saying that, whatever outcome is arrived at, it must be channeled through such-and-such a system, one designed to insure that certain types of facts have been gathered and considered, and that certain values have received their due weight.

Oddly, while the influencing of policy through mandatory structural and procedural requirements is commonplace in the design of public agencies, we only rarely and marginally use that approach where corporations—our "private governments"—are concerned. At present we leave it almost entirely up to the corporation to determine what offices it shall establish and how the functions of the various offices are to be spelled out. This is not to deny that the corporation's choices undoubtedly reflect, albeit indirectly, the pressures of the outside world. The passage of labor legislation, for example, may cause the corporation to create, after a period of time, a vice-president for labor relations. Social protests may bring about, amid much fanfare, the appointment of a vice-president for social policy. But when we rely on such indirect pressures, there is no reason to be confident that the corporation's response—the roles "it" chooses to set up, and the way "it" chooses to define them—will neatly conform to the socially ideal solution; anyone who feels that it will is taking too little account of the corporation's ability to buffer its core processes from the puny threats we strew about its environment.

We thus have to consider the possibility of impacting corporate behavior directly by, for example, mandating the addition of specified roles, for example, laying down by law that companies of a certain class *must* establish vice-presidents for environmental affairs, or vice-presidents for consumer affairs, and undertaking to establish—ourselves—the functions for these various roles so as to make them effective.

If, for example, we feel reasonably confident that computer-aided frauds like the Equity Funding scandal could be headed off if someone within the corporation were performing certain specific audit functions, might we require the corporations to establish the appropriate role, spelling out the desirable activity as part of the "job description" (and . . . making failure to abide by the specified functions an offense answerable to sources outside as well as inside the company)? Are there corporate problems of such a nature that it would be fruitful to mandate roles and role requirements for various positions in the organizational hierarchy? Could "graftings" of either sort "take," that is, would the balance of the corporation produce antibodies to reject or circumvent these alien intrusions?

Disclosure

The disclosure of corporate social responsibility undertakings has been suggested as a way of institutionalizing corporate social performance.

So far, several corporations in the United States have voluntarily instituted social reports. Only in France is social reporting required in the form of a legislatively mandated *bilan social* ("social balance sheet").

In the United States the Securities and Exchange Commission (SEC) has imposed requirements for limited social disclosure. These requirements stemmed from a petition submitted in 1971 by the Nadar Project on Corporate Responsibility and the Natural Resources Defense Council that the SEC hold hearings about requiring disclosure on corporate involvement in litigation over civil rights and environmental issues. The hearings were denied, but the SEC later imposed limited disclosure requirements on corporations involved in legal proceedings on the environment and equal employment opportunity. The denial of the National Resources Defense Council's petition resulted in litigation, and the SEC was ordered to hold public hearings regarding its authority to require disclosure of corporate social responsibility data. The outcome of the hearings was a refusal by the SEC to require further social disclosure, because the SEC found that the costs and burdens of such disclosure would be grossly disproportionate to the benefits it would bring to investors. The SEC's chilling tone strongly suggests its reluctance to be a conduit for change in this area. However, it conceded that social information might be economically significant to investors. Thus, it is arguably within the SEC's authority to require social disclosure to some extent.

Because France is the only nation that requires corporate social disclosure, the following excerpts illustrate what forms social disclosure can take.

The French Social Balance Sheet*

II Social Accounting

The French legislation is based upon the assumption that corporate social performance can be measured. The idea is not new to the United States or to France. American federal agencies have long required corporate gathering of what can be viewed as social information, and French management had already compiled a great deal of the information that the French balance sheet now requires. The innovation of social accounting, however, is its transformation of raw social statistics into a measurement of the social impacts of business actions on various environments. This transformation involves application of traditional financial accounting techniques to the social implications of corporate business actions in order to monitor what the corporation is doing in the area of social responsibility. This process, called the social audit in the United States, has as its unifying principle the qualification of the social efforts taken, or the social effects created, by a corporation in the pursuit of its business.

A social audit, or social balance sheet, necessarily includes some value judgments about social performance. Therefore, a means of comparing different aspects of a corporation's social performance is needed. Social accounting authorities suggest a

* *Blackburn and Newman,* 48 *Cincinnati Law Review* 972 (1981). Reprinted with permission of the publisher.

number of techniques, such as monetization (assignment of money values) of various social assets and liabilities, application of a cost-benefit analysis to determine the opportunity cost of various social programs, and the tabulation of points to measure positive or negative variations from a base performance fixed in different social areas.

The approach taken by the French legislation has been to assemble various indicators of social performance into social credits and debits, to measure them against each other, and then to compare the performance of one year with that of previous years. For example, the number of accidents at the plant in one year, a social debit, would be compared with those occurring during previous years. The legislation itself makes no attempt to give correlative values to different types of social performance in order to evaluate the allocation of resources in social efforts at any one time. This type of judgment is left to the recipients of the balance sheet, particularly the employee committee, which issues an opinion on each balance sheet. The legislation does not preclude more sophisticated systems of social accounting, however, and management and labor are free to modify the balance sheet as long as they fulfill the requirements of the legislated indicators.

The social balance sheet is intended to fulfill three functions. First, it is designed to be an informational tool, providing its recipients (the works committee, union representatives and shareholders) with data concerning the social performance of the plant. Second, it will form a basis for negotiation between labor and management on improving working conditions, including a mutual attempt at fixing a hierarchy of goals in the social environment of the plant. Third, the balance sheet is designed to further corporate planning of social programs. The pursuit of these goals undoubtedly

heightens the sensibility of management and individual employees to the social responsibility of the enterprise.

The social audit has been described as "an attempt to define the moving target called social responsibility." This characterization emphasizes the definitional requirements involved in the institution of a social audit. Before setting up a system for measuring the social impact of business actions on a given environment, the drafters must decide what impacts and business actions to measure, as well as which environments to consider. The parameters of social accounting are called the dimensions of the social audit.

The French Legislation

*　*　*　*　*

B. The contents of the social balance sheet. According to the text of the French legislation, the social balance sheet "sums up in a single document the principal numerical data that will facilitate an appraisal of the social situation of the plant, the recording of results achieved and the measurement of changes that have occurred during the preceding year and during the two years prior thereto." The legislation requires the compilation of information in seven general areas: employment, salary and benefits, health and safety, other conditions of work (such as organization and type of work performed), training, professional relations and "the living conditions of the employees and their families to the extent that these conditions depend upon the corporation." Implementing decrees and regulations issued by the Council of State and various ministries have afforded considerable specificity to these general categories. The Council of State has the power to determine the information required in the balance sheet for the whole enterprise and for each individual establishment. In order to accommodate differences in the social environments of the sectors of the economy, individual ministries have issued rulings (*arrêtés*) governing information to be included in the balance sheets of companies under their jurisdictions. The content requirements vary according to the level of the reporting body (enterprise or establishment), its size and the activity of the entity. The last factor allows the indicators of the balance sheet to reflect individual characteristics of the sector of industry in which a company operates. Ministries have either issued or are in the process of drafting rulings concerning industry and agriculture, commerce, and services, building and public works, land and air transport and shipbuilding.

It is noteworthy that the legislation requires only measurement of the workplace's internal social environment and not measurement of a corporation's effects on the external environment, such as the amount of pollution generated by an industrial plant. Indeed, examination of the external environment only occurs when the enterprise compiles statistics on "other conditions of the work to the extent that these conditions depend upon the corporation." Such statistics, for example, old-age and sickness benefits, touch only the enterprise's employees. The limited content of the legislation was intentional and reflects a desire to define more precisely the responsibility of management to labor, and not necessarily management's responsibility to society as a whole. In contrast, the little social accounting attempted in the United States has dealt almost entirely with corporations' effect on the external environment.

Notwithstanding its limited examination of an enterprise's external environment, the balance sheet is intended to be a flexible document. Its contents are susceptible to modification in response to the opin-

ions of the works council and to the recommendations put forth in collective bargaining between unions and management. In addition to ensuring some responsiveness to employee judgments concerning improvement of the plant environment, this flexibility introduces the potential for expanding the contents of the balance sheet. By pressing demands through collective negotiation or the works council, socially conscious workers may be able to force measurement of the impact of business actions on the external environment as well as on the plant's internal environment. In this manner the French balance sheet may eventually embrace many of the areas of corporate activity that have been monitored in the United States, such as the effects of pollution, quality of products produced and compliance with consumer legislation.

C. The recipients of the balance sheet. The potential for effectiveness of the French social accounting concept lies in the availability of an employee forum to which management can report and be held responsible. That forum is the works council, a factory committee consisting of representatives of several unions, elected by the employees, and a management representative of the plant. The council advises management on employees' concerns regarding the work environment. Although its decisions are not binding on the corporation, the council has a consultative role in the policy-making of the corporation. The French legislation requires each enterprise to furnish its council with a copy of the balance sheet to aid the council in its advisory role.

The works council meets to examine the sheet for compliance with the government regulations and may confer on the relative importance of the indicators the sheet includes. Following this examination, the council issues an opinion on the company's progress in improving the social environment. The opinion may include proposals for modifications in the composition of the balance sheet itself. Once the opinion of the factory committee has been issued, it becomes a part of the balance sheet and the entire document is made available to the labor inspector, the shareholders, company employees, and union representatives.

That the works council has input concerning factors relied on to measure corporate social performance raises the possibility that workers' values will determine part of what constitutes a good performance in the social sphere. Because the council has only an advisory role, its advice is unlikely to have any concrete effect without management's cooperation.

CHAPTER PROBLEMS

1. Jim Davis is a research and development chemist employed by Acme Chemical Company. Acme has a range of chemical products that are marketed strictly in the northeastern region of the United States. Jim has developed a chemical that he knows will be highly demanded in the U.S. and perhaps worldwide. However, he feels Acme does not have the reputable name needed to market his discovery. Jim decided to approach a large Western-based chemical corporation. They are willing to hire him, provided they obtain the rights to produce and market the chemical. In return, Jim will be given a large block of the corporation's common stock and his salary will be tripled. Jim is considering the offer. He figures the most Acme will do is give him a bonus for his discovery. Do you feel that Davis is being unethical in considering an offer from the Western corporation? Explain. If you were in his position, would you feel obligated to notify Acme of your discovery and not search for alternatives? Explain.

2. Computer Technics of America (CTA) is one of several computer manufacturers bidding for a large government agency contract. The contract calls for the manufacture and sale of a complex unit composed of data processor, data storage, and a score of terminals. Ken Johnson, president of CTA, is determined to get this contract. He believes the average bid will be $22 million. Mr. Johnson has purposely withheld a bid from CTA. On the last day of bidding, he phones a "political interest" in Washington who is a member of the agency's board and offers to donate $250,000 to the politician's campaign fund in return for the computer contract. Would you consider Johnson's practice unethical? Would you go to this extreme to get a government contract? Explain.

3. King Foods, Inc., is a large supermarket chain that grew steadily over the past decade. King's President, Ben Morris, explains its success: "The supermarket industry is known to have low profit margins. To be successful in this business, a company must turn over large volumes of goods. King Foods has grown to its current proportions by doing just that." Upper management pushed for reinvestment of profits and obtained outside funds for further expansion. Morris adds, "Because of our size, we can now enter a market and offer the consumer lower prices than previously existed." It is no secret that some of King's pricing activities contribute to its success. When King opens a new store, a "grand opening sale" lasts for six months, during which time the prices are consistently lower than those of their area competitors. King maintains prices at a level that eventually forces small grocery stores to close. Once King has a dominant share of the new market, its prices gradually move up to the normal range. Do you feel King's techniques are unethical? Would you adhere to its market acquisition techniques? Explain.

4. Skyhigh Construction Corporation specializes in multi-floor office buildings located predominately in major cities through the United States. Skyhigh is a very reputable firm in the high-rise construction industry. They are known to complete all contracts on time and on budget. Frank Cook, a site supervisor for Skyhigh, comments, "Skyhigh employs an average of 240 construction workers per site. For those who work up on the beams, this is a high health risk occupation. There is a small but considerable number of serious and sometimes fatal accidents at every site before it is completed. In order to meet deadlines, I sometimes must send the crew up when weather conditions are not favorable. My crew members are working in a potentially dangerous environment, but they are compensated with attractive wages. If one of them complains about going up every time it gets a little windy, I fire him. When Skyhigh signs a contract, my job is to assure completion of it on time." Do you feel Skyhigh is unethical by employing laborers and exposing them to potentially dangerous working conditions? If you were a site supervisor, would you send a crew up if weather conditions were not favorable? Explain.

5. Carl Simms is a account manager for Transit Systems, a large distribution conglomerate. Simms was recently employed by one of Transit's clients, Americus Department Stores, Inc. While at Americus (Mr. Simms was a vice president), he warned that the Internal Revenue Service would discover their fradulent income reporting practices. When Simms noticed upper management was not going to make any changes, he left Americus for fear of being indicted for tax evasion. One year later Americus was charged with failure to report total taxable earnings. Simms was asked to attend an inquiry at the I.R.S. office. He feared "blowing the whistle" on Americus because then he would surely lose one of Transit's largest accounts. Do you feel Simms would be unethical if he withholds any information which could incriminate Americus? If you were in Simms's position, would you feel obligated to "blow the whistle" on Americus? Explain.

6. George Geary was employed by the U.S. Steel Corporation to sell tubular steel products to the oil and gas industry. Believing that a product was unsafe, Geary advised his immediate superior of the problem. When Geary's immediate supervisor proved unresponsive, Geary presented his misgivings to the vice president in charge of the product's sales. Apparently the management of U.S. Steel recognized the dangerousness of the product, since it was later with-

drawn from the market. Nevertheless, Geary was discharged. He sued his former employer for wrongful discharge. How should the court rule?

7. David W. Ewing has proposed a constitutional amendment, calling it "an employee bill of rights." In pertinent part, it provides:

> No public or private organization shall discriminate against an employee for criticizing the ethical, moral, or legal policies and practices of the organization; nor shall any organization discriminate against an employee for engaging in outside activities of his or her choice, or for objecting to a directive that violates common norms of morality.[8]

Do you favor Ewing's proposal? Would you favor the proposal if it called for a statute rather than a constitutional amendment?

8. You are an officer of a medium-sized manufacturer, Suburban Corporation. You operate two large plants in the suburbs of a city whose population exceeds 500,000. The city has been deteriorating for some time. Its unemployment rate is about 15 percent, while the unemployment rate in the surrounding suburbs is about 5 percent. The city's revenues have been declining for some time. In an effort to increase revenue the city has imposed an income tax of 2 percent on all residents and a tax of 0.5 percent on the income that nonresidents earn in the city. The worst blight in the city has been on the east side, where over 15 percent of the residential property lies vacant and condemned. The crime rate is quite high; insurance is almost impossible to obtain. The mayor has said on many occasions that the east side can come back only if there is a large influx of private capital and jobs.

Suburban Corporation has prospered, and the demand for its products continues to expand. It is clear that the company must build another plant to meet this rising demand. Plans have already been drafted for the new plant, which will employ about 1,000 persons. Where should the new plant be located? If you conclude that the socially responsible choice would be to locate

---

[8] Ewing, "Freedom Inside the Organization," in *Individual Rights in the Corporation: A Reader on Employee Rights* 67 at 69 (Westin and Salisbury, eds. 1980).

on the city's east side, how will your decision affect the community? How will it affect shareholders? Employees? Consumers?

9. Consider the position of large institutional investors that must decide whether to retain their holdings in companies operating in South Africa. In making this decision, should such investors consider the South African government's practice of apartheid? Should they consider whether the companies in question have formally subscribed to the Sullivan Principles which call for companies to follow nondiscriminary employment policies in South Africa? Should the institutional investors consider the

companies' actual practices in South Africa? Should they consider whether selling their holdings in these companies is likely to persuade the companies to pull out of South Africa? Should they consider whether such a pullout is likely to influence South Africa's policies? Finally, should they consider the effect that selling large blocks of stock will have on the stock market? Explain.

10. You have been asked to speak to the local chamber of commerce. Your speech is to be entitled "Corporate Social Responsibility: Theoretical Framework and Practical Application." Outline your remarks.

PART PROBLEMS

1. You are a vice president of Ace Aircraft, Inc., which manufactures jet passenger airplanes. Ace developed the enormously profitable ACE-000 (otherwise known as the "ace-in-the-hole"). Recently Ace entered into several contracts to supply the leading commercial airlines with planes over the next 10 years. In addition, it has a contract to supply the U.S. Army with 100 modified ACE-000s for use as troop transports. The environmental consequences of using the modified ACE-000s are unclear.

You have undertaken a review of Ace's existing production facilities to ascertain whether its productive capacity is sufficient to meet its present contractual commitments and the anticipated growth in demand for the ACE-000. A preliminary report by your staff indicates that some plant facilities and equipment will need to be expanded and modernized and that entirely new plants will need to be built.

The report reveals that the company's two factories for building the ACE-000, located in Newark, New Jersey, and Cleveland, Ohio, are rapidly becoming outdated. State and local taxes are relatively high. Both cities have high unemployment and crime rates, and their population has declined. These facts, coupled with the high cost of living in these cities, make it difficult for Ace to attract top-quality engineers and executives to work at these two factories.

Both facilities have also experienced labor unrest. The Newark plant is unionized. Negotiation of its last three contracts has resulted in lengthy strikes. At these times the company was able to rely on the nonunionized, Cleveland facility. However, a recent election at the Cleveland plant resulted in the certificaton of the same international union that represents the Newark plant as the bargaining representative of the Cleveland plant's employees.

At your request your staff has prepared the following preliminary proposals for Ace's expansion:

Alternative A. Ace will improve its existing facilities in both Newark and Cleveland. This will require expanding the existing plants and building one new plant in each city. Obtaining the land for this expansion is no problem because Ace owns the property adjacent to its facilities in both cities. The adjacent property at both locations consists of deteriorated residential buildings. The land is zoned for both residential and industrial purposes. Ace's expansion effort will displace the residents of its buildings.

The new factories, like the present factories, will have toxic by-products. The pollution of the rivers on which Ace's present factories are located is already at a toxic level. The plants would also emit noxious but not toxic airborne pollutants.

Alternative B. Ace will close its Newark and Cleveland plants and relocate on the outskirts of Connersville (population 17,000), in east-central Indiana. Connersville is situated on the Whitewater River, which is as clean as its name suggests. Connersville is an hour's drive from both Indianapolis and Cincinnati, and thus offers the pleasures of a small-town environment while being close to the shopping and cultural attractions of these larger communities. Closing Ace's Newark and Cleveland facilities will result in the unemployment of 5,000 workers, and Ace will incur certain expenses in relocating its facilities. However, labor costs will be lower in Connersville and Connersville's location will make it easier to attract engineers and executives who are looking for a small-town lifestyle. If Ace makes the move, Connersville's population will increase substantially, resulting in increased traffic congestion and related problems.

After reviewing the proposals, you decide to confer with your staff to discuss the implications of each alternative and to ascertain what additional information, if any, you will need before you present a report to the board of directors. Explain the legal and social responsibilities that you see in the staff's suggestions, and make a list of the questions that you would ask your staff to answer as a follow-up to its proposals.

2. Dump Services, Inc., is a company that operates landfills for the reception of hazardous wastes. It purchased a site three years ago on 130 acres of land located over an abandoned mine and surrounded by farmland. The site is covered with a gob pile whose contents are similar to those of the gob piles spread over much of the nearby acreage by mines that operated between 1917 and 1954.

Under the 130 acres purchased by Dump are strata of tight clay. The top stratum extends to a depth of 10 to 12 feet. Beneath that is a very thin layer of more permeable saturated clay called the Sangamon Paleosal. This layer is continuous under Dump's 130 acres. An additional clay stratum more than 10 feet deep lies under the Paleosal. The mine spoil contains much of this clay, and the company uses it as a sealing agent in its landfill.

The company applied to the state EPA for a landfill permit. The application contained extensive information on groundwater, soil permeability, soil subsidence, subsurface, and hydrogeologic conditions. Dump was granted a permit in May of the year in which it acquired the site. It dug trenches in the clay to a depth of 10–12 feet, a width of 50 feet, and a length of 75–350 feet, with a space of 10 feet between the trenches. Hazardous substances were placed in the trenches and covered with soil from the gob piles.

Previously, however, the hazardous substances were dissolved in a solvent. If the solvent contains no PCBs or other hydrocarbons, it will tend to remain in the soil in which it is deposited. This process for keeping hazardous substances in place is known as attenuation. Dump's permit application included a request for permission to bury PCBs, herbicides, and paint sludge. Because PCBs are soluble in paint thinner and water, Dump's application stated that it would not combine PCBs with paint thinner and would keep groundwater and surface water free from PCBs.

To eliminate the possibility that hazardous substances might interact and pollute the air by causing chemical explosions, fires, or emissions of poisonous gas, Dump's application stated that it would not store incompatible substances together, that it would use materials tending to prevent incompatible hazardous substances from coming into contact with each other (e.g., it would place lime on certain substances to prevent them from combining with other substances to form poisonous gases), and that it would store many substances whose inherent qualities deterred their migration. Two years ago the state EPA renewed Dump's permit after an on-site inspection of Dump's operations.

A study of the landfill's operations undertaken by Dr. Dirt, one of Dump's geologists, indicates that the following conditions have occurred:

1. Oxidized spots extending to a depth of 25 feet exist in the undersurface. These oxidized spots are more permeable than the surrounding matter. Dr. Dirt explains that the oxidation occurred because these areas came into contact with the atmosphere in some way, for example, when roots pushed through the soil and then decayed, leaving an air space. He reports that in inspecting the trenches, he found root holes and other channels as large in diameter as a finger.

2. The clay undersurface indicates silty and sandy loesses whose porosity is greater than that of the clay.

3. Water from an artesian source has entered several trenches. The pressure on the water has caused it to rise through the landfill to the top of several trenches instead of being absorbed through the sides of these trenches. Thereby hazardous substances have been transported out of the trenches and to the surface. Dr. Dirt doubts whether the landfill can be restored to its former tightness.

4. The ability of the undersurface to adequately contain hazardous substances has been jeopardized by a collapse that occurred in the underlying abandoned mine. As a result, subsidence of the surface with accompanying cracks in the soil has been taking place and will continue to do so. Dr. Dirt believes that a subsidence crack extending to the top of the mine might develop. The existence of an underground crack indicates the

possibility of cracks that would give no warning of their presence and their need to be repaired. As the burial trenches at the site are only 10 feet apart, a crack of 100–150 feet long could severely impair the ability of the trenches to contain liquid.

5. Paint thinner has been deposited in the same trenches as PCBs.

Given the above conditions, respond to the following:

a. You are the vice president in charge of operations, and you have received Dr. Dirt's report. What will you do? Discuss the legal, ethical, and social responsibility implications of your response to the report.

b. You are Dr. Dirt. What will you do if the vice president in charge of operations fails to act on your report?

c. If Dr. Dirt does not have an employment contract with a stated period of duration, what are his rights if Dump terminates his employment?

d. Suppose that the neighboring landowners and residents of a village located less than a mile away file an action in a state court seeking an injunction to close the landfill. Using common-law principles, discuss the suit's probability of success.

e. Suppose that the state EPA calls a meeting attended by representatives of the state development department, the state department of health, the state department of natural resources, the state planning office, and the office of the governor, as well as you and other Dump officers, officers of other hazardous waste disposal companies, and representatives of the state's hazardous waste disposal trade association. At issue is the future disposal of hazardous wastes in a busy industrial state. The state officials are concerned about providing industry and its employees with a necessary service and at the same time protecting the public health. The hazardous waste disposal industry is interested in lawful economic survival. The purpose of the meeting is to explore possibilities. Because of your reputation as a brilliant, incisive, wide-ranging innovative thinker, you have been asked to make opening remarks in which you explore the possible legal alternatives. Justify your reputation.

3. Competitor Corporation filed an antitrust action against Conglomocorp, Inc., seeking $10 million in damages. The case was tried without a jury. The trial judge had the matter under advisement. He wrote an opinion finding in favor of Competitor Corporation and awarding that company $9 million in damages. Three days before releasing the opinion, he called the lawyers into his chambers and advised them of his decision. The case had received a large amount of publicity, and the judge wished to allow the parties time to prepare for the public announcement. He informed them that his decision would be announced in three days.

Your spouse, the secretary to the president of Competitor Corporation, typed a memorandum that explained the impending decision to the Competitor board of directors. Your spouse disclosed its contents to you. You realized that when the decision was released, the price of Competitor's stock would rise and that of Conglomocorp stock would fall. You also realized that you could make a large profit by purchasing puts in Conglomocorp and calls in Competitor. (A *put* allows the purchaser to sell a specified number of shares in a stock at a specified price at any time for a specified duration. If the price then falls, the purchaser can buy the stock at its new price and resell it at the higher specified price. A *call* allows the purchaser to buy a specified number of shares of a stock at a specified price at any time for a specified duration. If the price rises, the purchaser can buy the stock at the specified price and resell it at its higher current price.)

Would it be unethical for you to do this? Would your answer be different if instead of learning of the decision from your spouse, you learned of it in your capacity as president of Competitor? Would it be different if instead of trading for your own account, you were a stockbroker advising a client on investments? How would you answer a client who owned stock in both Competitor and Conglomocorp, needed to raise cash, and asked you which to sell?

Now place yourself in the position of the sellers of the puts and calls. Do you think they would feel cheated if they learned that you were aware of the impending decision when you and your client entered into the transaction? If a substantial number of persons traded stock upon receiving such information, what would be the impact of their transactions upon the credibility of the securities markets?

APPENDIX A

THE CONSTITUTION OF THE UNITED STATES OF AMERICA

PREAMBLE

We the People of the United States, in Order to form a more perfect Union, establish Justice, insure domestic Tranquility, provide for the common defence, promote the general Welfare, and secure the Blessings of Liberty to ourselves and our Posterity, do ordain and establish this Constitution for the United States of America.

Article I

BICAMERAL LEGLISLATURE

Section 1 All legislative Powers herein granted shall be vested in a Congress of the United States, which shall consist of a Senate and House of Representatives.

HOUSE OF REPRESENTATIVES

Section 2 The House of Representatives shall be composed of Members chosen every second Year by the People of the several States, and the Electors in each State shall have the Qualifications requisite for Electors of the most numerous Branch of the State Legislature.

No Person shall be a Representative who shall not have attained to the age of twenty five Years, and been seven Years a Citizen of the United States, and who shall not, when elected, be an Inhabitant of that State in which he shall be chosen.

Representatives and direct Taxes shall be apportioned among the several States which may be included within this Union, according to their respective Numbers, which shall be determined by adding to the whole Number of free Persons, including those bound to Service for a Term of Years, and excluding Indians not taxed, three fifths of all other Persons.[1] The actual Enumeration shall be made within three Years after the first Meeting of the Congress of the United States, and within every subsequent Term of ten Years, in such Manner as they shall by Law direct. The Number of Representatives shall not exceed one for every thirty Thousand, but each State shall have at Least one Representative; and until such enumeration shall be made, the State of New Hampshire shall be entitled to chuse three, Massachusetts eight, Rhode-Island and Providence Plantations one, Connecticut five, New-York six, New Jersey four, Pennsylvania eight, Delaware one, Maryland six, Virginia ten, North Carolina five, South Carolina five, and Georgia three.

When vacancies happen in the Representation from any State, the Executive Authority thereof shall issue Writs of Election to fill such Vacancies.

[1] Changed by the Fourteenth Amendment.

The House of Representative shall chuse their Speaker and other Officers; and shall have the sole Power of Impeachment.

SENATE

Section 3 The Senate of the United States shall be composed of two Senators from each State, chosen by the Legislature thereof,[2] for six Years; and each Senator shall have one Vote.

Immediately after they shall be assembled in Consequence of the first Election, they shall be divided as equally as may be into three Classes. The Seats of the Senators of the first Class shall be vacated at the Expiration of the second Year, of the second Class at the Expiration of the fourth Year, and of the third Class at the Expiration of the sixth Year, so that one third may be chosen every second Year; and if Vacancies happen by Resignation, or otherwise, during the Recess of the Legislature of any State, the Executive thereof may make temporary Appointments until the next Meeting of the Legislature, which shall then fill such Vacancies.[3]

No Person shall be a Senator who shall not have attained to the Age of third Years, and been nine Years a Citizen of the United States, and who shall not, when elected, be an Inhabitant of that State for which he shall be chosen.

The Vice President of the United States shall be President of the Senate, but shall have no Vote, unless they be equally divided.

The Senate shall chuse their other Officers, and also a President pro tempore, in the Absence of the Vice President, or when he shall exercise the Office of President of the United States.

The Senate shall have the sole Power to try all Impeachments. When sitting for that Purpose, they shall be on Oath or Affirmation. When the President of the United States is tried the Chief Justice shall preside: And no Person shall be convicted without the Concurrence of two thirds of the Members present.

Judgment in Cases of Impeachment shall not extend further than to removal from Office, and disqualification to hold and enjoy any Office of honor, Trust or Profit under the United States: but the Party convicted shall nevertheless be liable and subject to Indictment, Trial, Judgment and Punishment, according to Law.

CONGRES- SIONAL ELECTIONS

Section 4 The Times, Places and Manner of holding Elections for Senators and Representatives, shall be prescribed in each State by the Legislature thereof; but the Congress may at any time by Law make or alter such Regulations, except as to the Places of chusing Senators.

The Congress shall assemble at least once in every Year, and such Meeting shall be on the first Monday in December, unless they shall by Law appoint a different Day.[4]

POWERS AND DUTIES OF CONGRESS

Section 5 Each House shall be the Judge of the Elections, Returns and Qualifications of its own Members, and a Majority of each shall constitute a Quorum to do Business; but a smaller Number may adjourn from day to day, and may be authorized to compel the Attendance of absent Members, in such Manner, and under such Penalties as each House may provide.

---

[2] Changed by the Seventeenth Amendment.

[3] Changed by the Seventeenth Amendment

[4] Changed by the Twentieth Amendment.

Each House may determine the Rules of its Proceedings, punish its Members for disorderly Behavior, and, with the Concurrence of two thirds, expel a Member.

Each House shall keep a Journal of its Proceedings, and from time to time publish the same, excepting such Parts as may in their Judgment require Secrecy; and the Yeas and Nays of the Members of either House on any question shall, at the Desire of one fifth of those Present, be entered on the Journal.

Neither House, during the Session of Congress, shall, without the Consent of the other, adjourn for more than three days, not to any other Place than that in which the two Houses shall be sitting.

COMPENSA-TION, IMMU-NITIES, RESTRIC-TIONS— MEMBERS OF CONGRESS

Section 6 The Senators and Representatives shall receive a Compensation for their Services, to be ascertained by Law, and paid out of the Treasury of the United States. They shall in all Cases, except Treason, Felony and Breach of the Peace, be privileged from Arrest during their Attendance at the Session of their respective Houses, and in going to and returning from the same; and for any Speech or Debate in either House, they shall not be questioned in any other Place.

No Senator or Representative shall, curing the Time for which he was elected, be appointed to any civil Office under the Authority of the United States, which shall have been created, or the Emoluments whereof shall have been encreased during such time; and no Person holding any Office under the United States, shall be a Member of either House during his continuance in Office.

LEGISLATIVE PROCEDURES

Section 7 All Bills for raising Revenue shall originate in the House of Representatives; but the Senate may propose or concur with Amendments as on other Bills.

Every Bill which shall have passed the House of Representatives and the Senate, shall, before it become a Law, be presented to the President of the United States; If he approve he shall sign it, but if not he shall return it, with his Objections to that House in which it shall have originated, who shall enter the Objections at large on their Journal, and proceed to reconsider it. If after such Reconsideration two thirds of that House shall agree to pass the Bill, it shall be sent, together with the Objections, to the other House, by which it shall likewise be reconsidered, and if approved by two thirds of that House, it shall become a Law. But in all such Cases the Votes of both Houses shall be determined by Yeas and Nays, and the Names of the Persons voting for and against the Bill shall be entered on the Journal of each House respectively. If any Bill shall not be returned by the President within ten Days (Sundays excepted) after it shall have been presented to him, the Same shall be a Law, in like Manner as if he had signed it, unless the Congress by their Adjournment prevent its Return, in which Case it shall not be a Law.

Every order, Resolution, or Vote to which the Concurrence of the Senate and House of Representatives may be necessary (except on a question of Adjournment) shall be presented to the President of the United States; and before the Same shall take Effect, shall be approved by him, or being disapproved by him, shall be repassed by two thirds of the Senate and House of Representatives, according to the Rules and Limitations prescribed in the Case of a Bill.

POWERS OF CONGRESS

Section 8 The Congress shall have Power To lay and collect Taxes, Duties, Imposts and Excises, to pay the Debts and provide for the common Defence and general Welfare of the United States; but all Duties, Imposts and Excises shall be uniform throughout the United States;

To borrow Money on the credit of the United States;

To regulate Commerce with foreign Nations, and among the several States, and with the Indian Tribes;

To establish an uniform Rule of Naturalization, and uniform Laws on the subject of Bankruptcies throughout the United States;

To coin Money, regulate the Value thereof, and of foreign Coin, and fix the Standard of Weights and Measures;

To provide for the Punishment of counterfeiting the Securities and current Coin of the United States;

To establish Post Offices and post Roads;

To promote the Progress of Science and useful Arts, by securing for limited Times to Authors and Inventors the exclusive Right to their respective Writings and Discoveries;

To constitute Tribunals inferior to the supreme Court;

To define and punish Piracies and Felonies committed on the high Seas, and Offences against the Law of Nations;

To declare War, grant Letters of Marque and Reprisal, and make Rules concerning Captures on Land and Water;

To raise and support Armies, but no Appropriation of Money to that Use shall be for a longer Term than two Years;

To provide and maintain a Navy;

To make Rules for the Government and Regulation of the land and naval Forces;

To provide for calling forth the Militia to execute the Laws of the Union, suppress Insurrections and repel Invasions;

To provide for organizing, arming, and disciplining, the Militia, and for governing such Part of them as may be employed in the Service of the United States, reserving to the States respectively, the Appointment of the Officers, and the Authority of training the Militia according to the discipline prescribed by Congress;

To exercise exclusive Legislation in all Cases whatsoever, over such District (not exceeding ten Miles square) as may, by Cession of Particular States, and the Acceptance of Congress, become the Seat of the Government of the United States, and to exercise like Authority over all Places purchased by the Consent of the Legislature of the State in which the Same shall be, for the Erection of Forts, Magazines, Arsenals, dock-Yards, and other needful Buildings;—And

To make all Laws which shall be necessary and proper for carrying into Execution the foregoing Powers, and all other Powers vested by this Constitution in the Government of the United States, or in any Department or Officer thereof.

LIMITS ON CONGRES-SIONAL POWERS

Section 9 The Migration or Importation of such Persons as any of the States now existing shall think proper to admit, shall not be prohibited by the Congress prior to the Year one thousand eight hundred and eight, but a Tax or duty may be imposed on such Importation, not exceeding ten dollars for each Person.

The Privilege of the Writ of Habeas Corpus shall not be suspended, unless when in Cases of Rebellion or Invasion the public Safety may require it.

No Bill of Attainder or ex post facto Law shall be passed.

No Capitation, or other direct, Tax shall be laid, unless in Proportion to the Census of Enumeration herein before directed to be taken.[5]

---

[5] Changed by the Sixteenth Amendment.

No Tax or Duty shall be laid on Articles exported from any State.

No Preference shall be given by any Regulation of Commerce or Revenue to the Ports of one State over those of another; nor shall Vessels bound to, or from, one State, be obliged to enter, clear or pay Duties in another.

No Money shall be drawn from the Treasury, but on Consequence of Appropriations made by Law; and a regular Statement and Account of the Receipts and Expenditures of all public Money shall be published from time to time.

No Title of Nobility shall be granted by the United States: And no Person holding any Office of Profit or Trust under them, shall, without the Consent of the Congress, accept of any present, Emolument, Office, or Title, of any kind whatever, from any King, Prince, or foreign State.

LIMITS ON POWERS OF STATES

Section 10 No State shall enter into any Treaty, Alliance, or Confederation; grant Letters of Marque and Reprisal; coin Money; emit Bills of Credit; make any Thing but gold and silver Coin a Tender in Payment of Debts; pass any Bill of Attainder, ex post facto Law, or Law impairing the Obligation of Contracts, or grant any Title of Nobility.

No State shall, without the Consent of the Congress, lay any Imposts or Duties on Imports or Exports, except what may be absolutely necessary for executing its inspection Laws: and the net Produce of all Duties and Imposts, laid by any State on Imports or Exports, shall be for the Use of the Treasury of the United States; and all such Laws shall be subject to the Revision and Control of the Congress.

No State shall, without the consent of Congress, lay any Duty of Tonnage, keep Troops, or Ships of War in time of Peace, enter into any Agreement or Compact with another State, or with a foreign Power, or engage in War, unless actually invaded, or in such imminent Danger as will not admit of delay.

Article II

PRESIDENCY

Section 1 The executive Power shall be vested in a President of the United States of America. He shall hold his Office during the Term of four Years, and, together with the Vice President, chosen for the same Term, be elected, as follows

Each State shall appoint, in such Manner as the Legislature thereof may direct, a Number of Electors, equal to the whole Number of Senators and Representatives to which the State may be entitled in Congress: but no Senator or Representative, or Person holding an Office of Trust or Profit under the United States, shall be appointed an Elector.

The Electors shall meet in their respective States, and vote by Ballot for two Persons, of whom one at least shall not be an Inhabitant of the same State with themselves. And they shall make a List of all the Persons voted for, and of the Number of Votes for each; which List they shall sign and certify, and transmit sealed to the Seat of the Government of the United States, directed to the President of the Senate. The President of the Senate shall, in the Presence of the Senate and House of Representatives, open all the Certificates, and the Votes shall then be counted. The Person having the greatest Number of Votes shall be the President, if such Number be a Majority of the whole Number of Electors appointed; and if there be more than one who have such Majority, and have an equal Number of Votes, then the House of Representatives shall immediately chuse by Ballot one of them for President; and if no Person have a Majority, then from the five highest on the List the said House shall in like Manner chuse the President. But in chusing the President, the Votes shall be taken by States, the Representation from each State having one Vote; a quorum for this Purpose shall consist of a Member or Members from two thirds of the States, and a Majority of all the States shall be necessary to a Choice. In every Case, after the Choice of the President, the Person having the greatest Number of Votes of the Electors shall be the Vice President. But if there should remain two or more who have equal Votes, the Senate shall chuse from them by Ballot the Vice President.[6]

The Congress may determine the Time of chusing the Electors, and the Day on which they shall be given their Votes; which Day shall be the same throughout the United States.

No Person except a natural born Citizen, or a Citizen of the United States, at the time of the Adoption of this Constitution, shall be eligible to the Office of President; neither shall any person be eligible to that Office who shall not have attained to the Age of thirty five Years, and been fourteen Years a Resident within the United States.

In Case of the Removal of the President from Office, or of his Death, Resignation, or Inability to discharge the Powers and Duties of the said Office, the Same shall devolve on the Vice President, and the Congress may by Law provide for the Case of Removal, Death, Resignation or Inability, both of the President and Vice President, declaring what Officer shall then act as President, and such Officer shall act accordingly, until the Disability be removed, or a President shall be elected.[7]

The President shall, at stated Times, receive for his Services, a Compensation, which shall neither be increased nor diminished during the period for which he shall have been elected, and he shall not receive within that Period any other Emolument from the United States, or any of them.

Before he enter on the Execution of his Office, he shall take the following Oath or Affirmation:—"I do solemnly swear (or affirm) that I will faithfully execute the Office of President of the United States, and will to the best of my Ability, preserve, protect and defend the Constitution of the United States."

PRESIDENTIAL POWERS

Section 2 The President shall be Commander in Chief of the Army and Navy of the United States, and of the Militia of the several States, when called into the actual Service of the United States; he may require the Opinion, in writing, of the principal Officer in each of the executive Departments, upon any Subject relating to the Duties of their respective Offices, and he shall have Power to grant Reprieves and Pardons for Offences against the United States, except in Cases of Impeachment.

He shall have Power, by and with the Advice and Consent of the Senate, to make Treaties, provided two thirds of the Senators present concur; and he shall nominate, and by and with the Advice and Consent of the Senate, shall appoint Ambassadors, other public Ministers and Consuls, Judges of the supreme Court, and all other Officers of the United States, whose Appointments are not herein otherwise provided for, and which shall be established by Law: but the Congress may by Law vest the Appointment of such inferior Officers, as they

---

[6] Changed by the Twelfth Amendment.

[7] Changed by the Twenty-fifth Amendment.

think proper, in the President alone, in the Courts of Law, or in the Heads of Departments.

The President shall have Power to fill up all Vacancies that may happen during the Recess of the Senate, by granting Commissions which shall expire at the End of their next Session.

Section 3 He shall from time to time give to the Congress Information of the State of the Union, and recommend to their Consideration such Measures as he shall judge necessary and expedient; he may, on extraordinary Occasions, convene both Houses, or either of them, and in Case of Disagreement between them, with Respect to the Time of Adjournment, he may adjourn them to such Time as he shall think proper; he shall receive Ambassadors and other public Ministers; he shall take Care that the Laws be faithfully executed, and shall Commission all the Officers of the United States.

IMPEACHMENT *Section 4* The President, Vice President and all civil Officers of the United States, shall be removed from Office on Impeachment for, and Conviction of, Treason, Bribery, or other high Crimes and Misdemeanors.

Article III

JUDICIARY *Section 1* The judicial Power of the United States, shall be vested in one supreme Court, and in such inferior Courts as the Congress may from time to time ordain and establish. The Judges, both of the supreme and inferior Courts, shall hold their Offices during good Behaviour, and shall, at stated Times, receive for their Services, a Compensation, which shall not be diminished during their Continuance in Office.

JURISDICTION *Section 2* The judicial Power shall extend to all Cases, in Law and Equity, arising under this Constitution, the Laws of the United States, and Treaties made, or which shall be made, under their Authority;—to all Cases affecting Ambassadors, other public Ministers and Consuls;—to all Cases of admiralty and maritime Jurisdiction;—to Controversies to which the United States shall be a party;—to Controversies between two or more States;—between a State and Citizens of another State,[8] —between Citizens of different States;—between Citizens of the same State claiming Lands under Grants of different States, and between a State, or the Citizens thereof, and foreign States, Citizens or Subjects.

In all Cases affecting Ambassadors, other public Ministers and Consuls, and those in which a State shall be Part, the supreme Court shall have original Jurisdiction. In all the other Cases before mentioned, the supreme Court shall have appellate Jurisdiction, both as to Law and Fact, with such Exceptions, and under such Regulations as the Congress shall make.

The Trial of all Crimes, except in Cases of Impeachment, shall be by Jury; and such Trial shall be held in the State where the said Crimes shall have been committed; but when not committed within any State, the Trial shall be at such Place or Places as the Congress may by Law have directed.

TREASON *Section 3* Treason against the United States, shall consist only in levying War against them, or in adhering to the Enemies, giving them Aid and Comfort. No

---

[8] Changed by the Eleventh Amendment.

Person shall be convicted of Treason unless on the Testimony of two Witnesses to the same overt Act, or on Confession in open Court.

The Congress shall have Power to declare the Punishment of Treason, but no Attainder of Treason shall work Corruption of Blood, or Forfeiture except during the Life of the Person attainted.

Article IV

FULL FAITH AND CREDIT

Section 1 Full Faith and Credit shall be given in each State to the public Acts, Records, and judicial Proceedings of every other State. And the Congress may by general Laws prescribe the Manner in which such Acts, Records and Proceedings shall be proved, and the Effect thereof.

PRIVILEGES AND IMMUNITIES, EXTRADITION

Section 2 The Citizens of each State shall be entitled to all Privileges and Immunities of Citizens in the several States.

A person charged in any State with Treason, Felony, or other Crime, who shall flee from Justice, and be found in another State, shall on Demand of the executive Authority of the State from which he fled, be delivered up, to be removed to the State having Jurisdiction of the Crime.

No Person held to Service or Labour in one State, under the Laws thereof, escaping into another, shall, in Consequence of any Law or Regulation therein, be discharged from such Service or Labour, but shall be delivered up on Claim of the Party to whom such Service or Labour may be due.[9]

NEW STATES

Section 3 New States may be admitted by the Congress into this Union; but no new State shall be formed or erected within the Jurisdiction of any other State; nor any State be formed by the Junction of two or more States, or Parts of States, without the Consent of the Legislatures of the States concerned as well as of the Congress.

The Congress shall have Power to dispose of and make all needful Rules and Regulations respecting the Territory or other Property belonging to the United States; and nothing in this Constitution shall be so construed as to Prejudice any Claims of the United States, or of any particular State.

PROTECTION OF STATES

Section 4 The United States shall guarantee to every State in this Union a Republican Form of Government, and shall protect each of them against Invasion; and on Application of the Legislature, or of the Executive (when the Legislature cannot be convened) against domestic Violence.

Article V

AMENDMENT PROCEDURES

The Congress, whenever two thirds of both Houses shall deem it necessary, shall propose Amendments to this Constitution, or, on the Application of the Legislatures of two thirds of the several States, shall call a Convention for proposing Amendments, which, in either Case, shall be valid to all Intents and Purposes, as Part of this Constitution, when ratified by the Legislatures of three fourths of the several States, or by Conventions in three fourths thereof, as the one or the other Mode of Ratification may be proposed by the Congress; Provided that no Amendment which may be made prior to the Year One thousand eight hundred and eight

---

[9] Changed by the Thirteenth Amendment.

shall in any Manner affect the first and fourth Clauses in the Ninth Section of the first Article; and that no State, without its Consent, shall be deprived of its equal Suffrage in the Senate.

Article VI

SUPREMACY OF FEDERAL LAWS

All Debts contracted and Engagements entered into, before the Adoption of this Constitution, shall be as valid against the United States under this Constitution, as under the Confederation.

This Constitution, and the Laws of the United States which shall be made in Pursuance thereof; and all Treaties made, or which shall be made, under the Authority of the United States, shall be the supreme Law of the Land; and the Judges in every State shall be bound thereby, any Thing in the Constitution or Laws of any State to the Contrary notwithstanding.

The Senators and Representatives before mentioned, and the Members of the several State Legislatures, and all executive and judicial Officers, both of the United States and of the several States, shall be bound by Oath or Affirmation, to support this Constitution; but no religious Test shall ever be required as a Qualification to any Office or public Trust under the United States.

Article VII

RATIFICATION

The Ratification of the Conventions of nine States, shall be sufficient for the Establishment of this Constitution between the States so ratifying the Same.

Done in Convention by the Unanimous Consent of the States present the Seventeenth Day of September in the Year of our Lord one thousand seven hundred and Eighty seven and of the Independence of the United States of America the Twelfth In witness whereof We have hereunto subscribed our Names.

The first ten amendments, the "Bill of Rights," were ratified in 1791.

Amendment 1

FREEDOM OF RELIGION, SPEECH, PRESS, ASSEMBLY

Congress shall make no law respecting an establishment of religion, or prohibiting the free exercise thereof; or abridging the freedom of speech, or of the press; or the right of the people peaceably to assemble, and to petition the Government for a redress of grievances.

Amendment 2

RIGHT TO BEAR ARMS

A well regulated Militia, being necessary to the security of a free State, the right of the people to keep and bear Arms, shall not be infringed.

Amendment 3

QUARTERING SOLDIERS

No Soldier shall, in time of peace be quartered in any house, without the consent of the Owner, not in time of war, but in a manner to be prescribed by law.

Amendment 4

SEARCHES AND SEIZURES

The right of the people to be secure in their persons, houses, papers, and effects, against unreasonable searches and seizures, shall not be violated, and no Warrants shall issue, but upon probable cause, supported by Oath or affirmation, and particularly describing the place to be searched, and the persons or things to be seized.

Amendment 5

RIGHTS OF ACCUSED, DUE PROCESS

No person shall be held to answer for a capital, or otherwise infamous crime, unless on a presentment or indictment of a Grand Jury, except in cases arising in the land or naval forces, or in the Militia, when in actual service in time of War or public danger; nor shall any person be subject for the same offence to be twice put in jeopardy of life or limb; nor shall be compelled in any criminal case to be a witness against himself, nor be deprived of life, liberty, or property, without due process of law; nor shall private property be taken for public use, without just compensation.

Amendment 6

CRIMINAL PROSECU- TIONS

In all criminal prosecutions, the accused shall enjoy the right to a speedy and public trial, by an impartial jury of the State and district wherein the crime shall have been committed, which district shall have been previously ascertained by law, and to be informed of the nature and cause of the accusation; to be confronted with the witnesses against him; to have compulsory process for obtaining witnesses in his favor, and to have Assistance of Counsel for his defence.

Amendment 7

COMMON- LAW SUITS

In Suits at common law, where the value in controversy shall exceed twenty dollars, the right of trial by jury shall be preserved, and no fact tried by a jury, shall be otherwise reexamined in any Court of the United States, than according to the rules of the common law.

Amendment 8

BAIL, CRUEL AND UNUSUAL PUNISHMENT UNENUMER- ATED RIGHTS

Excessive bail shall not be required, nor excessive fines imposed, nor cruel and unusual punishments inflicted.

Amendment 9

The enumeration in the Constitution, of certain rights, shall not be construed to deny or disparage others retained by the people.

Amendment 10

POWERS RESERVED TO STATES

The powers not delegated to the United States by the Constitution, nor prohibited by it to the States, are reserved to the States respectively, or to the people.

Amendment 11 [*Ratified 1795*]

SUITS AGAINST STATES

The Judicial power of the United States shall not be construed to extend to any suit in law or equity, commenced or prosecuted against one of the United States by Citizens of another State, or by Citizens or Subjects of any Foreign State.

Amendment 12 [*Ratified 1804*]

PRESIDENTIAL ELECTIONS

The Electors shall meet in their respective states and vote by ballot for President and Vice President, one of whom, at least, shall not be an inhabitant of the same state with themselves; they shall name in their ballots the person voted for as President, and in distinct ballots the person voted for as Vice President, and they shall make distinct lists of all persons voted for as President, and of all persons voted for as Vice President, and of the number of votes for each, which lists they shall sign and certify, and transmit sealed to the seat of the government of the United States, directed to the President of the Senate;—The President of the Senate shall, in the presence of the Senate and House of Representatives, open all the certificates and the votes shall then be counted;—The person having the greatest number of votes for President, shall be the President, if such number be a majority of the whole number of Electors appointed; and if no person have such majority, then from the persons having the highest numbers not exceeding three on the list of those voted for as President, the House of Representatives shall choose immediately, by ballot, the President. But in choosing the President, the votes shall be taken by states, the representation from each state having one vote; a quorum for this purpose shall consist of a member or members from two-thirds of the states, and a majority of all the states shall be necessary to a choice. And if the House of Representatives shall not choose a President whenever the right of choice shall devolve upon them, before the fourth day of March next following, then the Vice President shall act as President, as in the case of the death or other constitutional disability of the President.—[10] The person having the greatest number of votes as Vice President, shall be the Vice President, if such number be a majority of the whole number of Electors appointed, and if no person have a majority, then from the two highest numbers on the list, the Senate shall choose the Vice President; a quorum for the purpose shall consist of two-thirds of the whole number of Senators, and a majority of the whole number shall be necessary to a choice. But no person constitutionally ineligible to the office of President shall be eligible to that of Vice President of the United States.

Amendment 13   [*Ratified 1865*]

PROHIBITION OF SLAVERY

Section 1   Neither slavery nor involuntary servitude, except as a punishment for crime whereof the party shall have been duly convicted, shall exist within the United States, or any place subject to their jurisdiction.

Section 2   Congress shall have power to enforce this article by appropriate legislation.

Amendment 14   [*Ratified 1868*]

CITIZENSHIP, DUE PROCESS APPLIED TO THE STATES, EQUAL PROTECTION OF THE LAWS

Section 1   All persons born or naturalized in the United States and subject to the jurisdiction thereof, are citizens of the United States and of the State wherein they reside. No State shall make or enforce any law which shall abridge the privileges or immunities of citizens of the United States; nor shall any State deprive any person of life, liberty, or property, without due process of law; nor deny to any person within its jurisdiction the equal protection of the laws.

Section 2   Representatives shall be apportioned among the several States according to their respective numbers, counting the whole number of persons in each State, excluding Indians not taxed. But when the right to vote at any election for the choice of electors for President and Vice President of the Unitd States, Representatives in Congress, the Executive and Judicial officers of a State, or the members of the Legislature thereof, is denied to any of the male inhabitants of such State, being twenty-one[11] years of age, and citizens of the United States,

---

[10] Changed by the Twentieth Amendment.
[11] Changed by the Twenty-sixth Amendment.

or in any way abridged, except for participation in rebellion, or other crime, the basis of representation therein shall be reduced in the proportion which the number of such male citizens shall bear to the whole number of male citizens twenty-one years of age in such State.

Section 3   No person shall be a Senator or Representative in Congress, or elector of President and Vice President, or hold any office, civil or military, under the United States, or under any State, who, having previously taken an oath, as a member of Congress, or as an officer of the United States, or as a member of any State legislature, or as an executive or judicial officer of any State, to support the Constitution of the United States, shall have engaged in insurrection or rebellion against the same, or given aid or comfort to the enemies thereof. But Congress may by a vote of two-thirds of each House, remove such disability.

Section 4   The validity of the public debt of the United States, authorized by law, including debts incurred for payment of pensions and bounties for services in suppressing insurrection or rebellion, shall not be questioned. But neither the United States nor any State shall assume or pay any debt or obligation incurred in aid of insurrection or rebellion against the United States, or any claim for the loss or emancipation of any slave; but all such debts, obligations and claims shall be held illegal and void.

Section 5   The Congress shall have power to enforce, by appropriate legislation, the provisions of this article.

Amendment 15   [*Ratified 1870*]

RIGHT TO VOTE

Section 1   The right of citizens of the United States to vote shall not be denied or abridged by the United States or by any State on account of race, color, or previous condition of servitude.

Section 2   The Congress shall have power to enforce this article by appropriate legislation.

Amendment 16   [*Ratified 1913*]

INCOME TAXES

The Congress shall have power to lay and collect taxes on incomes, from whatever source derived, without apportionment among the several States, and without regard to any census or enumeration.

Amendment 17   [*Ratified 1913*]

DIRECT ELECTION OF SENATORS

The Senate of the United States shall be composed of two Senators from each State, elected by the people thereof, for six years; and each Senator shall have one vote. The electors in each State shall have the qualifications requisite for electors of the most numerous branch of the State legislatures.

When vacancies happen in the representation of any State in the Senate, the executive authority of such State shall issue writs of election to fill such vacancies: *Provided,* That the legislature of any State may empower the executive thereof to make temporary appointments until the people fill the vacancies by election as the legislature may direct.

This amendment shall not be so construed as to affect the election or term of any Senator chosen before it becomes valid as part of the Constitution.

Amendment 18   [*Ratified 1919*]

PROHIBITION   *Section 1*   After one year from the ratification of this article the manufacture, sale, or transportation of intoxicating liquors within, the importation thereof into, or the exportation thereof from the United States and all territory subject to the jurisdiction thereof for beverage purposes is hereby prohibited.

Section 2   The Congress and the several States shall have concurrent power to enforce this article by appropriate legislation.

Section 3   This article shall be inoperative unless it shall have been ratified as an amendment to the Constitution by the legislatures of the several States, as provided in the Constitution, within seven years from the date of the submission hereof to the States by the Congress.[12]

Amendment 19   [*Ratified 1920*]

RIGHT TO VOTE FOR WOMEN   The right of citizens of the United States to vote shall not be denied or abridged by the United States or by any State on account of sex.

Congress shall have power to enforce this article by appropriate legislation.

Amendment 20   [*Ratified 1933*]

TERMS OF OFFICE   *Section 1*   The terms of the President and Vice President shall end at noon on the 20th day of January, and the terms of Senators and Representatives at noon on the 3d day of January, of the years in which such terms would have ended if this article had not been ratified; and the terms of their successors shall then begin.

Section 2   The Congress shall assemble at least once in every year, and such meeting shall begin at noon on the 3d day of January, unless they shall by law appoint a different day.

EMERGENCY PRESIDENTIAL SUCCESSION   *Section 3*   If, at the time fixed for the beginning of the term of the President, the President elect shall have died, the Vice President elect shall become President. If a President shall not have been chosen before the time fixed for the beginning of his term, or if the President elect shall have failed to qualify, then the Vice President elect shall act as President until a President shall have qualified; and the Congress may by law provide for the case wherein neither a President elect nor a Vice President elect shall have qualified, declaring who shall then act as President, or the manner in which one who is to act shall be selected, and such person shall act accordingly until a President or Vice President shall have qualified.

Section 4   The Congress may by law provide for the case of the death of any of the persons from whom the House of Representatives may choose a President whenever the right of choice shall have devolved upon them, and for the case of the death of any of the persons from whom the Senate may choose a Vice President whenever the right of choice shall have devolved upon them.

Section 5   Sections 1 and 2 shall take effect on the 15th day of October following the ratification of this article.

---

[12] Repealed by the Twenty-first Amendment.

Section 6   This article shall be inoperative unless it shall have been ratified as an amendment to the Constitution by the legislatures of three-fourths of the several States within seven years from the date of its submission.

Amendment 21   [Ratified 1933]

REPEAL OF PROHIBITION

Section 1   The eighteenth article of amendment to the Constitution of the United States is hereby repealed.

Section 2   The transportation or importation into any State, Territory, or possession of the United States for delivery or use therein of intoxicating liquors, in violation of the laws thereof, is hereby prohibted.

Section 3   This article shall be inoperative unless it shall have been ratified as an amendment to the Constitution by conventions in the several States, as provided in the Constitution, within seven years from the date of the submission hereof to the States by the Congress.

Amendment 22   [Ratified 1951]

NUMBER OF TERMS FOR PRESIDENT

Section 1   No person shall be elected to the office of the President more than twice, and no person who has held the office of President, or acted as President, for more than two years of a term to which some other person was elected President shall be elected to the office of the President more than once. But this Article shall not apply to any person holding the office of President when this Article was proposed by the Congress, and shall not prevent any person who may be holding the office of President, or acting as President, during the term within which this Article becomes operative from holding the office of President or acting as President during the remainder of such term.

Section 2   This Article shall be inoperative unless it shall have been ratified as an amendment to the Constitution by the legislatures of three-fourths of the several States within seven years from the date of its submission to the States by the Congress.

Amendment 23   [Ratified 1961]

PRESIDENTIAL ELECTIONS, DISTRICT OF COLUMBIA

Section 1   The District constituting the seat of Government of the United States shall appoint in such manner as the congress may direct:
   A number of electors of President and Vice President equal to the whole number of Senators and Representatives in Congress to which the District would be entitled if it were a State, but in no event more than the least populous State; they shall be in addition to those appointed by the States, but they shall be considered, for the purposes of the election of President and Vice President, to be electors appointed by a State; and they shall meet in the District and perform such duties as provided by the twelfth article of amendment.

Section 2   The Congress shall have power to enforce this article by appropriate legislation.

Amendment 24   [Ratified 1964]

PROHIBITION OF POLL TAXES

Section 1 The right of citizens of the United States to vote in any primary or other election for President or Vice President, for electors for President or Vice President, or for Senator or Representative in Congress, shall not be denied or abridged by the United States or any State by reason of failure to pay any poll tax or other tax.

Section 2 The Congress shall have power to enforce this article by appropriate legislation.

Amendment 25 [*Ratified 1967*]

PRESIDENTIAL DISABILITY AND SUCCESSION

Section 1 In case of the removal of the President from office or of his death or resignation, the Vice President shall become President.

Section 2 Whenever there is a vacancy in the office of the Vice President, the President shall nominate a Vice president who shall take office upon confirmation by a majority vote of both Houses of Congress.

Section 3 Whenever the President transmits to the President pro tempore of the Senate and the Speaker of the House of Representatives his written declaration that he is unable to discharge the powers and duties of his office, and until he transmits to them a written declaration to the contrary, such powers and duties shall be discharged by the Vice President as Acting President.

Section 4 Whenever the Vice President and a majority of either the principal officers of the executive departments or of such other body as Congress may by law provide, transmit to the President pro tempore of the Senate and the Speaker of the House of Representatives their written declaration that the President is unable to discharge the powers and duties of his office, the Vice President shall immediately assume the powers and duties of the office as Acting President.

Thereafter, when the President transmits to the President pro tempore of the Senate and the Speaker of the House of Representatives his written declaration that no inability exists, he shall resume the powers and duties of his office unless the Vice President and a majority of either the principal officers of the executive department or of such other body as Congress may by law provide, transmit within four days to the President pro tempore of the Senate and the Speaker of the House of Representatives their written declaration that the President is unable to discharge the powers and duties of his office. Thereupon Congress shall decide the issue, assembling within forty-eight hours for that purpose if not in session. If the Congress, within twenty-one days after receipt of the latter written declaration, or, if Congress is not in session, within twenty-one days after Congress is required to assemble, determines by two-thirds vote of both Houses that the President is unable to discharge the powers and duties of his office, the Vice President shall continue to discharge the same as Acting President; otherwise, the President shall resume the powers and duties of his office.

Amendment 26 [*Ratified 1971*]

EIGHTEEN-YEAR-OLD VOTING AGE

Section 1 The right of citizens of the United States, who are eighteen years of age or older, to vote shall not be denied or abridged by the United States or by any State on account of age.

Section 2 The Congress shall have power to enforce this article by appropriate legislation.

APPENDIX B

SECURITIES ACT OF 1933*

DEFINITIONS   *Section 2*   When used in this title, unless the context requires—

(1) The term "security" means any note, stock, treasury stock, bond, debenture, evidence of indebtedness, certificate of interest or participation in any profit-sharing agreement, collateral-trust certificate, preorganization certificate or subscription, transferable share, investment contract, voting-trust certificate, certificate of deposit for a security, fractional undivided interest in oil, gas, or other mineral rights, any put, call, straddle, option, or privilege on any security, certificate of deposit, or group or index of securities (including any interest therein or based on the value thereof), or any put, call, straddle, option, or privilege entered into on a national securities exchange relating to foreign currency, or, in general, any interest or instrument commonly known as a "security," or any certificate of interest or participation in, temporary or interim certificate for, receipt for, guarantee of, or warrant or right to subscribe to or purchase, any of the foregoing.

EXEMPTED
SECURITIES   *Section 3*   (a) Except as hereinafter expressly provided the provisions of this title shall not apply to any of the following classes of securities:

*   *   *   *   *

(2) Any security issued or guaranteed by the United States or any territory thereof, or by the District of Columbia, or by any State of the United States, or by any political subdivision of a State or Territory, or by any public instrumentality of one or more States or Territories, or by any person controlled or supervised by and acting as an instrumentality of the Government of the United States pursuant to authority granted by the Congress of the United States; or any certificate of deposit for any of the foregoing; or any security issued or guaranteed by any bank; or any security issued by or representing an interest in or a direct obligation of a Federal Reserve bank. . . .

(3) Any note, draft, bill of exchange, or banker's acceptance which arises out of a current transaction or the proceeds of which have been or are to be used for current transactions, and which has a maturity at the time of issuance of not exceeding nine months, exclusive of days of grace, or any renewal thereof the maturity of which is likewise limited;

(4) Any security issued by a person organized and operated exclusively for religious, educational, benevolent, fraternal, charitable, or reformatory purposes

---

* This material is excerpted from the Securities Act of 1933, as amended.

and not for pecuniary profit, and no part of the net earnings of which inures to the benefit of any person, private stockholder, or individual;

*   *   *   *   *

(11) Any security which is a part of an issue offered and sold only to persons resident within a single State or Territory, where the issuer of such security is a person resident and doing business within, or, if a corporation, incorporated by and doing business within, such State or Territory.

(b) The Commission may from time to time by its rules and regulations and subject to such terms and conditions as may be described therein, add any class of securities to the securities exempted as provided in this section, if it finds that the enforcement of this title with respect to such securities is not necessary in the public interest and for the protection of investors by reason of the small amount involved or the limited character of the public offering; but no issue of securities shall be exempted under this subsection where the aggregate amount at which such issue is offered to the public exceeds $5,000,000.

EXEMPTED TRANSACTIONS

Section 4   The provisions of section 5 shall not apply to—

(1) transactions by any person other than an issuer, underwriter, or dealer.

(2) transactions by an issuer not involving any public offering.

(3) transactions by a dealer (including an underwriter no longer acting as an underwriter in respect of the security involved in such transactions), except—

> (A) transactions taking place prior to the expiration of forty days after the first date upon which the security was bona fide offered to the public by the issuer or by or through an underwriter,
>
> (B) transactions in a security as to which a registration statement has been filed taking place prior to the expiration of forty days after the effective date of such registration statement or prior to the expiration of forty days after the first date upon which the security was bona fide offered to the public by the issuer or by or through an underwriter after such effective date, whichever is later (excluding in the computation of such forty days any time during which a stop order issued under section 8 is in effect as to the security), or such shorter period as the Commission may specify by rules and regulations or order, and
>
> (C) transactions as to securities constituting the whole or a part of an unsold allotment to or subscription by such dealer as a participant in the distribution of such securities by the issuer or by or through an underwriter.

With respect to transactions referred to in clause (B), if securities of the issuer have not previously been sold pursuant to an earlier effective registration statement the applicable period, instead of forty days, shall be ninety days, or such shorter period as the Commission may specify by rules and regulations or order.

(4) brokers' transactions, executed upon customers' orders on any exchange or in the over-the-counter market but not the solicitation of such orders.

*   *   *   *   *

(6) transactions involving offers or sales by an issuer solely to one or more accredited investors, if the aggregate offering price of an issue of securities offered in reliance on this paragraph does not exceed the amount allowed under section 3(b) of this title, if there is no advertising or public solicitation in connection with the transaction by the issuer or anyone acting on the issuer's behalf, and if the issuer files such notice with the Commission as the Commission shall prescribe.

PROHIBITIONS RELATING TO INTERSTATE COMMERCE AND THE MAILS

Section 5 (a) Unless a registration statement is in effect as to a security, it shall be unlawful for any person, directly or indirectly—

(1) to make use of any means or instruments of transportation or communication in interstate commerce or of the mails to sell such security through the use or medium of any prospectus or otherwise; or

(2) to carry or cause to be carried through the mails or in interstate commerce, by any means or instruments of transportation, any such security for the purpose of sale or for delivery after sale.

(b) It shall be unlawful for any person, directly or indirectly—

(1) to make use of any menas or instuments of transportation or communication in interstate commerce or of the mails to carry or transmit any prospectus relating to any security with respect to which a registration statement has been filed under this title, unless such prospectus meets the requirements of section 10, or

(2) to carry or to cause to be carried through the mails or in interstate commerce any such security for the purpose of sale or for delivery after sale, unless accompanied or preceded by a prospectus that meets the requirements of subsection (a) of section 10.

(c) It shall be unlawful for any person, directly or indirectly, to make use of any means or instruments of transportation or communication in interstate commerce or of the mails to offer to sell or offer to buy through the use or medium of any prospectus or otherwise any security, unless a registration statement has been filed as to such security, or while the registration statement is the subject of a refusal order or stop order or (prior to the effective date of the registration statement) any public proceeding of examination under section 8.

APPENDIX C

SECURITIES EXCHANGE ACT OF 1934*

DEFINITIONS AND APPLICATION OF TITLE

Section 3 (a) When used in this title, unless the context otherwise requires—

* * * * *

(4) The term "broker" means any person engaged in the business of effecting transactions in securities for the account of others, but does not include a bank.

(5) The term "dealer" means any person engaged in the business of buying and selling securities for his own account, through a broker or otherwise, but does not include a bank, or any person insofar as he buys or sells securities for his own account, either individually or in some fiduciary capacity, but not as part of a regular business.

* * * * *

(7) The term "director" means any director of a corporation or any person performing similar functions with respect to any organization, whether incorporated or unincorporated.

(8) The term "issuer" means any person who issues or proposes to issue any security; except that with respect to certificates of deposit for securities, voting-trust certificates, or collateral-trust certificates, or with respect to certificates of interest or shares in an unincorporated investment trust not having a board of directors or the fixed, restricted management, or unit type, the term "issuer" means the person or persons performing the acts and assuming the duties of depositor or manager pursuant to the provisions of the trust or other agreement or instrument under which such securities are issued; and except that with respect to equipment-trust certificates or like securities, the term "issuer" means the person by whom the equipment or property is, or is to be, used.

(9) The term "person" means a natural person, company, government, or political subdivision, agency, or instrumentality of a government.

REGULATION OF THE USE OF MANIPULATIVE AND DECEPTIVE DEVICES

Section 10 It shall be unlawful for any person, directly or indirectly, by the use of any means or instrumentality of interstate commerce or of the mails, or of any facility of any national securities exchange—

(a) To effect a short sale, or to use or employ any stop-loss order in connection with the purchase or sale, of any security registered on a national securities exchange, in contravention of such rules and regulations as the Commission may prescribe as necessary or appropriate in the public interest or for the protection of investors.

(b) To use or employ, in connection with the purchase or sale of any security registered on a national securities exchange or any security not so registered, any manipulative or deceptive device or contrivance in contravention of such rules and regulations as the Commission may prescribe as necessary or appropriate in the public interest or for the protection of investors.

---

* This material is excerpted from the Securities Exchange Act of 1934, as amended.

APPENDIX D

THE SHERMAN ACT*

RESTRAINTS OF TRADE PROHIBITED

Section 1   Trusts, etc., in restraint of trade illegal; penalty.   Every contract, combination in the form of trust or otherwise, or conspiracy, in restraint of trade or commerce among the several States, or with foreign nations, is declared to be illegal. Every person who shall make any contract or engage in any combination or conspiracy declared by sections 1 to 7 of this title to be illegal shall be deemed guilty of a felony, and, on conviction thereof, shall be punished by fine not exceeding one million dollars if a corporation, or if any other person, one hundred thousand dollars, or by imprisonment not exceeding three years, or both said punishments, in the discretion of the court.

MONOPO- LIZING PROHIBITED

Section 2   Monopolizing trade a felony; penalty.   Every person who shall monopolize, or attempt to monopolize, or combine or conspire with any other person or persons, to monopolize any part of the trade or commerce among the several States, or with foreign nations, shall be deemed guilty of a felony, and, on conviction thereof, shall be punished by fine not exceeding one million dollars if a corporation, or, if any other person, one hundred thousand dollars, or by imprisonment not exceeding three years, or by both said punishments, in the discretion of the court.

* This material is excerpted from the Sherman Act, as amended.

THE CLAYTON ACT*

REFUSALS TO DEAL

Section 3 Sale, etc., on agreement not to use goods of competitor. It shall be unlawful for any person engaged in commerce, in the course of such commerce, to lease or make a sale or contract for sale of goods, wares, merchandise, machinery, supplies, or other commodities, whether patented or unpatented, for use, consumption, or resale within the United States or any Territory thereof or the District of Columbia or any insular possession or other place under the jurisdiction of the United States, or fix a price charged thereof, or discount from, or rebate upon, such price, on the condition, agreement, or understanding that the lessee or purchaser thereof shall not use or deal in the goods, wares, merchandise, machinery, supplies, or other commodities of a competitor or competitors of the lessor or seller, where the effect of such lease, sale, or contract for sale or such condition, agreement or understanding may be to substantially lessen competition or tend to create a monopoly in any line of commerce.

PRIVATE SUITS

Section 4 Suits by persons injured; amount of recovery. Any person who shall be injured in his business or property by reason of anything forbidden in the antitrust laws may sue therefor in any district court of the United States in the district in which the defendant resides or is found or has an agent, without respect to the amount in controversy, and shall recover threefold the damages by him sustained, and the cost of suit, including a reasonable attorney's fee. . . .

MERGERS

Section 7 Acquisition by one corporation of stock of another. No corporation engaged in commerce shall acquire, directly or indirectly, the whole or any part of the stock or other share capital and no corporation subject to the jurisdiction of the Federal Trade Commission shall acquire the whole or any part of the assets of another corporation engaged also in commerce, where in any line of commerce in any section of the country, the effect of such acquisition may be substantially to lessen competition, or to tend to create a monopoly.

No corporation shall acquire, directly or indirectly, the whole or any part of the stock or other share capital and no corporation subject to the jurisdiction of the Federal Trade Commission shall acquire the whole or any part of the assets of one or more corporations engaged in commerce, where in any line of commerce in any section of the country, the effect of such acquisition, of such stocks or assets, or of the use of such stock by the voting or granting of proxies or otherwise, may be substantially to lessen competition, or to tend to create a monopoly.

---

* This material is excerpted from the Clayton Act, as amended.

This section shall not apply to corporations purchasing such stock solely for investment and not using the same by voting or otherwise to bring about, or in attempting to bring about, the substantial lessening of competition. Nor shall anything contained in this section prevent a corporation engaged in commerce from causing the formation of subsidiary corporations for the actual carrying on of their immediate lawful business, or the natural and legitimate branches or extensions thereof, or from owning and holding all or part of the stock of such subsidiary corporations, when the effect of such formation is not to substantially lessen competition.

INTERLOCK-ING DIREC-TORATES

Section 8   Interlocking directorates and officers. . . .

No person at the same time shall be a director in any two or more corporations, any one of which has capital, surplus, and undivided profits aggregating more than $1,000,000, engaged in whole or in part in commerce, other than banks, banking associations, trust companies, and common carriers subject to the Act to regulate commerce approved February fourth, eighteen hundred and eighty-seven, if such corporations are or shall have been theretofore, by virtue of their business and location or operation, competitors, so that the elimination of competition by agreement between them would constitute a violation of any of the provisions of any of the antitrust laws. The eligibility of a director under the foregoing provision shall be determined by the aggregate amount of the capital, surplus, and undivided profits, exclusive of dividends declared but not paid to stockholders, at the end of the fiscal year of said corporation next preceding the election of directors, and when a director has been elected in accordance with the provisions of this Act it shall be lawful for him to continue as such for one year thereafter.

APPENDIX F

THE FEDERAL TRADE COMMISSION ACT*

UNFAIR METHODS OF COMPETITION PROHIBITED

Section 5   Unfair methods of competition unlawful; prevention by Commission— declaration. Declaration of unlawfulness; power to prohibit unfair practices.

(a) (1) Unfair methods of competition in or affecting commerce, and unfair or deceptive acts or practices in or affecting commerce, are declared unlawful. . . .

Penalty for violation of order, injunctions and other appropriate equitable relief.

(b) Any person, partnership, or corporation who violates an order of the Commission to cease and desist after it has become final, and while such order is in effect, shall forfeit and pay to the United States a civil penalty of not more than $5,000 for each violation, which shall accrue to the United States and may be recovered in a civil action brought by the Attorney General of the United States. Each separate violation of such an order shall be a separate offense, except that in the case of a violation through continuing failure or neglect to obey a final order of the Commission each day of continuance of such failure or neglect shall be deemed a separate offense.

---

* This material is excerpted from the Federal Trade Commission Act, as amended.

APPENDIX G

THE ROBINSON–PATMAN ACT*

PRICE DISCRIMINATION; COST JUSTIFICATION; CHANGING CONDITIONS

Section 2 Discrimination in price, services, or facilities.

(a) Price; selection of customers.

It shall be unlawful for any person engaged in commerce, in the course of such commerce, either directly or indirectly, to discriminate in price between different purchases of commodities of like grade and quality, where either or any of the purchasers involved in such discrimination are in commerce, where such commodities are sold for use, consumption, or resale within the United States or any Territory thereof or the District of Columbia or any insular possession or other place under the jurisdiction of the United States, and where the effect of such discrimination may be substantially to lessen competition or tend to create a monopoly in any line of commerce, or to injure, destroy, or prevent competition with any person who either grants or knowingly receives the benefit of such discrimination, or with customers of either of them: *Provided,* That nothing herein contained shall prevent differentials which make only due allowance for differences in the cost of manufacture, sale, or delivery resulting from the differing methods or quantitites in which such commodities are to such purchasers sold or delivered: *Provided, however,* That the Federal Trade Commission may, after due investigation and hearing to all interested parties, fix and establish quantity limits, and revise the same as it finds necessary as to particular commodities or classes of commodities, where it finds that available purchasers in greater quantitites are so few as to render differentials on account thereof unjustly discriminatory or promotive of monopoly in any line of commerce; and the foregoing shall then not be construed to permit differentials based on differences in quantities greater than those so fixed and established: *And provided further,* That nothing herein contained shall prevent persons engaged in selling goods, wares, or merchandise in commerce from selecting their own customers in bona fide transactions and not in restraint of trade: *And provided further,* That nothing herein contained shall prevent price changes from time to time where in response to changing conditions affecting the market for or the market-ability of the goods concerned, such as but not limited to actual or imminent deterioration of perishable goods, obsolescence of seasonal goods, distress sales under court process, or sales in good faith in discontinuance of business in the goods concerned.

MEETING COMPETITION

(b) Burden of rebutting prima-facie case of discrimination.

Upon proof being made, at any hearing on a complaint under this section, that there has been discrimination in price or services or facilities furnished,

---

* This material is excerpted from the Robinson–Patman Act, as amended.

the burden of rebutting the prima-facie case thus made by showing justification shall be upon the person charged with a violation of this section, and unless justification shall be affirmatively shown, the Commission is authorized to issue an order terminating the discrimination: *Provided, however,* That nothing herein contained shall prevent a seller rebutting the prima-facie case thus made by showing that his lower price or the furnishing of services or facilities to any purchaser or purchasers was made in good faith to meet an equally low price of a competitor, or the services or facilities furnished by a competitor.

BROKERAGE PAYMENTS

(c) Payment or acceptance of commission, brokerage or other compensation.

It shall be unlawful for any person engaged in commerce, in the course of such commerce, to pay or grant, or to receive or accept, anything of value as a commission, brokerage, or other compensation, or any allowance of discount in lieu thereof, except for services rendered in connection with the sale or purchase of goods, wares, or merchandise, either to the other party to such transaction or to an agent, representative, or other intermediary therein where such intermediary is acting in fact for or in behalf, or is subject to the direct or indirect control, of any party to such transaction other than the person by whom such compensation is so granted or paid.

PROMO-TIONAL ALLOWANCES

(d) Payment for services or facilities for processing or sale.

It shall be unlawful for any person engaged in commerce to pay or contract for the payment of anything of value to or for the benefit of a customer of such person in the course of such commerce as compensation or in consideration for any services or facilities furnished by or through such customer in connection with the processing, handling, sale, or offering for sale of any products or commodities manufactured, sold, or offered for sale by such person, unless such payment of consideration is available on proportionally equal terms to all other customers competing in the distribution of such products or commodities.

PROMO-TIONAL SERVICES

(e) Furnishing services or facilities for processing, handling, etc.

It shall be unlawful for any person to discriminate in favor of one purchaser against another purchaser or purchasers of a commodity bought for resale, with or without processing, by contracting to furnish or furnishing, or by contributing to the furnishing of, any services or facilities connected with the processing, handling, sale, or offering for sale of such commodity so purchased upon terms not accorded to all purchasers on proportionally equal terms.

BUYER DISCRIMINA-TION

(f) Knowingly inducing or receiving discriminatory price.

It shall be unlawful for any person engaged in commerce, in the course of such commerce, knowingly to induce or receive a discrimination in price which is prohibited by this section.

PREDATORY PRACTICES

Section 3 Discrimination in rebates, discounts, or advertising service charges; underselling in particular localities; penalties. It shall be unlawful for any person engaged in commerce, in the course of such commerce, to be a party to, or assist in, any transaction of sale, or contract to sell, which discriminates to his knowledge against competitors of the purchaser, in that, any discount, rebate, allowance, or advertising service charge is granted to the purchaser over and above any discount, rebate, allowance, or advertising service charge available at the time of such transaction to said competitors in respect of a sale of goods of like grade, quality, and quantity; to sell, or contract to sell, goods in any part of the United States at prices lower than those exacted by said person elsewhere in the United States for the purpose of destroying competition, or eliminating a competitor in such part of the United States; or, to sell, or contract to sell, goods at unreasonably low prices for the purpose of destroying competition or eliminating a competitor.

Any person violating any of the provisions of this section shall, upon conviction thereof, be fined not more than $5,000 or imprisoned not more than one year, or both.

NATIONAL LABOR RELATIONS ACT*

DEFINITIONS   *Section 2*   When used in this Act—

(2) The term "employer" includes any person acting as an agent of an employer, directly or indirectly, but shall not include the United States or any wholly owned Government corporation, or any Federal Reserve Bank, or any State or political subdivision thereof, or any person subject to the Railway Labor Act, as amended from time to time, or any labor organization (other than when acting as an employer), or anyone acting in the capacity of officer or agent of such labor organization.

(3) The term "employee" shall include any employee, and shall not be limited to the employees of a particular employer, unless the Act explicitly states otherwise, and shall include any individual whose work has ceased as a consequence of, or in connection with, any current labor dispute or because of any unfair labor practice, and who has not obtained any other regular and substantially equivalent employment, but shall not include any individual employed as an agricultural laborer, or in the domestic service of any family or person at his home, or any individual employed by his parent or spouse, or any individual having the status of an independent contractor, or any individual employed as a supervisor, or any individual employed by an employer subject to the Railway Labor Act, as amended from time to time, or by any other person who is not an employer as herein defined.

(11) The term "supervisor" means any individual having authority, in the interest of the employer, to hire, transfer, suspend, lay off, recall, promote, discharge, assign, reward, or discipline other employees, or responsibly to direct them, or to adjust their grievances, or effectively to recommend such action, if in connection with the foregoing the exercise of such authority is not of a merely routine or clerical nature, but requires the use of independent judgment.

(12) The term "professional employee" means—

(a) any employee engaged in work (i) predominantly intellectual and varied in character as opposed to routine mental, manual, mechanical, or physical work; (ii) involving the consistent exercise of discretion and judgment in its performance; (iii) of such a character that the output produced or the result accomplished cannot be standardized in relation to a given period of time; (iv) requiring knowledge of an advanced type in a field of science or learning customarily acquired by a prolonged course of specialized intellectual instruction and study in an institution of higher learning or a hospital, as distinguished from a general academic educa-

---

* This material is excerpted from the National Labor Relations Act, as amended.

tion or from an apprenticeship or from training in the performance of routine mental, manual, or physical processes; or

(b) any employee, who (i) has completed the courses of specialized intellectual instruction and study described in clause (iv) of paragraph (a), and (ii) is performing related work under the supervision of a professional person to qualify himself to become a professional employee as defined in paragraph (a).

RIGHTS OF EMPLOYEES

Section 7 Employees shall have the right to self-organization, to form, join, or assist labor organizations, to bargain collectively through representatives of their own choosing, and to engage in other concerted activities for the purpose of collective bargaining or other mutual aid or protection, and shall also have the right to refrain from any or all of such activities except to the extent that such right may be affected by an agreement requiring membership in a labor organization as a condition of employment as authorized in section 8(a)(3).

UNFAIR LABOR PRACTICES

Section 8 (a) It shall be an unfair labor practice for an employer—

(1) to interfere with, restrain, or coerce employees in the exercise of the rights guaranteed in section 7;

(2) to dominate or interfere with the formation or administration of any labor organization or contribute financial or other support to it: *Provided,* That subject to rules and regulations made and published by the Board pursuant to section 6, an employer shall not be prohibited from permitting employees to confer with him during working hours without loss of time or pay;

(3) by discriminatoin in regard to hire or tenure of employment or any term or condition of employment to encourage or discourage membership in any labor organization: *Provided,* That nothing in this Act, or in any other statute of the United States, shall preclude an employer from making an agreement with a labor organization (not established, maintained, or assisted by any action defined in section 8(a) of this Act as an unfair labor practice) to require as a condition of employment membership therein on or after the thirtieth day following the beginning of such employment or the effective date of such agreement, whichever is the later, (i) if such labor organization is the representative of the employees as provided in section 9(a), in the appropriate collective-bargaining unit covered by such agreement when made, and (ii) unless following an election held as provided in section 9(e) within one year preceding the effective date of such agreement, the Board shall have certified that at least a majority of the employees eligible to vote in such election have voted to rescind the authority of such labor organization to make such an agreement: *Provided further,* That no employer shall justify any discrimination against an employee for nonmembership in a labor organization (A) if he has reasonable grounds for believing that such membership was not available to the employee on the same terms and conditions generally applicable to other members, or (B) if he had reasonable grounds for believing that membership was denied or terminated for reasons other than the failure of the employee to tender the periodic dues and the initiation fees uniformly required as a condition of acquiring or retaining membership;

(4) to discharge or otherwise discriminate against an employee because he has filed charges or given testimony under this Act;

(5) to refuse to bargain collectively with the representatives of his employees, subject to the provisions of section 9(a).

(b) It shall be an unfair labor practice for a labor organization or its agents—

(1) to restrain or coerce (A) employees in the exercise of the rights guaranteed in section 7: *Provided,* That this paragraph shall not impair the right of a labor organization to prescribe its own rules with respect to the acquisition or retention of membership therein; or (B) an employer in the selection of his representatives for the purposes of collective bargaining or the adjustment of grievances;

(2) to cause or attempt to cause an employer to discriminate against an employee in violation of subsection (a)(3) or to discriminate against an employee with respect to whom membership in such organization has been denied or terminated on some ground other than his failure to tender the periodic dues and the initiation fees uniformly required as a condition of acquiring or retaining membership;

(3) to refuse to bargain collectively with an employer, provided it is the representative of his employees subject to the provisions of section 9(a);

(4) (i) to engage in, or to induce or encourage any individual employed by any person engaged in commerce or in an industry affecting commerce to engage in, a strike or a refusal in the course of his employment to use, manufacture, process, transport, or otherwise handle or work on any goods, articles, materials, or commodities or to perform any services; or (ii) to threaten, coerce, or restrain any person engaged in commerce or in an industry affecting commerce, where in either case an object thereof is—

(A) forcing or requiring any employer or self-employed person to join any labor or employer organization or to enter into any agreement which is prohibited by section 8(e);

(B) forcing or requiring any person to cease using, selling, handling, transporting, or otherwise dealing in the products of any other producer, processor, or manufacturer, or to cease doing business with any other person, or forcing or requiring any other employer to recognize or bargain with a labor organization as the representative of his employees unless such labor organization has been certified as the representative of such employees under the provisions of section 9: *Provided,* That nothing contained in this clause (B) shall be construed to make unlawful, where not otherwise unlawful, any primary strike or primary picketing;

(C) forcing or requiring any employer to recognize or bargain with a particular labor organization as the representative of his employees if another labor organization has been certified as the representative of such employees under the provisions of section 9;

(D) forcing or requiring any employer to assign particular work to employees in a particular labor organization or in a particular trade, craft, or class rather than to employees in another labor organization or in another trade, craft, or class, unless such employer is failing to conform to an order or certification of the Board determining the bargaining representative for employees performing such work:

Provided, That nothing contained in this subsection (b) shall be construed to make unlawful a refusal by any person to enter upon the premises of any employer (other than his own employer), if the employees of such employer are engaged in a strike ratified or approved by a representative of such employees whom such employer is required to recognize under this Act: *Provided further,* That for the purposes of this paragraph (4) only, nothing contained in such paragraph shall be construed to prohibit publicity, other than picketing, for the purpose of truthfully advising the public, including consumers and members of a labor organization, that a product or products are produced by an employer with whom the labor organization has a primary dispute and are distributed by another employer, as long as such publicity does not have an effect of inducing any individual employed by any person other than the primary employer in the course of his employment to refuse to pick up, deliver, or transport any goods, or not to perform any services, at the establishment of the employer engaged in such distribution:

(5) to require of employees covered by an agreement authorized under subsection (a)(3) the payment, as a condition precedent to becoming a member of such organization, of a fee in an amount which the Boards finds excessive or discriminatory under all the circumstances. In making such a finding, the Borad shall consider, among other relevant factors, the practices and customs of labor organizations in the particular industry, and the wages currently paid to the employees affected;

(6) to cause or attempt to cause an employer to pay or deliver or agree to pay or deliver any money or other thing of value, in the nature of an exaction, for services which are not performed or not to be performed; and

(7) To picket or cause to be picketed, or threatened to picket or cause to be picketed, any employer where an object thereof is forcing or requiring an employer to recognize or bargain with a labor organization as the representative of his employees, or forcing or requiring the employees of an employer to accept or select such labor organization as their collective bargaining representative, unless such labor organization is currently certified as the representative of such employees:

> (A) where the employer has lawfully recognized in accordance with this Act any other labor organization and a question concerning representation may not appropriately be raised under section 9(c) of this Act;
> (B) where within the preceding twelve months a valid election under section 9(c) of this Act has been conducted, or
> (C) where such picketing has been conducted without a petition under section 9(c) being filed within a reasonable period of time not to exceed thirty days from the commencement of such picketing; *Provided,* That when such a petition has been filed the Board shall forthwith, without regard to the provisions of section 9(c)(1) or the absence of a showing of a substantial interest on the part of the labor organization, direct an election in such unit as the Board finds to be appropriate and shall certify the results thereof: *Provided further,* That nothing in this subparagraph (C) shall be construed to prohibit any picketing or other publicity for the purpose of truthfully advising the public (including consumers) that an employer does not employ members of, or have a contract with, a labor organization, unless an effect of such picketing is to induce any individual employed by any other person in the course of his employment, not to pick up, deliver or transport any goods or not to perform any services.

Nothing in this paragraph (7) shall be construed to permit any act which would otherwise be an unfair labor practice under this section 8(b).

(c) The expressing of any views, argument, or opinion, or the dissemination thereof, whether in written, printed, graphic, or visual form, shall not constitute or be evidence of an unfair labor practice under any of the provisions of this Act, if such expression contains no threat of reprisal or force or promise of benefit.

(d) For the purposes of this section, to bargain collectively is the performance of the mutual obligation of the employer and the representative of the employees to meet at reasonable times and confer in good faith with respect to wages, hours, and other terms and conditions of employment, or the negotiation of an agreement, or any question arising thereunder, and the execution of a written contract incorporating any agreement reached if requested by either party, but such obligation does not compel either party to agree to a proposal or require the making of a concession: *Provided,* That where there is in effect a collective-bargaining contract covering employees in an industry affecting commerce, the duty to bargain collectively shall also mean that no party to such contract shall terminate or modify such contract, unless the party desiring such termination or modification—

(1) serves a written notice upon the other party to the contract of the proposed termination or modification sixty days prior to the expiration date thereof, or in the event such contract contains no expiration date, sixty days prior to the time it is proposed to make such termination or modification;

(2) offers to meet and confer with the other party for the purpose of negotiating a new contract or a contract containing the proposed modifications;

(3) notifies the Federal Mediation and Conciliation Service within thirty days after such notice of the existence of a dispute, and simultaneously therewith notifies any State or Territorial agency established to mediate and conciliate disputes within the State or Territory where the dispute occurred, provided no agreement has been reached by that time; and

(4) continues in full force and effect, without resorting to strike or lockout, all the terms and conditions of the existing contract for a period of sixty days after such notice is given or until the expiration date of such contract, whichever occurs later:

The duties imposed upon employers, employees, and labor organizations by paragraphs (2), (3), and (4) shall become inapplicable upon an intervening certification of the Board, under which the labor organization or individual, which is a party to the contract, has been superseded as or ceased to be the representative of the employees subject to the provisions of section 9(a), and the duties so imposed shall not be construed as requiring either party to discuss or agree to any modification of the terms and conditions contained in a contract for a fixed period, if such modification is to become effective before such terms and conditions can be reopened under the provisions of the contract. Any employee who engages in a strike within any notice periods specified in this subsection, or who engages in any strike within the appropriate period specified in subsection (g) of this section, shall lose his status as an employee of the employer engaged in the particular labor dispute, for the purposes of sections 8, 9, and 10 of this Act, but such loss of status for such employee shall terminate if and when he is reemployed by such employer. Whenever the collective bargaining involves employees of a health care institution, the provisions of this section 8(d) shall be modified as follows:

(A) The notice of section 8(d)(1) shall be ninety days; the notice of section 8(d)(3) shall be sixty days; and the contract period of section 8(d)(4) shall be ninety days.

(B) Where the bargaining is for an initial agreement following certification or recognition, at least thirty days' notice of the existence of a dispute shall be given by the labor organization to the agencies set forth in section 8(d)(3).

(C) After notice is given to the Federal Mediation and Conciliation Service under either clause (A) or (B) of this sentence, the Service shall promptly communicate with the parties and use its best efforts, by mediation and conciliation, to bring them to agreement. The parties shall participate fully and promptly in such meetings as may be undertaken by the Service for the purpose of aiding in a settlement of the dispute.

(e) It shall be an unfair labor practice for any labor organization and any employer to enter into any contract or agreement, express or implied, whereby such employer ceases or refrains or agrees to cease or refrain from handling, using, selling, transporting, or otherwise dealing in any of the products of any other employer, or to cease doing business with any other person, and any contract or agreement entered into heretofore or hereafter containing such an agreement shall be to such extent unenforcable and void: *Provided,* That nothing in this subsection (e) shall apply to an agreement between a labor organization and an employer in the construction industry relating to the contracting or subcontracting of work to be done at the site of the construction, alteration, painting, or repair of a building, structure, or other work: *Provided further,* That for the purposes of this subsection (e) and section 8(b)(4)(B) the terms "any employer," "any person engaged in commerce or any industry affecting other producer, processor, or manufacturer," "any other employer," or "any other person" shall not include persons in the relation of a jobber, manufacturer, contractor, or subcontractor working on the goods or premises of the jobber or manufacturer or performing parts of an integrated process of production in the apparel and clothing industry: *Provided further,* That nothing in this Act shall prohibit the enforcement of any agreement which is within the foregoing exception.

(f) It shall not be an unfair labor practice under subsections (a) and (b) of this section for an employer engaged primariy in the building and construction industry to make an agreement covering employees engaged (or who, upon their employment, will be engaged) in the building and construction industry with a labor organization of which building and construction employees are members (not established, maintained, or assisted by any action defined in section 8(a) of this Act as an unfair labor practice) because (1) the majority status of such labor organizations has not been established under the provisions of section 9 of this Act prior to the making of such agreement, or (2) such agreement requires as a condition of employment, membership in such labor organization after the seventh day following the beginning of such employment or the effective date of the agreement, whichever is later, or (3) such agreement requires the employer to notify such labor organization of opportunities for employment with such employer, or gives such labor organization an opportunity to refer qualified applicants for such employment, or (4) such agreement specifies minimum training or experience qualifications for employment or provides for priority in opportunities for employment based upon length of service with such employer, in the industry or in the particular geographical area: *Provided,* That nothing in this subsection shall set aside the final proviso to section 8(a)(3) of this Act: *Provided further,* That any agreement which would be invalid, but for clause (1) of this subsection, shall not be a bar to a petition filed pursuant to section 9(c) or 9(e).

(g) A labor organization before engaging in any strike, picketing, or other concerted refusal to work at any health care institution shall, not less than ten days prior to such action, notify the institution in writing and the Federal Mediation and Conciliation Service of that intention, except that in the case of bargaining for an initial agreement following certification or recognition the notice required by this subsection shall not be given until the expiration of the period specified in clause (b) of the last sentence of section 8(d) of this Act. The notice shall state the date and time that such action will commence. The notice, once given, may be extended by the written agreement of both parties.

REPRESENTA-TIVES AND ELECTIONS

Section 9   (a) Representatives designated or selected for the purposes of collective bargaining by the majority of the employees in a unit appropriate for such purposes, shall be the exclusive representatives of all the employees in such unit for the purposes of collective bargaining in respect to rates of pay, wages, hours of employment, or other conditions of employment: *Provided*, That any individual employee or a group of employees shall have the right at any time to present grievances to their employer and to have such grievances adjusted, without the intervention of the bargaining representative, as long as the adjustment is not inconsistent with the terms of a collective-bargaining contract or agreement then in effect: *Provided further*, That the bargaining representative has been given opportunity to be present at such adjustment.

(b) The Board shall decide in each case whether, in order to assure to employees the fullest freedom in exercising the rights guaranteed by this Act, the unit appropriate for the purposes of collective bargaining shall be the employer unit, craft unit, plant unit, or subdivision thereof: *Provided*, That the Board shall not (1) decide that any unit is appropriate for such purposes if such unit included both professional employees and employees who are not professional employees unless a majority of such professional employees vote for inclusion in such unit; or (2) decide that any craft unit is inappropriate for such purposes on the ground that a different unit has been established by a prior Board determination, unless a majority of the employees in the proposed craft unit vote against separate representation or (3) decide that any unit is appropriate for such purposes if it includes, together with other employees, any individual employed as a guard to enforce against employees and other persons rules to protect property of the employer or to protect the safety of persons on the employer's premises; but no later organization shall be certified as the representative of employees in a bargaining unit of guards if such organization admits to membership, or is affiliated directly or indirectly with an organization which admits to membership, employees other than guards.

(c)(1) Whenever a petition shall have been filed, in accordance with such regulations as may be prescribed by the Board—

(A) by an employee or group of employees or an individual or labor organization acting in their behalf alleging that a substantial number of employees (i) wish to be represented for collective bargaining and that their employer declines to recognize their representative as the representative defined in section 9(a), or (ii) assert that the individual or labor organization, which has been certified or is being currently recognized by their employer as the bargaining representative, is no longer a representative as defined in section 9(a); or

(B) by an employer, alleging that one or more individuals or labor organizations have presented to him a claim to be recognized as the representative defined in section 9(a); the Board shall investigate such petition and if it has reasonable cause to believe that a question of representation affecting commerce exists shall provide for an appropriate hearing upon due notice. Such hearing may be conducted by an officer or employee of the regional office, who shall not make any recommendations with respect thereto. If the Board finds upon the record of such hearing that such a question of representation exists, it shall direct an election by secret ballot and shall certify the results thereof.

(2) In determining whether or not a question of representation affecting commerce exists, the same regulations and rules of decision shall apply irrespective of the identity of the persons filing the petition or the kind of relief sought and in no case shall the Board deny a labor organization a place on the ballot by reason of an order with respect to such labor organization or its predecessor not issued in conformity with section 10(c).

(3) No election shall be directed in any bargaining unit or any subdivision within which, in the preceding twelve-month period, a valid election shall have been held. Employees engaged in an economic strike who are not entitled to reinstatement shall be eligible to vote under such regulations as the Board shall find are consistent with the purposes and provisions of this Act in any election conducted within twelve months after the commencement of the strike. In any election where none of the choices on the ballot receives a majority, a run-off shall be conducted, the ballot providing for a selection between the two choices receiving the largest and second largest number of valid votes cast in the election.

(4) Nothing in this section shall be construed to prohibit the waiving of hearings by stipulation for the purpose of a consent election in conformity with regulations and rules of decision of the Board.

(5) In determining whether a unit is appropriate for the purposes specified in subsection (b) the extent to which the employees have organized shall not be controlling.

(d) Whenever an order of the Board made pursuant to section 10(c) is based in whole or in part upon facts certified following an investigation pursuant to subsection (c) of this section and there is a petition for the enforcement or review of such order, such certification and the record of such investigation shall be included in the transcript of the entire record required to be filed under section 10(e) or 10(f), and thereupon the decree of the court enforcing, modifying, or setting aside in whole or in part the order of the Board shall be made and entered upon the pleadings, testimony, and proceedings set forth in such transcript.

(e)(1) Upon the filing with the Board, by 30 per centum or more of the employees in a bargaining unit covered by an agreement between their employer and a labor organization made pursuant to section 8(a)(3), of a petition alleging they desire that such authority be rescinded, the Board shall take a secret ballot of the employees in such unit, and shall certify the results thereof to such labor organization and to the employer.

(2) No election shall be conducted pursuant to this subsection in any bargaining unit or any subdivision within which, in the preceding twelve-month period, a valid election shall have been held.

TITLE VII OF CIVIL RIGHTS ACT OF 1964*

DEFINITIONS

Section 701

(j) The term "religion" includes all aspects of religious observance and practice, as well as belief, unless an employer demonstrates that he is unable to reasonably accommodate to an employee's or prospective employee's religious observance or practice without undue hardship on the conduct of the employer's business.

(k) The terms "because of sex" or "on the basis of sex" include, but are not limited to, because of or on the basis of pregnancy, childbirth or related medical conditions; and women affected by pregnancy, childbirth, or related medical conditions shall be treated the same for all employment-related purposes, including receipt of benefits under fringe benefit programs, as other persons not so affected but similar in their ability or inability to work, and nothing in Section 703(h) of this title shall not be interpreted to permit otherwise. This subsection shall not require an employer to pay for health insurance benefits for abortion, except where the life of the mother would be endangered if the fetus were carried to term, or except where medical complications have arisen from an abortion: *Provided,* That nothing herein shall preclude an employer from providing abortion benefits or otherwise effect bargaining agreements in regard to abortion.

DISCRIMINATION BECAUSE OF RACE, COLOR, RELIGION, SEX, OR NATIONAL ORIGIN

Section 703   (a) It shall be an unlawful employment practice for an employer—

(1) to fail or refuse to hire or to discharge any individual, or otherwise to discriminate against any individual with respect to his compensation, terms, conditions, or privileges of employment, because of such individual's race, color, religion, sex, or national origin; or

(2) limit, segregate, or classify his employees or applicants for employment in any way which would deprive or tend to deprive any individual of employment opportunities or otherwise adversely affect his status as an employee, because of such individual's race, color, religion, sex, or national origin.

(b) It shall be an unlawful employment practice for an employment agency to fail or refuse to refer for employment, or otherwise to discriminate against, an individual because of his race, color, religion, sex, or national origin, or to classify or refer for employment any individual on the basis of his race, color, religion, sex, or national origin.

(c) It shall be an unlawful employment practice for a labor organization—

---

* This material is excerpted from Title VII of the Civil Rights Act of 1964.

(1) to exclude or to expel from its membership, or otherwise to discriminate against, any individual because of his race, color, religion, sex, or national origin;

(2) to limit, segregate, or classify its membership or applicants for membership or to classify or fail or refuse to refer for employment any individual, in any way which would deprive or tend to deprive any individual of employment opportunities, or would limit such employment opportunities or otherwise adversely affect his status as an employee or as an applicant for employment, because of such individual's race, color, religion, sex, or national origin; or

(3) to cause or attempt to cause an employer to discriminate against an individual in violation of this section.

(d) It shall be an unlawful employment practice for any employer, labor organization, or joint labor-management committee controlling apprenticeship or other training or retraining, including on-the-job training programs to discriminate against any individual because of his race, color, religion, sex, or national origin in admission to, or employment in, any program established to provide apprenticeship or other training.

(e) Notwithstanding any other provision of this title, (1) it shall not be an unlawful employment practice for an employer to hire and employ employees, for an employment agency to classify, or refer for employment any individual, or for any employer, labor organization, or joint labor-management committee controlling apprenticeship or other training or retraining programs to admit or employ any individual in any such program, on the basis of his religion, sex, or national origin in those certain instances where religion, sex, or national origin is a bona fide occupational qualification reasonably necessary to the normal operation of that particular business or enterprise, and (2) it shall not be an unlawful employment practice for a school, college, university, or other educational institution or institution of learning to hire and employ employees of a particular religion if such school, college, university, or other educational institution or institution of learning is, in whole or in substantial part, owned, supported, controlled, or managed by a particular religion or by a particular religious corporation, association, or society, or if the curriculum of such school, college, university, or other educational institution or institution of learning is directed toward the propagation of a particular religion.

(f) As used in this title, the phrase "unlawful employment practice" shall not be deemed to include any action or measure taken by an employer, labor organization, joint labor-management committee, or employment agency with respect to an individual who is a member of the Communist Party of the United States or of any other organization required to register as a Communist-action or Communist-front organization by final order of the Subversive Activities Control Act of 1950.

(g) Notwithstanding any other provision of this title, it shall not be an unlawful employment practice for an employer to fail or refuse to hire and employ any individual for any position, for an employer to discharge an individual from any position, or for any employment agency to fail or refuse to refer any individual for employment in any position, or for a labor organization to fail or refuse any individual for employment in any position, if—

(1) the occupancy of such position, or access to the premises in or upon which any part of the duties of such position is performed or is to be performed, is subject to any requirement imposed in the interest of the national security of the United States under any security program in effect pursuant to or administered

under any statute of the United States or any Executive order of the President; and

(2) such individual has not fulfilled or has ceased to fulfill that requirement.

(h) Notwithstanding any other provision of this title, it shall not be an unlawful employment practice for an employer to apply different standards of compensation, or different terms, conditions, or privileges of employment pursuant to a bona fide seniority or merit system, or a system which measures earnings by quantity or quality of production or to employees who work in different locations, provided that such differences are not the result of an intention to discriminate because of race, color, religion, sex, or national origin; nor shall it be an unlawful employment practice for an employer to give and to act upon the results of any professionally developed ability test provided that such test, its administration or action upon the results is not designed, intended, or used to discriminate because of race, color, religion, sex, or national origin. It shall not be an unlawful employment practice under this title for any employer to differentiate upon the basis of sex in determining the amount of wages or compensation paid or to be paid to employees of such employer if such differentiation is authorized by the provision of Section 6(d) of the Fair Labor Standards Act of 1938 as amended (29 U.S.C. 206(d)).

(i) Nothing contained in this title shall apply to any business or enterprise on or near an Indian reservation with respect to any publicly announced employment practice of such business or enterprise under which a preferential treatment is given to any individual because he is an Indian living on or near a reservation.

(j) Nothing contained in this title shall be interpreted to require any employer, employment agency, labor organization, or joint labor-management committee subject to this title to grant preferential treatment to any individual or to any group because of the race, color, religion, sex, or national origin of such individual or group on account of an imbalance which may exist with respect to the total number or percentage of persons of any race, color, religion, sex, or national origin employed by any employer, referred or classified for employment by any employment agency or labor organization, admitted to membership or classified by any labor organization, or admitted to, or employed in, any apprenticeship or other training program, in comparison with the total number or percentage of persons of such race, color, religion, sex, or national origin in any community, State, section, or other area, or in the available work force in any community, State, section, or other area.

OTHER UNLAWFUL EMPLOYMENT PRACTICES

Section 704 (a) It shall be an unlawful employment practice for an employer to discriminate against any of his employees or applicants for employment, for an employment agency, or joint labor-management committee controlling apprenticeship or other training or retraining, including on-the-job training programs, to discriminate against any individual, or for a labor organization to discriminate against any member thereof or applicant for membership, because he has opposed any practice, made an unlawful employment practice by this title, or because he has made a charge, testified, assisted, or participated in any manner in an investigation, proceeding, or hearing under this title.

(b) It shall be an unlawful employment practice for an employer, labor organization, employment agency, or joint labor-management committee controlling apprenticeship or other training or retraining, including on-the-job training programs, to print or cause to be printed or published any notice or advertisement relating to employment by such an employer or membership in or any classification or referral for employment by such a labor organization, or relating to any classification or referral for employment by such an employment agency, or relating to admission to, or employment in, any program established to provide apprenticeship or other training by such a joint labor-management committee indicating any preference, limitation, specification, or discrimination, based on race, color, religion, sex or national origin, except that such a notice or advertisement may indicate a preference, limitation, specification, or discrimination based on religion, sex or national origin when religion, sex, or national origin is a bona fide occupational qualification for employment.

GLOSSARY

Abusive discharge. A tort, recognized in some states, committed when an employer discharges an employee in violation of a clear expression of public policy.

Acceleration clause. A provision in a credit agreement that allows the creditor to demand full payment of the debt if the debtor does not make timely payments or otherwise fails to comply with the terms of the agreement.

Acceptance. The offeree's assent to the terms of an offer to enter into a contract.

Action. A suit brought in a court.

Actionable. A term used to show that acts provide a basis or legal reason for a lawsuit.

Adequate protection. Usually an amount of money paid by the trustee in bankruptcy to a secured creditor to compensate for depreciation or other loss to property in which the secured creditor has a security interest.

Adjudication. The determination of a controversy and pronouncement of a judgment or decree in a case.

Administrative agency. An agency of the government charged with administering particular legislation.

Administrative law judge. An officer who presides at the initial hearing on matters litigated before a federal agency. He or she is chosen by civil service exam and is independent of the agency staff.

Administrative Procedure Act. A statute establishing the procedural rules governing how federal agencies operate.

Affectation doctrine. A doctrine, developed by the Supreme Court in interpreting the Commerce Clause of the Constitution of the United States, whereby Congress has the power to regulate any activity that has an appreciable effect upon interstate commerce.

Affidavit. A written declaration or statement of facts, sworn before a person who has the authority to administer such an oath.

Affirm. To agree with. An appellate court affirms a lower court decision when it declares the decision valid.

Affirmative action. An obligation undertaken by federal contractors to undertake special efforts to hire women and minorities. It is also a remedy which a court may decree under Title VII of the Civil Rights Act of 1964 and which the National Labor Relations Board is authorized to make under the National Labor Relations Act to effectuate the policies of those statutes.

Affirmative defense.   An assertion that, if true, relieves a defendant of liabliity or limits a plaintiff's recovery.

Allegation.   In a pleading, a declaration or statement by a party to a suit.

Allege.   To make a statement of fact, an assertion, or a charge.

Amicus curiae.   Latin, "Friend of the court." An individual or corporation that, because of strong interest in a case, petitions the court for permission to file a brief.

Answer.   A pleading of the defendant which responds to a complaint by either admitting or denying the allegations contained in the complaint.

Appeal.   The process by which a party asks a higher court to review alleged errors made by a lower court or an agency.

Appellant.   The party that takes an appeal from one court to another.

Appellate court.   A court having jurisdiction of appeal and review.

Appellee.   The party in a case against which an appeal is taken; that is, the party with an interest adverse to setting aside or reversing a judgment.

Arbitrary and capricious.   A description of a decision or action taken by an administrative agency which clearly disregards facts or principles of law.

Arbitration.   A process wherein a dispute is submitted to a mutually acceptable person or board, each party to the dispute having agreed beforehand to comply with the decision.

Arguendo.   For the sake of the purposes of argument. A statement or observation made as a matter of argument or hypothetical illustration.

Arraignment.   A proceeding wherein the accused is formally informed of the charge(s) and is asked to plead guilty, not guilty, or nolo contendere.

Articles of Confederation.   The name of the document embodying the compact made between the 13 original states of the Union, before the adoption of the present Constitution.

Assumption of the risk.   An affirmative defense raised by the defendant that defeats the plaintiff's recovery because the plaintiff knowingly and voluntarily exposed himself or herself to the danger that caused the injury.

Attachment.   The act or process of taking, apprehending, or seizing persons or property by virtue of a judicial process for the purpose of securing satisfaction of a judgment.

Attempt.   In criminal law, an effort to accomplish a crime, amounting to more than mere preparation or planning for it, which, if not prevented, would have resulted in the full consummation of the attempted act, but which, in fact, does not bring to pass the party's ultimate design. In civil matters, an attempt ordinarily means an intent combined with an act falling short of the thing intended.

At-will employee.   An employee who may be discharged by the employer for any reason without liability.

Aver.   To set out, assert, or allege in a formal complaint before a court of law.

Bailment.   A delivery of goods by one person (bailor) to another (bailee) in trust for the accomplishment of a specific purpose involving the goods (e.g., repair) upon an express or implied contract to carry out such trust and subsequently return the goods to the bailor.

Bailor. One who entrusts goods to another under a bailment.

Bait and switch advertising. A method of selling in which a seller advertises at a low price a product that the seller does not intend to sell (the bait) and then disparages that product to the prospective buyer and directs the buyer to a higher-priced product (the switch) which the seller intended to sell all along.

Banc. French, "The full court." A court sits *en banc* when all the judges making up the court hear the case in contradistinction to having the case decided by one judge or a portion of the judges of the court.

Bargaining order. An order of the National Labor Relations Board directing an employer to bargain with a union. A bargaining order is made to remedy employer conduct during a board conducted election to decide whether the employees want a union to be their representative. The employer's conduct must be so serious an interference with employee free choice as to render a new election incapable of being conducted.

Barred. Obstructed; subject to a hindrance that will prevent legal redress or recovery.

Beneficiary. One for whose benefit a trust is created.

Best efforts underwriting. A type of underwriting whereby an underwriter agrees to use its best efforts to sell securities of an issuer to brokers in return for a commission on the sales that it makes. Under this type of distribution the underwriter is not obligated to sell any designated quantity of securities.

Bill. The draft of an act of the legislature before it becomes law.

Bill of information. A formal accusation of the commission of a crime made by a prosecutor in place of a grand jury indictment.

Blue sky laws. State statutes regulating the sale of securities.

Bona fide. Latin, "In good faith." Honestly, sincerely.

Bond (security). A certificate issued by a governmental body or a corporation to represent a debt owed to the bondholder as well as a promise to pay interest.

Boycott. A conspiracy or confederation to prevent anyone from carrying on business, or to injure anyone's business, by preventing potential customers from doing business with him or her.

Breach of contract. Failure, without legal excuse, to perform any promise which forms the whole or part of a contract.

Bribe. Anything given in value with the corrupt intent to induce or influence a public official in the performance of his or her duties.

Broker. An agent who bargains, carries on negotiations, and makes contracts on behalf of his or her employer for compensation; also, a dealer in securities issued by others.

Brokerage. The compensation of a broker, including wages and commission.

Burden of proof. The necessity or duty of affirmatively proving the fact or facts in dispute on an issue raised between the parties to a suit in court.

Canons of ethics. Standards for the professional conduct expected of a lawyer, comprising the Code of Professional Responsibility. Initially adopted by the American Bar Association, it has been enacted into law in most states.

Case law.   The law as developed or laid down in decided cases, as opposed to statutes.

Cause of action.   The facts which evidence a civil wrong, thereby giving rise to a right to judicial relief.

Cease and desist order.   An order by an agency or a court directing someone to stop doing something.

Certiorari.   A means of obtaining appellate review; a writ issued by an appellate court to an inferior court commanding the record to be certified to the appellate court for judicial review.

Charging party.   A person who files a complaint with a government agency alleging that there has been a violation of law. In labor law, the person who files an unfair labor practice charge with the National Labor Relations Board is called a charging party. Also, a person who files a charge with the Equal Employment Opportunity Commission, alleging that someone has violated one of the federal employment laws prohibiting employment discrimination, is called the charging party.

Churning.   Abuse of a customer's confidence by a broker who initiates excessive transactions for the customer for personal gain.

Circumstantial evidence.   Evidence of an indirect nature; evidence from which the existence of a fact is inferred.

Civil law.   That body of law which is concerned with civil or private rights. Contrast *Criminal law.*

Claim.   A cause of action.

Class action.   An action brought by one or more persons as representatives of a large group of similarly situated persons.

Codetermination.   A process of management in which employers and employees share in the decision making.

Collateral.   Property which is pledged as security for the satisfaction of a debt.

Collusion.   An agreement between two or more persons to commit a wrongful act.

Commerce.   The exchange of goods, products, or property of any kind.

Commercial speech.   A term used in constitutional law to refer to economic speech, such as advertising.

Commodity.   A movable article of commerce, especially merchandise.

Common carrier.   One that transports persons or property for compensation, providing such services to the general public.

Common law.   As distinguished from law created by the enactment of legislatures, the common law comprises the principles and rules which derive solely from custom or from the judgments and decisions of courts. It is judge-made law.

Comparative negligence.   The doctrine under which a plaintiff's negligence as a factor in his or her own injury is assigned a percentage value, and his or her recovery from the defendant is reduced proportionately. Contrast with *Contributory negligence.*

Compensable. Capable of being compensated.

Compensable damages. Damages which compensate the victim for a loss; damages that put the victim in the position he or she was in before the injury occurred.

Compensable injury. Within workers' compensation statutes is one which results in compensation to an employee for injury arising out of and in the course of employment.

Compensatory damages. Damages that will compensate an injured party for the injury sustained, and nothing more; such compensation as will simply make good or replace the loss caused by a wrong or injury.

Competitive injury. An injury to competition or to a competitor.

Complaint. The first pleading by the plaintiff in a civil case. Its purpose is to give the defendant the information on which the plaintiff relies to support its demand. In a complaint, the plaintiff sets out a cause of action, consisting of a formal allegation or charge presented to the appropriate court.

Concerted action. Action that has been planned, arranged, adjusted, agreed on, or settled between parties acting together pursuant to some design or scheme.

Conciliation. The proceeding in which litigants are brought together by a third party.

Concur. To agree.

Concurring opinion. A printed opinion in which a judge agrees with the decision of the majority of the court for a different reason. With reference to appellate court opinions, a concurring opinion is one written by a judge who may agree with the majority opinion's conclusion, but for different reasons, and therefore writes a separate opinion.

Confederation. A league or compact for mutual support, particularly of nations or states. Such was the colonial government during the American Revolution.

Confucianism. Relating to the Chinese philosopher Confucius, his teachings, and his followers.

Conglomerate merger. A merger among firms that operate in separate or distinct markets.

Consent decree. A decree entered by consent of the parties. It is not a judicial sentence, but is an agreement of the parties made under the sanction of the court.

Consent order. An agreement by the defendant to cease activities which the government asserts are illegal. Also known as consent decree.

Consequential damages. Damage or injury which is not a direct, immediate, or predictable result of a party's act, but is nevertheless shown to be a consequence of it.

Consignee. One to whom goods are consigned for sale or safekeeping.

Consignment. Property delivered by a consignor to an agent for sale where title is held by the consignor until the property is sold.

Consignor. One who delivers goods to another on consignment.

Conspiracy. A combination or confederation between two or more persons formed for the purpose of committing, by their joint efforts, some unlawful or criminal act.

Construction defect. In a product liability action, a defect which results from the negligent manufacture of a particular item rather than from a defect in its design.

Consumer credit. Credit that is extended primarily for personal, family, or household purposes.

Contempt. A willful disregard or disobedience of a public authority.

Contempt of court. An act which disturbs or obstructs a court or is intended to detract from its authority or dignity.

Continuing trespass. A type of trespass that occurs over an extended period of time.

Contract. An agreement that a court will enforce.

Contributory negligence. Conduct by the plaintiff which is a contributing factor in his or her injury, thus barring any recovery against the defendant. Contrast *Comparative negligence.*

Conversion. An unauthorized assumption and exercise of ownership over goods belonging to another, to the alteration of their condition or the exclusion of the owner's rights.

Conviction. The result of a criminal trial which ends in a judgment or sentence that the prisoner is guilty as charged.

Corporate takeover bid. An attempt to assume control or management of a corporation by purchasing a controlling portion of its stock.

Corrective advertising. A remedy of the Federal Trade Commission by which one found guilty of violating the Federal Trade Commission Act with regard to unlawful advertising is ordered to correct the lasting impression of the advertising upon the public by engaging in advertising that repudiates the earlier advertising.

Counterclaim. A claim presented by a defendant which, if successful, defeats or reduces the plaintiff's recovery.

Court judgment. The official decision of a court determining the respective rights and claims of the parties in a lawsuit.

Credit bureau. An establishment that makes a business of collecting information relating to the credit, character, responsibility, and reputation of individuals and businesses for the purpose of furnishing the information to subscribers.

Creditor. A person to whom a debt is owed.

Criminal law. That body of law, commonly codified into penal codes, which declares what conduct is criminal and provides punishment for such conduct in order to protect society from harm. Contrast *Civil law.*

Criminal penalty. Punishment attached to the conviction of a crime.

Cross claim. A claim made in the course of an action by a defendant against a codefendant or by a plaintiff against a coplaintiff.

Cross elasticity of demand. An economic measure that measures the relationship between price changes and demand changes for a particular good.

Cross-examination. The examination of a witness at a trial or hearing, or upon taking a deposition, by the party opposed to the one that produced said witness, upon his or her evidence given in chief, to test its truth, to further develop it, or for other purposes.

Data. Facts from which to draw a conclusion.

De facto. In fact, in deed, actually.

De minimis. Something small or trifling.

De novo. Latin, "To begin anew." Usually refers to the necessity of a new hearing on the same facts and law previously litigated.

Debt security. Bonds, notes, debentures, and any other corporate securities which represent a debt owed to the holder.

Deceit. A fraudulent misrepresentation used by one person to deceive or trick another, who is ignorant of the facts, to the damage of the latter.

Decertify. In labor law, to decertify a union is to take away its status as the exclusive bargaining agent of the employees of an employer. Decertification occurs usually after an election is conducted by the National Labor Relations Board to determine whether the employees wish to continue to have a particular union act as their exclusive bargaining agent.

Declaratory judgment. A judgment which simply declares the rights of the parties or expresses the opinion of the court on a question of law without ordering anything to be done.

Defamation. The disparagement of one's reputation; the offense of injuring a person's character, fame, or reputation by false and malicious statements.

Default. Failure; omission to perform a legal or contractual duty; the failure of a party to appear in court after being properly served with process.

Defendant. The party against which an action is brought in a civil case; the accused in a criminal case.

Defense. An assertion offered by a defendant which, if successful, relieves him or her of liability, reduces the plaintiff's recovery, or defeats a criminal charge.

Defined benefit plans. A retirement plan that provides specific retirement benefits based on age and length of employment.

Demand. The amount of a particular good that consumers will buy in a given period of time.

Deposition. Pretrial testimony of a witness taken orally and under oath before an officer of the court (but not in open court), subject to cross-examination, reduced to writing, and intended to be used at trial.

Design defect. In the law of product liability, a defect in a product resulting from its design, so that every one produced is similarly defective. Contrast with *Construction defect.*

Dicta. Plural of *dictum.* Opinions of a judge that do not embody the resolution or determination of the court.

Dictum. The word is generally used as an abbreviated form of *obiter dictum* ("a remark by the way"). An observation or remark made by a judge in pronouncing an opinion in a case, concerning some rule, principle, or application of law, or the solution of a question suggested by the case, but not necessarily involved in the case or essential to its determination.

Disclosure. The act of disclosing. In several areas of government regulation of business, it refers to the act of revealing required information to consumers, investors, and employees.

Discovery. Devices that may be used by one party, as part of its preparation for trial, to obtain information about the case from the other party.

Disparagement. An untrue or misleading statement about a competitor's business or goods which is made to influence or tends to influence the public not to buy from the competitor.

Disposable earnings. That portion of a person's income that he is free to spend or invest as he or she sees fit after payment of taxes and other obligations.

Dissenting opinion. An opinion wherein a judge disagrees with the result reached by the majority of the court. Contrast *Concurring opinion.*

Distress sale. A "going out of business" sale in which the seller receives less for the goods than would be received under normal conditions.

Diversity of citizenship. A phrase used with reference to the jurisdiction of the federal courts, which, under Article III, Section 2, of the Constitution of the United States, extends to cases between citizens of different states. See *diversity jurisdiction.*

Diversity jurisdiction. The jurisdiction of the federal courts to hear cases in which the parties are citizens of different states or one of the parties is an alien and the amount in controversy exceeds $10,000.

Dividend. The share allotted to each of several persons entitled to participate in a division of profits or property. Dividends are what a shareholder earns from the stock owned in a corporation.

Eminent domain. The power of a sovereign to take private property for public use.

Enabling legislation. A term applied to any statute that enables agencies, corporations, or persons to do something they could not do before. Such statutes confer a lawful power upon an agency to act on a given matter.

Enactment. The process by which a bill becomes a statute. Sometimes used with reference to the statute itself.

Enterprise coverage. A type of coverage of the federal Fair Labor Standards Act whereby that act covers all the employees of a firm that engages in commerce.

Entrepreneur. Someone who organizes, manages, or assumes the risk of a business.

Equitable relief. Injunction, specific performance, restraining orders, and the like, as opposed to money damages.

Equity security. A share in a corporation, usually referred to as stock.

Escrow. A writing, deed, stock, or property delivered to a third person, to be held by that person until the fulfillment of a condition and then delivered to its owner.

Ex parte. On the application of one party only. A judicial proceeding is ex parte when it is taken or granted at the request of or for the benefit of one party only, and without notice to, or contestation by, any person adversely interested.

Exclusive dealing agreements. Contracts on which the buyer is obligated to purchase all of its requirements of a given commodity from the seller.

Executive agencies. Federal agencies that are under the direct control of the president. Appointments to executive agencies do not need Senate approval.

Executive order. An order by the chief executive of a government affecting the administration of the executive branch of government.

Exhaustion. A doctrine requiring that a party utilize remedies provided within an agency before seeking review by a court.

Exonerate. To exculpate; to remove a responsibility or duty.

Express warranty. A warranty which the seller creates by making a representation or a promise relating to goods or by showing the buyer a sample or model of them, regardless of whether such words as *guaranty*, or *warranty* are used.

Expunge. To destroy; to strike out wholly. "Expungement of the record" refers to the process whereby a record of a criminal conviction is sealed or destroyed after a designated period of time.

Federal question jurisdiction. The jurisdiction of the federal courts to hear cases arising under the U.S. Constitution, acts of Congress, or treaties.

Federal Register. A federal publication providing notice of federal rulemaking by federal agencies.

Federalism. The relationship between the states and the federal government whereby responsibility and autonomy is divided between them.

Fellow servant doctrine. A common-law doctrine, now abrogated by all workers' compensation acts, that an employee injured by the negligent act of a fellow employee cannot recover damages from his or her employer.

Fiduciary. A person having a duty, created by his or her undertaking, to act primarily for another's benefit.

Fiduciary duty. The duty which arises whenever one person is in a special relationship of trust to another, such as the duty an attorney owes to a client.

Firm commitment underwriting. A type of underwriting of securities whereby the underwriter is obligated to purchase a designated number of shares of securities from an issuer at a specified price.

Foreign corporation. A corporation doing business in any state other than the one in which it is incorporated.

Forum non conveniens, doctrine of. The power of a court to decline jurisdiction when the convenience of the parties and the ends of justice would be better served by bringing the action in another court.

Franchise. A special privilege conferred upon someone.

Franchisee. A holder of a franchise.

Franchisor. A party granting a franchise.

Fungible goods. Goods of any type which are by nature considered to be the equivalent of any other goods of that type.

Garnishee. The person on whom a garnishment is served; one who has in his or her possession the property of someone who owes a debt to another person.

Garnishment. A proceeding in which money, property, or credits of a debtor in possession of a third person, the garnishee, are applied to the payment of debts. The process if available only where it is authorized by statute.

General intent. An intention, purpose, or design, either without a specific plan or without a particular object.

Goodwill. The propensity of customers to return to a business. The patronage of a particular business. As such, it is an intangible asset of a business.

Good faith. An intangible quality encompassing honesty, sincerity, and the lack of intent to defraud or take advantage of another.

Gratuity. A gift.

Gross negligence. A conscious or intentional act or omission which is likely to result in harm to a person or property; a higher level of culpability than simple negligence.

Horizontal merger. Acquisition of one company by another company producing the same product or similar product and selling it in the same geographic market.

Imminent hazard. An immediate danger resulting from a product defect.

Impeach. To challenge the credibility of a witness.

Impleader. A procedure whereby a defendant brings a new party into an action on the basis that the new party may be liable to that party.

Implied contract. A contract not explicitly created by the parties, but inferred, as a matter of reason and justice, from the circumstances.

Implied warranty. A warranty which arises by operation of law although the seller does not express it, e.g., that a good is fit for the purpose for which it is intended.

In camera. In chambers; in private. A cause is said to be heard in camera either when the hearing is held before a judge or agency official in his or her private office or when all spectators are excluded from the courtroom or agency hearing room.

In personam jurisdiction. The power which a court has over the defendant's person as opposed to the power of a court over property.

Incidental damages. Damages resulting from a buyer's breach of contract, such as the costs of stopping delivery and reselling the goods; damages resulting from a seller's breach, including the expenses incurred in returning rightfully rejected goods and procuring a replacement.

Incorporation doctrine. A doctrine developed by the Supreme Court whereby it has interpreted the Due Process Clause of the 14th Amendment of the Constitution of the United States as incorporating, or absorbing, selected provisions of the Bill of Rights (the first 10 amendments) and thus applying them to the states. Prior to the incorporation doctrine, the Bill of Rights applied only to the federal government.

Independent agency. A federal agency to which appointments require Senate approval.

Indict. See *indictment*.

Indictment. A formal accusation made by a grand jury which charges that a person has commited a crime.

Information. See *Bill of Information*.

Injunction. An order of the court directing someone to do or not to do something.

Insider.   With respect to federal regulation of securities, an insider is anyone who has knowledge of facts not available to the general public. With regard to Section 16 of the Exchange Act of 1934, an insider is specifically defined as an officer, director, or any security holder owning more than 10 percent of the stock of a corporation.

Intent.   A state of mind with which a person acts.

Intentional infliction of emotional distress.   An intentional tort action providing redress to the victims of outrageous conduct that causes severe psychological injury.

Intentional torts.   A category of civil wrongs giving redress to the victims of willful wrongdoing.

Interpretive rules.   Rules of a federal agency rendering interpretations of the agency's enabling legislation. Such rules are not binding on the courts. Such rules do not need to be issued according to the procedures of the federal Administrative Procedure Act.

Interpretivism.   A theory of constitutional law maintaining that the Constitution should be interpreted by resort to its literal language or the intent of the framers, as found in historical accounts of the drafting of the Constitution.

Interrogatories.   A discovery device consisting of a series of written questions directed by one party to another party.

Interstate commerce.   Commercial trading, traffic, or the transportation of persons or property from a point in one state to points in other states.

Intrastate commerce.   Commerce that is carried out wholly within the limits of a single state.

Invasion of privacy.   An intentional tort providing redress to the victims whose privacy has been unreasonably intruded upon.

Judgment non obstante verdicto (judgment n.o.v.).   See *Judgment notwithstanding the verdict.*

Judgment notwithstanding the verdict.   A judge's judgment that is contrary to the verdict of the jury.

Judicial review.   The process by which the Supreme Court of the United States reviews legislation and refuses to enforce those laws that it declares to be unconstitutional.

Jurisdiction.   The power of a court or a judicial officer to decide a case; the geographic area of a court's authority.

Jurisdictional standards.   Standards issued by the National Labor Relations Board for particular industries for purposes of determining whether the board will assert jurisdiction.

Jurisprudence.   The philosophy of law; the science which studies the principles of law and legal relations.

Labeling defect.   In the law of product liability, a defect in a product resulting from inadequate labeling.

Labeling standard.   A standard issued by the Consumer Product Safety Commission requiring that a warning label be attached to a product.

Labor organization.   An organization of employees organized for the purpose of dealing with their employer.

Laissez-faire economics.   A policy whereby government takes a hands-off posture toward economic planning.

Legal relief.   Money damages. Contrast *Equitable relief.*

Legislation.   The act of enacting laws; the making of laws by express decree. Sometimes used as a noun to mean a statute or statutes.

Legislative history.   The background and events leading up to the enactment of a statute, e.g., committee reports and floor debates. Courts use the legislative history of a statute in determining the legislature's intent in enacting it.

Legislative rules.   Regulations issued by federal agencies pursuant to the federal Administrative Procedure Act. Such rules are binding upon courts.

Legislator.   One who makes laws; a member of a legislative body.

Legislature.   The department, assembly, or body of government that makes laws for a state or nation.

Libel.   To defame or injure a person's reputation by a published writing.

Lien.   A security interest in another's property, usually exercisable upon the non-payment of a debt.

Liquidation.   The act or process by which a party settles his or her debt by converting all assets into cash and making distribution to creditors. The term is also used in connection with a Chapter 7 straight bankruptcy proceeding.

Lobbying.   Attempts, including personal solicitation, to induce legislators to vote in a certain way or to introduce legislation.

Long arm statute.   A state statute which subjects a nonresident or a foreign corporation to the state's jurisdiction if the person or corporation has committed a tortious wrong or conducted business within the state, or has otherwise had "minimal contacts" within the state.

Magistrate.   A term for a public officer. Commonly, however, the term is used to apply to judicial officers with limited authority, such as justices of the peace.

Mao Zedong.   Communist revolutionary. Leader of the People's Republic of China from 1949–1976.

Mediation.   The act of a third person who attempts to persuade disputing parties to adjust their positions so as to resolve their dispute.

Merchantable.   Of good quality; of the quality fit for the purpose for which the good is intended.

Merger.   The fusion or absorption of one thing or right into another. For example, a merger occurs when one corporation becomes a part of another corporation.

Misrepresentation.   An untrue statement that justifies the rescission of a contract.

Modification.   A change.

Monopoly.   The ownership or control of so large a part of the market supply of a given commodity as to stifle competition and insure control over prices and competition.

Moot. A question which is no longer a controversy because the issue involved is no longer in dispute.

Mortgage. A pledge or security of particular property for the payment of a debt.

Motion. A request to a court or judge for a rule or order favorable to the requesting party, generally made within the course of an existing lawsuit.

Motion for directed verdict. A request that the judge order the entry of a verdict for one party on the grounds that the opposing party has failed to present sufficient evidence for any other verdict.

Natural law. Conception of law as a system of rules and principles for the guidance of human conduct which, independently of enacted law or of the systems peculiar to any one people, might be discovered by the rational intelligence of man, and would be found to grow out of and conform to man's nature.

Necessary and Proper Clause. Clause in U.S. Constitution which authorizes Congress to make all laws necessary and proper to carry out the enumerated powers of Congress and all other powers vested in the federal government.

Negligence. The omission to do something that a reasonable and prudent person, guided by those considerations which ordinarily regulate human affairs, would do, or the doing of something that a reasonable and prudent person would not do.

Nolo contendere. Latin, "I will not contest it." A plea in a criminal action often having the same effect as a guilty plea, except that it may not be used against the defendant in a subsequent civil action. Also known as a non-contest plea.

Nonattainment area. An area that has not met the national standards for air quality established under the federal Clean Air Act.

Noninterpretivism. A theory of constitutional interpretation that maintains that the Supreme Court may make the determination of constitutionality by referring to values other than those constitutionalized by the framers.

Nuisance. A class of torts that arise from the unreasonable, unwarrantable, or unlawful use by a person of his or her property, or from unlawful personal conduct, which obstructs or injures the right of another.

Offer. An act on the part of one person whereby he or she gives to another the legal power of creating a contract.

Offeror. Someone who makes an offer.

Oligopoly. The economic condition existing where a few sellers sell only a standardized product.

Open-end credit. Revolving charges and credit cards which permit the consumer to pay a part of what is owed.

Opinion of the court. The statement by a judge or court of the decision reached in regard to a cause tried or argued before them, expounding the law as applied to the case, and detailing the reasons upon which the judgment is based.

Order. A command or direction authoritatively given.

Order for relief. An order of a court or an administrative agency providing a remedy to someone.

Over-the-counter market. The market for securities traded off the floor of a stock exchange and usually sold through brokerage houses.

Palming off.   To impose by fraud; to pass off a product as another product by unfair means.

Parent corporation.   A company which owns over 50 percent of the voting stock of another company, known as its subsidiary.

Parliament.   The supreme legislative assembly of Great Britain.

Per curiam.   Latin, "By the court." Used to indicate an opinion by the entire court rather than a single judge. Sometimes refers to a brief statement of the court's decision unaccompanied by any written opinion.

Per se.   Latin, "By itself." Inherently.

Performance standard.   A standard issued by the Consumer Product Safety Commission specifying minimum performance criteria for a product.

Petitioner.   A party that files a petition with a court, applying in writing for a court order; a party that takes an appeal from a judgment; a party that initiates an equity action.

Plaintiff.   A person who brings an action or complaint against a defendant; the party who initiates a suit.

Plea.   An answer to a complaint or to a material allegation of fact therein. In criminal procedure, the answer of the accused in response to the criminal charge.

Pleadings.   The formal allegations by the parties of their respective claims and defenses; the complaint, answer and reply.

Plenary.   Full; entire; complete; absolute; perfect.

Police power.   The inherent power of a state over persons and property which enables the state to regulate the health, safety, and welfare of society.

Positive Law.   Law actually or specifically enacted or adopted by proper authority for the government of a society.

Possession.   The control or custody of property, for one's use and enjoyment, to the exclusion of all others.

Post hoc.   Hereafter; after this time.

Precedent.   A previously decided court case which serves as authority for a subsequent similar case.

Predatory intent.   An attempt to drive competitors out of business by sacrificing present revenues in the hope of recouping losses through future high prices.

Preemption doctrine.   The doctrine adopted by the U.S. Supreme Court holding that certain matters are of such a national, as opposed to local, character that federal laws preempt or take precedence over state laws. As such, a state may not pass a law inconsistent with the federal law.

Prejudicial error.   An error made during a trial which materially affects the rights of a party and thus may be ground for a reversal of judgment or a new trial.

Premises rule.   A rule of workers' compensation law that holds that an employee who is injured while on the employer's premises may recover even though the employee was going to or coming from the work site.

Point source.   Any discernible and confined conveyance of water, such as a pipe, ditch, well, or canal.

Price discrimination. Selling to one at a price and refusing to sell to another at the same price by one engaged in interstate commerce, in the absence of reason for the refusal.

Price fix. The act of establishing a price.

Prima facie. Latin, "At first sight." A fact presumed to be true unless disproved by evidence to the contrary.

Prima facie case. A case which has proceeded upon sufficient proof to that stage at which it will support a judicial finding if evidence to the contrary is disregarded. A litigating party is said to have a prima facie case when the evidence in its favor is sufficiently strong for its opponent to be called on to answer it. A prima facie case, then, is one which is established by sufficient evidence and which can be overthrown only by rebutting evidence adduced on the other side.

Private law. As used in contrast to public law, the term means that part of the law which is administered between citizen and citizen or which is concerned with the definition and enforcement of rights in cases where both the person in whom the right inheres and the person upon whom the obligation is incident are private individuals.

Privilege. A right or advantage particular to an individual or a class.

Privity. A mutual or successive relationship, for example, the relationship between the parties to a contract.

Pro rata. Proportionately.

Probable cause. Reasonable grounds for belief in the existence of facts. In criminal procedure, reasonable grounds for the belief that a person should be arrested or a warrant issued.

Procedural law. That part of law which concerns the method or process of enforcing rights.

Procedural rules. Rules adopted by an administrative agency to govern its internal procedures, such as the handling of charges, the holding of hearings, and the timing of investigations and hearings.

Prosecution. A criminal action. The term is also frequently used with respect to civil litigation, and includes every step in action, from commencement to its final determination.

Proximate cause. Event(s) or action which, in natural and unbroken sequence, produce an injury that would not have occurred absent the event(s) or action.

Proxy. Written authorization given by a shareholder to vote his or her shares at a shareholders' meeting.

Public law. The branch of law which is concerned with administrative and constitutional law.

Punitive damages. Damages awarded to a plaintiff which are greater than the amount necessary to compensate his or her loss. Generally granted where the wrong involved intent, violence, fraud, malice, or other aggravated circumstances.

Quid pro quo. The giving of one valuable thing for another.

Realist conception. A conception of law that holds that law is not embodied in abstract principles but in the process of deciding disputes.

Reconstruction period. Period following the Civil War during which the states of the former Confederacy were reintegrated into the Union.

Red herring prospectus. In securities law, an advance copy of the statement (prospectus) to be filed with the Securities and Exchange Commission preceding an issue of securities. The copy is marked in red ink, "not a solicitation, for information only."

Redress. The receiving of satisfaction for an injury sustained.

Relevant market. The geographic market composed of products that have reasonable interchangeability for purposes for which they are produced, considering their price, use, and quality. The term, in relation to a case involving an alleged violation of the Sherman Act or the Clayton Act, consists of both a product market and a geographic market.

Remand. To send back. The sending of a case back to the same court out of which it came, for the purpose of having some action taken on it.

Res ipsa loquitur. Latin, "The thing speaks for itself." Rule of evidence whereby negligence of the defendant is inferred from the circumstances as the result of a reasonable belief that the injury could not have happened without such negligence.

Res judicata. Latin, "A matter adjudged." A thing judicially acted upon or decided; a rule that a final judgment or decree on the merits by a court of competent jurisdiction is conclusive of the rights of the parties or their privies in all later suits on points and matters determined in the former suit.

Respondeat superior. Latin, "Let the master answer." Doctrine which provides that an employer or master is responsible for the acts of an employee or servant committed within the scope of the employment.

Respondent. The party that contends against an appeal.

Restatement. A book published by the American Law Institute consisting of that body's "restatement" of the law in one of several areas of law, such as torts, contracts, agency, etc.

Restraining order. An injunction; a court order prohibiting a party from doing something.

Restraint of trade. Contracts or combinations which tend or are designed to eliminate or stifle competition, effect a monopoly, artificially maintain prices, or otherwise obstruct commerce as it would be carried on if left to the control of natural or economic forces.

Reverse. To overthrow, vacate, set aside, make void, annul, repeal, or revoke, as to reverse a judgment.

Reviewability. A term addressing whether a court has the power to review an administrative agency's action.

Revocation. The recall of some power, authority, or thing granted.

Rulemaking. A function of most federal agencies that allows interested parties to comment upon proposed binding rules of an agency before their promulgation.

Scalping. The practice of a securities broker whereby the broker recomends the purchase of a stock for the purpose of inflating its value so that the broker, who had purchased the same stock previously, capitalizes on its sale.

Scienter. Knowledge; intent to deceive or defraud.

Secondary boycott. In labor law, the term refers to a refusal by union employees to work for, purchase from, or handle products of a secondary employer with whom the union has no dispute, with the object of forcing such employer to stop doing business with the primary employer with whom the union has a dispute.

Security. A stock, bond, note, investment contract, or other interest involving an investment in a common enterprise with the expectation of a profit to be derived from the efforts of someone other than the investor; an obligation given by a debtor to assure payment of a debt by providing the creditor with a resource that the creditor can use if the debtor defaults on the debt.

Security interest. A type of interest held by a creditor in a debtor's property such that the property could be sold upon the debtor's default in order to satisfy the debt.

Seniority. Represents in the highest degree the right to work. By seniority, the oldest worker in point of service, ability, and fitness for the job is the first to be given a choice of jobs, is the first to be promoted within a range of jobs subject to seniority, and is the last to be laid off. This proceeding is followed down the line to the youngest worker in point of service.

Separation of powers. A phrase referring to the division of the federal government into three departments or branches: the legislative, which is empowered to make laws; the executive, which is required to carry out the laws; and the judiciary, which is charged with interpreting the laws and adjudicating disputes under the laws. One branch is not permitted to intrude on the domain of another.

Shareholder. A person who owns stock in a corporation.

Short-swing profits. Profits made by an insider through the sale or other disposition of the corporate stock within six months after purchase.

Single trespass. A trespass of a limited duration, a single instance.

Situs. Situation or location.

Social audit. A report of a company's social behavior.

Social balance sheet. A report, required by French law, in which a company shares information on its social behavior with its workers.

Sovereign. An independent body or state; a chief ruler with supreme power, such as a king.

Specific intent. Exercise of intelligent will to commit a crime.

Speluncean. Having to do with the hobby of exploring caves.

Standing. A stake in a controversy sufficient to entitle a person to sue and obtain judicial resolution of the controversy.

Stare decisis. Latin, "Let the decision stand." Doctrine under which courts stand by precedent and do not disturb a settled point. Under this doctrine, once a court has laid down a principle of law as applied to a certain state of facts, the court will adhere to that principle and apply it to all future cases in which the facts are substantially the same. (Stare decisis does *not* mean "The decision is in the stars.")

State action.   In constitutional law, the term is used to designate governmental action that is necessary for purposes of bringing a constitutional challenge to such action.

State right-to-work statute.   A state statute authorized by the Taft-Hartley Act whereby an employee may lawfully refuse to join a union that has been certified as the bargaining representative of the employer's employees.

Status quo ante.   Latin, "The state of things before."

Statute.   An act of a legislature declaring, commanding, or prohibiting something; a particular law enacted by the legislative department of government. Sometimes the word is used to designate codified law as opposed to case law.

Statute of limitations.   A statute prescribing the length of time after an event in which a suit must be brought or a criminal charge filed.

Statutory law.   Law consisting of statutes as opposed to common law, which is judge-made law.

Stay.   To stop, arrest, or forbear. To stay an order or decree means to hold it in abeyance or to refrain from enforcing it.

Stop order.   The name of a Securities and Exchange Commission order directing that the effectiveness of a registration statement be suspended. The order also suspends a security issuer's license to use the mails and warns the investing public that the SEC has found the registration statement to be unreliable.

Strict liability.   Liability without fault. A case is one of strict liability when neither care nor negligence, neither good nor bad faith, neither knowledge nor ignorance will exonerate the defendant.

Subject matter jurisdiction.   A court's authority to hear a particular type of case.

Subpoena.   A writ ordering a person to appear and give testimony or to bring documents which are in his or her control.

Subsidiary corporation.   A corporation at least a majority of whose shares are owned by another corporation, which thus has control over it.

Substantive law.   That part of law which creates, defines, and regulates rights, as opposed to procedural law, which prescribes the methods for enforcing the rights.

Summary judgment.   A pretrial decision reached by a trial court, after considering the pleadings, affidavits, depositions, and other documents, on the ground that no genuine issue of fact has been raised.

Summons.   An instrument served on a defendant in a civil proceeding to give the defendant notice that he or she has been sued.

Sunset legislation.   A statute which provides that an agency's authority shall expire on a given date unless the legislative body acts to extend it.

Supremacy Clause.   A clause in the U.S. Constitution which provides that all laws made by the federal government pursuant to the Constitution are the supreme law of the land and are superior to any conflicting state law.

Takeover bid.   A bid to assume control or management of a corporation; a tender offer.

Target company.   The company intended to be taken over in a takeover bid.

Tender offer. An offer to purchase shares of stock, usually made in an attempt to obtain a controlling interest in a corporation.

Tombstone ad. An advertisement of a stock offering containing language to the effect that the announcement is neither an offer to sell nor a solicitation of an offer to buy any of the securities listed. The actual offer is made only by the prospectus.

Tort. A civil wrong or injury, other than a breach of contract, committed against the person or property of another.

Tortfeasor. A person who has committed a tort.

Treatise. A book that expounds upon a broad area of a subject.

Treaty. An agreement between nations.

Treble damages. Three times actual damages. The remedy provided to a successful plaintiff in certain actions, including antitrust suits.

Trespass. A tort action affording redress for injury committed to the plaintiff by the immediate force and violence of the defendant.

Trust. A legal arrangement whereby property or other assets are secured for beneficiaries by placing legal title and usually management responsibility in a trustee.

Trustee. The person appointed to execute a trust.

Unconscionable. So unfair or one-sided as to oppress or unfairly surprise a party.

Uniform Commercial Code. A comprehensive code, drafted by the National Conference of Commissioners on Uniform State Laws, which has been enacted in all of the states.

Union certification. The process by which the National Labor Relations Board certifies a union as the exclusive bargaining representative of a unit of employees in the employer's work force.

Variance. Permission to depart from the literal requirements of an administrative regulation.

Venue. The particular county or geographic location in which a court with jurisdiction may hear a case.

Vertical merger. A merger between two firms that have a buyer-seller relationship.

Vested. Fixed, settled, absolute. Having the character of absolute ownership. With regard to pension plan benefits, "vested benefits" are not contingent upon the employee continuing to work for the employer.

Veto. Latin, "I forbid." The refusal of assent by the executive officer whose assent is necessary to perfect a law which a legislative body has passed.

Vis-à-vis. Face to face. One of two things or persons opposite or corresponding to each other. In relation to each other.

Void. Null; ineffectual; having no legal force.

Warrant. A writ from a competent authority in pursuance of law which directs the doing of an act, is addressed to an officer or person competent to do the act, and affords that officer or person protection from damage if he or she does it. In particular, writs are issued by a magistrate or justice, and addressed to a sheriff, constable, or other officer, requiring the latter to arrest someone or to search someone's person or property and seize items of evidence.

Warranty.   A promise that a statement is true. In contracts, a written or verbal undertaking or stipulation that a certain statement in relation to the subject matter of the contract is or shall be as it is stated or promised to be.

Work-product doctrine.   The doctrine by which certain material prepared by an attorney in anticipation of litigation is protected from discovery.

Works councils.   Plant-level committees consisting of supervisory personnel and workers, which decide plant-level matters.

Writ.   A court order directing a person to do something.

INDEX OF COURT CASES

Principal cases are in italic type; roman type indicates cases cited or discussed.

SUBJECT INDEX

This book has been set VideoComp, in 10 and 9 point Aster, leaded 2 points. Part numbers are 16 point Times Roman (initial cap is 20 points) and part titles are 20 point Times Roman Bold (initial cap is 27 points). Chapter numbers are 13 point Aster (initial cap is 18 points) and chapter titles are 13 point Aster Bold (initial cap is 16 points). The size of the type page is 36 by 46 picas.